Avizandum Statutes on

Scots Commercial and Consumer Law
2011–2012

Ninth edition

Editor

Ross Gilbert Anderson LLB (Hons), PhD, Solicitor, NP
Lecturer in Corporate and Financial Law, University of Glasgow

Avizandum Publishing Ltd
Edinburgh
2011

Avizandum Publishing Ltd
58 Candlemaker Row
Edinburgh EH1 2QE

First published   2003
2nd edition   2004
3rd edition   2005
4th edition   2006
5th edition   2007
6th edition   2008
7th edition   2009
8th edition   2010
9th edition   2011

ISBN 978-1-904968-46-7

© Avizandum Publishing Ltd 2011

Parliamentary material is reproduced with the permission of the Controller of HMSO on behalf of Parliament and of the Office of the Queen's Printer for Scotland on behalf of the Scottish Parliament.

EC materials © European Communities 1998–2011

British Library Cataloguing in Publication Data
A catalogue record for this book is available from the British Library

Typeset by AFS Image Setters Ltd, Glasgow
Printed and bound by Bell & Bain Ltd, Glasgow

EDITOR'S PREFACE

Avizandum Statutes on Scots Commercial and Consumer Law are aimed at students of commercial and consumer law in Scotland. The statutes selected for inclusion are those which relate to subjects which fall within the commercial law syllabus of the Law Society of Scotland.

Inevitably, because of the broad sweep of 'commercial and consumer law', decisions have to be made about what material to include, include in part, or omit altogether. The desire to be as comprehensive as possible has to be balanced against issues of length and cost, bearing in mind that this collection is aimed primarily at undergraduate students. So where, for example, European directives have been implemented in domestic law, the original text of the directives has not been included. Similarly, the many consumer regulations that create criminal offences but do not confer private law rights have not been included.

This year sees some additional minor amendments to the Consumer Credit Act 1974, while the amendments to that Act first included in last year's volume are now all in force. Two additional Scottish provisions have been added. One is the Diligence Act 1661. The other is the short Contract (Scotland) Act 1997, the provisions of which are particularly important in commercial contract cases. Prospective amendments are indicated by *italic* type.

There is also, in response to users' requests, the addition of the European Insolvency Regulation which, it is hoped, will render the volume useful for Honours and LLM students.

There is still no word on when the Third Parties (Rights against Insurers) Act 2010 is likely to come into force: the last official statement remains that given by Vince Cable MP in June 2010 (see *Hansard*, House of Commons, 9 June 2010: col 153W). In this state of affairs, it has been thought best to postpone the inclusion of the 2010 Act until the announcement of a commencement date.

I would like to thank George Gretton and Scott Wortley for helpful suggestions; Katie Fitzpatrick for checking through the legislative amendments; and, above all, Margaret Cherry, for her characteristic diligence in bringing the collection to publication.

Ross Gilbert Anderson
Mainz, Germany
July 2011

CONTENTS

Part III. EC Materials

PART I
STATUTES

COMPENSATION ACT 1592
(APS III, 573, c 61; 12mo c 143)

Oure Souerane Lord and estaitis of parliament statutis and Ordanis that ony debt de liquido ad liquidum instantlie verifiet be wreit or aith of the partie befoir the geving of decreit be admittit be all Jugis within this realme be way of exceptioun Bot nocht eftir the geving thairof in the suspensioun or in reductioun of the same decreit.

DILIGENCE ACT 1661*
(RPS 1661/1/433; APS VII, 317, c 344)

[A]ll compriseings deduced . . . befor the first effectuall compriseing or after but within yeer and day of the same Shall come in pari passu together [. . .].

* As applied to adjudications by Adjudications Act 1672 (RPS 1672/6/55; APS VIII, 93, c 45).

LIFE ASSURANCE ACT 1774
(14 Geo 3, c 48)

1   No Insurance to be made on the lives of persons having no interest, &c
From and after the passing of this Act no insurance shall be made by any person or persons, bodies politick or corporate, on the life or lives of any person, or persons, or on any other event or events whatsoever, wherein the person or persons for whose use, benefit, or on whose account such policy or policies shall be made, shall have no interest, or by way of gaming or wagering; and every assurance made contrary to the true intent and meaning hereof shall be null and void to all intents and purposes whatsoever.

2   No policies on lives without inserting the persons names, &c
And it shall not be lawful to make any policy or policies on the life or lives of any person or persons, or other event or events, without inserting in such policy or policies the person or persons name or names interested therein, or for whose use, benefit, or on whose account such policy is so made or underwrote.

3   How much may be recovered where the insured hath interest in lives
And in all cases where the insured hath interest in such life or lives, event or events, no greater sum shall be recovered or received from the insurer or insurers than the amount of value of the interest of the insured in such life or lives, or other event or events.

4   Not to extend to insurances on ships, goods, &c
Provided always, that nothing herein contained shall extend or be construed to extend to insurances bona fide made by any person or persons on ships, goods, or merchandises, but every such insurance shall be as valid and effectual in the law as if this Act had not been made.

1

TRANSMISSION OF MOVEABLE PROPERTY (SCOTLAND) ACT 1862
(25 & 26 Vict, c 85)

1   Personal bond or conveyance of moveable estate may be assigned in the form set forth in schedule A

It shall be competent to any party, in right of a personal bond or of a conveyance of moveable estate, to assign such bond or conveyance by assignation in or as nearly as may be in the form set forth in schedule A. hereto annexed; and it shall be competent to write the assignation or assignations on the bond or conveyance itself in or as nearly as may be in the form set forth in schedule B. hereto annexed; which assignation shall be registrable in the books of any court, in terms of any clause of registration contained in the bond or conveyance so assigned; and such assignation, upon being duly stamped and duly intimated, shall have the same force and effect as a duly stamped and duly intimated assignation according to the forms at present in use.

2   Certified copy to be delivered to person or persons to whom intimation may in any case be requisite

An assignation shall be validly intimated (1) by a notary public delivering a copy thereof, certified as correct, to the person or persons to whom intimation may in any case be requisite, or (2) by the holder of such assignation, or any person authorized by him, transmitting a copy thereof certified as correct by post to such person; and (in the first case) a certificate by such notary public in or as nearly as may be in the form set forth in schedule C. hereto annexed, and (in the second case) a written acknowledgment by the person to whom such copy may have been transmitted by post as aforesaid of the receipt of the copy, shall be sufficient evidence of such intimation having been duly made: Provided always, that if the deed or instrument containing such assignation shall likewise contain other conveyances or declarations of trust purposes, it shall not be necessary to deliver or transmit a full copy thereof, but only a copy of such part thereof as respects the subject matter of such assignation.

3   As to transmission of personal bond, &c

Nothing in this Act contained shall prevent the transmission of any personal bond or conveyance of moveable estate, or the intimation of any assignation according to the forms at present in use.

4   Interpretation of terms

The following words in this Act, and in the schedules annexed to this Act, shall have the several meanings hereby assigned to them, unless there by something in the subject or context repugnant to such construction; that is to say, the word 'bond' and the word 'conveyance' shall extend to and include personal bonds for payment or performance, bonds of caution, bonds of guarantee, bonds of relief, bonds and assignations in security of every kind, decreets of any court, policies of assurance of any assurance company or association in Scotland, whether held by parties resident in Scotland or elsewhere, protests of bills or of promissory notes, dispositions, assignations, or other conveyances of moveable or personal property or effects, assignations, translations, and retrocessions, and also probative extracts of all such deeds from the books of any competent court; the word 'assignation' shall also include translations and retrocessions, and probative extracts thereof; the words 'moveable estate' shall extend to and include all personal debts and obligations, and moveable or personal property or effects of every kind.

5   Short title

This Act may be cited for all purposes as the 'Transmission of Moveable Property (Scotland) Act, 1862.'

SCHEDULES REFERRED TO IN THE FOREGOING ACT

SCHEDULE A

I, A.B., in consideration of, &c [or otherwise, as the case may be], do hereby assign to C.D. and his heirs or assignees [or otherwise, as the case may be,] the bond [or other deed, describing it], granted by E.F., dated, &c, by which [here specify the nature of the deed, and specify also any connecting title, and any circumstances requiring to be stated in regard to the nature and extent of the right required], [Testing clause†

†Note—Subscription of the document by the granter of it will be sufficient for the document to be formally valid, but witnessing of it may be necessary or desirable for other purposes (see the Requirements of Writing (Scotland) Act 1995).]

SCHEDULE B

I, A.B., in consideration of, &c [or otherwise, as the case may be], do hereby assign to C.D. and his heirs or assignees [or otherwise, as the case may be,] the foregoing [or within-written] bond [or other writ or deed, describing it,] granted in my favour [or otherwise, as the case may be, specifying any connecting title, and any circumstances requiring to be stated in regard to the nature and extent of the right assigned] [Testing clause†

†Note—Subscription of the document by the granter of it will be sufficient for the document to be formally valid, but witnessing of it may be necessary or desirable for other purposes (see the Requirements of Writing (Scotland) Act 1995).]

SCHEDULE C

I (A.), of the city of notary public, do hereby attest and declare, that upon the day of , and between the hours of and , I duly intimated to B. [here describe the party] the within-written assignation [or otherwise, as the case may be], or an assignation granted by [here describe it] ,and that by delivering to the said A. personally [or otherwise] by leaving for the said A. within his dwelling house at E., in the hands of [here describe the party], a full copy thereof, [or if a partial copy here quote the portion of the deed which has been delivered], to be given to him; all of which was done in presence of C. [Testing clause]

TITLES TO LAND CONSOLIDATION (SCOTLAND) ACT 1868
(31 & 32 Vict, c 101)

59 Unnecessary to libel and conclude for decree of special adjudication
Whereas it is inconvenient in practice to libel and conclude for general adjudication of lands as the alternative only of special adjudication, in terms of an Act of the Parliament of Scotland passed in the year one thousand six hundred and seventy-two: It shall not be necessary to libel or conclude for special adjudication, and it shall be lawful to libel and conclude and decern for general adjudication without such alternative, anything in the said last-recited Act of the Parliament of Scotland, or in any other Act or Acts of the Parliament of Scotland or of Great Britain or of the United Kingdom of Great Britain and Ireland, to the contrary notwithstanding.

[62 Effect of a decree of adjudication or sale
In all cases a decree of adjudication whether for debt or in implement, or a decree of constitution and adjudication whether for debt or in implement, if duly obtained in the form prescribed by this Act, or obtained, if prior to the commencement of this

Act, in the form then in use, or a decree of declarator and adjudication, or a decree of sale, shall, except in the case where the subjects contained in the decree of adjudication, or of constitution and adjudication, or of declarator and adjudication, are heritable securities, be held equivalent to and shall have the legal operation and effect of a conveyance in ordinary form of the lands therein contained granted in favour of the adjudger or purchaser by the ancestor of such apparent heir, or by the owner or proprietor in trust or otherwise, and whether in life or deceased, of the lands adjudged, or by the seller of the lands sold, although [under legal disability by reason of nonage] or [mental or other incapacity] and it shall be lawful and competent to such adjudger or purchaser to complete [by recording the decree as a conveyance or by using the decree as a midcouple or link of title.]

[155   Date on which inhibition takes effect
   (1)   An inhibition has effect from the beginning of the day on which it is registered unless the circumstances referred to in subsection (2) below apply.
   (2)   Those circumstances are—
      (a)   a notice of inhibition is registered in the Register of Inhibitions;
      (b)   the schedule of inhibition is served on the debtor after that notice is registered; and
      (c)   the inhibition is registered before the expiry of the period of 21 days beginning with the day on which the notice is registered.
   (3)   In those circumstances the inhibition has effect from the beginning of the day on which the schedule of inhibition is served.
   (4)   A notice of inhibition must be in (or as nearly as may be in) the form prescribed.]

157   No inhibition to have effect against acquirenda, unless in case of heir under entail or other indefeasible title
No inhibition to be recorded from and after the thirty-first day of December one thousand eight hundred and sixty-eight shall have any force or effect as against any lands to be acquired by the person or persons against whom such inhibition is used after the date of recording such inhibition, or of recording the previous notice thereof prescribed by this Act, as the case may be: Provided always, that where such inhibition is used against a person or persons who shall thereafter succeed to any lands which, at the date of recording the inhibition or previous notice thereof, as the case may be, were destined to such person or persons by a deed of entail, or by a similar indefeasible title, then and in that case such inhibition shall affect the said person or persons in so far as regards the lands so destined, and to which he or they shall succeed as aforesaid, but no further.

159   Litigiosity not to begin before date of registration of notice of summons
It shall be competent to register in the general register of inhibitions a notice of any signeted summons of reduction of any conveyance or deed of or relating to lands, and in the register of adjudications a notice of any signeted summons of adjudication or of constitution and adjudication combined [. . .] in implement, which notice shall [be in (or as nearly as may be in) the form prescribed]; and no summons of reduction, constitution, adjudication, or constitution and adjudication combined, shall have any effect in rendering litigious the lands to which such summons relates, except from and after the date of the registration of such notice.

[159A   Registration of notice of summons of action of reduction
   (1)   This section applies where a pursuer raises an action of reduction of a conveyance or deed of or relating to lands granted in breach of an inhibition.
   (2)   The pursuer shall, as soon as is reasonably practicable after the summons in the action is signeted—
      (a)   register a notice of that signeted summons in accordance with section 159 of this Act; and

(b)   register in the Land Register of Scotland or, as the case may be, record in the Register of Sasines a copy of that notice.

(3)   Where a decree of reduction is not obtained in the action to which the notice relates, the pursuer shall, as soon as is reasonably practicable—

(a)   register in the Register of Inhibitions; and

(b)   register in the Land Register of Scotland or, as the case may be, record in the Register of Sasines,

a discharge of that notice in (or as nearly as may be in) the form prescribed.]

BILLS OF EXCHANGE ACT 1882
(45 & 46 Vict, c 61)

PART I
PRELIMINARY

1   Short title
This Act may be cited as the Bills of Exchange Act, 1882.

2   Interpretation of terms
In this Act, unless the context otherwise requires,—

'Acceptance' means an acceptance completed by delivery or notification.

'Action' includes a counter claim and set off.

'Banker' includes a body of persons whether incorporated or not who carry on the business of banking.

'Bankrupt' includes any person whose estate is vested in a trustee or assignee under the law for the time being in force relating to bankruptcy.

'Bearer' means the person in possession of a bill or note which is payable to bearer.

'Bill' means bill of exchange, and 'note' means promissory note.

'Delivery' means transfer of possession, actual or constructive, from one person to another.

'Holder' means the payee or indorsee of a bill or note who is in possession of it, or the bearer thereof.

'Indorsement' means an indorsement completed by delivery.

'Issue' means the first delivery of a bill or note, complete in form to a person who takes it as a holder.

'Person' includes a body of persons whether incorporated or not.

['Postal operator' has the meaning given by section 125(1) of the Postal Services Act 2000.]

'Value' means valuable consideration.

'Written' includes printed, and 'writing' includes print.

PART II
BILLS OF EXCHANGE

Form and interpretation

3   Bill of exchange defined
(1)   A bill of exchange is an unconditional order in writing, addressed by one person to another, signed by the person giving it, requiring the person to whom it is addressed to pay on demand or at a fixed or determinable future time a sum certain in money to or to the order of a specified person, or to bearer.

(2)   An instrument which does not comply with these conditions, or which orders any act to be done in addition to the payment of money, is not a bill of exchange.

(3)   An order to pay out of a particular fund is not unconditional within the

meaning of this section; but an unqualified order to pay, coupled with (a) an indication of a particular fund out of which the drawee is to reimburse himself or a
particular account to be debited with the amount, or (b) a statement of the transaction which gives rise to the bill, is unconditional.
  (4)   A bill is not invalid by reason—
      (a)   That it is not dated;
      (b)   That it does not specify the value given, or that any value has been given
  therefor;
      (c)   That it does not specify the place where it is drawn or the place where it
  is payable.

4 Inland and foreign bills
  (1)   An inland bill is a bill which is or on the face of it purports to be (a) both
drawn and payable within the British Islands, or (b) drawn within the British
Islands upon some person resident therein. Any other bill is a foreign bill.
  For the purposes of this Act 'British Islands' means any part of the United Kingdom of Great Britain and Ireland, the islands of Man, Guernsey, Jersey, Alderney,
and Sark, and the islands adjacent to any of them being part of the dominions of
Her Majesty.
  (2)   Unless the contrary appear on the face of the bill the holder may treat it as
an inland bill.

5 Effect where different parties to bill are the same person
  (1)   A bill may be drawn payable to, or to the order of, the drawer; or it may be
drawn payable to, or to the order of, the drawee.
  (2)   Where in a bill drawer and drawee are the same person, or where the
drawee is a fictitious person or a person not having capacity to contract, the holder
may treat the instrument, at his option, either as a bill of exchange or as a promissory note.

6 Address to drawee
  (1)   The drawee must be named or otherwise indicated in a bill with reasonable
certainty.
  (2)   A bill may be addressed to two or more drawees whether they are partners
or not, but an order addressed to two drawees in the alternative or to two or more
drawees in succession is not a bill of exchange.

7 Certainty required as to payee
  (1)   Where a bill is not payable to bearer, the payee must be named or otherwise indicated therein with reasonable certainty.
  (2)   A bill may be made payable to two or more payees jointly, or it may be
made payable in the alternative to one of two, or one or some of several payees. A
bill may also be made payable to the holder of an office for the time being.
  (3)   Where the payee is a fictitious or non-existing person the bill may be
treated as payable to bearer.

8 What bills are negotiable?
  (1)   When a bill contains words prohibiting transfer, or indicating an intention
that it should not be transferable, it is valid as between the parties thereto, but is
not negotiable.
  (2)   A negotiable bill may be payable either to order or to bearer.
  (3)   A bill is payable to bearer which is expressed to be so payable, or on which
the only or last indorsement is an indorsement in blank.
  (4)   A bill is payable to order which is expressed to be so payable, or which is
expressed to be payable to a particular person, and does not contain words prohibiting transfer or indicating an intention that it should not be transferable.
  (5)   Where a bill, either originally or by indorsement, is expressed to be payable

to the order of a specified person, and not to him or his order, it is nevertheless payable to him or his order at his option.

9 Sum payable

(1) The sum payable by a bill is a sum certain within the meaning of this Act, although it is required to be paid—

(a) With interest.

(b) By stated instalments.

(c) By stated instalments, with a provision that upon default in payment of any instalment the whole shall become due.

(d) According to an indicated rate of exchange or according to a rate of exchange to be ascertained as directed by the bill.

(2) Where the sum payable is expressed in words and also in figures, and there is a discrepancy between the two, the sum denoted by the words is the amount payable.

(3) Where a bill is expressed to be payable with interest, unless the instrument otherwise provides, interest runs from the date of the bill, and if the bill is undated from the issue thereof.

10 Bill payable on demand

(1) A bill is payable on demand—

(a) Which is expressed to be payable on demand, or at sight, or on presentation; or

(b) In which no time for payment is expressed.

(2) Where a bill is accepted or indorsed when it is overdue, it shall, as regards the acceptor who so accepts, or any indorser who so indorses it, be deemed a bill payable on demand.

11 Bill payable at a future time

A bill is payable at a determinable future time within the meaning of this Act which is expressed to be payable—

(1) At a fixed period after date or sight.

(2) On or at a fixed period after the occurrence of a specified event which is certain to happen, though the time of happening may be uncertain.

An instrument expressed to be payable on a contingency is not a bill, and the happening of the event does not cure the defect.

12 Omission of date in bill payable after date

Where a bill expressed to be payable at a fixed period after date is issued undated, or where the acceptance of a bill payable at a fixed period after sight is undated, any holder may insert therein the true date of issue or acceptance, and the bill shall be payable accordingly.

Provided that (1) where the holder in good faith and by mistake inserts a wrong date, and (2) in every case where a wrong date is inserted, if the bill subsequently comes into the hands of a holder in due course the bill shall not be avoided thereby, but shall operate and be payable as if the date so inserted had been the true date.

13 Ante-dating and post-dating

(1) Where a bill or an acceptance or any indorsement on a bill is dated, the date shall, unless the contrary be proved, be deemed to be the true date of the drawing, acceptance, or indorsement, as the case may be.

(2) A bill is not invalid by reason only that it is ante-dated or post-dated, or that it bears date on a Sunday.

14 Computation of time of payment

Where a bill is not payable on demand the day on which it falls due is determined as follows:

[(1) The bill is due and payable in all cases on the last day of the time of payment as fixed by the bill or, if that is a non-business day, on the succeeding business day.]

(2)   Where a bill is payable at a fixed period after date, after sight, or after the happening of a specified event, the time of payment is determined by excluding the day from which the time is to begin to run and by including the day of payment.

(3)   Where a bill is payable at a fixed period after sight, the time begins to run from the date of the acceptance if the bill be accepted, and from the date of noting or protest if the bill be noted or protested for non-acceptance, or for non-delivery.

15   Case of need

The drawer of a bill and any indorser may insert therein the name of a person to whom the holder may resort in case of need, that is to say, in case the bill is dishonoured by non-acceptance or non-payment. Such person is called the referee in case of need. It is in the option of the holder to resort to the referee in case of need or not as he may think fit.

16   Optional stipulations by drawer or indorser

The drawer of a bill, and any indorser, may insert therein an express stipulation—
(1)   Negativing or limiting his own liability to the holder;
(2)   Waiving as regards himself some or all of the holder's duties.

17   Definition and requisites of acceptance

(1)   The acceptance of a bill is the signification by the drawee of his assent to the order of the drawer.

(2)   An acceptance is invalid unless it complies with the following conditions, namely:
    (a)   It must be written on the bill and be signed by the drawee. The mere signature of the drawee without additional words is sufficient.
    (b)   It must not express that the drawee will perform his promise by any other means than the payment of money.

18   Time for acceptance

A bill may be accepted—
(1)   Before it has been signed by the drawer, or while otherwise incomplete;
(2)   When it is overdue, or after it has been dishonoured by a previous refusal to accept, or by non-payment;
(3)   When a bill payable after sight is dishonoured by non-acceptance, and the drawee subsequently accepts it, the holder, in the absence of any different agreement, is entitled to have the bill accepted as of the date of first presentment to the drawee for acceptance.

19   General and qualified acceptance

(1)   An acceptance is either (a) general, or (b) qualified.

(2)   A general acceptance assents without qualification to the order of the drawer. A qualified acceptance in express terms varies the effect of the bill as drawn.

In particular an acceptance is qualified which is—
    (a)   conditional, that is to say, which makes payment by the acceptor dependent on the fulfilment of a condition therein stated;
    (b)   partial, that is to say, an acceptance to pay part only of the amount for which the bill is drawn;
    (c)   local, that is to say, an acceptance to pay only at a particular specified place;
An acceptance to pay at a particular place is a general acceptance, unless it expressly states that the bill is to be paid there only and not elsewhere:
    (d)   qualified as to time;
    (e)   the acceptance of some one or more of the drawees, but not of all.

20 Inchoate instruments

(1) Where a simple signature on a blank paper is delivered by the signer in order that it may be converted into a bill, it operates as a prima facie authority to fill it up as a complete bill for any amount [. . .] using the signature for that of the drawer, or the acceptor, or an indorser; and, in like manner, when a bill is wanting in any material particular, the person in possession of it has a prima facie authority to fill up the omission in any way he thinks fit.

(2) In order that any such instrument when completed may be enforceable against any person who became a party thereto prior to its completion, it must be filled up within a reasonable time, and strictly in accordance with the authority given. Reasonable time for this purpose is a question of fact.

Provided that if any such instrument after completion is negotiated to a holder in due course it shall be valid and effectual for all purposes in his hands and he may enforce it as if it had been filled up within a reasonable time and strictly in accordance with the authority given.

21 Delivery

(1) Every contract on a bill, whether it be the drawer's, the acceptor's, or an indorser's is incomplete and revocable, until delivery of the instrument in order to give effect thereto.

Provided that where an acceptance is written on a bill, and the drawee gives notice to or according to the directions of the person entitled to the bill that he has accepted it, the acceptance then becomes complete and irrevocable.

(2) As between immediate parties, and as regards a remote party other than a holder in due course, the delivery—

    (a) in order to be effectual must be made either by or under the authority of the party drawing, accepting, or indorsing, as the case may be:

    (b) may be shown to have been conditional or for a special purpose only, and not for the purpose of transferring the property in the bill.

But if the bill be in the hands of a holder in due course a valid delivery of the bill by all parties prior to him so as to make them liable to him is conclusively presumed.

(3) Where a bill is no longer in the possession of a party who has signed it as drawer, acceptor, or indorser, a valid and unconditional delivery by him is presumed until the contrary is proved.

Capacity and authority of parties

22 Capacity of parties

(1) Capacity to incur liability as a party to a bill is co-extensive with capacity to contract.

Provided that nothing in this section shall enable a corporation to make itself liable as drawer, acceptor, or indorser of a bill unless it is competent to do so under the law for the time being in force relating to corporations.

(2) Where a bill is drawn or indorsed by an infant, minor, or corporation having no capacity or power to incur liability on a bill, the drawing or indorsement entitles the holder to receive payment of the bill, and to enforce it against any other party thereto.

23 Signature essential to liability

No person is liable as drawer, indorser, or acceptor of a bill who has not signed it as such: Provided that

(1) Where a person signs a bill in a trade or assumed name, he is liable thereon as if he had signed it in his own name:

(2) The signature of the name of a firm is equivalent to the signature by the person so signing of the names of all persons liable as partners in that firm.

24 Forged or unauthorised signature

Subject to the provisions of this Act, where a signature on a bill is forged or placed thereon without the authority of the person whose signature it purports to be, the forged or unauthorised signature is wholly inoperative, and no right to retain the bill or to give a discharge therefor or to enforce payment thereof against any party thereto can be acquired through or under that signature, unless the party against whom it is sought to retain or enforce payment of the bill is precluded from setting up the forgery or want of authority.

Provided that nothing in this section shall affect the ratification of an unauthorised signature not amounting to a forgery.

25 Procuration signatures

A signature by procuration operates as notice that the agent has but a limited authority to sign, and the principal is only bound by such signature if the agent in so signing was acting within the actual limits of his authority.

26 Person signing as agent or in representative capacity

(1) Where a person signs a bill as drawer, indorser, or acceptor, and adds words to his signature, indicating that he signs for or on behalf of a principal, or in a representative character, he is not personally liable thereon; but the mere addition to his signature of words describing him as an agent, or as filling a representative character, does not exempt him from personal liability.

(2) In determining whether a signature on a bill is that of the principal or that of the agent by whose hand it is written, the construction most favourable to the validity of the instrument shall be adopted.

The consideration for a bill

27 Value and holder for value

(1) Valuable consideration for a bill may be constituted by,—

(a) Any consideration sufficient to support a simple contract;

(b) An antecedent debt or liability. Such a debt or liability is deemed valuable consideration whether the bill is payable on demand or at a future time.

(2) Where value has at any time been given for a bill the holder is deemed to be a holder for value as regards the acceptor and all parties to the bill who became parties prior to such time.

(3) Where the holder of a bill has a lien on it, arising either from contract or by implication of law, he is deemed to be a holder for value to the extent of the sum for which he has a lien.

28 Accommodation bill or party

(1) An accommodation party to a bill is a person who has signed a bill as drawer, acceptor, or indorser, without receiving value therefor, and for the purpose of lending his name to some other person.

(2) An accommodation party is liable on the bill to a holder for value; and it is immaterial whether, when such holder took the bill, he knew such party to be an accommodation party or not.

29 Holder in due course

(1) A holder in due course is a holder who has taken a bill, complete and regular on the face of it, under the following conditions, namely,

(a) That he became the holder of it before it was overdue, and without notice that it had been previously dishonoured, if such was the fact;

(b) That he took the bill in good faith and for value, and that at the time the bill was negotiated to him he had no notice of any defect in the title of the person who negotiated it.

(2) In particular the title of a person who negotiates a bill is defective within

the meaning of this Act when he obtained the bill, or the acceptance thereof, by fraud, duress or force and fear, or other unlawful means, or for an illegal consideration, or when he negotiates it in breach of faith, or under such circumstances as amount to a fraud.

(3) A holder (whether for value or not), who derives his title to a bill through a holder in due course, and who is not himself a party to any fraud or illegality affecting it, has all the rights of that holder in due course as regards the acceptor and all parties to the bill prior to that holder.

30 Presumption of value and good faith

(1) Every party whose signature appears on a bill is prima facie deemed to have become a party thereto for value.

(2) Every holder of a bill is prima facie deemed to be a holder in due course; but if in an action on a bill it is admitted or proved that the acceptance, issue, or subsequent negotiation of the bill is affected with fraud, duress, or force and fear, or illegality, the burden of proof is shifted, unless and until the holder proves that, subsequent to the alleged fraud or illegality, value has in good faith been given for the bill.

Negotiation of bills

31 Negotiation of bill

(1) A bill is negotiated when it is transferred from one person to another in such a manner as to constitute the transferee the holder of the bill.

(2) A bill payable to bearer is negotiated by delivery.

(3) A bill payable to order is negotiated by the indorsement of the holder completed by delivery.

(4) Where the holder of a bill payable to his order transfers it for value without indorsing it, the transfer gives the transferee such title as the transferor had in the bill, and the transferee in addition acquires the right to have the indorsement of the transferor.

(5) Where any person is under obligation to indorse a bill in a representative capacity, he may indorse a bill in such terms as to negative personal liability.

32 Requisites of a valid indorsement

An indorsement in order to operate as a negotiation must comply with the following conditions, namely:—

(1) It must be written on the bill itself and signed by the indorser. The simple signature of the indorser on the bill, without additional words, is sufficient.

An indorsement written on an allonge, or a 'copy' of a bill issued or negotiated in a country where 'copies' are recognised, is deemed to have been written on the bill itself.

(2) It must be an indorsement of the entire bill. A partial indorsement, that is to say, an indorsement which purports to transfer to the indorsee a part only of the amount payable, or which purports to transfer the bill to two or more indorsees severally, does not operate as a negotiation of the bill.

(3) Where a bill is payable to the order of two or more payees or indorsees who are not partners all must indorse, unless the one indorsing has authority to indorse for the others.

(4) Where, in a bill payable to order, the payee or indorsee is wrongly designated, or his name is mis-spelt, he may indorse the bill as therein described, adding, if he think fit, his proper signature.

(5) Where there are two or more indorsements on a bill, each indorsement is deemed to have been made in the order in which it appears on the bill, until the contrary is proved.

(6) An indorsement may be made in blank or special. It may also contain terms making it restrictive.

33 Conditional indorsement
Where a bill purports to be indorsed conditionally the condition may be disregarded by the payer, and payment to the indorsee is valid whether the condition has been fulfilled or not.

34 Indorsement in blank and special indorsement
(1) An indorsement in blank specifies no indorsee, and a bill so indorsed becomes payable to bearer.

(2) A special indorsement specifies the person to whom, or to whose order, the bill is to be payable.

(3) The provisions of this Act relating to a payee apply with the necessary modifications to an indorsee under a special indorsement.

(4) When a bill has been indorsed in blank, any holder may convert the blank indorsement into a special indorsement by writing above the indorser's signature a direction to pay the bill to or to the order of himself or some other person.

35 Restrictive indorsement
(1) An indorsement is restrictive which prohibits the further negotiation of the bill or which expresses that it is a mere authority to deal with the bill as thereby directed and not a transfer of ownership thereof, as, for example, if a bill be indorsed 'Pay D. only', or 'Pay D. for the account of X.,' or 'Pay D. or order for collection.'

(2) A restrictive indorsement gives the indorsee the right to receive payment of the bill and to sue any party thereto that his indorser could have sued, but gives him no power to transfer his rights as indorsee unless it expressly authorises him to do so.

(3) Where a restrictive indorsement authorises further transfer, all subsequent indorsees take the bill with the same rights and subject to the same liabilities as the first indorsee under the restrictive indorsement.

36 Negotiation of overdue or dishonoured bills
(1) Where a bill is negotiable in its origin it continues to be negotiable until it has been (a) restrictively indorsed or (b) discharged by payment or otherwise.

(2) Where an overdue bill is negotiated, it can only be negotiated subject to any defect of title affecting it at its maturity, and thenceforward no person who takes it can acquire or give a better title than that which the person from whom he took it had.

(3) A bill payable on demand is deemed to be overdue within the meaning and for the purposes of this section, when it appears on the face of it to have been in circulation for an unreasonable length of time. What is an unreasonable length of time for this purpose is a question of fact.

(4) Except where an indorsement bears date after the maturity of the bill, every negotiation is prima facie deemed to have been effected before the bill was overdue.

(5) Where a bill which is not overdue has been dishonoured any person who takes it with notice of the dishonour takes it subject to any defect of title attaching thereto at the time of dishonour, but nothing in this sub-section shall affect the rights of a holder in due course.

37 Negotiation of bill to party already liable thereon
Where a bill is negotiated back to the drawer, or to a prior indorser or to the acceptor, such party may, subject to the provisions of this Act, reissue and further negotiate the bill, but he is not entitled to enforce payment of the bill against any intervening party to whom he was previously liable.

38 Rights of the holder
The rights and powers of the holder of a bill are as follows:

(1) He may sue on the bill in his own name:

(2)   Where he is a holder in due course, he holds the bill free from any defect of title of prior parties, as well as from mere personal defences available to prior parties among themselves, and may enforce payment against all parties liable on the bill:

(3)   Where his title is defective (a) if he negotiates the bill to a holder in due course, that holder obtains a good and complete title to the bill, and (b) if he obtains payment of the bill the person who pays him in due course gets a valid discharge for the bill.

General duties of the holder

39   When presentment for acceptance is necessary

(1)   Where a bill is payable after sight, presentment for acceptance is necessary in order to fix the maturity of the instrument.

(2)   Where a bill expressly stipulates that it shall be presented for acceptance, or where a bill is drawn payable elsewhere than at the residence or place of business of the drawee, it must be presented for acceptance before it can be presented for payment.

(3)   In no other case is presentment for acceptance necessary in order to render liable any party to the bill.

(4)   Where the holder of a bill, drawn payable elsewhere than at the place of business or residence of the drawee, has not time, with the exercise of reasonable diligence, to present the bill for acceptance before presenting it for payment on the day that it falls due, the delay caused by presenting the bill for acceptance before presenting it for payment is excused, and does not discharge the drawer and the indorsers.

40   Time for presenting bill payable after sight

(1)   Subject to the provisions of this Act, when a bill payable after sight is nego-tiated, the holder must either present it for acceptance or negotiate it within a reasonable time.

(2)   If he do not do so, the drawer and all indorsers prior to that holder are discharged.

(3)   In determining what is a reasonable time within the meaning of this section, regard shall be had to the nature of the bill, the usage of trade with respect to similar bills, and the facts of the particular case.

41   Rules as to presentment for acceptance and excuses for non-presentment

(1)   A bill is duly presented for acceptance which is presented in accordance with the following rules:

(a)   The presentment must be made by or on behalf of the holder to the drawee or to some person authorised to accept or refuse acceptance on his behalf at a reasonable hour on a business day and before the bill is overdue:

(b)   Where a bill is addressed to two or more drawees, who are not partners, presentment must be made to them all, unless one has authority to accept for them all, then presentment must be made to him only:

(c)   Where the drawee is dead, presentment may be made to his personal representative:

(d)   Where the drawee is bankrupt, presentment may be made to him or to his trustee:

(e)   Where authorised by agreement or usage, a presentment through [a postal operator] is sufficient.

(2)   Presentment in accordance with these rules is excused, and a bill may be treated as dishonoured by non-acceptance—

(a)   Where the drawee is dead or bankrupt, or is a fictitious person or a person not having capacity to contract by bill:

(b)   Where, after the exercise of reasonable diligence, such presentment cannot be effected:

(c)   Where although the presentment has been irregular, acceptance has been refused on some other ground.

(3)   The fact that the holder has reason to believe that the bill, on presentment, will be dishonoured does not excuse presentment.

42   Non-acceptance

(1)   When a bill is duly presented for acceptance and is not accepted within the customary time, the person presenting it must treat it as dishonoured by non-acceptance. If he does not, the holder shall lose his right of recourse against the drawer and indorsers.

43   Dishonour by non-acceptance and its consequences

(1)   A bill is dishonoured by non-acceptance—

(a)   when it is duly presented for acceptance, and such an acceptance as is prescribed by this Act is refused or cannot be obtained; or

(b)   when presentment for acceptance is excused and the bill is not accepted.

(2)   Subject to the provisions of this Act when a bill is dishonoured by non-acceptance an immediate right of recourse against the drawer and indorsers accrues to the holder, and no presentment for payment is necessary.

44   Duties as to qualified acceptances

(1)   The holder of a bill may refuse to take a qualified acceptance, and if he does not obtain an unqualified acceptance may treat the bill as dishonoured by non-acceptance.

(2)   Where a qualified acceptance is taken, and the drawer or an indorser has not expressly or impliedly authorised the holder to take a qualified acceptance, or does not subsequently assent thereto, such drawer or indorser is discharged from his liability on the bill.

The provisions of this sub-section do not apply to a partial acceptance, whereof due notice has been given. Where a foreign bill has been accepted as to part, it must be protested as to the balance.

(3)   When the drawer or indorser of a bill receives notice of a qualified acceptance, and does not within a reasonable time express his dissent to the holder he shall be deemed to have assented thereto.

45   Rules as to presentment for payment

Subject to the provisions of this Act a bill must be duly presented for payment. If it be not so presented the drawer and indorsers shall be discharged.

A bill is duly presented for payment which is presented in accordance with the following rules:—

(1)   Where the bill is not payable on demand, presentment must be made on the day it falls due.

(2)   Where the bill is payable on demand then, subject to the provisions of this Act, presentment must be made within a reasonable time after its issue in order to render the drawer liable, and within a reasonable time after the indorsement, in order to render the indorser liable.

In determining what is a reasonable time, regard shall be had to the nature of the bill, the usage of trade with regard to similar bills, and the facts of the particular case.

(3)   Presentment must be made by the holder or by some person authorised to receive payment on his behalf at a reasonable hour on a business day, at the proper place as hereinafter defined, either to the person designated by the bill as payer, or to some person authorised to pay or refuse payment on his behalf if with the exercise of reasonable diligence such person can there be found.

(4)   A bill is presented at the proper place:—

(a)   Where a place of payment is specified in the bill and the bill is there presented.

(b)   Where no place of payment is specified, but the address of the drawee or acceptor is given in the bill, and the bill is there presented.

(c)   Where no place of payment is specified and no address given, and the bill is presented at the drawee's or acceptor's place of business if known, and if not, at his ordinary residence if known.

(d)   In any other case if presented to the drawer or acceptor wherever he can be found, or if presented at his last known place of business or residence.

(5)   Where a bill is presented at the proper place, and after the exercise of reasonable diligence no person authorised to pay or refuse payment can be found there, no further presentment to the drawee or acceptor is required.

(6)   Where a bill is drawn upon, or accepted by two or more persons who are not partners, and no place of payment is specified, presentment must be made to them all.

(7)   Where the drawee or acceptor of a bill is dead, and no place of payment is specified, presentment must be made to a personal representative, if such there be, and with the exercise of reasonable diligence he can be found.

(8)   Where authorised by agreement or usage a presentment through [a postal operator] is sufficient.

46   Excuses for delay or non-presentment for payment

(1)   Delay in making presentment for payment is excused when the delay is caused by circumstances beyond the control of the holder, and not imputable to his default, misconduct, or negligence. When the cause of delay ceases to operate presentment must be made with reasonable diligence.

(2)   Presentment for payment is dispensed with,—

(a)   Where, after the exercise of reasonable diligence presentment, as required by this Act, cannot be effected.

The fact that the holder has reason to believe that the bill will, on presentment, be dishonoured, does not dispense with the necessity for presentment.

(b)   Where the drawee is a fictitious person.

(c)   As regards the drawer where the drawee or acceptor is not bound, as between himself and the drawee, to accept or pay the bill, and the drawer has no reason to believe that the bill would be paid if presented.

(d)   As regards an indorser, where the bill was accepted or made for the accommodation of the indorser, and he has no reason to expect that the bill would be paid if presented.

(e)   By waiver of presentment, express or implied.

47   Dishonour by non-payment

(1)   A bill is dishonoured by non-payment (a) when it is duly presented for payment and payment is refused or cannot be obtained, or (b) when presentment is excused and the bill is overdue and unpaid.

(2)   Subject to the provisions of this Act, when a bill is dishonoured by non-payment, an immediate right of recourse against the drawer and indorsers accrues to the holder.

48   Notice of dishonour and effect of non-notice

Subject to the provisions of this Act, when a bill has been dishonoured by non-acceptance or by non-payment, notice of dishonour must be given to the drawer and each indorser, and any drawer or indorser to whom such notice is not given is discharged; Provided that—

(1)   Where a bill is dishonoured by non-acceptance, and notice of dishonour is not given, the rights of the holder in due course subsequent to the omission, shall not be prejudiced by the omission.

(2)   Where a bill is dishonoured by non-acceptance and due notice of dishonour is given, it shall not be necessary to give notice of a subsequent dishonour by non-payment unless the bill shall in the meantime have been accepted.

49   Rules as to notice of dishonour
Notice of dishonour in order to be valid and effectual must be given in accordance with the following rules:—
(1)   The notice must be given by or on behalf of the holder, or by or on behalf of an indorser who, at the time of giving it, is himself liable on the bill.
(2)   Notice of dishonour may be given by an agent either in his own name, or in the name of any party entitled to give notice whether that party be his principal or not.
(3)   Where the notice is given by or on behalf of the holder, it enures for the benefit of all subsequent holders and all prior indorsers who have a right of recourse against the party to whom it is given.
(4)   Where notice is given by or on behalf of an indorser entitled to give notice as herein-before provided, it enures for the benefit of the holder and all indorsers subsequent to the party to whom notice is given.
(5)   The notice may be given in writing or by personal communication, and may be given in any terms which sufficiently identify the bill, and intimate that the bill has been dishonoured by non-acceptance or non-payment.
(6)   The return of a dishonoured bill to the drawer or an indorser is, in point of form, deemed a sufficient notice of dishonour.
(7)   A written notice need not be signed, and an insufficient written notice may be supplemented and validated by verbal communication. A misdescription of the bill shall not vitiate the notice unless the party to whom the notice is given is in fact misled thereby.
(8)   Where notice of dishonour is required to be given to any person, it may be given either to the party himself, or to his agent in that behalf.
(9)   Where the drawer or indorser is dead, and the party giving notice knows it, the notice must be given to a personal representative if such there be, and with the exercise of reasonable diligence he can be found.
(10)   Where the drawer or indorser is bankrupt, notice may be given either to the party himself or to the trustee.
(11)   Where there are two or more drawers or indorsers who are not partners, notice must be given to each of them, unless one of them has authority to receive such notice for the others.
(12)   The notice may be given as soon as the bill is dishonoured and must be given within a reasonable time thereafter.
In the absence of special circumstances notice is not deemed to have been given within a reasonable time, unless—
(a)   where the person giving and the person to receive notice reside in the same place, the notice is given or sent off in time to reach the latter on the day after the dishonour of the bill.
(b)   where the person giving and the person to receive notice reside in different places, the notice is sent off on the day after the dishonour of the bill, if there be a post at a convenient hour on that day, and if there be no such post on that day then by the next post thereafter.
(13)   Where a bill when dishonoured is in the hands of an agent, he may either himself give notice to the parties liable on the bill, or he may give notice to his principal. If he gives notice to his principal, he must do so within the same time as if he were the holder, and the principal upon receipt of such notice has himself the same time for giving notice as if the agent had been an independent holder.
(14)   Where a party to a bill receives due notice of dishonour, he has after the receipt of such notice the same period of time for giving notice to antecedent parties that the holder has after the dishonour.

(15)   Where a notice of dishonour is duly addressed and posted, the sender is deemed to have given due notice of dishonour, notwithstanding any miscarriage by the [postal operator concerned].

50   Excuses for non-notice and delay
(1)   Delay in giving notice of dishonour is excused where the delay is caused by circumstances beyond the control of the party giving notice, and not imputable to his default, misconduct, or negligence. When the cause of delay ceases to operate the notice must be given with reasonable diligence.
(2)   Notice of dishonour is dispensed with—
    (a)   When, after the exercise of reasonable diligence, notice as required by this Act cannot be given to or does not reach the drawer or indorser sought to be charged:
    (b)   By waiver express or implied. Notice of dishonour may be waived before the time of giving notice has arrived, or after the omission to give due notice:
    (c)   As regards the drawer in the following cases, namely, (1) where drawer and drawee are the same person, (2) where the drawee is a fictitious person or a person not having capacity to contract, (3) where the drawer is the person to whom the bill is presented for payment, (4) where the drawee or acceptor is as between himself and the drawer under no obligation to accept or pay the bill, (5) where the drawer has countermanded payment:
    (d)   As regards the indorser in the following cases, namely, (1) where the drawee is a fictitious person or a person not having the capacity to contract and the indorser was aware of the fact at the time he indorsed the bill, (2) where the indorser is the person to whom the bill is presented for payment, (3) where the bill was accepted or made for his accommodation.

51   Noting or protest of bill
(1)   Where an inland bill has been dishonoured it may, if the holder think fit, be noted for non-acceptance or non-payment, as the case may be; but it shall not be necessary to note or protest any such bill in order to preserve the recourse against the drawer or indorser.
(2)   Where a foreign bill, appearing on the face of it to be such, has been dishonoured by non-acceptance it must be duly protested for non-acceptance and where such a bill, which has not been previously dishonoured by non-acceptance, is dishonoured by non-payment it must be duly protested for non-payment. If it be not so protested the drawer and indorsers are discharged. Where a bill does not appear on the face of it to be a foreign bill, protest thereof in the case of dishonour is unnecessary.
(3)   A bill which has been protested for non-acceptance may be subsequently protested for non-payment.
(4)   Subject to the provisions of this Act, when a bill is noted or protested, [it may be noted on the day of its dishonour and must be noted not later than the next succeeding business day]. When a bill has been duly noted, the protest may be subsequently extended as of the date of the noting.
(5)   Where the acceptor of the bill becomes bankrupt or insolvent or suspends payment before it matures, the holder may cause the bill to be protested for better security against the drawer and indorsers.
(6)   A bill must be protested at the place where it is dishonoured: Provided that—
    (a)   When a bill is presented through [a postal operator], and returned by post dishonoured, it may be protested at the place to which it is returned and on the day of its return if received during business hours, and if not received during business hours, then not later than the next business day:
    (b)   When a bill drawn payable at the place of business or residence of some person other than the drawee, has been dishonoured by non-acceptance, it must be protested for non-payment at the place where it is expressed to be payable,

and no further presentment for payment to, or demand on, the drawee is necessary.

(7)   A protest must contain a copy of the bill, and must be signed by the notary making it, and must specify—

(a)   The person at whose request the bill is protested:

(b)   The place and date of protest, the cause or reason for protesting the bill, the demand made, and the answer given, if any, or the fact that the drawee or acceptor could not be found.

[(7A)   In subsection (7) 'notary' includes a person who, for the purposes of the Legal Services Act 2007, is an authorised person in relation to any activity which constitutes a notarial activity (within the meaning of that Act).]

(8)   Where a bill is lost or destroyed, or is wrongly detained from the person entitled to hold it, protest may be made on a copy or written particulars thereof.

(9)   Protest is dispensed with by any circumstance which would dispense with notice of dishonour. Delay in noting or protesting is excused when the delay is caused by circumstances beyond the control of the holder, and not imputable to his default, misconduct, or negligence. When the cause of delay ceases to operate the bill must be noted or protested with reasonable diligence.

52   Duties of holder as regards drawee or acceptor

(1)   When a bill is accepted generally presentment for payment is not necessary in order to render the acceptor liable.

(2)   When by the terms of a qualified acceptance presentment for payment is required, the acceptor, in the absence of an express stipulation to that effect, is not discharged by the omission to present the bill for payment on the day that it matures.

(3)   In order to render the acceptor of a bill liable it is not necessary to protest it, or that notice of dishonour should be given to him.

(4)   Where the holder of a bill presents it for payment, he shall exhibit the bill to the person from whom he demands payment, and when a bill is paid the holder shall forthwith deliver it up to the party paying it.

Liabilities of parties

53   Funds in hands of drawee

(1)   [*Does not apply to Scotland.*]

(2)   In Scotland, where the drawee of a bill [other than a cheque] has in his hands funds available for the payment thereof, the bill operates as an assignment of the sum for which it is drawn in favour of the holder, from the time when the bill is presented to the drawee.

54   Liability of acceptor

The acceptor of a bill, by accepting it—

(1)   Engages that he will pay it according to the tenour of his acceptance:

(2)   Is precluded from denying to a holder in due course:

(a)   The existence of the drawer, the genuineness of his signature, and his capacity and authority to draw the bill;

(b)   In the case of a bill payable to drawer's order, the then capacity of the drawer to indorse, but not the genuineness or validity of his indorsement;

(c)   In the case of a bill payable to the order of a third person, the existence of the payee and his then capacity to indorse, but not the genuineness or validity of his indorsement.

55   Liability of drawer or indorser

(1)   The drawer of a bill by drawing it—

(a)   Engages that on due presentment it shall be accepted and paid according to its tenour, and that if it be dishonoured he will compensate the holder or any indorser who is compelled to pay it, provided that the requisite proceedings on dishonour be duly taken;

(b)   Is precluded from denying to a holder in due course the existence of the payee and his then capacity to indorse.

(2)   The indorser of a bill by indorsing it—

(a)   Engages that on due presentment it shall be accepted and paid according to its tenour, and that if it be dishonoured he will compensate the holder or a subsequent indorser who is compelled to pay it, provided that the requisite proceedings on dishonour be duly taken;

(b)   Is precluded from denying to a holder in due course the genuineness and regularity in all respects of the drawer's signature and all previous indorsements;

(c)   Is precluded from denying to his immediate or a subsequent indorsee that the bill was at the time of his indorsement a valid and subsisting bill, and that he had then a good title thereto.

56   Stranger signing bill liable as indorser

Where a person signs a bill otherwise than as drawer or acceptor, he thereby incurs the liabilities of an indorser to a holder in due course.

57   Measure of damages against parties to dishonoured bill

Where a bill is dishonoured, the measure of damages, which shall be deemed to be liquidated damages, shall be as follows:

(1)   The holder may recover from any party liable on the bill, and the drawer who has been compelled to pay the bill may recover from the acceptor, and an indorser who has been compelled to pay the bill may recover from the acceptor or from the drawer, or from a prior indorser—

(a)   The amount of the bill:

(b)   Interest thereon from the time of presentment for payment if the bill is payable on demand, and from the maturity of the bill in any other case:

(c)   The expenses of noting, or, when protest is necessary, and the protest has been extended, the expenses of protest.

[. . .]

(3)   Where by this Act interest may be recovered as damages, such interest may, if justice require it, be withheld wholly or in part, and where a bill is expressed to be payable with interest at a given rate, interest as damages may or may not be given at the same rate as interest proper.

58   Transferor by delivery and transferee

(1)   Where the holder of a bill payable to bearer negotiates it by delivery without indorsing it, he is called a 'transferor by delivery'.

(2)   A transferor by delivery is not liable on the instrument.

(3)   A transferor by delivery who negotiates a bill thereby warrants to his immediate transferee being a holder for value that the bill is what it purports to be, that he has a right to transfer it, and that at the time of the transfer he is not aware of any fact which renders it valueless.

Discharge of bill

59   Payment in due course

(1)   A bill is discharged by payment in due course by or on behalf of the drawee or acceptor.

'Payment in due course' means payment made at or after the maturity of the bill to the holder thereof in good faith and without notice that his title to the bill is defective.

(2)   Subject to the provisions herein-after contained, when a bill is paid by the drawer or an indorser it is not discharged; but

(a)   Where a bill payable to, or to the order of, a third party is paid by the drawer, the drawer may enforce payment thereof against the acceptor, but may not re-issue the bill.

(b)   Where a bill is paid by an indorser, or where a bill payable to drawer's order is paid by the drawer, the party paying it is remitted to his former rights as regards the acceptor or antecedent parties, and he may, if he thinks fit, strike out his own and subsequent indorsements, and again negotiate the bill.

(3)   Where an accommodation bill is paid in due course by the party accommodated the bill is discharged.

60   Banker paying demand draft whereon indorsement is forged

When a bill payable to order on demand is drawn on a banker, and the banker on whom it is drawn pays the bill in good faith and in the ordinary course of business, it is not incumbent on the banker to show that the indorsement of the payee or any subsequent indorsement was made by or under the authority of the person whose indorsement it purports to be, and the banker is deemed to have paid the bill in due course, although such indorsement has been forged or made without authority.

61   Acceptor the holder at maturity

When the acceptor of a bill is or becomes the holder of it at or after its maturity, in his own right, the bill is discharged.

62   Express waiver

(1)   When the holder of a bill at or after its maturity absolutely and unconditionally renounces his rights against the acceptor the bill is discharged.

The renunciation must be in writing, unless the bill is delivered up to the acceptor.

(2)   The liabilities of any party to a bill may in like manner be renounced by the holder before, at, or after its maturity; but nothing in this section shall affect the rights of a holder in due course without notice of the renunciation.

63   Cancellation

(1)   Where a bill is intentionally cancelled by the holder or his agent, and the cancellation is apparent thereon, the bill is discharged.

(2)   In like manner any party liable on a bill may be discharged by the intentional cancellation of his signature by the holder or his agent. In such case any indorser who would have had a right of recourse against the party whose signature is cancelled, is also discharged.

(3)   A cancellation made unintentionally, or under a mistake, or without the authority of the holder is inoperative; but where a bill or any signature thereon appears to have been cancelled the burden of proof lies on the party who alleges that the cancellation was made unintentionally, or under a mistake, or without authority.

64   Alteration of bill

(1)   Where a bill or acceptance is materially altered without the assent of all parties liable on the bill, the bill is avoided except as against a party who has himself made, authorised, or assented to the alteration, and subsequent indorsers.

Provided that,

Where a bill has been materially altered, but the alteration is not apparent, and the bill is in the hands of a holder in due course, such holder may avail himself of the bill as if it had not been altered, and may enforce payment of it according to its original tenour.

(2)   In particular the following alterations are material, namely, any alteration of the date, the sum payable, the time of payment, the place of payment, and where a bill has been accepted generally, the addition of a place of payment without the acceptor's assent.

Acceptance and payment for honour

65 Acceptance for honour supra protest

(1) Where a bill of exchange has been protested for dishonour by non-acceptance, or protested for better security, and is not overdue, any person, not being a party already liable thereon, may, with the consent of the holder, intervene and accept the bill supra protest, for the honour of any party liable thereon, or for the honour of the person for whose account the bill is drawn.

(2) A bill may be accepted for honour for part only of the sum for which it is drawn.

(3) An acceptance for honour supra protest in order to be valid must—

(a) be written on the bill, and indicate that it is an acceptance for honour;

(b) be signed by the acceptor for honour.

(4) Where an acceptance for honour does not expressly state for whose honour it is made, it is deemed to be an acceptance for the honour of the drawer.

(5) Where a bill payable after sight is accepted for honour, its maturity is calculated from the date of the noting for non-acceptance, and not from the date of the acceptance for honour.

66 Liability of acceptor for honour

(1) The acceptor for honour of a bill by accepting it engages that he will, on due presentment, pay the bill according to the tenour of his acceptance, if it is not paid by the drawee, provided it has been duly presented for payment, and protested for non-payment, and that he receives notice of these facts.

(2) The acceptor for honour is liable to the holder and to all parties to the bill subsequent to the party for whose honour he has accepted.

67 Presentment to acceptor for honour

(1) Where a dishonoured bill has been accepted for honour supra protest, or contains a reference in case of need, it must be protested for non-payment before it is presented for payment to the acceptor for honour, or referee in case of need.

(2) Where the address of the acceptor for honour is in the same place where the bill is protested for non-payment, the bill must be presented to him not later than the day following its maturity; and where the address of the acceptor for honour is in some place other than the place where it was protested for non-payment, the bill must be forwarded not later than the day following its maturity for presentment to him.

(3) Delay in presentment or non-presentment is excused by any circumstances which would excuse delay in presentment for payment or non-presentment for payment.

(4) When a bill of exchange is dishonoured by the acceptor for honour it must be protested for non-payment by him.

68 Payment for honour supra protest

(1) Where a bill has been protested for non-payment any person may intervene and pay it supra protest for the honour of any party liable thereon, or for the honour of the person for whose account the bill is drawn.

(2) Where two or more persons offer to pay a bill for the honour of different parties, the person whose payment will discharge most parties to the bill shall have the preference.

(3) Payment for honour supra protest, in order to operate as such and not as a mere voluntary payment, must be attested by a notarial act of honour which may be appended to the protest or form an extension of it.

(4) The notarial act of honour must be founded on a declaration made by the payer for honour, or his agent in that behalf, declaring his intention to pay the bill for honour, and for whose honour he pays.

(5) Where a bill has been paid for honour, all parties subsequent to the party for whose honour it is paid are discharged, but the payer for honour is subrogated

for, and succeeds to both the rights and duties of, the holder as regards the party
for whose honour he pays, and all parties liable to that party.

(6)   The payer for honour on paying to the holder the amount of the bill and
the notarial expenses incidental to its dishonour is entitled to receive both the bill
itself and the protest. If the holder do not on demand deliver them up he shall be
liable to the payer for honour in damages.

(7)   Where the holder of a bill refuses to receive payment supra protest he shall
lose his right of recourse against any party who would have been discharged by
such payment.

Lost instruments

69   Holder's right to duplicate of lost bill

Where a bill has been lost before it is overdue, the person who was the holder of it
may apply to the drawer to give him another bill of the same tenour, giving security to the drawer if required to indemnify him against all persons whatever in
case the bill alleged to have been lost shall be found again.

If the drawer on request as aforesaid refuses to give such duplicate bill, he may
be compelled to do so.

70   Action on lost bill

In any action or proceeding upon a bill, the court or a judge may order that the
loss of the instrument shall not be set up, provided an indemnity be given to the
satisfaction of the court or judge against the claims of any other person upon the
instrument in question.

Bill in a set

71   Rules as to sets

(1)   Where a bill is drawn in a set, each part of the set being numbered and
containing a reference to the other parts, the whole of the parts constitute one bill.

(2)   Where the holder of a set indorses two or more parts to different persons,
he is liable to every such part, and every indorser subsequent to him is liable on
the part he has himself indorsed as if the said parts were separate bills.

(3)   Where two or more parts of a set are negotiated to different holders in due
course, the holder whose title first accrues is as between such holders deemed the
true owner of the bill; but nothing in this sub-section shall affect the rights of a
person who in due course accepts or pays the part first presented to him.

(4)   The acceptance may be written on any part, and it must be written on one
part only.

If the drawee accepts more than one part, and such accepted parts get into the
hands of different holders in due course, he is liable on every such part as if it
were a separate bill.

(5)   When the acceptor of a bill drawn in a set pays it without requiring the part
bearing the acceptance to be delivered up to him, and that part at maturity is outstanding in the hands of a holder in due course, he is liable to the holder thereof.

(6)   Subject to the preceding rules, where any one part of a bill drawn in a set is
discharged by payment or otherwise, the whole bill is discharged.

Conflict of laws

72   Rules where laws conflict

Where a bill drawn in one country is negotiated, accepted, or payable in another,
the rights, duties, and liabilities of the parties thereto are determined as follows:

(1)   The validity of a bill as regards requisites in form is determined by the law
of the place of issue, and the validity as regards requisites in form of the super-
vening contracts, such as acceptance, or indorsement, or acceptance supra protest,
is determined by the law of the place where such contract was made.

Provided that—

(a)   Where a bill is issued out of the United Kingdom it is not invalid by reason only that it is not stamped in accordance with the law of the place of issue:

(b)   Where a bill, issued out of the United Kingdom, conforms, as regards requisites in form, to the law of the United Kingdom, it may, for the purpose of enforcing payment thereof, be treated as valid as between all persons who negotiate, hold, or become parties to it in the United Kingdom.

(2)   Subject to the provisions of this Act, the interpretation of the drawing, indorsement, acceptance, or acceptance supra protest of a bill, is determined by the law of the place where such contract is made.

Provided that where an inland bill is indorsed in a foreign country the indorsement shall as regards the payer be interpreted according to the law of the United Kingdom.

(3)   The duties of the holder with respect to presentment for acceptance or payment and the necessity for or sufficiency of a protest or notice of dishonour, or otherwise, are determined by the law of the place where the act is done or the bill is dishonoured.

[. . .]

(5)   Where a bill is drawn in one country and is payable in another, the due date thereof is determined according to the law of the place where it is payable.

PART III

CHEQUES ON A BANKER

73   Cheque defined

A cheque is a bill of exchange drawn on a banker payable on demand. Except as otherwise provided in this Part, the provisions of this Act applicable to a bill of exchange payable on demand apply to a cheque.

74   Presentment of cheque for payment

Subject to the provisions of this Act—

(1)   Where a cheque is not presented for payment within a reasonable time of its issue, and the drawer or the person on whose account it is drawn had the right at the time of such presentment as between him and the banker to have the cheque paid and suffers actual damage through the delay, he is discharged to the extent of such damage, that is to say, to the extent to which such drawer or person is a creditor of such banker to a larger amount than he would have been had such cheque been paid.

(2)   In determining what is a reasonable time regard shall be had to the nature of the instrument, the usage of trade and of bankers, and the facts of the particular case.

(3)   The holder of such cheque as to which such drawer or person is discharged shall be a creditor, in lieu of such drawer or person, of such banker to the extent of such discharge, and entitled to recover the amount from him.

[. . .]

[74B   Presentment of cheque for payment: alternative means of presentment by banker

(1)   A banker may present a cheque for payment to the banker on whom it is drawn by notifying him of its essential features by electronic means or otherwise, instead of by presenting the cheque itself.

(2)   If a cheque is presented for payment under this section, presentment need not be made at the proper place or at a reasonable hour on a business day.

(3)   If, before the close of business on the next business day following presentment of a cheque under this section, the banker on whom the cheque is drawn requests the banker by whom the cheque was presented to present the cheque itself—

    (a)   the presentment under this section shall be disregarded, and

    (b)   this section shall not apply in relation to the subsequent presentment of the cheque.

    (4)   A request under subsection (3) above for the presentment of a cheque shall not constitute dishonour of the cheque by non-payment.

    (5)   Where presentment of a cheque is made under this section, the banker who presented the cheque and the banker on whom it is drawn shall be subject to the same duties in relation to the collection and payment of the cheque as if the cheque itself had been presented for payment.

    (6)   For the purposes of this section, the essential features of a cheque are—

    (a)   the serial number of the cheque,

    (b)   the code which identifies the banker on whom the cheque is drawn,

    (c)   the account number of the drawer of the cheque, and

    (d)   the amount of the cheque is entered by the drawer of the cheque.]

[74C Cheques presented for payment under section 74B: disapplication of section 52(4)

Section 52(4) above—

    (a)   so far as relating to presenting a bill for payment, shall not apply to presenting a cheque for payment under section 74B above, and

    (b)   so far as relating to a bill which is paid, shall not apply to a cheque which is paid following presentment under that section.]

75 Revocation of banker's authority

The duty and authority of a banker to pay a cheque drawn on him by his customer are determined by—

    (1)   Countermand of payment:

    (2)   Notice of the customer's death.

[. . .]

Crossed cheques

76 General and special crossings defined

    (1)   Where a cheque bears across its face an addition of—

    (a)   The words 'and company' or any abbreviation thereof between two parallel transverse lines either with or without the words 'not negotiable'; or

    (b)   Two parallel transverse lines simply, either with or without the words 'not negotiable';

that addition constitutes a crossing, and the cheque is crossed generally.

    (2)   Where a cheque bears across its face an addition of the name of a banker, either with or without the words 'not negotiable', that addition constitutes a crossing, and the cheque is crossed specially and to that banker.

77 Crossing by drawer or after issue

    (1)   A cheque may be crossed generally or specially by the drawer.

    (2)   Where a cheque is uncrossed, the holder may cross it generally or specially.

    (3)   Where a cheque is crossed generally, the holder may cross it specially.

    (4)   Where a cheque is crossed generally or specially, the holder may add the words 'not negotiable'.

    (5)   Where a cheque is crossed specially, the banker to whom it is crossed may again cross it specially to another banker for collection.

    (6)   Where an uncrossed cheque, or a cheque crossed generally is sent to a banker for collection, he may cross it specially to himself.

78 Crossing a material part of cheque

A crossing authorised by this Act is a material part of the cheque; it shall not be lawful for any person to obliterate or, except as authorised by this Act, to add to or alter the crossing.

79 Duties of banker as to crossed cheques

(1) Where a cheque is crossed specially to more than one banker except when crossed to an agent for collection being a banker, the banker on whom it is drawn shall refuse payment thereof.

(2) Where the banker on whom a cheque is drawn which is so crossed nevertheless pays the same, or pays a cheque crossed generally otherwise than to a banker, or if crossed specially otherwise than to the banker to whom it is crossed, or his agent for collection being a banker, he is liable to the true owner of the cheque for any loss he may sustain owing to the cheque having been so paid.

Provided that where a cheque is presented for payment which does not at the time of presentment appear to be crossed, or to have had a crossing which had been obliterated, or to have been added to or altered otherwise than as authorised by this Act, the banker paying the cheque in good faith and without negligence shall not be responsible or incur any liability, nor shall the payment be questioned by reason of the cheque having been crossed, or of the crossing having been obliterated on having been added to or altered otherwise than as authorised by this Act, and of payment having been made otherwise than to a banker or to the banker to whom the cheque is or was crossed, or to his agent for collection being a banker as the case may be.

80 Protection to banker and drawer where cheque is crossed

Where the banker, on whom a crossed cheque [(including a cheque which under section 81A below or otherwise is not transferable)] is drawn in good faith and without negligence pays it, if crossed generally to a banker, and if crossed specially, to the banker to whom it is crossed, or his agent for collection being a banker, the banker paying the cheque, and, if the cheque has come into the hands of the payee, the drawer, shall respectively be entitled to the same rights and be placed in the same position as if payment of the cheque had been made to the true owner thereof.

81 Effect of crossing on holder

Where a person takes a crossed cheque which bears on it the words 'not negotiable', he shall not have and shall not be capable of giving a better title to the cheque than that which the person from whom he took it had.

[81A Non-transferable cheques

(1) Where a cheque is crossed and bears across its face the words 'account payee' or 'a/c payee', either with or without the words 'only', the cheque shall not be transferable, but shall only be valid as between the parties thereto.

(2) A banker is not to be treated for the purposes of section 80 above as having been negligent by reason only of his failure to concern himself with any purported indorsement of a cheque which under subsection (1) above or otherwise is not transferable.]

[. . .]

PART IV
PROMISSORY NOTES

83 Promissory note defined

(1) A promissory note is an unconditional promise in writing made by one person to another signed by the maker, engaging to pay, on demand or at a fixed or determinable future time, a sum certain in money, to, or to the order of, a specified person or to bearer.

(2) An instrument in the form of a note payable to maker's order is not a note within the meaning of this section unless and until it is indorsed by the maker.

(3) A note is not invalid by reason only that it contains also a pledge of collateral security with authority to sell or dispose thereof.

(4)   A note which is, or on the face of it purports to be, both made and payable within the British Islands is an inland note. Any other note is a foreign note.

84   Delivery necessary
A promissory note is inchoate and incomplete until delivery thereof to the payee or bearer.

85   Joint and several notes
(1)   A promissory note may be made by two or more makers, and they may be liable thereon jointly, or jointly and severally according to its tenour.

(2)   Where a note runs 'I promise to pay' and is signed by two or more persons it is deemed to be their joint and several note.

86   Note payable on demand
(1)   Where a note payable on demand has been indorsed, it must be presented for payment within a reasonable time of the indorsement. If it be not so presented the indorser is discharged.

(2)   In determining what is a reasonable time, regard shall be had to the nature of the instrument, the usage of trade, and the facts of the particular case.

(3)   Where a note payable on demand is negotiated, it is not deemed to be overdue for the purpose of affecting the holder with defects of title of which he had no notice, by reason that it appears that a reasonable time for presenting it for payment has elapsed since its issue.

87   Presentment of note for payment
(1)   Where a promissory note is in the body of it made payable at a particular place, it must be presented for payment at that place in order to render the maker liable. In any other case, presentment for payment is not necessary to render the maker liable.

(2)   Presentment for payment is necessary in order to render the indorser of a note liable.

(3)   Where a note is in the body of it made payable at a particular place, presentment at that place is necessary in order to render an indorser liable; but when a place of payment is indicated by way of memorandum only, presentment at that place is sufficient to render the indorser liable, but a presentment to the maker elsewhere, if sufficient in other respects, shall also suffice.

88   Liability of maker
The maker of a promissory note by making it—
(1)   Engages that he will pay it according to its tenour;

(2)   Is precluded from denying to a holder in due course the existence of the payee and his then capacity to indorse.

89   Application of Part II to notes
(1)   Subject to the provisions in this part and, except as by this section provided, the provisions of this Act relating to bills of exchange apply, with the necessary modifications, to promissory notes.

(2)   In applying those provisions the maker of a note shall be deemed to correspond with the acceptor of a bill, and the first indorser of a note shall be deemed to correspond with the drawer of an accepted bill payable to drawer's order.

(3)   The following provisions as to bills do not apply to notes; namely, provisions relating to—
  (a)   Presentment for acceptance;
  (b)   Acceptance;
  (c)   Acceptance supra protest;
  (d)   Bills in a set.
(4)   Where a foreign note is dishonoured, protest thereof is unnecessary.

PART V
SUPPLEMENTARY

90 Good faith
A thing is deemed to be done in good faith, within the meaning of this Act, where it is in fact done honestly, whether it is done negligently or not.

91 Signature
(1) Where, by this Act, any instrument or writing is required to be signed by any person, it is not necessary that he should sign it with his own hand, but it is sufficient if his signature is written thereon by some other person by or under his authority.

(2) In the case of a corporation, where, by this Act, any instrument or writing is required to be signed, it is sufficient if the instrument or writing be sealed with the corporate seal.

But nothing in this section shall be construed as requiring the bill or note of a corporation to be under seal.

92 Computation of time
Where, by this Act, the time limited for doing any act or thing is less than three days, in reckoning time, non-business days are excluded.

'Non-business days' for the purposes of this Act mean—

(a) [Saturday,] Sunday, Good Friday, Christmas Day;

(b) A bank holiday under [the Banking and Financial Dealings Act 1971];

(c) A day appointed by Royal proclamation as a public fast or thanksgiving day;

[(d) A day declared by an order under section 2 of the Banking and Financial Dealings Act 1971 to be a non-business day.]

Any other day is a business day.

93 When noting equivalent to protest
For the purposes of this Act, where a bill or note is required to be protested within a specified time or before some further proceeding is taken, it is sufficient that the bill has been noted for protest before the expiration of the specified time or the taking of the proceeding; and the formal protest may be extended at any time thereafter as of the date of the noting.

94 Protest when notary not accessible
[(1)] Where a dishonoured bill or note is authorised or required to be protested, and the services of a notary cannot be obtained at the place where the bill is dishonoured, any householder, or substantial resident of the place may, in the presence of two witnesses, give a certificate, signed by them, attesting to the dishonour of the bill, and the certificate shall in all respects operate as if it were a formal protest of the bill.

The form given in Schedule I to this Act may be used with necessary modifications, and if used shall be sufficient.

[(2) In subsection (1) 'notary' includes a person who, for the purposes of the Legal Services Act 2007, is an authorised person in relation to any activity which constitutes a notarial activity (within the meaning of that Act).]

95 Dividend warrants may be crossed
The provisions of this Act as to crossed cheques shall apply to a warrant for payment of dividend.

[. . .]

97 Savings
(1) The rules in bankruptcy relating to bills of exchange, promissory notes, and cheques, shall continue to apply thereto notwithstanding anything in this Act contained.

(2)   The rules of common law including the law merchant, save in so far as they are inconsistent with the express provisions of this Act, shall continue to apply to bills of exchange, promissory notes, and cheques.

(3)   Nothing in this Act or in any repeal effected thereby shall affect—

(a)   [. . .] any law or enactment for the time being in force relating to the revenue:

(b)   The provisions of the Companies Act, 1862, or Acts amending it, or any Act relating to joint stock banks or companies:

(c)   The provisions of any Act relating to or confirming the privileges of the Bank of England or the Bank of Ireland respectively:

(d)   The validity of any usage relating to dividend warrants, or the indorsements thereof.

98   Saving of summary diligence in Scotland

Nothing in this Act or in any repeal effected thereby shall extend or restrict, or in any way alter the law and practice in Scotland in regard to summary diligence.

99   Construction with other Acts, etc

Where any Act or document refers to any enactment repealed by this Act, the Act or document shall be construed, and shall operate as if it referred to the corresponding provisions of this Act.

100   Parole evidence allowed in certain judicial proceedings in Scotland

In any judicial proceeding in Scotland, any fact relating to a bill of exchange, bank cheque, or promissory note, which is relevant to any question of liability thereon, may be proved by parole evidence: Provided that this enactment shall not in any way affect the existing law and practice whereby the party who is, according to the tenour of any bill of exchange, bank cheque, or promissory note, debtor to the holder in the amount thereof, may be required, as a condition of obtaining a sist of diligence, or suspension of a charge, or threatened charge, to make such consignation, or to find such caution as the court or judge before whom the cause is depending may require. [. . .]

SCHEDULES

FIRST SCHEDULE

Section 94

Form of protest which may be used when the services of a notary cannot be obtained

Know all men that I, *A. B.* [householder], of   in the county of   in the United Kingdom, at the request of *C. D.,* there being no notary public available, did on the   day of   188   at_____ demand payment [*or* acceptance] of the bill of exchange hereunder written, from *E. F.,* to which demand he made answer [state answer, if any] wherefore I now, in the presence of *G. H.* and *J. K.* do protest the said bill of exchange.

(Signed)   A. B. ⎫
              G. H. ⎬ *Witnesses*
              J. K. ⎭

N.B.—The bill itself should be annexed, or a copy of the bill and all that is written thereon should be underwritten.

FACTORS ACT 1889
(52 & 53 Vict, c 45)

Preliminary

1 Definitions
For the purposes of this Act—

(1)   The expression 'mercantile agent' shall mean a mercantile agent having in the customary course of his business as such agent authority either to sell goods or to consign goods for the purpose of sale, or to buy goods, or to raise money on the security of goods:

(2)   A person shall be deemed to be in possession of goods or of the documents of title to goods, where the goods or documents are in the actual custody or are held by any other person subject to his control or for him or on his behalf:

(3)   The expression 'goods' shall include wares and merchandise:

(4)   The expression 'document of title' shall include any bill of lading, dock warrant, warehouse-keeper's certificate, and warrant or order for the delivery of goods, and any other document used in the ordinary course of business as proof of the possession or control of goods, or authorising or purporting to authorise, either by endorsement or by delivery, the possessor of the document to transfer or receive goods thereby represented:

(5)   The expression 'pledge' shall include any contract pledging, or giving a lien or security on, goods, whether in consideration of an original advance or of any further or continuing advance or of any pecuniary liability:

(6)   The expression 'person' shall include any body of persons corporate or unincorporated.

Dispositions by mercantile agents

2 Powers of mercantile agent with respect to disposition of goods
(1)   Where a mercantile agent is, with the consent of the owner, in possession of goods or of the documents of title to goods, any sale, pledge, or other disposition of the goods, made by him when acting in the ordinary course of business of a mercantile agent, shall, subject to the provisions of this Act, be as valid as if he were expressly authorised by the owner of the goods to make the same; provided that the person taking under the disposition acts in good faith, and has not at the time of the disposition notice that the person making the disposition has not authority to make the same.

(2)   Where a mercantile agent has, with the consent of the owner, been in possession of goods or of the documents of title to goods, any sale, pledge, or other disposition, which would have been valid if the consent had continued, shall be valid notwithstanding the determination of the consent; provided that the person taking under the disposition has not at the time thereof notice that the consent has been determined.

(3)   Where a mercantile agent has obtained possession of any documents of title to goods by reason of his being or having been, with the consent of the owner, in possession of the goods represented thereby, or of any other documents of title to the goods, his possession of the first-mentioned documents shall, for the purposes of this Act, be deemed to be with the consent of the owner.

(4)   For the purposes of this Act the consent of the owner shall be presumed in the absence of evidence to the contrary.

Dispositions by sellers and buyers of goods

8 Disposition by seller remaining in possession
Where a person, having sold goods, continues, or is, in possession of the goods or of the documents of title to the goods, the delivery or transfer by that person, or by

a mercantile agent acting for him, of the goods or documents of title under any sale, pledge, or other disposition thereof, or under any agreement for sale, pledge, or other disposition thereof, to any person receiving the same in good faith and without notice of the previous sale, shall have the same effect as if the person making the delivery or transfer were expressly authorised by the owner of the goods to make the same.

9 Disposition by buyer obtaining possession
Where a person, having bought or agreed to buy goods, obtains with the consent of the seller possession of the goods or the documents of title to the goods, the delivery or transfer, by that person or by a mercantile agent acting for him, of the goods or documents of title under any sale, pledge, or other disposition thereof, or under any agreement for sale, pledge, or other disposition thereof, to any person receiving the same in good faith and without notice of any lien or other right of the original seller in respect of the goods, shall have the same effect as if the person making the delivery or transfer were a mercantile agent in possession of the goods or documents of title with the consent of the owner.
   [For the purposes of this section—
   (i) the buyer under a conditional sale agreement shall be deemed not to be a person who has bought or agreed to buy goods, and
   (ii) 'conditional sale agreement' means an agreement for the sale of goods which is a consumer credit agreement within the meaning of the Consumer Credit Act 1974 under which the purchase price or part of it is payable in instalments, and the property in the goods is to remain in the seller (notwithstanding that the buyer is to be in possession of the goods) until such conditions as to the payment of instalments or otherwise as may be specified in the agreement are fulfilled.]

PARTNERSHIP ACT 1890
(53 & 54 Vict, c 39)

Nature of partnership

1 Definition of partnership
   (1) Partnership is the relation which subsists between persons carrying on a business in common with a view of profit.
   (2) But the relation between members of any company or association which is—
   [(a) Registered under the Companies Act 2006,] or
   (b) Formed or incorporated by or in pursuance of any other Act of Parliament or letters patent, or Royal Charter
   [. . .]
is not a partnership within the meaning of this Act.

2 Rules for determining existence of partnership
In determining whether a partnership does or does not exist, regard shall be had to the following rules:
   (1) joint tenancy, tenancy in common, joint property, common property, or part ownership does not of itself create a partnership as to anything so held or owned, whether the tenants or owners do or do not share any profits made by the use thereof.
   (2) The sharing of gross returns does not of itself create a partnership, whether the persons sharing such returns have or have not a joint or common right or interest in any property from which or from the use of which the returns are derived.
   (3) The receipt by a person of a share of the profits of a business is prima facie

evidence that he is a partner in the business, but the receipt of such a share, or of a payment contingent on or varying with the profits of a business, does not of itself make him a partner in the business; and in particular—

(a)   The receipt by a person of a debt or other liquidated amount by instalments, or otherwise out of the accruing profits of a business does not of itself make him a partner in the business or liable as such:

(b)   A contract for the remuneration of a servant or agent of a person engaged in a business by a share of the profits of the business does not of itself make the servant or agent a partner in the business or liable as such:

(c)   A person being the widow [, widower, surviving civil partner] or child of a deceased partner, and receiving by way of annuity a portion of the profits made in the business in which the deceased person was a partner, is not by reason only of such receipt a partner in the business or liable as such:

(d)   The advance of money by way of loan to a person engaged or about to engage in any business on a contract with that person that the lender shall receive a rate of interest varying with the profits, or shall receive a share of the profits arising from carrying on the business, does not of itself make the lender a partner with the person or persons carrying on the business or liable as such. Provided that the contract is in writing, and signed by or on behalf of all the parties thereto:

(e)   A person receiving by way of annuity or otherwise a portion of the profits of a business in consideration of the sale by him of the goodwill of the business is not by reason only of such receipt a partner in the business or liable as such.

3   Postponement of rights of person lending or selling in consideration of share of profits in case of insolvency
In the event of any person to whom money has been advanced by way of loan upon such a contract as is mentioned in the last foregoing section, or of any buyer of a goodwill in consideration of a share of the profits of the business, being adjudged a bankrupt, entering into an arrangement to pay his creditors less than [100p] in the pound, or dying in insolvent circumstances, the lender of the loan shall not be entitled to recover anything in respect of the loan, and the seller of the goodwill shall not be entitled to recover anything in respect of the share of profits contracted for, until the claims of the other creditors of the borrower or buyer for valuable consideration in money or money's worth have been satisfied.

4   Meaning of firm
(1)   Persons who have entered into partnership with one another are for the purposes of this Act called collectively a firm, and the name under which their business is carried on is called the firm-name.

(2)   In Scotland a firm is a legal person distinct from the partners of whom it is composed, but an individual partner may be charged on a decree or diligence directed against the firm, and on payment of the debts is entitled to relief pro rata from the firm and its other members.

Relations of partners to persons dealing with them

5   Power of partner to bind the firm
Every partner is an agent of the firm and his other partners for the purpose of the business of the partnership; and the acts of every partner who does any act for carrying on in the usual way business of the kind carried on by the firm of which he is a member bind the firm and his partners, unless the partner so acting has in fact no authority to act for the firm in the particular matter, and the person with whom he is dealing either knows that he has no authority, or does not know or believe him to be a partner.

6 Partners bound by acts on behalf of firm

An act or instrument relating to the business of the firm and done or executed in the firm-name, or in any other manner showing an intention to bind the firm, by any person thereto authorised, whether a partner or not, is binding on the firm and all the partners.

Provided that this section shall not affect any general rule of law relating to the execution of deeds or negotiable instruments.

7 Partner using credit of firm for private purposes

Where one partner pledges the credit of the firm for a purpose apparently not connected with the firm's ordinary course of business, the firm is not bound, unless he is in fact specially authorised by the other partners; but this section does not affect any personal liability incurred by an individual partner.

8 Effect of notice that firm will not be bound by acts of partner

If it has been agreed between the partners that any restriction shall be placed on the power of any one or more of them to bind the firm, no act done in contravention of the agreement is binding on the firm with respect to persons having notice of the agreement.

9 Liability of partners

Every partner in a firm is liable jointly with the other partners, and in Scotland severally also, for all debts and obligations of the firm incurred while he is a partner; and after his death his estate is also severally liable in a due course of administration for such debts and obligations, so far as they remain unsatisfied, but subject in England or Ireland to the prior payment of his separate debts.

10 Liability of the firm for wrongs

Where, by any wrongful act or omission of any partner acting in the ordinary course of the business of the firm, or with the authority of his co-partners, loss or injury is caused to any person not being a partner in the firm, or any penalty is incurred, the firm is liable therefor to the same extent as the partner so acting or omitting to act.

11 Misapplication of money or property received for or in custody of the firm

In the following cases; namely—

(a) Where one partner acting within the scope of his apparent authority receives the money or property of a third person and misapplies it; and

(b) Where a firm in the course of its business receives money or property of a third person, and the money or property so received is misapplied by one or more of the partners while it is in the custody of the firm;

the firm is liable to make good the loss.

12 Liability for wrongs joint and several

Every partner is liable jointly with his co-partners and also severally for everything for which the firm while he is a partner therein becomes liable under either of the two last preceding sections.

13 Improper employment of trust-property for partnership purposes

If a partner, being a trustee, improperly employs trust property in the business or on the account of the partnership, no other partner is liable for the trust-property to the persons beneficially interested therein.

Provided as follows:—

(1) This section shall not affect any liability incurred by any partner by reason of his having notice of a breach of trust; and

(2) Nothing in this section shall prevent trust money from being followed and recovered from the firm if still in its possession or under its control.

14 Persons liable by 'holding out'
(1) Every one who by words spoken or written or by conduct represents himself, or who knowingly suffers himself to be represented, as a partner in a particular firm, is liable as a partner to one who has on the faith of any such representation given credit to the firm, whether the representation has or has not been made or communicated to the person so giving credit by or with the knowledge of the apparent partner making the representation or suffering it to be made.
(2) Provided that where after a partner's death the partnership business is continued in the old firm-name, the continued use of that name or of the deceased partner's name as part thereof shall not of itself make his executors' or administrators' estate or effects liable for any partnership debts contracted after his death.

15 Admissions and representations of partners
An admission or representation made by any partner concerning the partnership affairs, and in the ordinary course of its business, is evidence against the firm.

16 Notice to acting partner to be notice to the firm
Notice to any partner who habitually acts in the partnership business of any matter relating to partnership affairs operates as a notice to the firm, except in the case of a fraud on the firm committed by or with the consent of that partner.

17 Liabilities of incoming and outgoing partners
(1) A person who is admitted as a partner into an existing firm does not thereby become liable to the creditors of the firm for anything done before he became a partner.
(2) A partner who retires from a firm does not thereby cease to be liable for partnership debts or obligations incurred before his retirement.
(3) A retiring partner may be discharged from any existing liabilities, by an agreement to that effect between himself and the members of the firm as newly constituted and the creditors, and this agreement may be either express or inferred, as a fact from the course of dealing between the creditors and the firm as newly constituted.

18 Revocation of continuing guaranty by change in firm
A continuing guaranty or cautionary obligation given either to a firm or to a third person in respect of the transactions of a firm is, in the absence of agreement to the contrary, revoked as to future transactions by any change in the constitution of the firm to which, or of the firm in respect of the transactions of which, the guaranty or obligation was given.

Relations of partners to one another

19 Variation by consent of terms of partnership
The mutual rights and duties of partners, whether ascertained by agreement or defined by this Act, may be varied by the consent of all the partners, and such consent may be either express or inferred from a course of dealing.

20 Partnership property
(1) All property and rights and interests in property originally brought into the partnership stock or acquired, whether by purchase or otherwise, on account of the firm or for the purposes and in the course of the partnership business, are called in this Act partnership property, and must be held and applied by the partners exclusively for the purposes of the partnership and in accordance with the partnership agreement.
(2) Provided that the legal estate or interest in any land, or in Scotland the title to and interest in any heritable estate, which belongs to the partnership shall devolve according to the nature and tenure thereof, and the general rules of law thereto applicable, but in trust, so far as necessary, for the persons beneficially interested in the land under this section.

(3)   Where co-owners of an estate or interest in any land, or in Scotland of any heritable estate, not being itself partnership property, are partners as to profits made by the use of that land or estate, and purchase other land or estate out of the profits to be used in like manner, the land or estate so purchased belongs to them, in the absence of an agreement to the contrary, not as partners but as co-owners for the same respective estates and interests as are held by them in the land or estate first mentioned at the date of the purchase.

21   Property bought with partnership money
Unless the contrary intention appears, property bought with money belonging to the firm is deemed to have been bought on account of the firm.

22 Conversion into personal estate of land held as partnership property
Where land or any heritable interest therein has become partnership property, it shall, unless the contrary intention appears, be treated as between the partners (including the representatives of a deceased partner), and also as between the heirs of a deceased partner and his executors or administrators, as personal or moveable and not real or heritable estate.

23   [Does not apply to Scotland]

24   Rules as to interests and duties of partners subject to special agreement
The interests of partners in the partnership property and their rights and duties in relation to the partnership shall be determined, subject to any agreement express or implied between the partners, by the following rules:
   (1)   All the partners are entitled to share equally in the capital and profits of the business, and must contribute equally towards the losses whether of capital or otherwise sustained by the firm.
   (2)   The firm must indemnify every partner in respect of payments made and personal liabilities incurred by him—
      (a)   In the ordinary and proper conduct of the business of the firm-, or,
      (b)   In or about anything necessarily done for the preservation of the business or property of the firm.
   (3)   A partner making, for the purpose of the partnership, any actual payment or advance beyond the amount of capital which he has agreed to subscribe, is entitled to interest at the rate of five per cent. per annum from the date of the payment or advance.
   (4)   A partner is not entitled, before the ascertainment of profits, to interest on the capital subscribed by him.
   (5)   Every partner may take part in the management of the partnership business.
   (6)   No partner shall be entitled to remuneration for acting in the partnership business.
   (7)   No person may be introduced as a partner without the consent of all existing partners.
   (8)   Any difference arising as to ordinary matters connected with the partnership business may be decided by a majority of the partners, but no change may be made in the nature of the partnership business without the consent of all existing partners.
   (9)   The partnership books are to be kept at the place of business of the partnership (or the principal place, if there is more than one), and every partner may, when he thinks fit, have access to and inspect and copy any of them.

25   Expulsion of partner
No majority of the partners can expel any partner unless a power to do so has been conferred by express agreement between the partners.

26   Retirement from partnership at will
   (1)   Where no fixed term has been agreed upon for the duration of the partner-

ship, any partner may determine the partnership at any time on giving notice of his intention so to do to all the other partners.

(2)   Where the partnership has originally been constituted by deed, a notice in writing, signed by the partner giving it, shall be sufficient for this purpose.

27   Where partnership for term is continued over, continuance on old terms presumed

(1)   Where a partnership entered into for a fixed term is continued after the term has expired, and without any express new agreement, the rights and duties of the partners remain the same as they were at the expiration of the term, so far as is consistent with the incidents of a partnership at will.

(2)   A continuance of the business by the partners or such of them as habitually acted therein during the term, without any settlement or liquidation of the partnership affairs, is presumed to be a continuance of the partnership.

28   Duty of partners to render accounts, &c

Partners are bound to render true accounts and full information of all things affecting the partnership to any partner or his legal representatives.

29   Accountability of partners for private profits

(1)   Every partner must account to the firm for any benefit derived by him without the consent of the other partners from any transaction concerning the partnership, or from any use by him of the partnership property name or business connexion.

(2)   This section applies also to transactions undertaken after a partnership has been dissolved by the death of a partner, and before the affairs thereof have been completely wound up, either by any surviving partner or by the representatives of the deceased partner.

30   Duty of partner not to compete with firm

If a partner, without the consent of the other partners, carries on any business of the same nature as and competing with that of the firm, he must account for and pay over to the firm all profits made by him in that business.

31   Rights of assignee of share in partnership

(1)   An assignment by any partner of his share in the partnership, either absolute or by way of mortgage or redeemable charge, does not, as against the other partners, entitle the assignee, during the continuance of the partnership, to interfere in the management or administration of the partnership business or affairs, or to require any accounts of the partnership transactions, or to inspect the partnership books, but entitles the assignee only to receive the share of profits to which the assigning partner would otherwise be entitled, and the assignee must accept the account of profits agreed to by the partners.

(2)   In the case of a dissolution of the partnership, whether as respects all the partners or as respects the assigning partner, the assignee is entitled to receive the share of the partnership assets to which the assigning partner is entitled as between himself and the other partners, and, for the purpose of ascertaining that share, to an account as from the date of the dissolution.

Dissolution of partnership, and its consequences

32   Dissolution by expiration or notice

Subject to any agreement between the partners a partnership is dissolved—

(a)   If entered into for a fixed term, by the expiration of that term:

(b)   If entered into for a single adventure or undertaking, by the termination of that adventure or undertaking:

(c)   If entered into for an undefined time, by any partner giving notice to the other or others of his intention to dissolve the partnership.

In the last-mentioned case the partnership is dissolved as from the date mentioned in the notice as the date of dissolution, or, if no date is so mentioned, as from the date of the communication of the notice.

33 Dissolution by bankruptcy, death, or charge
(1) Subject to any agreement between the partners, every partnership is dissolved as regards all partners by the death or bankruptcy of any partner.

(2) A partnership may, at the option of the other partners, be dissolved if any partner suffers his share of the partnership property to be charged under this Act for his separate debt.

34 Dissolution by illegality of partnership
A partnership is in every case dissolved by the happening of any event which makes it unlawful for the business of the firm to be carried on or for the members of the firm to carry it on in partnership.

35 Dissolution by the Court
On application by a partner the Court may decree a dissolution of the partnership in any of the following cases:

(a) When a partner is found lunatic by inquisition, or in Scotland by cognition, or is shown to the satisfaction of the Court to be of permanently unsound mind, in either of which cases the application may be made as well on behalf of that partner by his committee or next friend or person having title to intervene as by any other partner:

(b) When a partner, other than the partner suing, becomes in any other way permanently incapable of performing his part of the partnership contract:

(c) When a partner, other than the partner suing, has been guilty of such conduct as, in the opinion of the Court, regard being had to the nature of the business, is calculated to prejudicially affect the carrying on of the business:

(d) When a partner, other than the partner suing, wilfully or persistently commits a breach of the partnership agreement, or otherwise so conducts himself in matters relating to the partnership business that it is not reasonably practicable for the other partner or partners to carry on the business in partnership with him:

(e) When the business of the partnership can only be carried on at a loss:

(f) Whenever in any case circumstances have arisen which, in the opinion of the Court, render it just and equitable that the partnership be dissolved.

36 Rights of persons dealing with firm against apparent members of firm
(1) Where a person deals with a firm after a change in its constitution he is entitled to treat all apparent members of the old firm as still being members of the firm until he has notice of the change.

(2) An advertisement in the London Gazette as to a firm whose principal place of business is in England or Wales, in the Edinburgh Gazette as to a firm whose principal place of business is in Scotland, and in the [Belfast Gazette] as to a firm whose principal place of business is in Ireland, shall be notice as to persons who had not dealings with the firm before the date of the dissolution or change so advertised.

(3) The estate of a partner who dies, or who becomes bankrupt, or of a partner who, not having been known to the person dealing with the firm to be a partner, retires from the firm, is not liable for partnership debts contracted after the date of the death, bankruptcy, or retirement respectively.

37 Right of partners to notify dissolution
On dissolution of a partnership or retirement of a partner any partner may publicly notify the same, and may require the other partner or partners to concur for that purpose in all necessary or proper acts, if any, which cannot be done without his or their concurrence.

38 Continuing authority of partners for purposes of winding up

After the dissolution of a partnership the authority of each partner to bind the firm, and the other rights and obligations of the partners, continue notwithstanding the dissolution so far as may be necessary to wind up the affairs of the partnership, and to complete transactions begun but unfinished at the time of the dissolution, but not otherwise.

Provided that the firm is in no case bound by the acts of a partner who has become bankrupt; but this proviso does not affect the liability of any person who has after the bankruptcy represented himself or knowingly suffered himself to be represented as a partner of the bankrupt.

39 Rights of partners as to application of partnership property

On the dissolution of a partnership every partner is entitled, as against the other partners in the firm, and all persons claiming through them in respect of their interests as partners, to have the property of the partnership applied in payment of the debts and liabilities of the firm, and to have the surplus assets after such payment applied in payment of what may be due to the partners respectively after deducting what may be due from them as partners to the firm; and for that purpose any partner or his representatives may on the termination of the partnership apply to the Court to wind up the business and affairs of the firm.

40 Apportionment of premium where partnership prematurely dissolved

Where one partner has paid a premium to another on entering into a partnership for a fixed term, and the partnership is dissolved before the expiration of that term otherwise than by the death of a partner, the Court may order the repayment of the premium, or of such part thereof as it thinks just, having regard to the terms of the partnership contract and to the length of time during which the partnership has continued; unless

(a) the dissolution is, in the judgment of the Court, wholly or chiefly due to the misconduct of the partner who paid the premium, or

(b) the partnership has been dissolved by an agreement containing no provision for a return of any part of the premium.

41 Rights where partnership dissolved for fraud or misrepresentation

Where a partnership contract is rescinded on the ground of fraud or misrepresentation of one of the parties thereto, the party entitled to rescind is, without prejudice to any other right, entitled—

(a) to a lien on, or right of retention of, the surplus of the partnership assets, after satisfying the partnership liabilities, for any sum of money paid by him for the purchase of a share in the partnership and for any capital contributed by him, and is

(b) to stand in the place of the creditors of the firm for any payments made by him in respect of the partnership liabilities, and

(c) to be indemnified by the person guilty of the fraud or making the representation against all the debts and liabilities of the firm.

42 Right of outgoing partner in certain cases to share in profits made after dissolution

(1) Where any member of a firm has died or otherwise ceased to be a partner, and the surviving or continuing partners carry on the business of the firm with its capital or assets without any final settlement of accounts as between the firm and the outgoing partner or his estate, then, in the absence of any agreement to the contrary, the outgoing partner or his estate is entitled at the option of himself or his representatives to such share of the profits made since the dissolution as the Court may find to be attributable to the use of his share of the partnership assets, or to interest at the rate of five per cent. per annum on the amount of his share of the partnership assets.

(2) Provided that where by the partnership contract an option is given to sur-

viving or continuing partners to purchase the interest of a deceased or outgoing partner, and that option is duly exercised, the estate of the deceased partner, or the outgoing partner or his estate, as the case may be, is not entitled to any further or other share of profits; but if any partner assuming to act in exercise of the option does not in all material respects comply with the terms thereof, he is liable to account under the foregoing provisions of this section.

43   Retiring or deceased partner's share to be a debt
Subject to any agreement between the partners, the amount due from surviving or continuing partners to an outgoing partner or the representatives of a deceased partner in respect of the outgoing or deceased partner's share is a debt accruing at the date of the dissolution or death.

44   Rule for distribution of assets on final settlement of accounts
In settling accounts between the partners after a dissolution of partnership, the following rules shall, subject to any agreement, be observed:
   (a)   Losses, including losses and deficiencies of capital, shall be paid first out of profits, next out of capital, and lastly, if necessary, by the partners individually in the proportion in which they were entitled to share profits:
   (b)   The assets of the firm including the sums, if any, contributed by the partners to make up losses or deficiencies of capital, shall be applied in the following manner and order:
      1   In paying the debts and liabilities of the firm to persons who are not partners therein:
      2   In paying to each partner rateably what is due from the firm to him for advances as distinguished from capital:
      3   In paying to each partner rateably what is due from the firm to him in respect of capital:
      4   The ultimate residue, if any, shall be divided among the partners in the proportion in which the profits are divisible.

Supplemental

45   Definitions of 'court' and 'business'
In this Act, unless the contrary intention appears—
   The expression 'court' includes every court and judge having jurisdiction in the case:
   The expression 'business' includes every trade, occupation or profession.

46   Saving for rules of equity and common law
The rules of equity and of common law applicable to partnership shall continue in force except so far as they are inconsistent with the express provisions of this Act.

47   Provision as to bankruptcy in Scotland
   (1)   In the application of this Act to Scotland the bankruptcy of a firm or of an individual shall mean sequestration under the Bankruptcy (Scotland) Acts, and also in the case of an individual the issue against him of a decree of cessio bonorum.
   (2)   Nothing in this Act shall alter the rules of the law of Scotland relating to the bankruptcy of a firm or of the individual partners thereof.

[. . .]

50   Short title
This Act may be cited as the Partnership Act, 1890.

FACTORS (SCOTLAND) ACT 1890
(53 & 54 Vict, c 40)

1 Application of 52 & 53 Vict c 45 to Scotland

Subject to the following provisions, the Factors Act, 1889, shall apply to Scotland—

(1) The expression 'lien' shall mean and include right of retention; the expression 'vendor's lien' shall mean and include any right of retention competent to the original owner or vendor; and the expression 'set off' shall mean and include compensation.

(2) In the application of section five of the recited Act, a sale, pledge, or other disposition of goods shall not be valid unless made for valuable consideration.

MARINE INSURANCE ACT 1906
(6 Edw 7, c 41)

Marine insurance

1 Marine insurance defined

A contract of marine insurance is a contract whereby the insurer undertakes to indemnify the assured, in manner and to the extent thereby agreed, against marine losses, that is to say, the losses incident to marine adventure.

2 Mixed sea and land risks

(1) A contract of marine insurance may, by its express terms, or by usage of trade, be extended so as to protect the assured against losses on inland waters or on any land risk which may be incidental to any sea voyage.

(2) Where a ship in course of building, or the launch of a ship, or any adventure analogous to marine adventure, is covered by a policy in the form of a marine policy, the provisions of this Act, in so far as applicable, shall apply thereto; but, except as by this section provided, nothing in this Act shall alter or affect any rule of law applicable to any contract of insurance other than a contract of marine insurance as by this Act defined.

3 Marine adventure and maritime perils defined

(1) Subject to the provisions of this Act, every lawful marine adventure may be the subject of marine insurance.

(2) In particular there is a marine adventure where—

(a) Any ship goods or other moveables are exposed to maritime perils. Such property is in this Act referred to as 'insurable property';

(b) The earning or acquisition of any freight, passage money, commission, profit, or other pecuniary benefit, or the security for any advances, loan or disbursements, is endangered by the exposure of insurable property to maritime perils;

(c) Any liability to a third party may be incurred by the owner of, or other person interested in or responsible for, insurable property, by reason of maritime perils.

'Maritime perils' means the perils consequent on, or incidental to, the navigation of the sea, that is to say, perils of the seas, fire, war perils, pirates, rovers, thieves, captures, seizures, restraints, and detainments of princes and peoples, jettisons, barratry, and any other perils, either of the like kind or which may be designated by the policy.

Insurable interest

4 Avoidance of wagering or gaming contracts

(1) Every contract of marine insurance by way of gaming or wagering is void.

(2) A contract of marine insurance is deemed to be a gaming or wagering contract—

(a)   Where the assured has not an insurable interest as defined by this Act, and the contract is entered into with no expectation of acquiring such an interest; or

(b)   Where the policy is made 'interest or no interest', or 'without further proof of interest than the policy itself', or 'without benefit of salvage to the insurer', or subject to any other like term:

Provided that, where there is no possibility of salvage, a policy may be effected without benefit of salvage to the insurer.

5   Insurable interest defined

(1)   Subject to the provisions of this Act, every person has an insurable interest who is interested in a marine adventure.

(2)   In particular a person is interested in a marine adventure where he stands in any legal or equitable relation to the adventure or to any insurable property at risk therein, in consequence of which he may benefit by the safety or due arrival of insurable property, or may be prejudiced by its loss, or damage thereto, or by the detention thereof, or may incur liability in respect thereof.

6   When interest must attach

(1)   The assured must be interested in the subject-matter insured at the time of the loss though he need not be interested when the insurance is effected:

Provided that where the subject-matter is insured 'lost or not lost', the assured may recover although he may not have acquired his interest until after the loss, unless at the time of effecting the contract of insurance the assured was aware of the loss, and the insurer was not.

(2)   Where the assured has no interest at the time of the loss, he cannot acquire interest by any act or election after he is aware of the loss.

7   Defeasible or contingent interest

(1)   A defeasible interest is insurable, as also is a contingent interest.

(2)   In particular, where the buyer of goods has insured them, he has an insurable interest, notwithstanding that he might, at his election, have rejected the goods, or have treated them as at the seller's risk, by reason of the latter's delay in making delivery or otherwise.

8   Partial interest

A partial interest of any nature is insurable.

9   Re-insurance

(1)   The insurer under a contract of marine insurance has an insurable interest in his risk, and may re-insure in respect of it.

(2)   Unless the policy otherwise provides, the original assured has no right or interest in respect of such re-insurance.

10   Bottomry

The lender of money on bottomry or respondentia has an insurable interest in respect of the loan.

11   Master's and seamen's wages

The master or any member of the crew of a ship has an insurable interest in respect of his wages.

12   Advance freight

In the case of advance freight, the person advancing the freight has an insurable interest, in so far as such freight is not repayable in case of loss.

13   Charges of insurance

The assured has an insurable interest in the charges of any insurance which he may effect.

14 Quantum of interest

(1) Where the subject-matter insured is mortgaged, the mortgagor has an insurable interest in the full value thereof, and the mortgagee has an insurable interest in respect of any sum due or to become due under the mortgage.

(2) A mortgagee, consignee, or other person having an interest in the subject-matter insured may insure on his own behalf and for the benefit of other persons interested as well as for his own benefit.

(3) The owner of insurable property has an insurable interest in respect of the full value thereof, notwithstanding that some third person may have agreed, or be liable, to indemnify him in case of loss.

15 Assignment of interest

Where the assured assigns or otherwise parts with his interest in the subject-matter insured, he does not thereby transfer to the assignee his rights under the contract of insurance, unless there be an express or implied agreement with the assignee to that effect.

But the provisions of this section do not affect a transmission of interest by operation of law.

Insurable value

16 Measure of insurable value

Subject to any express provision or valuation in the policy, the insurable value of the subject-matter insured must be ascertained as follows:—

(1) In insurance on ship, the insurable value is the value, at the commencement of the risk, of the ship, including her outfit, provisions and stores for the officers and crew, money advanced for seamen's wages, and other disbursements (if any) incurred to make the ship fit for the voyage or adventure contemplated by the policy, plus the charges of insurance upon the whole.

The insurable value, in the case of a steamship, includes also the machinery, boilers, and coals and engine stores if owned by the assured, and, in the case of a ship engaged in a special trade, the ordinary fittings requisite for that trade.

(2) In insurance on freight, whether paid in advance or otherwise, the insurable value is the gross amount of freight at the risk of the assured, plus the charges of insurance.

(3) In insurance on goods or merchandise, the insurable value is the prime cost of the property insured, plus the expenses of and incidental to shipping and the charges of insurance upon the whole.

(4) In insurance on any other subject-matter, the insurable value is the amount at the risk of the assured when the policy attaches, plus the charges of insurance.

Disclosure and representations

17 Insurance is uberrimae fidei

A contract of marine insurance is a contract based upon the utmost good faith, and, if the utmost good faith is not observed by either party, the contract may be avoided by the other party.

18 Disclosure by assured

(1) Subject to the provisions of this section, the assured must disclose to the insurer, before the contract is concluded, every material circumstance which is known to the assured, and the assured is deemed to know every circumstance which, in the ordinary course of business, ought to be known by him. If the assured fails to make such disclosure, the insurer may avoid the contract.

(2) Every circumstance is material which would influence the judgment of a prudent insurer in fixing the premium, or determining whether he will take the risk.

(3)   In the absence of inquiry the following circumstances need not be disclosed, namely:—

(a)   Any circumstance which diminishes the risk;

(b)   Any circumstance which is known or presumed to be known to the insurer. The insurer is presumed to know matters of common notoriety or knowledge, and matters which an insurer in the ordinary course of his business, as such, ought to know;

(c)   Any circumstance as to which information is waived by the insurer;

(d)   Any circumstance which it is superfluous to disclose by reason of any express or implied warranty.

(4)   Whether any particular circumstance, which is not disclosed, be material or not is, in each case, a question of fact.

(5)   The term 'circumstance' includes any communication made to, or information received by, the assured.

19   Disclosure by agent effecting insurance
Subject to the provisions of the preceding section as to circumstances which need not be disclosed, where an insurance is effected for the assured by an agent, the agent must disclose to the insurer—

(a)   Every material circumstance which is known to himself, and an agent to insure is deemed to know every circumstance which, in the ordinary course of business, ought to be known by, or to have been communicated to, him; and

(b)   Every material circumstance which the assured is bound to disclose, unless it come to his knowledge too late to communicate it to the agent.

20   Representations pending negotiation of contract
(1)   Every material representation made by the assured or his agent to the insurer during the negotiations for contract, and before the contract is concluded, must be true. If it be untrue the insurer may avoid the contract.

(2)   A representation is material which would influence the judgment of a prudent insurer in fixing the premium, or determining whether he will take the risk.

(3)   A representation may be either a representation as to a matter of fact, or as to a matter of expectation or belief.

(4)   A representation as to matter of fact is true, if it be substantially correct, that is to say, if the difference between what is represented and what is actually correct would not be considered material by a prudent insurer.

(5)   A representation as to a matter of expectation or belief is true if it be made in good faith.

(6)   A representation may be withdrawn or corrected before the contract is concluded.

(7)   Whether a particular representation be material or not is, in each case, a question of fact.

21   When contract is deemed to be concluded
A contract of marine insurance is deemed to be concluded when the proposal of the assured is accepted by the insurer, whether the policy be then issued or not; and, for the purpose of showing when the proposal was accepted, reference may be made to the slip or covering note or other customary memorandum of the contract. [. . .]

The policy

22   Contract must be embedded in policy
Subject to the provisions of any statute, a contract of marine insurance is inadmissible in evidence unless it is embodied in a marine policy in accordance with this Act. The policy may be executed and issued either at the time when the contract is concluded or afterwards.

23 What policy must specify
A marine policy must specify—

(1)   The name of the assured, or of some person who effects the insurance on his behalf.

[. . .]

24 Signature of insurer

(1)   A marine policy must be signed by or on behalf of the insurer, provided that in the case of a corporation the corporate seal may be sufficient, but nothing in this section shall be construed as requiring the subscription of a corporation to be under seal.

(2)   Where a policy is subscribed by or on behalf of two or more insurers, each subscription, unless the contrary be expressed, constitutes a distinct contract with the assured.

25 Voyage and time policies

(1)   Where the contract is to insure the subject-matter 'at and from', or from one place to another or others, the policy is called a 'voyage policy', and where the contract is to insure the subject-matter for a definite period of time the policy is called a 'time policy'. A contract for both voyage and time may be included in the same policy.

[. . .]

26 Designation of subject-matter

(1)   The subject-matter insured must be designated in a marine policy with reasonable certainty.

(2)   The nature and extent of the interest of the assured in the subject-matter insured need not be specified in the policy.

(3)   Where the policy designates the subject-matter insured in general terms, it shall be construed to apply to the interest intended by the assured to be covered.

(4)   In the application of this section regard shall be had to any usage regulating the designation of the subject-matter insured.

27 Valued policy

(1)   A policy may be either valued or unvalued.

(2)   A valued policy is a policy which specifies the agreed value of the subject-matter insured.

(3)   Subject to the provisions of this Act, and in the absence of fraud, the value fixed by the policy is, as between the insurer and the assured, conclusive of the insurable value of the subject intended to be insured, whether the loss be total or partial.

(4)   Unless the policy otherwise provides, the value fixed by the policy is not conclusive for the purpose of determining whether there has been a constructive total loss.

28 Unvalued policy
An unvalued policy is a policy which does not specify the value of the subject-matter insured, but, subject to the limit of the sum insured, leaves the insurable value to be subsequently ascertained, in the manner herein-before specified.

29 Floating policy by ship or ships

(1)   A floating policy is a policy which describes the insurance in general terms, and leaves the name of the ship or ships and other particulars to be defined by subsequent declaration.

(2)   The subsequent declaration or declarations may be made by indorsement on the policy, or in other customary manner.

(3)   Unless the policy otherwise provides, the declarations must be made in the order of dispatch or shipment. They must, in the case of goods, comprise all consignments within the terms of the policy, and the value of the goods or other prop-

erty must be honestly stated, but an omission or erroneous declaration may be rectified even after loss or arrival, provided the omission or declaration was made in good faith.

(4)   Unless the policy otherwise provides, where a declaration of value is not made until after notice of loss or arrival, the policy must be treated as an unvalued policy as regards the subject-matter of that declaration.

30   Construction of terms in policy

(1)   A policy may be in the form in the First Schedule to this Act.

(2)   Subject to the provisions of this Act, and unless the context of the policy otherwise requires, the terms and expressions mentioned in the First Schedule to this Act shall be construed as having the scope and meaning in that schedule assigned to them.

31   Premium to be arranged

(1)   Where an insurance is effected at a premium to be arranged, and no arrangement is made, a reasonable premium is payable.

(2)   Where an insurance is effected on the terms that an additional premium is to be arranged in a given event, and that event happens but no arrangement is made, then a reasonable additional premium is payable.

Double insurance

32   Double insurance

(1)   Where two or more policies are effected by or on behalf of the assured on the same adventure and interest or any part thereof, and the sums insured exceed the indemnity allowed by this Act, the assured is said to be over-insured by double insurance.

(2)   Where the assured is over-insured by double insurance—

(a)   The assured, unless the policy otherwise provides, may claim payment from the insurers in such order as he may think fit, provided that he is not entitled to receive any sum in excess of the indemnity allowed by this Act;

(b)   Where the policy under which the assured claims is a valued policy, the assured must give credit as against the valuation for any sum received by him under any other policy without regard to the actual value of the subject-matter insured;

(c)   Where the policy under which the assured claims is an unvalued policy he must give credit, as against the full insurable value, for any sum received by him under any other policy.

(d)   Where the assured receives any sum in excess of the indemnity allowed by this Act, he is deemed to hold such sum in trust for the insurers, according to their right of contribution among themselves.

Warranties, etc

33   Nature of warranty

(1)   A warranty, in the following sections relating to warranties, means a promissory warranty, that is to say, a warranty by which the assured undertakes that some particular thing shall or shall not be done, or that some condition shall be fulfilled, or whereby he affirms or negatives the existence of a particular state of facts.

(2)   A warranty may be express or implied.

(3)   A warranty, as above defined, is a condition which must be exactly complied with, whether it be material to the risk or not. If it be not so complied with, then, subject to any express provision in the policy, the insurer is discharged from liability as from the date of the breach of warranty, but without prejudice to any liability incurred by him before that date.

34 When breach of warranty excused

(1) Non-compliance with a warranty is excused when, by reason of a change of circumstances, the warranty ceases to be applicable to the circumstances of the contract, or when compliance with the warranty is rendered unlawful by any subsequent law.

(2) Where a warranty is broken, the assured cannot avail himself of the defence that the breach has been remedied, and the warranty complied with, before loss.

(3) A breach of warranty may be waived by the insurer.

35 Express warranties

(1) An express warranty may be in any form of words from which the intention to warrant is to be inferred.

(2) An express warranty must be included in, or written upon, the policy, or must be contained in some document incorporated by reference into the policy.

(3) An express warranty does not exclude an implied warranty, unless it be inconsistent therewith.

36 Warranty of neutrality

(1) Where insurable property, whether ship or goods, is expressly warranted neutral, there is an implied condition that the property shall have a neutral character at the commencement of the risk, and that, so far as the assured can control the matter, its neutral character shall be preserved during the risk.

(2) Where a ship is expressly warranted 'neutral' there is also an implied condition that, so far as the assured can control the matter, she shall be properly documented, that is to say, that she shall carry the necessary papers to establish her neutrality, and that she shall not falsify or suppress her papers, or use simulated papers. If any loss occurs through breach of this condition, the insurer may avoid the contract.

37 No implied warranty of nationality

There is no implied warranty as to the nationality of a ship, or that her nationality shall not be changed during the risk.

38 Warranty of good safety

Where the subject-matter insured is warranted 'well' or 'in good safety' on a particular day, it is sufficient if it be safe at any time during that day.

39 Warranty of seaworthiness of ship

(1) In a voyage policy there is an implied warranty that at the commencement of the voyage the ship shall be seaworthy for the purpose of the particular adventure insured.

(2) Where the policy attaches while the ship is in port, there is also an implied warranty that she shall, at the commencement of the risk, be reasonably fit to encounter the ordinary perils of the port.

(3) Where the policy relates to a voyage which is performed in different stages, during which the ship requires different kinds of or further preparation or equipment, there is an implied warranty that at the commencement of each stage the ship is seaworthy in respect of such preparation or equipment for the purposes of that stage.

(4) A ship is deemed to be seaworthy when she is reasonably fit in all respects to encounter the ordinary perils of the seas of the adventure insured.

(5) In a time policy there is no implied warranty that the ship shall be seaworthy at any stage of the adventure, but where, with the privity of the assured, the ship is sent to sea in an unseaworthy state, the insurer is not liable for any loss attributable to unseaworthiness.

40 No implied warranty that goods are seaworthy

(1) In a policy on goods or other moveables there is no implied warranty that the goods or moveables are seaworthy.

(2) In a voyage policy on goods or other moveables there is an implied warranty that at the commencement of the voyage the ship is not only seaworthy as a ship, but also that she is reasonably fit to carry the goods or other moveables to the destination contemplated by the policy.

41 Warranty of legality
There is an implied warranty that the adventure insured is a lawful one, and that, so far as the assured can control the matter, the adventure shall be carried out in a lawful manner.

The voyage

42 Implied condition as to commencement of risk
(1) Where the subject-matter is insured by a voyage policy 'at and from' or 'from' a particular place, it is not necessary that the ship should be at that place when the contract is concluded, but there is an implied condition that the adventure shall be commenced within a reasonable time, and that if the adventure be not so commenced the insurer may avoid the contract.

(2) The implied condition may be negatived by showing that the delay was caused by circumstances known to the insurer before the contract was concluded, or by showing that he waived the condition.

43 Alteration of port of departure
Where the place of departure is specified by the policy, and the ship instead of sailing from that place sails from any other place, the risk does not attach.

44 Sailing for different destination
Where the destination is specified in the policy, and the ship, instead of sailing for that destination, sails for any other destination, the risk does not attach.

45 Change of voyage
(1) Where, after the commencement of the risk, the destination of the ship is voluntarily changed from the destination contemplated by the policy, there is said to be a change of voyage.

(2) Unless the policy otherwise provides, where there is a change of voyage, the insurer is discharged from liability as from the time of the change, that is to say, as from the time when the determination to change it is manifested; and it is immaterial that the ship may not have left the course of voyage contemplated by the policy when the loss occurs.

46 Deviation
(1) Where a ship, without lawful excuse, deviates from the voyage contemplated by the policy, the insurer is discharged from liability as from the time of deviation, and it is immaterial that the ship may have regained her route before any loss occurs.

(2) There is a deviation from the voyage contemplated by the policy—

(a) Where the course of the voyage is specifically designated by the policy, and that course is departed from; or

(b) Where the course of the voyage is not specifically designated by the policy, but the usual and customary course is departed from.

(3) The intention to deviate is immaterial; there must be a deviation in fact to discharge the insurer from his liability under the contract.

47 Several ports of discharge
(1) Where several ports of discharge are specified by the policy, the ship may proceed to all or any of them, but, in the absence of any usage or sufficient cause to the contrary, she must proceed to them, or such of them as she goes to, in the order designated by the policy. If she does not there is a deviation.

(2) Where the policy is to 'ports of discharge', within a given area, which are

not named, the ship must, in the absence of any usage or sufficient cause to the contrary, proceed to them, or such of them as she goes to, in their geographical order. If she does not there is a deviation.

48 Delay in voyage

In the case of a voyage policy, the adventure insured must be prosecuted throughout its course with reasonable dispatch, and, if without lawful excuse it is not so prosecuted, the insurer is discharged from liability as from the time when the delay becomes unreasonable.

49 Excuses for deviation or delay

(1) Deviation or delay in prosecuting the voyage contemplated by the policy is excused—

(a) Where authorised by any special term in the policy; or

(b) Where caused by circumstances beyond the control of the master and his employer; or

(c) Where reasonably necessary in order to comply with an express or implied warranty; or

(d) Where reasonably necessary for the safety of the ship or subject-matter insured; or

(e) For the purpose of saving human life, or aiding a ship in distress where human life may be in danger; or

(f) Where reasonably necessary for the purpose of obtaining medical or surgical aid for any person on board the ship; or

(g) Where caused by the barratrous conduct of the master or crew, if barratry be one of the perils insured against.

(2) When the cause excusing the deviation or delay ceases to operate, the ship must resume her course, and prosecute her voyage, with reasonable dispatch.

Assignment of policy

50 When and how policy is assignable

(1) A marine policy is assignable unless it contains terms expressly prohibiting assignment. It may be assigned either before or after loss.

(2) Where a marine policy has been assigned so as to pass the beneficial interest in such policy, the assignee of the policy is entitled to sue thereon in his own name; and the defendant is entitled to make any defence arising out of the contract which he would have been entitled to make if the action had been brought in the name of the person by or on behalf of whom the policy was effected.

(3) A marine policy may be assigned by indorsement thereon or in other customary manner.

51 Assured who has no interest cannot assign

Where the assured has parted with or lost his interest in the subject-matter insured, and has not, before or at the time of so doing, expressly or impliedly agreed to assign the policy, any subsequent assignment of the policy is inoperative:

Provided that nothing in this section affects the assignment of a policy after loss.

The premium

52 When premium payable

Unless otherwise agreed, the duty of the assured or his agent to pay the premium, and the duty of the insurer to issue the policy to the assured or his agent, are concurrent conditions, and the insurer is not bound to issue the policy until payment or tender of the premium.

53 Policy effected through broker

(1) Unless otherwise agreed, where a marine policy is effected on behalf of the assured by a broker, the broker is directly responsible to the insurer for the

premium, and the insurer is directly responsible to the assured for the amount which may be payable in respect of losses, or in respect of returnable premium.

(2) Unless otherwise agreed, the broker has, as against the assured, a lien upon the policy for the amount of the premium and his charges in respect of effecting the policy; and, where he has dealt with the person who employs him as a principal, he has also a lien on the policy in respect of any balance on any insurance account which may be due to him from such person, unless when the debt was incurred he had reason to believe that such person was only an agent.

54 Effect of receipt on policy

Where a marine policy effected on behalf of the assured by a broker acknowledges the receipt of the premium, such acknowledgement is, in the absence of fraud, conclusive as between the insurer and the assured, but not as between the insurer and broker.

Loss and abandonment

55 Included and excluded losses

(1) Subject to the provisions of this Act, and unless the policy otherwise provides, the insurer is liable for any loss proximately caused by a peril insured against, but, subject as aforesaid, he is not liable for any loss which is not proximately caused by a peril insured against.

(2) In particular,—

(a) The insurer is not liable for any loss attributable to the wilful misconduct of the assured, but, unless the policy otherwise provides, he is liable for any loss proximately caused by a peril insured against, even though the loss would not have happened but for the misconduct or negligence of the master or crew;

(b) Unless the policy otherwise provides, the insurer on ship or goods is not liable for any loss proximately caused by delay, although the delay be caused by a peril insured against.

(c) Unless the policy otherwise provides, the insurer is not liable for ordinary wear and tear, ordinary leakage and breakage, inherent vice or nature of the subject-matter insured, or for any loss proximately caused by rats or vermin, or for any injury to machinery not proximately caused by maritime perils.

56 Partial and total loss

(1) A loss may be either total or partial. Any loss other than a total loss, as herein-after defined, is a partial loss.

(2) A total loss may be either an actual total loss, or a constructive total loss.

(3) Unless a different intention appears from the terms of the policy, an insurance against total loss includes a constructive, as well as an actual, total loss.

(4) Where the assured brings an action for a total loss and the evidence proves only a partial loss, he may, unless the policy otherwise provides, recover for a partial loss.

(5) Where goods reach their destination in specie, but by reason of obliteration of marks, or otherwise, they are incapable of identification, the loss, if any, is partial, and not total.

57 Actual total loss

(1) Where the subject-matter insured is destroyed, or so damaged as to cease to be a thing of the kind insured, or where the assured is irretrievably deprived thereof, there is an actual total loss.

(2) In the case of an actual total loss no notice of abandonment need be given.

58 Missing ship

Where the ship concerned in the adventure is missing, and after the lapse of a reasonable time no news of her has been received, an actual total loss may be presumed.

59   Effect of transhipment, etc

Where, by a peril insured against, the voyage is interrupted at any intermediate port or place, under such circumstances as apart from any special stipulation in the contract of affreightment, to justify the master in landing and re-shipping the goods or other moveables, or in transhipping them, and sending them on to their destination, the liability of the insurer continues, notwithstanding the landing or transhipment.

60   Constructive total loss defined

(1)   Subject to any express provision in the policy, there is a constructive total loss where the subject-matter insured is reasonably abandoned on account of its total loss appearing to be unavoidable, or because it could not be preserved from the actual total loss without an expenditure which would exceed its value when the expenditure had been incurred.

(2)   In particular, there is a constructive total loss—

(i)   Where the assured is deprived of the possession of his ship or goods by a peril insured against, and (a) it is unlikely that he can recover the ship or goods, as the case may be, or (b) the cost of recovering the ship or goods, as the case may be, would exceed their value when recovered; or

(ii)   In the case of damage to a ship, where she is so damaged by a peril insured against that the cost of repairing the damage would exceed the value of the ship when repaired.

In estimating the cost of repairs, no deduction is to be made in respect of general average contributions to those repairs payable by other interests, but account is to be taken of the expense of future salvage operations and of any future general average contributions to which the ship would be liable if repaired; or

(iii)   In the case of damage to goods, where the cost of repairing the damage and forwarding the goods to their destination would exceed their value on arrival.

61   Effect of constructive total loss

Where there is a constructive total loss the assured may either treat the loss as a partial loss, or abandon the subject-matter insured to the insurer and treat the loss as if it were an actual total loss.

62   Notice of abandonment

(1)   Subject to the provisions of this section, where the assured elects to abandon the subject-matter insured to the insurer, he must give notice of the abandonment. If he fails to do so the loss can only be treated as a partial loss.

(2)   Notice of abandonment may be given in writing, or by word of mouth, or partly in writing and partly by word of mouth, and may be given in terms which indicate the intention of the assured to abandon his insured interest in the subject-matter insured unconditionally to the insurer.

(3)   Notice of abandonment must be given with reasonable diligence after the receipt of reliable information of the loss, but where the information is of a doubtful character the assured is entitled to a reasonable time to make inquiry.

(4)   Where notice of abandonment is properly given, the rights of the assured are not prejudiced by the fact that the insurer refuses to accept the abandonment.

(5)   The acceptance of an abandonment may be either express or implied from the conduct of the insurer. The mere silence of the insurer after notice is not an acceptance.

(6)   Where a notice of abandonment is accepted the abandonment is irrevocable. The acceptance of the notice conclusively admits liability for the loss and the sufficiency of the notice.

(7)   Notice of abandonment is unnecessary where, at the time when the assured

receives information of the loss, there would be no possibility of benefit to the insurer if notice were given to him.

(8)   Notice of abandonment may be waived by the insurer.

(9)   Where an insurer has re-insured his risk, no notice of abandonment need be given by him.

63   Effect of abandonment

(1)   Where there is a valid abandonment the insurer is entitled to take over the interest of the assured in whatever may remain of the subject-matter insured, and all proprietary rights incidental thereto.

(2)   Upon the abandonment of a ship, the insurer thereof is entitled to any freight in course of being earned, and which is earned by her subsequent to the casualty causing the loss, less the expenses of earning it incurred after the casualty; and, where a ship is carrying the owner's goods, the insurer is entitled to a reasonable remuneration for the carriage of them subsequent to the casualty causing the loss.

Partial losses (including salvage and general average and particular charges)

64   Particular average loss

(1)   A particular average loss is a partial loss of the subject-matter insured, caused by a peril insured against, and which is not a general average loss.

(2)   Expenses incurred by or on behalf of the assured for the safety or preservation of the subject-matter insured, other than general average and salvage charges, are called particular charges. Particular charges are not included in particular average.

65   Salvage charges

(1)   Subject to any express provision in the policy, salvage charges incurred in preventing a loss by perils insured against may be recovered as a loss by those perils.

(2)   'Salvage charges' means the charges recoverable under maritime law by a salvor independently of contract. They do not include the expenses of services in the nature of salvage rendered by the assured or his agents, or any person employed for hire by them, for the purpose of averting a peril insured against. Such expenses, where properly incurred, may be recovered as particular charges or as a general average loss, according to the circumstances under which they were incurred.

66   General average loss

(1)   A general average loss is a loss caused by or directly consequential on a general average act. It includes a general average expenditure as well as a general average sacrifice.

(2)   There is a general average act where any extraordinary sacrifice or expenditure is voluntarily and reasonably made or incurred in the time of peril for the purpose of preserving the property imperilled in the common adventure.

(3)   Where there is a general average loss, the party on whom it falls is entitled, subject to the conditions imposed by maritime law, to a rateable contribution from the other parties interested, and such contribution is called a general average contribution.

(4)   Subject to any express provision in the policy, where the assured has incurred a general average expenditure, he may recover from the insurer in respect of the proportion of the loss which falls upon him; and, in the case of a general average sacrifice, he may recover from the insurer in respect of the whole loss without having enforced his right of contribution from the other parties liable to contribute.

(5)   Subject to any express provision in the policy, where the assured has paid,

or is liable to pay, a general average contribution in respect of the subject insured, he may recover therefor from the insurer.

(6)   In the absence of express stipulation, the insurer is not liable for any general average loss or contribution where the loss was not incurred for the purpose of avoiding, or in connexion with the avoidance of, a peril insured against.

(7)   Where ship, freight, and cargo, or any two of those interests, are owned by the same assured, the liability of the insurer in respect of general average losses or contributions is to be determined as if those subjects were owned by different persons.

Measure of indemnity

67   Extent of liability of insurer for loss

(1)   The sum which the assured can recover in respect of a loss on a policy by which he is insured, in the case of an unvalued policy to the full extent of the insurable value, or in the case of a valued policy to the full extent of the value fixed by the policy, is called the measure of indemnity.

(2)   Where there is a loss recoverable under the policy, the insurer, or each insurer if there be more than one, is liable for such proportion of the measure of indemnity as the amount of his subscription bears to the value fixed by the policy in the case of a valued policy, or to the insurable value in the case of an unvalued policy.

68   Total loss

Subject to the provisions of this Act and to any express provision in the policy, where there is a total loss of the subject-matter insured,—

(1)   If the policy be a valued policy, the measure of indemnity is the sum fixed by the policy.

(2)   If the policy be an unvalued policy, the measure of indemnity is the insurable value of the subject-matter insured.

69   Partial loss of ship

Where a ship is damaged, but not totally lost, the measure of indemnity, subject to any express provision in the policy, is as follows:—

(1)   Where the ship has been repaired, the assured is entitled to the reasonable cost of the repairs, less the customary deductions, but not exceeding the sum insured in respect of any one casualty.

(2)   Where the ship has been only partially repaired, the assured is entitled to the reasonable cost of such repairs, computed as above, and also to be indemnified for the reasonable depreciation, if any, arising from the unrepaired damage, provided that the aggregate amount shall not exceed the cost of repairing the whole damage, computed as above.

(3)   Where the ship has not been repaired, and has not been sold in her damaged state during the risk, the assured is entitled to be indemnified for the reasonable depreciation arising from the unrepaired damage, but not exceeding the reasonable cost of repairing such damage, computed as above.

70   Partial loss of freight

Subject to any express provision in the policy, where there is a partial loss of freight, the measure of indemnity is such proportion of the sum fixed by the policy in the case of a valued policy, or of the insurable value in the case of an unvalued policy, as the proportion of freight lost by the assured bears to the whole freight at the risk of the assured under the policy.

71   Partial loss of goods, merchandise, etc

Where there is a partial loss of goods, merchandise, or other moveables, the measure of indemnity, subject to any express provision in the policy, is as follows:—

(1)   Where part of the goods, merchandise, or other moveables insured by a valued policy is totally lost, the measure of indemnity is such proportion of the sum fixed by the policy as the insurable value of the part lost bears to the insurable value of the whole, ascertained as in the case of an unvalued policy.

(2)   Where part of the goods, merchandise, or other moveables insured by an unvalued policy is totally lost, the measure of indemnity is the insurable value of the part lost, ascertained as in the case of total loss.

(3)   Where the whole or any part of the goods or merchandise insured has been delivered damaged at its destination, the measure of indemnity is such proportion of the sum fixed by the policy in the case of a valued policy, or of the insurable value in the case of an unvalued policy, as the difference between the gross sound and damaged values at the place of arrival bears to the gross sound value.

(4)   'Gross value' means the wholesale price or, if there be no such price, the estimated value, with, in either case, freight, landing charges, and duty paid beforehand; provided that, in the case of goods or merchandise customarily sold in bond, the bonded price is deemed to be the gross value. 'Gross proceeds' means the actual price obtained at a sale where all charges on sale are paid by the sellers.

72   Apportionment of valuation

(1)   Where different species of property are insured under a single valuation, the valuation must be apportioned over the different species in proportion to their respective insurable values, as in the case of an unvalued policy. The insured value of any part of a species is such proportion of the total insured value of the same as the insurable value of the part bears to the insurable value of the whole, ascertained in both cases as provided by this Act.

(2)   Where a valuation has to be apportioned, and particulars of the prime cost of each separate species, quality, or description of goods cannot be ascertained, the division of the valuation may be made over the net arrived sound values of the different species, qualities, or descriptions of goods.

73   General average contributions and salvage charges

(1)   Subject to any express provision in the policy, where the assured has paid, or is liable for, any general average contribution, the measure of indemnity is the full amount of such contribution, if the subject-matter liable to contribution is insured for its full contributory value; but, if such subject-matter be not insured for its full contributory value, or if only part of it be insured, the indemnity payable by the insurer must be reduced in proportion to the under insurance, and where there has been a particular average loss which constitutes a deduction from the contributory value, and for which the insurer is liable, that amount must be deducted from the insured value in order to ascertain what the insurer is liable to contribute.

(2)   Where the insurer is liable for salvage charges the extent of his liability must be determined on the like principle.

74   Liabilities to third parties

Where the assured has effected an insurance in express terms against any liability to a third party, the measure of indemnity, subject to any express provision in the policy, is the amount paid or payable by him to such third party in respect of such liability.

75   General provisions as to measure of indemnity

(1)   Where there has been a loss in respect of any subject-matter not expressly provided for in the foregoing provisions of this Act, the measure of indemnity shall be ascertained, as nearly as may be, in accordance with those provisions, in so far as applicable to the particular case.

(2)   Nothing in the provisions of this Act relating to the measure of indemnity shall affect the rules relating to double insurance, or prohibit the insurer from dis-

(f)   Subject to the foregoing provisions, where the assured has over-insured by double insurance, a proportionate part of the several premiums is returnable:

Provided that, if the policies are effected at different times, and any earlier policy has at any time borne the entire risk, or if a claim has been paid on the policy in respect of the full sum insured thereby, no premium is returnable in respect of that policy, and when the double insurance is effected knowingly by the assured no premium is returnable.

Mutual insurance

85   Modification of Act in case of mutual insurance

(1)   Where two or more persons mutually agree to insure each other against marine losses there is said to be a mutual insurance.

(2)   The provisions of this Act relating to the premium do not apply to mutual insurance, but a guarantee, or such other arrangement as may be agreed upon, may be substituted for the premium.

(3)   The provisions of this Act, in so far as they may be modified by the agreement of the parties, may in the case of mutual insurance be modified by the terms of the policies issued by the association, or by the rules and regulations of the association.

(4)   Subject to the expectations mentioned in this section, the provisions of this Act apply to a mutual insurance.

Supplemental

86   Ratification by assured

Where a contract of marine insurance is in good faith effected by one person on behalf of another, the person on whose behalf it is effected may ratify the contract even after he is aware of a loss.

87   Implied obligations varied by agreement or usage

(1)   Where any right, duty, or liability would arise under a contract of marine insurance by implication of law, it may be negatived or varied by express agreement or by usage, if the usage be such as to bind both parties to the contract.

(2)   The provisions of this section extend to any right, duty, or liability declared by this Act which may be lawfully modified by agreement.

88   Reasonable time, etc, a question of fact

Where by this Act any reference is made to reasonable time, reasonable premium, or reasonable diligence, the question what is reasonable is a question of fact.

89   Slip as evidence

Where there is a duly stamped policy, reference may be made, as heretofore, to the slip or covering note, in any legal proceeding.

90   Interpretation of terms

In this Act, unless the context or subject-matter otherwise requires,—

'Action' includes counter-claim and set off:

'Freight' includes the profit derivable by a shipowner from the employment of his ship to carry his own goods or moveables, as well as freight payable by a third party, but does not include passage money:

'Moveables' means any moveable tangible property, other than the ship, and includes money, valuable securities, and other documents:

'Policy' means a marine policy.

91   Savings

(1)   Nothing in this Act, or in any repeal effected thereby, shall affect—

(a)   The provisions of the Stamp Act 1891, or any enactment for the time being in force relating to the revenue;

(b)   The provisions of the Companies Act 1862, or any enactment amending or substituted for the same;

(c)   The provisions of any statute not expressly repealed by this Act.

(2)   The rules of the common law including the law merchant, save in so far as they are inconsistent with the express provisions of this Act, shall continue to apply to contracts of marine insurance.

94   Short title

This Act may be cited as the Marine Insurance Act 1906.

SCHEDULES

SCHEDULE 1
FORM OF POLICY

Section 30

BE IT KNOWN THAT .. .. .. as well in .. .. own name as for and in the name and names of all and every other person or persons to whom the same doth, may, or shall appertain, in part or in all doth make assurance and cause .. .. and them, and every of them, to be insured lost or not lost, at and from .. ..

Upon any kind of goods and merchandise, and also upon the body, tackle, apparel, ordnance, munition, artillery, boat, and other furniture, of and in the good ship or vessel called the .. .. whereof is master under God, for this present voyage, ... or whosoever else shall go for master in the said ship, or by whatsoever other name or names the said ship, or the master thereof, is or shall be named or called; beginning the adventure upon the said goods and merchandises from the loading thereof aboard the said ship, ... upon the said ship, ... etc and so shall continue and endure, during her abode there, upon the said ship, etc. And further, until the said ship, with all her ordnance, tackle, apparel, etc, and goods and merchandises whatsoever shall be arrived at .. .. upon the said ship, etc, until she hath moored at anchor for twenty-four hours in good safety; and upon the goods and merchandises, until the same be there discharged and safely landed. And it shall be lawful for the said ship, etc, in this voyage, to proceed and sail to and touch and stay at any ports or places whatsoever without prejudice to this insurance. The said ship, etc, goods and merchandises, etc, for so much as concerns the assured by agreement between the assured and assurers in this policy, are and shall be valued at .. ..

Touching the adventures and perils which we the assurers are contented to bear and do take upon us in this voyage: they are of the seas, men of war, fire, enemies, pirates, rovers, thieves, jettisons, letters of mart and countermart, surprisals, takings at sea, arrests, restraints, and detainments of all kings, princes, and people, of what nation, condition, or quality soever, barratry of the master and mariners, and of all other perils, losses, and misfortunes, that have or shall come to the hurt, detriment, or damage of the said goods and merchandises, and ship, etc, or any part thereof. And in case of any loss or misfortune it shall be lawful to the assured, their factors, servants and assigns, to sue, labour, and travel for, in and about the defence, safeguards, and recovery of the said goods and merchandises, and ship, etc, or any part thereof, without prejudice to this insurance; to the charges whereof we, the assurers, will contribute each one according to the rate and quantity of his sum herein assured. And it is especially declared and agreed that no acts of the insurer or insured in recovering, saving, or preserving the property insured shall be considered as a waiver, or acceptance of abandonment. And it is agreed by us, the insurers, that this writing or policy of assurance shall be of as much force and effect as the surest writing or policy of assurance heretofore made in Lombard Street, or in the Royal Exchange, or elsewhere in London. And so we, the assurers, are contented, and do hereby promise and bind ourselves, each one for his own part, our heirs, executors, and goods to the assured, their executors, administrators, and assigns, for the true performance of the premises, confessing ourselves paid the consideration due unto us for this assurance by the assured, at and after the rate of .. ..

In Witness whereof we, the assurers, have subscribed our names and sums assured in London.

N.B.—Corn, fish, salt, fruit, flour, and seed are warranted free from average, unless general, or the ship be stranded—sugar, tobacco, hemp, flax, hides and skins are warranted free from average, under five pounds per cent, and all other goods, also the ship and freight, are warranted free from average, under three pounds per cent unless general, or the ship be stranded.

Rules for construction of policy

The following are the rules referred to by this Act for the construction of a policy in the above or other like form, where the context does not otherwise require:—

1   Where the subject-matter is insured 'lost or not lost', and the loss has occurred before the contract is concluded, the risk attaches, unless at such time the assured was aware of the loss, and the insurer was not.

2   Where the subject-matter is insured 'from' a particular place, the risk does not attach until the ship starts on the voyage insured.

3   (a)   Where a ship is insured 'at and from' a particular place, and she is at that place in good safety when the contract is concluded, the risk attaches immediately.

(b)   If she be not at that place when the contract is concluded, the risk attaches as soon as she arrives there in good safety, and, unless the policy otherwise provides, it is immaterial that she is covered by another policy for a specified time after arrival.

(c)   Where chartered freight is insured 'at and from' a particular place, and the ship is at that place in good safety when the contract is concluded the risk attaches immediately. If she be not there when the contract is concluded, the risk attaches as soon as she arrives there in good safety.

(d)   Where freight, other than chartered freight, is payable without special conditions and is insured 'at and from' a particular place, the risk attaches pro rata as the goods or merchandise are shipped; provided that if there be cargo in readiness which belongs to the shipowner, or which some other person has contracted with him to ship, the risk attaches as soon as the ship is ready to receive such cargo.

4   Where goods or other moveables are insured 'from the loading thereof', the risk does not attach until such goods or moveables are actually on board, and the insurer is not liable for them while in transit from shore to ship.

5   Where the risk on goods or other moveables continues until they are 'safely landed', they must be landed in the customary manner and within a reasonable time after arrival at the port of discharge, and if they are not so landed the risk ceases.

6   In the absence of any further license or usage, the liberty to touch and stay 'at any port or place whatsoever' does not authorise the ship to depart from the course of her voyage from the port of departure to the port of destination.

7   The term 'perils of the seas' refers only to fortuitous accidents or casualties of the seas. It does not include the ordinary action of the winds and waves.

8   The term 'pirates' includes passengers who mutiny and rioters who attack the ship from the shore.

9   The term 'thieves' does not cover clandestine theft or a theft committed by anyone of the ship's company, whether crew or passengers.

10   The term 'arrests, etc, of kings, princes, and people' refers to political or

executive acts, and does not include a loss caused by riot or by ordinary judicial process.

11   The term 'barratry' includes every wrongful act wilfully committed by the master or crew to the prejudice of the owner, or, as the case may be, the charterer.

12   The term 'all other perils' includes only perils similar in kind to the perils specifically mentioned in the policy.

13   The term 'average unless general' means a partial loss of the subject-matter insured other than a general average loss, and does not include 'particular charges'.

14   Where the ship has stranded, the insurer is liable for the excepted losses, although the loss is not attributable to the stranding, provided that when the stranding takes place the risk has attached and, if the policy be on goods, that the damaged goods are on board.

15   The term 'ship' includes the hull, materials and outfit, stores and provisions for the officers and crew, and, in the case of vessels engaged in a special trade, the ordinary fittings requisite for the trade, and also, in the case of a steamship, the machinery, boilers, and coals and engine stores, if owned by the assured.

16   The term 'freight' includes the profit derivable by a shipowner from the employment of his ship to carry his own goods or moveables, as well as freight payable by a third party, but does not include passage money.

17   The term 'goods' means goods in the nature of merchandise, and does not include personal effects or provisions and stores for use on board.

In the absence of any usage to the contrary, deck cargo and living animals must be insured specifically, and not under the general denomination of goods.

LIMITED PARTNERSHIPS ACT 1907
(7 Edw 7, c 24)

3   Interpretation of terms
In the construction of this Act the following words and expressions shall have the meanings respectively assigned to them in this section, unless there be something in the subject or context repugnant to such construction:—

'Firm,' 'firm name,' and 'business' have the same meanings as in the Partnership Act 1890:

'General partner' shall mean any partner who is not a limited partner as defined by this Act.

4   Definition and constitution of limited partnership
(1)   [. . .] Limited partnerships may be formed in the manner and subject to the conditions by this Act provided.

(2)   A limited partnership [. . .] must consist of one or more persons called general partners, who shall be liable for all debts and obligations of the firm, and one or more persons to be called limited partners, who shall at the time of entering into such partnership contribute thereto a sum or sums as capital or property valued at a stated amount, and who shall not be liable for the debts or obligations of the firm beyond the amount so contributed.

(3)   A limited partner shall not during the continuance of the partnership, either directly or indirectly, draw out or receive back any part of his contribution, and if he does so draw out or receive back any such part shall be liable for the debts and obligations of the firm up to the amount so drawn out or received back.

(4)   A body corporate may be a limited partner.

5   Registration of limited partnership required
Every limited partnership must be registered as such in accordance with the provisions of this Act [. . .].

6   Modifications of general law in case of limited partnerships

(1)   A limited partner shall not take part in the management of the partnership business, and shall not have power to bind the firm:

Provided that a limited partner may by himself or his agent at any time inspect the books of the firm and examine into the state and prospects of the partnership business, and may advise with the partners thereon.

If a limited partner takes part in the management of the partnership business he shall be liable for all debts and obligations of the firm incurred while he so takes part in the management as though he were a general partner.

(2)   A limited partnership shall not be dissolved by the death or bankruptcy of a limited partner, and the lunacy of a limited partner shall not be a ground for dissolution of the partnership by the court unless the lunatic's share cannot be otherwise ascertained and realised.

(3)   In the event of the dissolution of a limited partnership its affairs shall be wound up by the general partners unless the court otherwise orders.

[. . .]

(5)   Subject to any agreement expressed or implied between the partners—

(a)   Any difference arising as to ordinary matters connected with the partnership business may be decided by a majority of the general partners;

(b)   A limited partner may, with the consent of the general partners, assign his share in the partnership, and upon such an assignment the assignee shall become a limited partner with all the rights of the assignor;

(c)   The other partners shall not be entitled to dissolve the partnership by reason of any limited partner suffering his share to be charged for his separate debt;

(d)   A person may be introduced as a partner without the consent of the existing limited partners;

(e)   A limited partner shall not be entitled to dissolve the partnership by notice.

7   Law as to private partnerships to apply where not excluded by this Act

Subject to the provisions of this Act, the Partnership Act 1890, and the rules of equity and of common law applicable to partnerships, except so far as they are inconsistent with the express provisions of the last-mentioned Act, shall apply to limited partnerships.

[8   Duty to register

The registrar shall register a limited partnership if an application is made to the registrar in accordance with section 8A.]

[8A   Application for registration

(1)   An application for registration must—

(a)   specify the firm name, complying with section 8B, under which the limited partnership is to be registered,

(b)   contain the details listed in subsection (2),

(c)   be signed or otherwise authenticated by or on behalf of each partner, and

(d)   be made to the registrar for the part of the United Kingdom in which the principal place of business of the limited partnership is to be situated.

(2)   The required details are—

(a)   the general nature of the partnership business,

(b)   the name of each general partner,

(c)   the name of each limited partner,

(d)   the amount of the capital contribution of each limited partner (and whether the contribution is paid in cash or in another specified form),

(e)   the address of the proposed principal place of business of the limited partnership, and

(f)   the term (if any) for which the limited partnership is to be entered into (beginning with the date of registration).]

[8B   Name of limited partnership

(1)   This section sets out conditions which must be satisfied by the firm name of a limited partnership as specified in the application for registration.

(2)   The name must end with—

(a)   the words 'limited partnership' (upper or lower case, or any combination), or

(b)   the abbreviation 'LP' (upper or lower case, or any combination, with or without punctuation).

(3)   But if the principal place of business of a limited partnership is to be in Wales, its firm name may end with—

(a)   the words 'partneriaeth cyfyngedig' (upper or lower case, or any combination), or

(b)   the abbreviation 'PC' (upper or lower case, or any combination, with or without punctuation).]

[8C   Certificate of registration

(1)   On registering a limited partnership the registrar shall issue a certificate of registration.

(2)   The certificate must be—

(a)   signed by the registrar, or

(b)   authenticated with the registrar's seal.

(3)   The certificate must state—

(a)   the firm name of the limited partnership given in the application for registration,

(b)   the limited partnership's registration number,

(c)   the date of registration, and

(d)   that the limited partnership is registered as a limited partnership under this Act.

(4)   The certificate is conclusive evidence that a limited partnership came into existence on the date of registration.]

9   Registration of changes in partnerships

(1)   If during the continuance of a limited partnership any change is made or occurs in—

(a)   the firm name,

(b)   the general nature of the business,

(c)   the principal place of business,

(d)   the partners or the name of any partner,

(e)   the term of character of the partnership,

(f)   the sum contributed by any limited partner,

(g)   the liability of any partner by reason of his becoming a limited instead of a general partner or a general instead of a limited partner,

a statement, signed by the firm, specifying the nature of the change, shall within seven days be sent by post or delivered to the registrar [. . .].

(2)   If default is made in compliance with the requirements of this section each of the general partners shall, on conviction under [the Magistrates' Courts Act 1952], be liable to a fine not exceeding one pound for each day during which the default continues.

10   Advertisement in Gazette of statement of general partner becoming a limited partner and of assignment of share of limited partner

(1)   Notice of any arrangement or transaction under which any person will cease to be a general partner in any firm, and will become a limited partner in that firm, or under which the share of a limited partner in a firm will be assigned to any person, shall be forthwith advertised in the Gazette, and until notice of the

arrangement or transaction is so advertised the arrangement or transaction shall, for the purposes of this Act, be deemed to be of no effect.

(2)   For the purposes of this section, the expression 'the Gazette' means—

In the case of a limited partnership registered in England, the London Gazette;

In the case of a limited partnership registered in Scotland, the Edinburgh Gazette;

In the case of a limited partnership registered in [Northern Ireland], the [Belfast] Gazette.

[. . .]

13   Registrar to file statement and issue certificate of registration

On receiving any statement made in pursuance of this Act the registrar shall cause the same to be filed, and he shall send by post to the firm from whom such statement shall have been received a certificate of the registration thereof.

14   Register and index to be kept

[. . .] the registrar shall keep [. . .] a register and an index of all the limited partnerships registered as aforesaid, and of all the statements registered in relation to such partnerships.

[15   The registrar

(1)   The registrar of companies is the registrar of limited partnerships.

(2)   In this Act—

(a)   references to the registrar in relation to the registration of a limited partnership are to the registrar to whom the application for registration is to be made (see section 8A(1)(d));

(b)   references to registration in a particular part of the United Kingdom are to registration by the registrar for that part of the United Kingdom;

(c)   references to the registrar in relation to any other matter relating to a limited partnership are to the registrar for the part of the United Kingdom in which the partnership is registered.]

16   Inspection of statements registered

(1)   Any person may inspect the statements filed by the registrar [. . .]; and any person may require a certificate of the registration of any limited partnership, or a copy of or extract from any registered statement, to be certified by the registrar [. . .].

(2)   A certificate of registration, or a copy of or extract from any statement registered under this Act, if duly certified to be a true copy under the hand of the registrar [. . .] (whom it shall not be necessary to prove to be the registrar [. . .]) shall, in all legal proceedings, civil or criminal, and in all cases whatsoever be received in evidence.

CONVEYANCING (SCOTLAND) ACT 1924
(14 & 15 Geo 5, c 27)

44   General Register of Inhibitions and Register of Adjudications to be combined; limitation of effect of entries therein

(1)   The General Register of Inhibitions and Interdictions and the Register of Adjudications shall be combined, and the Keeper thereof shall keep only one register for inhibitions, interdictions, adjudications, reductions, and notices of litigiosity, and such register shall be called the Register of Inhibitions and Adjudications; and a reference in any public, general or local Act to the General Register of Inhibitions or the Register of Adjudications shall be deemed to mean and include such Register of Inhibitions and Adjudications.

(2)(a)   No action whether raised before or after the commencement of this Act relating to land or to a lease or to a heritable security, shall be deemed to have had or shall have the effect of making such land, lease or heritable security litigious, unless and until [—

(i)] a notice relative to such action in or as nearly as may be in the form of Schedule RR annexed to the Titles to Land Consolidation (Scotland) Act, 1868, shall have been or shall be registered in the Register of Inhibitions [. . .] in the manner provided by section one hundred and fifty-nine of that Act [; or

(ii) a notice of an application under section 8 of the Law Reform (Miscellaneous Provisions)(Scotland) Act 1985 has been registered in the said register.]

(b) No decree in any action of adjudication of land or of a lease or of a heritable security, whether pronounced before or after the commencement of this Act, and no abbreviate of any such decree shall be deemed to have had or to have any effect in making such land, lease or heritable security litigious.

(3)(a) All inhibitions and all notices of litigiosity registered in terms of section one hundred and fifty-nine of the Titles to Land Consolidation (Scotland) Act, 1868, subsisting at the commencement of this Act shall prescribe and be of no effect on the lapse of five years after such commencement or at such earlier date as they would prescribe according to the present law and practice; and all [. . .] [, notices of litigiosity and notices of applications under section 8 of the Law Reform (Miscellaneous Provisions)(Scotland) Act 1985] which relate to land or to a lease or to a heritable security and which shall be first registered after the commencement of this Act, shall prescribe and be of no effect on the lapse of five years from the date on which the same shall respectively take effect: Provided that in no case shall litigiosity be pleadable or be founded on to any effect after the expiry of six months from and after final decree is pronounced in the action creating such litigiosity.

[(aa) all inhibitions shall cease to have effect on the lapse of five years from the date on which they take effect.]

(b) From and after the commencement of this Act interdiction, whether judicial or voluntary, shall be incompetent, and any interdiction which is legally operative at such commencement shall remain legally operative for not longer than the period of five years thereafter.

(4) [. . .]

(c) No deed, decree, instrument or writing granted or expede by a person whose estates have been sequestrated under the Bankruptcy (Scotland) Act, 1856, or the Bankruptcy (Scotland) Act, 1913 [or the Bankruptcy (Scotland) Act 1985], or the heirs, executors, successors or assignees of such person relative to any land or lease or heritable security belonging to such person at the date of such sequestration or subsequently acquired by him shall be challengeable or denied effect on the ground of such sequestration if such deed, decree, instrument or writing shall have been granted or expede, or shall come into operation at a date when the effect of recording [(a)] the abbreviate provided for under section forty-four of the said Act of 1913, as amended by this Act, shall have expired in terms of the said section as amended as aforesaid [; or (b) under subsection (1)(a) of section 14 of the Bankruptcy (Scotland) Act 1985 the certified copy of an order shall have expired by virtue of subsection (3) of that section], unless the trustee in such sequestration shall before the recording of such deed, decree, instrument or writing in the appropriate Register of Sasines have completed his title to such land, lease or heritable security by recording the same in such register [or have recorded a memorandum in such register [in the form provided by Schedule O to this Act]] Provided always, in the case of sequestrations awarded under the Bankruptcy (Scotland) Act, 1856, that the provisions of this section shall not apply to any deed, decree, instrument or writing dated within five years after the commencement of this Act.

(5) The provisions of this section shall not affect the ranking of adjudgers inter se, or any real right obtained in virtue of a decree of adjudication, or in virtue of a

decree pronounced in an action creating litigiosity, or by a trustee in bankruptcy, if such right has been completed by the recording in the appropriate Register of Sasines of any deed, decree, abbreviate, or instrument necessary to effect the completion of such right.

(6) Section one hundred and fifty-nine of the Titles to Land Consolidation (Scotland) Act, 1868, and sections sixteen and seventeen of the Land Registers (Scotland) Act, 1868, [. . .] are hereby amended in accordance with this section, and section forty-two of the Conveyancing (Scotland) Act, 1874, and Schedule J thereto annexed, are hereby repealed.

THIRD PARTIES (RIGHTS AGAINST INSURERS) ACT 1930
(20 & 21 Geo 5, c 25)

1 Rights of third parties against insurers on bankruptcy &c of the insured

(1)   Where under any contract of insurance a person (hereinafter referred to as the insured) is insured against liabilities to third parties which he may incur, then—

(a)   in the event of the insured becoming bankrupt or making a composition or arrangement with his creditors; or

(b)   in the case of the insured being a company, in the event of a winding-up order being made, or a resolution for a voluntary winding-up being passed, with respect to the company, [or of the company entering administration,] or of a receiver or manager of the company's business or undertaking being duly appointed, or of possession being taken, by or on behalf of the holders of any debentures secured by a floating charge, of any property comprised in or subject to the charge [or of a voluntary arrangement proposed for the purposes of Part I of the Insolvency Act 1986 being approved under that Part];

if, either before or after that event, any such liability as aforesaid is incurred by the insured, his rights against the insurer under the contract in respect of the liability shall, notwithstanding anything in any Act or rule of law to the contrary, be transferred to and vest in the third party to whom the liability was so incurred.

(2)   Where [the estate of any person falls to be administered in accordance with an order under section 421 of the Insolvency Act 1986], then, if any debt provable in bankruptcy [(in Scotland, any claim accepted in the sequestration)] is owing by the deceased in respect of a liability against which he was insured under a contract of insurance as being a liability to a third party, the deceased debtor's rights against the insurer under the contract in respect of that liability shall, notwithstanding anything in [any such order], be transferred to and vest in the person to whom the debt is owing.

(3)   In so far as any contract of insurance made after the commencement of this Act in respect of any liability of the insured to third parties purports, whether directly or indirectly, to avoid the contract or to alter the rights of the parties thereunder upon the happening to the insured of any of the events specified in paragraph (a) or paragraph (b) of subsection (1) of this section or upon the [estate of any person falling to be administered in accordance with an order under section 421 of the Insolvency Act 1986], the contract shall be of no effect.

(4)   Upon a transfer under subsection (1) or subsection (2) of this section, the insurer shall, subject to the provisions of section three of this Act, be under the same liability to the third party as he would have been under to the insured, but—

(a)   if the liability of the insurer exceeds the liability of the insured to the third party, nothing in this Act shall affect the rights of the insured against the insurer in respect of the excess; and

(b)   if the liability of the insurer to the insured is less than the liability of the insured to the third party, nothing in this Act shall affect the rights of the third party against the insured in respect of the balance.

(5)　For the purposes of this Act, the expression 'liabilities to third parties', in relation to a person insured under any contract of insurance, shall not include any liability of that person in the capacity of insurer under some other contract of insurance.

(6)　This Act shall not apply—

(a)　where a company is wound up voluntarily merely for the purposes of reconstruction or of amalgamation with another company; or

(b)　to any case to which subsections (1) and (2) of section seven of the Workmen's Compensation Act 1925, applies.

2　Duty to give necessary information to third parties

(1)　In the event of any person becoming bankrupt or making a composition or arrangement with his creditors, or in the event of [the estate of any person falling to be administered in accordance with an order under section 421 of the Insolvency Act 1986], or in the event of a winding-up order being made, or a resolution for a voluntary winding-up being passed, with respect to any company [or of the company entering administration] or of a receiver or manager of the company's business or undertaking being duly appointed or of possession being taken by or on behalf of the holders of any debentures secured by a floating charge of any property comprised in or subject to the charge it shall be the duty of the bankrupt, debtor, personal representative of the deceased debtor or company, and, as the case may be, of the trustee in bankruptcy, trustee, liquidator, [administrator,] receiver, or manager, or person in possession of the property to give at the request of any person claiming that the bankrupt, debtor, deceased debtor, or company is under a liability to him such information as may reasonably be required by him for the purpose of ascertaining whether any rights have been transferred to and vested in him by this Act and for the purpose of enforcing such rights, if any, and any contract of insurance, in so far as it purports, whether directly or indirectly, to avoid the contract or to alter the rights of the parties thereunder upon the giving of any such information in the events aforesaid or otherwise to prohibit or prevent the giving thereof in the said events shall be of no effect.

[(1A)　The reference in subsection (1) of this section to a trustee includes a reference to the supervisor of a [voluntary arrangement proposed for the purposes of, and approved under, Part I or Part VIII of the Insolvency Act 1986]].

(2)　If the information given to any person in pursuance of subsection (1) of this section discloses reasonable ground for supposing that there have or may have been transferred to him under this Act rights against any particular insurer, that insurer shall be subject to the same duty as is imposed by the said subsection on the persons therein mentioned.

(3)　The duty to give information imposed by this section shall include a duty to allow all contracts of insurance, receipts for premiums, and other relevant documents in the possession or power of the person on whom the duty is so imposed to be inspected and copies thereof to be taken.

3　Settlement between insurers and insured persons

Where the insured has become bankrupt or where in the case of the insured being a company, a winding-up order [or an administrative order] has been made or a resolution for a voluntary winding-up has been passed, with respect to the company, no agreement made between the insurer and the insured after liability has been incurred to a third party and after the commencement of the bankruptcy or winding-up [or the day of the making of the administration order], as the case may be, nor any waiver, assignment, or other disposition made by, or payment made to the insured after the commencement [or day] aforesaid shall be effective to defeat or affect the rights transferred to the third party under this Act, but those rights shall be the same as if no such agreement, waiver, assignment, disposition or payment had been made.

[3A   Application to limited liability partnerships
   (1)   This Act applies to limited liability partnerships as it applies to companies.
   (2)   In its application to limited liability partnerships, references to a resolution for a voluntary winding-up being passed are references to a determination for a voluntary winding-up being made.]

4   Application to Scotland
In the application of this Act to Scotland—
   [. . .]
   (b)   any reference to [an estate falling to be administered in accordance with an order under section 421 of the Insolvency Act 1986], shall be deemed to include a reference to an award of sequestration of the estate of a deceased debtor, and a reference to an appointment of a judicial factor, under section [11A of the Judicial Factors (Scotland) Act 1889], on the insolvent estate of a deceased person.

5   Short title
This Act may be cited as the Third Parties (Rights against Insurers) Act 1930.

CHEQUES ACT 1957
(5 & 6 Eliz 2, c 36)

1   Protection of bankers paying unindorsed or irregularly indorsed cheques, etc
   (1)   Where a banker in good faith and in the ordinary course of business pays a cheque drawn on him which is not indorsed or is irregularly indorsed, he does not in doing so, incur any liability by reason only of the absence of, or irregularly in indorsement, and he is deemed to have paid it in due course.
   (2)   Where a banker in good faith and in the ordinary course of business pays any such instrument as the following namely—
   (a)   a document issued by a customer of his which, though not a bill of exchange, is intended to enable a person to obtain payment from him of the sum mentioned in the document;
   (b)   a draft payable on demand drawn by him upon himself, whether payable at the head office or some other office of his bank; he does not, in so doing, incur any liability by reason only of the absence of, or irregularity in, indorsement, and the payment discharges the instrument.

2   Rights of bankers collecting cheques not indorsed by holders
A banker who gives value for, or has a lien on, a cheque payable to order which the holder delivers to him for collection without indorsing it, has such (if any) rights as he would have had if, upon delivery, the holder had indorsed it in blank.

3   Unindorsed cheques as evidence of payment
   [(1)]   An unindorsed cheque which appears to have been paid by the banker on whom it is drawn is evidence of the receipt by the payee of the sum payable by the cheque.
   [(2)   For the purposes of subsection (1) above, a copy of a cheque to which that subsection applies is evidence of the cheque if—
   (a)   the copy is made by the banker in whose possession the cheque is after presentment and,
   (b)   it is certified by him to be a true copy of the original.]

4   Protection of bankers collecting payment of cheques, etc
   (1)   Where a banker, in good faith and without negligence—
   (a)   receives payment for a customer of an instrument to which this section applies; or

(b)   having credited a customer's account with the amount of such an instrument, receives payment thereof for himself;
and the customer has no title, or a defective title, to the instrument, the banker
does not incur any liability to the true owner of the instrument by reason only of
having received payment thereof.

(2)   This section applies to the following instruments, namely:—

(a)   cheques [(including cheques which under section 81A(1) of the Bills of
Exchange Act 1882 or otherwise are not transferable)];

(b)   any document issued by a customer of a banker which, though not a bill
of exchange, is intended to enable a person to obtain payment from that banker
of the sum mentioned in the document;

(c)   any document issued by a public officer is intended to enable a person to
obtain payment from the Paymaster General or the Queen's and Lord
Treasurer's Remembrancer of the sum mentioned in the document but is not a
bill of exchange;

(d)   any draft payable on demand drawn by a banker upon himself whether
payable at the head office or some other office of his bank.

(3)   A banker is not to be treated for the purposes of this section as having been
negligent by reason only of his failure to concern himself with absence of, or
irregularity in, indorsement of an instrument.

5   Application of certain provisions of Bills of Exchange Act, 1882, to instruments not being bills of exchange

The provisions of the Bills of Exchange Act, 1882, relating to crossed cheques shall,
so far as applicable, have effect in relation to instruments (other than cheques) to
which the last foregoing section applies as they have effect in relation to cheques.

6   Construction, saving and repeal

(1)   This Act shall be construed as one with the Bills of Exchange Act, 1882.

(2)   The foregoing provisions of this Act do not make negotiable any instrument
which, apart from them, is not negotiable.

[. . .]

HIRE-PURCHASE ACT 1964
(1964, c 53)

[PART III
TITLE TO MOTOR VEHICLES ON HIRE-PURCHASE OR CONDITIONAL SALE

27   Protection of purchasers of motor vehicles

(1)   This section applies where a motor vehicle has been bailed or (in Scotland)
hired under a hire-purchase agreement, or has been agreed to be sold under a conditional sale agreement, and, before the property in the vehicle has become vested
in the debtor, he disposes of the vehicle to another person.

(2)   Where the disposition referred to in subsection (1) above is to a private purchaser, and he is a purchaser of the motor vehicle in good faith without notice of
the hire-purchase or conditional sale agreement (the 'relevant agreement') that disposition shall have effect as if the creditor's title to the vehicle has been vested in
the debtor immediately before that disposition.

(3)   Where the person to whom the disposition referred to in subsection (1)
above is made (the 'original purchaser') is a trade or finance purchaser, then if the
person who is the first private purchaser of the motor vehicle after that disposition
(the 'first private purchaser') is a purchaser of the vehicle in good faith without
notice of the relevant agreement, the disposition of the vehicle to the first private
purchaser shall have effect as if the title of the creditor to the vehicle had been
vested in the debtor immediately before he disposed of it to the original purchaser.

(4)   Where, in a case within subsection (3) above—

(a)   the disposition by which the first private purchaser becomes a purchaser of the motor vehicle in good faith without notice of the relevant agreement is itself a bailment or hiring under a hire-purchase agreement, and

(b)   the person who is the creditor in relation to that agreement disposes of the vehicle to the first private purchaser, or a person claiming under him, by transferring to him the property in the vehicle in pursuance of a provision in the agreement in that behalf, the disposition referred to in paragraph (b) above (whether or not the person to whom it is made is a purchaser in good faith without notice of the relevant agreement) shall as well as the disposition referred to in paragraph (a) above, have effect as mentioned in subsection (3) above.

(5)   The preceding provisions of this section apply—

(a)   notwithstanding anything in [section 21 of the Sale of Goods Act 1979] (sale of goods by a person not the owner), but

(b)   without prejudice to the provisions of the Factors Acts (as defined by [section 61(1) of the said Act of 1979]) or any other enactment enabling the apparent owner of goods to dispose of them as if he were the true owner.

(6)   Nothing in this section shall exonerate the debtor from any liability (whether criminal or civil) to which he would be subject apart from this section; and, in a case where the debtor disposes of the motor vehicle to a trade or finance purchaser, nothing in this section shall exonerate—

(a)   that trade or finance purchaser, or

(b)   any other trade or finance purchaser who becomes a purchaser of the vehicle and is not a person claiming under the first private purchaser,

from any liability (whether criminal or civil) to which he would be subject apart from this section.

28   Presumptions relating to dealings with motor vehicles

(1)   Where in any proceedings (whether criminal or civil) relating to a motor vehicle it is proved—

(a)   that the vehicle was bailed or (in Scotland) hired under a hire-purchase agreement, or was agreed to be sold under a conditional sale agreement, and

(b)   that a person (whether a party to the proceedings or not) became a private purchaser of the vehicle in good faith without notice of the hire-purchase or conditional sale agreement (the 'relevant agreement'), this section shall have effect for the purposes of the operation of section 27 of this Act in relation to those proceedings.

(2)   It shall be presumed for those purposes unless the contrary is proved, that the disposition of the vehicle to the person referred to in subsection (1)(b) above (the 'relevant purchaser') was made by the debtor.

(3)   If it is proved that that disposition was not made by the debtor, then it shall be presumed for those purposes, unless the contrary is proved—

(a)   that the debtor disposed of the vehicle to a private purchaser purchasing in good faith without notice of the relevant agreement, and

(b)   that the relevant purchaser is or was a person claiming under the person to whom the debtor so disposed of the vehicle.

(4)   If it is proved that the disposition of the vehicle to the relevant purchaser was not made by the debtor, and that the person to whom the debtor disposed of the vehicle (the 'original purchaser') was a trade or finance purchaser, then it shall be presumed for those purposes, unless the contrary is proved—   .

(a)   that the person who, after the disposition of the vehicle to the original purchaser, first became a private purchaser of the vehicle was a purchaser in good faith without notice of the relevant agreement, and

(b)   that the relevant purchaser is or was a person claiming under the original purchaser.

(5)   Without prejudice to any other method of proof, where in any proceedings

a party thereto admits a fact, that fact shall, for the purposes of this section, be taken as against him to be proved in relation to those proceedings.

29 Interpretation of Part III

(1) In this Part of this Act—

'conditional sale agreement' means an agreement for the sale of goods under which the purchase price or part of it is payable by instalments, and the property in the goods is to remain in the seller (notwithstanding that the buyer is to be in possession of the goods) until such conditions as to the payment of instalments or otherwise as may be specified in the agreement are fulfilled;

'creditor' means the person by whom goods are bailed or (in Scotland) hired under a hire-purchase agreement or as the case may be, the seller under a conditional sale agreement, or the person to whom his rights and duties have passed by assignment or operation of law;

'disposition' means any sale or contract of sale (including a conditional sale agreement), any bailment or (in Scotland) hiring under a hire-purchase agreement and any transfer of the property of goods in pursuance of a provision in that behalf contained in a hire-purchase agreement, and includes any transaction purporting to be a disposition (as so defined), and 'dispose of' shall be construed accordingly;

'hire-purchase agreement' means an agreement, other than a conditional sale agreement, under which—

(a) goods are bailed or (in Scotland) hired in return for periodical payments by the person to whom they are bailed or hired, and

(b) the property in the goods will pass to that person if the terms of the agreement are complied with and one or more of the following occurs—

(i) the exercise of an option to purchase by that person,

(ii) the doing of any other specified act by any party to the agreement,

(iii) the happening of any other specified events; and

'motor vehicle' means a mechanically propelled vehicle intended or adapted for use on roads to which the public has access.

(2) In this Part of this Act 'trade or finance purchaser' means a purchaser who, at the time of the disposition made to him, carries on a business which consists, wholly or partly—

(a) of purchasing motor vehicles for the purpose of offering or exposing them for sale, or

(b) of providing finance by purchasing motor vehicles for the purpose of bailing or (in Scotland) hiring them under hire-purchase agreements or agreeing to sell them under conditional sale agreements,

and 'private purchaser' means a purchaser who, at the time of the disposition made to him, does not carry on any such business.

(3) For the purposes of this Part of this Act a person becomes a purchaser of a motor vehicle if, and at the time when, a disposition of the vehicle is made to him; and a person shall be taken to be a purchaser of a motor vehicle without notice of a hire-purchase agreement or conditional sale agreement if, at the time of the disposition made to him, he has no actual notice that the vehicle is or was the subject of any such agreement.

(4) In this Part of this Act the 'debtor' in relation to a motor vehicle which has been bailed or hired under a hire-purchase agreement, or, as the case may be, agreed to be sold under a conditional sale agreement, means the person who at the material time (whether the agreement has before that time been terminated or not) either—

(a) is the person to whom the vehicle is bailed or hired under that agreement, or

(b) is, in relation to the agreement, the buyer,

including a person who at that time is, by virtue of section 130(4) of the

Consumer Credit Act 1974 treated as a bailee or (in Scotland) a custodier of the vehicle.

(5)   In this Part of this Act any reference to the title of the creditor to a motor vehicle which has been bailed or (in Scotland) hired under a hire-purchase agreement or agreed to be sold under a conditional sale agreement, and is disposed of by the debtor, is a reference to such title (if any) to the vehicle as, immediately before that disposition, was vested in the person who then was the creditor in relation to the agreement.]

CARRIAGE OF GOODS BY ROAD ACT 1965
(1965, c 37)

1   Convention to have force of law
Subject to the following provisions of this Act, the provisions of the Convention on the Contract for the International Carriage of Goods by Road (in this Act referred to as 'the Convention'), as set out in the Schedule to this Act, shall have the force of law in the United Kingdom so far as they relate to the rights and liabilities of persons concerned in the carriage of goods by road under a contract to which the Convention applies.

2   Designation of High Contracting Parties
(1)   Her Majesty may by Order in Council from time to time certify who are the High Contracting Parties to the Convention and in respect of what territories they are respectively parties.

(2)   An Order in Council under this section shall, except so far as it has been superseded by a subsequent Order, be conclusive evidence of the matters so certified.

3   Power of court to take account of other proceedings
(1)   A court before which proceedings are brought to enforce a liability which is limited by article 23 in the Schedule to this Act may at any stage of the proceedings make any such order as appears to the court to be just and equitable in view of the provisions of the said article 23 and of any other proceedings which have been, or are likely to be, commenced in the United Kingdom or elsewhere to enforce the liability in whole or in part.

(2)   Without prejudice to the preceding subsection, a court before which proceedings are brought to enforce a liability which is limited by the said article 23 shall, where the liability is, or may be, partly enforceable in other proceedings in the United Kingdom or elsewhere, have jurisdiction to award an amount less than the court would have awarded if the limitation applied solely to the proceedings before the court, or to make any part of its award conditional on the result of any other proceedings.

4   Registration of foreign judgments
(1)   Subject to the next following subsection, Part I of the Foreign Judgments (Reciprocal Enforcement) Act 1933 (in this section referred to as 'the Act of 1933') shall apply whether or not it would otherwise have so applied, to any judgment which—

(a)   has been given in any such action as is referred to in paragraph 1 of article 31 in the Schedule to this Act, and

(b)   has been so given by any court or tribunal of a territory in respect of which one of the High Contracting Parties other than the United Kingdom, is a party to the Convention, and

(c)   has become enforceable in that territory.

(2)   In the application of Part I of the Act of 1933 in relation to any such judg-

ment as is referred to in the preceding subsection, section 4 of that Act shall have effect with the omission of subsections (2) and (3).

(3)   The registration, in accordance with Part I of the Act of 1933, of any such judgment as is referred to in subsection (1) of this section shall constitute, in relation to that judgment compliance with the formalities for the purposes of paragraph 3 of article 31 in the Schedule to this Act.

5   Contribution between carriers

(1)   Where a carrier under a contract to which the Convention applies is liable in respect of any loss or damage for which compensation is payable under the Convention, nothing in [section 1 of the Civil Liability (Contribution) Act 1978] or section 3(2) of the Law Reform (Miscellaneous Provisions) (Scotland) Act 1940 shall confer on him any right to recover contribution in respect of that loss or damage from any other carrier who, in accordance with article 34 in the Schedule to this Act, is a party to the contract of carriage.

(2)   The preceding subsection shall be without prejudice to the operation of article 37 in the Schedule to this Act.

6   Actions against High Contracting Parties

Every High Contracting Party to the Convention shall, for the purpose of any proceedings brought in a court in the United Kingdom in accordance with the provisions of article 31 in the Schedule to this Act to enforce a claim in respect of carriage undertaken by that Party, be deemed to have submitted to the jurisdiction of that court, and accordingly rules of court may provide for the manner in which any such action is to be commenced and carried on; but nothing in this section shall authorise the issue of execution, or in Scotland the execution of diligence, against the property of any High Contracting Party.

7   Arbitrations

(1)   Any reference in the preceding provisions of this Act to a court includes a reference to an arbitration tribunal acting by virtue of article 33 in the Schedule to this Act.

(2)   For the purposes of article 32 in the Schedule to this Act, as it has effect (by virtue of the said article 33) in relation to arbitrations,—

[(a)   as respects England and Wales and Northern Ireland, the provisions of section 14(3) to (5) of the Arbitration Act 1996 (which determine the time at which an arbitration is commenced) apply;]

(c)   as respects Scotland, an arbitration shall be deemed to be commenced when one party to the arbitration serves on the other party or parties a notice requiring him or them to appoint an arbiter or to agree to the appointment of an arbiter or, where the arbitration agreement provides that the reference shall be to a person named or designated in the agreement, requiring him or them to submit the dispute to the person so named or designated.

8   Resolution of conflicts between Conventions on carriage of goods

(1)   If it appears to Her Majesty in Council that there is any conflict between the provisions of this Act (including the provisions of the Convention as set out in the Schedule to this Act) and any provisions relating to the carriage of goods for reward by land, sea or air contained in—

(a)   any other Convention which has been signed or ratified by or on behalf of Her Majesty's Government in the United Kingdom before the passing of this Act, or

(b)   any enactment of the Parliament of the United Kingdom giving effect to such a Convention,

Her Majesty may by Order in Council make such provision as may seem to her to be appropriate for resolving that conflict by amending or modifying this Act or any such enactment.

(2)   Any statutory instrument made by virtue of this section shall be subject to annulment in pursuance of a resolution of either House of Parliament.

[8A   Amendments consequential on revision of Convention
(1)   If at any time it appears to Her Majesty in Council that Her Majesty's Government in the United Kingdom have agreed to any revision of the Convention, Her Majesty may by Order in Council make such amendment of—
    [(a)   this Act; and]
    (c)   section 5(1) of the Carriage by Air and Road Act 1979,
as appear to Her to be appropriate in consequence of the revision.

(2)   In the preceding subsection 'revision' means an omission from, addition to or alteration of the Convention and includes replacement of the Convention or part of it by another Convention.

(3)   An Order in Council under this section shall not be made unless a draft of the Order has been laid before Parliament and approved by a resolution of each House of Parliament. [. . .]

9   Application to British possessions, etc
Her Majesty may by Order in Council direct that this Act shall extend, subject to such exceptions, adaptations and modifications as may be specified in the Order, to—
    (a)   the Isle of Man;
    (b)   any of the Channel Islands;
    (c)   any colony.

10   Application to Scotland
In its application to Scotland, the Schedule to this Act shall have effect as if—
    (a)   any reference therein to a plaintiff included a reference to a pursuer;
    (b)   any reference therein to a defendant included a defender; and
    (c)   any reference to security for costs included a reference to caution for expenses.

11   [Applies to Northern Ireland]

12   Orders in Council
An Order in Council made under any of the preceding provisions of this Act may contain such transitional and supplementary provisions as appear to Her Majesty to be expedient and may be varied or revoked by a subsequent Order in Council made under that provision.

13   Application to Crown
This Act shall bind the Crown.

14   Short title, interpretation and commencement
(1)   This Act may be cited as the Carriage of Goods by Road Act 1965.

(2)   The persons who, for the purposes of this Act, are persons concerned in the carriage of goods by road under a contract to which the Convention applies are—
    (a)   the sender,
    (b)   the consignee,
    (c)   any carrier who, in accordance with article 34 in the Schedule to this Act or otherwise, is a party to the contract of carriage,
    (d)   any person for whom such a carrier is responsible by virtue of article 3 in the Schedule to this Act,
    (e)   any person to whom the rights and liabilities of any of the persons referred to in paragraphs (a) to (d) of this subsection have passed (whether by assignment or assignation or by operation of law).

(3)   Except in so far as the context otherwise requires, any reference in this Act

to an enactment shall be construed as a reference to that enactment as amended or extended by or under any other enactment.

(4) This Act shall come into operation on such day as Her Majesty may by Order in Council appoint; but nothing in this Act shall apply in relation to any contract for the carriage of goods by road made before the day so appointed.

SCHEDULE
CONVENTION ON THE CONTRACT FOR THE INTERNATIONAL CARRIAGE
OF GOODS BY ROAD (CMR)
Section 1

CHAPTER I
Scope of application

Article 1

1 This Convention shall apply to every contract for the carriage of goods by road in vehicles for reward, when the place of taking over of the goods and the place designated for delivery, as specified in the contract, are situated in two different countries, of which at least one is a contracting country, irrespective of the place of residence and the nationality of the parties.

2 For the purposes of this Convention, 'vehicles' means motor vehicles, articulated vehicles, trailers and semi-trailers as defined in article 4 of the Convention on Road Traffic dated 19th September 1949.

3 This Convention shall apply also where carriage coming within its scope is carried out by States or by governmental institutions or organisations.

4 This Convention shall not apply:

(a) to carriage performed under the terms of any international postal convention;

(b) to funeral consignments;

(c) to furniture removal.

5 The Contracting Parties agree not to vary any of the provisions of this Convention by special agreements between two or more of them, except to make it inapplicable to their frontier traffic or to authorise the use in transport operations entirely confined to their territory of consignment notes representing a title to the goods.

Article 2

1 Where the vehicle containing the goods is carried over part of the journey by sea, rail, inland waterways or air, and except where the provisions of article 14 are applicable, the goods are not unloaded from the vehicle, this Convention shall nevertheless apply to the whole of the carriage. Provided that to the extent that it is proved that any loss, damage or delay in delivery of the goods which occurs during the carriage by the other means of transport was not caused by an act or omission of the carrier by road, but by some event which could only have occurred in the course of and by reason of the carriage by that other means of transport, the liability of the carrier by road shall be determined not by this Convention but in the manner in which the liability of the carrier by the other means of transport would have been determined if a contract for the carriage of the goods alone had been made by the sender with the carrier by the other means of transport in accordance with the conditions prescribed by law for the carriage of goods by that means of transport. If, however, there be no such prescribed conditions, the liability of the carrier by road shall be determined by this Convention.

2 If the carrier by road is also himself the carrier by the other means of transport, his liability shall also be determined in accordance with the provisions of paragraph 1 of this article, but as if, in his capacities as carrier by road and as carrier by the other means of transport, he were two separate persons.

CHAPTER II
Persons for whom the carrier is responsible

Article 3
For the purposes of this Convention the carrier shall be responsible for the acts and omissions of his agents and servants and of any other persons of whose services he makes use for the performance of the carriage, when such agents, servants or other persons are acting within the scope of their employment, as if such acts or omissions were his own.

CHAPTER III
Conclusion and performance of the contract of carriage

Article 4
The contract of carriage shall be confirmed by the making out of a consignment note. The absence, irregularity or loss of the consignment note shall not affect the existence or the validity of the contract of carriage which shall remain subject to the provisions of this Convention.

Article 5
1 The consignment note shall be made out in three original copies signed by the sender and by the carrier. These signatures may be printed or replaced by the stamps of the sender and the carrier if the law of the country in which the consignment note has been made out so permits. The first copy shall be handed to the sender, the second shall accompany the goods and the third shall be retained by the carrier.
2 When the goods which are to be carried have to be loaded in different vehicles, or are of different kinds or are divided into different lots, the sender or the carrier shall have the right to require a separate consignment note to be made out for each vehicle used, or for each kind or lot of goods.

Article 6
1 The consignment note shall contain the following particulars:
  (a) the date of the consignment note and the place at which it is made out;
  (b) the name and address of the sender;
  (c) the name and address of the carrier;
  (d) the place and the date of taking over of the goods and the place designated for delivery;
  (e) the name and address of the consignee;
  (f) the description in common use of the nature of the goods and the method of packing, and, in the case of dangerous goods, their generally recognised description;
  (g) the number of packages and their special marks and numbers;
  (h) the gross weight of the goods or their quantity otherwise expressed;
  (i) charges relating to the carriage (carriage charges, supplementary charges, customs duties and other charges incurred from the making of the contract to the time of delivery);
  (j) the requisite instructions for Customs and other formalities;
  (k) a statement that the carriage is subject, notwithstanding any clause to the contrary, to the provisions of this Convention.
2 Where applicable, the consignment note shall also contain the following particulars:
  (a) a statement that transhipment is not allowed;
  (b) the charges which the sender undertakes to pay;
  (c) the amount of 'cash on delivery' charges;
  (d) a declaration of the value of the goods and the amount representing special interest on delivery;
  (e) the sender's instructions to the carrier regarding insurance of the goods;

(f)   the agreed time-limit within which the carriage is to be carried out;

(g)   a list of documents handed to the carrier.

3   The parties may enter in the consignment note any other particulars which they deem useful.

Article 7

1   The sender shall be responsible for all expenses, loss and damage sustained by the carrier by reason of the inaccuracy or inadequacy of:

(a)   the particulars specified in article 6, paragraph 1, (b), (d), (e), (f), (g), (h) and (j);

(b)   the particulars specified in article 6, paragraph 2;

(c)   any other particulars or instructions given by him to enable the consignment note to be made out or for the purpose of their being entered therein.

2   If, at the request of the sender, the carrier enters in the consignment note the particulars referred to in paragraph 1 of this article, he shall be deemed, unless the contrary is proved to have done so on behalf of the sender.

3   If the consignment note does not contain the statement specified in article 6, paragraph 1(k), the carrier shall be liable for all expenses, loss and damage sustained through such omission by the person entitled to dispose of the goods.

Article 8

1   On taking over the goods, the carrier shall check:

(a)   the accuracy of the statements in the consignment note as to the number of packages and their marks and numbers, and

(b)   the apparent condition of the goods and their packaging.

2   Where the carrier has no reasonable means of checking the accuracy of the statements referred to in paragraph 1(a) of this article, he shall enter his reservations in the consignment note together with the grounds on which they are based. He shall likewise specify the grounds for any reservations which he makes with regard to the apparent condition of the goods and their packaging. Such reservations shall not bind the sender unless he has expressly agreed to be bound by them in the consignment note.

3   The sender shall be entitled to require the carrier to check the gross weight of the goods or their quantity otherwise expressed. He may also require the contents of the packages to be checked. The carrier shall be entitled to claim the cost of such checking. The result of the checks shall be entered in the consignment note.

Article 9

1   The consignment note shall be prima facie evidence of the making of the contract of carriage, the conditions of the contract and the receipt of the goods by the carrier.

2   If the consignment note contains no specific reservations by the carrier, it shall be presumed, unless the contrary is proved, that the goods and their packaging appeared to be in good condition when the carrier took them over and that the number of packages, their marks and numbers corresponded with the statements in the consignment note.

Article 10

The sender shall be liable to the carrier for damage to persons, equipment or other goods, and for any expenses due to defective packing of the goods, unless the defect was apparent or known to the carrier at the time when he took over the goods and he made no reservations concerning it.

Article 11

1   For the purposes of the Customs or other formalities which have to be completed before delivery of the goods, the sender shall attach the necessary docu-

ments to the consignment note or place them at the disposal of the carrier and shall furnish him with all the information which he requires.

2 The carrier shall not be under any duty to enquire into either the accuracy or the adequacy of such documents and information. The sender shall be liable to the carrier for any damage caused by the absence, inadequacy or irregularity of such documents and information, except in the case of some wrongful act or neglect on the part of the carrier.

3 The liability of the carrier for the consequences arising from the loss or incorrect use of the documents specified in and accompanying the consignment note or deposited with the carrier shall be that of an agent, provided that the compensation payable by the carrier shall not exceed that payable in the event of loss of the goods.

Article 12

1 The sender has a right to dispose of the goods, in particular by asking the carrier to stop the goods in transit, to change the place at which delivery is to take place or to deliver the goods to a consignee other than the consignee indicated in the consignment note.

2 This right shall cease to exist when the second copy of the consignment note is handed to the consignee or when the consignee exercises his right under article 13, paragraph 1; from that time onwards the carrier shall obey the orders of the consignee.

3 The consignee shall, however, have the right of disposal from the time when the consignment note is drawn up, if the sender makes an entry to that effect in the consignment note.

4 If in exercising his right of disposal the consignee has ordered the delivery of the goods to another person, that other person shall not be entitled to name other consignees.

5 The exercise of the right of disposal shall be subject to the following conditions:

(a) that the sender or, in the case referred to in paragraph 3 of this article, the consignee who wishes to exercise the right produces the first copy of the consignment note on which the new instructions to the carrier have been entered and indemnifies the carrier against all expenses, loss and damage involved in carrying out such instructions;

(b) that the carrying out of such instructions is possible at the time when the instructions reach the person who is to carry them out and does not either interfere with the normal working of the carrier's undertaking or prejudice the senders or consignees of other consignments;

(c) that the instructions do not result in a division of the consignment.

6 When, by reason of the provisions of paragraph 5(b) of this article, the carrier cannot carry out the instructions which he receives he shall immediately notify the person who gave him such instructions.

7 A carrier who has not carried out the instructions given under the conditions provided for in this article, or who has carried them out without requiring the first copy of the consignment note to be produced, shall be liable to the person entitled to make a claim for any loss or damage caused thereby.

Article 13

1 After arrival of the goods at the place designated for delivery, the consignee shall be entitled to require the carrier to deliver to him, against a receipt, the second copy of the consignment note and the goods. If the loss of the goods is established or if the goods have not arrived after the expiry of the period provided for in article 19, the consignee shall be entitled to enforce in his own name against the carrier any rights arising from the contract of carriage.

2 The consignee who avails himself of the rights granted to him under paragraph 1 of this article shall pay the charges shown to be due on the consignment

note, but in the event of dispute on this matter the carrier shall not be required to deliver the goods unless security has been furnished by the consignee.

Article 14

1   If for any reason it is or becomes impossible to carry out the contract in accordance with the terms laid down in the consignment note before the goods reach the place designated for delivery, the carrier shall ask for instructions from the person entitled to dispose of the goods in accordance with the provisions of article 12.

2   Nevertheless, if circumstances are such as to allow the carriage to be carried out under conditions differing from those laid down in the consignment note and if the carrier has been unable to obtain instructions in reasonable time from the person entitled to dispose of the goods in accordance with the provisions of article 12, he shall take such steps as seem to him to be in the best interests of the person entitled to dispose of the goods.

Article 15

1   Where circumstances prevent delivery of the goods after their arrival at the place designated for delivery, the carrier shall ask the sender for his instructions. If the consignee refuses the goods the sender shall be entitled to dispose of them without being obliged to produce the first copy of the consignment note.

2   Even if he has refused the goods, the consignee may nevertheless require delivery so long as the carrier has not received instructions to the contrary from the sender.

3   When circumstances preventing delivery of the goods arise after the consignee, in exercise of his rights under article 12, paragraph 3, has given an order for the goods to be delivered to another person, paragraphs 1 and 2 of this article shall apply as if the consignee were the sender and that other person were the consignee.

Article 16

1   The carrier shall be entitled to recover the cost of his request for instructions and any expenses entailed in carrying out such instructions, unless such expenses were caused by the wrongful act or neglect of the carrier.

2   In the cases referred to in article 14, paragraph 1, and in article 15, the carrier may immediately unload the goods for account of the person entitled to dispose of them and thereupon the carriage shall be deemed to be at an end. The carrier shall then hold the goods on behalf of the person so entitled. He may however entrust them to a third party, and in that case he shall not be under any liability except for the exercise of reasonable care in the choice of such third party. The charges due under the consignment note and all other expenses shall remain chargeable against the goods.

3   The carrier may sell the goods, without awaiting instructions from the person entitled to dispose of them, if the goods are perishable or their condition warrants such a course, or when the storage expenses would be out of proportion to the value of the goods. He may also proceed to the sale of the goods in other cases if after the expiry of a reasonable period he has not received from the person entitled to dispose of the goods instructions to the contrary which he may reasonably be required to carry out.

4   If the goods have been sold pursuant to this article, the proceeds of sale, after deduction of the expenses chargeable against the goods, shall be placed at the disposal of the person entitled to dispose of the goods. If these charges exceed the proceeds of sale, the carrier shall be entitled to the difference.

5   The procedure in the case of sale shall be determined by the law or custom of the place where the goods are situated.

CHAPTER IV
Liability of the carrier

Article 17

1   The carrier shall be liable for the total or partial loss of the goods and for damage thereto occurring between the time when he takes over the goods and the time of delivery, as well as for any delay in delivery.

2   The carrier shall however be relieved of liability if the loss, damage or delay was caused by the wrongful act or neglect of the claimant, by the instructions of the claimant given otherwise than as the result of a wrongful act or neglect on the part of the carrier, by inherent vice of the goods or through circumstances which the carrier could not avoid and the consequences of which he was unable to prevent.

3   The carrier shall not be relieved of liability by reason of the defective condition of the vehicle used by him in order to perform the carriage, or by reason of the wrongful act or neglect of the person from whom he may have hired the vehicle or of the agents or servants of the latter.

4   Subject to article 18, paragraphs 2 to 5 the carrier shall be relieved of liability when the loss or damage arises from the special risks inherent in one or more of the following circumstances:

(a)   use of open unsheeted vehicles, when their use has been expressly agreed and specified in the consignment note;

(b)   the lack of, or defective condition of packing in the case of goods which, by their nature, are liable to wastage or to be damaged when not packed or when not properly packed;

(c)   handling, loading, stowage or unloading of the goods by the sender, the consignee or person acting on behalf of the sender or consignee;

(d)   the nature of certain kinds of goods which particularly exposes them to total or partial loss or to damage, especially through breakage, rust, decay, desiccation, leakage, normal wastage, or the action of moth or vermin;

(e)   insufficiency or inadequacy of marks or numbers on the packages;

(f)   the carriage of livestock.

5   Where under this article the carrier is not under any liability in respect of some of the factors causing the loss, damage or delay, he shall only be liable to the extent that those factors for which he is liable under this article have contributed to the loss, damage or delay.

Article 18

1   The burden of proving that loss, damage or delay was due to one of the causes specified in article 17, paragraph 2, shall rest upon the carrier.

2   When the carrier establishes that in the circumstances of the case, the loss or damage could be attributed to one or more of the special risks referred to in article 17, paragraph 4, it shall be presumed that it was so caused. The claimant shall however be entitled to prove that the loss or damage was not, in fact, attributable either wholly or partly to one of these risks.

3   This presumption shall not apply in the circumstances set out in article 17, paragraph 4(a), if there has been an abnormal shortage, or a loss of any package.

4   If the carriage is performed in vehicles specially equipped to protect the goods from the effects of heat, cold, variations in temperature or the humidity of the air, the carrier shall not be entitled to claim the benefit of article 17, paragraph 4(d) unless he proves that all steps incumbent on him in the circumstances with respect to the choice, maintenance and use of such equipment were taken and that he complied with any special instructions issued to him.

5   The carrier shall not be entitled to claim the benefit of article 17, paragraph 4(f), unless he proves that all steps normally incumbent on him in the circumstances were taken and that he complied with any special instructions issued to him.

Article 19

Delay in delivery shall be said to occur when the goods have not been delivered within the agreed time-limit or when, failing an agreed time-limit, the actual duration of the carriage having regard to the circumstances of the case, and in particular, in the case of partial loads, the time required for making up a complete load in the normal way, exceeds the time it would be reasonable to allow a diligent carrier.

Article 20

1   The fact that the goods have not been delivered within thirty days following the expiry of the agreed time-limit, or if there is no agreed time-limit, within sixty days from the time when the carrier took over the goods, shall be conclusive evidence of the loss of the goods, and the person entitled to make a claim may thereupon treat them as lost.

2   The person so entitled may, on receipt of compensation for the missing goods, request in writing that he shall be notified immediately should the goods be recovered in the course of the year following the payment of compensation. He shall be given a written acknowledgement of such request.

3   Within the thirty days following receipt of such notification, the person entitled as aforesaid may require the goods to be delivered to him against payment of the charges shown to be due on the consignment note and also against refund of the compensation he received less any charges included therein but without prejudice to any claims to compensation for delay in delivery under article 23 and, where applicable, article 26.

4   In the absence of the request mentioned in paragraph 2 or of any instructions given within the period of thirty days specified in paragraph 3, or if the goods are not recovered until more than one year after the payment of compensation, the carrier shall be entitled to deal with them in accordance with the law of the place where the goods are situated.

Article 21

Should the goods have been delivered to the consignee without collection of the 'cash on delivery' charge which should have been collected by the carrier under the terms of the contract of carriage, the carrier shall be liable to the sender for compensation not exceeding the amount of such charge without prejudice to his right of action against the consignee.

Article 22

1   When the sender hands goods of a dangerous nature to the carrier, he shall inform the carrier of the exact nature of the danger and indicate, if necessary, the precautions to be taken. If this information has not been entered in the consignment note, the burden of proving, by some other means, that the carrier knew the exact nature of the danger constituted by the carriage of the said goods shall rest upon the sender or the consignee.

2   Goods of a dangerous nature which, in the circumstances referred to in paragraph 1 of this article, the carrier did not know were dangerous, may, at any time or place, be unloaded, destroyed or rendered harmless by the carrier without compensation; further, the sender shall be liable for all expenses, loss or damage arising out of their handing over for carriage or of their carriage.

Article 23

1   When, under the provisions of this Convention, a carrier is liable for compensation in respect of total or partial loss of goods, such compensation shall be calculated by reference to the value of the goods at the place and time at which they were accepted for carriage.

2   The value of the goods shall be fixed according to the commodity exchange price or, if there is no such price, according to the current market price, or, if there

is no commodity exchange price or current market price, by reference to the normal value of goods of the same kind and quality.

[3   Compensation shall not, however, exceed 8.33 units of account per kilogram of gross weight short.]

4   In addition, the carriage charges, Customs duties and other charges incurred in respect of the carriage of the goods shall be refunded in full in case of total loss and in proportion to the loss sustained in case of partial loss, but no further damages shall be payable.

5   In the case of delay, if the claimant proves that damage has resulted therefrom the carrier shall pay compensation for such damage not exceeding the carriage charges.

6   Higher compensation may only be claimed where the value of the goods or a special interest in delivery has been declared in accordance with articles 24 and 26.

[7   The unit of account mentioned in this Convention is the Special Drawing Right as defined by the International Monetary Fund. The amount mentioned in paragraph 3 of this article shall be converted into the national currency of the State of the Court seised of the case on the basis of the value of that currency on the date of judgment or the date agreed upon by the Parties.]

Article 24
The sender may, against payment of a surcharge to be agreed upon, declare in the consignment note a value for the goods exceeding the limit laid down in article 23, paragraph 3, and in that case the amount of the declared value shall be substituted for that limit.

Article 25
1   In case of damage, the carrier shall be liable for the amount by which the goods have diminished in value, calculated by reference to the value of the goods fixed in accordance with article 23, paragraphs 1, 2 and 4.

2   The compensation may not, however, exceed:

(a)   if the whole consignment has been damaged, the amount payable in the case of total loss;

(b)   if part only of the consignment has been damaged, the amount payable in the case of loss of the part affected.

Article 26
1   The sender may, against payment of a surcharge to be agreed upon, fix the amount of a special interest in delivery in the case of loss or damage or of the agreed time-limit being exceeded, by entering such amount in the consignment note.

2   If a declaration of a special interest in delivery has been made, compensation for the additional loss or damage proved may be claimed, up to the total amount of the interest declared, independently of the compensation provided for in articles 23, 24 and 25.

Article 27
1   The claimant shall be entitled to claim interest on compensation payable. Such interest, calculated at five per centum per annum, shall accrue from the date on which the claim was sent in writing to the carrier or, if no such claim has been made, from the date on which legal proceedings were instituted.

2   When the amounts on which the calculation of the compensation is based are not expressed in the currency of the country in which payment is claimed, conversion shall be at the rate of exchange applicable on the day and at the place of payment of compensation.

Article 28
1   In cases where, under the law applicable, loss, damage or delay arising out of carriage under this Convention gives rise to an extra-contractual claim, the

carrier may avail himself of the provisions of this Convention which exclude his liability or which fix or limit the compensation due.

2   In cases where the extra-contractual liability for loss, damage or delay of one of the persons for whom the carrier is responsible under the terms of article 3 is in issue, such person may also avail himself of the provisions of this Convention which exclude the liability of the carrier or which fix or limit the compensation due.

Article 29

1   The carrier shall not be entitled to avail himself of the provisions of this chapter which exclude or limit his liability or which shift the burden of proof if the damage was caused by his wilful misconduct or by such default on his part as, in accordance with the law of the court or tribunal seised of the case, is considered as equivalent to misconduct.

2   The same provision shall apply if the wilful misconduct or default is committed by the agents or servants of the carrier or by any other persons of whose services he makes use for the performance of the carriage, when such agents, servants or other persons are acting within the scope of their employment. Furthermore, in such a case such agents, servants or other persons shall not be entitled to avail themselves, with regard to their personal liability, of the provisions of this chapter referred to in paragraph 1.

CHAPTER V

Claims and actions

Article 30

1   If the consignee takes delivery of the goods without duly checking their condition with the carrier or without sending him reservations giving a general indication of the loss or damage, not later than the time of delivery in the case of apparent loss or damage and within seven days of delivery, Sundays and public holidays excepted, in the case of loss or damage which is not apparent, the fact of his taking delivery shall be prima facie evidence that he has received the goods in the condition described in the consignment note. In the case of loss or damage which is not apparent the reservations referred to shall be made in writing.

2   When the condition of the goods has been duly checked by the consignee and the carrier, evidence contradicting the result of this checking shall only be admissible in the case of loss or damage which is not apparent and provided that the consignee has duly sent reservations in writing to the carrier within seven days, Sundays and public holidays excepted, from the date of checking.

3   No compensation shall be payable for delay in delivery unless a reservation has been sent in writing to the carrier, within twenty-one days from the time that the goods were placed at the disposal of the consignee.

4   In calculating the time-limits provided for in this article the date of delivery, or the date of checking, or the date when the goods were placed at the disposal of the consignee, as the case may be, shall not be included.

5   The carrier and the consignee shall give each other every reasonable facility for making the requisite investigations and checks.

Article 31

1   In legal proceedings arising out of carriage under this Convention, the plaintiff may bring an action in any court or tribunal of a contracting country designated by agreement between the parties and, in addition, in the courts or tribunals of a country within whose territory:

(a)   the defendant is ordinarily resident, or has his principal place of business, or the branch or agency through which the contract of carriage was made, or

(b)   the place where the goods were taken over by the carrier or the place designated for delivery is situated,
and in no other courts or tribunals.

2   Where in respect of a claim referred to in paragraph 1 of this article an action is pending before a court or tribunal competent under that paragraph, or where in respect of such a claim a judgment has been entered by such a court or tribunal no new action shall be started between the same parties on the same grounds unless the judgment of the court or tribunal before which the first action was brought is not enforceable in the country in which the fresh proceedings are brought.

3   When a judgment entered by a court or tribunal of a contracting country in any such action as is referred to in paragraph 1 of this article has become enforceable in that country, it shall also become enforceable in each of the other contracting States, as soon as the formalities required in the country concerned have been complied with. These formalities shall not permit the merits of the case to be reopened.

4   The provisions of paragraph 3 of this article shall apply to judgments after trial, judgments by default and settlements confirmed by an order of the court, but shall not apply to interim judgments or to awards of damages, in addition to costs against a plaintiff who wholly or partly fails in his action.

5   Security for costs shall not be required in proceedings arising out of carriage under this Convention from nationals of contracting countries resident or having their place of business in one of those countries.

Article 32

1   The period of limitation for an action arising out of carriage under this Convention shall be one year. Nevertheless, in the case of wilful misconduct, or such default as in accordance with the law of the court or tribunal seised of the case, is considered as equivalent to wilful misconduct, the period of limitation shall be three years. The period of limitation shall begin to run:
(a)   in the case of partial loss, damage or delay in delivery, from the date of delivery;
(b)   in the case of total loss, from the thirtieth day after the expiry of the agreed time-limit or where there is no agreed time-limit from the sixtieth day from the date on which the goods were taken over by the carrier;
(c)   in all other cases, on the expiry of a period of three months after the making of the contract of carriage.
The day on which the period of limitation begins to run shall not be included in the period.

2   A written claim shall suspend the period of limitation until such date as the carrier rejects the claim by notification in writing and returns the documents attached thereto. If a part of the claim is admitted the period of limitation shall start to run again only in respect of that part of the claim still in dispute. The burden of proof of the receipt of the claim, or of the reply and of the return of the documents, shall rest with the party relying upon these facts. The running of the period of limitation shall not be suspended by further claims having the same object.

3   Subject to the provisions of paragraph 2 above, the extension of the period of limitation shall be governed by the law of the court or tribunal seised of the case. That law shall also govern the fresh accrual rights of action.

4   A right of action which has become barred by lapse of time may not be exercised by way of counter-claim or set-off.

Article 33

The contract of carriage may contain a clause conferring competence on an arbitration tribunal if the clause conferring competence on the tribunal provides that the tribunal shall apply this Convention.

CHAPTER VI
Provisions relating to carriage performed by successive carriers

Article 34

If carriage governed by a single contract is performed by successive road carriers, each of them shall be responsible for the performance of the whole operation, the second carrier and each succeeding carrier becoming a party to the contract of carriage, under the terms of the consignment note, by reason of his acceptance of the goods and the consignment note.

Article 35

1   A carrier accepting the goods from a previous carrier shall give the latter a dated and signed receipt. He shall enter his name and address on the second copy of the consignment note. Where applicable, he shall enter on the second copy of the consignment note and on the receipt reservations of the kind provided for in article 8, paragraph 2.

2   The provisions of article 9 shall apply to the relations between successive carriers.

Article 36

Except in the case of a counter-claim or a set-off raised in an action concerning a claim based on the same contract of carriage, legal proceedings in respect of liability for loss, damage or delay may only be brought against the first carrier, the last carrier or the carrier who was performing that portion of the carriage during which the event causing the loss, damage or delay occurred; an action may be brought at the same time against several of these carriers.

Article 37

A carrier who has paid compensation in compliance with the provisions of this Convention, shall be entitled to recover such compensation, together with interest thereon and all costs and expenses incurred by reason of the claim, from the other carriers who have taken part in the carriage, subject to the following provisions:

   (a)   the carrier responsible for the loss or damage shall be solely liable for the compensation whether paid by himself or by another carrier;

   (b)   when the loss or damage has been caused by the action of two or more carriers, each of them shall pay an amount proportionate to his share of liability; should it be impossible to apportion the liability, each carrier shall be liable in proportion to the share of the payment for the carriage which is due to him;

   (c)   if it cannot be ascertained to which carriers liability is attributable for the loss or damage, the amount of the compensation shall be apportioned between all the carriers as laid down in (b) above.

Article 38

If one of the carriers is insolvent, the share of the compensation due from him and unpaid by him shall be divided among the other carriers in proportion to the share of the payment for the carriage due to them.

Article 39

1   No carrier against whom a claim is made under articles 37 and 38 shall be entitled to dispute the validity of the payment made by the carrier making the claim if the amount of the compensation was determined by judicial authority after the first mentioned carrier had been given due notice of the proceedings and afforded an opportunity of entering an appearance.

2   A carrier wishing to take proceedings to enforce his right of recovery may make his claim before the competent court or tribunal of the country in which one of the carriers concerned is ordinarily resident, or has his principal place of business or the branch or agency through which the contract of carriage was made. All the carriers concerned may be made defendants in the same action.

3   The provisions of article 31, paragraphs 3 and 4 shall apply to judgments entered in the proceedings referred to in articles 37 and 38.

4   The provisions of article 32 shall apply to claims between carriers. The period of limitation shall, however, begin to run either on the date of the final judicial decision fixing the amount of compensation payable under the provisions of this Convention, or, if there is no such judicial decision, from the actual date of payment.

Article 40
Carriers shall be free to agree among themselves on provisions other than those laid down in articles 37 and 38.

CHAPTER VII
Nullity of stipulations contrary to the Convention

Article 41
1   Subject to the provisions of article 40, any stipulation which would directly or indirectly derogate from the provisions of this Convention shall be null and void. The nullity of such a stipulation shall not involve the nullity of the other provisions of the contract.

2   In particular, a benefit of insurance in favour of the carrier or any other similar clause, or any clause shifting the burden of proof shall be null and void.

[Chapter VIII deals with the coming into force of the Convention, the settlement of disputes between the high contracting parties and related matters.]

CARRIAGE OF GOODS BY SEA ACT 1971
(1971, c 19)

1   Application of Hague Rules as amended
(1)   In this Act, 'the Rules' means the International Convention for the unification of certain rules of law relating to bills of lading signed at Brussels on 25th August 1924, as amended by the Protocol signed at Brussels on 23rd February 1968 [and by the protocol signed at Brussels on 21st December 1979].

(2)   The provisions of the Rules, as set out in the Schedule to this Act, shall have the force of law.

(3)   Without prejudice to subsection (2) above, the said provisions shall have effect (and have the force of law) in relation to and in connection with the carriage of goods by sea in ships where the port of shipment is a port in the United Kingdom, whether or not the carriage is between ports in two different States within the meaning of Article X of the Rules.

(4)   Subject to subsection (6) below, nothing in this section shall be taken as applying anything in the Rules to any contract for the carriage of goods by sea, unless the contract expressly or by implication provides for the issue of a bill of lading or any similar document of title.

[. . .]

(6)   Without prejudice to Article X(c) of the Rules, the Rules shall have the force of law in relation to—

(a)   any bill of lading if the contract contained in or evidenced by it expressly provides that the Rules shall govern the contract, and

(b)   any receipt which is a non-negotiable document marked as such if the contract contained in or evidenced by it is a contract for the carriage of goods by sea which expressly provides that the Rules are to govern the contract as if the receipt were a bill of lading, but subject, where paragraph (b) applies, to any necessary modifications and in particular with the omission in Article III of the Rules of the second sentence of paragraph 4 and of paragraph 7.

(7)   If and so far as the contract contained in or evidenced by a bill of lading or

receipt within paragraph (a) or (b) of subsection (6) above applies to deck cargo or live animals, the Rules as given the force of law by that subsection shall have effect as if Article I(c) did not exclude deck cargo and live animals.

In this subsection 'deck cargo' means cargo which by the contract of carriage is stated as being carried on deck and is so carried.

[1A Conversion of special drawing rights into sterling
(1) For the purposes of Article IV of the Rules the value on a particular day of one special drawing right shall be treated as equal to such a sum in sterling as the International Monetary Fund have fixed as being the equivalent of one special drawing right—

(a) for that day; or

(b) if no sum has been so fixed for that day, for the last day before that day for which a sum has been so fixed.

(2) A certificate given by or on behalf of the Treasury stating—

(a) that a particular sum in sterling has been fixed as aforesaid for a particular day; or

(b) that no sum has been so fixed for a particular day and that a particular sum in sterling has been so fixed for a day which is the last day for which a sum has been so fixed before the particular day,

shall be conclusive evidence of those matters for the purposes of subsection (1) above;

and a document purporting to be such a certificate shall in any proceedings be received in evidence and, unless the contrary is proved, be deemed to be such a certificate.

(3) The Treasury may charge a reasonable fee for any certificate given in pursuance of subsection (2) above, and any fee received by the Treasury by virtue of this subsection shall be paid into the Consolidated Fund.]

2 Contracting States, etc
(1) If Her Majesty by Order in Council certifies to the following effect, that is to say, that for the purposes of the Rules—

(a) a State specified in the Order is a contracting State, or is a contracting State in respect of any place or territory so specified; or

(b) any place or territory specified in the Order forms part of a State so specified (whether a contracting State or not),

the Order shall, except so far as it has been superseded by a subsequent Order, be conclusive evidence of the matters so certified.

(2) An Order in Council under this section may be varied or revoked by a subsequent Order in Council.

3 Absolute warranty of seaworthiness not to be implied in contracts to which Rules apply
There shall not be implied in any contract for the carriage of goods by sea to which the Rules apply by virtue of this Act any absolute undertaking by the carrier of the goods to provide a seaworthy ship.

4 Application of Act to British possessions, etc
(1) Her Majesty may by Order in Council direct that this Act shall extend, subject to such exceptions, adaptations and modifications as may be specified in the Order, to all or any of the following territories, that is—

(a) any colony (not being a colony for whose external relations a country other than the United Kingdom is responsible),

(b) any country outside Her Majesty's dominions in which Her Majesty has jurisdiction in right of Her Majesty's Government of the United Kingdom.

(2) An Order in Council under this section may contain such transitional and other consequential and incidental provisions as appear to Her Majesty to be expedient, including provisions amending or repealing any legislation about the

carriage of goods by sea forming part of the law of any of the territories mentioned in paragraphs (a) and (b) above.

(3)   An Order in Council under this section may be varied or revoked by a subsequent Order in Council.

5   Extension of application of Rules to carriage from ports in British possessions, etc

(1)   Her Majesty may by Order in Council provide that section 1(3) of this Act shall have effect as if the reference therein to the United Kingdom included a reference to all or any of the following territories, that is—

(a)   the Isle of Man;

(b)   any of the Channel Islands specified in the Order;

(c)   any colony specified in the Order (not being a colony for whose external relations a country other than the United Kingdom is responsible);

[. . .]

(e)   any country specified in the Order, being a country outside Her Majesty's dominions in which Her Majesty has jurisdiction in right of Her Majesty's Government of the United Kingdom.

(2)   An Order in Council under this section may be varied or revoked by a subsequent Order in Council.

6   Supplemental

(1)   This Act may be cited as the Carriage of Goods by Sea Act 1971.

(2)   It is hereby declared that this Act extends to Northern Ireland.

(3)   The following enactments shall be repealed, that is—

(a)   the Carriage of Goods by Sea Act 1924,

(b)   section 12(4)(a) of the Nuclear Installations Act 1965,

and without prejudice to section 38(1) of the Interpretation Act 1889, the reference to the said Act of 1924 in section 1(1)(i)(ii) of the Hovercraft Act 1968 shall include a reference to this Act.

(4)   It is hereby declared that for the purposes of Article VIII of the Rules [section 186 of the Merchant Shipping Act 1995 (which] entirely exempts shipowners and others in certain circumstances from liability for loss of, or damage to, goods) is a provision relating to limitation of liability.

(5)   This Act shall come into force on such day as Her Majesty may by Order in Council appoint, and, for the purposes of the transition from the law in force immediately before the day appointed under this subsection to the provisions of this Act, the Order appointing the day may provide that those provisions shall have effect subject to such transitional provisions as may be contained in the Order.

SCHEDULE

THE HAGUE RULES AS AMENDED BY
THE BRUSSELS PROTOCOL 1968

Article I

In these Rules the following words are employed, with the meanings set out below:—

(a)   'Carrier' includes the owner or the charterer who enters into a contract of carriage with a shipper.

(b)   'Contract of carriage' applies only to contracts of carriage covered by a bill of lading or any similar document of title, in so far as such document relates to the carriage of goods by sea, including any bill of lading or any similar document as aforesaid issued under or pursuant to a charter party from the moment at which such bill of lading or similar document of title regulates the relations between a carrier and a holder of the same.

(c)   'Goods' includes goods, wares, merchandise, and articles of every kind whatsoever except live animals and cargo which by the contract of carriage is stated as being carried on deck and is so carried.

(d) 'Ship' means any vessel used for the carriage of goods by sea.

(e) 'Carriage of goods' covers the period from the time when the goods are loaded on to the time they are discharged from the ship.

Article II
Subject to the provisions of Article VI, under every contract of carriage of goods by sea the carrier, in relation to the loading, handling, stowage, carriage, custody, care and discharge of such goods, shall be subject to the responsibilities and liabilities, and entitled to the rights and immunities hereinafter set forth.

Article III
(1) The carrier shall be bound before and at the beginning of the voyage to exercise due diligence to—

(a) Make the ship seaworthy.

(b) Properly man, equip and supply the ship.

(c) Make the holds, refrigerating and cool chambers, and all other parts of the ship in which goods are carried, fit and safe for their reception, carriage and preservation.

(2) Subject to the provisions of Article IV, the carrier shall properly and carefully load, handle, stow, carry, keep, care for, and discharge the goods carried.

(3) After receiving the goods into his charge the carrier or the master or agent of the carrier shall, on demand of the shipper, issue to the shipper a bill of lading showing among other things—

(a) The leading marks necessary for identification of the goods as the same are furnished in writing by the shipper before the loading of such goods starts, provided such marks are stamped or otherwise shown clearly upon the goods if uncovered, or on the cases or coverings in which such goods are contained, in such a manner as should ordinarily remain legible until the end of the voyage.

(b) Either the number of packages or pieces, or the quantity, or weight, as the case may be, as furnished in writing by the shipper.

(c) The apparent order and condition of the goods.

Provided that no carrier, master or agent of the carrier shall be bound to state or show in the bill of lading any marks, number, quantity, or weight which he has reasonable ground for suspecting not accurately to represent the goods actually received, or which be has had no reasonable means of checking.

(4) Such a bill of lading shall be prima facie evidence of the receipt by the carrier of the goods as therein described in accordance with paragraph 3(a), (b) and (c). However, proof to the contrary shall not be admissible when the bill of lading has been transferred to a third party acting in good faith.

(5) The shipper shall be deemed to have guaranteed to the carrier the accuracy at the time of shipment of the marks, number, quantity and weight, as furnished by him, and the shipper shall indemnify the carrier against all loss, damages and expenses arising or resulting from inaccuracies in such particulars. The right of the carrier to such indemnity shall in no way limit his responsibility and liability under the contract of carriage to any person other than the shipper.

(6) Unless notice of loss or damage and the general nature of such loss or damage be given in writing to the carrier or his agent at the port of discharge before or at the time of the removal of the goods into the custody of the person entitled to delivery thereof under the contract of carriage, or, if the loss or damage be not apparent, within three days, such removal shall be prima facie evidence of the delivery by the carrier of the goods as described in the bill of lading.

The notice in writing need not be given if the state of the goods has, at the time of their receipt, been the subject of joint survey or inspection.

Subject to paragraph 6bis the carrier and the ship shall in any event be discharged from all liability whatsoever in respect of the goods, unless suit is brought within one year of their delivery or of the date when they should have been delivered. This period may, however, be extended if the parties so agree after the cause of action has arisen.

In the case of any actual or apprehended loss or damage the carrier and the receiver shall give all reasonable facilities to each other for inspecting and tallying the goods.

(6*bis*) An action for indemnity against a third person may be brought even after the expiration of the year provided for in the preceding paragraph if brought within the time allowed by the law of the court seised of the case. However, the time allowed shall be not less than three months, commencing from the day when the person bringing such action for indemnity has settled the claim or has been served with process in the action against himself.

(7) After the goods are loaded the bill of lading to be issued by the carrier, master, or agent of the carrier, to the shipper shall, if the shipper so demands, be a 'shipped' bill of lading, provided that if the shipper shall have previously taken up any document of title to such goods, he shall surrender the same as against the issue of the 'shipped' bill of lading, but at the option of the carrier such document of title may be noted at the port of shipment by the carrier, master, or agent with the name or names of the ship or ships upon which the goods have been shipped and the date or dates of shipment, and when so noted if it shows the particulars mentioned in paragraph 3 of Article III, shall for the purpose of this article be deemed to constitute a 'shipped' bill of lading.

(8) Any clause, covenant, or agreement in a contract of carriage relieving the carrier or the ship from liability for loss or damage to, or in connection with, goods arising from negligence, fault, or failure in the duties and obligations provided in this article or lessening such liability otherwise than as provided in these Rules, shall be null and void and of no effect. A benefit of insurance in favour of the carrier or similar clause shall be deemed to be a clause relieving the carrier from liability.

Article IV

(1) Neither the carrier nor the ship shall be liable for loss or damage arising or resulting from unseaworthiness unless caused by want of due diligence on the part of the carrier to make the ship seaworthy, and to secure that the ship is properly manned, equipped and supplied, and to make the holds, refrigerating and cool chambers and all other parts of the ship in which goods are carried fit and safe for their reception, carriage and preservation in accordance with the provisions of paragraph 1 of Article III. Whenever loss or damage has resulted from unseaworthiness the burden of proving the exercise of due diligence shall be on the carrier or other person claiming exemption under this article.

(2) Neither the carrier nor the ship shall be responsible for loss or damage arising or resulting from—

(a) Act, neglect, or default of the master, mariner, pilot, or the servants of the carrier in the navigation or in the management of the ship.

(b) Fire, unless caused by the actual fault or privity of the carrier.

(c) Perils, dangers and accidents of the sea or other navigable waters.

(d) Act of God.

(e) Act of war.

(f) Act of public enemies.

(g) Arrest or restraint of princes, rulers or people, or seizure under legal process.

(h) Quarantine restrictions.

(i) Act or omission of the shipper or owner of the goods, his agent or representative.

(j) Strikes or lockouts or stoppage or restraint of labour from whatever cause, whether partial or general.

(k)   Riots and civil commotions.

(l)   Saving or attempting to save life or property at sea.

(m)   Wastage in bulk or weight or any other loss or damage arising from inherent defect, quality or vice of the goods.

(n)   Insufficiency of packing.

(o)   Insufficiency or inadequacy of marks.

(p)   Latent defects not discoverable by due diligence.

(q)   Any other cause arising without the actual fault or privity of the carrier, or without the fault or neglect of the agents or servants of the carrier, but the burden of proof shall be on the person claiming the benefit of this exception to show that neither the actual fault or privity of the carrier nor the fault or neglect of the agents or servants of the carrier contributed to the loss or damage.

(3)   The shipper shall not be responsible for the loss or damage sustained by the carrier or the ship arising or resulting from any cause without the act, fault or neglect of the shipper, his agents or his servants.

(4)   Any deviation in saving or attempting to save life or property at sea or any reasonable deviation shall not be deemed to be an infringement or breach of these Rules or of the contract of carriage, and the carrier shall not be liable for any loss or damage resulting therefrom.

(5)(a)   Unless the nature and value of such goods have been declared by the shipper before shipment and inserted in the bill of lading, neither the carrier nor the ship shall in any event be or become liable for any loss or damage to or in connection with the goods in an amount exceeding [666.67 units of account] per package or unit or [2 units of account per kilogramme] of gross weight of the goods lost or damaged, whichever is the higher.

(b)   The total amount recoverable shall be calculated by reference to the value of such goods at the place and time at which the goods are discharged from the ship in accordance with the contract or should have been so discharged.

The value of the goods shall be fixed according to the commodity exchange price, or, if there be no such price, according to the current market price, or, if there be no commodity exchange price or current market price, by reference to the normal value of goods of the same kind and quality.

(c)   Where a container, pallet or similar article of transport is used to consolidate goods, the number of packages or units enumerated in the bill of lading as packed in such article of transport shall be deemed the number of packages or units for the purpose of this paragraph as far as these packages or units are concerned. Except as aforesaid such article of transport shall be considered the package or unit.

[(d)   The unit of account mentioned in this Article is the special drawing right as defined by the International Monetary Fund. The amounts mentioned in sub-paragraph (a) of this paragraph shall be converted into national currency on the basis of the value of that currency on a date to be determined by the law of the court seised of the case.]

(e)   Neither the carrier nor the ship shall be entitled to the benefit of the limitation of liability provided for in this paragraph if it is proved that the damage resulted from an act or omission of the carrier done with intent to cause damage, or recklessly and with knowledge that damage would probably result.

(f)   The declaration mentioned in sub-paragraph (a) of this paragraph, if embodied in the bill of lading, shall be prima facie evidence, but shall not be binding or conclusive on the carrier.

(g)   By agreement between the carrier, master or agent of the carrier and the shipper other maximum amounts than those mentioned in sub-paragraph (a) of this paragraph may be fixed, provided that no maximum amount so fixed shall be less than the appropriate maximum mentioned in that sub-paragraph.

(h)   Neither the carrier nor the ship shall be responsible in any event for loss or damage to, or in connection with, goods if the nature or value thereof has been knowingly mis-stated by the shipper in the bill of lading.

(6) Goods of an inflammable, explosive or dangerous nature to the shipment whereof the carrier, master or agent of the carrier has not consented with knowledge of their nature and character, may at any time before discharge be landed at any place, or destroyed or rendered innocuous by the carrier without compensation and the shipper of such goods shall be liable for all damages and expenses directly or indirectly arising out of or resulting from such shipment. If any such goods shipped with such knowledge and consent shall become a danger to the ship or cargo, they may in like manner be landed at any place, or destroyed or rendered innocuous by the carrier without liability on the part of the carrier except to general average, if any.

Article IV bis

(1) The defences and limits of liability provided for in these Rules shall apply in any action against the carrier in respect of loss or damage to goods covered by a contract of carriage whether the action be founded in contract or in tort.

(2) If such an action is brought against a servant or agent of the carrier (such servant or agent not being an independent contractor), such servant or agent shall be entitled to avail himself of the defences and limits of liability which the carrier is entitled to invoke under these Rules.

(3) The aggregate of the amounts recoverable from the carrier, and such servants and agents, shall in no case exceed the limit provided for in these Rules.

(4) Nevertheless, a servant or agent of the carrier shall not be entitled to avail himself of the provisions of this article, if it is proved that the damage resulted from an act or omission of the servant or agent done with intent to cause damage or recklessly and with knowledge that damage would probably result.

Article V

A carrier shall be at liberty to surrender in whole or in part all or any of his rights and immunities or to increase any of his responsibilities and obligations under these Rules, provided such surrender or increase shall be embodied in the bill of lading issued to the shipper. The provisions of the Rules shall not be applicable to charter parties, but if bills of lading are issued in the case of a ship under a charter party they shall comply with the terms of these Rules. Nothing in these Rules shall be held to prevent the insertion in a bill of lading of any lawful provisions regarding general average.

Article VI

Notwithstanding the provisions of the preceding articles, a carrier, master or agent of the carrier and a shipper shall in regard to any particular goods be at liberty to enter into any agreement in any terms as to the responsibility and liability of the carrier for such goods, and as to the rights and immunities of the carrier in respect of such goods, or his obligation as to seaworthiness, so far as this stipulation is not contrary to public policy, or the care or diligence of his servants or agents in regard to the loading, handling, stowage, carriage, custody, care and discharge of the goods carried by sea, provided that in this case no bill of lading has been or shall be issued and that the terms agreed shall be embodied in a receipt which shall be a non-negotiable document and shall be marked as such.

Any agreement so entered into shall have full legal effect.

Provided that this article shall not apply to ordinary commercial shipment made in the ordinary course of trade, but only to other shipments where the character or condition of the property to be carried or the circumstances, terms and conditions under which the carriage is to be performed are such as reasonably to justify a special agreement.

Article VII

Nothing herein contained shall prevent a carrier or a shipper from entering into any agreement, stipulation, condition, reservation or exemption as to the responsibility and liability of the carrier or the ship for the loss or damage to, or in connection with, the custody and care and handling of goods prior to the loading on, and subsequent to the discharge from, the ship on which the goods are carried by sea.

Article VIII
The provisions of these Rules shall not affect the rights and obligations of the carrier under any statute for the time being in force relating to the limitation of the liability of owners of sea-going vessels.

Article IX
These rules shall not affect the provisions of any international Convention or national law governing liability for nuclear damage.

Article X
The provisions of these Rules shall apply to every bill of lading relating to the carriage of goods between ports in two different States if:
    (a)   the bill of lading is issued in a contracting State, or
    (b)   the carriage is from a port in a contracting State, or
    (c)   the contract contained in or evidenced by the bill of lading provides that these Rules or legislation of any State giving effect to them are to govern the contract, whatever may be the nationality of the ship, the carrier, the shipper, the consignee, or any other interested person.

[The last two paragraphs of this article require contracting States to apply the Rules to bills of lading mentioned in the article and authorise them to apply the Rules to other bills of lading.]
[Articles XI to XVI deal with the coming into force of the Convention, procedure for ratification, accession and denunciation and the right to call for a fresh conference to consider amendments to the Rules contained in the Convention.]

UNSOLICITED GOODS AND SERVICES ACT 1971
(1971, c 30)

[. . .]

2 Demands and threats regarding payment
(1) A person who, not having reasonable cause to believe there is a right to payment, in the course of any trade or business makes a demand for payment, or asserts a present or prospective right to payment, for what he knows are unsolicited goods sent (after the commencement of this Act) to another person with a view to his acquiring them [for the purposes of his trade or business], shall be guilty of an offence and on summary conviction shall be liable to a fine not exceeding [level 4 on the standard scale].
(2) A person who, not having reasonable cause to believe there is a right to payment, in the course of any trade or business and with a view to obtaining any payment for what he knows are unsolicited goods sent as aforesaid—
    (a)   threatens to bring any legal proceedings; or
    (b)   places or causes to be placed the name of any person on a list of defaulters or debtors or threatens to do so; or
    (c)   invokes or causes to be invoked any other collection procedure or threatens to do so,
shall be guilty of an offence and shall be liable on summary conviction to a fine not exceeding [level 5 on the standard scale].

3 Directory entries
[(1) A person ('the purchaser') shall not be liable to make any payment, and shall be entitled to recover any payment made by him, by way of charge for

including or arranging for the inclusion in a directory of an entry relating to that person or his trade or business, unless—

(a)   there has been signed by the purchaser or on his behalf an order complying with this section,

(b)   there has been signed by the purchaser or on his behalf a note complying with this section of his agreement to the charge and before the note was signed, a copy of it was supplied, for retention by him, to him or a person acting on his behalf,

(c)   there has been transmitted by the purchaser or a person acting on his behalf an electronic communication which includes a statement that the purchaser agrees to the charge and the relevant condition is satisfied in relation to that communication, [or

(d)   the charge arises under a contract in relation to which the conditions in section 3B(1) (renewed and extended contracts) are met.]

(2)   A person shall be guilty of an offence punishable on summary conviction with a fine not exceeding [level 5 on the standard scale] if, in a case where a payment in respect of a charge would [. . .] be recoverable from him in accordance with the terms of subsection (1) above, he demands payment, or asserts a present or prospective right to payment, of the charge or any part of it, without knowing or having reasonable cause to believe [that—

(a)   the entry to which the charge relates was ordered in accordance with this section,

(b)   a proper note of the agreement has been duly signed, or

(c)   the requirements set out in subsection (1)(c) [or (d)] above have been met.]

(3)   For the purposes of [this section—

(a)] an order for an entry in a directory must be made by means of an order form or other stationery belonging to the [purchaser, which may be sent electronically but which must bear his name and address (or one or more of his addresses)]; and

[b]   the note [of a person's agreement to a charge must—

(i)   specify the particulars set out in Part 1 of the Schedule to the Regulatory Reform (Unsolicited Goods and Services Act 1971) (Directory Entries and Demands for Payment) Order 2005, and

(ii)   give reasonable particulars of the entry in respect of which the charge would be payable].

[(3A)   In relation to an electronic communication which includes a statement that the purchaser agrees to a charge for including or arranging the inclusion in a directory of any entry, the relevant condition is that—

(a)   before the electronic communication was transmitted the information referred to in subsection (3B) below was communicated to the purchaser, and

(b)   the electronic communication can readily be produced and retained in a visible and legible form.

(3B)   that information is—

(a)   the following particulars—

(i)   the amount of the charge;

(ii)   the name of the directory or proposed directory;

(iii)   the name of the person producing the directory;

(iv)   the geographic address at which that person is established;

(v)   if the directory is or is to be available in printed form, the proposed date of publication of the directory or of the issue in which the entry is to be included;

(vi)   if the directory or the issue in which the entry is to be included is to be put on sale, the price at which it is to be offered for sale and the minimum number of copies which are to be available for sale;

(vii)   if the directory or the issue in which the entry is to be included is to be distributed free of charge (whether or not it is also to be put on sale), the minimum number of copies which are to be so distributed;

(viii) if the directory is or is to be available in a form other than in printed form, adequate details of how it may be accessed; and

(b) reasonable particulars of the entry in respect of which the charge would be payable.

(3C) In this section 'electronic communication' has the same meaning as in the Electronic Communications Act 2000.]

[. . .]

[3B Renewed and extended contracts

(1) The conditions referred to in section 3(1)(e) above are met in relation to a contract ('the new contract') if—

(a) a person ('the purchaser') has entered into an earlier contract ('the earlier contract') for including or arranging for the inclusion in a particular issue or version of a directory ('the earlier directory') of an entry ('the earlier entry') relating to him or his trade or business;

(b) the purchaser was liable to make a payment by way of a charge arising under the earlier contract for including or arranging for the inclusion of the earlier entry in the earlier directory;

(c) the new contract is a contract for including or arranging for the inclusion in a later issue or version of a directory ('the later directory') of an entry ('the later entry') relating to the purchaser or his trade or business;

(d) the form, content and distribution of the later directory is materially the same as the form, content and distribution of the earlier directory;

(e) the form and content of the later entry is materially the same as the form and content of the earlier entry;

(f) if the later directory is published other than in electronic form—

(i) the earlier directory was the last, or the last but one, issue or version of the directory to be published before the later directory, and

(ii) the date of publication of the later directory is not more than 13 months after the date of publication of the earlier directory;

(g) if the later directory is published in electronic form, the first date on which the new contract requires the later entry to be published is not more than the relevant period after the last date on which the earlier contract required the earlier entry to be published;

(h) if it was a term of the earlier contract that the purchaser renew or extend the contract—

(i) before the start of the new contract the relevant publisher has given notice in writing to the purchaser containing the information set out in Part 3 of the Schedule to the Regulatory Reform (Unsolicited Goods and Services Act 1971) (Directory Entries and Demands for Payment) Order 2005; and

(ii) the purchaser has not written to the relevant publisher withdrawing his agreement to the renewal or extension of the earlier contract within the period of 21 days starting when he receives the notice referred to in sub-paragraph (i); and

(i) if the parties to the earlier contract and the new contract are different—

(i) the parties to both contracts have entered into a novation agreement in respect of the earlier contract; or

(ii) the relevant publisher has given the purchaser the information set out in Part 4 of the Schedule to the Regulatory Reform (Unsolicited Goods and Services Act 1971) (Directory Entries and Demands for Payment) Order 2005.

(2) For the purposes of subsection (1)(d) and (e), the form, content or distribution of the later directory, or the form or content of the later entry, shall be taken to be materially the same as that of the earlier directory or the earlier entry (as the case may be), if a reasonable person in the position of the purchaser would—

(a)   view the two as being materially the same; or
(b)   view that of the later directory or the later entry as being an improvement on that of the earlier directory or the earlier entry.
(3)   For the purposes of subsection (1)(g) 'the relevant period' means the period of 13 months or (if shorter) the term of the earlier contract.
(4)   For the purposes of subsection (1)(h) and (i) 'the relevant publisher' is the person with whom the purchaser has entered into the new contract.
(5)   The information referred to in subsection (1)(i)(ii) must be given to the purchaser prior to the conclusion of the new contract.]

4   Unsolicited publications
(1)   A person shall be guilty of an offence if he sends or causes to be sent to another person any book, magazine or leaflet (or advertising material for any such publication) which he knows or ought reasonably to know is unsolicited and which describes or illustrates human sexual techniques.
(2)   A person found guilty of an offence under this section shall be liable on summary conviction to a fine not exceeding [level 5 on the standard scale].
(3)   A prosecution for an offence under this section shall not in England and Wales be instituted except by, or with the consent of, the Director of Public Prosecutions.

5   Offences by corporations
(1)   Where an offence under this Act which has been committed by a body corporate is proved to have been committed with the consent or connivance of, or to be attributable to any neglect on the part of, any director, manager, secretary, or other similar officer of the body corporate, or of any person who was purporting to act in any such capacity, he as well as the body corporate shall be guilty of that offence and shall be liable to be proceeded against and punished accordingly.
(2)   Where the affairs of a body corporate are managed by its members, this section shall apply in relation to the acts or defaults of a member in connection with his functions of management as if he were a director of the body corporate.

6   Interpretation
(1)   In this Act, unless the context or subject matter otherwise requires,—
'acquire' includes hire;
'send' includes deliver, and 'sender' shall be construed accordingly;
'unsolicited' means, in relation to goods sent to any person, that they are sent without any prior request made by him or on his behalf.
[(2)   For the purposes of this Act any invoice or similar document stating the amount of any payment shall be regarded as asserting a right to the payment unless it complies with the conditions set out in Part 2 of the Schedule to the Regulatory Reform (Unsolicited Goods and Services Act 1971) (Directory Entries and Demands for Payment) Order 2005.
(3)   Nothing in sections 3 or 3B shall affect the rights of any consumer under the Consumer Protection (Distance Selling) Regulations 2000.]

7   Citation, commencement and extent
(1)   This Act may be cited as the Unsolicited Goods and Services Act 1971.
(2)   This Act shall come into force at the expiration of three months beginning with the day on which it is passed.
(3)   This Act does not extend to Northern Ireland.

SUPPLY OF GOODS (IMPLIED TERMS) ACT 1973
(1973, c 13)

8   Implied terms as to title

[(1)   In every hire-purchase agreement, other than one to which subsection (2) below applies, there is—

(a)   an implied term on the part of the creditor that he will have a right to sell the goods at the time when the property is to pass; and

(b)   an implied term that—

(i)   the goods are free, and will remain free until the time when the property is to pass, from any charge or encumbrance not disclosed or known to the person to whom the goods are bailed or (in Scotland) hired before the agreement is made, and

(ii)   that person will enjoy quiet possession of the goods except so far as it may be disturbed by any person entitled to the benefit of any charge or encumbrance so disclosed or known.

(2)   In a hire-purchase agreement, in the case of which there appears from the agreement or is to be inferred from the circumstances of the agreement an intention that the creditor should transfer only such title as he or a third person may have, there is—

(a)   an implied term that all charges or encumbrances known to the creditor and not known to the person to whom the goods are bailed or hired have been disclosed to that person before the agreement is made; and

(b)   an implied term that neither—

(i)   the creditor; nor

(ii)   in a case where the parties to the agreement intend that any title which may be transferred shall be only such title as a third person may have, that person; nor

(iii)   anyone claiming through or under the creditor or that third person not otherwise than under a charge or encumbrance disclosed or known to the person to whom the goods are bailed or hired, before the agreement is made; will disturb the quiet possession of the person to whom the goods are bailed or hired.

(3)   As regards England and Wales and Northern Ireland, the term implied by subsection (1)(a) above is a condition and the terms implied by subsections (1)(b), (2)(a) and (2)(b) above are warranties.]

9   Bailing or hiring by description

[(1)   Where under a hire-purchase agreement goods are bailed or (in Scotland) hired by description, there is an implied term that the goods will correspond with the description, and if under the agreement the goods are bailed or hired by reference to a sample as well as a description, it is not sufficient that the bulk of the goods corresponds with the sample if the goods do not also correspond with the description.

(1A)   As regards England and Wales and Northern Ireland, the term implied by subsection (1) above is a condition.

(2)   Goods shall not be prevented from being bailed or hired by description by reason only that, being exposed for sale, bailment or hire, they are selected by the person to whom they are bailed or hired.]

10   Implied undertakings as to quality or fitness

[(1)   Except as provided by this section and section 11 below and subject to the provisions of any other enactment, including any enactment of the Parliament of Northern Ireland or the Northern Ireland Assembly, there is no implied term as to the quality or fitness for any particular purpose of goods bailed or (in Scotland) hired under a hire-purchase agreement.

(2)   Where the creditor bails or hires goods under a hire-purchase agreement in

the course of a business, there is an implied term that the goods supplied under the agreement are of satisfactory quality.

(2A) For the purposes of this Act, goods are of satisfactory quality if they meet the standard that a reasonable person would regard as satisfactory, taking account of any description of the goods, the price (if relevant) and all the other relevant circumstances.

(2B) For the purposes of this Act, the quality of goods includes their state and condition and the following (among others) are in appropriate cases aspects of the quality of goods—

(a) fitness for all the purposes for which goods of the kind in question are commonly supplied,

(b) appearance and finish,

(c) freedom from minor defects,

(d) safety, and

(e) durability.

(2C) The term implied by subsection (2) above does not extend to any matter making the quality of goods unsatisfactory—

(a) which is specifically drawn to the attention of the person to whom the goods are bailed or hired before the agreement is made,

(b) where that person examines the goods before the agreement is made, which that examination ought to reveal, or

(c) where the goods are bailed or hired by reference to a sample, which would have been apparent on a reasonable examination of the sample.

[(2D) If the person to whom the goods are bailed or hired deals as consumer or, in Scotland, if the goods are hired to a person under a consumer contract, the relevant circumstances mentioned in subsection (2A) above include any public statements on the specific characteristics of the goods made about them by the creditor, the producer or his representative, particularly in advertising or on labelling.

(2E) A public statement is not by virtue of subsection (2D) above a relevant circumstance for the purposes of subsection (2A) above in the case of a contract of hire-purchase, if the creditor shows that—

(a) at the time the contract was made, he was not, and could not reasonably have been, aware of the statement,

(b) before the contract was made, the statement had been withdrawn in public or, to the extent that it contained anything which was incorrect or misleading, it had been corrected in public, or

(c) the decision to acquire the goods could not have been influenced by the statement.

(2F) Subsections (2D) and (2E) above do not prevent any public statement from being a relevant circumstance for the purposes of subsection (2A) above (whether or not the person to whom the goods are bailed or hired deals as consumer or, in Scotland, whether or not the goods are hired to a person under a consumer contract) if the statement would have been such a circumstance apart from those subsections.]

(3) Where the creditor bails or hires goods under a hire-purchase agreement in the course of a business and the person to whom the goods are bailed or hired, expressly or by implication, makes known—

(a) to the creditor in the course of negotiations conducted by the creditor in relation to the making of the hire-purchase agreement, or

(b) to a credit-broker in the course of negotiations conducted by that broker in relation to goods sold by him to the creditor before forming the subject matter of the hire-purchase agreement,

any particular purpose for which the goods are being bailed or hired, there is an implied term that the goods supplied under the agreement are reasonably fit for that purpose, whether or not that is a purpose for which such goods are commonly supplied, except where the circumstances show that the person to whom the goods are bailed or hired does not rely, or that it is unreasonable for him to rely, on the skill or judgment of the creditor or credit-broker.

(4) An implied term as to quality or fitness for a particular purpose may be annexed to a hire-purchase agreement by usage.

(5) The preceding provisions of this section apply to a hire-purchase agreement made by a person who in the course of a business is acting as agent for the creditor as they apply to an agreement made by the creditor in the course of a business, except where the creditor is not bailing or hiring in the course of a business and either the person to whom the goods are bailed or hired knows that fact or reasonable steps are taken to bring it to the notice of that person before the agreement is made.

(6) In subsection (3) above and this subsection—

(a) 'credit-broker' means a person acting in the course of a business of credit brokerage;

(b) 'credit brokerage' means the effecting of introductions of individuals desiring to obtain credit—

(i) to persons carrying on any business so far as it relates to the provision of credit, or

(ii) to other persons engaged in credit brokerage.

(7) As regards England and Wales and Northern Ireland, the terms implied by subsections (2) and (3) above are conditions.

[(8) In Scotland, 'consumer contract' in this section has the same meaning as in section 12A(3) below.]

11   Samples

[(1) Where under a hire-purchase agreement goods are bailed or (in Scotland) hired by reference to a sample, there is an implied term—

(a) that the bulk will correspond with the sample in quality; and

(b) that the person to whom the goods are bailed or hired will have a reasonable opportunity of comparing the bulk with the sample; and

(c) that the goods will be free from any defect, making their quality unsatisfactory, which would not be apparent on reasonable examination of the sample.

(2) As regards England and Wales and Northern Ireland, the term implied by subsection (1) above is a condition.]

[12   Exclusion of implied terms

An express term does not negative a term implied by this Act unless inconsistent with it.]

[12A   Remedies for breach of hire-purchase agreement as respects Scotland

(1) Where in a hire-purchase agreement the creditor is in breach of any term of the agreement (express or implied), the person to whom the goods are hired shall be entitled—

(a) to claim damages, and

(b) if the breach is material, to reject any goods delivered under the agreement and treat it as repudiated.

(2) Where a hire-purchase agreement is a consumer contract, then, for the purposes of subsection (1) above, breach by the creditor of any term (express or implied)—

(a) as to the quality of the goods or their fitness for a purpose,

(b) if the goods are, or are to be, hired by description, that the goods will correspond with the description,

(c) if the goods are, or are to be, hired by reference to a sample, that the bulk will correspond with the sample in quality,

shall be deemed to be a material breach.

(3) In subsection (2) above 'consumer contract' has the same meaning as in

section 25(1) of the Unfair Contract Terms Act 1977; and for the purposes of that subsection the onus of proving that a hire-purchase agreement is not to be regarded as a consumer contract shall lie on the creditor.

(4)   This section applies to Scotland only.]

[. . .]

14   Special provisions as to conditional sale agreements

[(1)   Section 11(4) of the Sale of Goods Act 1979 (whereby in certain circumstances a breach of a condition in a contract of sale is treated only as a breach of warranty) shall not apply to [a conditional sale agreement] where the buyer deals as consumer within Part I of the Unfair Contract Terms Act 1977 or, in Scotland, the agreement is a consumer contract within Part II of that Act.]

15   Supplementary

[(1)   In sections 8 to 14 above and this section—

'business' includes a profession and the activities of any government department (including a Northern Ireland department), [or local or public authority];

'buyer' and 'seller' includes a person to whom rights and duties under a conditional sale agreement have passed by assignment or operation of law;

'conditional sale agreement' means an agreement for the sale of goods under which the purchase price or part of it is payable by instalments, and the property in the goods is to remain in the seller (notwithstanding that the buyer is to be in possession of the goods) until such conditions as to the payment of instalments or otherwise as may be specified in the agreement are fulfilled;

['consumer sale' has the same meaning as in section 55 of the Sale of Goods Act 1979 (as set out in paragraph 11 of Schedule 1 to that Act)];

'creditor' means the person by whom the goods are bailed or (in Scotland) hired under a hire-purchase agreement or the person to whom his rights and duties under the agreement have passed by assignment or operation of law; and

'hire-purchase agreement' means an agreement, other than conditional sale agreement, under which—

(a)   goods are bailed or (in Scotland) hired in return for periodical payments by the person to whom they are bailed or hired, and

(b)   the property in the goods will pass to that person if the terms of the agreement are complied with and one or more of the following occurs—

(i)   the exercise of an option to purchase by that person,

(ii)   the doing of any other specified act by any party to the agreement,

(iii)   the happening of any other specified event.

['producer' means the manufacturer of goods, the importer of goods into the European Economic Area or any person purporting to be a producer by placing his name, trade mark or other distinctive sign on the goods;]

(3)   In section 14(2) above 'corresponding hire-purchase agreement' means, in relation to a conditional sale agreement, a hire-purchase agreement relating to the same goods as the conditional sale agreement and made between the same parties and at the same time and in the same circumstances and, as nearly as may be, in the same terms as the conditional sale agreement.

(4)   Nothing in sections 8 to 13 above shall prejudice the operation of any other enactment including any enactment of the Parliament of Northern Ireland or the Northern Ireland Assembly or any rule of law whereby any term, other than one relating to quality or fitness, is to be implied in any hire-purchase agreement.]

CONSUMER CREDIT ACT 1974
(1974, c 39)

PART I
[OFFICE OF FAIR TRADING]

1   General functions of [OFT]
(1)   It is the duty of [the Office of Fair Trading ('the OFT')]—
(a)   to administer the licensing system set up by this Act,
(b)   to exercise the adjudicating functions conferred on [it] by this Act in relation to the issue, renewal, variation, suspension and revocation of licences, and other matters,
[(ba) to monitor, as it sees fit, businesses being carried on under licences;]
(c)   generally to superintend the working and enforcement of this Act, and regulations made under it, and
(d)   where necessary or expedient, [itself] to take steps to enforce this Act, and regulations so made.
(2)   It is the duty of the [OFT], so far as appears to [it] to be practicable and having regard both to the national interest and the interests of persons carrying on businesses to which this Act applies and their customers, to keep under review and from time to time advise the Secretary of State about—
(a)   social and commercial developments in the United Kingdom and elsewhere relating to the provision of credit or bailment or (in Scotland) hiring of goods to individuals, and related activities; and
(b)   the working and enforcement of this Act and orders and regulations made under it.

2   Powers of Secretary of State
(1)   The Secretary of State may by order—
(a)   confer on the [OFT] additional functions concerning the provision of credit or bailment or (in Scotland) hiring of goods to individuals, and related activities, and
(b)   regulate the carrying out by the [OFT] of [its] functions under this Act.
(2)   The Secretary of State may give general directions indicating considerations to which the [OFT] should have particular regard in carrying out [its] functions under this Act, and may give specific directions on any matter connected with the carrying out by the [OFT] of those functions.
(3)   The Secretary of State, on giving any directions under subsection (2), shall arrange for them to be published in such manner as he thinks most suitable for drawing them to the attention of interested persons.
(4)   With the approval of the Secretary of State and the Treasury, the [OFT] may charge, for any service or facility provided by [it] under this Act, a fee of an amount specified by general notice (the 'specified fee').
(5)   Provision may be made under subsection (4) for reduced fees, or no fees at all, to be paid for certain services or facilities by persons of a specified description, and references in this Act to the specified fee shall, in such cases, be construed accordingly.
(6)   An order under subsection (1)(a) shall be made by statutory instrument and shall be of no effect unless a draft of the order has been laid before and approved by each House of Parliament.
(7)   References in subsection (2) to the functions of the [OFT] under this Act do not include the making of a determination to which section 41 [. . .] (appeals from [OFT] to [the [First-tier] Tribunal]) applies.

[. . .]

4 Dissemination of information and advice

The [OFT] shall arrange for the dissemination, in such form and manner as [it] considers appropriate, of such information and advice as it may appear to [it] expedient to give to the public in the United Kingdom about the operation of this Act, [the consumer credit jurisdiction under Part 16 of the Financial Services and Markets Act 2000,] the credit facilities available to them, and other matters within the scope of [its] functions under this Act.

6 Form etc of applications

(1)   An application to the [OFT] under this Act is of no effect unless the requirements of this section are satisfied.

(2)   The application must be in writing, and in such form, and accompanied by such [information and documents], as the [OFT] may specify [or describe in a] general notice [. . .].

   [(2A)   The application must also be accompanied—

   (a)   in the case of an application for a licence or for the renewal of a licence, by the charge payable by virtue of section 6A;

   (b)   in any other case, by the specified fee.]

(3)   [Where the OFT receives an application, it may by notice to the applicant at any time before the determination of the application require him to provide such information or documents relevant to the application as may be specified or described in the notice.]

(4)   The [OFT] may by notice require the applicant to publish details of his application at a time or times and in a manner specified in the notice.

   [(5)   Subsection (6) applies where a general notice under subsection (2) comes into effect—

   (a)   after an application has been made; but

   (b)   before its determination.

(6)   The applicant shall, within such period as may be specified in the general notice, provide the OFT with any information or document—

   (a)   which he has not previously provided in relation to the application by virtue of this section;

   (b)   which he would have been required to provide with his application had it been made after the general notice came into effect; and

   (c)   which the general notice requires to be provided for the purposes of this subsection.

(7)   An applicant shall notify the OFT, giving details, if before his application is determined—

   (a)   any information or document provided by him in relation to the application by virtue of this section is, to any extent, superseded or otherwise affected by a change in circumstances; or

   (b)   he becomes aware of an error in or omission from any such information or document.

(8)   A notification for the purposes of subsection (7) shall be given within the period of 28 days beginning with the day on which (as the case may be)—

   (a)   the information or document is superseded;

   (b)   the change in circumstances occurs; or

   (c)   the applicant becomes aware of the error or omission.

(9)   Subsection (7) does not require an applicant to notify the OFT about—

   (a)   anything of which he is required to notify it under section 36; or

   (b)   an error in or omission from any information or document which is a clerical error or omission not affecting the substance of the information or document.]

[6A   Charge on applicants for licences etc

(1)   An applicant for a licence, or for the renewal of a licence, shall pay the OFT a charge towards the costs of carrying out its functions under this Act.

(2)   The amount of the charge payable by an applicant shall be determined in accordance with provision made by the OFT by general notice.

(3)   The provision that may be made by the OFT under subsection (2) includes—

(a)   different provision in relation to persons of different descriptions;

(b)   provision for no charge at all to be payable by persons of specified descriptions.

(4)   The approval of the Secretary of State and the Treasury is required for a general notice under subsection (2).]

[7   Penalty for false information

A person commits an offence if, for the purposes of, or in connection with, any requirement imposed or other provision made by or under this Act, he knowingly or recklessly gives information to the OFT, or to an officer of the OFT, which, in a material particular, is false or misleading.]

PART II
CREDIT AGREEMENTS, HIRE AGREEMENTS AND LINKED TRANSACTIONS

8   Consumer credit agreements

(1)   A [consumer] credit agreement is an agreement between an individual ('the debtor') and any other person ('the creditor') by which the creditor provides the debtor with credit of any amount.

[. . .]

(3)   A consumer credit agreement is a regulated agreement within the meaning of this Act if it is not an agreement (an 'exempt agreement') specified in or under section 16 [, 16A, 16B or 16C].

9   Meaning of credit

(1)   In this Act 'credit' includes a cash loan, and any other form of financial accommodation.

(2)   Where credit is provided otherwise than in sterling it shall be treated for the purposes of this Act as provided in sterling of an equivalent amount.

(3)   Without prejudice to the generality of subsection (1), the person by whom goods are bailed or (in Scotland) hired to an individual under a hire-purchase agreement shall be taken to provide him with fixed-sum credit to finance the transaction of an amount equal to the total price of the goods less the aggregate of the deposit (if any) and the total charge for credit.

(4)   For the purposes of this Act, an item entering into the total charge for credit shall not be treated as credit even though time is allowed for its payment.

10   Running-account credit and fixed-sum credit

(1)   For the purposes of this Act—

(a)   running-account credit is a facility under a [consumer] credit agreement whereby the debtor is enabled to receive from time to time (whether in his own person, or by another person) from the creditor or a third party cash, goods and services (or any of them) to an amount or value such that, taking into account payments made by or to the credit of the debtor, the credit limit (if any) is not at any time exceeded; and

(b)   fixed-sum credit is any other facility under a [consumer] credit agreement whereby the debtor is enabled to receive credit (whether in one amount or by instalments).

(2)   In relation to running-account credit, 'credit limit' means, as respects any period, the maximum debit balance which, under the credit agreement, is allowed to stand on the account during that period, disregarding any term of the agreement allowing that maximum to be exceeded merely temporarily.

(3)   For the purposes of [any provision of this Act that specifies an amount of

credit (except section 17(1)(a))], running-account credit shall be taken not to exceed the amount specified in [that provision] ('the specified amount') if—
    (a)   the credit limit does not exceed the specified amount; or
    (b)   whether or not there is a credit limit, and if there is, notwithstanding that it exceeds the specified amount,—
        (i)   the debtor is not enabled to draw at any one time an amount which, so far as (having regard to section 9(4)) it represents credit, exceeds the specified amount, or
        (ii)   the agreement provides that, if the debit balance rises above a given amount (not exceeding the specified amount), the rate of the total charge for credit increases or any other condition favouring the creditor or his associate comes into operation, or
        (iii)   at the time the agreement is made it is probable, having regard to the terms of the agreement and any other relevant considerations, that the debit balance will not at any time rise above the specified amount.

11   Restricted-use credit and unrestricted-use credit

(1)   A restricted-use credit agreement is a regulated consumer credit agreement—
    (a)   to finance a transaction between the debtor and the creditor, whether forming part of that agreement or not, or
    (b)   to finance a transaction between the debtor and a person (the 'supplier') other than the creditor, or
    (c)   to refinance any existing indebtedness of the debtor's, whether to the creditor or another person, and 'restricted-use credit' shall be construed accordingly.
(2)   An unrestricted-use credit agreement is a regulated consumer credit agreement not falling within subsection (1), and 'unrestricted-use credit' shall be construed accordingly.
(3)   An agreement does not fall within subsection (1) if the credit is in fact provided in such a way as to leave the debtor free to use it as he chooses, even though certain uses would contravene that or any other agreement.
(4)   An agreement may fall within subsection (1)(b) although the identity of the supplier is unknown at the time the agreement is made.

12   Debtor-creditor-supplier agreements

A debtor-creditor-supplier agreement is a regulated consumer credit agreement being—
    (a)   a restricted-use credit agreement which falls within section 11(1)(a), or
    (b)   a restricted-use credit agreement which falls within section 11(1)(b) and is made by the creditor under pre-existing arrangements, or in contemplation of future arrangements, between himself and the supplier, or
    (c)   an unrestricted-use credit agreement which is made by the creditor under pre-existing arrangements between himself and a person (the 'supplier') other than the debtor in the knowledge that the credit is to be used to finance a transaction between the debtor and the supplier.

13   Debtor-creditor agreements

A debtor-creditor agreement is a regulated consumer credit agreement being—
    (a)   a restricted-use credit agreement which falls within section 11(1)(b) but is not made by the creditor under pre-existing arrangements, or in contemplation of future arrangements, between himself and the supplier, or
    (b)   a restricted-use credit agreement which falls within section 11(1)(c), or
    (c)   an unrestricted-use credit agreement which is not made by the creditor under pre-existing arrangements between himself and a person (the 'supplier') other than the debtor in the knowledge that the credit is to be used to finance a transaction between the debtor and the supplier.

14   Credit-token agreements

(1)   A credit-token is a card, check, voucher, coupon, stamp, form, booklet or other document or thing given to an individual by a person carrying on a consumer credit business, who undertakes—

(a)   that on the production of it (whether or not some other action is also required) he will supply cash, goods and services (or any of them) on credit, or

(b)   that where, on the production of it to a third party (whether or not any other action is also required), the third party supplies cash, goods and services (or any of them), he will pay the third party for them (whether or not deducting any discount or commission), in return for payment to him by the individual.

(2)   A credit-token agreement is a regulated agreement for the provision of credit in connection with the use of a credit-token.

(3)   Without prejudice to the generality of section 9(1), the person who gives to an individual an undertaking falling within subsection (1)(b) shall be taken to provide him with credit drawn on whenever a third party supplies him with cash, goods or services.

(4)   For the purposes of subsection (1), use of an object to operate a machine provided by the person giving the object or a third party shall be treated as the production of the object to him.

15   Consumer hire agreements

(1)   A consumer hire agreement is an agreement made by a person with an individual (the 'hirer') for the bailment or (in Scotland) the hiring of goods to the hirer, being an agreement which—

(a)   is not a hire-purchase agreement, and

(b)   is capable of subsisting for more than three months, [. . .].

(2)   A consumer hire agreement is a regulated agreement if it is not an exempt agreement.

16   Exempt agreements

(1)   This Act does not regulate a consumer credit agreement where the creditor is a local authority [. . .], or a body specified, or of a description specified, in an order made by the Secretary of State, being—

(a)   [an insurer],

(b)   a friendly society,

(c)   an organisation of employers or organisation of workers,

(d)   a charity,

(e)   a land improvement company,

(f)   a body corporate named or specifically referred to in any public general Act,

[(ff)   a body corporate named or specifically referred to in an order made under—

section 156(4), 444(1) or 447(2)(a) of the Housing Act 1985,

section 156(4) of that Act as it has effect by virtue of section 17 of the Housing Act 1996 (the right to acquire),

section 223 or 229 of the Housing (Scotland) Act 1987, or

Article 154(1)(a) or 156AA of the Housing (Northern Ireland) Order 1981

Article 10(6A) of the Housing (Northern Ireland) Order 1983; or

(g)   a building society, or

(h)   a deposit-taker.]

(2)   Subsection (1) applies only where the agreement is—

(a)   a debtor-creditor-supplier agreement financing—

(i)   the purchase of land, or

(ii)   the provision of dwellings on any land, and secured by a land mortgage on that land; or

(b)   a debtor-creditor agreement secured by any land mortgage; or

(c)   a debtor-creditor-supplier agreement financing a transaction which is a linked transaction in relation to—

    (i)   an agreement falling within paragraph (a), or

    (ii)   an agreement falling within paragraph (b) financing—

       (aa)   the purchase of any land, or

       (bb)   the provision of dwellings on any land, and secured by a land mortgage on the land referred to in paragraph (a) or, as the case may be, the land referred to in sub-paragraph (ii).

[(3)   Before he makes, varies or revokes an order under subsection (1), the Secretary of State must undertake the necessary consultation.

(3A)   The necessary consultation means consultation with the bodies mentioned in the following table in relation to the provision under which the order is to be made, varied or revoked:

Provision of subsection (1)	Consultee
Paragraph (a) or (b)	The Financial Services Authority
Paragraph (d)	The [Charity Commission]
Paragraph (e), (f) or (ff)	Any Minister of the Crown with responsibilities in relation to the body in question
Paragraph (g) or (h)	The Treasury and the Financial Services Authority]

(4)   An order under subsection (1) relating to a body may be limited so as to apply only to agreements by that body of a description specified in the order.

(5)   The Secretary of State may by order provide that this Act shall not regulate other consumer credit agreements where—

    (a)   the number of payments to be made by the debtor does not exceed the number specified for that purpose in the order, or

    (b)   the rate of the total charge for credit does not exceed the rate so specified, or

    (c)   an agreement has a connection with a country outside the United Kingdom.

(6)   The Secretary of State may by order provide that this Act shall not regulate consumer hire agreements of a description specified in the order where—

    (a)   the owner is a body corporate authorised by or under any enactment to supply electricity, gas or water, and

    (b)   the subject of the agreement is a meter or metering equipment [or where the owner is a provider of a public electronic communications service who is specified in the order].

[(6A)   This Act does not regulate a consumer credit agreement where the creditor is a housing authority and the agreement is secured by a land mortgage of a dwelling.

(6B)   In subsection (6A) 'housing authority' means—

    (a)   as regards England and Wales, [the Homes and Communities Agency, the Welsh new towns residuary body, the Regulator of Social Housing] and an authority or body within section 80(1) of the Housing Act 1985 (the landlord condition for secure tenancies), other than a housing association or a housing trust which is a charity;

    (b)   as regards Scotland, a development corporation established under an order made, or having effect as if made under the New Towns (Scotland) Act 1968, the Scottish Special Housing Association or the Housing Corporation;

(c)   as regards Northern Ireland, the Northern Ireland Housing Executive.]
[(6C)   This Act does not regulate a consumer credit agreement if—
(a)   it is secured by a land mortgage and entering into the agreement as lender is a regulated activity for the purposes of the Financial Services and Markets Act 2000; or
(b)   it is or forms part of a regulated home purchase plan and entering into the agreement as home purchase provider is a regulated activity for the purposes of that Act.]
[(6D)   But section 126, and any other provision so far as it related to section 126, applies to an agreement which would (but for [subsection (6C)(a)]) be a regulated agreement.
(6E)   Subsection (6C) must be read with—
(a)   section 22 of the Financial Services and Markets Act 2000 (regulated activities; power to specify classes of activity and categories of investment);
(b)   any order for the time being in force under that section; and
(c)   Schedule 2 to that Act.]
[. . .]
[(7A)   Nothing in this section affects the application of sections 140A to 140C.]
(8)   [In the application of this section to Scotland subsection (3A) shall have effect as if the reference to the Charity Commissioners were a reference to the Lord Advocate.]
(9)   In the application of this section to Northern Ireland subsection [(3A)] shall have effect as if any reference to a Minister of the Crown were a reference to a Northern Ireland department, [. . .] and any reference to the Charity Commissioners were a reference to the Department of Finance for Northern Ireland.
[(10)   In this section—
(a)   'deposit-taker' means—
(i)   a person who has permission under Part 4 of the Financial Services and Markets Act 2000 to accept deposits,
(ii)   an EEA firm of the kind mentioned in paragraph 5(b) of Schedule 3 to that Act which has permission under paragraph 15 of that Schedule (as a result of qualifying for authorisation under paragraph 12 of that Schedule) to accept deposits,
(iii)   any wholly owned subsidiary (within the meaning of [the Companies Acts (see section 1159 of the Companies Act 2006)]) of a person mentioned in sub-paragraph (i), or
(iv)   any undertaking which, in relation to a person mentioned in sub-paragraph (ii), is a subsidiary undertaking within the meaning of any rule of law in force in the EEA State in question for purposes connected with the implementation of the European Council Seventh Company Law Directive of 13 June 1983 on consolidated accounts (No 83/349/EEC), and which has no members other than that person;
(b)   'insurer' means—
(i)   a person who has permission under Part 4 of the Financial Services and Markets Act 2000 to effect or carry out contracts of insurance, or
(ii)   an EEA firm of the kind mentioned in paragraph 5(d) of Schedule 3 to that Act, which has permission under paragraph 15 of that Schedule (as a result of qualifying for authorisation under paragraph 12 of that Schedule) to effect or carry out contracts of insurance,
but does not include a friendly society or an organisation of workers or of employers.
(11)   Subsection (10) must be read with—
(a)   section 22 of the Financial Services and Markets Act 2000;
(b)   any relevant order under that section; and
(c)   Schedule 2 to that Act.]

[16A Exemption relating to high net worth debtors and hirers

(1) The Secretary of State may by order provide that this Act shall not regulate a consumer credit agreement or a consumer hire agreement where—

(a) the debtor or hirer is a natural person;

(b) the agreement includes a declaration made by him to the effect that he agrees to forgo the protection and remedies that would be available to him under this Act if the agreement were a regulated agreement;

(c) a statement of high net worth has been made in relation to him; and

(d) that statement is current in relation to the agreement and a copy of it was provided to the creditor or owner before the agreement was made.

(2) For the purposes of this section a statement of high net worth is a statement to the effect that, in the opinion of the person making it, the natural person in relation to whom it is made—

(a) received during the previous financial year income of a specified description totalling an amount of not less than the specified amount; or

(b) had throughout that year net assets of a specified description with a total value of not less than the specified value.

(3) Such a statement—

(a) may not be made by the person in relation to whom it is made;

(b) must be made by a person of a specified description; and

(c) is current in relation to an agreement if it was made during the period of one year ending with the day on which the agreement is made.

(4) An order under this section may make provision about—

(a) how amounts of income and values of net assets are to be determined for the purposes of subsection (2)(a) and (b);

(b) the form, content and signing of—

(i) statements of high net worth;

(ii) declarations for the purposes of subsection (1)(b).

(5) Where an agreement has two or more debtors or hirers, for the purposes of paragraph (c) of subsection (1) a separate statement of high net worth must have been made in relation to each of them; and paragraph (d) of that subsection shall have effect accordingly.

(6) In this section—

'previous financial year' means, in relation to a statement of high net worth, the financial year immediately preceding the financial year during which the statement is made;

'specified' means specified in an order under this section.

(7) In subsection (6) 'financial year' means a period of one year ending with 31st March.

(8) Nothing in this section affects the application of sections 140A to 140C.]

[16B Exemption relating to businesses

(1) This Act does not regulate—

(a) a consumer credit agreement by which the creditor provides the debtor with credit exceeding £25,000, or

(b) a consumer hire agreement that requires the hirer to make payments exceeding £25,000,

if the agreement is entered into by the debtor or hirer wholly or predominantly for the purposes of a business carried on, or intended to be carried on, by him.

(2) If an agreement includes a declaration made by the debtor or hirer to the effect that the agreement is entered into by him wholly or predominantly for the purposes of a business carried on, or intended to be carried on, by him, the agreement shall be presumed to have been entered into by him wholly or predominantly for such purposes.

(3) But that presumption does not apply if, when the agreement is entered into—

(a)   the creditor or owner, or

(b)   any person who has acted on his behalf in connection with the entering into of the agreement,

knows, or has reasonable cause to suspect, that the agreement is not entered into by the debtor or hirer wholly or predominantly for the purposes of a business carried on, or intended to be carried on, by him.

(4)   The Secretary of State may by order make provision about the form, content and signing of declarations for the purposes of subsection (2).

(5)   Where an agreement has two or more creditors or owners, in subsection (3) references to the creditor or owner are references to any one or more of them.

(6)   Nothing in this section affects the application of sections 140A to 140C.]

[16C   Exemption relating to investment properties

(1)   This Act does not regulate a consumer credit agreement if, at the time the agreement is entered into, any sums due under it are secured by a land mortgage on land where the condition in subsection (2) is satisfied.

(2)   The condition is that less than 40% of the land is used, or is intended to be used, as or in connection with a dwelling—

(a)   by the debtor or a person connected with the debtor, or

(b)   in the case of credit provided to trustees, by an individual who is the beneficiary of the trust or a person connected with such an individual.

(3)   For the purposes of subsection (2) the area of any land which comprises a building or other structure containing two or more storeys is to be taken to be the aggregate of the floor areas of each of those storeys.

(4)   For the purposes of subsection (2) a person is 'connected with' the debtor or an individual who is the beneficiary of a trust if he is—

(a)   that person's spouse or civil partner;

(b)   a person (whether or not of the opposite sex) whose relationship with that person has the characteristics of the relationship between husband and wife; or

(c)   that person's parent, brother, sister, child, grandparent or grandchild.

(5)   Section 126 (enforcement of land mortgages) applies to an agreement which would but for this section be a regulated agreement.

(6)   Nothing in this section affects the application of sections 140A to 140C.]

17   Small agreements

(1)   A small agreement is—

(a)   a regulated consumer credit agreement for credit not exceeding [£50], other than a hire-purchase or conditional sale agreement; or

(b)   a regulated consumer hire agreement which does not require the hirer to make payments exceeding [£50],

being an agreement which is either unsecured or secured by a guarantee or indemnity only (whether or not the guarantee or indemnity is itself secured).

[(2)   For the purposes of paragraph (a) of subsection (1), running-account credit shall be taken not to exceed the amount specified in that paragraph if the credit limit does not exceed that amount.]

(3)   Where—

(a)   two or more small agreements are made at or about the same time between the same parties, and

(b)   it appears probable that they would instead have been made as a single agreement but for the desire to avoid the operation of provisions of this Act which would have applied to that single agreement but, apart from this subsection, are not applicable to the small agreements,

this Act applies to the small agreements as if they were regulated agreements other small agreements.

(4)   If, apart from this subsection, subsection (3) does not apply to any agreements but would apply if, for any party or parties to any of the agreements, there

were substituted an associate of that party, or associates of each of those parties, as the case may be, then subsection (3) shall apply to the agreements.

18 Multiple agreements

(1) This section applies to an agreement (a 'multiple agreement') if its terms are such as—

(a) to place a part of it within one category of agreement mentioned in this Act, and another part of it within a different category of agreement so mentioned, or within a category of agreement not so mentioned, or

(b) to place it, or a part of it, within two or more categories of agreement so mentioned.

(2) Where a part of an agreement falls within subsection (1), that part shall be treated for the purposes of this Act as a separate agreement.

(3) Where an agreement falls within subsection (1)(b), it shall be treated as an agreement in each of the categories in question, and this Act shall apply to it accordingly.

(4) Where under subsection (2) a part of a multiple agreement is to be treated as a separate agreement, the multiple agreement shall (with any necessary modifications) be construed accordingly; and any sum payable under the multiple agreement, if not apportioned by the parties, shall for the purposes of proceedings in any court relating to the multiple agreement be apportioned by the court as may be requisite.

(5) In the case of an agreement for running-account credit, a term of the agreement allowing the credit limit to be exceeded merely temporarily shall not be treated as a separate agreement or as providing fixed-sum credit in respect of the excess.

(6) This Act does not apply to a multiple agreement so far as the agreement relates to goods if under the agreement payments are to be made in respect of the goods in the form of rent (other than a rentcharge) issuing out of land.

19 Linked transactions

(1) A transaction entered into by the debtor or hirer, or a relative of his, with any other person ('the other party'), except one for the provision of security, is a linked transaction in relation to an actual or prospective regulated agreement (the 'principal agreement') of which it does not form part if—

(a) the transaction is entered into in compliance with a term of the principal agreement; or

(b) the principal agreement is a debtor-creditor-supplier agreement and the transaction is financed, or to be financed, by the principal agreement; or

(c) the other party is a person mentioned in subsection (2), and a person so mentioned initiated the transaction by suggesting it to the debtor or hirer, or his relative, who enters into it—

(i) to induce the creditor or owner to enter into the principal agreement, or

(ii) for another purpose related to the principal agreement, or

(iii) where the principal agreement is a restricted-use credit agreement, for a purpose related to a transaction financed, or to be financed, by the principal agreement.

(2) The persons referred to in subsection (1)(c) are—

(a) the creditor or owner, or his associate;

(b) a person who, in the negotiation of the transaction, is represented by a credit-broker who is also a negotiator in antecedent negotiations for the principal agreement;

(c) a person who, at the time the transaction is initiated, knows that the principal agreement has been made or contemplates that it might be made.

(3) A linked transaction entered into before the making of the principal agreement has no effect until such time (if any) as that agreement is made.

(4)   Regulations may exclude linked transactions of the prescribed description from the operation of subsection (3).

20   Total charge for credit

(1)   The Secretary of State shall make regulations containing such provisions as appear to him appropriate for determining the true cost to the debtor of the credit provided or to be provided under an actual or prospective consumer credit agreement (the 'total charge for credit'), and regulations so made shall prescribe—

(a)   what items are to be treated as entering into the total charge for credit, and how their amount is to be ascertained;

(b)   the method of calculating the rate of the total charge for credit.

(2)   Regulations under subsection (1) may provide for the whole or part of the amount payable by the debtor or his relative under any linked transaction to be included in the total charge for credit, whether or not the creditor is a party to the transaction or derives benefit from it.

PART III
LICENSING OF CREDIT AND HIRE BUSINESSES

Licensing principles

21   Businesses needing a licence

(1)   Subject to this section, a licence is required to carry on a consumer credit business [a consumer hire business or an ancillary credit business].

(2)   A local authority does not need a licence to carry on a business.

(3)   A body corporate empowered by a public general Act naming it to carry on a business does not need a licence to do so.

22   Standard and group licences

(1)   A licence may be—

(a)   a standard licence, that is a licence issued by the [OFT] to a person named in the licence on an application made by him, which, [whilst the licence is in effect], covers such activities as are described in the licence, or

(b)   a group licence, that is a licence issued by the [OFT] (whether on the application of any person or of [its] own motion), which, [whilst the licence is in effect], covers such persons and activities as are described in the licence.

[(1A)   The terms of a licence shall specify—

(a)   whether it has effect indefinitely or only for a limited period; and

(b)   if it has effect for a limited period, that period.

(1B)   For the purposes of subsection (1A)(b) the period specified shall be such period not exceeding the prescribed period as the OFT thinks fit (subject to subsection (1E)).

(1C)   A standard licence shall have effect indefinitely unless—

(a)   the application for its issue requests that it have effect for a limited period only; or

(b)   the OFT otherwise thinks there is good reason why it should have effect for such a period only.

(1D)   A group licence shall have effect for a limited period only unless the OFT thinks there is good reason why it should have effect indefinitely.

(1E)   Where a licence which has effect indefinitely is to be varied under section 30 or 31 for the purpose of limiting the licence's duration, the variation shall provide for the licence to expire—

(a)   in the case of a variation under section 30, at the end of such period from the time of the variation as is set out in the application for the variation; or

(b)   in the case of a variation under section 31, at the end of such period from the time of the variation as the OFT thinks fit;

but a period mentioned in paragraph (a) or (b) shall not exceed the prescribed period.]

(2) A licence is not assignable or, subject to section 37, transmissible on death or in any other way.

(3) Except in the case of a partnership or an unincorporated body of persons, a standard licence shall not be issued to more than one person.

(4) A standard licence issued to a partnership or an unincorporated body of persons shall be issued in the name of the partnership or body.

(5) The [OFT] may issue a group licence only if it appears to [it] that the public interest is better served by doing so than by obliging the persons concerned to apply separately for standard licences.

[(5A) A group licence to carry on a business may limit the activities it covers in any way the OFT thinks fit.]

(6) The persons covered by a group licence may be described by general words, whether or not coupled with the exclusion of named persons, or in any other way the [OFT] thinks fit.

(7) The fact that a person is covered by a group licence in respect of certain activities does not prevent a standard licence being issued to him in respect of those activities or any of them.

(8) A group licence issued on the application of any person shall be issued to that person, and general notice shall be given of the issue of any group licence (whether on application or not).

[. . .]

23 Authorisation of specific activities

(1) Subject to [the terms of the licence], a licence to carry on a business covers all lawful activities done in the course of that business, whether by the licensee or other persons on his behalf.

[. . .]

(3) A licence covers the canvassing off trade premises of debtor-creditor-supplier agreements or regulated consumer hire agreements only if, and to the extent that, the licence specifically so provides; and such provision shall not be included in a group licence.

(4) [The OFT may by general notice specify] other activities which, if engaged in by or on behalf of the person carrying on a business, require to be covered by an express term in his licence.

24 Control of name of business

A standard licence authorises the licensee to carry on a business under the name or names specified in the licence, but not under any other name.

[24A Applications for standard licences

(1) An application for a standard licence shall, in relation to each type of business which is covered by the application, state whether the applicant is applying—

(a) for the licence to cover the carrying on of that type of business with no limitation; or

(b) for the licence to cover the carrying on of that type of business only so far as it falls within one or more descriptions of business.

(2) An application within subsection (1)(b) in relation to a type of business shall set out the description or descriptions of business in question.

(3) References in this Part to a type of business are references to a type of business within subsection (4).

(4) The types of business within this subsection are—

(a) a consumer credit business;

(b) a consumer hire business;

(c) a business so far as it comprises or relates to credit brokerage;

(d)   a business so far as it comprises or relates to debt-adjusting;

(e)   a business so far as it comprises or relates to debt-counselling;

(f)   a business so far as it comprises or relates to debt-collecting;

(g)   a business so far as it comprises or relates to debt administration;

(h)   a business so far as it comprises or relates to the provision of credit information services;

(i)   a business so far as it comprises or relates to the operation of a credit reference agency.

(5)   The OFT—

(a)   shall by general notice specify the descriptions of business which can be set out in an application for the purposes of subsection (2) in relation to a type of business;

(b)   may by general notice provide that applications within subsection (1)(b) cannot be made in relation to one or more of the types of business within subsection (4)(c) to (i).

(6)   The power of the OFT under subsection (5) includes power to make different provision for different cases or classes of case.]

25   Licensee to be a fit person

[(1)   If an applicant for a standard licence—

(a)   makes an application within section 24A(1)(a) in relation to a type of business, and

(b)   satisfies the OFT that he is a fit person to carry on that type of business with no limitation,

he shall be entitled to be issued with a standard licence covering the carrying on of that type of business with no limitation.

(1AA)   If such an applicant—

(a)   makes an application within subsection (1)(b) of section 24A in relation to a type of business, and

(b)   satisfies the OFT that he is a fit person to carry on that type of business so far as it falls within the description or descriptions of business set out in his application in accordance with subsection (2) of that section,

he shall be entitled to be issued with a standard licence covering the carrying on of that type of business so far as it falls within the description or descriptions in question.

(1AB)   If such an applicant makes an application within section 24A(1)(a) or (b) in relation to a type of business but fails to satisfy the OFT as mentioned in subsection (1) or (1AA) (as the case may be), he shall nevertheless be entitled to be issued with a standard licence covering the carrying on of that type of business so far as it falls within one or more descriptions of business if—

(a)   he satisfies the OFT that he is a fit person to carry on that type of business so far as it falls within the description or descriptions in question;

(b)   he could have applied for the licence to be limited in that way; and

(c)   the licence would not cover any activity which was not covered by his application.

(1AC)   In this section 'description of business' means, in relation to a type of business, a description of business specified in a general notice under section 24A(5)(a).

(1AD)   An applicant shall not, by virtue of this section, be issued with a licence unless he satisfies the OFT that the name or names under which he would be licensed is or are not misleading or otherwise undesirable.]

[. . .]

(1B)   If an application for the grant of a standard licence—

(a)   is made by a person with permission under Part 4 of the Financial Services and Markets Act 2000 to accept deposits, and

(b)   relates to a listed activity,

the Financial Services Authority may, if it considers that the [OFT] ought to refuse the application, notify [it] of that fact.

(1C) In subsection (1B) 'listed activity' means an activity listed in [Annex I to Directive 2006/48/EC of the European Parliament and of the Council of 14 June 2006 relating to the taking up and pursuit of the business of credit institutions] or in [Annex I to the markets in financial instruments directive (2004/39/EC)] and references to deposits and to their acceptance must be read with—

(a) section 22 of the Financial Services and Markets Act 2000;

(b) any relevant order under that section; and

(c) Schedule 2 to that Act.]

[(2) In determining whether an applicant for a licence is a fit person for the purposes of this section the OFT shall have regard to any matters appearing to it to be relevant including (amongst other things)—

(a) the applicant's skills, knowledge and experience in relation to consumer credit businesses, consumer hire businesses or ancillary credit businesses;

(b) such skills, knowledge and experience of other persons who the applicant proposes will participate in any business that would be carried on by him under the licence;

(c) practices and procedures that the applicant proposes to implement in connection with any such business;

(d) evidence of the kind mentioned in subsection (2A).

(2A) That evidence is evidence tending to show that the applicant, or any of the applicant's employees, agents or associates (whether past or present) or, where the applicant is a body corporate, any person appearing to the OFT to be a controller of the body corporate or an associate of any such person, has—

(a) committed any offence involving fraud or other dishonesty or violence;

(b) contravened any provision made by or under—

(i) this Act;

(ii) Part 16 of the Financial Services and Markets Act 2000 so far as it relates to the consumer credit jurisdiction under that Part;

(iii) any other enactment regulating the provision of credit to individuals or other transactions with individuals;

(c) contravened any provision in force in an EEA State which corresponds to a provision of the kind mentioned in paragraph (b);

(d) practised discrimination on grounds of sex, colour, race or ethnic or national origins in, or in connection with, the carrying on of any business; or

(e) engaged in business practices appearing to the OFT to be deceitful or oppressive or otherwise unfair or improper (whether unlawful or not).

(2B) For the purposes of subsection (2A)(e), the business practices which the OFT may consider to be deceitful or oppressive or otherwise unfair or improper include practices in the carrying on of a consumer credit business that appear to the OFT to involve irresponsible lending.]

(3) In subsection [(2A)], 'associate', in addition to the persons specified in section 184, includes a business associate.

[25A Guidance on fitness test

(1) The OFT shall prepare and publish guidance in relation to how it determines, or how it proposes to determine, whether persons are fit persons as mentioned in section 25.

(2) If the OFT revises the guidance at any time after it has been published, the OFT shall publish it as revised.

(3) The guidance shall be published in such manner as the OFT thinks fit for the purpose of bringing it to the attention of those likely to be affected by it.

(4) In preparing or revising the guidance the OFT shall consult such persons as it thinks fit.

(5)   In carrying out its functions under this Part the OFT shall have regard to the guidance as most recently published.]

[26   Conduct of business
(1)   Regulations may be made as to—
    (a)   the conduct by a licensee of his business; and
    (b)   the conduct by a consumer credit EEA firm of its business in the United Kingdom.
(2)   The regulations may in particular specify—
    (a)   the books or other records to be kept by any person to whom the regulations apply;
    (b)   the information to be furnished by such a person to those persons with whom—
        (i)   that person does business, or
        (ii)   that person seeks to do business,
and the way in which that information is to be furnished.]

Issue of licences

27   Determination of applications
(1)   Unless the [OFT] determines to issue a licence in accordance with an application [it] shall, before determining the application by notice—
    (a)   inform the applicant, giving [its] reasons, that, as the case may be, [it] is minded to refuse the application, or to grant it in terms different from those applied for, describing them, and
    (b)   invite the applicant to submit to the [OFT] representations in support of his application in accordance with section 34.
(2)   If the [OFT] grants the application in terms different from those applied for then, whether or not the applicant appeals, the [OFT] shall issue the licence in the terms approved by [it] unless the applicant by notice informs [it] that he does not desire a licence in those terms.

[27A   Consumer credit EEA firms
(1)   Where—
    (a)   a consumer credit EEA firm makes an application for a standard licence, and
    (b)   the activities covered by the application are all permitted activities,
the OFT shall refuse the application.
(2)   Subsection (3) applies where—
    (a)   a consumer credit EEA firm makes an application for a standard licence; and
    (b)   some (but not all) of the activities covered by the application are permitted activities.
(3)   In order to be entitled to be issued with a standard licence in accordance with section 25(1) to (1AB) in relation to a type of business, the firm need not satisfy the OFT that it is a fit person to carry on that type of business so far as it would involve any of the permitted activities covered by the application.
(4)   A standard licence held by a consumer credit EEA firm does not at any time authorise the carrying on of an activity which is a permitted activity at that time.
(5)   In this section 'permitted activity' means, in relation to a consumer credit EEA firm, an activity for which the firm has, or could obtain, permission under paragraph 15 of Schedule 3 to the Financial Services and Markets Act 2000.]

28   Exclusion from group licence
Where the [OFT] is minded to issue a group licence (whether on the application of any person or not), and in doing so to exclude any person from the group by name, [it] shall, before determining the matter,—

(a)   give notice of that fact to the person proposed to be excluded, giving [its] reasons, and

(b)   invite that person to submit to the [OFT] representations against his exclusion in accordance with section 34.

[Charges for indefinite licences

[28A   Charges to be paid by licensees etc before end of payment periods

(1)   The licensee under a standard licence which has effect indefinitely shall, before the end of each payment period of his, pay the OFT a charge towards the costs of carrying out its functions under this Act.

(2)   The original applicant for a group licence which has effect indefinitely shall, before the end of each payment period of his, pay the OFT such a charge.

(3)   The amount of the charge payable by a person under subsection (1) or (2) before the end of a payment period shall be determined in accordance with pro-vision which—

(a)   is made by the OFT by general notice; and

(b)   is current on such day as may be determined in accordance with provision made by regulations.

(4)   The provision that may be made by the OFT under subsection (3)(a) includes—

(a)   different provision in relation to persons of different descriptions (including persons whose payment periods end at different times);

(b)   provision for no charge at all to be payable by persons of specified descriptions.

(5)   The approval of the Secretary of State and the Treasury is required for a general notice under subsection (3)(a).

(6)   For the purposes of this section a person's payment periods are to be deter-mined in accordance with provision made by regulations.]

[28B   Extension of period to pay charge under s 28A

(1)   A person who is required under section 28A to pay a charge before the end of a period may apply once to the OFT for that period to be extended.

(2)   The application shall be made before such day as may be determined in accordance with provision made by the OFT by general notice.

(3)   If the OFT is satisfied that there is a good reason—

(a)   why the applicant has not paid that charge prior to his making of the application, and

(b)   why he cannot pay that charge before the end of that period,

it may, if it thinks fit, by notice to him extend that period by such time as it thinks fit having regard to that reason.

(4)   The power of the OFT under this section to extend a period in relation to a charge—

(a)   includes the power to extend the period in relation to a part of the charge only;

(b)   may be exercised even though the period has ended.]

[28C   Failure to pay charge under s 28A

(1)   This section applies if a person (the 'defaulter') fails to pay a charge—

(a)   before the end of a period (the 'payment period') as required under section 28A; or

(b)   where the payment period is extended under section 28B, before the end of the payment period as extended (subject to subsection (2)).

(2)   Where the payment period is extended under section 28B in relation to a part of the charge only, this section applies if the defaulter fails—

(a)   to pay so much of the charge as is not covered by the extension before the end of the payment period disregarding the extension; or

(b)   to pay so much of the charge as is covered by the extension before the end of the payment period as extended.

(3)   Subject to subsection (4), if the charge is a charge under section 28A(1), the defaulter's licence terminates.

(4)   If the defaulter has applied to the OFT under section 28B for the payment period to be extended and that application has not been determined—

(a)   his licence shall not terminate before the application has been determined and the OFT has notified him of the determination; and

(b)   if the OFT extends the payment period on that application, this section shall have effect accordingly.

(5)   If the charge is a charge under section 28A(2), the charge shall be recoverable by the OFT.]]

Renewal, variation, suspension and revocation of licences

29   Renewal

(1)   If the licensee under a standard licence [of limited duration], or the original applicant for, or any licensee under, a group licence of limited duration, wishes the [OFT] to renew the licence, whether on the same terms (except as to expiry) or on varied terms, he must, during the period specified by the [OFT] by general notice or such longer period as the [OFT] may allow, make an application to the [OFT] for its renewal.

(2)   The [OFT] may of [its] own motion renew any group licence.

(3)   The preceding provisions of this Part apply to the renewal of a licence as they apply to the issue of a licence, except that section 28 does not apply to a person who was already excluded in the licence up for renewal.

[(3A)   In its application to the renewal of standard licences by virtue of subsection (3) of this section, section 27(1) shall have effect as if for paragraph (b) there were substituted—

'(b)   invite the applicant to submit to the OFT in accordance with section 34 representations—

(i)   in support of his application; and

(ii)   about the provision (if any) that should be included under section 34A as part of the determination were the OFT to refuse the application or grant it in terms different from those applied for.']

(4)   Until the determination of an application under subsection (1) and, where an appeal lies from the determination, until the end of the appeal period, the licence shall continue [to have effect], notwithstanding that apart from this subsection it would expire earlier.

[. . .]

(6)   General notice shall be given of the renewal of a group licence.

30   Variation by request

(1)   [If it thinks fit, the OFT may by notice to the licensee under a standard licence—

(a)   in the case of a licence which covers the carrying on of a type of business only so far as it falls within one or more descriptions of business, vary the licence by—

(i)   removing that limitation;

(ii)   adding a description of business to that limitation; or

(iii)   removing a description of business from that limitation;

(b)   in the case of a licence which covers the carrying on of a type of business with no limitation, vary the licence so that it covers the carrying on of that type of business only so far as it falls within one or more descriptions of business;

(c)   vary the licence so that it no longer covers the carrying on of a type of business at all;

(d)   vary the licence so that a type of business the carrying on of which is not covered at all by the licence is covered either—
    (i)   with no limitation; or
    (ii)   only so far as it falls within one or more descriptions of business; or
(e)   vary the licence in any other way except for the purpose of varying the descriptions of activities covered by the licence.]
[(1A)   The OFT may vary a licence under subsection (1) only in accordance with an application made by the licensee.
(1B)   References in this section to a description of business in relation to a type of business—
(a)   are references to a description of business specified in a general notice under section 24A(5)(a); and
(b)   in subsection (1)(a) (apart from sub-paragraph (ii)) include references to a description of business that was, but is no longer, so specified.]
(2)   In the case of a group licence issued on the application of any person, the [OFT], on an application made by that person, may if [it] thinks fit by notice to that person vary the terms of the licence in accordance with the application; but the [OFT] shall not vary a group licence under this subsection by excluding a named person, other than the person making the request, unless that named person consents in writing to his exclusion.
(3)   In the case of a group licence from which (whether by name or description) a person is excluded, the [OFT], on an application made by that person, may if [it] thinks fit, by notice to that person, vary the terms of the licence so as to remove the exclusion.
(4)   Unless the [OFT] determines to vary a licence in accordance with an application [it] shall, before determining the application, by notice—
(a)   inform the applicant, giving [its] reasons, that [it] is minded to refuse the application, and
(b)   invite the applicant to submit to the [OFT] representations in support of his application in accordance with section 34.
[. . .]

31   Compulsory variation
(1)   Where at a time during the currency of a licence the [OFT] is of the opinion that, if the licence had expired at that time, [(assuming, in the case of a licence which has effect indefinitely, that it were a licence of limited duration)], it would on an application for its renewal or further renewal on the same terms (except as to expiry), have been minded to grant the application but on different terms, and that therefore [it should take steps mentioned in subsection (1A)], [it] shall proceed as follows.
[(1A)   Those steps are—
(a)   in the case of a standard licence, steps mentioned in section 30(1)(a)(ii) and (iii), (b), (c) and (e);
(b)   in the case of a group licence, the varying of terms of the licence.
(1B)   The OFT shall also proceed as follows if, having regard to section 22(1B) to (1E), it is of the opinion—
(a)   that a licence which has effect indefinitely should have its duration limited; or
(b)   in the case of a licence of limited duration, that the period during which it has effect should be shortened.]
(2)   In the case of a standard licence the [OFT] shall, by notice—
(a)   inform the licensee of the variations the [OFT] is minded to make in the terms of the licence, stating [its] reasons, and
[(b)   invite him to submit to the OFT in accordance with section 34 representations—
    (i)   as to the proposed variations; and

(ii)   about the provision (if any) that should be included under section 34A as part of the determination were the OFT to vary the licence.]

(3)   In the case of a group licence the [OFT] shall—

(a)   give general notice of the variations [it] is minded to make in the terms of the licence, stating [its] reasons, and

(b)   in the notice invite any licensee to submit to [it] representations as to the proposed variations in accordance with section 34.

(4)   In the case of a group licence issued on application the [OFT] shall also—

(a)   inform the original applicant of the variations the [OFT] is minded to make in the terms of the licence, stating [its] reasons, and

(b)   invite him to submit to the [OFT] representations as to the proposed variations in accordance with section 34.

(5)   If the [OFT] is minded to vary a group licence by excluding any person (other than the original applicant) from the group by name the [OFT] shall, in addition, take the like steps under section 28 as are required in the case mentioned in that section.

(6)   General notice shall be given that a variation of any group licence has been made under this section.

(7)   A variation under this section shall not take effect before the end of the appeal period.

[(8)   Subsection (1) shall have effect in relation to a standard licence as if an application could be made for the renewal or further renewal of the licence on the same terms (except as to expiry) even if such an application could not be made because of provision made in a general notice under section 24A(5).

(9)   Accordingly, in applying subsection (1AA) of section 25 in relation to the licence for the purposes of this section, the OFT shall treat references in that subsection to the description or descriptions of business in relation to a type of business as references to the description or descriptions of business included in the licence in relation to that type of business, notwithstanding that provision under section 24A(5).]

32   Suspension and revocation

(1)   Where at a time during the currency of a licence the [OFT] is of the opinion that if the licence had expired at that time [(assuming, in the case of a licence which has effect indefinitely, that it were a licence of limited duration)] it would have been minded not to renew it, and that therefore it should be revoked or suspended, [it] shall proceed as follows.

(2)   In the case of a standard licence the [OFT] shall, by notice—

(a)   inform the licensee that, as the case may be, the [OFT] is minded to revoke the licence, or suspend it until a specified date or indefinitely, stating [its] reasons, and

[(b)   invite him to submit to the OFT in accordance with section 34 representations—

(i)   as to the proposed revocation or suspension; and

(ii)   about the provision (if any) that should be included under section 34A as part of the determination were the OFT to revoke or suspend the licence.]

(3)   In the case of a group licence the [OFT] shall—

(a)   give general notice that, as the case may be, [it] is minded to revoke the licence, or suspend it until a specified date or indefinitely, stating [its] reasons, and

(b)   in the notice invite any licensee to submit to [it] representations as to the proposed revocation or suspension in accordance with section 34.

(4)   In the case of a group licence issued on application the [OFT] shall also—

(a)   inform the original applicant that, as the case may be, the [OFT] is minded to revoke the licence, or suspend it until a specified date or indefinitely, stating [its] reasons, and

(b)   invite him to submit representations as to the proposed revocation or suspension in accordance with section 34.
[. . .]
(6)   General notice shall be given of the revocation or suspension of a group licence.
(7)   A revocation or suspension under this section shall not take effect before the end of the appeal period.
(8)   Except for the purposes of section 29, a licensee under a suspended licence shall be treated, in respect of the period of suspension, as if the licence had not been issued; and where the suspension is not expressed to end on a specified date it may, if the [OFT] thinks fit, be ended by notice given by [it] to the licensee or, in the case of a group licence, by general notice.
[(9)   The OFT has no power to revoke or to suspend a standard licence simply because, by virtue of provision made in a general notice under section 24A(5), a person cannot apply for the renewal of such a licence on terms which are the same as the terms of the licence in question.]

33   Application to end suspension

(1)   On an application made by a licensee the [OFT] may, if [it] thinks fit, by notice to the licensee end the suspension of a licence, whether the suspension was for a fixed or indefinite period.
(2)   Unless the [OFT] determines to end the suspension in accordance with the application [it] shall, before determining the application, by notice—
(a)   inform the applicant, giving [its] reasons, that [it] is minded to refuse the application, and
(b)   invite the applicant to submit to the [OFT] representations in support of his application in accordance with section 34.
(3)   General notice shall be given that a suspension of a group licence has been ended under this section.
(4)   In the case of a group licence issued on application—
(a)   the references in subsection (1) to a licensee include the original applicant;
(b)   the [OFT] shall inform the original applicant that a suspension of a group licence has been ended under this section.

[Further powers of OFT to regulate conduct of licensees etc

[33A   Power of OFT to impose requirements on licensees

(1)   This section applies where the OFT is dissatisfied with any matter in connection with—
(a)   a business being carried on, or which has been carried on, by a licensee or by an associate or a former associate of a licensee;
(b)   a proposal to carry on a business which has been made by a licensee or by an associate or a former associate of a licensee; or
(c)   any conduct not covered by paragraph (a) or (b) of a licensee or of an associate or a former associate of a licensee.
(2)   The OFT may by notice to the licensee require him to do or not to do (or to cease doing) anything specified in the notice for purposes connected with—
(a)   addressing the matter with which the OFT is dissatisfied; or
(b)   securing that matters of the same or a similar kind do not arise.
(3)   A requirement imposed under this section on a licensee shall only relate to a business which the licensee is carrying on, or is proposing to carry on, under the licence under which he is a licensee.
(4)   Such a requirement may be framed by reference to a named person other than the licensee.
(5)   For the purposes of subsection (1) it is immaterial whether the matter with which the OFT is dissatisfied arose before or after the licensee became a licensee.

(6)   If—

(a)   a person makes an application for a standard licence, and

(b)   while dealing with that application the OFT forms the opinion that, if such a licence were to be issued to that person, it would be minded to impose on him a requirement under this section,

the OFT may, before issuing such a licence to that person, do (in whole or in part) anything that it must do under section 33D or 34(1) or (2) in relation to the imposing of the requirement.

(7)   In this section 'associate', in addition to the persons specified in section 184, includes a business associate.]

[33B   Power of OFT to impose requirements on supervisory bodies

(1)   This section applies where the OFT is dissatisfied with the way in which a responsible person in relation to a group licence—

(a)   is regulating or otherwise supervising, or has regulated or otherwise supervised, persons who are licensees under that licence; or

(b)   is proposing to regulate or otherwise to supervise such persons.

(2)   The OFT may by notice to the responsible person require him to do or not to do (or to cease doing) anything specified in the notice for purposes connected with—

(a)   addressing the matters giving rise to the OFT's dissatisfaction; or

(b)   securing that matters of the same or a similar kind do not arise.

(3)   A requirement imposed under this section on a responsible person in relation to a group licence shall only relate to practices and procedures for regulating or otherwise supervising licensees under the licence in connection with their carrying on of businesses under the licence.

(4)   For the purposes of subsection (1) it is immaterial whether the matters giving rise to the OFT's dissatisfaction arose before or after the issue of the group licence in question.

(5)   If—

(a)   a person makes an application for a group licence, and

(b)   while dealing with that application the OFT forms the opinion that, if such a licence were to be issued to that person, it would be minded to impose on him a requirement under this section,

the OFT may, before issuing such a licence to that person, do (in whole or in part) anything that it must do under section 33D or 34(1) or (2) in relation to the imposing of the requirement.

(6)   For the purposes of this Part a person is a responsible person in relation to a group licence if—

(a)   he is the original applicant for it; and

(b)   he has a responsibility (whether by virtue of an enactment, an agreement or otherwise) for regulating or otherwise supervising persons who are licensees under the licence.]

[33C   Supplementary provision relating to requirements

(1)   A notice imposing a requirement under section 33A or 33B may include provision about the time at or by which, or the period during which, the requirement is to be complied with.

(2)   A requirement imposed under section 33A or 33B shall not have effect after the licence by reference to which it is imposed has itself ceased to have effect.

(3)   A person shall not be required under section 33A or 33B to compensate, or otherwise to make amends to, another person.

(4)   The OFT may by notice to the person on whom a requirement has been imposed under section 33A or 33B vary or revoke the requirement (including any provision made under subsection (1) of this section in relation to it) with effect from such date as may be specified in the notice.

(5)   The OFT may exercise its power under subsection (4) in relation to a

requirement either on its own motion or on the application of a person falling within subsection (6) or (7) in relation to the requirement.

(6)   A person falls within this subsection in relation to a requirement if he is the person on whom the requirement is imposed.

(7)   A person falls within this subsection in relation to a requirement if—

(a)   the requirement is imposed under section 33A;

(b)   he is not the person on whom the requirement is imposed;

(c)   the requirement is framed by reference to him by name; and

(d)   the effect of the requirement is—

(i)   to prevent him being an employee of the person on whom the requirement is imposed;

(ii)   to restrict the activities that he may engage in as an employee of that person; or

(iii)   otherwise to prevent him from doing something, or to restrict his doing something, in connection with a business being carried on by that person.]

[33D   Procedure in relation to requirements

(1)   Before making a determination—

(a)   to impose a requirement on a person under section 33A or 33B,

(b)   to refuse an application under section 33C(5) in relation to a requirement imposed under either of those sections, or

(c)   to vary or to revoke a requirement so imposed,

the OFT shall proceed as follows.

(2)   The OFT shall give a notice to every person to whom subsection (3) applies in relation to the determination—

(a)   informing him, with reasons, that it is minded to make the determination; and

(b)   inviting him to submit to it representations as to the determination under section 34.

(3)   This subsection applies to a person in relation to the determination if he falls within, or as a consequence of the determination would fall within, section 33C(6) or (7) in relation to the requirement in question.

(4)   This section does not require the OFT to give a notice to a person if the determination in question is in the same terms as a proposal made to the OFT by that person (whether as part of an application under this Part or otherwise).]

[33E   Guidance on requirements

(1)   The OFT shall prepare and publish guidance in relation to how it exercises, or how it proposes to exercise, its powers under sections 33A to 33C.

(2)   If the OFT revises the guidance at any time after it has been published, the OFT shall publish it as revised.

(3)   The guidance shall be published in such manner as the OFT thinks fit for the purpose of bringing it to the attention of those likely to be affected by it.

(4)   In preparing or revising the guidance the OFT shall consult such persons as it thinks fit.

(5)   In exercising its powers under sections 33A to 33C the OFT shall have regard to the guidance as most recently published.]]

Miscellaneous

34   Representations to [OFT]

(1)   Where this section applies to an invitation by the [OFT] to any person to submit representations, the [OFT] shall invite that person, within 21 days after the notice containing the invitation is given to him or published, or such longer period as the [OFT] may allow—

(a)   to submit his representations in writing to the [OFT], and

(b)   to give notice to the [OFT], if he thinks fit, that he wishes to make representations orally,

and where notice is given under paragraph (b) the [OFT] shall arrange for the oral representations to be heard.

(2)   In reaching [its] determination the [OFT] shall take into account any representations submitted or made under this section.

(3)   The [OFT] shall give notice of [its] determination to the persons who were required to be invited to submit representations about it or, where the invitation to submit representations was required to be given by general notice, shall give general notice of the determination.

[34A   Winding-up of standard licensee's business

(1)   If it thinks fit, the OFT may, for the purpose of enabling the licensee's business, or any part of his business, to be transferred or wound up, include as part of a determination to which subsection (2) applies provision authorising the licensee to carry on for a specified period—

(a)   specified activities, or

(b)   activities of specified descriptions,

which, because of that determination, the licensee will no longer be licensed to carry on.

(2)   This subsection applies to the following determinations—

(a)   a determination to refuse to renew a standard licence in accordance with the terms of the application for its renewal;

(b)   a determination to vary such a licence under section 31;

(c)   a determination to suspend or revoke such a licence.

(3)   Such provision—

(a)   may specify different periods for different activities or activities of different descriptions;

(b)   may provide for persons other than the licensee to carry on activities under the authorisation;

(c)   may specify requirements which must be complied with by a person carrying on activities under the authorisation in relation to those activities;

and, if a requirement specified under paragraph (c) is not complied with, the OFT may by notice to a person carrying on activities under the authorisation terminate the authorisation (in whole or in part) from a specified date.

(4)   Without prejudice to the generality of paragraph (c) of subsection (3), a requirement specified under that paragraph may have the effect of—

(a)   preventing a named person from being an employee of a person carrying on activities under the authorisation, or restricting the activities he may engage in as an employee of such a person;

(b)   preventing a named person from doing something, or restricting his doing something, in connection with activities being carried on by a person under the authorisation;

(c)   securing that access to premises is given to officers of the OFT for the purpose of enabling them to inspect documents or to observe the carrying on of activities.

(5)   Activities carried on under an authorisation shall be treated for the purposes of sections 39(1), 40, 148 and 149 as if carried on under a standard licence.]

35   The register

(1)   The [OFT] shall establish and maintain a register, in which [it] shall cause to be kept particulars of—

(a)   applications not yet determined for the issue, variation or renewal of licences, or for ending the suspension of a licence;

(b)   licences which are in [effect], or have at any time been suspended or revoked [or terminated by section 28C], with details of any variation of the terms of a licence;

[(ba)   requirements imposed under section 33A or 33B which are in effect or which have been in effect, with details of any variation of such a requirement;]

(c)   decisions given by [it] under this Act, and any appeal from those decisions; and

(d)   such other matters (if any) as [it] thinks fit.

[(1A)   The [OFT] shall also cause to be kept in the register any copy of any notice or other document relating to a consumer credit EEA firm which is given to the [OFT] by the Financial Services Authority for inclusion in the register.]

(2)   The [OFT] shall give general notice of the various matters required to be entered in the register, and of any change in them made under subsection (1)(d).

(3)   Any person shall be entitled on payment of the specified fee—

(a)   to inspect the register during ordinary office hours and take copies of any entry, or

(b)   to obtain from the [OFT] a copy, certified by the [OFT] to be correct, of any entry in the register.

(4)   The [OFT] may, if [it] thinks fit, determine that the right conferred by subsection (3)(a) shall be exercisable in relation to a copy of the register instead of, or in addition to, the original.

(5)   The [OFT] shall give general notice of the place or places where, and times when, the register or a copy of it may be inspected.

36   Duty to notify changes

(1)   Within 21 working days after change takes place in any particulars entered in the register in respect of a standard licence or the licensee under section 35(1)(d) (not being a change resulting from action taken by the [OFT]), the licensee shall give the [OFT] notice of the change; and the [OFT] shall cause any necessary amendment to be made in the register.

(2)   Within 21 working days after—

(a)   any change takes place in the officers of—

(i)   a body corporate, or an unincorporated body of persons, which is the licensee under a standard licence, or

(ii)   a body corporate which is a controller of a body corporate which is such a licensee, or

(b)   a body corporate which is such a licensee becomes aware that a person has become or ceased to be a controller of the body corporate, or

(c)   any change takes place in the members of a partnership which is such a licensee (including a change on the amalgamation of the partnership with another firm, or a change whereby the number of partners is reduced to one), the licensee shall give the [OFT] notice of the change.

(3)   Within 14 working days after any change takes place in the officers of a body corporate which is a controller of another body corporate which is a licensee under a standard licence, the controller shall give the licensee notice of the change.

(4)   Within 14 working days after a person becomes or ceases to be a controller of a body corporate which is a licensee under a standard licence, that person shall give the licensee notice of the fact.

(5)   Where a change in a partnership has the result that the business ceases to be carried on under the name, or any of the names, specified in a standard licence the licence shall cease to have effect.

[. . .]

[36A   Further duties to notify changes etc

(1)   Subsections (2) to (4) apply where a general notice under section 6(2) comes into effect.

(2)   A person who is the licensee under a standard licence or who is the original applicant for a group licence shall, in relation to each relevant application which he has made and which was determined before the general notice came into effect, provide the OFT with any information or document—

(a)   which he would have been required to provide with the application had the application been made after the general notice came into effect; and

(b)   which the general notice requires to be provided for the purposes of this subsection.

(3)   Any such information or document shall be provided within such period as may be specified in the general notice.

(4)   Subsection (2) does not require a person to provide any information or document—

(a)   which he provided in relation to the application by virtue of section 6;

(b)   which he has previously provided in relation to the application by virtue of this section; or

(c)   which he would have been required to provide in relation to the application by virtue of subsection (5) but for subsection (6).

(5)   A person who is the licensee under a standard licence or who is the original applicant for a group licence shall, in relation to each relevant application which he has made, notify the OFT giving details if, after the application is determined, any information or document which he—

(a)   provided in relation to the application by virtue of section 6, or

(b)   has so provided by virtue of this section,

is, to any extent, superseded or otherwise affected by a change in circumstances.

(6)   Subsection (5) does not require a person to notify the OFT about a matter unless it falls within a description of matters specified by the OFT in a general notice.

(7)   A description may be specified for the purposes of subsection (6) only if the OFT is satisfied that the matters which would fall within that description are matters which would be relevant to the question of—

(a)   whether, having regard to section 25(2), a person is a fit person to carry on a business under a standard licence; or

(b)   whether the public interest is better served by a group licence remaining in effect than by obliging the licensees under it to apply separately for standard licences.

(8)   A person who is the licensee under a standard licence or who is the original applicant for a group licence shall, in relation to each relevant application which he has made, notify the OFT about every error or omission—

(a)   in or from any information or document which he provided by virtue of section 6, or which he has provided by virtue of this section, in relation to the application; and

(b)   of which he becomes aware after the determination of the application.

(9)   A notification for the purposes of subsection (5) or (8) shall be given within the period of 28 days beginning with the day on which (as the case may be)—

(a)   the information or document is superseded;

(b)   the change in circumstances occurs; or

(c)   the licensee or the original applicant becomes aware of the error or omission.

(10)   This section does not require a person to notify the OFT about—

(a)   anything of which he is required to notify it under section 36; or

(b)   an error in or omission from any information or document which is a clerical error or omission not affecting the substance of the information or document.

(11)   In this section 'relevant application' means, in relation to a person who is the licensee under a standard licence or who is the original applicant for a group licence—

(a)   the original application for the licence; or

(b)   an application for its renewal or for its variation.]

[36B   Power of OFT to require information generally

(1)   The OFT may by notice to a person require him—

(a)   to provide such information as may be specified or described in the notice; or

(b)   to produce such documents as may be so specified or described.

(2)   The notice shall set out the reasons why the OFT requires the information or documents to be provided or produced.

(3)   The information or documents shall be provided or produced—

(a)   before the end of such reasonable period as may be specified in the notice; and

(b)   at such place as may be so specified.

(4)   A requirement may be imposed under subsection (1) on a person who is—

(a)   the licensee under a standard licence, or

(b)   the original applicant for a group licence,

only if the provision or production of the information or documents in question is reasonably required for purposes connected with the OFT's functions under this Act.

(5)   A requirement may be imposed under subsection (1) on any other person only if—

(a)   an act or omission mentioned in subsection (6) has occurred or the OFT has reason to suspect that such an act or omission has occurred; and

(b)   the provision or production of the information or documents in question is reasonably required for purposes connected with—

(i)   the taking by the OFT of steps under this Part as a consequence; or

(ii)   its consideration of whether to take such steps as a consequence.

(6)   Those acts or omissions are acts or omissions which—

(a)   cast doubt on whether, having regard to section 25(2), a person is a fit person to carry on a business under a standard licence;

(b)   cast doubt on whether the public interest is better served by a group licence remaining in effect, or being issued, than by obliging the persons who are licensees under it, or who would be licensees under it, to apply separately for standard licences;

(c)   give rise, or are likely to give rise, to dissatisfaction for the purposes of section 33A(1) or 33B(1); or

(d)   constitute or give rise to a failure of the kind mentioned in section 39A(1).]

[36C   Power of OFT to require access to premises

(1)   The OFT may by notice to a licensee under a licence require him to secure that access to the premises specified or described in the notice is given to an officer of an enforcement authority in order for the officer—

(a)   to observe the carrying on of a business under the licence by the licensee; or

(b)   to inspect such documents of the licensee relating to such a business as are—

(i)   specified or described in the notice; and

(ii)   situated on the premises.

(2)   The notice shall set out the reasons why the access is required.

(3)   The premises which may be specified or described in the notice—

(a)   include premises which are not premises of the licensee if they are premises from which he carries on activities in connection with the business in question; but

(b)   do not include premises which are used only as a dwelling.

(4)   The licensee shall secure that the required access is given at such times as the OFT reasonably requires.

(5)   The OFT shall give reasonable notice of those times.

(6)   Where an officer is given access to any premises by virtue of this section, the licensee shall also secure that persons on the premises give the officer such assistance or information as he may reasonably require in connection with his observation or inspection of documents (as the case may be).

(7)   The assistance that may be required under subsection (6) includes (amongst other things) the giving to the officer of an explanation of a document which he is inspecting.

(8)   A requirement may be imposed under subsection (1) on a person who is—

(a)   the licensee under a standard licence, or

(b)   the original applicant for a group licence,

only if the observation or inspection in question is reasonably required for purposes connected with the OFT's functions under this Act.

(9)   A requirement may be imposed under subsection (1) on any other person only if—

(a)   an act or omission mentioned in section 36B(6) has occurred or the OFT has reason to suspect that such an act or omission has occurred; and

(b)   the observation or inspection in question is reasonably required for purposes connected with—

(i)   the taking by the OFT of steps under this Part as a consequence; or

(ii)   its consideration of whether to take such steps as a consequence.

(10)   In this section—

(a)   references to a licensee under a licence include, in relation to a group licence issued on application, references to the original applicant; and

(b)   references to a business being carried on under a licence by a licensee include, in relation to the original applicant for a group licence, activities being carried on by him for the purpose of regulating or otherwise supervising (whether by virtue of an enactment, an agreement or otherwise) licensees under that licence in connection with their carrying on of businesses under that licence.]

[36D   Entry to premises under warrant

(1)   A justice of the peace may issue a warrant under this section if satisfied on information on oath given on behalf of the OFT that there are reasonable grounds for believing that the following conditions are satisfied.

(2)   Those conditions are—

(a)   that there is on the premises specified in the warrant information or documents in relation to which a requirement could be imposed under section 36B; and

(b)   that if such a requirement were to be imposed in relation to the information or documents—

(i)   it would not be complied with; or

(ii)   the information or documents would be tampered with.

(3)   A warrant under this section shall authorise an officer of an enforcement authority—

(a)   to enter the premises specified in the warrant;

(b)   to search the premises and to seize and detain any information or documents appearing to be information or documents specified in the warrant or information or documents of a description so specified;

(c)   to take any other steps which may appear to be reasonably necessary for preserving such information or documents or preventing interference with them; and

(d)   to use such force as may be reasonably necessary.

(4)   An officer entering premises by virtue of this section may take such persons and equipment with him as he thinks necessary.

(5)   In the application of this section to Scotland—

(a)   the reference to a justice of the peace includes a reference to a sheriff;

(b)   for 'information on oath' there is substituted 'evidence on oath'.

(6)   In the application of this section to Northern Ireland the reference to a justice of the peace shall be construed as a reference to a lay magistrate.]

[36E   Failure to comply with information requirement

(1)   If on an application made by the OFT it appears to the court that a person (the 'information defaulter') has failed to do something that he was required to do by virtue of section 36B or 36C, the court may make an order under this section.

(2)   An order under this section may require the information defaulter—

(a)   to do the thing that it appears he failed to do within such period as may be specified in the order;

(b)   otherwise to take such steps to remedy the consequences of the failure as may be so specified.

(3)   If the information defaulter is a body corporate, a partnership or an unincorporated body of persons which is not a partnership, the order may require any officer who is (wholly or partly) responsible for the failure to meet such costs of the application as are specified in the order.

(4)   In this section—

'court' means—

(a)   in England and Wales and Northern Ireland, the High Court or the county court;

(b)   in Scotland, the Court of Session or the sheriff;

'officer' means—

(a)   in relation to a body corporate, a person holding a position of director, manager or secretary of the body or any similar position;

(b)   in relation to a partnership or to an unincorporated body of persons, a member of the partnership or body.

(5)   In subsection (4) 'director' means, in relation to a body corporate whose affairs are managed by its members, a member of the body.]

[36F   Officers of enforcement authorities other than OFT

(1)   A relevant officer may only exercise powers by virtue of section 36C or 36D in pursuance of arrangements made with the OFT by or on behalf of the enforcement authority of which he is an officer.

(2)   Anything done or omitted to be done by, or in relation to, a relevant officer in the exercise or purported exercise of a power by virtue of section 36C or 36D shall be treated for all purposes as having been done or omitted to be done by, or in relation to, an officer of the OFT.

(3)   Subsection (2) does not apply for the purposes of any criminal proceedings brought against the officer, the enforcement authority of which he is an officer or the OFT in respect of anything done or omitted to be done by the officer.

(4)   A relevant officer shall not disclose to a person other than the OFT information obtained by his exercise of a power by virtue of section 36C or 36D unless—

(a)   he has the approval of the OFT to do so; or

(b)   he is under a duty to make the disclosure.

(5)   In this section 'relevant officer' means an officer of an enforcement authority other than the OFT.]

37   Death, bankruptcy etc of licensee

(1)   A licence held by one individual terminates if he—

(a)   dies,

[(b)   has his estate sequestrated, or]

[(c)   becomes incapable of managing his own affairs.]

[(1A)   A licence terminates if the licensee gives the OFT a notice under subsection (1B).

(1B)   A notice under this subsection shall—
    (a)   be in such form as the OFT may by general notice specify;
    (b)   contain such information as may be so specified;
    (c)   be accompanied by the licence or give reasons as to why it is not accompanied by the licence; and
    (d)   be signed by or on behalf of the licensee.]
(2)   In relation to a licence held by one individual, or a partnership or other unincorporated body of persons, or a body corporate, regulations may specify other events relating to the licensee on the occurrence of which the licence is to terminate.
(3)   Regulations may—
    (a)   provide for the termination of a licence by subsection (1) [or (1A)], or under subsection (2), to be deferred for a period not exceeding 12 months, and
    (b)   authorise the business of the licensee to be carried on under the licence by some other person during the period of deferment, subject to such conditions as may be prescribed.
(4)   This section does not apply to group licences.

38   Application of s 37 to Scotland and Northern Ireland
(1)   [*Scottish provisions incorporated in s 37 above.*]

39   Offences against Part III
(1)   A person who engages in any activities for which a licence is required when he is not a licensee under a licence covering those activities commits an offence.
(2)   A licensee under a standard licence who carries on business under a name not specified in the licence commits an offence.
(3)   A person who fails to give the [OFT] or a licensee notice under section 36 within the period required commits an offence.

[39A   Power of OFT to impose civil penalties
(1)   Where the OFT is satisfied that a person (the 'defaulter') has failed or is failing to comply with a requirement imposed on him by virtue of section 33A, 33B or 36A, it may by notice to him (a 'penalty notice') impose on him a penalty of such amount as it thinks fit.
(2)   The penalty notice shall—
    (a)   specify the amount of the penalty that is being imposed;
    (b)   set out the OFT's reasons for imposing a penalty and for specifying that amount;
    (c)   specify how the payment of the penalty may be made to the OFT; and
    (d)   specify the period within which the penalty is required to be paid.
(3)   The amount of the penalty shall not exceed £50,000.
(4)   The period specified in the penalty notice for the purposes of subsection (2)(d) shall not end earlier than the end of the period during which an appeal may be brought against the imposition of the penalty under section 41.
(5)   If the defaulter does not pay the penalty to the OFT within the period so specified—
    (a)   the unpaid balance from time to time shall carry interest at the rate for the time being specified in section 17 of the Judgments Act 1838; and
    (b)   the penalty and any interest payable on it shall be recoverable by the OFT.]

[39B   Further provision relating to civil penalties
(1)   Before determining to impose a penalty on a person under section 39A the OFT shall give a notice to that person—
    (a)   informing him that it is minded to impose a penalty on him;
    (b)   stating the proposed amount of the penalty;

(c)   setting out its reasons for being minded to impose a penalty on him and for proposing that amount;

(d)   setting out the proposed period for the payment of the penalty; and

(e)   inviting him to submit representations to it about the matters mentioned in the preceding paragraphs in accordance with section 34.

(2)   In determining whether and how to exercise its powers under section 39A in relation to a person's failure, the OFT shall have regard to (amongst other things)—

(a)   any penalty or fine that has been imposed on that person by another body in relation to the conduct giving rise to the failure;

(b)   other steps that the OFT has taken or might take under this Part in relation to that conduct.

(3)   General notice shall be given of the imposition of a penalty under section 39A on a person who is a responsible person in relation to a group licence.

(4)   That notice shall include the matters set out in the notice imposing the penalty in accordance with section 39A(2)(a) and (b).]

[39C   Statement of policy in relation to civil penalties

(1)   The OFT shall prepare and publish a statement of policy in relation to how it exercises, or how it proposes to exercise, its powers under section 39A.

(2)   If the OFT revises the statement of policy at any time after it has been published, the OFT shall publish it as revised.

(3)   No statement of policy shall be published without the approval of the Secretary of State.

(4)   The statement of policy shall be published in such manner as the OFT thinks fit for the purpose of bringing it to the attention of those likely to be affected by it.

(5)   In preparing or revising the statement of policy the OFT shall consult such persons as it thinks fit.

(6)   In determining whether and how to exercise its powers under section 39A in relation to a person's failure, the OFT shall have regard to the statement of policy as most recently published at the time the failure occurred.

(7)   The OFT shall not impose a penalty on a person under section 39A in relation to a failure occurring before it has published a statement of policy.]

40   Enforcement of agreements made by unlicensed trader

[(1)   A regulated agreement is not enforceable against the debtor or hirer by a person acting in the course of a consumer credit business or a consumer hire business (as the case may be) if that person is not licensed to carry on a consumer credit business or a consumer hire business (as the case may be) of a description which covers the enforcement of the agreement.

(1A)   Unless the OFT has made an order under subsection (2) which applies to the agreement, a regulated agreement is not enforceable against the debtor or hirer if—

(a)   it was made by the creditor or owner in the course of a consumer credit business or a consumer hire business (as the case may be); and

(b)   at the time the agreement was made he was not licensed to carry on a consumer credit business or a consumer hire business (as the case may be) of a description which covered the making of the agreement.

(2)   Where—

(a)   during any period a person (the 'trader') has made regulated agreements in the course of a consumer credit business or a consumer hire business (as the case may be), and

(b)   during that period he was not licensed to carry on a consumer credit business or a consumer hire business (as the case may be) of a description which covered the making of those agreements,

he or his successor in title may apply to the OFT for an order that the agreements are to be treated for the purposes of subsection (1A) as if he had been licensed as required.]

(3) Unless the [OFT] determines to make an order under subsection (2) in accordance with the application, [it] shall, before determining the application, by notice—

(a) inform the applicant, giving [its] reasons, that, as the case may be, [it] is minded to refuse the application, or to grant it in terms different from those applied for, describing them, and

(b) invite the applicant to submit to the [OFT] representations in support of his application in accordance with section 34.

(4) In determining whether or not to make an order under subsection (2) in respect of any period the [OFT] shall consider, in addition to any other relevant factors—

(a) how far, if at all, debtors or hirers under [the regulated agreements in question] made by the trader during that period were prejudiced by the trader's conduct,

(b) whether or not the [OFT] would have been likely to grant a licence covering [the making of those agreements during] that period on an application by the trader, and

(c) the degree of culpability for the failure to [be licensed as required].

(5) If the [OFT] thinks fit, [it] may in an order under subsection (2)—

(a) limit the order to specified agreements, or agreements of a specified description or made at a specified time;

(b) make the order conditional on the doing of specified acts by the applicant.

[(6) This section [(apart from subsection (1))] does not apply to a regulated agreement [. . .] made by a consumer credit EEA firm unless at the time it was made that firm was precluded from entering into it as a result of—

(a) a consumer credit prohibition imposed under section 203 of the Financial Services and Markets Act 2000; or

(b) a restriction imposed on the firm under section 204 of that Act.]

[(7) Subsection (1) does not apply to the enforcement of a regulated agreement by a consumer credit EEA firm unless that firm is precluded from enforcing it as a result of a prohibition or restriction mentioned in subsection (6)(a) or (b).

(8) This section (apart from subsection (1)) does not apply to a regulated agreement made by a person if by virtue of section 21(2) or (3) he was not required to be licensed to make the agreement.

(9) Subsection (1) does not apply to the enforcement of a regulated agreement by a person if by virtue of section 21(2) or (3) he is not required to be licensed to enforce the agreement.]

[*Appeals*

[. . .]

41 Appeals to [First-tier Tribunal] under Part III

(1) If, in the case of a determination by the [OFT] such as is mentioned in column 1 of the table set out at the end of this section, a person mentioned in relation to that determination in column 2 of the table is aggrieved by the determination he may, within the [specified period, appeal to the [First-tier] Tribunal].

[. . .]

TABLE

Determination	*Appellant*
Refusal to issue, renew or vary licence in accordance with terms of application.	The applicant.
Exclusion of person from group licence.	The person excluded.
[. . .]	[. . .]
Compulsory variation, or suspension or revocation, of standard licence.	The licensee.
Compulsory variation, or suspension or revocation, of group licence.	The original applicant or any licensee.
Refusal to end suspension of licence in accordance with terms of application.	The applicant.

[Determination—
    (a) to impose a requirement under section 33A or 33B;
    (b) to refuse an application under section 33C(5) in relation to a requirement imposed under either of those sections;
    (c) to vary or revoke a requirement so imposed.
	A person who falls within section 33C(6) or (7) in relation to the requirement unless the OFT was not required to give a notice to him in relation to the determination by virtue of section 33D(4).

Imposition of penalty under section 39A	The person on whom the penalty is imposed.]
Refusal to make order under section 40(2) [, 148(2) or 149(2)] in accordance with terms of application.	The applicant.
[Imposition of, or refusal to withdraw, consumer credit prohibition under section 203 of the Financial Services and Markets Act 2000.	The consumer credit EEA firm concerned.
Imposition of, or refusal to withdraw, a restriction under section 204 of the Financial Services and Markets Act 2000.	The consumer credit EEA firm concerned.]

[41ZA Tribunal Procedure Rules: suspension of OFT determinations

In the case of appeals to the First-tier Tribunal under section 41, Tribunal Procedure Rules may make provision for the suspension of determinations of the OFT.]

[41ZB Disposal of appeals

(1) The First-tier Tribunal shall decide an appeal under section 41 by way of a rehearing of the determination appealed against.

(2) In disposing of an appeal under section 41 the First-tier Tribunal may do one or more of the following—

   (a) confirm the determination appealed against;

   (b) quash that determination;

   (c) vary that determination;

   (d) remit the matter to the OFT for reconsideration and determination in accordance with the directions (if any) given to it by the tribunal;

   (e) give the OFT directions for the purpose of giving effect to its decision.

(3) In the case of an appeal under section 41 against a determination to impose a penalty, the First-tier Tribunal—

   (a) has no power by virtue of subsection (2)(c) to increase the penalty;

   (b) may extend the period within which the penalty is to be paid (including in cases where that period has already ended).

(4)   Subsection (3) does not affect—

(a)   the tribunal's power to give directions to the OFT under subsection (2)(d); or

(b)   what the OFT can do where a matter is remitted to it under subsection (2)(d).

(5)   Where the First-tier Tribunal remits a matter to the OFT, it may direct that the requirements of section 34 of this Act are not to apply, or are only to apply to a specified extent, in relation to the OFT's reconsideration of the matter.

(6)   Subject to subsections (7) and (8), where the First-tier Tribunal remits an application to the OFT, section 6(1) and (3) to (9) of this Act shall apply as if the application had not been previously determined by the OFT.

(7)   In the case of a general notice which came into effect after the determination appealed against was made but before the application was remitted, the applicant shall provide any information or document which he is required to provide under section 6(6) within—

(a)   the period of 28 days beginning with the day on which the application was remitted; or

(b)   such longer period as the OFT may allow.

(8)   In the case of—

(a)   any information or document which was superseded,

(b)   any change in circumstances which occurred, or

(c)   any error or omission of which the applicant became aware,

after the determination appealed against was made but before the application was remitted, any notification that is required to be given by the applicant under section 6(7) shall be given within the period of 28 days beginning with the day on which the application was remitted.]

[. . .]

PART IV
SEEKING BUSINESS

Advertising

43   Advertisements to which Part IV applies

(1)   This Part applies to any advertisement, published for the purposes of a business carried on by the advertiser, indicating that he is willing—

(a)   to provide credit, or

(b)   to enter into an agreement for the bailment or (in Scotland) the hiring of goods by him.

(2)   An advertisement does not fall within subsection (1) if the advertiser does not carry on—

(a)   a consumer credit business or consumer hire business, or

(b)   a business in the course of which he provides credit to individuals secured on land, or

(c)   a business which comprises or relates to unregulated agreements where—

(i)   the [law applicable to] the agreement is the law of a country outside the United Kingdom, and

(ii)   if the [law applicable to] the agreement were the law of a part of the United Kingdom it would be a regulated agreement.

(3)   An advertisement does not fall within subsection (1)(a) if it indicates—

[. . .]

(b)   that the credit is available only to a body corporate.

[(3A)   An advertisement does not fall within subsection (1)(a) in so far as it is a communication of an invitation or inducement to engage in investment activity within the meaning of section 21 of the Financial Services and Markets Act 2000, other than an exempt generic communication.

(3B) An 'exempt generic communication' is a communication to which subsection (1) of section 21 of the Financial Services and Markets Act 2000 does not apply, as a result of an order under subsection (5) of that section, because it does not identify a person as providing an investment or as carrying on an activity to which the communication relates.]

(4) An advertisement does not fall within subsection (1)(b) if it indicates that the advertiser is not willing to enter into a consumer hire agreement.

(5) The Secretary of State may by order provide that this Part shall not apply to other advertisements of a description specified in the order.

44 Form and content of advertisements

(1) The Secretary of State shall make regulations as to the form and content of advertisements to which this Part applies, and the regulations shall contain such provisions as appear to him appropriate with a view to ensuring that, having regard to its subject-matter and the amount of detail included in it, an advertisement conveys a fair and reasonably comprehensive indication of the nature of the credit or hire facilities offered by the advertiser and of their true cost to persons using them.

(2) Regulations under subsection (1) may in particular—

(a) require specified information to be included in the prescribed manner in advertisements, and other specified material to be excluded;

(b) contain requirements to ensure that specified information is clearly brought to the attention of persons to whom advertisements are directed, and that one part of an advertisement is not given insufficient or excessive prominence compared with another.

45 Prohibition of advertisement where goods etc not sold for cash

If an advertisement to which this Part applies indicates that the advertiser is willing to provide credit under a restricted-use credit agreement relating to goods or services to be supplied by any person, but at the time when the advertisement is published that person is not holding himself out as prepared to sell the goods or provide the services (as the case may be) for cash, the advertiser commits an offence.

[. . .]

47 Advertising infringements

(1) Where an advertiser commits an offence against regulations made under section 44 or against section 45 [. . .] or would be taken to commit such an offence but for the defence provided by section 168, a like offence is committed by—

(a) the publisher of the advertisement, and

(b) any person who, in the course of a business carried on by him, devised the advertisement, or a part of it relevant to the first-mentioned offence, and

(c) where the advertiser did not procure the publication of the advertisement, the person who did procure it.

(2) In proceedings for an offence under subsection (1)(a) it is a defence for the person charged to prove that—

(a) the advertisement was published in the course of a business carried on by him, and

(b) he received the advertisement in the course of that business, and did not know and had no reason to suspect that its publication would be an offence under this Part.

Canvassing, etc

48 Definition of canvassing off trade premises (regulated agreements)

(1) An individual (the 'canvasser') canvasses a regulated agreement off trade premises if he solicits the entry (as debtor or hirer) of another individual (the 'consumer') into the agreement by making oral representations to the consumer, or any other individual, during a visit by the canvasser to any place (not excluded by subsection (2)) where the consumer, or that other individual, as the case may be, is, being a visit—

(a) carried out for the purpose of making such oral representations to individuals who are at that place, but

(b) not carried out in response to a request made on a previous occasion.

(2) A place is excluded from subsection (1) if it is a place where a business is carried on (whether on a permanent or temporary basis) by—

(a) the creditor or owner, or

(b) a supplier, or

(c) the canvasser, or the person whose employee or agent the canvasser is, or

(d) the consumer.

49 Prohibition of canvassing debtor-creditor agreements off trade premises

(1) It is an offence to canvass debtor-creditor agreements off trade premises.

(2) It is also an offence to solicit the entry of an individual (as debtor) into a debtor-creditor agreement during a visit carried out in response to a request made on a previous occasion, where—

(a) the request was not in writing signed by or on behalf of the person making it, and

(b) if no request for the visit had been made, the soliciting would have constituted the canvassing of a debtor-creditor agreement off trade premises.

(3) Subsections (1) and (2) do not apply to any soliciting for an agreement enabling the debtor to overdraw on a current account of any description kept with the creditor, where—

(a) the [OFT] has determined that current accounts of that description kept with the creditor are excluded from subsections (1) and (2), and

(b) the debtor already keeps an account with the creditor (whether a current account or not).

(4) A determination under subsection (3)(a)—

(a) may be made subject to such conditions as the [OFT] thinks fit, and

(b) shall be made only where the [OFT] is of opinion that it is not against the interests of debtors.

(5) If soliciting is done in breach of a condition imposed under subsection (4)(a), the determination under subsection (3)(a) does not apply to it.

50 Circulars to minors

(1) A person commits an offence who, with a view to financial gain, sends to a minor any document inviting him to—

(a) borrow money, or

(b) obtain goods on credit or hire, or

(c) obtain services on credit, or

(d) apply for information or advice on borrowing money or otherwise obtaining credit, or hiring goods.

(2) In proceedings under subsection (1) in respect of the sending of a document to a minor, it is a defence for the person charged to prove that he did not know, and had no reasonable cause to suspect, that he was a minor.

(3) Where a document is received by a minor at any school or other educational establishment for minors, a person sending it to him at that establishment

knowing or suspecting it to be such an establishment shall be taken to have reasonable cause to suspect that he is a minor.

51 Prohibition of unsolicited credit-tokens

(1)   It is an offence to give a person a credit-token if he has not asked for it.

(2)   To comply with subsection (1) a request must be contained in a document signed by the person making the request, unless the credit-token agreement is a small debtor-creditor-supplier agreement.

(3)   Subsection (1) does not apply to the giving of a credit-token to a person—

(a)   for use under a credit-token agreement already made, or

(b)   in renewal or replacement of a credit-token previously accepted by him under a credit-token agreement which continues in force, whether or not varied.

Miscellaneous

52 Quotations

(1)   Regulations may be made—

(a)   as to the form and content of any document (a 'quotation') by which a person who carries on a consumer credit business or consumer hire business, or a business in the course of which he provides credit to individuals secured on land, gives prospective customers information about the terms on which he is prepared to do business;

(b)   requiring a person carrying on such a business to provide quotations to such persons and in such circumstances as are prescribed.

(2)   Regulations under subsection (1)(a) may in particular contain provisions relating to quotations such as are set out in relation to advertisements in section 44.

[(3)   In this section, 'quotation' does not include—

(a)   any document which is a communication of an invitation or inducement to engage in investment activity within the meaning of section 21 of the Financial Services and Markets Act 2000; or

(b)   any document (other than one falling within paragraph (a)) provided by an authorised person (within the meaning of that Act) in connection with an agreement which would or might be an exempt agreement as a result of section 16(6C).]

53 Duty to display information

Regulations may require a person who carries on a consumer credit business or consumer hire business, or a business in the course of which he provides credit to individuals secured on land [(other than credit provided under an agreement which is an exempt agreement as a result of [section 16(6C)(a)], to display in the prescribed manner, at any premises where the business is carried on to which the public have access, prescribed information about the business.

54 Conduct of business regulations

Without prejudice to the generality of section 26, regulations under that section may include provisions further regulating the seeking of business by [a person to whom the regulations apply] who carries on a consumer credit business or a consumer hire business.

PART V
ENTRY INTO CREDIT OR HIRE AGREEMENTS

Preliminary matters

55 Disclosure of information

(1)   Regulations may require specified information to be disclosed in the prescribed manner to the debtor or hirer before a regulated agreement is made.

[(2)   If regulations under subsection (1) are not complied with, the agreement is enforceable against the debtor or hirer on an order of the court only (and for these purposes a retaking of goods or land to which the agreement relates is an enforcement of the agreement).]

[55A   Pre-contractual explanations etc
(1)   Before a regulated consumer credit agreement, other than an excluded agreement, is made, the creditor must—
(a)   provide the debtor with an adequate explanation of the matters referred to in subsection (2) in order to place him in a position enabling him to assess whether the agreement is adapted to his needs and his financial situation,
(b)   advise the debtor—
(i)   to consider the information which is required to be disclosed under section 55(1), and
(ii)   where this information is disclosed in person to the debtor, that the debtor is able to take it away,
(c)   provide the debtor with an opportunity to ask questions about the agreement, and
(d)   advise the debtor how to ask the creditor for further information and explanation.
(2)   The matters referred to in subsection (1)(a) are—
(a)   the features of the agreement which may make the credit to be provided under the agreement unsuitable for particular types of use,
(b)   how much the debtor will have to pay periodically and, where the amount can be determined, in total under the agreement,
(c)   the features of the agreement which may operate in a manner which would have a significant adverse effect on the debtor in a way which the debtor is unlikely to foresee,
(d)   the principal consequences for the debtor arising from a failure to make payments under the agreement at the times required by the agreement including legal proceedings and, where this is a possibility, repossession of the debtor's home, and
(e)   the effect of the exercise of any right to withdraw from the agreement and how and when this right may be exercised.
(3)   The advice and explanation may be given orally or in writing except as provided in subsection (4).
(4)   Where the explanation of the matters specified in paragraphs (a), (b) or (e) of subsection (2) is given orally or in person to a debtor, the explanation of the other matters specified in that paragraph, and the advice required to be given by subsection (1)(b), must be given orally to him.
(5)   Subsections (1) to (4) do not apply to a creditor if a credit intermediary (see section 160A) has complied with those subsections in respect of the agreement.
(6)   For the purposes of this section an agreement is an excluded agreement if it is—
(a)   an agreement under which the creditor provides the debtor with credit which exceeds £60, 260, or
(b)   an agreement secured on land.
(7)   Where the regulated consumer credit agreement is an agreement under which a person takes an article in pawn—
(a)   the obligation in subsection (1)(a) only relates to the matters listed in paragraphs (d) and (e) of subsection (2), and
(b)   the obligations in subsection (1)(b) and (d) do not apply.]

[55B   Assessment of creditworthiness
(1)   Before making a regulated consumer credit agreement, other than an excluded agreement, the creditor must undertake an assessment of the creditworthiness of the debtor.

(2)   Before significantly increasing—

(a)   the amount of credit to be provided under a regulated consumer credit agreement, other than an excluded agreement, or

(b)   a credit limit for running-account credit under a regulated consumer credit agreement, other than an excluded agreement,

the creditor must undertake an assessment of the debtor's creditworthiness.

(3)   A creditworthiness assessment must be based on sufficient information obtained from—

(a)   the debtor, where appropriate, and

(b)   a credit reference agency, where necessary.

(4)   For the purposes of this section an agreement is an excluded agreement if it is—

(a)   an agreement secured on land, or

(b)   an agreement under which a person takes an article in pawn.]

[55C   Copy of draft consumer credit agreement

(1)   Before a regulated consumer credit agreement, other than an excluded agreement, is made, the creditor must, if requested, give to the debtor without delay a copy of the prospective agreement (or such of its terms as have at that time been reduced to writing).

(2)   Subsection (1) does not apply if at the time the request is made, the creditor is unwilling to proceed with the agreement.

(3)   A breach of the duty imposed by subsection (1) is actionable as a breach of statutory duty.

(4)   For the purposes of this section an agreement is an excluded agreement if it is—

(a)   an agreement secured on land,

(b)   an agreement under which a person takes an article in pawn,

(c)   an agreement under which the creditor provides the debtor with credit which exceeds £60,260, or

(d)   an agreement entered into by the debtor wholly or predominantly for the purposes of a business carried on, or intended to be carried on, by him.

(5)   Subsections (2) to (5) of section 16B (declaration by the debtor as to the purposes of the agreement) apply for the purposes of subsection (4)(d).]

56   Antecedent negotiations

(1)   In this Act 'antecedent negotiations' means any negotiations with the debtor or hirer—

(a)   conducted by the creditor or owner in relation to the making of any regulated agreement, or

(b)   conducted by a credit-broker in relation to goods sold or proposed to be sold by the credit-broker to the creditor before forming the subject-matter of a debtor-creditor-supplier agreement within section 12(a), or

(c)   conducted by the supplier in relation to a transaction financed or proposed to be financed by a debtor-creditor-supplier agreement within section 12(b) or (c), and 'negotiator' means the person by whom negotiations are so conducted with the debtor or hirer.

(2)   Negotiations with the debtor in a case falling within subsection (1)(b) or (c) shall be deemed to be conducted by the negotiator in the capacity of agent of the creditor as well as in his actual capacity.

(3)   An agreement is void if, and to the extent that, it purports in relation to an actual or prospective regulated agreement—

(a)   to provide that a person acting as, or on behalf of, a negotiator is to be treated as the agent of the debtor or hirer, or

(b)   to relieve a person from liability for acts or omissions of any person acting as, or on behalf of, a negotiator.

(4)   For the purposes of this Act, antecedent negotiations shall be taken to

begin when the negotiator and the debtor or hirer first enter into communication (including communication by advertisement), and to include any representations made by the negotiator to the debtor or hirer and any other dealings between them.

57 Withdrawal from prospective agreement

(1) The withdrawal of a party from a prospective regulated agreement shall operate to apply this Part to the agreement, any linked transaction and any other thing done in anticipation of the making of the agreement as it would apply if the agreement were made and then cancelled under section 69.

(2) The giving to a party of a written or oral notice which, however expressed, indicates the intention of the other party to withdraw from a prospective regulated agreement operates as a withdrawal from it.

(3) Each of the following shall be deemed to be the agent of the creditor or owner for the purpose of receiving a notice under subsection (2)—

(a) a credit-broker or supplier who is the negotiator in antecedent negotiations, and

(b) any person who, in the course of a business carried on by him, acts on behalf of the debtor or hirer in any negotiations for the agreement.

(4) Where the agreement, if made, would not be a cancellable agreement, subsection (1) shall nevertheless apply as if the contrary were the case.

58 Opportunity for withdrawal from prospective land mortgage

(1) Before sending to the debtor or hirer, for his signature, an unexecuted agreement in a case where the prospective regulated agreement is to be secured on land (the 'mortgaged land'), the creditor or owner shall give the debtor or hirer a copy of the unexecuted agreement which contains a notice in the prescribed form indicating the right of the debtor or hirer to withdraw from the prospective agreement, and how and when the right is exercisable, together with a copy of any other document referred to in the unexecuted agreement.

(2) Subsection (1) does not apply to—

(a) a restricted-use credit agreement to finance the purchase of the mortgaged land, or

(b) an agreement for a bridging loan in connection with the purchase of the mortgaged land or other land.

59 Agreement to enter future agreement void

(1) An agreement is void if, and to the extent that, it purports to bind a person to enter as debtor or hirer into a prospective regulated agreement.

(2) Regulations may exclude from the operation of subsection (1) agreements such as are described in the regulations.

Making the agreement

60 Form and content of agreements

(1) The Secretary of State shall make regulations as to the form and content of documents embodying regulated agreements, and the regulations shall contain such provisions as appear to him appropriate with a view to ensuring that the debtor or hirer is made aware of—

(a) the rights and duties conferred or imposed on him by the agreement,

(b) the amount and rate of the total charge for credit (in the case of a consumer credit agreement),

(c) the protection and remedies available to him under this Act, and

(d) any other matters which, in the opinion of the Secretary of State, it is desirable for him to know about in connection with the agreement.

(2) Regulations under subsection (1) may in particular—

(a) require specified information to be included in the prescribed manner in documents, and other specified material to be excluded;

(b)   contain requirements to ensure that specified information is clearly brought to the attention of the debtor or hirer, and that one part of a document is not given insufficient or excessive prominence compared with another.

(3)   If, on an application made to the [OFT] by a person carrying on a consumer credit business or a consumer hire business, it appears to the [OFT] impracticable for the applicant to comply with any requirement of regulations under subsection (1) in a particular case, [it] may, by notice to the applicant direct that the requirement be waived or varied in relation to such agreements, and subject to such conditions (if any), as [it] may specify, and this Act and the regulations shall have effect accordingly.

(4)   The [OFT] shall give a notice under subsection (3) only if [it] is satisfied that to do so would not prejudice the interests of debtors or hirers.

[(5)   An application may be made under subsection (3) only if it relates to—
(a)   a consumer credit agreement secured on land,
(b)   a consumer credit agreement under which a person takes an article in pawn,
(c)   a consumer credit agreement under which the creditor provides the debtor with credit which exceeds £60,260,
(d)   a consumer credit agreement entered into by the debtor wholly or predominantly for the purposes of a business carried on, or intended to be carried on, by him, or
(e)   a consumer hire agreement.

(6)   Subsections (2) to (5) of section 16B (declaration by the debtor as to the purposes of the agreement) apply for the purposes of subsection (5)(d).]

61   Signing of agreement

(1)   A regulated agreement is not properly executed unless—
(a)   a document in the prescribed form itself containing all the prescribed terms and conforming to regulations under section 60(1) is signed in the prescribed manner both by the debtor or hirer and by or on behalf of the creditor or owner, and
(b)   the document embodies all the terms of the agreement, other than implied terms, and
(c)   the document is, when presented or sent to the debtor or hirer for signature, in such a state that all its terms are readily legible.

(2)   In addition, where the agreement is one to which section 58(1) applies, it is not properly executed unless—
(a)   the requirements of section 58(1) were complied with, and
(b)   the unexecuted agreement was sent, for his signature, to the debtor or hirer [by an appropriate method] not less than seven days after a copy of it was given to him under section 58(1), and
(c)   during the consideration period, the creditor or owner refrained from approaching the debtor or hirer (whether in person, by telephone or letter, or in any other way) except in response to a specific request made by the debtor or hirer after the beginning of the consideration period, and
(d)   no notice of withdrawal by the debtor or hirer was received by the creditor or owner before the sending of the unexecuted agreement.

(3)   In subsection (2)(c), 'the consideration period' means the period beginning with the giving of the copy under section 58(1) and ending—
(a)   at the expiry of seven days after the day on which the unexecuted agreement is sent, for his signature, to the debtor or hirer, or
(b)   on its return by the debtor or hirer after signature by him, whichever first occurs.

(4)   Where the debtor or hirer is a partnership or an unincorporated body of persons, subsection (1)(a) shall apply with the substitution for 'by the debtor or hirer' of 'by or on behalf of the debtor or hirer'.

[61A   Duty to supply copy of executed consumer credit agreement

(1)   Where a regulated consumer credit agreement, other than an excluded agreement, has been made, the creditor must give a copy of the executed agreement, and any other document referred to in it, to the debtor.

(2)   Subsection (1) does not apply if—

(a)   a copy of the unexecuted agreement (and of any other document referred to in it) has already been given to the debtor, and

(b)   the unexecuted agreement is in identical terms to the executed agreement.

(3)   In a case referred to in subsection (2), the creditor must inform the debtor in writing—

(a)   that the agreement has been executed,

(b)   that the executed agreement is in identical terms to the unexecuted agreement a copy of which has already been given to the debtor, and

(c)   that the debtor has the right to receive a copy of the executed agreement if the debtor makes a request for it at any time before the end of the period referred to in section 66A(2).

(4)   Where a request is made under subsection (3)(c) the creditor must give a copy of the executed agreement to the debtor without delay.

(5)   If the requirements of this section are not observed, the agreement is not properly executed.

(6)   For the purposes of this section, an agreement is an excluded agreement if it is—

(a)   a cancellable agreement, or

(b)   an agreement—

(i)   secured on land,

(ii)   under which the creditor provides the debtor with credit which exceeds £60,260, or

(iii)   entered into by the debtor wholly or predominantly for the purposes of a business carried on, or intended to be carried on, by him,

unless the creditor or a credit intermediary has complied with or purported to comply with regulation 3(2) of the Consumer Credit (Disclosure of Information) Regulations 2010.

(7)   Subsections (2) to (5) of section 16B (declaration by the debtor as to the purposes of the agreement) apply for the purposes of subsection (6)(b)(iii).]

[61B   Duty to supply copy of overdraft agreement

(1)   Where an authorised business overdraft agreement or an authorised non-business overdraft agreement has been made, a document containing the terms of the agreement must be given to the debtor.

(2)   The creditor must provide the document referred to in subsection (1) to the debtor before or at the time the agreement is made unless—

(a)   the creditor has provided the debtor with the information referred to in regulation 10(3) of the Consumer Credit (Disclosure of Information) Regulations 2010, in which case it [may] be provided after the agreement is made,

(b)   the creditor has provided the debtor with the information referred to in regulation 10(3)(c), (e), (f), (h) and (k) of those Regulations, in which case it must be provided immediately after the agreement is made, or

(c)   the agreement is an agreement of a description referred to in regulation 10(4)(b) of those Regulations, in which case it must be provided immediately after the agreement is made.

(3)   If the requirements of this section are not observed, the agreement is enforceable against the debtor on an order of the court only (and for these purposes a retaking of goods or land to which the agreement relates is an enforcement of the agreement).]

62   Duty to supply copy of unexecuted agreement [: excluded agreement]

(1)   If [in the case of a regulated agreement which is an excluded agreement] the unexecuted agreement is presented personally to the debtor or hirer for his signature, but on the occasion when he signs it the document does not become an executed agreement, a copy of it, and of any other document referred to in it, must be there and then delivered to him.

(2)   If the unexecuted agreement is sent to the debtor or hirer for his signature, a copy of it, and of any other document referred to in it, must be sent to him at the same time.

(3)   A regulated agreement [which is an excluded agreement] is not properly executed if the requirements of this section are not observed.

[(4)   In this section, 'excluded agreement' has the same meaning as in section 61A.]

63   Duty to supply copy of executed agreement [: excluded agreements]

(1)   If [in the case of a regulated agreement which is an excluded agreement] the unexecuted agreement is presented personally to the debtor or hirer for his signature, and on the occasion when he signs it the document becomes an executed agreement, a copy of the executed agreement, and of any other document referred to in it, must be there and then delivered to him.

(2)   A copy of the executed agreement, and of any other document referred to in it, must be given to the debtor or hirer within the seven days following the making of the agreement unless—

(a)   subsection (1) applies, or

(b)   the unexecuted agreement was sent to the debtor or hirer for his signature and, on the occasion of his signing it, the document became an executed agreement.

(3)   In the case of a cancellable agreement, a copy under subsection (2) must be sent [by an appropriate method].

(4)   In the case of a credit-token agreement, a copy under subsection (2) need not be given within the seven days following the making of the agreement if it is given before or at the time when the credit-token is given to the debtor.

(5)   A regulated agreement [which is an excluded agreement] is not properly executed if the requirements of this section are not observed.

[(6)   In this section, 'excluded agreement' has the same meaning as in section 61A.]

64   Duty to give notice of cancellation rights

(1)   In the case of a cancellable agreement, a notice in the prescribed form indicating the right of the debtor or hirer to cancel the agreement, how and when that right is exercisable, and the name and address of a person to whom notice of cancellation may be given,—

(a)   must be included in every copy given to the debtor or hirer under section 62 or 63, and

(b)   except where section 63(2) applied, must also be sent [by an appropriate method] to the debtor or hirer within the seven days following the making of the agreement.

(2)   In the case of a credit-token agreement, a notice under subsection (1)(b) need not be sent [by an appropriate method] within the seven days following the making of the agreement if either—

(a)   it is sent [by an appropriate method] to the debtor or hirer before the credit-token is given to him, or

(b)   it is sent [by an appropriate method] to him together with the credit-token.

(3)   Regulations may provide that except where section 63(2) applied a notice sent under subsection (1)(b) shall be accompanied by a further copy of the executed agreement, and of any other document referred to in it.

(4)   Regulations may provide that subsection (1)(b) is not to apply in the case of

agreements such as are described in the regulations, being agreements made by a particular person, if—

(a)   on an application by that person to the [OFT], the [OFT] has determined that, having regard to—

(i)   the manner in which antecedent negotiations for agreements with the applicant of that description are conducted, and

(ii)   the information provided to debtors or hirers before such agreements are made, the requirement imposed by subsection (1)(b) can be dispensed with without prejudicing the interests of debtors or hirers, and

(b)   any conditions imposed by the [OFT] in making the determination are complied with.

(5)   A cancellable agreement is not properly executed if the requirements of this section are not observed.

65   Consequences of improper execution

(1)   An improperly-executed regulated agreement is enforceable against the debtor or hirer on an order of the court only.

(2)   A retaking of goods or land to which a regulated agreement relates is an enforcement of the agreement.

66   Acceptance of credit-tokens

(1)   The debtor shall not be liable under a credit-token agreement for use made of the credit-token by any person unless the debtor had previously accepted the credit-token, or the use constituted an acceptance of it by him.

(2)   The debtor accepts a credit-token when—

(a)   it is signed, or

(b)   a receipt for it is signed, or

(c)   it is first used,

either by the debtor himself or by a person who, pursuant to the agreement, is authorised by him to use it.

[Withdrawal from certain agreements]

[66A   Withdrawal from consumer credit agreement

(1)   The debtor under a regulated consumer credit agreement, other than an excluded agreement, may withdraw from the agreement, without giving any reason, in accordance with this section.

(2)   To withdraw from an agreement under this section the debtor must give oral or written notice of the withdrawal to the creditor before the end of the period of 14 days beginning with [the day after] the relevant day.

(3)   For the purposes of subsection (2) the relevant day is whichever is the latest of the following—

(a)   the day on which the agreement is made;

(b)   where the creditor is required to inform the debtor of the credit limit under the agreement, the day on which the creditor first does so;

(c)   in the case of an agreement to which section 61A (duty to supply copy of executed consumer credit agreement) applies, the day on which the debtor receives a copy of the agreement under that section or on which the debtor is informed as specified in subsection (3) of that section;

(d)   in the case of an agreement to which section 63 (duty to supply copy of executed agreement: excluded agreements) applies, the day on which the debtor receives a copy of the agreement under that section.

(4)   Where oral notice under this section is given to the creditor it must be given in a manner specified in the agreement.

(5)   Where written notice under this section is given by facsimile transmission or electronically—

(a)   it must be sent to the number or electronic address specified for the purpose in the agreement, and

(b)   where it is so sent, it is to be regarded as having been received by the creditor at the time it is sent (and section 176A does not apply).

(6)   Where written notice under this section is given in any other form—

(a)   it must be sent by post to, or left at, the postal address specified for the purpose in the agreement, and

(b)   where it is sent by post to that address, it is to be regarded as having been received by the creditor at the time of posting (and section 176 does not apply).

(7)   Subject as follows, where the debtor withdraws from a regulated consumer credit agreement under this section—

(a)   the agreement shall be treated as if it had never been entered into, and

(b)   where an ancillary service relating to the agreement is or is to be provided by the creditor, or by a third party on the basis of an agreement between the third party and the creditor, the ancillary service contract shall be treated as if it had never been entered into.

(8)   In the case referred to in subsection (7)(b) the creditor must without delay notify any third party of the fact that the debtor has withdrawn from the agreement.

(9)   Where the debtor withdraws from an agreement under this section—

(a)   the debtor must repay to the creditor any credit provided and the interest accrued on it (at the rate provided for under the agreement), but

(b)   the debtor is not liable to pay to the creditor any compensation, fees or charges except any non-returnable charges paid by the creditor to a public administrative body.

(10)   An amount payable under subsection (9) must be paid without undue delay and no later than the end of the period of 30 days beginning with the day after the day on which the notice of withdrawal was given (and if not paid by the end of that period may be recovered by the creditor as a debt).

(11)   Where a regulated consumer credit agreement is a conditional sale, hire-purchase or credit-sale agreement and—

(a)   the debtor withdraws from the agreement under this section after the credit has been provided, and

(b)   the sum payable under subsection (9)(a) is paid in full by the debtor,

title to the goods purchased or supplied under the agreement is to pass to the debtor on the same terms as would have applied had the debtor not withdrawn from the agreement.

(12)   In subsections (2), (4), (5), (6) and (9)(a) references to the creditor include a person specified by the creditor in the agreement.

(13)   In subsection (7)(b) the reference to an ancillary service means a service that relates to the provision of credit under the agreement and includes in particular an insurance or payment protection policy.

(14)   For the purposes of this section, an agreement is an excluded agreement if it is—

(a)   an agreement for credit exceeding £60, 260,

(b)   an agreement secured on land,

(c)   a restricted-use credit agreement to finance the purchase of land, or

(d)   an agreement for a bridging loan in connection with the purchase of land.]

Cancellation of certain agreements within cooling-off period

67   Cancellable agreements

[(1)   Subject to subsection (2)] a regulated agreement may be cancelled by the debtor or hirer in accordance with this Part if the antecedent negotiations included oral representations made when in the presence of the debtor or hirer by an individual acting as, or on behalf of, the negotiator, unless—

(a)   the agreement is secured on land, or is a restricted-use credit agreement to finance the purchase of land or is an agreement for a bridging loan in connection with the purchase of land, or

(b)   the unexecuted agreement is signed by the debtor or hirer at premises at which any of the following is carrying on any business (whether on a permanent or temporary basis)—

(i)   the creditor or owner;

(ii)   any party to a linked transaction (other than the debtor or hirer or a relative of his);

(iii)   the negotiator in any antecedent negotiations.

[(2)   This section does not apply where section 66A applies.]

68   Cooling-off period

The debtor or hirer may serve notice of cancellation of a cancellable agreement between his signing of the unexecuted agreement and—

(a)   the end of the fifth day following the day on which he received a copy under section 63(2) or a notice under section 64(1)(b), or

(b)   if (by virtue of regulations made under section 64(4)) section 64(1)(b) does not apply, the end of the fourteenth day following the day on which he signed the unexecuted agreement.

69   Notice of cancellation

(1)   If within the period specified in section 68 the debtor or hirer under a cancellable agreement serves on—

(a)   the creditor or owner, or

(b)   the person specified in the notice under section 64(1), or

(c)   a person who (whether by virtue of subsection (6) or otherwise) is the agent of the creditor or owner, a notice (a 'notice of cancellation') which, however expressed and whether or not conforming to the notice given under section 64(1), indicates the intention of the debtor or hirer to withdraw from the agreement, the notice shall operate—

(i)   to cancel the agreement, and any linked transaction, and

(ii)   to withdraw any offer by the debtor or hirer, or his relative, to enter into a linked transaction.

(2)   In the case of a debtor-creditor-supplier agreement for restricted-use credit financing—

(a)   the doing of work or supply of goods to meet an emergency, or

(b)   the supply of goods which, before service of the notice of cancellation, had by the act of the debtor or his relative become incorporated in any land or thing not comprised in the agreement or any linked transaction,

subsection (1) shall apply with the substitution of the following for paragraph (i)—

'(i)   to cancel only such provisions of the agreement and any linked transaction as—

(aa)   relate to the provision of credit, or

(bb)   require the debtor to pay an item in the total charge for credit, or

(cc)   subject the debtor to any obligation other than to pay for the doing of the said work, or the supply of the said goods.'

(3)   Except so far as is otherwise provided, references in this Act to the cancellation of an agreement or transaction do not include a case within subsection (2).

(4)   Except as otherwise provided by or under this Act, an agreement or transaction cancelled under subsection (1) shall be treated as if it had never been entered into.

(5)   Regulations may exclude linked transactions of the prescribed description from subsection (1)(i) or (ii).

(6) Each of the following shall be deemed to be the agent of the creditor or owner for the purpose of receiving a notice of cancellation—

(a) a credit-broker or supplier who is the negotiator in antecedent negotiations, and

(b) any person who, in the course of a business carried on by him, acts on behalf of the debtor or hirer in any negotiations for the agreement.

[(7) Whether or not it is actually received by him, a notice of cancellation sent to a person shall be deemed to be served on him—

(a) in the case of a notice sent by post, at the time of posting, and

(b) in the case of a notice transmitted in the form of an electronic communication in accordance with section 17A(1), at the time of the transmission.]

70 Cancellation: recovery of money paid by debtor or hirer

(1) On the cancellation of a regulated agreement, and of any linked transaction,—

(a) any sum paid by the debtor or hirer, or his relative, under or in contemplation of the agreement or transaction, including any item in the total charge for credit, shall become repayable, and

(b) any sum, including any item in the total charge for credit, which but for the cancellation is, or would or might become, payable by the debtor or hirer, or his relative, under the agreement or transaction shall cease to be, or shall not become, so payable, and

(c) in the case of a debtor-creditor-supplier agreement falling within section 12(b), any sum paid on the debtor's behalf by the creditor to the supplier shall become repayable to the creditor.

(2) If, under the terms of a cancelled agreement or transaction, the debtor or hirer, or his relative, is in possession of any goods, he shall have a lien on them for any sum repayable to him under subsection (1) in respect of that agreement or transaction, or any other linked transaction.

(3) A sum repayable under subsection (1) is repayable by the person to whom it was originally paid, but in the case of a debtor-creditor-supplier agreement falling within section 12(b) the creditor and the supplier shall be under a joint and several liability to repay sums paid by the debtor, or his relative, under the agreement or under a linked transaction falling within section 19(1)(b) and accordingly, in such a case, the creditor shall be entitled, in accordance with rules of court, to have the supplier made a party to any proceedings brought against the creditor to recover any such sums.

(4) Subject to any agreement between them, the creditor shall be entitled to be indemnified by the supplier for loss suffered by the creditor in satisfying his liability under subsection (3), including costs reasonably incurred by him in defending proceedings instituted by the debtor.

(5) Subsection (1) does not apply to any sum which, if not paid by a debtor, would be payable by virtue of section 71, and applies to a sum paid or payable by a debtor for the issue of a credit-token only where the credit-token has been returned to the creditor or surrendered to a supplier.

(6) If the total charge for credit includes an item in respect of a fee or commission charged by a credit-broker, the amount repayable under subsection (1) in respect of that item shall be the excess over [£5] of the fee or commission.

(7) If the total charge for credit includes any sum payable or paid by the debtor to a credit-broker otherwise than in respect of a fee or commission charged by him, that sum shall for the purposes of subsection (6) be treated as if it were such a fee or commission.

(8) So far only as is necessary to give effect to section 69(2), this section applies to an agreement or transaction within that subsection as it applies to a cancelled agreement or transaction.

71 Cancellation: repayment of credit

(1) Notwithstanding the cancellation of a regulated consumer credit agreement, other than a debtor-creditor-supplier agreement for restricted-use credit, the agreement shall continue in force so far as it relates to repayment of credit and payment of interest.

(2) If, following the cancellation of a regulated consumer credit agreement, the debtor repays the whole or a portion of the credit—

(a) before the expiry of one month following service of the notice of cancellation, or

(b) in the case of a credit repayable by instalments, before the date on which the first instalment is due,

no interest shall be payable on the amount repaid.

(3) If the whole of a credit repayable by instalments is not repaid on or before the date specified in subsection (2)(b), the debtor shall not be liable to repay any of the credit except on receipt of a request in writing in the prescribed form, signed by or on behalf of the creditor, stating the amounts of the remaining instalments (recalculated by the creditor as nearly as may be in accordance with the agreement and without extending the repayment period), but excluding any sum other than principal and interest.

(4) Repayment of a credit, or payment of interest, under a cancelled agreement shall be treated as duly made if it is made to any person on whom, under section 69, a notice of cancellation could have been served, other than a person referred to in section 69(6)(b).

72 Cancellation: return of goods

(1) This section applies where any agreement or transaction relating to goods, being—

(a) a restricted-use debtor-creditor-supplier agreement, a consumer hire agreement, or a linked transaction to which the debtor or hirer under any regulated agreement is a party, or

(b) a linked transaction to which a relative of the debtor or hirer under any regulated agreement is a party,

is cancelled after the debtor or hirer (in a case within paragraph (a)) or the relative (in a case within paragraph (b)) has acquired possession of the goods by virtue of the agreement or transaction.

(2) In this section—

(a) 'the possessor' means the person who has acquired possession of the goods as mentioned in subsection (1),

(b) 'the other party' means the person from whom the possessor acquired possession, and

(c) 'the pre-cancellation period' means the period beginning when the possessor acquired possession and ending with the cancellation.

(3) The possessor shall be treated as having been under a duty throughout the pre-cancellation period—

(a) to retain possession of the goods, and

(b) to take reasonable care of them.

(4) On the cancellation, the possessor shall be under a duty, subject to any lien to restore the goods to the other party in accordance with this section, and meanwhile to retain possession of the goods and take reasonable care of them.

(5) The possessor shall not be under any duty to deliver the goods except at his own premises and in pursuance of a request in writing signed by or on behalf of the other party and served on the possessor either before, or at the time when, the goods are collected from those premises.

(6) If the possessor—

(a) delivers the goods (whether at his own premises or elsewhere) to any person on whom, under section 69, a notice of cancellation could have been served (other than a person referred to in section 69(6)(b)), or

(b)   sends the goods at his own expense to such a person, he shall be discharged from any duty to retain the goods or deliver them to any person.

(7)   Where the possessor delivers the goods as mentioned in subsection (6)(a), his obligation to take care of the goods shall cease; and if he sends the goods as mentioned in subsection (6)(b), he shall be under a duty to take reasonable care to see that they are received by the other party and not damaged in transit, but in other respects his duty to take care of the goods shall cease.

(8)   Where, at any time during the period of 21 days following the cancellation, the possessor receives such a request as is mentioned in subsection (5), and unreasonably refuses or unreasonably fails to comply with it, his duty to take reasonable care of the goods shall continue until he delivers or sends the goods as mentioned in subsection (6), but if within that period he does not receive such a request his duty to take reasonable care of the goods shall cease at the end of that period.

(9)   The preceding provisions of this section do not apply to—

(a)   perishable goods, or

(b)   goods which by their nature are consumed by use and which, before the cancellation, were so consumed, or

(c)   goods supplied to meet an emergency, or

(d)   goods which, before the cancellation, had become incorporated in any land or thing not comprised in the cancelled agreement or a linked transaction.

(10)   Where the address of the possessor is specified in the executed agreement, references in this section to his own premises are to that address and no other.

(11)   Breach of a duty imposed by this section is actionable as a breach of statutory duty.

73   Cancellation: goods given in part-exchange

(1)   This section applies on the cancellation of a regulated agreement where, in antecedent negotiations, the negotiator agreed to take goods in part-exchange (the 'part-exchange goods') and those goods have been delivered to him.

(2)   Unless, before the end of the period of ten days beginning with the date of cancellation, the part-exchange goods are returned to the debtor or hirer in a condition substantially as good as when they were delivered to the negotiator, the debtor or hirer shall be entitled to recover from the negotiator a sum equal to the part-exchange allowance (as defined in subsection (7)(b)).

(3)   In the case of a debtor-creditor-supplier agreement within section 12(b), the negotiator and the creditor shall be under a joint and several liability to pay to the debtor a sum recoverable under subsection (2).

(4)   Subject to any agreement between them, the creditor shall be entitled to be indemnified by the negotiator for loss suffered by the creditor in satisfying his liability under subsection (3), including costs reasonably incurred by him in defending proceedings instituted by the debtor.

(5)   During the period of ten days beginning with the date of cancellation, the debtor or hirer, if he is in possession of goods to which the cancelled agreement relates, shall have a lien on them for—

(a)   delivery of the part-exchange goods, in a condition substantially as good as when they were delivered to the negotiator; or

(b)   a sum equal to the part-exchange allowance;

and if the lien continues to the end of that period it shall thereafter subsist only as a lien for a sum equal to the part-exchange allowance.

(6)   Where the debtor or hirer recovers from the negotiator or creditor, or both of them jointly, a sum equal to the part-exchange allowance, then, if the title of the

debtor or hirer to the part-exchange goods has not vested in the negotiator, it shall so vest on the recovery of that sum.

(7)   For the purposes of this section—

(a)   the negotiator shall be treated as having agreed to take goods in part-exchange if, in pursuance of the antecedent negotiations, he either purchased or agreed to purchase those goods or accepted or agreed to accept them as part of the consideration for the cancelled agreement, and

(b)   the part-exchange allowance shall be the sum agreed as such in the antecedent negotiations or, if no such agreement was arrived at, such sum as it would have been reasonable to allow in respect of the part-exchange goods if no notice of cancellation had been served.

(8)   In an action brought against the creditor for a sum recoverable under sub-section (2), he shall be entitled, in accordance with rules of court, to have the nego-tiator made a party to the proceedings.

Exclusion of certain agreements from Part V

74   Exclusion of certain agreements from Part V

[(1)   Except as provided in subsections (1A) to (2), this Part does not apply to—

(a)   a non-commercial agreement,

(b)   a debtor-creditor agreement enabling the debtor to overdraw on a current account,

(c)   a debtor-creditor agreement to finance the making of such payments arising on, or connected with, the death of a person as may be prescribed, or

(d)   a small debtor-creditor-supplier agreement for restricted-use credit.

(1A)   Section 56 (antecedent negotiations) applies to a non-commercial agreement.

(1B)   Where an agreement that falls within subsection (1)(b) is an authorised business overdraft agreement the following provisions apply—

(a)   section 55B (assessment of creditworthiness);

(b)   section 56 (antecedent negotiations);

(c)   section 60 (regulations on form and content of agreements);

(d)   section 61B (duty to supply copy of overdraft agreement).

(1C)   Where an agreement that falls within subsection (1)(b) is an authorised non-business overdraft agreement the following provisions apply—

(a)   section 55 (regulations on disclosure of information);

(b)   section 55B (assessment of creditworthiness);

(c)   section 55C (copy of draft consumer credit agreement);

(d)   section 56 (antecedent negotiations);

(e)   section 60 (regulations on form and content of agreements);

(f)   section 61B (duty to supply copy of overdraft agreement).

(1D)   Where an agreement that falls within subsection (1)(b) would be an authorised non-business overdraft agreement but for the fact that the credit is not repayable on demand or within three months the following provisions apply—

(a)   section 55 (regulations on disclosure of information);

(b)   section 55A (adequate explanations);

(c)   section 55B (credit assessment);

(d)   section 55C (copy of draft consumer credit agreement);

(e)   section 56 (antecedent negotiations);

(f)   section 60 (regulations on form and content of agreements);

(g)   section 61 (signing of agreement);

(h)   section 61A (duty to supply copy of executed agreement);

(i)   section 66A (withdrawal from consumer credit agreement).

(1E)   In the case of an agreement that falls within subsection (1)(b) but does not fall within subsection (1B), (1C) or (1D), section 56 (antecedent negotiations) applies.

(1F) The following provisions apply to a debtor-creditor agreement to finance the making of such payments arising on, or connected with, the death of a person as may be prescribed—

(a)   section 55 (regulations on disclosure of information);
(b)   section 55A (adequate explanations);
(c)   section 55B (assessment of creditworthiness);
(d)   section 55C (copy of draft consumer credit agreement);
(e)   section 56 (antecedent negotiations);
(f)   section 60 (regulations on form and content of agreements);
(g)   section 61 (signing of agreement);
(h)   section 61A (duty to supply copy of executed agreement);
(i)   section 66A (withdrawal from consumer credit agreement).]

[(2) The following provisions apply to a small debtor-creditor-supplier agreement for restricted-use credit—

(a)   section 55 (regulations on disclosure of information);
(b)   section 56 (antecedent negotiations);
(c)   section 66A (withdrawal from consumer credit agreement).]

[(2A) In the case of an agreement to which the [Cancellation of Contracts made in a Consumer's Home or Place of Work etc Regulations 2008] apply the reference in subsection (2) to a small agreement shall be construed as if in section 17(1)(a) and (b) '£35' were substituted for '£50'.]

(3) [Subsection (1)(c) applies] only where the [OFT] so determines, and such a determination—

(a)   may be made subject to such conditions as the [OFT] thinks fit, and
(b)   shall be made only if the [OFT] is of opinion that it is not against the interests of debtors.

[. . .]

(4) If any term of an agreement falling within subsection [(1)(d)] is expressed in writing, regulations under section 60(1) shall apply to that term (subject to section 60(3)) as if the agreement were a regulated agreement not falling within subsection [(1)(d)].

[PART VA
CURRENT ACCOUNT OVERDRAFTS

[74A   Information to be provided on a current account agreement

[(1)   This section applies to a current account agreement where—

(a)   there is the possibility that the account-holder may be allowed to overdraw on the current account without a pre-arranged overdraft or exceed a pre-arranged overdraft limit, and
(b)   if the account-holder did so, this would be a regulated consumer credit agreement.]

(2)   The current account agreement must include the following information at the time it is made—

(a)   the rate of interest charged on the amount by which an account-holder overdraws on the current account or exceeds the pre-arranged overdraft limit,
(b)   any conditions applicable to that rate,
(c)   any reference rate on which that rate is based,
(d)   information on any changes to the rate of interest (including the periods that the rate applies and any conditions or procedure applicable to changing that rate), and
(e)   any other charges payable by the debtor under the agreement (and the conditions under which those charges may be varied).

(3)   The account-holder must be informed [in writing] at least annually of the information in subsection (2).

(4)   For the purposes of subsections (2) and (3) where different rates of interest are charged in different circumstances, the creditor must provide the information in subsection (2)(a) to (d) in respect of each rate.

(5)   Subsection (3) does not apply where the overdraft or excess would be secured on land.]

[74B   Information to be provided on significant overdrawing without prior arrangement

[(1)   Where—

(a)   the holder of a current account overdraws on the account without a pre-arranged overdraft, or exceeds a pre-arranged overdraft limit, for a period exceeding one month,

(b)   the amount of that overdraft or excess is significant throughout that period,

(c)   that overdraft or excess is a regulated consumer credit agreement, and

(d)   the account-holder has not been informed in writing of the matters mentioned in subsection (2) within that period,

the account-holder must be informed in writing of those matters without delay.]

(2)   The matters referred to in subsection (1) are—

(a)   the fact that the current account is overdrawn or the overdraft limit has been exceeded,

(b)   the amount of that overdraft or excess,

(c)   the rate of interest charged on it, and

(d)   any other charges payable by the debtor in relation to it (including any penalties and any interest on those charges).

(3)   For the purposes of subsection (1)(b) the amount of the overdraft or excess is to be treated as significant if—

(a)   the account-holder is liable to pay a charge for which he would not otherwise be liable,

(b)   the overdraft or excess is likely to have an adverse effect on the debtor's ability to receive further credit (including any effect on the information about the debtor held by a credit reference agency), or

(c)   it otherwise appears significant, having regard to all the circumstances.

(4)   Where the overdraft or excess is secured on land, subsection (1)(a) is to be read as if the reference to one month were a reference to three months.]]

PART VI
MATTERS ARISING DURING CURRENCY OF CREDIT OR HIRE AGREEMENTS

75   Liability of creditor for breaches by supplier

(1)   If the debtor under a debtor-creditor-supplier agreement falling within section 12(b) or (c) has, in relation to a transaction financed by the agreement, any claim against the supplier in respect of a misrepresentation or breach of contract, he shall have a like claim against the creditor, who, with the supplier, shall accordingly be jointly and severally liable to the debtor.

(2)   Subject to any agreement between them, the creditor shall be entitled to be indemnified by the supplier for loss suffered by the creditor in satisfying his liability under subsection (1), including costs reasonably incurred by him in defending proceedings instituted by the debtor.

(3)   Subsection (1) does not apply to a claim—

(a)   under a non-commercial agreement,

(b)   so far as the claim relates to any single item to which the supplier has attached a cash price not exceeding [£100] or more than [£30,000] [, or

[(c)   under a debtor-creditor-supplier agreement for running-account credit—

(i)   which provides for the making of payments by the debtor in relation to specified periods which, in the case of an agreement which is not secured on land, do not exceed three months, and

(ii) which requires that the number of payments to be made by the debtor in repayments of the whole amount of the credit provided in each such period shall not exceed one.]

(4) This section applies notwithstanding that the debtor, in entering into the transaction, exceeded the credit limit or otherwise contravened any term of the agreement.

(5) In an action brought against the creditor under subsection (1) he shall be entitled, in accordance with rules of court, to have the supplier made a party to the proceedings.

[75A Further provision for liability of creditor for breaches by supplier

(1) If the debtor under a linked credit agreement has a claim against the supplier in respect of a breach of contract the debtor may pursue that claim against the creditor where any of the conditions in subsection (2) are met.

(2) The conditions in subsection (1) are—

(a) that the supplier cannot be traced,

(b) that the debtor has contacted the supplier but the supplier has not responded,

(c) that the supplier is insolvent, or

(d) that the debtor has taken reasonable steps to pursue his claim against the supplier but has not obtained satisfaction for his claim.

(3) The steps referred to in subsection (2)(d) need not include litigation.

(4) For the purposes of subsection (2)(d) a debtor is to be deemed to have obtained satisfaction where he has accepted a replacement product or service or other compensation from the supplier in settlement of his claim.

(5) In this section 'linked credit agreement' means a regulated consumer credit agreement which serves exclusively to finance an agreement for the supply of specific goods or the provision of a specific service and where—

(a) the creditor uses the services of the supplier in connection with the preparation or making of the credit agreement, or

(b) the specific goods or provision of a specific service are explicitly specified in the credit agreement.

(6) This section does not apply where—

(a) the cash value of the goods or service is £30, 000 or less,

(b) the linked credit agreement is for credit which exceeds £60, 260, or

(c) the linked credit agreement is entered into by the debtor wholly or predominantly for the purposes of a business carried on, or intended to be carried on, by him.

(7) Subsections (2) to (5) of section 16B (declaration by the debtor as to the purposes of the agreement) apply for the purposes of subsection (6)(c).]

[(8) This section does not apply to an agreement secured on land.]

76 Duty to give notice before taking certain action

(1) The creditor or owner is not entitled to enforce a term of a regulated agreement by—

(a) demanding earlier payment of any sum, or

(b) recovering possession of any goods or land, or

(c) treating any right conferred on the debtor or hirer by the agreement as terminated, restricted or deferred,

except by or after giving the debtor or hirer not less than seven days' notice of his intention to do so.

(2) Subsection (1) applies only where—

(a) a period for the duration of the agreement is specified in the agreement, and

(b) that period has not ended when the creditor or owner does an act mentioned in subsection (1), but so applies notwithstanding that, under the agreement, any party is entitled to terminate it before the end of the period so specified.

(3)   A notice under subsection (1) is ineffective if not in the prescribed form.

(4)   Subsection (1) does not prevent a creditor from treating the right to draw on any credit as restricted or deferred and taking such steps as may be necessary to make the restriction or deferment effective.

(5)   Regulations may provide that subsection (1) is not to apply to agreements described by the regulations.

(6)   Subsection (1) does not apply to a right of enforcement arising by reason of any breach by the debtor or hirer of the regulated agreement.

77   Duty to give information to debtor under fixed-sum credit agreement

(1)   The creditor under a regulated agreement for fixed-sum credit, within the prescribed period after receiving a request in writing to that effect from the debtor and payment of a fee of [£1], shall give the debtor a copy of the executed agreement (if any) and of any other document referred to in it, together with a statement signed by or on behalf of the creditor showing, according to the information to which it is practicable for him to refer,—

(a)   the total sum paid under the agreement by the debtor;

(b)   the total sum which has become payable under the agreement by the debtor but remains unpaid, and the various amounts comprised in that total sum, with the date when each became due; and

(c)   the total sum which is to become payable under the agreement by the debtor, and the various amounts comprised in that total sum, with the date, or mode of determining the date, when each becomes due.

(2)   If the creditor possesses insufficient information to enable him to ascertain the amounts and dates mentioned in subsection (1)(c), he shall be taken to comply with that paragraph if his statement under subsection (1) gives the basis on which, under the regulated agreement, they would fall to be ascertained.

(3)   Subsection (1) does not apply to—

(a)   an agreement under which no sum is, or will or may become, payable by the debtor, or

(b)   a request made less than one month after a previous request under that subsection relating to the same agreement was complied with.

(4)   If the creditor under an agreement fails to comply with subsection (1)—

(a)   he is not entitled, while the default continues, to enforce the agreement [. . .]

(5)   This section does not apply to a non-commercial agreement.

[77A   Statements to be provided in relation to fixed-sum credit agreements

[(1)   The creditor under a regulated agreement for fixed-sum credit must give the debtor statements under this section.

(1A)   The statements must relate to consecutive periods.

(1B)   The first such period must begin with either—

(a)   the day on which the agreement is made, or

(b)   the day the first movement occurs on the debtor's account with the creditor relating to the agreement.

(1C)   No such period may exceed a year.

(1D)   For the purposes of subsection (1C), a period of a year which expires on a non-working day may be regarded as expiring on the next working day.

(1E)   Each statement under this section must be given to the debtor before the end of the period of thirty days beginning with the day after the end of the period to which the statement relates.]

(2)   Regulations may make provision about the form and content of statements under this section.

(3)   The debtor shall have no liability to pay any sum in connection with the preparation or the giving to him of a statement under this section.

(4)   The creditor is not required to give the debtor any statement under this section once the following conditions are satisfied—

(a)   that there is no sum payable under the agreement by the debtor; and

(b)   that there is no sum which will or may become so payable.

(5)   Subsection (6) applies if at a time before the conditions mentioned in sub-section (4) are satisfied the creditor fails to give the debtor—

(a)   a statement under this section within the period mentioned in subsection [(1E)].

[. . .]

(6)   Where this subsection applies in relation to a failure to give a statement under this section to the debtor—

(a)   the creditor shall not be entitled to enforce the agreement during the period of non-compliance;

(b)   the debtor shall have no liability to pay any sum of interest to the extent calculated by reference to the period of non-compliance or to any part of it; and

(c)   the debtor shall have no liability to pay any default sum which (apart from this paragraph)—

(i)   would have become payable during the period of non-compliance; or

(ii)   would have become payable after the end of that period in connection with a breach of the agreement which occurs during that period (whether or not the breach continues after the end of that period).

(7)   In this section 'the period of non-compliance' means, in relation to a failure to give a statement under this section to the debtor, the period which—

(a)   begins immediately after the end of the period mentioned in [. . .] subsection (5); and

(b)   ends at the end of the day on which the statement is given to the debtor or on which the conditions mentioned in subsection (4) are satisfied, whichever is earlier.

(8)   This section does not apply in relation to a non-commercial agreement or to a small agreement.]

[(9)   This section does not apply where the holder of a current account over-draws on the account without a pre-arranged overdraft or exceeds a pre-arranged overdraft limit.]

[77B   Fixed-sum credit agreement: statement of account to be provided on request

(1)   This section applies to a regulated consumer credit agreement—

(a)   which is for fixed-sum credit,

(b)   which is of fixed duration,

(c)   where the credit is repayable in instalments by the debtor, and

(d)   which is not an excluded agreement.

(2)   Upon a request from the debtor, the creditor must as soon as reasonably practicable give to the debtor a statement in writing which complies with subsec-tions (3) to (5).

(3)   The statement must include a table showing the details of each instalment owing under the agreement as at the date of the request.

(4)   Details to be provided under subsection (3) must include—

(a)   the date on which the instalment is due,

(b)   the amount of the instalment,

(c)   any conditions relating to payment of the instalment, and

(d)   a breakdown of the instalment showing how much of it is made up of capital repayment, interest payment and other charges.

(5)   Where the rate of interest is variable or the charges under the agreement may be varied, the statement must also indicate clearly and concisely that the information in the table is valid only until the rate of interest or charges are varied.

(6)   The debtor may make a request under subsection (2) at any time that the

agreement is in force unless a previous request has been made less than a month before and has been complied with.

(7)   The debtor shall have no liability to pay any sum in connection with the preparation or the giving of a statement under this section.

(8)   A breach of the duty imposed by this section is actionable as a breach of statutory duty.

(9)   For the purposes of this section, an agreement is an excluded agreement if it is—

(a)   an agreement secured on land,

(b)   an agreement under which a person takes an article in pawn,

(c)   an agreement under which the creditor provides the debtor with credit which exceeds £60,260, or

(d)   an agreement entered into by the debtor wholly or predominantly for the purpose of a business carried on, or intended to be carried on, by him.

(10)   Subsections (2) to (5) of section 16B (declaration by the debtor as to the purposes of the agreement) apply for the purposes of subsection (9)(d).]

78   Duty to give information to debtor under running-account credit agreement

(1)   The creditor under a regulated agreement for running-account credit, within the prescribed period after receiving a request in writing to that effect from the debtor and payment of a fee of [£1], shall give the debtor a copy of the executed agreement (if any) and of any other document referred to in it, together with a statement signed by or on behalf of the creditor showing, according to the information to which it is practicable for him to refer,—

(a)   the state of the account, and

(b)   the amount, if any, currently payable under the agreement by the debtor to the creditor, and

(c)   the amounts and due dates of any payments which, if the debtor does not draw further on the account, will later become payable under the agreement by the debtor to the creditor.

(2)   If the creditor possesses insufficient information to enable him to ascertain the amounts and dates mentioned in subsection (1)(c), he shall be taken to comply with that paragraph if his statement under subsection (1) gives the basis on which, under the regulated agreement, they would fall to be ascertained.

(3)   Subsection (1) does not apply to—

(a)   an agreement under which no sum is, or will or may become, payable by the debtor, or

(b)   a request made less than one month after a previous request under that subsection relating to the same agreement was complied with.

(4)   Where running-account credit is provided under a regulated agreement, the creditor shall give the debtor statements in the prescribed form, and with the prescribed contents—

(a)   showing according to the information to which it is practicable for him to refer, the state of the account at regular intervals of not more than twelve months, and

(b)   where the agreement provides, in relation to specified periods, for the making of payments by the debtor, or the charging against him of interest or any other sum, showing according to the information to which it is practicable for him to refer the state of the account at the end of each of those periods during which there is any movement in the account.

[(4A)   Regulations may require a statement under subsection (4) to contain also information in the prescribed terms about the consequences of the debtor—

(a)   failing to make payments as required by the agreement; or

(b)   only making payments of a prescribed description in prescribed circumstances.]

(5)   A statement under subsection (4) shall be given within the prescribed period after the end of the period to which the statement relates.

(6)   If the creditor under an agreement fails to comply with subsection (1)—

(a)   he is not entitled, while the default continues, to enforce the agreement [. . .]

(7)   This section does not apply to a non-commercial agreement, and subsections [(4) to (5)] do not apply to a small agreement.

[78A   Duty to give information to debtor on change of rate of interest

(1)   Where the rate of interest charged under a regulated consumer credit agreement, other than an excluded agreement, is to be varied, the creditor must inform the debtor in writing of the matters mentioned in subsection (3) before the variation can take effect.

(2)   But subsection (1) does not apply where—

(a)   the agreement provides that the creditor is to inform the debtor in writing periodically of the matters mentioned in subsection (3) in relation to any variation, at such times as may be provided for in the agreement,

(b)   the agreement provides that the rate of interest is to vary according to a reference rate,

(c)   the reference rate is publicly available,

(d)   information about the reference rate is available on the premises of the creditor, and

(e)   the variation of the rate of interest results from a change to the reference rate.

(3)   The matters referred to in subsections (1) and (2)(a) are—

(a)   the variation in the rate of interest,

(b)   the amount of any payments that are to be made after the variation has effect, if different, expressed as a sum of money where practicable, and

(c)   if the number or frequency of payments changes as a result of the variation, the new number or frequency.

(4)   In the case of an agreement mentioned in subsection (5) this section applies as follows—

(a)   the obligation in subsection (1) only applies if the rate of interest increases, and

(b)   subsection (3) is to be read as if paragraphs (b) and (c) were omitted.

(5)   The agreements referred to in subsection (4) are—

(a)   an authorised business overdraft agreement,

(b)   an authorised non-business overdraft agreement, or

(c)   an agreement which would be an authorised non-business overdraft agreement but for the fact that the credit is not repayable on demand or within three months.

(6)   For the purposes of this section an agreement is an excluded agreement if it is—

(a)   a debtor-creditor agreement arising where the holder of a current account overdraws on the account without a pre-arranged overdraft or exceeds a pre-arranged overdraft limit, or

(b)   an agreement secured on land.]

79   Duty to give hirer information

(1)   The owner under a regulated consumer hire agreement, within the prescribed period after receiving a request in writing to that effect from the hirer and payment of a fee of [£1], shall give to the hirer a copy of the executed agreement and of any other document referred to in it, together with a statement signed by or on behalf of the owner showing, according to the information to which it is practicable for him to refer, the total sum which has become payable under the agreement by the hirer but remains unpaid and the various amounts comprised in that total sum, with the date when each became due.

(2)   Subsection (1) does not apply to—
   (a)   an agreement under which no sum is, or will or may become, payable by
the hirer, or
   (b)   a request made less than one month after a previous request under that
subsection relating to the same agreement was complied with.
(3)   If the owner under an agreement fails to comply with subsection (1)—
   (a)   he is not entitled, while the default continues, to enforce the agreement
[. . .]
(4)   This section does not apply to a non-commercial agreement.

80   Debtor or hirer to give information about goods

(1)   Where a regulated agreement, other than a non-commercial agreement,
requires the debtor or hirer to keep goods to which the agreement relates in his
possession or control, he shall, within seven working days after he has received a
request in writing to that effect from the creditor or owner, tell the creditor or
owner where the goods are.
(2)   If the debtor or hirer fails to comply with subsection (1), and the default
continues for 14 days, he commits an offence.

81   Appropriation of payments

(1)   Where a debtor or hirer is liable to make to the same person payments in
respect of two or more regulated agreements, he shall be entitled, on making any
payment in respect of the agreements which is not sufficient to discharge the total
amount then due under all the agreements, to appropriate the sum so paid by
him—
   (a)   in or towards the satisfaction of the sum due under any one of the
agreements, or
   (b)   in or towards the satisfaction of the sums due under any two or more of
the agreements in such proportions as he thinks fit.
(2)   If the debtor or hirer fails to make any such appropriation where one or
more of the agreements is—
   (a)   a hire-purchase agreement or conditional sale agreement, or
   (b)   a consumer hire agreement, or
   (c)   an agreement in relation to which any security is provided,
the payment shall be appropriated towards the satisfaction of the sums due under
the several agreements respectively in the proportions which those sums bear to
one another.

82   Variation of agreements

(1)   Where, under a power contained in a regulated agreement, the creditor or
owner varies the agreement, the variation shall not take effect before notice of it is
given to the debtor or hirer in the prescribed manner.
[(1A)   Subsection (1) does not apply to a variation in the rate of interest charged
under an agreement not secured on land (see section 78A).
(1B)   Subsection (1) does not apply to a variation in the rate of interest charged
under an agreement secured on land if—
   (a)   the agreement falls within subsection (1D), and
   (b)   the variation is a reduction in the rate.
(1C)   Subsection (1) does not apply to a variation in any other charge under an
agreement if—
   (a)   the agreement falls within subsection (1D), and
   (b)   the variation is a reduction in the charge.
(1D)   The agreements referred to in subsections (1B) and (1C) are—
   (a)   an authorised business overdraft agreement,
   (b)   an authorised non-business overdraft agreement, or

(c)   an agreement which would be an authorised non-business overdraft agreement but for the fact that the credit is not repayable on demand or within three months.

(1E) Subsection (1) does not apply to a debtor-creditor agreement arising where the holder of a current account overdraws on the account without a pre-arranged overdraft or exceeds a pre-arranged overdraft limit.]

(2)   Where an agreement (a 'modifying agreement') varies or supplements an earlier agreement, the modifying agreement shall for the purposes of this Act be treated as—

(a)   revoking the earlier agreement, and

(b)   containing provisions reproducing the combined effect of the two agreements, and obligations outstanding in relation to the earlier agreement shall accordingly be treated as outstanding instead in relation to the modifying agreement.

[(2A) Subsection (2) does not apply if [the earlier agreement or] the modifying agreement is an exempt agreement as a result of section 16(6C) [or 16C].]

[(2B) Subsection (2) does not apply if the modifying agreement varies—

(a)   the amount of the repayment to be made under the earlier agreement, or

(b)   the duration of the agreement,

as a result of the discharge of part of the debtor's indebtedness under the earlier agreement by virtue of section 94(3).]

(3)   If the earlier agreement is a regulated agreement but (apart from this subsection) the modifying agreement is not then, [unless the modifying agreement is—

(a)   for running account credit; or

(b)   an exempt agreement as a result of section 16(6C) [or 16C], it shall be treated as a regulated agreement.]

(4)   If the earlier agreement is a regulated agreement for running-account credit, and by the modifying agreement the creditor allows the credit limit to be exceeded but intends the excess to be merely temporary, Part V (except section 56) shall not apply to the modifying agreement.

(5)   If—

(a)   the earlier agreement is a cancellable agreement, and

(b)   the modifying agreement is made within the period applicable under section 68 to the earlier agreement,

then, whether or not the modifying agreement would, apart from this subsection, be a cancellable agreement, it shall be treated as a cancellable agreement in respect of which a notice may be served under section 68 not later than the end of the period applicable under that section to the earlier agreement.

[(5A) Subsection (5) does not apply where the modifying agreement is an exempt agreement as a result of section 16(6C) [or 16C].]

(6)   Except under subsection (5), a modifying agreement shall not be treated as a cancellable agreement.

[(6A) If—

(a)   the earlier agreement is an agreement to which section 66A (right of withdrawal) applies, and

(b)   the modifying agreement is made within the period during which the debtor may give notice of withdrawal from the earlier agreement (see section 66A(2)),

then, whether or not the modifying agreement would, apart from this subsection, be an agreement to which section 66A applies, it shall be treated as such an agreement in respect of which notice may be given under subsection (2) of that section within the period referred to in paragraph (b) above.

(6B) Except as provided for under subsection (6A) section 66A does not apply to a modifying agreement.]

(7)   This section does not apply to a non-commercial agreement.

[82A   Assignment of rights

(1)   Where rights of a creditor under a regulated consumer credit agreement are assigned to a third party, the assignee must arrange for notice of the assignment to be given to the debtor—

(a)   as soon as reasonably possible, or

(b)   if, after the assignment, the arrangements for servicing the credit under the agreement do not change as far as the debtor is concerned, on or before the first occasion that they do.

(2)   This section does not apply to an agreement secured on land.]

83   Liability for misuse of credit facilities

(1)   The debtor under a regulated consumer credit agreement shall not be liable to the creditor for any loss arising from use of the credit facility by another person not acting, or to be treated as acting, as the debtor's agent.

(2)   This section does not apply to a non-commercial agreement, or to any loss in so far as it arises from misuse of an instrument to which section 4 of the Cheques Act 1957 applies.

84   Misuse of credit-tokens

(1)   Section 83 does not prevent the debtor under a credit-token agreement from being made liable to the extent of [£50] (or the credit limit if lower) for loss to the creditor arising from use of the credit-token by other persons during a period beginning when the credit-token ceases to be in the possession of any authorised person and ending when the credit-token is once more in the possession of an authorised person.

(2)   Section 83 does not prevent the debtor under a credit-token agreement from being made liable to any extent for loss to the creditor from use of the credit-token by a person who acquired possession of it with the debtor's consent.

(3)   Subsections (1) and (2) shall not apply to any use of the credit-token after the creditor has been given oral or written notice that it is lost or stolen, or is for any other reason liable to misuse.

[(3A)   Subsections (1) and (2) shall not apply to any use, in connection with a distance contract (other than an excepted contract), of a card which is a credit-token.

(3B)   In subsection (3A), 'distance contract' and 'excepted contract' have the meanings given in the Consumer Protection (Distance Selling) Regulations 2000.

(3C)   Subsections (1) and (2) shall not apply to any use, in connection with a distance contract within the meaning of the Financial Services (Distance Marketing) Regulations 2004, of a card which is a credit-token.

(3D)   In subsection (3C), 'distance contract' and 'excepted contract' have the meanings given in the Financial Services (Distance Marketing) Regulations 2004.]

(4)   Subsections (1) and (2) shall not apply unless there are contained in the credit-token agreement in the prescribed manner particulars of the name, address and telephone number of a person stated to be the person to whom notice is to be given under subsection (3).

(5)   Notice under subsection (3) takes effect when received, but where it is given orally, and the agreement so requires, it shall be treated as not taking effect if not confirmed in writing within seven days.

(6)   Any sum paid by the debtor for the issue of the credit-token to the extent (if any) that it has not been previously offset by use made of the credit-token, shall be treated as paid towards satisfaction of any liability under subsection (1) or (2).

(7)   The debtor, the creditor, and any person authorised by the debtor to use the credit-token, shall be authorised persons for the purposes of subsection (1).

(8)   Where two or more credit-tokens are given under one credit-token agreement, the preceding provisions of this section apply to each credit-token separately.

85   Duty on issue of new credit-tokens

(1)   Whenever, in connection with a credit-token agreement, a credit-token (other than the first) is given by the creditor to the debtor, the creditor shall give the debtor a copy of the executed agreement (if any) and of any other document referred to in it.

(2)   If the creditor fails to comply with this section—

(a)   he is not entitled, while the default continues, to enforce the agreement [. . .]

(3)   This section does not apply to a small agreement.

86   Death of debtor or hirer

(1)   The creditor or owner under a regulated agreement is not entitled, by reason of the death of the debtor or hirer, to do an act specified in paragraphs (a) to (e) of section 87(1) if at the death the agreement is fully secured.

(2)   If at the death of the debtor or hirer a regulated agreement is only partly secured or is unsecured, the creditor or owner is entitled, by reason of the death of the debtor or hirer, to do an act specified in paragraphs (a) to (e) of section 87(1) on an order of the court only.

(3)   This section applies in relation to the termination of an agreement only where—

(a)   a period for its duration is specified in the agreement, and

(b)   that period has not ended when the creditor or owner purports to terminate the agreement,

but so applies notwithstanding that, under the agreement, any party is entitled to terminate it before the end of the period so specified.

(4)   The section does not prevent the creditor from treating the right to draw on any credit as restricted or deferred, and taking such steps as may be necessary to make the restriction or deferment effective.

(5)   This section does not affect the operation of any agreement providing for payment of sums—

(a)   due under the regulated agreement, or

(b)   becoming due under it on the death of the debtor or hirer,

out of the proceeds of a policy of assurance on his life.

(6)   For the purposes of this section an act is done by reason of the death of the debtor or hirer if it is done under a power conferred by the agreement which is—

(a)   exercisable on his death, or

(b)   exercisable at will and exercised at any time after his death.

PART VII
DEFAULT AND TERMINATION

[Information sheets

[86A   OFT to prepare information sheets on arrears and default

(1)   The OFT shall prepare, and give general notice of, an arrears information sheet and a default information sheet.

(2)   The arrears information sheet shall include information to help debtors and hirers who receive notices under section 86B or 86C.

(3)   The default information sheet shall include information to help debtors and hirers who receive default notices.

(4)   Regulations may make provision about the information to be included in an information sheet.

(5)   An information sheet takes effect for the purposes of this Part at the end of the period of three months beginning with the day on which general notice of it is given.

(6)   If the OFT revises an information sheet after general notice of it has been given, it shall give general notice of the information sheet as revised.

(7)   A revised information sheet takes effect for the purposes of this Part at the end of the period of three months beginning with the day on which general notice of it is given.]]

[*Sums in arrears and default sums*

[86B   Notice of sums in arrears under fixed-sum credit agreements etc
(1)   This section applies where at any time the following conditions are satisfied—

(a)   that the debtor or hirer under an applicable agreement is required to have made at least two payments under the agreement before that time;

(b)   that the total sum paid under the agreement by him is less than the total sum which he is required to have paid before that time;

(c)   that the amount of the shortfall is no less than the sum of the last two payments which he is required to have made before that time;

(d)   that the creditor or owner is not already under a duty to give him notices under this section in relation to the agreement; and

(e)   if a judgment has been given in relation to the agreement before that time, that there is no sum still to be paid under the judgment by the debtor or hirer.

(2)   The creditor or owner—

(a)   shall, within the period of 14 days beginning with the day on which the conditions mentioned in subsection (1) are satisfied, give the debtor or hirer a notice under this section; and

(b)   after the giving of that notice, shall give him further notices under this section at intervals of not more than six months.

(3)   The duty of the creditor or owner to give the debtor or hirer notices under this section shall cease when either of the conditions mentioned in subsection (4) is satisfied; but if either of those conditions is satisfied before the notice required by subsection (2)(a) is given, the duty shall not cease until that notice is given.

(4)   The conditions referred to in subsection (3) are—

(a)   that the debtor or hirer ceases to be in arrears;

(b)   that a judgment is given in relation to the agreement under which a sum is required to be paid by the debtor or hirer.

(5)   For the purposes of subsection (4)(a) the debtor or hirer ceases to be in arrears when—

(a)   no [payments], which he has ever failed to [make] under the agreement when required, [are] still owing;

(b)   no default sum, which has ever become payable under the agreement in connection with his failure to pay any sum under the agreement when required, is still owing;

(c)   no sum of interest, which has ever become payable under the agreement in connection with such a default sum, is still owing; and

(d)   no other sum of interest, which has ever become payable under the agreement in connection with his failure to pay any sum under the agreement when required, is still owing.

(6)   A notice under this section shall include a copy of the current arrears information sheet under section 86A.

(7)   The debtor or hirer shall have no liability to pay any sum in connection with the preparation or the giving to him of a notice under this section.

(8)   Regulations may make provision about the form and content of notices under this section.

(9)   In the case of an applicable agreement under which the debtor or hirer must make all payments he is required to make at intervals of one week or less,

this section shall have effect as if in subsection (1)(a) and (c) for 'two' there were substituted 'four'.

(10)   If an agreement mentioned in subsection (9) was made before the beginning of the relevant period, only amounts resulting from failures by the debtor or hirer to make payments he is required to have made during that period shall be taken into account in determining any shortfall for the purposes of subsection (1)(c).

(11)   In subsection (10) 'relevant period' means the period of 20 weeks ending with the day on which the debtor or hirer is required to have made the most recent payment under the agreement.

(12)   In this section 'applicable agreement' means an agreement which—
(a)   is a regulated agreement for fixed-sum credit or a regulated consumer hire agreement; and
(b)   is neither a non-commercial agreement nor a small agreement.

[(13)   In this section—
(a)   'payments' in relation to an applicable agreement which is a regulated agreement for fixed-sum credit means payments to be made at predetermined intervals provided for under the terms of the agreement; and
(b)   'payments' in relation to an applicable agreement which is a regulated consumer hire agreement means any payments to be made by the hirer in relation to any period in consideration of the bailment or hiring to him of goods under the agreement.]]

[86C   Notice of sums in arrears under running-account credit agreements

(1)   This section applies where at any time the following conditions are satisfied—
(a)   that the debtor under an applicable agreement is required to have made at least two payments under the agreement before that time;
(b)   that the last two payments which he is required to have made before that time have not been made;
(c)   that the creditor has not already been required to give a notice under this section in relation to either of those payments; and
(d)   if a judgment has been given in relation to the agreement before that time, that there is no sum still to be paid under the judgment by the debtor.

(2)   The creditor shall, no later than the end of the period within which he is next required to give a statement under section 78(4) in relation to the agreement, give the debtor a notice under this section.

(3)   The notice shall include a copy of the current arrears information sheet under section 86A.

(4)   The notice may be incorporated in a statement or other notice which the creditor gives the debtor in relation to the agreement by virtue of another provision of this Act.

(5)   The debtor shall have no liability to pay any sum in connection with the preparation or the giving to him of the notice.

(6)   Regulations may make provision about the form and content of notices under this section.

(7)   In this section 'applicable agreement' means an agreement which—
(a)   is a regulated agreement for running-account credit; and
(b)   is neither a non-commercial agreement nor a small agreement.

[(8)   In this section 'payments' means payments to be made at predetermined intervals provided for under the terms of the agreement.]]

[86D   Failure to give notice of sums in arrears

(1)   This section applies where the creditor or owner under an agreement is under a duty to give the debtor or hirer notices under section 86B but fails to give him such a notice—
(a)   within the period mentioned in subsection (2)(a) of that section; or

(b)   within the period of six months beginning with the day after the day on which such a notice was last given to him.

(2)   This section also applies where the creditor under an agreement is under a duty to give the debtor a notice under section 86C but fails to do so before the end of the period mentioned in subsection (2) of that section.

(3)   The creditor or owner shall not be entitled to enforce the agreement during the period of non-compliance.

(4)   The debtor or hirer shall have no liability to pay—

(a)   any sum of interest to the extent calculated by reference to the period of non-compliance or to any part of it; or

(b)   any default sum which (apart from this paragraph)—

(i)   would have become payable during the period of non-compliance; or

(ii)   would have become payable after the end of that period in connection with a breach of the agreement which occurs during that period (whether or not the breach continues after the end of that period).

(5)   In this section 'the period of non-compliance' means, in relation to a failure to give a notice under section 86B or 86C to the debtor or hirer, the period which—

(a)   begins immediately after the end of the period mentioned in (as the case may be) subsection (1)(a) or (b) or (2); and

(b)   ends at the end of the day mentioned in subsection (6).

(6)   That day is—

(a)   in the case of a failure to give a notice under section 86B as mentioned in subsection (1)(a) of this section, the day on which the notice is given to the debtor or hirer;

(b)   in the case of a failure to give a notice under that section as mentioned in subsection (1)(b) of this section, the earlier of the following—

(i)   the day on which the notice is given to the debtor or hirer;

(ii)   the day on which the condition mentioned in subsection (4)(a) of that section is satisfied;

(c)   in the case of a failure to give a notice under section 86C, the day on which the notice is given to the debtor.]

[86E   Notice of default sums

(1)   This section applies where a default sum becomes payable under a regulated agreement by the debtor or hirer.

(2)   The creditor or owner shall, within the prescribed period after the default sum becomes payable, give the debtor or hirer a notice under this section.

(3)   The notice under this section may be incorporated in a statement or other notice which the creditor or owner gives the debtor or hirer in relation to the agreement by virtue of another provision of this Act.

(4)   The debtor or hirer shall have no liability to pay interest in connection with the default sum to the extent that the interest is calculated by reference to a period occurring before the 29th day after the day on which the debtor or hirer is given the notice under this section.

(5)   If the creditor or owner fails to give the debtor or hirer the notice under this section within the period mentioned in subsection (2), he shall not be entitled to enforce the agreement until the notice is given to the debtor or hirer.

(6)   The debtor or hirer shall have no liability to pay any sum in connection with the preparation or the giving to him of the notice under this section.

(7)   Regulations may—

(a)   provide that this section does not apply in relation to a default sum which is less than a prescribed amount;

(b)   make provision about the form and content of notices under this section.

(8)   This section does not apply in relation to a non-commercial agreement or to a small agreement.]

[86F   Interest on default sums

(1)   This section applies where a default sum becomes payable under a regulated agreement by the debtor or hirer.

(2)   The debtor or hirer shall only be liable to pay interest in connection with the default sum if the interest is simple interest.]]

Default notices

87   Need for default notice

(1)   Service of a notice on the debtor or hirer in accordance with section 88 (a 'default notice') is necessary before the creditor or owner can become entitled, by reason of any breach by the debtor or hirer of a regulated agreement,—

(a)   to terminate the agreement, or

(b)   to demand earlier payment of any sum, or

(c)   to recover possession of any goods or land, or

(d)   to treat any right conferred on the debtor or hirer by the agreement as terminated, restricted or deferred, or

(e)   to enforce any security.

(2)   Subsection (1) does not prevent the creditor from treating the right to draw upon any credit as restricted or deferred, and taking such steps as may be necessary to make the restriction or deferment effective.

(3)   The doing of an act by which a floating charge becomes fixed is not enforcement of a security.

(4)   Regulations may provide that section (1) is not to apply to agreements described by the regulations.

[(5)   Subsection (1)(d) does not apply in a case referred to in section 98A(4) (termination or suspension of debtor's right to draw on credit under open-end agreement).]

88   Contents and effect of default notice

(1)   The default notice must be in the prescribed form and specify—

(a)   the nature of the alleged breach;

(b)   if the breach is capable of remedy, what action is required to remedy it and the date before which that action is to be taken;

(c)   if the breach is not capable of remedy, the sum (if any) required to be paid as compensation for the breach, and the date before which it is to be paid.

(2)   A date specified under subsection (1) must not be less than [14] days after the date of service of the default notice, and the creditor or owner shall not take action such as is mentioned in section 87(1) before the date so specified or (if no requirement is made under subsection (1)) before those [14] days have elapsed.

(3)   The default notice must not treat as a breach failure to comply with a provision of the agreement which becomes operative only on breach of some other provision, but if the breach of that other provision is not duly remedied or compensation demanded under subsection (1) is not duly paid, or (where no requirement is made under subsection (1)) if the [14] days mentioned in subsection (2) have elapsed, the creditor or owner may treat the failure as a breach and section 87(1) shall not apply to it.

(4)   The default notice must contain information in the prescribed terms about the consequences of failure to comply with it [and any other prescribed matters relating to the agreement].

[(4A)   The default notice must also include a copy of the current default information sheet under section 86A.]

(5)   A default notice making a requirement under subsection (1) may include a provision for the taking of action such as is mentioned in section 87(1) at any time after the restriction imposed by subsection (2) will cease, together with a statement that the provision will be ineffective if the breach is duly remedied or the compensation duly paid.

89 Compliance with default notice
If before the date specified for that purpose in the default notice the debtor or hirer takes the action specified under section 88(1)(b) or (c) the breach shall be treated as not having occurred.

Further restriction of remedies for default

90 Retaking of protected hire-purchase etc goods
(1) At any time when—
(a) the debtor is in breach of a regulated hire-purchase or a regulated conditional sale agreement relating to goods, and
(b) the debtor has paid to the creditor one-third or more of the total price of the goods, and
(c) the property in the goods remains in the creditor,
the creditor is not entitled to recover possession of the goods from the debtor except on an order of the court.
(2) Where under a hire-purchase or conditional sale agreement the creditor is required to carry out any installation and the agreement specifies, as part of the total price, the amount to be paid in respect of the installation (the 'installation charge') the reference in subsection (1)(b) to one-third of the total price shall be construed as a reference to the aggregate of the installation charge and one-third of the remainder of the total price.
(3) In a case where—
(a) subsection (1)(a) is satisfied, but not subsection (1)(b), and
(b) subsection (1)(b) was satisfied on a previous occasion in relation to an earlier agreement, being a regulated hire-purchase or regulated conditional sale agreement, between the same parties, and relating to any of the goods comprised in the later agreement (whether or not other goods were also included),
subsection (1) shall apply to the later agreement with the omission of paragraph (b).
(4) If the later agreement is a modifying agreement, subsection (3) shall apply with the substitution, for the second reference to the later agreement, of a reference to the modifying agreement.
(5) Subsection (1) shall not apply, or shall cease to apply, to an agreement if the debtor has terminated, or terminates, the agreement.
(6) Where subsection (1) applies to an agreement at the death of the debtor, it shall continue to apply (in relation to the possessor of the goods) until the grant of probate or administration, or (in Scotland) confirmation (on which the personal representative would fall to be treated as the debtor).
(7) Goods falling within this section are in this Act referred to as 'protected goods'.

91 Consequences of breach of s 90
If goods are recovered by the creditor in contravention of section 90—
(a) the regulated agreement, if not previously terminated, shall terminate, and
(b) the debtor shall be released from all liability under the agreement, and shall be entitled to recover from the creditor all sums paid by the debtor under the agreement.

92 Recovery of possession of goods or land
(1) Except under an order of the court, the creditor or owner shall not be entitled to enter any premises to take possession of goods subject to a regulated hire-purchase agreement, regulated conditional sale agreement or regulated consumer hire agreement.
(2) At any time when the debtor is in breach of a regulated conditional sale

agreement relating to land, the creditor is entitled to recover possession of the land from the debtor, or any person claiming under him, on an order of the court only.

(3)   An entry in contravention of subsection (1) or (2) is actionable as a breach of statutory duty.

93   Interest not to be increased on default
The debtor under a regulated consumer credit agreement shall not be obliged to pay interest on sums which, in breach of the agreement, are unpaid by him at a rate—
  (a)   where the total charge for credit includes an item in respect of interest, exceeding the rate of that interest, or
  (b)   in any other case, exceeding what would be the rate of the total charge for credit if any items included in the total charge for credit by virtue of section 20(2) were disregarded.

[93A   Summary diligence not competent in Scotland
Summary diligence shall not be competent in Scotland to enforce payment of a debt due under a regulated agreement or under any security related thereto.]

Early payment by debtor

94   Right to complete payments ahead of time
(1)   The debtor under a regulated consumer credit agreement is entitled at any time, by notice to the creditor and the payment to the creditor of all amounts payable by the debtor to him under the agreement [and any amount which the creditor claims under section 95A(2)] (less any rebate allowable under section 95), to discharge the debtor's indebtedness under the agreement.

(2)   A notice under subsection (1) may embody the exercise by the debtor of any option to purchase goods conferred on him by the agreement, and deal with any other matter arising on, or in relation to, the termination of the agreement.

[(3)   The debtor under a regulated consumer credit agreement, other than an agreement secured on land, is entitled at any time to discharge part of his indebtedness by taking the steps in subsection (4).

(4)   The steps referred to in subsection (3) are as follows—
  (a)   he provides notice to the creditor,
  (b)   he pays to the creditor some of the amount payable by him to the creditor under the agreement before the time fixed by the agreement, and
  (c)   he makes the payment—
    (i)   before the end of the period of 28 days beginning with the day following that on which notice under paragraph (a) was received by the creditor, or
    (ii)   on or before any later date specified in the notice.

(5)   Where a debtor takes the steps in subsection (4) his indebtedness shall be discharged by an amount equal to the sum of the amount paid and any rebate allowable under section 95 less any amount which the creditor claims under section 95A(2).

(6)   A notice—
  (a)   under subsection (1), other than a notice relating to a regulated consumer credit agreement secured on land, or
  (b)   under subsection (4)(a),
need not be in writing.]

95   Rebate on early settlement
(1)   Regulations may provide for the allowance of a rebate of charges for credit to the debtor under a regulated consumer credit agreement where, under section 94, on refinancing, on breach of the agreement, or for any other reason, his indebtedness is discharged [or is discharged in part] or becomes payable before the

time fixed by the agreement, or any sum becomes payable by him before the time so fixed.

(2)   Regulations under subsection (1) may provide for calculation of the rebate by reference to any sums paid or payable by the debtor or his relative under or in connection with the agreement (whether to the creditor or some other person), including sums under linked transactions and other items in the total charge for credit.

[95A   Compensatory amount

(1)   This section applies where—

(a)   a regulated consumer credit agreement, other than an agreement secured on land, provides for the rate of interest on the credit to be fixed for a period of time, and

(b)   under section 94 the debtor discharges all or part of his indebtedness during that period.

(2)   The creditor may claim an amount equal to the cost which the creditor has incurred as a result only of the debtor's indebtedness being discharged during that period if—

(a)   the amount of the payment under section 94 exceeds £8,000 or, where more than one such payment is made in any 12 month period, the total of those payments exceeds £8,000,

(b)   the agreement is not a debtor-creditor agreement enabling the debtor to overdraw on a current account, and

(c)   the amount of the payment under section 94 is not paid from the proceeds of a contract of payment protection insurance.

(3)   The amount in subsection (2)—

(a)   must be fair,

(b)   must be objectively justified, and

(c)   must not exceed whichever is the higher of—

(i)   the relevant percentage of the amount of the payment under section 94, and

(ii)   the total amount of interest that would have been paid by the debtor under the agreement in the period from the date on which the debtor makes the payment under section 94 to the date fixed by the agreement for the discharge of the indebtedness of the debtor.

(4)   In subsection (3)(c)(i) 'relevant percentage' means—

(a)   1%, where the period from the date on which the debtor makes the payment under section 94 to the date fixed by the agreement for the discharge of the indebtedness of the debtor is more than one year, or

(b)   0.5%, where that period is equal to or less than one year.]

96   Effect on linked transactions

(1)   Where for any reason the indebtedness of the debtor under a regulated consumer credit agreement is discharged before the time fixed by the agreement, he, and any relative of his, shall at the same time be discharged from any liability under a linked transaction, other than a debt which has already become payable.

(2)   Subsection (1) does not apply to a linked transaction which is itself an agreement providing the debtor or his relative with credit.

(3)   Regulations may exclude linked transactions of the prescribed description from the operation of subsection (1).

97   Duty to give information

(1)   The creditor under a regulated consumer credit agreement, within the prescribed period after he has received a request [. . .] to that effect from the debtor, shall give the debtor a statement in the prescribed form indicating, according to the information to which it is practicable for him to refer, the amount of the pay-

ment required to discharge the debtor's indebtedness under the agreement, to-gether with the prescribed particulars showing how the amount is arrived at.

(2)   Subsection (1) does not apply to a request made less than one month after a previous request under that subsection relating to the same agreement was complied with.

[(2A)   A request under subsection (1) need not be in writing unless the agreement is secured on land.]

(3)   If the creditor fails to comply with subsection (1)—

(a)   he is not entitled, while the default continues, to enforce the agreement [. . .]

[97A Duty to give information on partial repayment

(1)   Where a debtor under a regulated consumer credit agreement—

(a)   makes a payment by virtue of which part of his indebtedness is discharged under section 94, and

(b)   at the same time or subsequently requests the creditor to give him a statement concerning the effect of the payment on the debtor's indebtedness,

the creditor must give the statement to the debtor before the end of the period of seven working days beginning with the day following that on which the creditor receives the request.

(2)   The statement shall be in writing and shall contain the following particulars—

(a)   a description of the agreement sufficient to identify it,

(b)   the name, postal address and, where appropriate, any other address of the creditor and the debtor,

(c)   where the creditor is claiming an amount under section 95A(2), that amount and the method used to determine it,

(d)   the amount of any rebate to which the debtor is entitled—

(i)   under the agreement, or

(ii)   by virtue of section 95 where that is higher,

(e)   where the amount of the rebate mentioned in paragraph (d)(ii) is given, a statement indicating that this amount has been calculated having regard to the Consumer Credit (Early Settlement) Regulations 2004,

(f)   where the debtor is not entitled to any rebate, a statement to this effect,

(g)   any change to—

(i)   the number, timing or amount of repayments to be made under the agreement, or

(ii)   the duration of the agreement,

which results from the partial discharge of the indebtedness of the debtor, and

(h)   the amount of the debtor's indebtedness remaining under the agreement at the date the creditor gives the statement.]

Termination of agreements

98 Duty to give notice of termination (non-default cases)

(1)   The creditor or owner is not entitled to terminate a regulated agreement except by or after giving the debtor or hirer not less than seven days' notice of the termination.

(2)   Subsection (1) applies only where—

(a)   a period for the duration of the agreement is specified in the agreement, and

(b)   that period has not ended when the creditor or owner does an act mentioned in subsection (1),

but so applies notwithstanding that, under the agreement, any party is entitled to terminate it before the end of the period so specified.

(3)   A notice under subsection (1) is ineffective if not in the prescribed form.

(4)   Subsection (1) does not prevent a creditor from treating the right to draw on any credit as restricted or deferred and taking such steps as may be necessary to make the restriction or deferment effective.

(5)   Regulations may provide that subsection (1) is not to apply to agreements described by the regulations.

(6)   Subsection (1) does not apply to the termination of a regulated agreement by reason of any breach by the debtor or hirer of the agreement.

[98A   Termination etc of open-end consumer credit agreements

(1)   The debtor under a regulated open-end consumer credit agreement, other than an excluded agreement, may by notice terminate the agreement, free of charge, at any time, subject to any period of notice not exceeding one month provided for by the agreement.

(2)   Notice under subsection (1) need not be in writing unless the creditor so requires.

(3)   Where a regulated open-end consumer credit agreement, other than an excluded agreement, provides for termination of the agreement by the creditor—
(a)   the termination must be by notice served on the debtor, and
(b)   the termination may not take effect until after the end of the period of two months, or such longer period as the agreement may provide, beginning with the day after the day on which notice is served.

(4)   Where a regulated open-end consumer credit agreement, other than an excluded agreement, provides for termination or suspension by the creditor of the debtor's right to draw on credit—
(a)   to terminate or suspend the right to draw on credit the creditor must serve a notice on the debtor before the termination or suspension or, if that is not practicable, immediately afterwards,
(b)   the notice must give reasons for the termination or suspension, and
(c)   the reasons must be objectively justified.

(5)   Subsection (4)(a) and (b) does not apply where giving the notice—
(a)   is prohibited by an EU obligation, or
(b)   would, or would be likely to, prejudice—
(i)   the prevention or detection of crime,
(ii)   the apprehension or prosecution of offenders, or
(iii)   the administration of justice.

(6)   An objectively justified reason under subsection (4)(c) may, for example, relate to—
(a)   the unauthorised or fraudulent use of credit, or
(b)   a significantly increased risk of the debtor being unable to fulfil his obligation to repay the credit.

(7)   Subsections (1) and (3) do not affect any right to terminate an agreement for breach of contract.

(8)   For the purposes of this section an agreement is an excluded agreement if it is—
(a)   an authorised non-business overdraft agreement,
(b)   an authorised business overdraft agreement,
(c)   a debtor-creditor agreement arising where the holder of a current account overdraws on the account without a pre-arranged overdraft or exceeds a pre-arranged overdraft limit, or
(d)   an agreement secured on land.]

99   Right to terminate hire-purchase etc agreements

(1)   At any time before the final payment by the debtor under a regulated hire-purchase or regulated conditional sale agreement falls due, the debtor shall be entitled to terminate the agreement by giving notice to any person entitled or authorised to receive the sums payable under the agreement.

(2)   Termination of an agreement under subsection (1) does not affect any liability under the agreement which has accrued before the termination.

(3)   Subsection (1) does not apply to a conditional sale agreement relating to land after the title to the land has passed to the debtor.

(4)   In the case of a conditional sale agreement relating to goods, where the property in the goods, having become vested in the debtor, is transferred to a person who does not become the debtor under the agreement, the debtor shall not thereafter be entitled to terminate the agreement under subsection (1).

(5)   Subject to subsection (4), where a debtor under a conditional sale agreement relating to goods terminates the agreement under this section after the property in the goods has become vested in him, the property in the goods shall thereupon vest in the person (the 'previous owner') in whom it was vested immediately before it became vested in the debtor:

Provided that if the previous owner has died, or any other event has occurred whereby that property, if vested in him immediately before that event, would thereupon have vested in some other person, the property shall be treated as having devolved as if it had been vested in the previous owner immediately before his death or immediately before that event, as the case may be.

100   Liability of debtor on termination of hire-purchase etc agreement

(1)   Where a regulated hire-purchase or regulated conditional sale agreement is terminated under section 99 the debtor shall be liable, unless the agreement provides for a smaller payment, or does not provide for any payment, to pay to the creditor the amount (if any) by which one-half of the total price exceeds the aggregate of the sums paid and the sums due in respect of the total price immediately before the termination.

(2)   Where under a hire-purchase or conditional sale agreement the creditor is required to carry out any installation and the agreement specifies, as part of the total price, the amount to be paid in respect of the installation (the 'installation charge') the reference in subsection (1) to one-half of the total price shall be construed as a reference to the aggregate of the installation charge and one-half of the remainder of the total price.

(3)   If in any action the court is satisfied that a sum less than the amount specified in subsection (1) would be equal to the loss sustained by the creditor in consequence of the termination of the agreement by the debtor, the court may make an order for the payment of that sum in lieu of the amount specified in subsection (1).

(4)   If the debtor has contravened an obligation to take reasonable care of the goods or land, the amount arrived at under subsection (1) shall be increased by the sum required to recompense the creditor for that contravention, and subsection (2) shall have effect accordingly.

(5)   Where the debtor, on the termination of the agreement, wrongfully retains possession of goods to which the agreement relates, then, in any action brought by the creditor to recover possession of the goods from the debtor, the court, unless it is satisfied that having regard to the circumstances it would not be just to do so, shall order the goods to be delivered to the creditor without giving the debtor an option to pay the value of the goods.

101   Right to terminate hire agreement

(1)   The hirer under a regulated consumer hire agreement is entitled to terminate the agreement by giving notice to any person entitled or authorised to receive the sums payable under the agreement.

(2)   Termination of an agreement under subsection (1) does not affect any liability under the agreement which has accrued before the termination.

(3)   A notice under subsection (1) shall not expire earlier than eighteen months after the making of the agreement, but apart from that the minimum period of

notice to be given under subsection (1), unless the agreement provides for a shorter period, is as follows.

(4) If the agreement provides for the making of payments by the hirer to the owner at equal intervals, the minimum period of notice is the length of one interval or three months, whichever is less.

(5) If the agreement provides for the making of such payments at differing intervals, the minimum period of notice is the length of the shortest interval or three months, whichever is less.

(6) In any other case, the minimum period of notice is three months.

(7) This section does not apply to—

(a) any agreement which provides for the making by the hirer of payments which in total (and without breach of the agreement) exceed [£1,500] in any year, or

(b) any agreement where—

(i) goods are bailed or (in Scotland) hired to the hirer for the purposes of a business carried on by him, or the hirer holds himself out as requiring the goods for those purposes, and

(ii) the goods are selected by the hirer, and acquired by the owner for the purposes of the agreement at the request of the hirer from any person other than the owner's associate, or

(c) any agreement where the hirer requires, or holds himself out as requiring, the goods for the purpose of bailing or hiring them to other persons in the course of a business carried on by him.

(8) If, on an application made to the [OFT] by a person carrying on a consumer hire business, it appears to the [OFT] that it would be in the interest of hirers to do so, [it] may by notice to the applicant direct that [, subject to such conditions (if any) as it may specify, this section shall not apply to consumer hire agreements made by the applicant; and this Act shall have effect accordingly].

[(8A) If it appears to the OFT that it would be in the interest of hirers to do so, it may by general notice direct that, subject to such conditions (if any) as it may specify, this section shall not apply to a consumer hire agreement if the agreement falls within a specified description; and this Act shall have effect accordingly.]

(9) In the case of a modifying agreement, subsection (3) shall apply with the substitution for 'the making of the agreement' of 'the making of the original agreement'.

102 Agency for receiving notice of rescission

(1) Where the debtor or hirer under a regulated agreement claims to have a right to rescind the agreement, each of the following shall be deemed to be the agent of the creditor owner for the purpose of receiving any notice rescinding the agreement which is served by the debtor or hirer—

(a) a credit-broker or supplier who was the negotiator in antecedent negotiations, and

(b) any person who, in the course of a business carried on by him, acted on behalf of the debtor or hirer in any negotiations for the agreement.

(2) In subsection (1) 'rescind' does not include—

(a) service of a notice of cancellation, or

(b) termination of an agreement under section 99 or 101 or by the exercise of a right or power in that behalf expressly conferred by the agreement.

103 Termination statements

(1) If an individual (the 'customer') serves on any person (the 'trader') a notice—

(a) stating that—

(i) the customer was the debtor or hirer under a regulated agreement described in the notice, and the trader was the creditor or owner under the agreement, and

(ii) the customer has discharged his indebtedness to the trader under the agreement, and

(iii) the agreement has ceased to have any operation; and

(b) requiring the trader to give the customer a notice, signed by or on behalf of the trader, confirming that those statements are correct,

the trader shall, within the prescribed period after receiving the notice, either comply with it or serve on the customer a counter-notice stating that, as the case may be, he disputes the correctness of the notice or asserts that the customer is not indebted to him under the agreement.

(2) Where the trader disputes the correctness of the notice he shall give particulars of the way in which he alleges it to be wrong.

(3) Subsection (1) does not apply in relation to any agreement if the trader has previously complied with that subsection on the service of a notice under it with respect to that agreement.

(4) Subsection (1) does not apply to a non-commercial agreement.

[. . .]

[(6) A breach of the duty imposed by subsection (1) is actionable as a breach of statutory duty.]

104 Goods not to be treated as subject to landlord's hypothec in Scotland

Goods comprised in a hire-purchase agreement or goods comprised in a conditional sale agreement which have not become vested in the debtor shall not be treated in Scotland as subject to the landlord's hypothec—

(a) during the period between the service of a default notice in respect of the goods and the date on which the notice expires or is earlier complied with; or

(b) if the agreement is enforceable on an order of the court only, during the period between the commencement and termination of an action by the creditor to enforce the agreement.

PART VIII
SECURITY

General

105 Form and content of securities

(1) Any security provided in relation to a regulated agreement shall be expressed in writing.

(2) Regulations may prescribe the form and content of documents ('security instruments') to be made in compliance with subsection (1).

(3) Regulations under subsection (2) may in particular—

(a) require specified information to be included in the prescribed manner in documents, and other specified material to be excluded;

(b) contain requirements to ensure that specified information is clearly brought to the attention of the surety, and that one part of a document is not given insufficient or excessive prominence compared with another.

(4) A security instrument is not properly executed unless—

(a) a document in the prescribed form, itself containing all the prescribed terms and conforming to regulations under subsection (2), is signed in the prescribed manner by or on behalf of the surety, and

(b) the document embodies all the terms of the security, other than implied terms, and

(c) the document, when presented or sent for the purpose of being signed by or on behalf of the surety, is in such state that its terms are readily legible, and

(d) when the document is presented or sent for the purpose of being signed by or on behalf of the surety there is also presented or sent a copy of the document.

(5)   A security instrument is not properly executed unless—

(a)   where the security is provided after, or at the time when, the regulated agreement is made, a copy of the executed agreement, together with a copy of any other document referred to in it, is given to the surety at the time the security is provided, or

(b)   where the security is provided before the regulated agreement is made, a copy of the executed agreement, together with a copy of any other document referred to in it, is given to the surety within seven days after the regulated agreement is made.

(6)   Subsection (1) does not apply to a security provided by the debtor or hirer.

(7)   If—

(a)   in contravention of subsection (1) a security is not expressed in writing, or

(b)   a security instrument is improperly executed,

the security, so far as provided in relation to a regulated agreement, is enforceable against the surety on an order of the court only.

(8)   If an application for an order under subsection (7) is dismissed (except on technical grounds only) section 106 (ineffective securities) shall apply to the security.

(9)   Regulations under section 60(1) shall include provision requiring documents embodying regulated agreements also to embody any security provided in relation to a regulated agreement by the debtor or hirer.

106   Ineffective securities

Where, under any provision of this Act, this section is applied to any security provided in relation to a regulated agreement, then, subject to section 177 (saving for registered charges)—

(a)   the security, so far as it is so provided, shall be treated as never having effect;

(b)   any property lodged with the creditor or owner solely for the purposes of the security as so provided shall be returned by him forthwith;

(c)   the creditor or owner shall take any necessary action to remove or cancel an entry in any register, so far as the entry relates to the security as so provided; and

(d)   any amount received by the creditor or owner on realisation of the security shall, so far as it is referable to the agreement, be repaid to the surety.

107   Duty to give information to surety under fixed-sum credit agreement

(1)   The creditor under a regulated agreement for fixed-sum credit in relation to which security is provided, within the prescribed period after receiving a request in writing to that effect from the surety and payment of a fee of [£1], shall give to the surety (if a different person from the debtor)—

(a)   a copy of the executed agreement (if any) and of any other document referred to in it;

(b)   a copy of the security instrument (if any); and

(c)   a statement signed by or on behalf of the creditor showing, according to the information to which it is practicable for him to refer,—

(i)   the total sum paid under the agreement by the debtor,

(ii)   the total sum which has become payable under the agreement by the debtor but remains unpaid, and the various amounts comprised in that total sum, with the date when each became due, and

(iii)   the total sum which is to become payable under the agreement by the debtor, and the various amounts comprised in that total sum, with the date, or mode of determining the date, when each becomes due.

(2)   If the creditor possesses insufficient information to enable him to ascertain the amounts and dates mentioned in subsection (1)(c)(iii), he shall be taken to

comply with that sub-paragraph if his statement under subsection (1)(c) gives the basis on which, under the regulated agreement, they would fall to be ascertained.

(3)   Subsection (1) does not apply to—

(a)   an agreement under which no sum is, or will or may become, payable by the debtor, or

(b)   a request made less than one month after a previous request under that subsection relating to the same agreement was complied with.

(4)   If the creditor under an agreement fails to comply with subsection (1)—

(a)   he is not entitled, while the default continues, to enforce the security, so far as provided in relation to the agreement [. . .]

(5)   This section does not apply to a non-commercial agreement.

108   Duty to give information to surety under running-account credit agreement

(1)   The creditor under a regulated agreement for running-account credit in relation to which security is provided, within the prescribed period after receiving a request in writing to that effect from the surety and payment of a fee of [£1], shall give to the surety (if a different person from the debtor)—

(a)   a copy of the executed agreement (if any) and of any other document referred to in it;

(b)   a copy of the security instrument (if any); and

(c)   a statement signed by or on behalf of the creditor showing, according to the information to which it is practicable for him to refer,—

(i)   the state of the account, and

(ii)   the amount if any, currently payable under the agreement by the debtor to the creditor, and

(iii)   the amounts and due dates of any payments which, if the debtor does not draw further on the account, will later become payable under the agreement by the debtor to the creditor.

(2)   If the creditor possesses insufficient information to enable him to ascertain the amounts and dates mentioned in subsection (1)(c)(iii), he shall be taken to comply with that sub-paragraph if his statement under subsection (1)(c) gives the basis on which, under the regulated agreement, they would fall to be ascertained.

(3)   Subsection (1) does not apply to—

(a)   an agreement under which no sum is, or will or may become, payable by the debtor, or

(b)   a request made less than one month after a previous request under that subsection relating to the same agreement was complied with.

(4)   If the creditor under an agreement fails to comply with subsection (1)—

(a)   he is not entitled, while the default continues, to enforce the security, so far as provided in relation to the agreement [. . .]

(5)   This section does not apply to a non-commercial agreement.

109   Duty to give information to surety under consumer hire agreement

(1)   The owner under a regulated consumer hire agreement in relation to which security is provided, within the prescribed period after receiving a request in writing to that effect from the surety and payment of a fee of [£1], shall give to the surety (if a different person from the hirer)—

(a)   a copy of the executed agreement and of any other document referred to in it;

(b)   a copy of the security instrument (if any); and

(c)   a statement signed by or on behalf of the owner showing, according to the information to which it is practicable for him to refer, the total sum which has become payable under the agreement by the hirer but remains unpaid and the various amounts comprised in that total sum, with the date when each became due.

(2)   Subsection (1) does not apply to—
   (a)   an agreement under which no sum is, or will or may become, payable by the hirer, or
   (b)   a request made less than one month after a previous request under that subsection relating to the same agreement was complied with.
(3)   If the owner under an agreement fails to comply with subsection (1)—
   (a)   he is not entitled, while the default continues, to enforce the security, so far as provided in relation to the agreement [. . .]
(4)   This section does not apply to a non-commercial agreement.

110   Duty to give information to debtor or hirer
(1)   The creditor or owner under a regulated agreement, within the prescribed period after receiving a request in writing to that effect from the debtor or hirer and payment of a fee of [£1], shall give the debtor or hirer a copy of any security instrument executed in relation to the agreement after the making of the agreement.
(2)   Subsection (1) does not apply to—
   (a)   a non-commercial agreement, or
   (b)   an agreement under which no sum is, or will or may become, payable by the debtor or hirer, or
   (c)   a request made less than one month after a previous request under subsection (1) relating to the same agreement was complied with.
(3)   If the creditor or owner under an agreement fails to comply with subsection (1)—
   (a)   he is not entitled, while the default continues, to enforce the security (so far as provided in relation to the agreement) [. . .]

111   Duty to give surety copy of default etc notice
(1)   When a default notice or a notice under section 76(1) or 98(1) is served on a debtor or hirer, a copy of the notice shall be served by the creditor or owner on any surety (if a different person from the debtor or hirer).
(2)   If the creditor or owner fails to comply with subsection (1) in the case of any surety, the security is enforceable against the surety (in respect of the breach or other matter to which the notice relates) on an order of the court only.

112   Realisation of securities
Subject to section 121, regulations may provide for any matters relating to the sale or other realisation, by the creditor or owner, of property over which any right has been provided by way of security in relation to an actual or prospective regulated agreement, other than a non-commercial agreement.

113   Act not to be evaded by use of security
(1)   Where a security is provided in relation to an actual or prospective regulated agreement, the security shall not be enforced so as to benefit the creditor or owner, directly or indirectly, to an extent greater (whether as respects the amount of any payment or the time or manner of its being made) than would be the case if the security were not provided and any obligations of the debtor or hirer, or his relative, under or in relation to the agreement were carried out to the extent (if any) to which they would be enforced under this Act.
(2)   In accordance with subsection (1), where a regulated agreement is enforceable on an order of the court or the [OFT] only, any security provided in relation to the agreement is enforceable (so far as provided in relation to the agreement) where such an order has been made in relation to the agreement, but not otherwise.
(3)   Where—
   (a)   a regulated agreement is cancelled under section 69(1) or becomes subject to section 69(2), or
   (b)   a regulated agreement is terminated under section 91, or

(c)   in relation to any agreement an application for an order under section 40(2), 65(1), 124(1) or 149(2) is dismissed (except on technical grounds only), or

(d)   a declaration is made by the court under section 142(1) (refusal of enforcement order) as respects any regulated agreement,

section 106 shall apply to any security provided in relation to the agreement.

(4)   Where subsection (3)(d) applies and the declaration relates to a part only of the regulated agreement, section 106 shall apply to the security only so far as it concerns that part.

(5)   In the case of a cancelled agreement, the duty imposed on the debtor or hirer by section 71 or 72 shall not be enforceable before the creditor or owner has discharged any duty imposed on him by section 106 (as applied by subsection (3)(a)).

(6)   If the security is provided in relation to a prospective agreement or transaction, the security shall be enforceable in relation to the agreement or transaction only after the time (if any) when the agreement is made; and until that time the person providing the security shall be entitled, by notice to the creditor or owner, to require that section 106 shall thereupon apply to the security.

(7)   Where an indemnity [or guarantee] is given in a case where the debtor or hirer is a minor, or [an indemnity is given in a case where he] is otherwise not of full capacity, the reference in subsection (1) to the extent to which his obligations would be enforced shall be read in relation to the indemnity [or guarantee] as a reference to the extent to which [those obligations] would be enforced if he were of full capacity.

(8)   Subsections (1) and (3) also apply where a security is provided in relation to an actual or prospective linked transaction, and in that case—

(a)   references to the agreement shall be read as references to the linked transaction, and

(b)   references to the creditor or owner shall be read as references to any person (other than the debtor or hirer, or his relative) who is a party, or prospective party, to the linked transaction.

Pledges

114   Pawn-receipts

(1)   At the time he receives the article, a person who takes any article in pawn under a regulated agreement shall give to the person from whom he receives it a receipt in the prescribed form (a 'pawn-receipt').

(2)   A person who takes any article in pawn from an individual whom he knows to be, or who appears to be and is, a minor commits an offence.

(3)   This section and sections 115 to 122 do not apply to—

(a)   a pledge of documents of title [or of bearer bonds], or

(b)   a non-commercial agreement.

115   Penalty for failure to supply copies of pledge agreement, etc

If the creditor under a regulated agreement to take any article in pawn fails to observe the requirements of section 62 to 64 or 114(1) in relation to the agreement he commits an offence.

116   Redemption period

(1)   A pawn is redeemable at any time within six months after it was taken.

(2)   Subject to subsection (1), the period within which a pawn is redeemable shall be the same as the period fixed by the parties for the duration of the credit secured by the pledge, or such longer period as they may agree.

(3)   If the pawn is not redeemed by the end of the period laid down by subsections (1) and (2) (the 'redemption period'), it nevertheless remains redeemable until it is realised by the pawnee under section 121 except where under section 120(1)(a) the property in it passes to the pawnee.

(4)   No special charge shall be made for redemption of a pawn after the end of the redemption period, and charges in respect of the safe keeping of the pawn shall not be at a higher rate after the end of the redemption period than before.

117   Redemption procedure

(1)   On surrender of the pawn-receipt, and payment of the amount owing, at any time when the pawn is redeemable, the pawnee shall deliver the pawn to the bearer of the pawn-receipt.

(2)   Subsection (1) does not apply if the pawnee knows or has reasonable cause to suspect that the bearer of the pawn-receipt is neither the owner of the pawn nor authorised by the owner to redeem it.

(3)   The pawnee is not liable to any person in tort or delict for delivering the pawn where subsection (1) applies, or refusing to deliver it where the person demanding delivery does not comply with subsection (1) or, by reason of subsection (2), subsection (1) does not apply.

118   Loss etc of pawn-receipt

(1)   A person (the 'claimant') who is not in possession of the pawn-receipt but claims to be the owner of the pawn, or to be otherwise entitled or authorised to redeem it, may do so at any time when it is redeemable by tendering to the pawnee in place of the pawn-receipt—

(a)   a statutory declaration made by the claimant in the prescribed form, and with the prescribed contents, or

(b)   where the pawn is security for fixed-sum credit not exceeding [£75] or running-account credit on which the credit limit does not exceed [£75], and the pawnee agrees, a statement in writing in the prescribed form, and with the prescribed contents, signed by the claimant.

(2)   On compliance by the claimant with subsection (1), section 117 shall apply as if the declaration or statement were the pawn-receipt, and the pawn-receipt itself shall become inoperative for the purposes of section 117.

119   Unreasonable refusal to deliver pawn

(1)   If a person who has taken a pawn under a regulated agreement refuses without reasonable cause to allow the pawn to be redeemed, he commits an offence.

(2)   On the conviction in England and Wales of a pawnee under subsection (1) where the offence does not amount to theft, [section 148 of the Powers of Criminal Courts (Sentencing) Act 2000 (restitution orders)] shall apply as if the pawnee had been convicted of stealing the pawn.

(3)   On the conviction in Northern Ireland of a pawnee under subsection (1) where the offence does not amount to theft, section 27 (orders for restitution) of the Theft Act (Northern Ireland) 1969, and any provision of the Theft Act (Northern Ireland) 1969 relating to that section, shall apply as if the pawnee had been convicted of stealing the pawn.

120   Consequence of failure to redeem

(1)   If at the end of the redemption period the pawn has not been redeemed—

(a)   notwithstanding anything in section 113, the property in the pawn passes to the pawnee where—

[(i)   the redemption period is six months,

(ii)   the pawn is security for fixed-sum credit not exceeding £75 or running-account credit on which the credit limit does not exceed £75, and

(iii)   the pawn was not immediately before the making of the regulated consumer credit agreement a pawn under another regulated consumer credit agreement in respect of which the debtor has discharged his indebtedness in part under section 94(3); or]

(b)   in any other case the pawn becomes realisable by the pawnee.

(2)   Where the debtor or hirer is entitled to apply to the court for a time order

under section 129, subsection (1) shall apply with the substitution, for 'at the end of the redemption period' of 'after the expiry of five days following the end of the redemption period'.

121 Realisation of pawn

(1) When a pawn has become realisable by him, the pawnee may sell it, after giving to the pawnor (except in such cases as may be prescribed) not less than the prescribed period of notice of the intention to sell, indicating in the notice the asking price and such other particulars as may be prescribed.

(2) Within the prescribed period after the sale takes place, the pawnee shall give the pawnor the prescribed information in writing as to the sale, its proceeds and expenses.

(3) Where the net proceeds of sale are not less than the sum which, if the pawn had been redeemed on the date of the sale, would have been payable for its redemption, the debt secured by the pawn is discharged and any surplus shall be paid by the pawnee to the pawnor.

(4) Where subsection (3) does not apply, the debt shall be treated as from the date of sale as equal to the amount by which the net proceeds of sale fall short of the sum which would have been payable for the redemption of the pawn on that date.

(5) In this section the 'net proceeds of sale' is the amount realised (the 'gross amount') less the expenses (if any) of the sale.

(6) If the pawnor alleges that the gross amount is less than the true market value of the pawn on the date of sale, it is for the pawnee to prove that he and any agents employed by him in the sale used reasonable care to ensure that the true market value was obtained, and if he fails to do so subsections (3) and (4) shall have effect as if the reference in subsection (5) to the gross amount were a reference to the true market value.

(7) If the pawnor alleges that the expenses of the sale were unreasonably high, it is for the pawnee to prove that they were reasonable, and if he fails to do so subsections (3) and (4) shall have effect as if the reference in subsection (5) to expenses were a reference to reasonable expenses.

122 Order in Scotland to deliver pawn

(1) As respects Scotland where—
    (a) a pawn is either—
        (i) an article which has been stolen, or
        (ii) an article which has been obtained by fraud, and a person is convicted
    of any offence in relation to the theft or, as the case may be, the fraud; or
    (b) a person is convicted of an offence under section 119(1), the court by which that person is so convicted may order delivery of the pawn to the owner or the person otherwise entitled thereto.

(2) A court making an order under subsection (1)(a) for delivery of a pawn may make the order subject to such conditions as to payment of the debt secured by the pawn as it thinks fit.

Negotiable instruments

123 Restrictions on taking and negotiating instruments

(1) A creditor or owner shall not take a negotiable instrument, other than a bank note or cheque, in discharge of any sum payable—
    (a) by the debtor or hirer under a regulated agreement, or
    (b) by any person as surety in relation to the agreement.

(2) The creditor or owner shall not negotiate a cheque taken by him in discharge of a sum payable as mentioned in subsection (1) except to a banker (within the meaning of the Bills of Exchange Act 1882).

(3)   The creditor or owner shall not take a negotiable instrument as security for the discharge of any sum payable as mentioned in subsection (1).

(4)   A person takes a negotiable instrument as security for the discharge of a sum if the sum is intended to be paid in some other way, and the negotiable instrument is to be presented for payment only if the sum is not paid in that way.

(5)   This section does not apply where the regulated agreement is a non-commercial agreement.

(6)   The Secretary of State may by order provide that this section shall not apply where the regulated agreement has a connection with a country outside the United Kingdom.

124   Consequences of breach of s 123

(1)   After any contravention of section 123 has occurred in relation to a sum payable as mentioned in section 123(1)(a), the agreement under which the sum is payable is enforceable against the debtor or hirer on an order of the court only.

(2)   After any contravention of section 123 has occurred in relation to a sum payable by any surety, the security is enforceable on an order of the court only.

(3)   Where an application for an order under subsection (2) is dismissed (except on technical grounds only) section 106 shall apply to the security.

125   Holders in due course

(1)   A person who takes a negotiable instrument in contravention of section 123(1) or (3) is not a holder in due course, and is not entitled to enforce the instrument.

(2)   Where a person negotiates a cheque in contravention of section 123(2), his doing so constitutes a defect in his title within the meaning of the Bills of Exchange Act 1882.

(3)   If a person mentioned in section 123(1)(a) and (b) ('the protected person') becomes liable to a holder in due course of an instrument taken from the protected person in contravention of section 123(1) or (3), or taken from the protected person and negotiated in contravention of section 123(2), the creditor or owner shall indemnify the protected person in respect of that liability.

(4)   Nothing in this Act affects the rights of the holder in due course of any negotiable instrument.

Land mortgages

126   Enforcement of land mortgages

A land mortgage securing a regulated agreement is enforceable (so far as provided in relation to the agreement) on an order of the court only.

PART IX
JUDICIAL CONTROL

Enforcement of certain regulated agreements and securities

127   Enforcement orders in cases of infringement

(1)   In the case of an application for an enforcement order under—

[(za)   section 55(2) (disclosure of information), or]

[(zb)   section 61B(3) (duty to supply copy of overdraft agreement), or]

(a)   section 65(1) (improperly executed agreements), or

(b)   section 105(7)(a) or (b) (improperly executed security instruments), or

(c)   section 111(2) (failure to serve copy of notice on surety), or

(d)   section 124(1) or (2) (taking of negotiable instrument in contravention of section 123),

the court shall dismiss the application if, but [. . .] only if, it considers it just to do so having regard to—

(i) prejudice caused to any person by the contravention in question, and the degree of culpability for it; and

(ii) the powers conferred on the court by subsection (2) and sections 135 and 136.

(2) If it appears to the court just to do so, it may in an enforcement order reduce or discharge any sum payable by the debtor or hirer, or any surety, so as to compensate him for prejudice suffered as a result of the contravention in question.

[. . .]

128   Enforcement orders on death of debtor or hirer

The court shall make an order under section 86(2) if, but only if, the creditor or owner proves that he has been unable to satisfy himself that the present and future obligations of the debtor or hirer under the agreement are likely to be discharged.

Extension of time

129   Time orders

(1) [Subject to subsection (3) below,] if it appears to the court just to do so—

(a) on an application for an enforcement order; or

(b) on an application made by a debtor or hirer under this paragraph after service on him of—

(i) a default notice, or

(ii) a notice under section 76(1) or 98(1); or

[(ba) on an application made by a debtor or hirer under this paragraph after he has been given a notice under section 86B or 86C; or]

(c) in an action brought by a creditor or owner to enforce a regulated agreement or any security, or recover possession of any goods or land to which a regulated agreement relates,

the court may make an order under this section (a 'time order').

(2) A time order shall provide for one or both of the following, as the court considers just—

(a) the payment by the debtor or hirer or any surety of any sum owed under a regulated agreement or a security by such instalments, payable at such times, as the court having regard to the means of the debtor or hirer and any surety, considers reasonable;

(b) the remedying by the debtor or hirer of any breach of a regulated agreement (other than non-payment of money) within such period as the court may specify.

[(3) Where in Scotland a time to pay direction or a time order has been made in relation to a debt, it shall not thereafter be competent to make a time order in relation to the same debt.]

[129A   Debtor or hirer to give notice of intent etc to creditor or owner

(1) A debtor or hirer may make an application under section 129(1)(ba) in relation to a regulated agreement only if—

(a) following his being given the notice under section 86B or 86C, he gave a notice within subsection (2) to the creditor or owner; and

(b) a period of at least 14 days has elapsed after the day on which he gave that notice to the creditor or owner.

(2) A notice is within this subsection if it—

(a) indicates that the debtor or hirer intends to make the application;

(b) indicates that he wants to make a proposal to the creditor or owner in relation to his making of payments under the agreement; and

(c) gives details of that proposal.]

130   Supplemental provisions about time orders

(1) Where in accordance with rules of court an offer to pay any sum by instalments is made by the debtor or hirer and accepted by the creditor or owner, the

court may in accordance with rules of court make a time order under section 129(2)(a) giving effect to the offer without hearing evidence of means.

(2)   In the case of a hire-purchase or conditional sale agreement only, a time order under section 129(2)(a) may deal with sums which, although not payable by the debtor at the time the order is made, would if the agreement continued in force become payable under it subsequently.

(3)   A time order under section 129(2)(a) shall not be made where the regulated agreement is secured by a pledge if, by virtue of regulations made under section 76(5), 87(4) or 98(5), service of a notice is not necessary for enforcement of the pledge.

(4)   Where, following the making of a time order in relation to a regulated hire-purchase or conditional sale agreement or a regulated consumer hire agreement, the debtor or hirer is in possession of the goods, he shall be treated (except in the case of a debtor to whom the creditor's title has passed) as a bailee or (in Scotland) a custodier of the goods under the terms of the agreement, notwithstanding that the agreement has been terminated.

(5)   Without prejudice to anything done by the creditor or owner before the commencement of the period specified in a time order made under section 129(2)(b) ('the relevant period'),—

(a)   he shall not while the relevant period subsists take in relation to the agreement any action such as is mentioned in section 87(1);

(b)   where—

(i)   a provision of the agreement ('the secondary provision') becomes operative only on breach of another provision of the agreement ('the primary provision'), and

(ii)   the time order provides for the remedying of such a breach of the primary provision within the relevant period,

he shall not treat the secondary provision as operative before the end of that period;

(c)   if while the relevant period subsists the breach to which the order relates is remedied it shall be treated as not having occurred.

(6)   On the application of any person affected by a time order, the court may vary or revoke the order.

[Interest

[130A   Interest payable on judgment debts etc

(1)   If the creditor or owner under a regulated agreement wants to be able to recover from the debtor or hirer post-judgment interest in connection with a sum that is required to be paid under a judgment given in relation to the agreement (the 'judgment sum'), he—

(a)   after the giving of that judgment, shall give the debtor or hirer a notice under this section (the 'first required notice'); and

(b)   after the giving of the first required notice, shall give the debtor or hirer further notices under this section at intervals of not more than six months.

(2)   The debtor or hirer shall have no liability to pay post-judgment interest in connection with the judgment sum to the extent that the interest is calculated by reference to a period occurring before the day on which he is given the first required notice.

(3)   If the creditor or owner fails to give the debtor or hirer a notice under this section within the period of six months beginning with the day after the day on which such a notice was last given to the debtor or hirer, the debtor or hirer shall have no liability to pay post-judgment interest in connection with the judgment sum to the extent that the interest is calculated by reference to the whole or to a part of the period which—

(a)   begins immediately after the end of that period of six months; and

(b)   ends at the end of the day on which the notice is given to the debtor or hirer.

(4)   The debtor or hirer shall have no liability to pay any sum in connection with the preparation or the giving to him of a notice under this section.

(5)   A notice under this section may be incorporated in a statement or other notice which the creditor or owner gives the debtor or hirer in relation to the agreement by virtue of another provision of this Act.

(6)   Regulations may make provision about the form and content of notices under this section.

(7)   This section does not apply in relation to post-judgment interest which is required to be paid by virtue of any of the following—

(a)   section 4 of the Administration of Justice (Scotland) Act 1972;

(b)   Article 127 of the Judgments Enforcement (Northern Ireland) Order 1981;

(c)   section 74 of the County Courts Act 1984.

(8)   This section does not apply in relation to a non-commercial agreement or to a small agreement.

(9)   In this section 'post-judgment interest' means interest to the extent calculated by reference to a period occurring after the giving of the judgment under which the judgment sum is required to be paid.]]

Protection of property pending proceedings

131   Protection orders

The court, on application of the creditor or owner under a regulated agreement, may make such orders as it thinks just for protecting any property of the creditor or owner, or property subject to any security, from damage or depreciation pending the determination of any proceedings under this Act, including orders restricting or prohibiting use of the property or giving directions as to its custody.

Hire and hire-purchase etc agreements

132   Financial relief for hirer

(1)   Where the owner under a regulated consumer hire agreement recovers possession of goods to which the agreement relates otherwise than by action, the hirer may apply to the court for an order that—

(a)   the whole or part of any sum paid by the hirer to the owner in respect of the goods shall be repaid, and

(b)   the obligation to pay the whole or part of any sum owed by the hirer to the owner in respect of the goods shall cease,

and if it appears to the court just to do so, having regard to the extent of the enjoyment of the goods by the hirer, the court shall grant the application in full or in part.

(2)   Where in proceedings relating to a regulated consumer hire agreement the court makes an order for the delivery to the owner of goods to which the agreement relates the court may include in the order the like provision as may be made in an order under subsection (1).

133   Hire-purchase etc agreements: special powers of court

(1)   If, in relation to a regulated hire-purchase or conditional sale agreement, it appears to the court just to do so—

(a)   on an application for an enforcement order or time order; or

(b)   in an action brought by the creditor to recover possession of goods to which the agreement relates,

the court may—

(i)   make an order (a 'return order') for the return to the creditor of goods to which the agreement relates;

(ii)   make an order (a 'transfer order') for the transfer to the debtor of the creditor's title to certain goods to which the agreement relates ('the transferred goods'), and the return to the creditor of the remainder of the goods.

(2)   In determining for the purposes of this section how much of the total price has been paid ('the paid-up sum'), the court may—

(a)   treat any sum paid by the debtor, or owed by the creditor, in relation to the goods as part of the paid-up sum;

(b)   deduct any sum owed by the debtor in relation to the goods (otherwise than as part of the total price) from the paid-up sum,

and make corresponding reductions in amounts so owed.

(3)   Where a transfer order is made, the transferred goods shall be such of the goods to which the agreement relates as the court thinks just; but a transfer order shall be made only where the paid-up sum exceeds the part of the total price referable to the transferred goods by an amount equal to at least one-third of the unpaid balance of the total price.

(4)   Notwithstanding the making of a return order or transfer order, the debtor may at any time before the goods enter the possession of the creditor, on payment of the balance of the total price and the fulfilment of any other necessary conditions, claim the goods ordered to be returned to the creditor.

(5)   When, in pursuance of a time order or under this section, the total price of goods under a regulated hire-purchase agreement or regulated conditional sale agreement is paid and any other necessary conditions are fulfilled, the creditor's title to the goods vests in the debtor.

(6)   If, in contravention of a return order or transfer order, any goods to which the order relates are not returned to the creditor, the court, on the application of the creditor, may—

(a)   revoke so much of the order as relates to those goods, and

(b)   order the debtor to pay the creditor the unpaid portion of so much of the total price as is referable to those goods.

(7)   For the purposes of this section, the part of the total price referable to any goods is the part assigned to those goods by the agreement or (if no such assignment is made) the part determined by the court to be reasonable.

134   Evidence of adverse detention in hire-purchase etc cases

(1)   Where goods are comprised in a regulated hire-purchase agreement, regulated conditional sale agreement or regulated consumer hire agreement, and the creditor or owner—

(a)   brings an action or makes an application to enforce a right to recover possession of the goods from the debtor or hirer, and

(b)   proves that a demand for the delivery of the goods was included in the default notice under section 88(5), or that, after the right to recover possession of the goods accrued but before the action was begun or the application was made, he made a request in writing to the debtor or hirer to surrender the goods,

then, for the purposes of the claim of the creditor or owner to recover possession of the goods, the possession of them by the debtor or hirer shall be deemed to be adverse to the creditor or owner.

(2)   In subsection (1) 'the debtor or hirer' includes a person in possession of the goods at any time between the debtor's or hirer's death and the grant of probate or administration, or (in Scotland) confirmation.

(3)   Nothing in this section affects a claim for damages for conversion or (in Scotland) for delict.

Supplemental provisions as to orders

135   Power to impose conditions, or suspend operation of order

(1)   If it considers it just to do so, the court may in an order made by it in relation to a regulated agreement include provisions—

(a)   making the operation of any term of the order conditional on the doing of specified acts by any party to the proceedings;

(b)   suspending the operation of any term of the order either—

(i)   until such time as the court subsequently directs, or

(ii)   until the occurrence of a specified act or omission.

(2)   The court shall not suspend the operation of a term requiring the delivery up of goods by any person unless satisfied that the goods are in his possession or control.

(3)   In the case of a consumer hire agreement, the court shall not so use its powers under subsection (1)(b) as to extend the period for which, under the terms of the agreement, the hirer is entitled to possession of the goods to which the agreement relates.

(4)   On the application of any person affected by a provision included under subsection (1), the court may vary the provision.

136   Power to vary agreements and securities

(1)   The court may in an order made by it under this Act include such provision as it considers just for amending any agreement or security in consequence of a term of the order.

[. . .]

[Unfair relationships

[140A   Unfair relationships between creditors and debtors

(1)   The court may make an order under section 140B in connection with a credit agreement if it determines that the relationship between the creditor and the debtor arising out of the agreement (or the agreement taken with any related agreement) is unfair to the debtor because of one or more of the following—

(a)   any of the terms of the agreement or of any related agreement;

(b)   the way in which the creditor has exercised or enforced any of his rights under the agreement or any related agreement;

(c)   any other thing done (or not done) by, or on behalf of, the creditor (either before or after the making of the agreement or any related agreement).

(2)   In deciding whether to make a determination under this section the court shall have regard to all matters it thinks relevant (including matters relating to the creditor and matters relating to the debtor).

(3)   For the purposes of this section the court shall (except to the extent that it is not appropriate to do so) treat anything done (or not done) by, or on behalf of, or in relation to, an associate or a former associate of the creditor as if done (or not done) by, or on behalf of, or in relation to, the creditor.

(4)   A determination may be made under this section in relation to a relationship notwithstanding that the relationship may have ended.

(5)   An order under section 140B shall not be made in connection with a credit agreement which is an exempt agreement by virtue of section 16(6C).]

[140B   Powers of court in relation to unfair relationships

(1)   An order under this section in connection with a credit agreement may do one or more of the following—

(a)   require the creditor, or any associate or former associate of his, to repay (in whole or in part) any sum paid by the debtor or by a surety by virtue of the agreement or any related agreement (whether paid to the creditor, the associate or the former associate or to any other person);

(b)   require the creditor, or any associate or former associate of his, to do or not to do (or to cease doing) anything specified in the order in connection with the agreement or any related agreement;

(c)   reduce or discharge any sum payable by the debtor or by a surety by virtue of the agreement or any related agreement;

(d)   direct the return to a surety of any property provided by him for the purposes of a security;

(e)   otherwise set aside (in whole or in part) any duty imposed on the debtor or on a surety by virtue of the agreement or any related agreement;

(f)   alter the terms of the agreement or of any related agreement;

(g)   direct accounts to be taken, or (in Scotland) an accounting to be made, between any persons.

(2)   An order under this section may be made in connection with a credit agreement only—

(a)   on an application made by the debtor or by a surety;

(b)   at the instance of the debtor or a surety in any proceedings in any court to which the debtor and the creditor are parties, being proceedings to enforce the agreement or any related agreement; or

(c)   at the instance of the debtor or a surety in any other proceedings in any court where the amount paid or payable under the agreement or any related agreement is relevant.

(3)   An order under this section may be made notwithstanding that its effect is to place on the creditor, or any associate or former associate of his, a burden in respect of an advantage enjoyed by another person.

(4)   An application under subsection (2)(a) may only be made—

(a)   in England and Wales, to the county court;

(b)   in Scotland, to the sheriff court;

(c)   in Northern Ireland, to the High Court (subject to subsection (6)).

(5)   In Scotland such an application may be made in the sheriff court for the district in which the debtor or surety resides or carries on business.

(6)   In Northern Ireland such an application may be made to the county court if the credit agreement is an agreement under which the creditor provides the debtor with—

(a)   fixed-sum credit not exceeding £15,000; or

(b)   running-account credit on which the credit limit does not exceed £15,000.

(7)   Without prejudice to any provision which may be made by rules of court made in relation to county courts in Northern Ireland, such rules may provide that an application made by virtue of subsection (6) may be made in the county court for the division in which the debtor or surety resides or carries on business.

(8)   A party to any proceedings mentioned in subsection (2) shall be entitled, in accordance with rules of court, to have any person who might be the subject of an order under this section made a party to the proceedings.

(9)   If, in any such proceedings, the debtor or a surety alleges that the relationship between the creditor and the debtor is unfair to the debtor, it is for the creditor to prove to the contrary.]

[140C   Interpretation of ss 140A and 140B

(1)   In this section and in sections 140A and 140B 'credit agreement' means any agreement between an individual (the 'debtor') and any other person (the 'creditor') by which the creditor provides the debtor with credit of any amount.

(2)   References in this section and in sections 140A and 140B to the creditor or to the debtor under a credit agreement include—

(a)   references to the person to whom his rights and duties under the agreement have passed by assignment or operation of law;

(b)   where two or more persons are the creditor or the debtor, references to any one or more of those persons.

(3)   The definition of 'court' in section 189(1) does not apply for the purposes of sections 140A and 140B.

(4)   References in sections 140A and 140B to an agreement related to a credit agreement (the 'main agreement') are references to—

(a)   a credit agreement consolidated by the main agreement;

(b)   a linked transaction in relation to the main agreement or to a credit agreement within paragraph (a);

(c)   a security provided in relation to the main agreement, to a credit agreement within paragraph (a) or to a linked transaction within paragraph (b).

(5)   In the case of a credit agreement which is not a regulated consumer credit agreement, for the purposes of subsection (4) a transaction shall be treated as being a linked transaction in relation to that agreement if it would have been such a transaction had that agreement been a regulated consumer credit agreement.

(6)   For the purposes of this section and section 140B the definitions of 'security' and 'surety' in section 189(1) apply (with any appropriate changes) in relation to—

(a)   a credit agreement which is not a consumer credit agreement as if it were a consumer credit agreement; and

(b)   a transaction which is a linked transaction by virtue of subsection (5).

(7)   For the purposes of this section a credit agreement (the 'earlier agreement') is consolidated by another credit agreement (the 'later agreement') if—

(a)   the later agreement is entered into by the debtor (in whole or in part) for purposes connected with debts owed by virtue of the earlier agreement; and

(b)   at any time prior to the later agreement being entered into the parties to the earlier agreement included—

(i)   the debtor under the later agreement; and

(ii)   the creditor under the later agreement or an associate or a former associate of his.

(8)   Further, if the later agreement is itself consolidated by another credit agreement (whether by virtue of this subsection or subsection (7)), then the earlier agreement is consolidated by that other agreement as well.]

[140D   Advice and information

The advice and information published by the OFT under section 229 of the Enterprise Act 2002 shall indicate how the OFT expects sections 140A to 140C of this Act to interact with Part 8 of that Act.]]

Miscellaneous

141   Jurisdiction and parties

(1)   In England and Wales the county court shall have jurisdiction to hear and determine—

(a)   any action by the creditor or owner to enforce a regulated agreement or any security relating to it;

(b)   any action to enforce any linked transaction against the debtor or hirer or his relative,

and such an action shall not be brought in any other court.

(2)   Where an action or application is brought in the High Court which, by virtue of this Act, ought to have been brought in the county court it shall not be treated as improperly brought, but shall be transferred to the county court.

[(3)   In Scotland the sheriff court shall have jurisdiction to hear and determine any action falling within subsection (1) and such an action shall not be brought in any other court.

(3A)   Subject to subsection (3B) an action which is brought in the sheriff court by virtue of subsection (3) shall be brought only in one of the following courts, namely—

(a)   the court for the place where the debtor or hirer is domiciled (within the meaning of section 41 or 42 of the Civil Jurisdiction and Judgments Act 1982);

(b)   the court for the place where the debtor or hirer carries on business; and

(c)   where the purpose of the action is to assert, declare or determine proprietary or possessory rights, or rights of security, in or over moveable property, or to obtain authority to dispose of moveable property, the court for the place where the property is situated.

(3B)   Subsection (3A) shall not apply—
  (a)   where rule 3 of Schedule 8 to the said Act of 1982 applies; or
  (b)   where the jurisdiction of another court has been prorogated by an agreement entered into after the dispute has arisen.]
(4)   In Northern Ireland the county court shall have jurisdiction to hear and determine any action or application falling within subsection (1).
(5)   Except as may be provided by rules of court, all the parties to a regulated agreement, and any surety, shall be made parties to any proceedings relating to the agreement.

142   Power to declare rights of parties
(1)   Where under any provision of this Act a thing can be done by a creditor or owner on an enforcement order only, and either—
  (a)   the court dismisses (except on technical grounds only) an application for an enforcement order, or
  (b)   where no such application has been made or such an application has been dismissed on technical grounds only an interested party applies to the court for a declaration under this subsection,
the court may if it thinks just make a declaration that the creditor or owner is not entitled to do that thing, and thereafter no application for an enforcement order in respect of it shall be entertained.
(2)   Where—
  (a)   a regulated agreement or linked transaction is cancelled under section 69(1), or becomes subject to section 69(2), or
  (b)   a regulated agreement is terminated under section 91, and an interested party applies to the court for a declaration under this subsection, the court may make a declaration to that effect.

143, 144   [*Apply to Northern Ireland*]

PART X
ANCILLARY CREDIT BUSINESSES

Definitions

145   Types of ancillary credit business
(1)   An ancillary credit business is any business so far as it comprises or relates to—
  (a)   credit brokerage,
  (b)   debt-adjusting,
  (c)   debt-counselling,
  (d)   debt-collecting,
  [(da) debt administration;
  (db) the provision of credit information services, or]
  (e)   the operation of a credit reference agency.
(2)   Subject to section 146(5) [and (5A)], credit brokerage is the effecting of introductions—
  (a)   of individuals desiring to obtain credit—
    (i) to persons carrying on businesses to which this sub-paragraph applies, or
    (ii) in the case of an individual desiring to obtain credit to finance the acquisition or provision of a dwelling occupied by himself or his relative, to any person carrying on a business in the course of which he provides credit secured on land, or
  (b)   of individuals desiring to obtain goods on hire to persons carrying on businesses to which this paragraph applies, or

(c)   of individuals desiring to obtain credit, or to obtain goods on hire, to other credit-brokers.

(3)   Subsection (2)(a)(i) applies to—

(a)   a consumer credit business;

(b)   a business which comprises or relates to consumer credit agreements being, otherwise than by virtue of section 16(5)(a), exempt agreements;

(c)   a business which comprises or relates to unregulated agreements where—

(i)   the [law applicable to] the agreement is the law of a country outside the United Kingdom, and

(ii)   if the [law applicable to] the agreement were the law of a part of the United Kingdom it would be a regulated consumer credit agreement.

(4)   Subsection (2)(b) applies to—

(a)   a consumer hire business;

[(aa)   a business which comprises or relates to consumer hire agreements being, otherwise than by virtue of section 16(6), exempt agreements,]

(b)   a business which comprises or relates to unregulated agreements where—

(i)   the [law applicable to] the agreement is the law of a country outside the United Kingdom, and

(ii)   if the [law applicable to] the agreement were the law of a part of the United Kingdom it would be a regulated consumer hire agreement.

(5)   Subject to section [146(5B) and (6)], debt-adjusting is, in relation to debts due under consumer credit agreements or consumer hire agreements,—

(a)   negotiating with the creditor or owner, on behalf of the debtor or hirer, terms for the discharge of a debt, or

(b)   taking over, in return for payments by the debtor or hirer, his obligation to discharge a debt, or

(c)   any similar activity concerned with the liquidation of a debt.

(6)   Subject to [section 146(5C) and (6)], debt-counselling is the giving of advice to debtors or hirers about the liquidation of debts due under consumer credit agreements or consumer hire agreements.

(7)   Subject to [section 146(6)], debt-collecting is the taking of steps to procure payment of debts due under consumer credit agreements or consumer hire agreements.

[(7A)   Subject to section 146(7), debt administration is the taking of steps—

(a)   to perform duties under a consumer credit agreement or a consumer hire agreement on behalf of the creditor or owner, or

(b)   to exercise or to enforce rights under such an agreement on behalf of the creditor or owner,

so far as the taking of such steps is not debt-collecting.

(7B)   A person provides credit information services if—

(a)   he takes any steps mentioned in subsection (7C) on behalf of an individual; or

(b)   he gives advice to an individual in relation to the taking of any such steps.

(7C)   Those steps are taken with a view—

(a)   to ascertaining whether a credit information agency (other than that person himself if he is one) holds information relevant to the financial standing of an individual;

(b)   to ascertaining the contents of such information held by such an agency;

(c)   to securing the correction of, the omission of anything from, or the making of any other kind of modification of, such information so held; or

(d)   to securing that such agency which holds such information—

(i)   stops holding it; or

(ii)   does not provide it to another person.

(7D)   In subsection (7C) 'credit information agency' means—

(a)   a person carrying on a consumer credit business or a consumer hire business;

(b)   a person carrying on a business so far as it comprises or relates to credit brokerage, debt-adjusting, debt-counselling, debt-collecting, debt administration or the operation of a credit reference agency;

(c)   a person carrying on a business which would be a consumer credit business except that it comprises or relates to consumer credit agreements being, otherwise than by virtue of section 16(5)(a), exempt agreements; or

(d)   a person carrying on a business which would be a consumer hire business except that it comprises or relates to consumer hire agreements being, otherwise than by virtue of section 16(6), exempt agreements.]

(8)   A credit reference agency is a person carrying on a business comprising the furnishing of persons with information relevant to the financial standing of individuals, being information collected by the agency for that purpose.

146   Exceptions from section 145

(1)   A barrister or advocate acting in that capacity is not to be treated as doing so in the course of any ancillary credit business.

(2)   A solicitor engaging in contentious business (as defined in [section 87(1) of the Solicitors Act 1974]) is not to be treated as doing so in the course of any ancillary credit business.

[(2A)   An authorised person (other than a barrister or solicitor) engaging in contentious business is not to be treated as doing so in the course of any ancillary credit business.

(2B)   In subsection (2A)—

'authorised person' means a person who, for the purposes of the Legal Services Act 2007, is an authorised person in relation to an activity which constitutes the exercise of a right of audience or the conduct of litigation (within the meaning of that Act);

'contentious business' means business done in or for the purposes of proceedings begun before a court or before an arbitrator, not being non-contentious or common form probate business (within the meaning of section 128 of the Supreme Court Act 1981).]

(3)   A solicitor within the meaning of the [Solicitors (Scotland) Act 1980] engaging in business done in or for the purposes of proceedings before a court or before an arbiter is not to be treated as doing so in the course of any ancillary credit business.

(4)   A solicitor in Northern Ireland engaging in [contentious business (as defined in Article 3(2) of the Solicitors (Northern Ireland) Order 1976], is not to be treated as doing so in the course of any ancillary credit business.

(5)   For the purposes of section 145(2), introductions effected by an individual by canvassing off trade premises either debtor-creditor-supplier agreements falling within section 12(a) or regulated consumer hire agreements shall be disregarded if—

(a)   the introductions are not effected by him in the capacity of an employee, and

(b)   he does not by any other method effect introductions falling within section 145(2).

[(5A)   It is not credit brokerage for a person to effect the introduction of an individual desiring to obtain credit if the introduction is made—

[(a)   to an authorised person, within the meaning of the 2000 Act, who has permission under that Act to enter into a relevant agreement as lender or home purchase provider (as the case may be); or]

(b)   to a qualifying broker,

with a view to that individual obtaining credit under [the relevant agreement].

(5B)   It is not debt-adjusting for a person to carry on an activity mentioned in paragraph (a), (b) or (c) of section 145(5) if—
    (a)   the debt in question is due under a relevant agreement; and
    (b)   that activity is a regulated activity for the purposes of the 2000 Act.
(5C)   It is not debt-counselling for a person to give advice to debtors about the liquidation of debts if—
    (a)   the debt in question is due under a relevant agreement; and
    (b)   giving that advice is a regulated activity for the purposes of the 2000 Act.
(5D)   In this section—
'the 2000 Act' means the Financial Services and Markets Act 2000;
['relevant agreement' means an agreement which—
    (a)   is secured by a land mortgage, or
    (b)   is or forms part of a regulated home purchase plan,
but only if entering into the agreement as lender or home purchase provider (as the case may be) is a regulated activity for the purposes of the 2000 Act;]
'qualifying broker' means a person who may effect introductions of the kind mentioned in subsection (5A) without contravening the general prohibition, within the meaning of section 19 of the 2000 Act,
    and references to 'regulated activities' [, 'regulated home purchase plan' and 'home purchase provider'] and the definition of 'qualifying broker' must be read with—
    (a)   section 22 of the 2000 Act (regulated activities: power to specify classes of activity and categories of investment);
    (b)   any order for the time being in force under that section; and
    (c)   Schedule 2 to that Act.].
(6)   It is not debt-adjusting, debt-counselling or debt-collecting for a person to do anything in relation to a debt arising under an agreement if [any of the following conditions is satisfied]—
    [(aa)   that he is the creditor or owner under the agreement, or]
    (c)   that he is the supplier in relation to the agreement, or
    (d)   that he is a credit-broker who has acquired the business of the person who was the supplier in relation to the agreement, or
    (e)   that he is a person prevented by subsection (5) from being treated as a credit-broker, and the agreement was made in consequence of an introduction (whether made by him or another person) which, under subsection (5), is to be disregarded.
    [(7)   It is not debt administration for a person to take steps to perform duties, or to exercise or enforce rights, under an agreement on behalf of the creditor or owner if any of the conditions mentioned in subsection (6)(aa) to (e) is satisfied in relation to that person.]

Licensing

147   Application of Part III
    [. . .]
(2)   Without prejudice to the generality of section 26, regulations under that section [. . .] may include provisions regulating the collection and dissemination of information by credit reference agencies.

148   Agreement for services of unlicensed trader
(1)   An agreement for the services of a person carrying on ancillary credit business (the 'trader'), if made when the trader was unlicensed, is enforceable against the other party (the 'customer') only where the [OFT] has made an order under subsection (2) which applies to the agreement.
(2)   The trader or his successor in title may apply to the [OFT] for an order that agreements within subsection (1) are to be treated as if made when the trader was licensed.

(3)   Unless the [OFT] determines to make an order under subsection (2) in accordance with the application, [it] shall, before determining the application, by notice—

(a)   inform the trader, giving [its] reasons, that, as the case may be, [it] is minded to refuse the application, or to grant it in terms different from those applied for, describing them, and

(b)   invite the trader to submit to the [OFT] representations in support of his application in accordance with section 34.

(4)   In determining whether or not to make an order under subsection (2) in respect of any period the [OFT] shall consider, in addition to any other relevant factors,—

(a)   how far, if at all, customers under agreements made by the trader during that period were prejudiced by the trader's conduct,

(b)   whether or not the [OFT] would have been likely to grant a licence covering that period on an application by the trader, and

(c)   the degree of culpability for the failure to obtain a licence.

(5)   If the [OFT] thinks fit, [it] may in an order under subsection (2)—

(a)   limit the order to specified agreements, or agreements of a specified description or made at a specified time;

(b)   make the order conditional on the doing of specified acts by the trader.

[(6)   This section does not apply to an agreement made by a consumer credit EEA firm unless at the time it was made that firm was precluded from entering into it as a result of—

(a)   a consumer credit prohibition imposed under section 203 of the Financial Services and Markets Act 2000; or

(b)   a restriction imposed on the firm under section 204 of that Act.]

149   Regulated agreements made on introductions by unlicensed credit-broker

(1)   A regulated agreement made by a debtor or hirer who, for the purpose of making that agreement, was introduced to the creditor or owner by an unlicensed credit-broker is enforceable against the debtor or hirer only where—

(a)   on the application of the credit-broker, the [OFT] has made an order under section 148(2) in respect of a period including the time when the introduction was made, and the order does not (whether in general terms or specifically) exclude the application of this paragraph to the regulated agreement, or

(b)   the [OFT] has made an order under subsection (2) which applies to the agreement.

(2)   Where during any period individuals were introduced to a person carrying on a consumer credit business or consumer hire business by an unlicensed credit-broker for the purpose of making regulated agreements with the person carrying on that business, that person or his successor in title may apply to the [OFT] for an order that regulated agreements so made are to be treated as if the credit-broker had been licensed at the time of the introduction.

(3)   Unless the [OFT] determines to make an order under subsection (2) in accordance with the application, [it] shall, before determining the application, by notice—

(a)   inform the applicant, giving [its] reasons, that, as the case may be, [it] is minded to refuse the application, or to grant it in terms different from those applied for, describing them, and

(b)   invite the applicant to submit to the [OFT] representations in support of his application in accordance with section 34.

(4)   In determining whether or not to make an order under subsection (2) the [OFT] shall consider, in addition to any other relevant factors—

(a)   how far, if at all, debtors or hirers under regulated agreements to which the application relates were prejudiced by the credit-broker's conduct, and

(b)   the degree of culpability of the applicant in facilitating the carrying on by the credit-broker of his business when unlicensed.

(5)   If the [OFT] thinks fit, [it] may in an order under subsection (2)—

(a)   limit the order to specified agreements, or agreements of a specified description or made at a specified time;

(b)   make the order conditional on the doing of specified acts by the applicant.

[(6)   For the purposes of this section 'unlicensed credit-broker' does not include a consumer credit EEA firm unless at the time the introduction was made that firm was precluded from making it as a result of—

(a)   a consumer credit prohibition imposed under section 203 of the Financial Services and Markets Act 2000; or

(b)   a restriction imposed on the firm under section 204 of that Act.]

[. . .]

Seeking business

151   Advertisements

(1)   Sections 44 to 47 apply to an advertisement published for the purposes of a business of credit brokerage carried on by any person, whether it advertises the services of that person or the services of persons to whom he effects introductions, as they apply to an advertisement to which Part IV applies.

(2)   Sections 44 [. . .] and 47 apply to an advertisement, published for the purposes of a business carried on by the advertiser, indicating that he is willing to advise on debts, [to] engage in transactions concerned with the liquidation of debts [or to provide credit information services], as they apply to an advertisement to which Part IV applies.

[(2A)   An advertisement does not fall within subsection (1) or (2) in so far as it is a communication of an invitation or inducement to engage in investment activity within the meaning of section 21 of the Financial Services and Markets Act 2000, other than an exempt generic communication (as defined in section 43(3B).]

(3)   The Secretary of State may by order provide that an advertisement published for the purposes of a business of credit brokerage, debt-adjusting [, debt-counselling or the provision of credit information services] shall not fall within subsection (1) or (2) if it is of a description specified in the order.

(4)   An advertisement [(other than one for credit information services)] does not fall within subsection (2) if it indicates that the advertiser is not willing to act in relation to consumer credit agreements and consumer hire agreements.

(5)   In subsections (1) and (3) 'credit brokerage' includes the effecting of introductions of individuals desiring to obtain credit to any person carrying on a business in the course of which he provides credit secured on land.

152   Application of sections 52 to 54 to credit brokerage etc

(1)   Sections 52 to 54 apply to a business of credit brokerage, debt-adjusting [, debt-counselling or the provision of credit information services] as they apply to a consumer credit business.

(2)   In their application to a business of credit brokerage, sections 52 and 53 shall apply to the giving of quotations and information about the business of any person to whom the credit-broker effects introductions as well as to the giving of quotations and information about his own business.

153   Definition of canvassing off trade premises (agreements for ancillary credit services)

(1)   An individual (the 'canvasser') canvasses off trade premises the services of a person carrying on an ancillary credit business if he solicits the entry of another individual (the 'consumer') into an agreement for the provision to the consumer of those services by making oral representations to the consumer, or any other indivi-

dual, during a visit by the canvasser to any place (not excluded by subsection (2)) where the consumer, or that other individual as the case may be, is, being a visit—
    (a)   carried out for the purpose of making such oral representations to individuals who are at that place, but
    (b)   not carried out in response to a request made on a previous occasion.
    (2)   A place is excluded from subsection (1) if it is a place where (whether on a permanent or temporary basis)—
    (a)   the ancillary credit business is carried on, or
    (b)   any business is carried on by the canvasser or the person whose employee or agent the canvasser is, or by the consumer.

154   Prohibition of canvassing certain ancillary credit services off trade premises

It is an offence to canvass off trade premises the services of a person carrying on a business of credit-brokerage, debt-adjusting [, debt-counselling or the provision of credit information services].

155   Right to recover brokerage fees

    (1)   [Subject to subsection (2A)] the excess over [£5] of a fee or commission for his services charged by a credit-broker to an individual to whom this subsection applies shall cease to be payable or, as the case may be, shall be recoverable by the individual if the introduction does not result in his entering into a relevant agreement within the six months following the introduction (disregarding any agreement which is cancelled under section 69(1) or becomes subject to section 69(2)).
    (2)   Subsection (1) applies to an individual who sought an introduction for a purpose which would have been fulfilled by his entry into—
    (a)   a regulated agreement, or
    (b)   in the case of an individual such as is referred to in section 145(2)(a)(ii), an agreement for credit secured on land, or
    (c)   an agreement such as is referred to in section 145(3)(b) or (c) or (4)(b).
    [(2A)   But subsection (1) does not apply where—
    (a)   the fee or commission relates to the effecting of an introduction of a kind mentioned in section 146(5A); and
    (b)   the person charging that fee or commission is an authorised person or an appointed representative, within the meaning of the Financial Services and Markets Act 2000.]
    (3)   An agreement is a relevant agreement for the purposes of subsection (1) in relation to an individual if it is an agreement such as is referred to in subsection (2) in relation to that individual.
    (4)   In the case of an individual desiring to obtain credit under a consumer credit agreement, any sum payable or paid by him to a credit-broker otherwise than as a fee or commission for the credit-broker's services shall for the purposes of subsection (1) be treated as such a fee or commission if it enters, or would enter, into the total charge for credit.

Entry into agreements

156   Entry into agreements

Regulations may make provision, in relation to agreements entered into in the course of a business of credit brokerage, debt-adjusting [, debt-counselling or the provision of credit information services], corresponding, with such modifications as the Secretary of State thinks fit, to the provision which is or may be made by or under sections 55, 60, 61, 62, 63, 65, 127, 179 or 180 in relation to agreements to which those sections apply.

Credit reference agencies

157 Duty to disclose name etc of agency

[(A1) Where a creditor under a prospective regulated agreement, other than an excluded agreement, decides not to proceed with it on the basis of information obtained by the creditor from a credit reference agency, the creditor must, when informing the debtor of the decision—

(a) inform the debtor that this decision has been reached on the basis of information from a credit reference agency, and

(b) provide the debtor with the particulars of the agency including its name, address and telephone number.]

(1) [In any other case,] a creditor, owner or negotiator, within the prescribed period after receiving a request in writing to that effect from the debtor or hirer, shall give him notice of the name and address of any credit reference agency from which the creditor, owner or negotiator has, during the antecedent negotiations, applied for information about his financial standing.

(2) Subsection (1) does not apply to a request received more than 28 days after the termination of the antecedent negotiations, whether on the making of the regulated agreement or otherwise.

[(2A) A creditor is not required to disclose information under this section if such disclosure—

(a) contravenes the Data Protection Act 1998,

(b) is prohibited by any EU obligation,

(c) would create or be likely to create a serious risk that any person would be subject to violence or intimidation, or

(d) would, or would be likely to, prejudice—

(i) the prevention or detection of crime,

(ii) the apprehension or prosecution of offenders, or

(iii) the administration of justice.]

(3) If the creditor, owner or negotiator fails to comply with subsection [(A1) or] (1) he commits an offence.

[(4) For the purposes of subsection (A1) an agreement is an excluded agreement if it is—

(a) a consumer hire agreement, or

(b) an agreement secured on land.]

158 Duty of agency to disclose filed information

(1) A credit reference agency, within the prescribed period after receiving,—

(a) [a request in writing to that effect from a consumer], and

(b) such particulars as the agency may reasonably require to enable them to identify the file, and

(c) a fee of [£2],

shall give the consumer a copy of the file relating to [it] kept by the agency.

(2) When giving a copy of the file under subsection (1), the agency shall also give the consumer a statement in the prescribed form of [the consumer's] rights under section 159.

(3) If the agency does not keep a file relating to [the consumer] it shall give the consumer notice of that fact, but need not return any money paid.

(4) If the agency contravenes any provision of this section it commits an offence.

[(4A) In this section 'consumer' means—

(a) a partnership consisting of two or three persons not all of whom are bodies corporate; or

(b) an unincorporated body of persons which does not consist entirely of bodies corporate and is not a partnership.]

(5) In this Act 'file', in relation to an individual, means all the information about him kept by a credit reference agency, regardless of how the information is

stored, and 'copy of the file', as respects information not in plain English, means a transcript reduced into plain English.

159 Correction of wrong information
[(1)   Any individual (the 'objector') given—
    (a)   information under section 7 of the Data Protection Act 1998 by a credit reference agency, or
    (b)   information under section 158,
who considers that an entry in his file is incorrect, and that if it is not corrected he is likely to be prejudiced, may give notice to the agency requiring it either to remove the entry from the file or amend it.]
    (2)   Within 28 days after receiving a notice under subsection (1), the agency shall by notice inform the [objector] that it has—
    (a)   removed the entry from the file, or
    (b)   amended the entry, or
    (c)   taken no action,
and if the notice states that the agency has amended the entry it shall include a copy of the file so far as it comprises the amended entry.
    (3)   Within 28 days after receiving a notice under subsection (2), or where no such notice was given, within 28 days after the expiry of the period mentioned in subsection (2), the [objector] may, unless he has been informed by the agency that it has removed the entry from his file, serve a further notice on the agency requiring it to add to the file an accompanying notice of correction (not exceeding 200 words) drawn up by the [objector], and include a copy of it when furnishing information included in or based on that entry.
    (4)   Within 28 days after receiving a notice under subsection (3), the agency, unless it intends to apply to the [the relevant authority] under subsection (5), shall by notice inform the [objector] that it has received the notice under subsection (3) and intends to comply with it.
    (5)   If—
    (a)   the [objector] has not received a notice under subsection (4) within the time required, or
    (b)   it appears to the agency that it would be improper for it to publish a notice of correction because it is incorrect, or unjustly defames any person, or is frivolous or scandalous, or is for any other reason unsuitable, the [objector] or, as the case may be, the agency may, in the prescribed manner and on payment of the specified fee, apply to [the relevant authority], who may make such order on the application as it thinks fit.
    (6)   If a person to whom an order under this section is directed fails to comply with it within the period specified in the order he commits an offence.
    [(7)   The Information Commissioner may vary or revoke any order made by him under this section.
    (8)   In this section 'the relevant authority' means—
    (a)   where the objector is a partnership or other unincorporated body of persons, the [OFT], and
    (b)   in any other case, the Information Commissioner.]

160 Alternative procedure for business consumers
    (1)   The [OFT], on an application made by a credit reference agency, may direct that this section shall apply to the agency if [it] is satisfied—
    (a)   that compliance with section 158 in the case of consumers who carry on a business would adversely affect the service provided to its customers by the agency, and
    (b)   that, having regard to the methods employed by the agency and to any other relevant facts, it is probable that consumers carrying on a business would not be prejudiced by the making of the direction.

(2) Where an agency to which this section applies receives a request, particulars and a fee under section 158(1) from a consumer who carries on a business and section 158(3) does not apply, the agency, instead of complying with section 158, may elect to deal with the matter under the following subsections.

(3) Instead of giving the consumer a copy of the file, the agency shall within the prescribed period give notice to the consumer that it is proceeding under this section, and by notice give the consumer such information included in or based on entries in the file as the [OFT] may direct, together with a statement in the prescribed form of the consumer's rights under subsections (4) and (5).

(4) If within 28 days after receiving the information given [to the consumer] under subsection (3), or such longer period as the [OFT] may allow, the consumer—

(a) gives notice to the [OFT] that [the consumer] is dissatisfied with the information, and

(b) satisfies the [OFT] that [the consumer] has taken such steps in relation to the agency as may be reasonable with a view to removing the cause of [the consumer's] dissatisfaction, and

(c) pays the [OFT] the specified fee,

the [OFT] may direct the agency to give the [OFT] a copy of the file, and the [OFT] may disclose to the consumer such of the information on the file as the [OFT] thinks fit.

(5) Section 159 applies with any necessary modifications to information given to the consumer under this section as it applies to information given under section 158.

(6) If an agency making an election under subsection (2) fails to comply with subsection (3) or (4) it commits an offence.

[(7) In this section 'consumer' has the same meaning as in section 158.]

[160A Credit intermediaries

(1) In this section 'credit intermediary' means a person who in the course of business—

(a) carries out any of the activities specified in subsection (2) for a consideration that is or includes a financial consideration, and

(b) does not do so as a creditor.

(2) The activities are—

(a) recommending or making available prospective regulated consumer credit agreements, other than agreements secured on land, to individuals,

(b) assisting individuals by undertaking other preparatory work in relation to such agreements, or

(c) entering into regulated consumer credit agreements, other than agreements secured on land, with individuals on behalf of creditors.

(3) A credit intermediary must in—

(a) advertising of his relating to an activity in subsection (2) which is intended for individuals not acting the course of a business, or

(b) documentation of his relating to an activity in subsection (2) which is intended for individuals,

indicate the extent to which the intermediary is acting independently and in particular whether he works exclusively with a creditor.

(4) Where a credit intermediary carries on an activity specified in subsection (2) for a debtor, the intermediary must secure that any financial consideration payable to him by the debtor for the activity is disclosed to the debtor and then agreed in writing before the regulated consumer credit agreement is concluded.

(5) Where a credit intermediary carries on an activity specified in subsection (2) for a debtor, the intermediary must disclose to the creditor the financial consideration for the activity payable by the debtor if the annual percentage rate of

the total charge for credit prescribed under section 20 is to be ascertained by the creditor.

(6)   A credit intermediary who fails to comply with a requirement of this section commits an offence.

(7)   An offence under this section is to be treated for the purposes of the definition of 'relevant offence' in section 38(1) and (2) of the Regulatory Enforcement and Sanctions Act 2008 as an offence contained in this Act immediately before the day on which that Act was passed.]

PART XI
ENFORCEMENT OF ACT

161   Enforcement authorities

(1)   The following authorities ('enforcement authorities') have a duty to enforce this Act and regulations made under it—
  (a)   the [OFT],
  (b)   in Great Britain, the local weights and measures authority,
  (c)   in Northern Ireland, the Department of Commerce for Northern Ireland.
[. . .]
(3)   Every local weights and measures authority shall, whenever the [OFT] requires, report to [it] in such form and with such particulars as [it] requires on the exercise of their functions under this Act.
[. . .]

162   Powers of entry and inspection

(1)   A duly authorised officer of an enforcement authority, at all reasonable hours and on production, if required, of his credentials, may—
  (a)   in order to ascertain whether a breach of any provision of or under this Act has been committed, inspect any goods and enter any premises (other than premises used only as a dwelling);
  (b)   if he has reasonable cause to suspect that a breach of any provision of or under this Act has been committed, in order to ascertain whether it has been committed, require any person—
      (i)   carrying on, or employed in connection with, a business to produce any [. . .] documents relating to it; or
      (ii)   having control of any information relating to a business [to provide him with that information] [. . .];
  (c)   if he has reasonable cause to believe that a breach of any provision of or under this Act has been committed, seize and detain any goods in order to ascertain (by testing or otherwise) whether such a breach has been committed;
  (d)   seize and detain any goods, [. . .] or documents which he has reason to believe may be required as evidence in proceedings for an offence under this Act;
  (e)   for the purpose of exercising his powers under this subsection to seize goods, [. . .] or documents, but only if and to the extent that it is reasonably necessary for securing that the provision of this Act and of any regulations made under it are duly observed, require any person having authority to do so to break open any container and, if that person does not comply, break it open himself.
(2)   An officer seizing goods, [. . .] or documents in exercise of his powers under this section shall not do so without informing the person he seizes them from.
(3)   If a justice of the peace, on sworn information in writing, or, in Scotland, a sheriff or a magistrate or justice of the peace, on evidence on oath,—
  (a)   is satisfied that there is reasonable ground to believe either—
      (i)   that any goods, [. . .] or documents which a duly authorised officer has power to inspect under this section are on any premises and their inspection

is likely to disclose evidence of a breach of any provision of or under this Act; or

(ii)   that a breach of any provision of or under this Act has been, is being or is about to be committed on any premises; and

(b)   is also satisfied either—

(i)   that admission to the premises has been or is likely to be refused and that notice of intention to apply for a warrant under this subsection has been given to the occupier; or

(ii)   that an application for admission, or the giving of such a notice, would defeat the object of the entry or that the premises are unoccupied or that the occupier is temporarily absent and it might defeat the object of the entry to wait for his return, the justice or, as the case may be, the sheriff or magistrate may by warrant under his hand, which shall continue in force for a period of one month, authorise an officer of an enforcement authority to enter the premises (by force if need be).

(4)   An officer entering premises by virtue of this section may take such other persons and equipment with him as he thinks necessary; and on leaving premises entered by virtue of a warrant under subsection (3) shall, if they are unoccupied or the occupier is temporarily absent, leave them as effectively secured against trespassers as he found them.

(5)   Regulations may provide that, in cases described by the regulations, an officer of a local weights and measures authority is not to be taken to be duly authorised for the purposes of this section unless he is authorised by the [OFT].

(6)   A person who is not a duly authorised officer of an enforcement authority, but purports to act as such under this section, commits an offence.

[. . .]

[(8)   References in this section to a breach of any provision of or under this Act do not include references to—

(a)   a failure to comply with a requirement imposed under section 33A or 33B;

(b)   a failure to comply with section 36A; or

(c)   a failure in relation to which the OFT can apply for an order under section 36E.]

163   Compensation for loss

(1)   Where, in exercising his powers under section 162, an officer of an enforcement authority seizes and detains goods and their owner suffers loss by reason of—

(a)   that seizure, or

(b)   the loss, damage or deterioration of the goods during detention, then, unless the owner is convicted of an offence under this Act committed in relation to the goods, the authority shall compensate him for the loss so suffered.

(2)   Any dispute as to the right to or amount of any compensation under subsection (1) shall be determined by arbitration.

164   Power to make test purchases etc

(1)   An enforcement authority may—

(a)   make, or authorise any of their officers to make on their behalf, such purchases of goods; and

(b)   authorise any of their officers to procure the provision of such services or facilities or to enter into such agreements or other transactions, as may appear to them expedient for determining whether any provisions made by or under this Act are being complied with.

(2)   Any act done by an officer authorised to do it under subsection (1) shall be treated for the purposes of this Act as done by him as an individual on his own behalf.

(3)   Any goods seized by an officer under this Act may be tested, and in the event of such a test he shall inform the person mentioned in section 162(2) of the test results.

(4)   Where any test leads to proceedings under this Act, the enforcement authority shall—

(a)   if the goods were purchased, inform the person they were purchased from of the test results, and

(b)   allow any person against whom the proceedings are taken to have the goods tested on his behalf if it is reasonably practicable to do so.

165   Obstruction of authorised officers

(1)   Any person who—

(a)   wilfully obstructs an officer of an enforcement authority acting in pursuance of this Act; or

(b)   wilfully fails to comply with any requirement properly made to him by such an officer under section 162; or

(c)   without reasonable cause fails to give such an officer (so acting) other assistance or information he may reasonably require in performing his functions under this Act, commits an offence.

[(1A)   A failure to give assistance or information shall not constitute an offence under subsection (1)(c) if it is also—

(a)   a failure to comply with a requirement imposed under section 33A or 33B;

(b)   a failure to comply with section 36A; or

(c)   a failure in relation to which the OFT can apply for an order under section 36E.]

(2)   If any person, in giving such information as is mentioned in subsection (1)(c), makes any statement which he knows to be false, he commits an offence.

(3)   Nothing in this section requires a person to answer any question or give any information if to do so might incriminate that person or (where that person is [married or a civil partner) the spouse or civil partner] of that person.

166   Notification of convictions and judgments to [OFT]

Where a person is convicted of an offence or has a judgment given against him by or before any court in the United Kingdom and it appears to the court—

(a)   having regard to the functions of the [OFT] under this Act, that the conviction or judgment should be brought to the [OFT's] attention, and

(b)   that it may not be brought to [its] attention unless arrangements for that purpose are made by the court,

the court may make such arrangements notwithstanding that the proceedings have been finally disposed of.

167   Penalties

(1)   An offence under a provision of this Act specified in column 1 of Schedule 1 is triable in the mode or modes indicated in column 3, and on conviction is punishable as indicated in column 4 (where a period of time indicates the maximum term of imprisonment, and a monetary amount indicates the maximum fine, for the offence in question).

(2)   A person who contravenes any regulations made under section 44, 52, 53, or 112, or made under section 26 by virtue of section 54, commits an offence.

168   Defences

(1)   In any proceedings for an offence under this Act it is a defence for the person charged to prove—

(a)   that his act or omission was due to a mistake, or to reliance on information supplied to him, or to an act or omission by another person, or to an accident or some other cause beyond his control, and

(b)   that he took all reasonable precautions and exercised all due diligence to avoid such an act or omission by himself or any person under his control.

(2)   If in any case the defence provided by subsection (1) involves the allegation that the act or omission was due to an act or omission by another person or to reliance on information supplied by another person, the person charged shall not, without leave of the court, be entitled to rely on that defence unless, within a period ending seven clear days before the hearing, he has served on the prosecutor a notice giving such information identifying or assisting in the identification of that other person as was then in his possession.

169   Offences by bodies corporate

Where at any time a body corporate commits an offence under this Act with the consent or connivance of, or because of neglect by, any individual, the individual commits the like offence if at that time—

(a)   he is a director, manager, secretary or similar officer of the body corporate, or

(b)   he is purporting to act as such an officer, or

(c)   the body corporate is managed by its members of whom he is one.

170   No further sanctions for breach of Act

(1)   A breach of any requirement made (otherwise than by any court) by or under this Act shall incur no civil or criminal sanction as being such a breach, except to the extent (if any) expressly provided by or under this Act.

(2)   In exercising [its] functions under this Act the [OFT] may take account of any matter appearing to [it] to constitute a breach of a requirement made by or under this Act, whether or not any sanction for that breach is provided by or under this Act and, if it is so provided, whether or not proceedings have been brought in respect of the breach.

(3)   Subsection (1) does not prevent the grant of an injunction, or the making of an order of certiorari, mandamus or prohibition or as respects Scotland the grant of an interdict or of an order under [section 45 of the Court of Session Act 1988] (order for specific performance of statutory duty).

171   Onus of proof in various proceedings

(1)   If an agreement contains a term signifying that in the opinion of the parties section 10(3)(b)(iii) does not apply to the agreement, it shall be taken not to apply unless the contrary is proved.

(2)   It shall be assumed in any proceedings, unless the contrary is proved, that when a person initiated a transaction as mentioned in section 19(1)(c) he knew the principal agreement had been made, or contemplated that it might be made.

(3)   Regulations under section 44 or 52 may make provision as to the onus of proof in any proceedings to enforce the regulations.

(4)   In proceedings brought by the creditor under a credit-token agreement—

(a)   it is for the creditor to prove that the credit-token was lawfully supplied to the debtor, and was accepted by him, and

(b)   if the debtor alleges that any use made of the credit-token was not authorised by him, it is for the creditor to prove either—

(i)   that the use was so authorised, or

(ii)   that the use occurred before the creditor had been given notice under section 84(3).

(5)   In proceedings under section 50(1) in respect of a document received by a minor at any school or other educational establishment for minors, it is for the person sending it to him at that establishment to prove that he did not know or suspect it to be such an establishment.

(6)   In proceedings under section 119(1) it is for the pawnee to prove that he had reasonable cause to refuse to allow the pawn to be redeemed.

[. . .]

172   Statements by creditor or owner to be binding

(1)   A statement by a creditor or owner is binding on him if given under—
section 77(1),
section 78(1),
section 79(1),
section 97(1),
section 107(1)(c),
section 108(1)(c), or
section 109(1)(c).

(2)   Where a trader—

(a)   gives a customer a notice in compliance with section 103(1)(b), or

(b)   gives a customer a notice under section 103(1) asserting that the customer is not indebted to him under an agreement,
the notice is binding on the trader.

(3)   Where in proceedings before any court—

(a)   it is sought to reply on a statement or notice given as mentioned in subsection (1) or (2), and

(b)   the statement or notice is shown to be incorrect, the court may direct such relief (if any) to be given to the creditor or owner from the operation of subsection (1) or (2) as appears to the court to be just.

173   Contracting-out forbidden

(1)   A term contained in a regulated agreement or linked transaction, or in any other agreement relating to an actual or prospective regulated agreement or linked transaction, is void if, and to the extent that, it is inconsistent with a provision for the protection of the debtor or hirer or his relative or any surety contained in this Act or in any regulation made under this Act.

(2)   Where a provision specifies the duty or liability of the debtor or hirer or his relative or any surety in certain circumstances, a term is inconsistent with that provision if it purports to impose, directly or indirectly, an additional duty or liability on him in those circumstances.

(3)   Notwithstanding subsection (1), a provision of this Act under which a thing may be done in relation to any person on an order of the court or the [OFT] only shall not be taken to prevent its being done at any time with that person's consent given at that time, but the refusal of such consent shall not give rise to any liability.

PART XII
SUPPLEMENTAL

[. . .]

[174A Powers to require provision of information or documents etc

(1)   Every power conferred on a relevant authority by or under this Act (however expressed) to require the provision or production of information or documents includes the power—

(a)   to require information to be provided or produced in such form as the authority may specify, including, in relation to information recorded otherwise than in a legible form, in a legible form;

(b)   to take copies of, or extracts from, any documents provided or produced by virtue of the exercise of the power;

(c)   to require the person who is required to provide or produce any information or document by virtue of the exercise of the power—

(i)   to state, to the best of his knowledge and belief, where the information or document is;

(ii)   to give an explanation of the information or document;

(iii)   to secure that any information provided or produced, whether in a document or otherwise, is verified in such manner as may be specified by the authority;

(iv) to secure that any document provided or produced is authenticated in such manner as may be so specified;

(d) to specify a time at or by which a requirement imposed by virtue of paragraph (c) must be complied with.

(2) Every power conferred on a relevant authority by or under this Act (however expressed) to inspect or to seize documents at any premises includes the power to take copies of, or extracts from, any documents inspected or seized by virtue of the exercise of the power.

(3) But a relevant authority has no power under this Act—

(a) to require another person to provide or to produce,

(b) to seize from another person, or

(c) to require another person to give access to premises for the purposes of the inspection of,

any information or document which the other person would be entitled to refuse to provide or produce in proceedings in the High Court on the grounds of legal professional privilege or (in Scotland) in proceedings in the Court of Session on the grounds of confidentiality of communications.

(4) In subsection (3) 'communications' means—

(a) communications between a professional legal adviser and his client;

(b) communications made in connection with or in contemplation of legal proceedings and for the purposes of those proceedings.

(5) In this section 'relevant authority' means—

(a) the OFT or an enforcement authority (other than the OFT);

(b) an officer of the OFT or of an enforcement authority (other than the OFT).]

175 Duty of persons deemed to be agents

Where under this Act a person is deemed to receive a notice or payment as agent of the creditor or owner under a regulated agreement, he shall be deemed to be under a contractual duty to the creditor or owner to transmit the notice, or remit the payment, to him forthwith.

176 Service of documents

(1) A document to be served under this Act by one person ('the server') on another person ('the subject') is to be treated as properly served on the subject if dealt with as mentioned in the following subsections.

(2) The document may be delivered or sent [by an appropriate method] to the subject, or addressed to him by name and left at his proper address.

(3) For the purposes of this Act, a document sent [by an appropriate method] to, or left at, the address last known to the server as the address of a person shall be treated as sent by post to, or left at, his proper address.

(4) Where the document is to be served on the subject as being the person having any interest in land, and it is not practicable after reasonable inquiry to ascertain the subject's name or address, the document may be served by—

(a) addressing it to the subject by the description of the person having that interest in the land (naming it), and

(b) delivering the document to some responsible person on the land or affixing it, or a copy of it, in a conspicuous position on the land.

(5) Where a document to be served on the subject as being a debtor, hirer or surety, or as having any other capacity relevant for the purposes of this Act, is served at any time on another person who—

(a) is the person last known to the server as having that capacity, but

(b) before that time had ceased to have it, the document shall be treated as having been served at that time on the subject.

(6) Anything done to a document in relation to a person who (whether to the

knowledge of the server or not) has died shall be treated for the purposes of sub-section (5) as service of the document on that person if it would have been so treated had he not died.

[(7)   The following enactments shall not be construed as authorising service on the Public Trustee (in England and Wales) or the Probate Judge (in Northern Ireland) of any document which is to be served under this Act—

   section 9 of the Administration of Estates Act 1925;

   section 3 of the Administration of Estates Act (Northern Ireland) 1955.]

(8)   References in the preceding subsections to the serving of a document on a person include the giving of the document to that person.

[176A   Electronic transmission of documents

   (1)   A document is transmitted in accordance with this subsection if—

   (a)   the person to whom it is transmitted agrees that it may be delivered to him by being transmitted to a particular electronic address in a particular electronic form,

   (b)   it is transmitted to that address in that form, and

   (c)   the form in which the document is transmitted is such that any information in the document which is addressed to the person to whom the document is transmitted is capable of being stored for future reference for an appropriate period in a way which allows the information to be reproduced without change.

(2)   A document transmitted in accordance with subsection (1) shall, unless the contrary is proved, be treated for the purposes of this Act, except section 69, as having been delivered on the working day immediately following the day on which it is transmitted.

(3)   In this section, 'electronic address' includes any number of addresses used for the purposes of receiving electronic communications.]

177   Saving for registered charges

   (1)   Nothing in this Act affects the rights of a creditor in a heritable security who—

   (a)   became the creditor under a transfer for value without notice of any defect in the title arising (apart from this section) by virtue of this Act; or

   (b)   derives title from such a creditor.

(2)   Nothing in this Act affects the operation of section 41 of the Conveyancing (Scotland) Act 1924 (protection of purchasers), or of that section as applied to standard securities by section 32 of the Conveyancing and Feudal Reform (Scotland) Act 1970.

(3)   Subsection (1) does not apply to a creditor carrying on [a consumer credit business, a consumer hire business or a business of debt-collecting or debt administration].

(4)   Where, by virtue of subsection (1), a land mortgage is enforced which apart from this section would be treated as never having effect, the original creditor or owner shall be liable to indemnify the debtor or hirer against any loss thereby suffered by him.

(5)   [Substitutes subsections (1) to (3) for Scotland.]

(6)   [Applies to Northern Ireland.]

178   Local Acts

The Secretary of State or the Department of Commerce for Northern Ireland may by order make such amendments or repeals of any provision of any local Act as appears to the Secretary of State or, as the case may be, the Department, necessary or expedient in consequence of the replacement by this Act of the enactments relating to pawnbrokers and moneylenders.

Regulations, orders, etc

179   Power to prescribe form etc of secondary documents

(1)   Regulations may be made as to the form and content of credit-cards, trading-checks, receipts, vouchers and other documents or things issued by creditors, owners or suppliers under or in connection with regulated agreements or by other persons in connection with linked transactions, and may in particular—

(a)   require specified information to be included in the prescribed manner in documents, and other specified material to be excluded;

(b)   contain requirements to ensure that specified information is clearly brought to the attention of the debtor or hirer, or his relative, and that one part of a document is not given insufficient or excessive prominence compared with another.

(2)   If a person issues any document or thing in contravention of regulations under subsection (1) then, as from the time of the contravention but without prejudice to anything done before it, this Act shall apply as if the regulated agreement had been improperly executed by reason of a contravention of regulations under section 60(1).

180   Power to prescribe form etc of copies

(1)   Regulations may be made as to the form and content of documents to be issued as copies of any executed agreement, security instrument or other document referred to in this Act, and may in particular—

(a)   require specified information to be included in the prescribed manner in any copy, and contain requirements to ensure that such information is clearly brought to the attention of a reader of the copy;

(b)   authorise the omission from a copy of certain material contained in the original, or the inclusion of such material in condensed form.

(2)   A duty imposed by any provision of this Act (except section 35) to supply a copy of any document—

(a)   is not satisfied unless the copy supplied is in the prescribed form and conforms to the prescribed requirements;

(b)   is not infringed by the omission of any material, or its inclusion in condensed form, if that is authorised by regulations;

and references in this Act to copies shall be construed accordingly.

(3)   Regulations may provide that a duty imposed by this Act to supply a copy of a document referred to in an unexecuted agreement or an executed agreement shall not apply to documents of a kind specified in the regulations.

181   Power to alter monetary limits etc

(1)   The Secretary of State may by order made by statutory instrument amend, or further amend, any of the following provisions of this Act so as to reduce or increase a sum mentioned in that provision, namely, sections [16B(1), 39A(3)], 70(6), 75(3)(b), 77(1), 78(1), 79(1), 84(1), 101(7)(a), 107(1), 108(1), 109(1), 110(1), 118(1)(b), 120(1)(a), 140B(6), [. . .], 155(1) and 158(1).

(2)   An order under subsection (1) amending section [16B(1), 39A(3)], 75(3)(b) or 140B(6), [. . .] shall be of no effect unless a draft of the order has been laid before and approved by each House of Parliament.

182   Regulations and orders

(1)   Any power of the Secretary of State to make regulations or orders under this Act, except the power conferred by sections 2(1)(a), 181 and 192 shall be exercisable by statutory instrument subject to annulment in pursuance of a resolution of either House of Parliament.

[. . .]

(2)   Where a power to make regulations or orders is exercisable by the Secretary of State by virtue of this Act, regulations or orders made in the exercise of that power may—

(a) make different provision in relation to different cases or classes of case, and

(b) exclude certain cases or classes of case, and

(c) contain such transitional provision as the [Secretary of State] thinks fit.

(3) Regulations may provide that specified expressions, when used as described by the regulations, are to be given the prescribed meaning, notwithstanding that another meaning is intended by the person using them.

(4) Any power conferred on the Secretary of State by this Act to make orders includes power to vary or revoke an order so made.

183 Determinations etc by OFT

[(1) The OFT may vary or revoke any determination made, or direction given, by it under this Act.

(2) Subsection (1) does not apply to—

(a) a determination to issue, renew or vary a licence;

(b) a determination to extend a period under section 28B or to refuse to extend a period under that section;

(c) a determination to end a suspension under section 33;

(d) a determination to make an order under section 40(2), 148(2) or 149(2);

(e) a determination mentioned in column 1 of the Table in section 41.]

Interpretation

184 Associates

[(1) A person is an associate of an individual if that person is—

(a) the individual's husband or wife or civil partner,

(b) a relative of—

(i) the individual, or

(ii) the individual's husband or wife or civil partner, or

(c) the husband or wife or civil partner of a relative of—

(i) the individual, or

(ii) the individual's husband or wife or civil partner.]

(2) A person is an associate of any person with whom he is in partnership, and of the husband or wife [or civil partner] or a relative of any individual with whom he is in partnership.

(3) A body corporate is an associate of another body corporate—

(a) if the same person is a controller of both, or a person is a controller of one and persons who are his associates, or he and persons who are his associates, are controllers of the other; or

(b) if a group of two or more persons is controller of each company, and the groups either consist of the same persons or could be regarded as consisting of the same persons by treating (in one or more cases) a member of either group as replaced by a person of whom he is an associate.

(4) A body corporate is an associate of another person if that person is a controller of it or if that person and persons who are his associates together are controllers of it.

(5) In this section 'relative' means brother, sister, uncle, aunt, nephew, niece, lineal ancestor or lineal descendant, references to a husband [or wife, and references to a civil partner include a former civil partner,] include a former husband or wife and a reputed husband or wife; and for the purposes of this subsection a relationship shall be established as if any illegitimate child, stepchild or adopted child of a person [were the legitimate child of the relationship in question].

185 Agreement with more than one debtor or hirer

(1) Where an actual or prosective regulated agreement has two or more debtors or hirers (not being a partnership or an unincorporated body of persons)—

(a)   anything required by or under this Act to be done to or in relation to the debtor or hirer shall be done to or in relation to each of them; and

(b)   anything done under this Act by or on behalf of one of them shall have effect as if done by or on behalf of all of them.

[(1A)   Notwithstanding subsection (1) above, subsection (4) of section 55A (pre-contractual explanations etc) does not require an oral explanation to be given to any debtor to whom an explanation of the matters referred to in subsection (2)(a), (b) and (e) of that section has not been given orally or in person.]

[(2)   Notwithstanding subsection (1)(a), where credit is provided under an agreement to two or more debtors jointly, in performing his duties—

(a)   in the case of fixed-sum credit, under section 77A, or

(b)   in the case of running-account credit, under section 78(4),

the creditor need not give statements to any debtor who has signed and given to him a notice (a 'dispensing notice') authorising him not to comply in the debtor's case with section 77A or (as the case may be) 78(4).

(2A)   A dispensing notice given by a debtor is operative from when it is given to the creditor until it is revoked by a further notice given to the creditor by the debtor.

(2B)   But subsection (2) does not apply if (apart from this subsection) dispensing notices would be operative in relation to all of the debtors to whom the credit is provided.

(2C)   Any dispensing notices operative in relation to an agreement shall cease to have effect if any of the debtors dies.

(2D)   A dispensing notice which is operative in relation to an agreement shall be operative also in relation to any subsequent agreement which, in relation to the earlier agreement, is a modifying agreement.]

(3)   Subsection (1)(b) does not apply for the purposes of section 61(1)(a) [. . .].

(4)   Where a regulated agreement has two or more debtors or hirers (not being a partnership or an unincorporated body of persons), section 86 applies to the death of any of them.

(5)   An agreement for the provision of credit, or the bailment or (in Scotland) the hiring of goods, to two or more persons jointly where—

(a)   one or more of those persons is an individual, and

(b)   one or more of them is [not an individual],

is a consumer credit agreement or consumer hire agreement if it would have been one had they all been individuals; and [each person within paragraph (b)] shall accordingly be included among the debtors or hirers under the agreement.

(6)   Where subsection (5) applies, references in this Act to the signing of any document by the debtor or hirer shall be construed in relation to a body corporate [within paragraph (b) of that subsection] as referring to a signing on behalf of the body corporate.

186   Agreement with more than one creditor or owner

Where an actual or prospective regulated agreement has two or more creditors or owners, anything required by or under this Act to be done to, or in relation to, or by, the creditor or owner shall be effective if done to, or in relation to, or by, any one of them.

187   Arrangements between creditor and supplier

(1)   A consumer credit agreement shall be treated as entered into under pre-existing arrangements between a creditor and a supplier if it is entered into in accordance with, or in furtherance of, arrangements previously made between persons mentioned in subsection (4)(a), (b) or (c).

(2)   A consumer credit agreement shall be treated as entered into in contemplation of future arrangements between a creditor and a supplier if it is entered into in the expectation that arrangements will subsequently be made between

persons mentioned in subsection (4)(a), (b) or (c) for the supply of cash, goods and services (or any of them) to be financed by the consumer credit agreement.

(3)   Arrangements shall be disregarded for the purposes of subsection (1) or (2) if—

   (a)   they are arrangements for the making, in specified circumstances, of payments to the supplier by the creditor, and

   (b)   the creditor holds himself out as willing to make, in such circumstances, payments of the kind to suppliers generally.

[(3A)   Arrangements shall also be disregarded for the purposes of subsections (1) and (2) if they are arrangements for the electronic transfer of funds from a current account at a bank within the meaning of the Bankers' Books Evidence Act 1879.]

(4)   The persons referred to in subsections (1) and (2) are—

   (a)   the creditor and the supplier;

   (b)   one of them and an associate of the other's;

   (c)   an associate of one and an associate of the other's.

(5)   Where the creditor is an associate of the supplier's, the consumer credit agreement shall be treated, unless the contrary is proved, as entered into under pre-existing arrangements between the creditor and the supplier.

[187A   Definition of 'default sum'

(1)   In this Act 'default sum' means, in relation to the debtor or hirer under a regulated agreement, a sum (other than a sum of interest) which is payable by him under the agreement in connection with a breach of the agreement by him.

(2)   But a sum is not a default sum in relation to the debtor or hirer simply because, as a consequence of his breach of the agreement, he is required to pay it earlier than he would otherwise have had to.]

188   Examples of use of new terminology

(1)   Schedule 2 shall have effect for illustrating the use of terminology employed in this Act.

(2)   The examples given in Schedule 2 are not exhaustive.

(3)   In the case of conflict between Schedule 2 and any other provision of this Act, that other provision shall prevail.

(4)   The Secretary of State may by order amend Schedule 2 by adding further examples or in any other way.

189   Definitions

(1)   In this Act, unless the context otherwise requires—

'advertisement' includes every form of advertising, whether in a publication, by television or radio, by display of notices, signs, labels, showcards or goods, by distribution of samples, circulars, catalogues, price lists or other material, by exhibition of pictures, models or films, or in any other way, and references to the publishing of advertisements shall be construed accordingly;

'advertiser' in relation to an advertisement, means any person indicated by the advertisement as willing to enter into transactions to which the advertisement relates;

'ancillary credit business' has the meaning given by section 145(1);

'antecedent negotiations' has the meaning given by section 56;

'appeal period' means the period beginning on the first day on which an appeal to the [First-tier Tribunal] may be brought and ending on the last day on which it may be brought or, if it is brought, ending on its final determination, or abandonment;

['appropriate method' means—

   (a)   post, or

   (b)   transmission in the form of an electronic communication [in accordance with section 176A(1)].]

'assignment', in relation to Scotland, means assignation;

'associate' shall be construed in accordance with section 184;

['authorised business overdraft agreement' means a debtor-creditor agreement which provides authorisation in advance for the debtor to overdraw on a current account, where the agreement is entered into by the debtor wholly or predominantly for the purposes of the debtor's business (see subsection (2A));

'authorised non-business overdraft agreement' means a debtor-creditor agreement which provides authorisation in advance for the debtor to overdraw on a current account where—

(a) the credit must be repaid on demand or within three months, and

(b) the agreement is not entered into by the debtor wholly or predominantly for the purposes of the debtor's business (see subsection (2A));]

[. . .]

'bill of sale' has the meaning given by section 4 of the Bills of Sale Act 1878 or, for Northern Ireland, by section 4 of the Bills of Sale (Ireland) Act 1879;

['building society' means a building society within the meaning of the Building Societies Act 1986;]

'business' includes profession or trade, and references to a business apply subject to subsection (2);

'cancellable agreement' means a regulated agreement which, by virtue of section 67, may be cancelled by the debtor or hirer;

'canvass' shall be construed in accordance with sections 48 and 153;

'cash' includes money in any form;

'charity' means as respects England and Wales a charity registered under [the Charities Act 1993] or an exempt charity (within the meaning of that Act), and as respects [. . .] Northern Ireland an institution or other organisation established for charitable purposes only ('organisation' including any persons administering a trust and 'charitable' being construed in the same way as if it were contained in the Income Tax Acts) [, and as respects Scotland a body entered in the Scottish Charity Register];

'conditional sale agreement' means an agreement for the sale of goods or land under which the purchase price or part of it is payable by instalments, and the property in the goods or land is to remain in the seller (notwithstanding that the buyer is to be in possession of the goods or land) until such conditions as to the payment of instalments or otherwise as may be specified in the agreement are fulfilled;

'consumer credit agreement' has the meaning given by section 8, and includes a consumer credit agreement which is cancelled under section 69(1), or becomes subject to section 69(2), so far as the agreement remains in force;

['consumer credit business' means any business being carried on by a person so far as it comprises or relates to—

(a) the provision of credit by him, or

(b) otherwise his being a creditor,

under regulated consumer credit agreements];

'consumer hire agreement' has the meaning given by section 15;

['consumer hire business' means any business being carried on by a person so far as it comprises or relates to—

(a) the bailment or (in Scotland) the hiring of goods by him, or

(b) otherwise his being an owner,

under regulated consumer hire agreements;]

'controller', in relation to a body corporate, means a person—

(a) in accordance with whose directions or instructions the directors of the body corporate or of another body corporate which is its controller (or any of them) are accustomed to act, or

(b) who, either alone or with any associate or associates, is entitled to exercise, or control the exercise of, one third or more of the voting power at any

general meeting of the body corporate or of another body corporate which is its
controller;
'copy' shall be construed in accordance with section 180;
[. . .]
'court' means in relation to England and Wales the county court, in relation to
Scotland the sheriff court and in relation to Northern Ireland the High Court or the
county court;
'credit' shall be construed in accordance with section 9;
'credit-broker' means a person carrying on a business of credit-brokerage;
'credit-brokerage' has the meaning given by section 145(2);
['credit information services' has the meaning given by section 145(7B);]
['credit intermediary' has the meaning given by section 160A;]
'credit limit' has the meaning given by section 10(2);
'creditor' means the person providing credit under a consumer credit agreement
or the person to whom his rights and duties under the agreement have passed by
assignment or operation of law, and in relation to a prospective consumer agreement, includes the prospective creditor;
'credit reference agency' has the meaning given by section 145(8);
'credit-sale agreement' means an agreement for the sale of goods, under which
the purchase price or part of it is payable by instalments, but which is not a conditional sale agreement;
'credit-token' has the meaning given by section 14(1);
'credit-token agreement' means a regulated agreement for the provision of credit
in connection with the use of a credit-token;
'debt-adjusting' has the meaning given by section 145(5);
['debt administration' has the meaning given by section 145(7A);]
'debt-collecting' has the meaning given by section 145(7);
'debt-counselling' has the meaning given by section 145(6);
'debtor' means the individual receiving credit under a consumer credit agreement or the person to whom his rights and duties under the agreement have
passed by assignment or operation of law, and in relation to a prospective consumer credit agreement includes the prospective debtor;
'debtor-creditor agreement' has the meaning given by section 13;
'debtor-creditor-supplier agreement' has the meaning given by section 12;
'default notice' has the meaning given by section 87(1);
['default sum' has the meaning given by section 187A;]
'deposit' means [(except in sections 16(10) and 25(1B))] any sum payable by a
debtor or hirer by way of deposit or downpayment, or credited or to be credited to
him on account of any deposit or downpayment, whether the sum is to be or has
been paid to the creditor or owner or any other person, or is to be or has been
discharged by a payment of money or a transfer or delivery of goods or by any
other means;
['documents' includes information recorded in any form;]
[. . .]
'electric line' has the meaning given by [the Electricity Act 1989] or, for Northern
Ireland the Electricity Supply (Northern Ireland) Order 1972;
['electronic communication' means an electronic communication within the
meaning of the Electronic Communications Act 2000 (c 7).]
'embodies' and related words shall be construed in accordance with subsection
(4);
'enforcement authority' has the meaning given by section 161(1);
'enforcement order' means an order under section 65(1), 105(7)(a) or (b), 111(2)
or 124(1) or (2);
'executed agreement' means a document, signed by or on behalf of the parties,
embodying the terms of a regulated agreement, or such of them as have been
reduced to writing;

'exempt agreement' means an agreement specified in or under section 16 [, 16A [, 16B or 16C]];

'finance' means to finance wholly or partly, and 'financed' and 'refinanced' shall be construed accordingly;

'file' and 'copy of the file' have the meanings given by section 158(5);

'fixed-sum credit' has the meaning given by section 10(1)(b);

'friendly society' means a society registered [or treated as registered under the Friendly Societies Act 1974 or the Friendly Societies Act 1992];

'future arrangements' shall be construed in accordance with section 187;

'general notice' means a notice published by the [OFT] at a time and in a manner appearing to [it] suitable for securing that the notice is seen within a reasonable time by persons likely to be affected by it;

'give' means deliver or send [by an appropriate method] to;

'goods' has the meaning given by [section 61(1) of the Sale of Goods Act 1979];

'group licence' has the meaning given by section 22(1)(b);

'High Court' means Her Majesty's High Court of Justice, or the Court of Session in Scotland or the High Court of Justice in Northern Ireland;

'hire-purchase agreement' means an agreement, other than a conditional sale agreement, under which—

(a)   goods are bailed or (in Scotland) hired in return for periodical payments by the person to whom they are bailed or hired, and

(b)   the property in the goods will pass to that person if the terms of the agreement are complied with and one or more of the following occurs—

(i)   the exercise of an option to purchase by that person,

(ii)   the doing of any other specified act by any party to the agreement,

(iii)   the happening of any other specified event;

'hirer' means the individual to whom goods are bailed or (in Scotland) hired under a consumer hire agreement, or the person to whom his rights and duties under the agreement have passed by assignment or operation of law, and in relation to a prospective consumer hire agreement includes the prospective hirer;

['individual' includes—

(a)   a partnership consisting of two or three persons not all of whom are bodies corporate; and

(b)   an unincorporated body of persons which does not consist entirely of bodies corporate and is not a partnership.]

'installation' means—

(a)   the installing of any electric line or any gas or water pipe,

(b)   the fixing of goods to the premises where they are to be used, and the alteration of premises to enable goods to be used on them,

(c)   where it is reasonably necessary that goods should be constructed or erected on the premises where they are to be used, any work carried out for the purpose of constructing or erecting them on those premises;

[. . .]

'judgment' includes an order or decree made by any court;

'land' includes an interest in land, and in relation to Scotland includes heritable subjects of whatever description;

'land improvement company' means an improvement company as defined by section 7 of the improvement of Land Act 1899;

'land mortgage' includes any security charged on land;

'licence' means a licence under Part III [. . .];

'licensed', in relation to any act, means authorised by a licence to do the act or cause or permit another person to do it;

'licensee', in the case of a group licence, includes any person covered by the licence;

'linked transaction' has the meaning given by section 19(1);

'local authority', in relation to England [. . .], means [. . .] a county council, a London borough council, a district council, the Common Council of the City of London, or the Council of the Isles of Scilly, [in relation to Wales means a county council or a county borough council,] and in relation to Scotland, means a [council constituted under section 2 of the Local Government etc (Scotland) Act 1994], and, in relation to Northern Ireland, means a district council;

'modifying agreement' has the meaning given by section 82(2);

'mortgage', in relation to Scotland, includes any heritable security;

'multiple agreement' has the meaning given by section 18(1);

'negotiator' has the meaning given by section 56(1);

'non-commercial agreement' means a consumer credit agreement or a consumer hire agreement not made by the creditor or owner in the course of a business carried on by him;

'notice' means notice in writing;

'notice of cancellation' has the meaning given by section 69(1);

['OFT' means the Office of Fair Trading;]

['open-end' in relation to a consumer credit agreement, means of no fixed duration;]

'owner' means a person who bails or (in Scotland) hires out goods under a consumer hire agreement or the person to whom his rights and duties under the agreement have passed by assignment or operation of law, and in relation to a prospective consumer hire agreement, includes the prospective bailor or person from whom the goods are to be hired;

'pawn' means any article subject to a pledge;

'pawn-receipt' has the meaning given by section 114;

'pawnee' and 'pawnor' include any person to whom the rights and duties of the original pawnee or the original pawnor, as the case may be, have passed by assignment or operation of law;

'payment' includes tender;

[. . .]

'pledge' means the pawnee's rights over an article taken in pawn;

'prescribed' means prescribed by regulations made by the Secretary of State;

'pre-existing arrangements' shall be construed in accordance with section 187;

'principal agreement' has the meaning given by section 19(1);

'protected goods' has the meaning given by section 90(7);

'quotation' has the meaning given by section 52(1)(a);

'redemption period' has the meaning given by section 116(3);

'register' means the register kept by the [OFT] under section 35;

'regulated agreement' means a consumer credit agreement, or consumer hire agreement, other than an exempt agreement, and 'regulated' and 'unregulated' shall be construed accordingly;

'regulations' means regulations made by the Secretary of State;

'relative', except in section 184, means a person who is an associate by virtue of section 184(1);

'representation' includes any condition or warranty, and any other statement or undertaking, whether oral or in writing;

'restricted-use credit agreement' and 'restricted-use credit' have the meanings given by section 11(1);

'rules of court', in relation to Northern Ireland means, in relation to the High Court, rules made under section 7 of the Northern Ireland Act 1962, and, in relation to any other court, rules made by the authority having for the time being power to make rules regulating the practice and procedure in that court;

'running-account credit' shall be construed in accordance with section 10;

'security', in relation to an actual or prospective consumer credit agreement or consumer hire agreement, or any linked transaction, means a mortgage, charge, pledge, bond, debenture, indemnity, guarantee, bill, note or other right provided by the debtor or hirer, or at his request (express or implied), to secure the carrying out of the obligations of the debtor or hirer under the agreement;

'security instrument' has the meaning given by section 105(2);

'serve on' means deliver or send [by an appropriate method] to;

'signed' shall be construed in accordance with subsection (3);

'small agreement' has the meaning given by section 17(1), and 'small' in relation to an agreement within any category shall be construed accordingly;

'specified fee' shall be construed in accordance with section 2(4) and (5);

'standard licence' has the meaning given by section 22(1)(a);

'supplier' has the meaning given by section 11(1)(b) or 12(c) or 13(c) or, in relation to an agreement falling within section 11(1)(a), means the creditor, and includes a person to whom the rights and duties of a supplier (as so defined) have passed by assignment or operation of law, or (in relation to a prospective agreement) the prospective supplier;

'surety' means the person by whom any security is provided, or the person to whom his rights and duties in relation to the security have passed by assignment or operation of law;

'technical grounds' shall be construed in accordance with subsection (5);

'time order' has the meaning given by section 129(1);

'total charge for credit' means a sum calculated in accordance with regulations under section 20(1);

'total price' means the total sum payable by the debtor under a hire-purchase agreement or a conditional sale agreement, including any sum payable on the exercise of an option to purchase, but excluding any sum payable as a penalty or as compensation or damages for a breach of the agreement;

[. . .]

'unexecuted agreement' means a document embodying the terms of a prospective regulated agreement, or such of them as it is intended to reduce to writing;

'unlicensed' means without a licence, but applies only in relation to acts for which a licence is required;

'unrestricted-use credit agreement' and 'unrestricted-use credit' have the meanings given by section 11(2);

'working day' means any day other than—

(a)   Saturday or Sunday,

(b)   Christmas Day or Good Friday,

(c)   a bank holiday within the meaning given by section 1 of the Banking and Financial Dealings Act 1971.

[(1A)   In sections 36E(3), 70(4), 73(4) and 75(2) [. . .] 'costs', in relation to proceedings in Scotland, means expenses.]

(2)   A person is not to be treated as carrying on a particular type of business merely because occasionally he enters into transactions belonging to a business of that type.

[(2A)   For the purpose of the definitions of 'authorised business overdraft agreement' and 'authorised non-business overdraft agreement' subsections (2) to (5) of section 16B (declaration by the debtor as to the purposes of the agreement) apply.]

(3)   Any provision of this Act requiring a document to be signed is complied with by a body corporate if the document is sealed by that body.

This subsection does not apply to Scotland.

(4)   A document embodies a provision if the provision is set out either in the document itself or in another document referred to in it.

(5)   An application dismissed by the court or the [OFT] shall, if the court or the [OFT] (as the case may be) so certifies, be taken to be dismissed on technical grounds only.

(6)   Except in so far as the context otherwise requires, any reference in this Act

to an enactment shall be construed as a reference to that enactment as amended by or under any other enactment, including this Act.

(7)   In this Act, except where otherwise indicated—

(a)   a reference to a numbered Part, section or Schedule is a reference to the Part or section of, or the Schedule to, this Act so numbered, and

(b)   a reference in a section to a numbered subsection is a reference to the subsection of that section so numbered, and

(c)   a reference in a section, subsection or Schedule to a numbered paragraph is a reference to the paragraph of that section, subsection or Schedule so numbered.

[**189A   Meaning of 'consumer credit EEA firm'**
In this Act 'consumer credit EEA firm' means an EEA firm falling within sub-paragraph (a), (b) or (c) of paragraph 5 of Schedule 3 to the Financial Services and Markets Act 2000 carrying on, or seeking to carry on, consumer credit business, consumer hire business or ancillary credit business for which a licence would be required under this Act but for paragraph 15(3) of Schedule 3 to the Financial Services and Markets Act 2000.]

190   Financial provisions
(1)   There shall be defrayed out of money provided by Parliament—

(a)   all expenses incurred by the Secretary of State in consequence of the provisions of this Act;

(b)   any expenses incurred in consequence of those provisions by any other Minister of the Crown or Government department;

(c)   any increase attributable to this Act in the sums payable out of money so provided under the Superannuation Act 1972 or the Fair Trading Act 1973.

(2)   Any fees [, charges, penalties or other sums] received by the Director under this Act shall be paid into the Consolidated Fund.

191   [*Applies to Northern Ireland*]

193   Short title and extent
(1)   This Act may be cited as the Consumer Credit Act 1974.

(2)   This Act extends to Northern Ireland.

SCHEDULES

[. . .]

SCHEDULE 1. PROSECUTION AND PUNISHMENT OF OFFENCES

Section 167

1 Section	2 Offence	3 Mode of prosecution	4 Imprisonment or fine
7	... Knowingly or recklessly giving false information to [the OFT].	(a) Summarily. (b) On indictment.	[The prescribed sum.] 2 years or a fine or both.
39(1)	... Engaging in activities requiring a licence when not a licensee.	(a) Summarily. (b) On indictment.	[The prescribed sum.] 2 years or a fine or both.
39(2)	... Carrying on a business under a name not specified in licence.	(a) Summarily. (b) On indictment.	[The prescribed sum.] 2 years or a fine or both.
39(3)	... Failure to notify changes in registered particulars.	(a) Summarily. (b) On indictment.	[The prescribed sum.] 2 years or a fine or both.
45	... Advertising credit where goods etc not available for cash.	(a) Summarily. (b) On indictment.	[The prescribed sum.] 2 years or a fine or both.
[. . .]			[. . .]
47(1)	... Advertising infringements.	(a) Summarily. (b) On indictment.	[The prescribed sum.] 2 years or a fine or both.
49(1)	... Canvassing debtor-creditor agreements off trade premises.	(a) Summarily. (b) On indictment.	[The prescribed sum.] 1 year or a fine or both.
49(2)	... Soliciting debtor-creditor agreements during visits made in response to previous oral requests.	(a) Summarily. (b) On indictment.	[The prescribed sum.] 1 year or a fine or both.
50(1)	... Sending circulars to minors.	(a) Summarily. (b) On indictment.	[The prescribed sum.] 1 year or a fine or both.
51(1)	... Supplying unsolicited credit-tokens.	(a) Summarily. (b) On indictment.	[The prescribed sum.] 2 years or a fine or both.
[. . .]			[. . .]
79(3)	... Failure of owner under consumer hire agreement to supply copies of documents etc.	Summarily.	[Level 4 on the standard scale.]
80(2)	... Failure to tell creditor or owner whereabouts of goods.	Summarily.	[Level 3 on the standard scale.]
[. . .]			[. . .]
114(2)	... Taking pledges from minors.	(a) Summarily. (b) On indictment.	[The prescribed sum.] 1 year or a fine or both.
115	... Failure to supply copies of a pledge agreement or pawn-receipt.	Summarily.	[Level 4 on the standard scale.]

1 Section	2 Offence	3 Mode of prosecution	4 Imprisonment or fine
119(1)	Unreasonable refusal to allow pawn to be redeemed.	Summarily.	[Level 4 on the standard scale.]
154	Canvassing ancillary credit services of trade premises.	(a) Summarily. (b) On indictment.	[The prescribed sum.] 1 year or a fine or both.
157(3)	Refusal to give name etc of credit reference agency.	Summarily.	[Level 4 on the standard scale.]
158(4)	Failure of credit reference agency to disclose filed information.	Summarily.	[Level 4 on the standard scale.]
159(6)	Failure of credit reference agency to correct information.	Summarily.	[Level 4 on the standard scale.]
160(6)	Failure of credit reference agency to comply with section 160(3) or (4).	Summarily.	[Level 4 on the standard scale.]
[160A	Failure of credit intermediary to comply with section 160A(3), (4) or (5).	Summarily.	Level 4 on the standard scale.]
162(6)	Impersonation of enforcement authority officers.	(a) Summarily. (b) On indictment.	[The prescribed sum.] 1 year or a fine or both.
165(1)	Obstruction of enforcement authority officers.	Summarily.	[Level 4 on the standard scale.]
165(2)	Giving false information to enforcement authority officers.	(a) Summarily. (b) On indictment.	[The prescribed sum.] 2 years or a fine or both.
167(2)	Contravention of regulations under section 44, 52, 53, 54, or 112.	(a) Summarily. (b) On indictment.	[The prescribed sum.] 2 years or a fine or both.
174(5)	Wrongful disclosure of information.	(a) Summarily. (b) On indictment.	[The prescribed sum.] 2 years or a fine or both.

SCHEDULE 2
EXAMPLES OF USE OF NEW TERMINOLOGY

Section 188(1)

PART I
LIST OF TERMS

Term	Defined in section	Illustrated by examples(s)
Advertisement	189(1)	2
Advertiser	189(1)	2
Antecedent negotiations	56	1, 2, 3, 4
Cancellable agreement	67	4
Consumer credit agreement	8	5, 6, 7, 15, 19, 21
Consumer hire agreement	15	20, 24
Credit	9	16, 19, 21
Credit-broker	189(1)	2
Credit limit	10(2)	6, 7, 19, 22, 23
Creditor	189(1)	1, 2, 3, 4
Credit-sale agreement	189(1)	5
Credit-token	14	3, 14, 16
Credit-token agreement	14	3, 14, 16, 22
Debtor-creditor agreement	13	8, 16, 17, 18
Debtor-creditor-supplier agreement	12	8, 16
Fixed-sum credit	10	9, 10, 17, 23
Hire-purchase agreement	189(1)	10
Individual	189(1)	19, 24
Linked transaction	19	11
Modifying agreement	82(2)	24
Multiple agreement	18	16, 18
Negotiator	56(1)	1, 2, 3, 4
[. . .]		
Pre-existing arrangements	187	8, 21
Restricted-use credit	11	10, 12, 13, 14, 16
Running-account credit	10	15, 16, 18, 23
Small agreement	17	16, 17, 22
Supplier	189(1)	3, 14
Total charge for credit	20	5, 10
Total price	189(1)	10
Unrestricted-use credit	11	8, 12, 16, 17, 18

PART II
EXAMPLES

Example 1

Facts Correspondence passes between an employee of a money-lending company (writing on behalf of the company) and an individual about the terms on which the company would grant him a loan under a regulated agreement.

Analysis The correspondence constitutes antecedent negotiations falling within section 56(1)(a), the money-lending company being both creditor and negotiator.

Example 2

Facts Representations are made about goods in a poster displayed by a shopkeeper near the goods, the goods being selected by a customer who has read the poster and then sold by the shopkeeper to a finance company introduced by him (with whom he has a business relationship). The goods are disposed of by the finance company to the customer under a regulated hire-purchase agreement.

Analysis The representations in the poster constitute antecedent negotiations falling within section 56(1)(b), the shopkeeper being the credit-broker and negotiator and the finance company being the creditor. The poster is an advertisement and the shopkeeper is the advertiser.

Example 3

Facts Discussions take place between a shopkeeper and a customer about goods the customer wishes to buy using a credit-card issued by the D Bank under a regulated agreement.

Analysis The discussions constitute antecedent negotiations falling within section 36(1)(c), the shopkeeper being the supplier and negotiator and the D Bank the creditor. The credit-card is a credit-token as defined in section 14(1), and the regulated agreement under which it was issued is a credit-token agreement as defined in section 14(2).

Example 4

Facts Discussions take place and correspondence passes between a second-hand car dealer and a customer about a car, which is then sold by the dealer to the customer under a regulated conditional sale agreement. Subsequently, on a revocation of that agreement by consent, the car is resold by the dealer to a finance company introduced by him (with whom he has a business relationship), who in turn dispose of it to the same customer under a regulated hire-purchase agreement.

Analysis The discussions and correspondence constitute antecedent negotiations in relation both to the conditional sale agreement and the hire-purchase agreement. They fall under section 56(1)(a) in relation to the conditional sale agreement, the dealer being the creditor and the negotiator. In relation to the hire-purchase agreement they fall within section 56(1)(b), the dealer continuing to be treated as the negotiator but the finance company now being the creditor. Both agreements are cancellable if the discussions took place when the individual conducting the negotiations (whether the 'negotiator' or his employee or agent) was in the presence of the debtor, unless the unexecuted agreement was signed by the debtor at trade premises (as defined in section 67(b)). If the discussions all took place by telephone however, or the unexecuted agreement was signed by the debtor on trade premises (as so defined) the agreements are not cancellable.

Example 5

Facts E agrees to sell to F (an individual) an item of furniture in return for 24 monthly instalments of £10 payable in arrear. The property in the goods passes to F immediately.

Analysis This is a credit-sale agreement (see definition of 'credit-sale agreement' in section 189(1)). The credit provided amounts to £240 less the amount which, according to regulations made under section 20(1), constitutes the total charge for credit. (This amount is required to be deducted by section 9(4).) Accordingly the agreement falls within section 8(2) and is a consumer credit agreement.

Example 6

Facts The G Bank grants H (an individual) an unlimited over-draft, with an increased rate of interest on so much of any debit balance as exceeds £2,000.

Analysis Although the overdraft purports to be unlimited, the stipulation for increased interest above £2,000 brings the agreement within section 10(3)(b)(ii) and it is a consumer credit agreement.

Example 7

Facts J is an individual who owns a small shop which usually carries a stock worth about £1,000. K makes a stocking agreement under which he undertakes to provide on short-term credit the stock needed from time to time by J without any specified limit.

Analysis Although the agreement appears to provide unlimited credit, it is probable, having regard to the stock usually carried by J, that his indebtedness to K will not at any time rise above £5,000. Accordingly the agreement falls within section 10(3)(b)(iii) and is a consumer credit agreement.

Example 8

Facts U, a moneylender, lends £500 to V (an individual) knowing he intends to use it to buy office equipment from W. W introduced V to U, it being his practice to introduce customers needing finance to him. Sometimes U gives W a commission for this and sometimes not. U pays the £500 direct to V.

Analysis Although this appears to fall under section 11(1)(b), it is excluded by section 11(3) and is therefore (by section 11(2)) an unrestricted-use credit agreement. Whether it is a debtor-creditor agreement (by section 13(c)) or a debtor-creditor-supplier agreement (by section 12(c)) depends on whether the previous dealings between U and W amount to 'pre-existing arrangements', that is whether the agreement can be taken to have been entered into 'in accordance with, or in furtherance of' arrangements previously made between U and W, as laid down in section 187(1).

Example 9

Facts A agrees to lend B (an individual) £4,500 in nine monthly instalments of £500.

Analysis This is a cash loan and is a form of credit (see section 9 and definition of 'cash' in section 189(1)). Accordingly it falls within section 10(1)(b) and is fixed-sum credit amounting to £4,500.

Example 10

Facts C (in England) agrees to bail goods to D (an individual) in return for periodical payments. The agreement provides for the property in the goods to pass to D on payment of a total of £7,500 and the exercise by D of an option to purchase. The sum of £7,500 includes a down-payment of £1,000. It also includes an amount which, according to regulations made under section 20(1), constitutes a total charge for credit of £1,500.

Analysis This is a hire-purchase agreement with a deposit of £1,000 and a total price of £7,500 (see definitions of 'hire-purchase agreement', 'deposit' and 'total price' in section 189(1)). By section 9(3), it is taken to provide credit amounting to £7,500 − (£1,500 + £1,000), which equals £5,000. Under section 8(2), the agreement is therefore a consumer credit agreement, and under sections 9(3) and 11(1) it is a restricted-use credit agreement for fixed-sum credit. A similar result would follow if the agreement by C had been a hiring agreement in Scotland.

Example 11

Facts X (an individual) borrows £500 from Y (Finance). As a condition of the granting of the loan X is required—
    (a)   to execute a second mortgage on his house in favour of Y (Finance), and
    (b)   to take out a policy of insurance on his life with Y (Insurances).
In accordance with the loan agreement, the policy is charged to Y (Finance) as collateral security for the loan. The two companies are associates within the meaning of section 184(3).

Analysis The second mortgage is a transaction for the provision of security and accordingly does not fall within section 19(1), but the taking out of the insurance policy is a linked transaction falling within section 19(1)(a). The charging of the policy is a separate transaction (made between different parties) for the provision of security and again is excluded from section 19(1). The only linked transaction is therefore the taking out of the insurance policy. If X had not been required by the loan agreement to take out the policy, but it had been done at the suggestion of Y (Finance) to induce them to enter into the loan agreement, it would have been a linked transaction under section 19(1)(c)(i) by virtue of section 19(2)(a).

Example 12

Facts   The N Bank agrees to lend O (an individual) £2,000 to buy a car from P. To make sure the loan is used as intended, the N Bank stipulates that the money must be paid by it direct to P.

Analysis   The agreement is a consumer credit agreement by virtue of section 8(2). Since it falls within section 11(1)(b), it is a restricted-use credit agreement, P being the supplier. If the N Bank had not stipulated for direct payment to the supplier, section 11(3) would have operated and made the agreement into one for unrestricted-use credit.

Example 13

Facts   Q, a debt-adjuster, agrees to pay off debts owed by R (an individual) to various moneylenders. For this purpose the agreement provides for the making of a loan by Q to R in return for R's agreeing to repay the loan by instalments with interest. The loan money is not paid over to R but retained by Q and used to pay off the money lenders.

Analysis   This is an agreement to refinance existing indebtedness of the debtor's, and if the loan by Q does not exceed £5,000 is a restricted-use credit agreement falling within section 11(1)(c).

Example 14

Facts   On payment of £1, S issues to T (an individual) a trading check under which T can spend up to £20 at any shop which has agreed, or in future agrees, to accept S's trading checks.

Analysis   The trading check is a credit-token falling within section 14(1)(b). The credit-token agreement is a restricted-use credit agreement within section 11(1)(b), any shop in which the credit-token is used being the 'supplier'. The fact that further shops may be added after the issue of the credit-token is irrelevant in view of section 11(4).

Example 15

Facts   A retailer L agrees with M (an individual) to open an account in M's name and, in return for M's promise to pay a specified minimum sum into the account each month and to pay a monthly charge for credit, agrees to allow to be debited to the account, in respect of purchases made by M from L, such sums as will not increase the debit balance at any time beyond the credit limit, defined in the agreement as a given multiple of the specified minimum sum.

Analysis   This agreement provides credit falling within the definition of running-account credit in section 10(1)(a). Provided the credit limit is not over £5,000, the agreement falls within section 8(2) and is a consumer credit agreement for running-account credit.

Example 16

Facts   Under an unsecured agreement, A (Credit), an associate of the A Bank, issues to B (an individual) a credit-card for use in obtaining cash on credit from A (Credit), to be paid by branches of the A Bank (acting as agent of A (Credit)), or goods or cash from suppliers or banks who have agreed to honour credit-cards issued by A (Credit). The credit limit is £30.

Analysis This is a credit-token agreement falling within section 14(1)(a) and (b). It is a regulated consumer credit agreement for running-account credit. Since the credit limit does not exceed £30, the agreement is a small agreement. So far as the agreement relates to goods it is a debtor-creditor-supplier agreement within section 12(b), since it provides restricted-use credit under section 11(1)(b). So far as it relates to cash it is a debtor-creditor agreement within section 13(c) and the credit it provides is unrestricted-use credit. This is therefore a multiple agreement. In that the whole agreement falls within several of the categories of agreement mentioned in this Act, it is, by section 18(3), to be treated as an agreement in each of those categories. So far as it is a debtor-creditor-supplier agreement providing restricted-use credit it is, by section 18(2), to be treated as a separate agreement; and similarly so far as it is a debtor-creditor agreement providing unrestricted-use credit. (See also Example 22.)

Example 17

Facts The manager of the C Bank agrees orally with D (an individual) to open a current account in D's name. Nothing is said about overdraft facilities. After maintaining the account in credit for some weeks, D draws a cheque in favour of E for an amount exceeding D's credit balance by £20. E presents the cheque and the Bank pay it.

Analysis In drawing the cheque D, by implication, requests the Bank to grant him an overdraft of £20 on its usual terms as to interest and other charges. In deciding to honour the cheque, the Bank by implication accept the offer. This constitutes a regulated small consumer credit agreement for unrestricted-use, fixed sum credit. It is a debtor-creditor agreement, and falls within section 74(1)(b) *if covered by a determination under section 74(3).* (Compare Example 18.)

Example 18

Facts F (an individual) has had a current account with the G Bank for many years. Although usually in credit, the account has been allowed by the Bank to become overdrawn from time to time. The maximum such overdraft has been is about £1,000. No explicit agreement has ever been made about overdraft facilities. Now, with a credit balance of £500, F draws a cheque for £1,300.

Analysis It might well be held that the agreement with F (express or implied) under which the Bank operate his account includes an implied term giving him the right to overdraft facilities up to say £1,000. If so, the agreement is a regulated consumer credit agreement for unrestricted-use, running-account credit. It is a debtor-creditor agreement, and falls within section 74(1)(b) *if covered by a direction under section 74(3).* It is also a multiple agreement, part of which (i.e. the part not dealing with the overdraft), as referred to in section 18(1)(a), falls within a category of agreement not mentioned in this Act. (Compare Example 17.)

Example 19

Facts H (a finance house) agrees with J (a partnership of individuals) to open an unsecured loan account in J's name on which the debit balance is not to exceed £7,500 (having regard to payments into the account made from time to time by J). Interest is to be payable in advance on this sum, with provision for yearly adjustments. H is entitled to debit the account with interest, a 'setting-up' charge, and other charges. Before J has an opportunity to draw on the account it is initially debited with £2,250 for advance interest and other charges.

Analysis This is a personal running-account credit agreement (see sections 8(1) and 10(1)(a), and definition of 'individual' in section 189(1)). By section 10(2) the credit limit is £7,000. By section 9(4) however the initial debit of £2,250, and any other charges later debited to the account by H, are not to be treated as credit even though time is allowed for their payment. Effect is given to this by section 10(3). Although the credit limit of £7,000 exceeds the amount (£5,000) specified in section 8(2) as the maximum for a consumer credit agreement, so that the agreement is not within section 10(3)(a), it is caught by section 10(3)(b)(i). At the beginning J can effectively draw (as credit) no more than £4,750, so the agreement is a consumer credit agreement.

Example 20

Facts   K (in England) agrees with L (an individual) to bail goods to L for a period of three years certain at £2,200 a year, payable quarterly. The agreement contains no provision for the passing of the property in the goods to L.

Analysis   This is not a hire-purchase agreement (see paragraph (b) of the definition of that term in section 189(1)), and is capable of subsisting for more than three months. Paragraphs (a) and (b) of section 15(1) are therefore satisfied, but paragraph (c) is not. The payments by L must exceed £5,000 if he conforms to the agreement. It is true that under section 101 L has a right to terminate the agreement on giving K three months' notice expiring not earlier than eighteen months after the making of the agreement, but that section applies only where the agreement is a regulated consumer hire agreement apart from the section (see subsection (1)). So the agreement is not a consumer hire agreement, though it would be if the hire charge were say £1,500 a year, or there were a 'break' clause in it operable by either party before the hire charges exceeded £5,000. A similar result would follow if the agreement by K had been a hiring agreement in Scotland.

Example 21

Facts   The P Bank decides to issue cheque cards to its customers under a scheme whereby the bank undertakes to honour cheques of up to £30 in every case where the payee has taken the cheque in reliance on the cheque card, whether the customer has funds in his account or not. The P Bank writes to the major retailers advising them of this scheme and also publicises it by advertising. The Bank issues a cheque card to Q (an individual), who uses it to pay by cheque for goods costing £20 bought by Q from R, a major retailer. At the time, Q has £500 in his account at the P Bank.

Analysis   The agreement under which the cheque card is issued to Q is a consumer credit agreement even though at all relevant times Q has more than £30 in his account. This is because Q is free to draw out his whole balance and then use the cheque card, in which case the Bank has bound itself to honour the cheque. In other words the cheque card agreement provides Q with credit, whether he avails himself of it or not. Since the amount of the credit is not subject to any express limit, the cheque card can be used any number of times. It may be presumed however that section 10(3)(b)(iii) will apply. The agreement is an unrestricted-use debtor-creditor agreement (by section 13(c)). Although the P Bank wrote to R informing R of the P Bank's willingness to honour any cheque taken by R in reliance on a cheque card, this does not constitute pre-existing arrangements as mentioned in section 13(c) because section 187(3) operates to prevent it. The agreement is not a credit-token agreement within section 14(1)(b) because payment by the P Bank to R, would be a payment of the cheque and not a payment for the goods.

Example 22

Facts   The facts are as in Example 16. On one occasion B uses the credit-card in a way which increases his debit balance with A (Credit) to £40. A (Credit) writes to B agreeing to allow the excess on that occasion only, but stating that it must be paid off within one month.

Analysis   In exceeding his credit limit B, by implication, requests A (Credit) to allow him a temporary excess (compare Example 17). A (Credit) is thus faced by B's action with the choice of treating it as a breach of contract or granting his implied request. He does the latter. If he had done the former, B would be treated as taking credit to which he was not entitled (see section 14(3)) and, subject to the terms of his contract with A (Credit), would be liable to damages for breach of contract. As it is, the agreement to allow the excess varies the original credit-token agreement by adding a new term. Under section 10(2), the new term is to be disregarded in arriving at the credit limit, so that the credit-token agreement at no time ceases to be a small agreement. By section 82(2) the later agreement is deemed to revoke the original agreement and contain provisions reproducing the combined effect of the two agreements. By section 82(4), this later agreement is exempted from Part V (except section 56).

Example 23

Facts   Under an oral agreement made on 10th January, X (an individual) has an overdraft on his current account at the Y bank with a credit limit of £100. On 15th February, when his overdraft stands at £90, X draws a cheque for £25. It is the first time that X has exceeded his credit limit, and on 16th February the bank honours the cheque.

Analysis   The agreement of 10th January is a consumer credit agreement for running-account credit. The agreement of 15th–16th February varies the earlier agreement by adding a term allowing the credit limit to be exceeded merely temporarily. By section 82(2) the later agreement is deemed to revoke the earlier agreement and reproduce the combined effect of the two agreements. By section 82(4), Part V of this Act (except section 56) does not apply to the later agreement. By section 18(5), a term allowing a merely temporary excess over the credit limit is not to be treated as a separate agreement, or as providing fixed-sum credit. The whole of the £115 owed to the bank by X on 16th February is therefore running-account credit.

Example 24

Facts   On 1st March 1975 Z (in England) enters into an agreement with A (an unincorporated body of persons) to bail to A equipment consisting of two components (component P and component Q). The agreement is not a hire-purchase agreement and is for a fixed term of 3 years, so paragraphs (a) and (b) of section 15(1) are both satisfied. The rental is payable monthly at a rate of £2,400 a year, but the agreement provides that this is to be reduced to £1,200 a year for the remainder of the agreement if at any time during its currency A returns component Q to the owner Z. On 5th May 1976 A is incorporated as A Ltd, taking over A's assets and liabilities. On 1st March 1977, A Ltd returns component Q. On 1st January 1978, Z and A Ltd agree to extend the earlier agreement by one year, increasing the rental for the final year by £250 to £1,450.

Analysis   When entered into on 1st March 1975, the agreement is a consumer hire agreement. A falls within the definition of 'individual' in section 189(1) and if A returns component Q before 1st May 1976 the total rental will not exceed £5,000 (see section 15(1)(c)). When this date is passed without component Q having been returned it is obvious that the total rental must now exceed £5,000. Does this mean that the agreement then ceases to be a consumer hire agreement? The answer is no, because there has been no change in the terms of the agreement, and without such a change the agreement cannot move from one category to the other. Similarly, the fact that A's rights and duties under the agreement pass to a body corporate on 5th May 1976 does not cause the agreement to cease to be a consumer hire agreement (see definition of 'hirer' in section 189(1)).

The effect of the modifying agreement of 1st January 1978 is governed by section 82(2), which requires it to be treated as containing provisions reproducing the combined effect of the two actual agreements, that is to say as providing that—

    (a)   obligations outstanding on 1st January 1978 are to be treated as outstanding under the modifying agreement;

(b)   the modifying agreement applies at the old rate of hire for the months of January and February 1978, and
(c)   for the year beginning 1st March 1978 A Ltd will be the bailee of component P at a rental of £1,450.
The total rental under the modifying agreement is £1,850. Accordingly the modifying agreement is a regulated agreement. Even if the total rental under the modifying agreement exceeded £5,000 it would still be regulated because of the provisions of section 82(3).

UNFAIR CONTRACT TERMS ACT 1977
(1977, c 50)

PART II
AMENDMENT OF LAW FOR SCOTLAND

15   Scope of Part II
(1)   This Part of this Act [. . .] is subject to Part III of this Act and does not affect the validity of any discharge or indemnity given by a person in consideration of the receipt by him of compensation in settlement of any claim which he has.
(2)   Subject to subsection (3) below, sections 16 to 18 of this Act apply to any contract only to the extent that the contract—
    (a)   relates to the transfer of the ownership or possession of goods from one person to another (with or without work having been done on them);
    (b)   constitutes a contract of service or apprenticeship;
    (c)   relates to services of whatever kind, including (without prejudice to the foregoing generality) carriage, deposit and pledge, care and custody, mandate, agency, loan and services relating to the use of land;
    (d)   relates to the liability of an occupier of land to persons entering upon or using that land;
    (e)   relates to a grant of any right or permission to enter upon or use land not amounting to an estate or interest in the land.
(3)   Notwithstanding anything in subsection (2) above, sections 16 to 18—
    (a)   do not apply to any contract to the extent that the contract—
        (i)   is a contract of insurance (including a contract to pay an annuity on human life);
        (ii)   relates to the formation, constitution or dissolution of any body corporate or unincorporated association or partnership;
    (b)   apply to—
    a contract of marine salvage or towage;
    a charter party of a ship or hovercraft;
    a contract for the carriage of goods by ship or hovercraft; or
    a contract to which subsection (4) below relates,
only to the extent that—
        (i)   both parties deal or hold themselves out as dealing in the course of a business (and then only in so far as the contract purports to exclude or restrict liability for breach of duty in respect of death or personal injury); or
        (ii)   the contract is a consumer contract (and then only in favour of the consumer).
(4)   This subsection relates to a contract in pursuance of which goods are carried by ship or hovercraft and which either—
    (a)   specifies ship or hovercraft as the means of carriage over part of the journey to be covered; or
    (b)   makes no provision as to the means of carriage and does not exclude ship or hovercraft as that means,
in so far as the contract operates for and in relation to the carriage of the goods by that means.

16   Liability for breach of duty

(1) [Subject to subsection (1A) below,] where a term of a contract [, or a provision of a notice given to persons generally or to particular persons,] purports to exclude or restrict liability for breach of duty arising in the course of any business or from the occupation of any premises used for business purposes of the occupier, that term [or provision]—

(a)   shall be void in any case where such exclusion or restriction is in respect of death or personal injury;

(b)   shall, in any other case, have no effect if it was not fair and reasonable to incorporate the term in the contract [or, as the case may be, if it is not fair and reasonable to allow reliance on the provision].

[(1A)   Nothing in paragraph (b) of subsection (1) above shall be taken as implying that a provision of a notice has effect in circumstances where, apart from that paragraph, it would not have effect.]

(2)   Subsection (1)(a) above does not affect the validity of any discharge and indemnity given by a person, on or in connection with an award to him of compensation for pneumoconiosis attributable to employment in the coal industry, in respect of any further claim arising from his contracting that disease.

(3)   Where under subsection (1) above a term of a contract [or a provision of a notice] is void or has no effect, the fact that a person agreed to, or was aware of, the term [or provision] shall not of itself be sufficient evidence that he knowingly and voluntarily assumed any risk.

17   Control of unreasonable exemptions in consumer or standard form contracts

(1)   Any term of a contract which is a consumer contract or a standard form contract shall have no effect for the purpose of enabling a party to the contract—

(a)   who is in breach of a contractual obligation, to exclude or restrict any liability of his to the consumer or customer in respect of the breach;

(b)   in respect of a contractual obligation, to render no performance, or to render a performance substantially different from that which the consumer or customer reasonably expected from the contract;

if it was not fair and reasonable to incorporate the term in the contract.

(2)   In this section 'customer' means a party to a standard form contract who deals on the basis of written standard terms of business of the other party to the contract who himself deals in the course of a business.

18   Unreasonable indemnity clauses in consumer contracts

(1)   Any term of a contract which is a consumer contract shall have no effect for the purpose of making the consumer indemnify another person (whether a party to the contract or not) in respect of liability which that other person may incur as a result of breach of duty or breach of contract, if it was not fair and reasonable to incorporate the term in the contract.

(2)   In this section 'liability' means liability arising in the course of any business or from the occupation of any premises used for business purposes of the occupier.

19   'Guarantee' of consumer goods

(1)   This section applies to a guarantee—

(a)   in relation to goods which are of a type ordinarily supplied for private use or consumption; and

(b)   which is not a guarantee given by one party to the other party to a contract under or in pursuance of which the ownership or possession of the goods to which the guarantee relates is transferred.

(2)   A term of a guarantee to which this section applies shall be void in so far as it purports to exclude or restrict liability for loss or damage (including death or personal injury)—

(a)   arising from the goods proving defective while—

(i)   in use otherwise than exclusively for the purposes of a business; or

(ii)   in the possession of a person for such use; and

(b)   resulting from the breach of duty of a person concerned in the manufacture or distribution of the goods.

(3)   For the purposes of this section, any document is a guarantee if it contains or purports to contain some promise or assurance (however worded or presented) that defects will be made good by complete or partial replacement, or by repair, monetary compensation or otherwise.

20   Obligations implied by law in sale and hire-purchase contracts

(1)   Any term of a contract which purports to exclude or restrict liability for breach of the obligations arising from—

(a)   section 12 of the Sale of Goods Act [1979] (seller's implied undertakings as to title etc);

(b)   section 8 of the Supply of Goods (Implied Terms) Act 1973 (implied terms as to title in hire-purchase agreements),

shall be void.

(2)   Any term of a contract which purports to exclude or restrict liability for breach of the obligations arising from—

(a)   section 13, 14 or 15 of the said Act of [1979] (seller's implied undertakings as to conformity of goods with description or sample, or as to their quality or fitness for a particular purpose);

(b)   section 9, 10 or 11 of the said Act of 1973 (the corresponding provisions in relation to hire-purchase),

shall—

(i)   in the case of a consumer contract, be void against the consumer;

(ii)   in any other case, have no effect if it was not fair and reasonable to incorporate the term in the contract.

21   Obligations implied by law in other contracts for the supply of goods

(1)   Any term of a contract to which this section applies purporting to exclude or restrict liability for breach of an obligation—

(a)   such as is referred to in subsection (3)(a) below—

(i)   in the case of a consumer contract, shall be void against the consumer, and

(ii)   in any other case, shall have no effect if it was not fair and reasonable to incorporate the term in the contract;

(b)   such as is referred to in subsection (3)(b) below, shall have no effect if it was not fair and reasonable to incorporate the term in the contract.

(2)   This section applies to any contract to the extent that it relates to any such matter as is referred to in section 15(2)(a) of this Act, but does not apply to—

(a)   a contract of sale of goods or a hire-purchase agreement; or

(b)   a charterparty of a ship or hovercraft unless it is a consumer contract (and then only in favour of the consumer).

(3)   An obligation referred to in this subsection is an obligation incurred under a contract in the course of a business and arising by implication of law from the nature of the contract which relates—

(a)   to the correspondence of goods with description or sample, or to the quality or fitness of goods for any particular purpose; or

(b)   to any right to transfer ownership or possession of goods, or to the enjoyment of quiet possession of goods.

[(3A)   Notwithstanding anything in the foregoing provisions of this section, any term of a contract which purports to exclude or restrict liability for breach of the obligations arising under section 11B of the Supply of Goods and Services Act 1982 (implied terms about title, freedom from encumbrances and quiet possession in certain contracts for the transfer of property in goods) shall be void.]

[. . .]

22 Consequence of breach

For the avoidance of doubt, where any provision of this Part of this Act requires that the incorporation of a term in a contract must be fair and reasonable for that term to have effect—

(a) if that requirement is satisfied, the term may be given effect to notwithstanding that the contract has been terminated in consequence of breach of that contract;

(b) for the term to be given effect to, that requirement must be satisfied even where a party who is entitled to rescind the contract elects not to rescind it.

23 Evasion by means of secondary contract

Any term of any contract shall be void which purports to exclude or restrict, or has the effect of excluding or restricting—

(a) the exercise, by a party to any other contract, of any right or remedy which arises in respect of that other contract in consequence of breach of duty, or of obligation, liability for which could not by virtue of the provisions of this Part of this Act be excluded or restricted by a term of that other contract;

(b) the application of the provisions of this Part of this Act in respect of that or any other contract.

24 The 'reasonableness' test

(1) In determining for the purposes of this Part of this Act whether it was fair and reasonable to incorporate a term in a contract, regard shall be had only to the circumstances which were, or ought reasonably to have been, known to or in the contemplation of the parties to the contract at the time the contract was made.

(2) In determining for the purposes of section 20 or 21 of this Act whether it was fair and reasonable to incorporate a term in a contract, regard shall be had in particular to the matters specified in Schedule 2 to this Act; but this sub-section shall not prevent a court or arbiter from holding in accordance with any rule of law, that a term which purports to exclude or restrict any relevant liability is not a term of the contract.

[(2A) In determining for the purposes of this Part of this Act whether it is fair and reasonable to allow reliance on a provision of a notice (not being a notice having contractual effect), regard shall be had to all the circumstances obtaining when the liability arose or (but for the provision) would have arisen.]

(3) Where a term in a contract [or a provision of a notice] purports to restrict liability to a specified sum of money, and the question arises for the purposes of this Part of this Act whether it was fair and reasonable to incorporate the term in the contract [or whether it is fair and reasonable to allow reliance on the provision], then, without prejudice to subsection (2) above [in the case of a term in a contract], regard shall be had in particular to—

(a) the resources which the party seeking to rely on that term [or provision] could expect to be available to him for the purpose of meeting the liability should it arise;

(b) how far it was open to that party to cover himself by insurance.

(4) The onus of proving that it was fair and reasonable to incorporate a term in a contract [or that it is fair and reasonable to allow reliance on a provision of a notice] shall lie on the party so contending.

25 Interpretation of Part II

(1) In this Part of this Act—

'breach of duty' means the breach—

(a) of any obligation, arising from the express or implied terms of a contract, to take reasonable care or exercise reasonable skill in the performance of the contract;

(b) of any common law duty to take reasonable care or exercise reasonable skill;

(c)   of the duty of reasonable care imposed by section 2(1) of the Occupiers' Liability (Scotland) Act 1960;

'business' includes a profession and the activities of any government department or local or public authority;

'consumer' has the meaning assigned to that expression in the definition in this section of 'consumer contract';

'consumer contract' means [subject to subsections (1A) and (1B) below] a contract [. . .] in which—

(a)   one party to the contract deals, and the other party to the contract ('the consumer') does not deal or hold himself out as dealing, in the course of a business, and

(b)   in the case of a contract such as is mentioned in section 15(2)(a) of this Act, the goods are of a type ordinarily supplied for private use or consumption; and for the purposes of this Part of this Act the onus of proving that a contract is not to be regarded as a consumer contract shall lie on the party so contending;

'goods' has the same meaning as in the Sale of Goods Act [1979];

'hire-purchase agreement' has the same meaning as in section 189(1) of the Consumer Credit Act 1974;

['notice' includes an announcement, whether or not in writing, and any other communication or pretended communication;]

'personal injury' includes any disease and any impairment of physical or mental condition.

[(1A)   Where the consumer is an individual, paragraph (b) in the definition of 'consumer contract' in subsection (1) must be disregarded.

(1B)   The expression of 'consumer contract' does not include a contract in which—

(a)   the buyer is an individual and the goods are second hand goods sold by public auction at which individuals have the opportunity of attending in person; or

(b)   the buyer is not an individual and the goods are sold by auction or competitive tender.]

(2)   In relation to any breach of duty or obligation, it is immaterial for any purpose of this Part of this Act whether the act or omission giving rise to that breach was inadvertent or intentional or whether liability for it arises directly or vicariously.

(3)   In this Part of this Act, any reference to excluding or restricting any liability includes—

(a)   making the liability or its enforcement subject to any restrictive or onerous conditions;

(b)   excluding or restricting any right or remedy in respect of the liability, or subjecting a person to any prejudice in consequence of his pursuing any such right or remedy;

(c)   excluding or restricting any rule of evidence or procedure;

[. . .]

(5)   In section 15 and 16 and 19 to 21 of this Act, any reference to excluding or restricting liability for breach of any obligation or duty shall include a reference to excluding or restricting the obligation or duty itself.

PART III
PROVISIONS APPLYING TO WHOLE OF UNITED KINGDOM

26   International supply contracts

(1)   The limits imposed by this Act on the extent to which a person may exclude or restrict liability by reference to a contract term do not apply to liability arising under such a contract as is described in subsection (3) below.

(2)   The terms of such a contract are not subject to any requirement of reasonableness under section 3 or 4: and nothing in Part II of this Act should

require the incorporation of the terms of such a contract to be fair and reasonable for them to have effect.

(3) Subject to subsection (4), that description of contract is one whose characteristics are the following—

(a) either it is a contract of sale of goods or it is one under or in pursuance of which the possession of ownership of goods passes, and

(b) it is made by parties whose places of business (or, if they have none, habitual residences) are in the territories of different States (the Channel Islands and the Isle of Man being treated for this purpose as different States from the United Kingdom).

(4) A contract falls within subsection (3) above only if either—

(a) the goods in question are, at the time of the conclusion of the contract, in the course of carriage, or will be carried, from the territory of one State to the territory of another; or

(b) the acts constituting the offer and acceptance have been done in the territories of different States; or

(c) the contract provides for the goods to be delivered to the territory of a state other than that within whose territory those acts were done.

27 Choice of law clauses

(1) Where the [law applicable to] a contract is the law of any part of the United Kingdom only by choice of the parties (and apart from that choice would be the law of some country outside the United Kingdom) sections 2 to 7 and 16 to 21 of this Act do not operate as part [of the law applicable to the contract].

(2) This Act has effect notwithstanding any contract term which applies or purports to apply the law of some country outside the United Kingdom, where (either or both)—

(a) the term appears to the court, or arbitrator or arbiter to have been imposed wholly or mainly for the purpose of enabling the party imposing it to evade the operation of this Act; or

(b) in the making of the contract one of the parties dealt as consumer, and he was then habitually resident in the United Kingdom, and the essential steps necessary for the making of the contract were taken there, whether by him or by others on his behalf.

29 Saving for other relevant legislation

(1) Nothing in this Act removes or restricts the effect of, or prevents reliance upon, any contractual provision which—

(a) is authorised or required by the express terms or necessary implication of an enactment; or

(b) being made with a view to compliance with an international agreement to which the United Kingdom is a party, does not operate more restrictively than is contemplated by the agreement.

(2) A contract term is to be taken—

(a) for the purposes of Part I of this Act, as satisfying the requirement of reasonableness [. . .]

if it is incorporated or approved by, or incorporated pursuant to a decision or ruling of, a competent authority acting in the exercise of any statutory jurisdiction or function and is not a term in a contract to which the competent authority is itself a party.

(3) In this section—

'competent authority' means any court, arbitrator or arbiter, government department or public authority;

'enactment' means any legislation (including subordinate legislation) of the United Kingdom or Northern Ireland and any instrument having effect by virtue of such legislation; and

'statutory' means conferred by an enactment.

SCHEDULE 2
'GUIDELINES' FOR APPLICATION OF REASONABLENESS TEST
Sections 11(2) and 24(2)

The matters to which regard is to be had in particular for the purposes of sections 6(3), 7(3) and (4), 20 and 21 are any of the following which appear to be relevant—

(a)   the strength of the bargaining positions of the parties relative to each other, taking into account (among other things) alternative means by which the customer's requirements could have been met;

(b)   whether the customer received an inducement to agree to the terms, or in accepting it had an opportunity of entering into a similar contract with other persons, but without having to accept similar terms;

(c)   whether the customer knew or ought reasonably to have known of the existence and extent of the term (having regard, among other things, to any customs of the trade and any previous course of dealing between the parties);

(d)   where the term excludes or restricts any relevant liability if some condition is not complied with, whether it was reasonable at the time of the contract to expect that compliance with that condition would be practicable;

(e)   whether the goods were manufactured, processed or adapted to the special order of the customer.

SALE OF GOODS ACT 1979
(1979, c 54)

PART I
CONTRACTS TO WHICH ACT APPLIES

1   Contracts to which Act applies

(1)   This Act applies to contracts of sale of goods made on or after (but not to those made before) 1 January 1894.

(2)   In relation to contracts made on certain dates, this Act applies subject to the modification of certain of its sections as mentioned in Schedule 1 below.

(3)   Any such modification is indicated in the section concerned by a reference to Schedule 1 below.

(4)   Accordingly, where a section does not contain such a reference, this Act applies in relation to the contract concerned without such modification of the section.

PART II
FORMATION OF THE CONTRACT

Contract of sale

2   Contract of sale

(1)   A contract of sale of goods is a contract by which the seller transfers or agrees to transfer the property in goods to the buyer for a money consideration, called the price.

(2)   There may be a contract of sale between one part owner and another.

(3)   A contract of sale may be absolute or conditional.

(4)   Where under a contract of sale the property in the goods is transferred from the seller to the buyer the contract is called a sale.

(5)   Where under a contract of sale the transfer of the property in the goods is to take place at a future time or subject to some condition later to be fulfilled the contract is called an agreement to sell.

(6)   An agreement to sell becomes a sale when the time elapses or the conditions are fulfilled subject to which the property in the goods is to be transferred.

3 Capacity to buy and sell

(1) Capacity to buy and sell is regulated by the general law concerning capacity to contract and to transfer and acquire property.

(2) Where necessaries are sold and delivered [. . .] to a person who by reason of mental incapacity or drunkenness is incompetent to contract, he must pay a reasonable price for them.

(3) In subsection (2) above 'necessaries' means goods suitable to the condition in life of the [. . .] person concerned and to his actual requirements at the time of the sale and delivery.

Formalities of contract

4 How contract of sale is made

(1) Subject to this and any other Act, a contract of sale may be made in writing (either with or without seal), or by word of mouth, or partly in writing and partly by word of mouth, or may be implied from the conduct of the parties.

(2) Nothing in this section affects the law relating to corporations.

Subject matter of contract

5 Existing or future goods

(1) The goods which form the subject of a contract of sale may be either existing goods, owned or possessed by the seller, or goods to be manufactured or acquired by him after the making of the contract of sale, in this Act called future goods.

(2) There may be a contract for the sale of goods the acquisition of which by the seller depends on a contingency which may or may not happen.

(3) Where by a contract of sale the seller purports to effect a present sale of future goods, the contract operates as an agreement to sell the goods.

6 Goods which have perished

Where there is a contract for the sale of specific goods, and the goods without the knowledge of the seller have perished at the time when a contract is made, the contract is void.

7 Goods perishing before sale but after agreement to sell

Where there is an agreement to sell specific goods and subsequently the goods, without any fault on the part of the seller or buyer, perish before the risk passes to the buyer, the agreement is avoided.

The price

8 Ascertainment of price

(1) The price in a contract of sale may be fixed by the contract, or may be left to be fixed in a manner agreed by the contract, or may be determined by the course of dealing between the parties.

(2) Where the price is not determined as mentioned in subsection (1) above the buyer must pay a reasonable price.

(3) What is a reasonable price is a question of fact dependent on the circumstances of each particular case.

9 Agreement to sell at valuation

(1) Where there is an agreement to sell goods on the terms that the price is to be fixed by the valuation of a third party, and he cannot or does not make the valuation, the agreement is avoided; but if the goods or any part of them have been delivered to and appropriated by the buyer he must pay a reasonable price for them.

(2) Where the third party is prevented from making the valuation by the fault

of the seller or buyer, the party not at fault may maintain an action for damages against the party at fault.

10   Stipulations about time

(1)   Unless a different intention appears from the terms of the contract, stipulations as to time of payment are not of the essence of a contract of sale.

(2)   Whether any other stipulation as to time is or is not of the essence of the contract depends on the terms of the contract.

(3)   In a contract of sale 'month' prima facie means calendar month.

11   [*Does not apply to Scotland.*]

12   Implied terms about title, etc

(1)   In a contract of sale, other than one to which subsection (3) below applies, there is an implied [term] on the part of the seller that in the case of a sale he has a right to sell the goods, and in the case of an agreement to sell he will have such a right at the time when the property is to pass.

(2)   In a contract of sale, other than one to which subsection (3) below applies, there is also an implied [term] that—

  (a)   the goods are free, and will remain free until the time when the property is to pass, from any charge or encumbrance not disclosed or known to the buyer before the contract is made, and

  (b)   the buyer will enjoy quiet possession of the goods except so far as it may be disturbed by the owner or other person entitled to the benefit of any charge or encumbrance so disclosed or known.

(3)   This subsection applies to a contract of sale in the case of which there appears from the contract or is to be inferred from its circumstances an intention that the seller should transfer only such title as he or a third person may have.

(4)   In a contract to which subsection (3) above applies there is an implied [term] that all charges or encumbrances known to the seller and not known to the buyer have been disclosed to the buyer before the contract is made.

(5)   In a contract to which subsection (3) above applies there is also an implied [term] that none of the following will disturb the buyer's quiet possession of the goods, namely—

  (a)   the seller;

  (b)   in a case where the parties to the contract intend that the seller should transfer only such title as a third person may have, that person;

  (c)   anyone claiming through or under the seller or that third person otherwise than under a charge or encumbrance disclosed or known to the buyer before the contract is made.

[(5A)   As regards England and Wales and Northern Ireland, the term implied by subsection (1) above is a condition and the terms implied by subsections (2), (4) and (5) above are warranties.]

(6)   Paragraph 3 of Schedule 1 below applies in relation to a contract made before 18 May 1973.

13   Sale by description

(1)   Where there is a contract for the sale of goods by description, there is an implied [term] that the goods will correspond with the description.

[(1A)   As regards England and Wales and Northern Ireland, the term implied by subsection (1) above is a condition.]

(2)   If the sale is by sample as well as by description it is not sufficient that the bulk of the goods corresponds with the sample if the goods do not also correspond with the description.

(3)   A sale of goods is not prevented from being a sale by description by reason only that, being exposed for sale or hire, they are selected by the buyer.

(4)   Paragraph 4 of Schedule 1 below applies in relation to a contract made before 18 May 1973.

14   Implied terms about quality or fitness

(1)   Except as provided by this section and section 15 below and subject to any other enactment, there is no implied [term] about the quality or fitness for any particular purpose of goods supplied under a contract of sale.

[(2)   Where the seller sells goods in the course of a business, there is an implied term that the goods supplied under the contract are of satisfactory quality.

(2A)   For the purposes of this Act, goods are of satisfactory quality if they meet the standard that a reasonable person would regard as satisfactory, taking account of any description of the goods, the price (if relevant) and all the other relevant circumstances.

(2B)   For the purposes of this Act, the quality of goods includes their state and condition and the following (among others) are in appropriate cases aspects of the quality of goods—

(a)   fitness for all the purposes for which goods of the kind in question are commonly supplied,

(b)   appearance and finish,

(c)   freedom from minor defects,

(d)   safety, and

(e)   durability.

(2C)   The term implied by subsection (2) above does not extend to any matter making the quality of goods unsatisfactory—

(a)   which is specifically drawn to the buyer's attention before the contract is made,

(b)   where the buyer examines the goods before the contract is made, which that examination ought to reveal, or

(c)   in the case of a contract for sale by sample, which would have been apparent on a reasonable examination of the sample.]

[(2D)   If the buyer deals as consumer or, in Scotland, if a contract of sale is a consumer contract, the relevant circumstances mentioned in subsection (2A) above include any public statements on the specific characteristics of the goods made about them by the seller, the producer or his representative, particularly in advertising or on labelling.

(2E)   A public statement is not by virtue of subsection (2D) above a relevant circumstance for the purposes of subsection (2A) above in the case of a contract of sale, if the seller shows that—

(a)   at the time the contract was made, he was not, and could not reasonably have been, aware of the statement,

(b)   before the contract was made, the statement had been withdrawn in public or, to the extent that it contained anything which was incorrect or misleading, it had been corrected in public, or

(c)   the decision to buy the goods could not have been influenced by the statement.

(2F)   Subsections (2D) and (2E) above do not prevent any public statement from being a relevant circumstance for the purposes of subsection (2A) above (whether or not the buyer deals as consumer or, in Scotland, whether or not the contract of sale is a consumer contract) if the statement would have been such a circumstance apart from those subsections.]

(3)   Where the seller sells goods in the course of a business and the buyer, expressly or by implication, makes known—

(a)   to the seller, or

(b)   where the purchase price or part of it is payable by instalments and the goods were previously sold by a credit-broker to the seller, to that credit-broker, any particular purpose for which the goods are being bought,

there is an implied [term] that the goods supplied under the contract are reasonably fit for that purpose, whether or not that is a purpose for which such goods are
commonly supplied, except where the circumstances show that the buyer does not
rely, or that it is unreasonable for him to rely, on the skill or judgment of the seller
or credit-broker.

(4)   An implied [term] about quality or fitness for a particular purpose may be
annexed to a contract of sale by usage.

(5)   The preceding provisions of this section apply to a sale by a person who in
the course of a business is acting as agent for another as they apply to a sale by a
principal in the course of a business, except where that other is not selling in the
course of a business and either the buyer knows that fact or reasonable steps are
taken to bring it to the notice of the buyer before the contract is made.

[(6)   As regards England and Wales and Northern Ireland, the terms implied by
subsections (2) and (3) above are conditions.]

(7)   Paragraph 5 of Schedule 1 below applies in relation to a contract made on
or after 18 May 1973 and before the appointed day, and paragraph 6 in relation to
one made before 18 May 1973.

(8)   In subsection (7) above and paragraph 5 of Schedule 1 below references to
the appointed day are to the day appointed for the purposes of those provisions
by an order of the Secretary of State made by statutory instrument.

Sale by sample

15   Sale by sample
(1)   A contract of sale is a contract for sale by sample where there is an express
or implied term to that effect in the contract.

(2)   In the case of a contract for sale by sample there is an implied [term]—
   (a)   that the bulk will correspond with the sample in quality;
   [. . .]
   (c)   that the goods will be free from any defect, making their quality
unsatisfactory, which would not be apparent on reasonable examination of the
sample.

[(3)   As regards England and Wales and Northern Ireland, the term implied by
subsection (2) above is a condition.]

(4)   Paragraph 7 of Schedule 1 below applies in relation to a contract made
before 18 May 1973.

Miscellaneous

15A   [*Does not apply to Scotland.*]

[15B   Remedies for breach of contract as respects Scotland
(1)   Where in a contract of sale the seller is in breach of any term of the contract
(express or implied), the buyer shall be entitled—
   (a)   to claim damages, and
   (b)   if the breach is material, to reject any goods delivered under the contract
and treat it as repudiated.

(2)   Where a contract of sale is a consumer contract, then, for the purposes of
subsection (1)(b) above, breach by the seller of any term (express or implied)—
   (a)   as to the quality of the goods or their fitness for a purpose,
   (b)   if the goods are, or are to be, sold by description, that the goods will
correspond with the description,
   (c)   if the goods are, or are to be, sold by reference to a sample, that the bulk
   will correspond with the sample in quality,
shall be deemed to be a material breach.

(3)   This section applies to Scotland only.]

PART III
EFFECTS OF THE CONTRACT

Transfer of property as between seller and buyer

16   Goods must be ascertained
[Subject to section 20A below] where there is a contract for the sale of unascertained goods no property in the goods is transferred to the buyer unless and until the goods are ascertained.

17   Property passes when intended to pass
(1)   Where there is a contract for the sale of specific or ascertained goods the property in them is transferred to the buyer at such time as the parties to the contract intend it to be transferred.

(2)   For the purpose of ascertaining the intention of the parties regard shall be had to the terms of the contract, the conduct of the parties and the circumstances of the case.

18   Rules for ascertaining intention
Unless a different intention appears, the following are rules for ascertaining the intention of the parties as to the time at which the property in the goods is to pass to the buyer.

Rule 1.—Where there is an unconditional contract for the sale of specific goods in a deliverable state the property in the goods passes to the buyer when the contract is made, and it is immaterial whether the time of payment or the time of delivery, or both, be postponed.

Rule 2.—Where there is a contract for the sale of specific goods and the seller is bound to do something to the goods for the purpose of putting them into a deliverable state, the property does not pass until the thing is done and the buyer has notice that it has been done.

Rule 3.—Where there is a contract for the sale of specific goods in a deliverable state but the seller is bound to weigh, measure, test, or do some other act or thing with reference to the goods for the purpose of ascertaining the price, the property does not pass until the act or thing is done and the buyer has notice that it has been done.

Rule 4.—When goods are delivered to the buyer on approval or on sale or return or other similar terms the property in the goods passes to the buyer:—

(a)   when he signifies his approval or acceptance to the seller or does any other act adopting the transaction;

(b)   if he does not signify his approval or acceptance to the seller but retains the goods without giving notice of rejection, then, if a time has been fixed for the return of the goods, on the expiration of that time, and, if no time has been fixed, on the expiration of a reasonable time.

Rule 5.—(1)   Where there is a contract for the sale of unascertained or future goods by description, and goods of that description and in a deliverable state are unconditionally appropriated to the contract, either by the seller with the assent of the buyer or by the buyer with the assent of the seller, the property in the goods then passes to the buyer; and the assent may be express or implied, and may be given either before or after the appropriation is made.

(2)   Where, in pursuance of the contract, the seller delivers the goods to the buyer or to a carrier or other bailee or custodier (whether named by the buyer or not) for the purpose of transmission to the buyer, and does not reserve the right of disposal, he is to be taken to have unconditionally appropriated the goods to the contract.

[(3)   Where there is a contract for the sale of a specified quantity of unascertained goods in a deliverable state forming part of a bulk which is identified either in the contract or by subsequent agreement between the parties and the bulk is reduced to (or to less than) that quantity, then, if the buyer under that contract is the only buyer to whom goods are then due out of the bulk—

(a)   the remaining goods are to be taken as appropriated to that contract at the time when the bulk is so reduced; and

(b)   the property in those goods then passes to that buyer.

(4)   Paragraph (3) above applies also (with the necessary modifications) where a bulk is reduced to (or to less than) the aggregate of the quantities due to a single buyer under separate contracts relating to that bulk and he is the only buyer to whom goods are then due out of that bulk.]

19   Reservation of right of disposal

(1)   Where there is a contract for the sale of specific goods or where goods are subsequently appropriated to the contract, the seller may, by the terms of the contract or appropriation, reserve the right of disposal of the goods until certain conditions are fulfilled; and in such a case, notwithstanding the delivery of the goods to the buyer, or to a carrier or other bailee or custodier for the purpose of transmission to the buyer, the property in the goods does not pass to the buyer until the conditions imposed by the seller are fulfilled.

(2)   Where goods are shipped, and by the bill of lading the goods are deliverable to the order of the seller or his agent, the seller is prima facie to be taken to reserve the right of disposal.

(3)   Where the seller of goods draws on the buyer for the price, and transmits the bill of exchange and bill of lading to the buyer together to secure acceptance or payment of the bill of exchange, the buyer is bound to return the bill of lading if he does not honour the bill of exchange, and if he wrongfully retains the bill of lading the property in the goods does not pass to him.

20   [Passing of risk]

(1)   Unless otherwise agreed, the goods remain at the seller's risk until the property in them is transferred to the buyer, but when the property in them is transferred to the buyer the goods are at the buyer's risk whether delivery has been made or not.

(2)   But where delivery has been delayed through the fault of either buyer or seller the goods are at the risk of the party at fault as regards any loss which might not have occurred but for such fault.

(3)   Nothing in this section affects the duties or liabilities of either seller or buyer as a bailee or custodier of the goods of the other party.

[(4)   In a case where the buyer deals as consumer or, in Scotland, where there is a consumer contract in which the buyer is a consumer, subsections (1) to (3) above must be ignored and the goods remain at the seller's risk until they are delivered to the consumer.]

[20A   Undivided shares in goods forming part of a bulk

(1)   This section applies to a contract for the sale of a specified quantity of unascertained goods if the following conditions are met—

(a)   the goods or some of them form part of a bulk which is identified either in the contract or by subsequent agreement between the parties; and

(b)   the buyer has paid the price for some or all of the goods which are the subject of the contract and which form part of the bulk.

(2)   Where this section applies, then (unless the parties agree otherwise), as soon as the conditions specified in paragraphs (a) and (b) of subsection (1) above are met or at such later time as the parties may agree—

(a)   property in an undivided share in the bulk is transferred to the buyer; and

(b)   the buyer becomes an owner in common of the bulk.

(3)   Subject to subsection (4) below, for the purposes of this section, the undivided share of a buyer in a bulk at any time shall be such share as the quantity

of goods paid for and due to the buyer out of the bulk bears to the quantity of goods in the bulk at that time.

(4) Where the aggregate of the undivided shares of buyers in a bulk determined under subsection (3) above would at any time exceed the whole of the bulk at that time, the undivided share in the bulk of each buyer shall be reduced proportionately so that the aggregate of the undivided shares is equal to the whole bulk.

(5) Where a buyer has paid the price for only some of the goods due to him out of a bulk, any delivery to the buyer out of the bulk shall, for the purposes of this section, be ascribed in the first place to the goods in respect of which payment has been made.

(6) For the purpose of this section payment of part of the price for any goods shall be treated as payment for a corresponding part of the goods.]

[20B Deemed consent by co-owner to dealings in bulk goods

(1) A person who has become an owner in common of a bulk by virtue of section 20A above shall be deemed to have consented to—

(a) any delivery of goods out of the bulk to any other owner in common of the bulk, being goods which are due to him under his contract;

(b) any removal, dealing with, delivery or disposal of goods in the bulk by any other person who is an owner in common of the bulk in so far as the goods fall within that co-owner's undivided share in the bulk at the time of the removal, dealing, delivery or disposal.

(2) No cause of action shall accrue to anyone against a person by reason of that person having acted in accordance with paragraph (a) or (b) of subsection (1) above in reliance on any consent deemed to have been given under that subsection.

(3) Nothing in this section or section 20A above shall—

(a) impose an obligation on a buyer of goods out of a bulk to compensate any other buyer of goods out of that bulk for any shortfall in the goods received by that other buyer;

(b) affects any contractual arrangement between buyers of goods out of a bulk for adjustments between themselves; or

(c) affect the rights of any buyer under his contract.]

Transfer of title

21 Sale by person not the owner

(1) Subject to this Act, where goods are sold by a person who is not their owner, and who does not sell them under the authority or with the consent of the owner, the buyer acquires no better title to the goods than the seller had, unless the owner of the goods is by his conduct precluded from denying the seller's authority to sell.

(2) Nothing in this Act affects—

(a) the provisions of the Factors Acts or any enactment enabling the apparent owner of goods to dispose of them as if he were their true owner;

(b) the validity of any contract of sale under any special common law or statutory power of sale or under the order of a court of competent jurisdiction.

22 [*Does not apply to Scotland.*]

23 Sale under voidable title

When the seller of goods has a voidable title to them, but his title has not been avoided at the time of the sale, the buyer acquires a good title to the goods, provided he buys them in good faith and without notice of the seller's defect of title.

24 Seller in possession after sale

Where a person having sold goods continues or is in possession of the goods, or of the documents of title to the goods, the delivery or transfer by that person, or by a mercantile agent acting for him, of the goods or documents of title under any sale, pledge, or other disposition thereof, to any person receiving the same in good faith and without notice of the previous sale, has the same effect as if the person making the delivery or transfer were expressly authorised by the owner of the goods to make the same.

25 Buyer in possession after sale

(1) Where a person having bought or agreed to buy goods obtains, with the consent of the seller, possession of the goods or the documents of title to the goods, the delivery or transfer by that person, or by a mercantile agent acting for him, of the goods or documents of title, under any sale, pledge, or other disposition thereof, to any person receiving the same in good faith and without notice of any lien or other right of the original seller in respect of the goods, has the same effect as if the person making the delivery or transfer were a mercantile agent in possession of the goods or documents of title with the consent of the owner.

(2) For the purposes of subsection (1) above—

(a) the buyer under a conditional sale agreement is to be taken not to be a person who has bought or agreed to buy goods, and

(b) 'conditional sale agreement' means an agreement for the sale of goods which is a consumer credit agreement within the meaning of the Consumer Credit Act 1974 under which the purchase price or part of it is payable by instalments, and the property in the goods is to remain in the seller (notwithstanding that the buyer is to be in possession of the goods) until such conditions as to the payment of instalments or otherwise as may be specified in the agreement are fulfilled.

(3) Paragraph 9 of Schedule 1 below applies in relation to a contract under which a person buys or agrees to buy goods and which is made before the appointed day.

(4) In subsection (3) above and paragraph 9 of Schedule 1 below references to the appointed day are to the day appointed for the purposes of those provisions by an order of the Secretary of State made by statutory instrument.

26 Supplementary to sections 24 and 25

In sections 24 and 25 above 'mercantile agent' means a mercantile agent having in the customary course of his business as such agent authority either—

(a) to sell goods, or
(b) to consign goods for the purpose of sale, or
(c) to buy goods, or
(d) to raise money on the security of goods.

PART IV

PERFORMANCE OF THE CONTRACT

27 Duties of seller and buyer

It is the duty of the seller to deliver the goods, and of the buyer to accept and pay for them, in accordance with the terms of the contract of sale.

28 Payment and delivery are concurrent conditions

Unless otherwise agreed, delivery of the goods and payment of the price are concurrent conditions, that is to say, the seller must be ready and willing to give possession of the goods to the buyer in exchange for the price and the buyer must be ready and willing to pay the price in exchange for possession of the goods.

29 Rules about delivery

(1) Whether it is for the buyer to take possession of the goods or for the seller to send them to the buyer is a question depending in each case on the contract, express or implied, between the parties.

(2) Apart from any such contract, express or implied, the place of delivery is the seller's place of business if he has one, and if not, his residence; except that, if the contract is for the sale of specific goods, which to the knowledge of the parties when the contract is made are in some other place, then that place is the place of delivery.

(3) Where under the contract of sale the seller is bound to send the goods to the buyer, but no time for sending them is fixed, the seller is bound to send them within a reasonable time.

(4) Where the goods at the time of sale are in the possession of a third person, there is no delivery by seller to buyer unless and until the third person acknowledges to the buyer that he holds the goods on his behalf; but nothing in this section affects the operation of the issue or transfer of any document of title to goods.

(5) Demand or tender of delivery may be treated as ineffectual unless made at a reasonable hour, and what is a reasonable hour is a question of fact.

(6) Unless otherwise agreed, the expenses of and incidental to putting the goods into a deliverable state must be borne by the seller.

30 Delivery of wrong quantity

(1) Where the seller delivers to the buyer a quantity of goods less than he contracted to sell, the buyer may reject them, but if the buyer accepts the goods so delivered he must pay for them at the contract rate.

(2) Where the seller delivers to the buyer a quantity of goods larger than he contracted to sell, the buyer may accept the goods included in the contract and reject the rest, or he may reject the whole.

. . .

[(2C) Subsections (2A) and (2B) above do not apply to Scotland.

(2D) Where the seller delivers a quantity of goods—

(a) less than he contracted to sell, the buyer shall not be entitled to reject the goods under subsection (1) above,

(b) larger than he contracted to sell, the buyer shall not be entitled to reject the whole under subsection (2) above,

unless the shortfall or excess is material.

(2E) Subsection (2D) above applies to Scotland only.]

(3) Where the seller delivers to the buyer a quantity of goods larger than he contracted to sell and the buyer accepts the whole of the goods so delivered he must pay for them at the contract rate.

[. . .]

(5) This section is subject to any usage of trade, special agreement, or course of dealing between the parties.

31 Instalment deliveries

(1) Unless otherwise agreed, the buyer of goods is not bound to accept delivery of them by instalments.

(2) Where there is a contract for the sale of goods to be delivered by stated instalments, which are to be separately paid for, and the seller makes defective deliveries in respect of one or more instalments, or the buyer neglects or refuses to take delivery of or pay for one or more instalments, it is a question in each case depending on the terms of the contract and the circumstances of the case whether the breach of contract is a repudiation of the whole contract or whether it is a severable breach giving rise to a claim for compensation but not to a right to treat the whole contract as repudiated.

32 Delivery to carrier

(1) Where, in pursuance of a contract of sale, the seller is authorised or required to send the goods to the buyer, delivery of the goods to a carrier (whether

named by the buyer or not) for the purpose of transmission to the buyer is prima facie deemed to be delivery of the goods to the buyer.

(2) Unless otherwise authorised by the buyer, the seller must make such contact with the carrier on behalf of the buyer as may be reasonable having regard to the nature of the goods and the other circumstances of the case; and if the seller omits to do so, and the goods are lost or damaged in course of transit, the buyer may decline to treat the delivery to the carrier as a delivery to himself or may hold the seller responsible in damages.

(3) Unless otherwise agreed, where goods are sent by the seller to the buyer by a route involving sea transit, under circumstances in which it is usual to insure, the seller must give such notice to the buyer as may enable him to insure them during their sea transit, and if the seller fails to do so, the goods are at his risk during such sea transit.

[(4) In a case where the buyer deals as consumer or, in Scotland, where there is a consumer contract in which the buyer is a consumer, subsections (1) to (3) above must be ignored, but if in pursuance of a contract of sale the seller is authorised or required to send the goods to the buyer, delivery of the goods to the carrier is not delivery of the goods to the buyer.]

33   Risk where goods are delivered at distant place
Where the seller of goods agrees to deliver them at his own risk at a place other than that where they are when sold, the buyer must nevertheless (unless otherwise agreed) take any risk of deterioration in the goods necessarily incident to the course of transit.

34   Buyer's right of examining the goods
[Unless otherwise agreed, when the seller tenders delivery of goods to the buyer, he is bound on request to afford the buyer a reasonable opportunity of examining the goods for the purpose of ascertaining whether they are in conformity with the contract and, in the case of a contract for sale by sample, of comparing the bulk with the sample.]

35   Acceptance
(1) The buyer is deemed to have accepted the goods [subject to subsection (2) below—
    (a)   when he intimates to the seller that he has accepted them, or
    (b)   when the goods have been delivered to him and he does any act in relation to them which is inconsistent with the ownership of the seller.
(2) Where goods are delivered to the buyer, and he has not previously examined them, he is not deemed to have accepted them under subsection (1) above until he has had a reasonable opportunity of examining them for the purpose—
    (a)   of ascertaining whether they are in conformity with the contract, and
    (b)   in the case of a contract for sale by sample, of comparing the bulk with the sample.
(3) Where the buyer deals as consumer or (in Scotland) the contract of sale is a consumer contract, the buyer cannot lose his right to rely on subsection (2) above by agreement, waiver or otherwise.
(4) The buyer is also deemed to have accepted the goods when after the lapse of a reasonable time he retains the goods without intimating to the seller that he has rejected them.
(5) The questions that are material in determining for the purposes of subsection (4) above whether a reasonable time has elapsed include whether the buyer has had a reasonable opportunity of examining the goods for the purpose mentioned in subsection (2) above.
(6) The buyer is not by virtue of this section deemed to have accepted the goods merely because—

(a)   he asks for, or agrees to, their repair by or under an arrangement with the seller, or

(b)   the goods are delivered to another under a sub-sale or other disposition.

(7)   Where the contract is for the sale of goods making one or more commercial units, a buyer accepting any goods included in a unit is deemed to have accepted all the goods making the unit; and in this subsection 'commercial unit' means a unit division of which would materially impair the value of the goods or the character of the unit.

(8)]   Paragraph 10 of Schedule 1 below applies in relation to a contract made before 22 April 1967 or (in the application of this Act to Northern Ireland) 28 July 1967.

[35A   Right of partial rejection

(1)   If the buyer—

(a)   has the right to reject the goods by reason of a breach on the part of the seller that affects some or all of them, but

(b)   accepts some of the goods, including, where there are any goods unaffected by the breach, all such goods,

he does not by accepting them lose his right to reject the rest.

(2)   In the case of a buyer having the right to reject an instalment of goods, subsection (1) above applies as if references to the goods were references to the goods comprised in the instalment.

(3)   For the purposes of subsection (1) above, goods are affected by a breach if by reason of the breach they are not in conformity with the contract.

(4)   This section applies unless a contrary intention appears in, or is to be implied from, the contract.]

36   Buyer not bound to return rejected goods

Unless otherwise agreed, where goods are delivered to the buyer, and he refuses to accept them, having the right to do so, he is not bound to return them to the seller, but it is sufficient if he intimates to the seller that he refuses to accept them.

37   Buyer's liability for not taking delivery of goods

(1)   When the seller is ready and willing to deliver the goods, and requests the buyer to take delivery, and the buyer does not within a reasonable time after such request take delivery of the goods, he is liable to the seller for any loss occasioned by his neglect or refusal to take delivery, and also for a reasonable charge for the care and custody of the goods.

(2)   Nothing in this section affects the rights of the seller where the neglect or refusal of the buyer to take delivery amounts to a repudiation of the contract.

PART V
RIGHTS OF UNPAID SELLER AGAINST THE GOODS

Preliminary

38   Unpaid seller defined

(1)   The seller of goods is an unpaid seller within the meaning of this Act—

(a)   when the whole of the price has not been paid or tendered;

(b)   when a bill of exchange or other negotiable instrument has been received as conditional payment, and the condition on which it was received has not been fulfilled by reason of the dishonour of the instrument or otherwise.

(2)   In this Part of this Act 'seller' includes any person who is in the position of a seller, as, for instance, an agent of the seller to whom the bill of lading has been indorsed, or a consignor or agent who has himself paid (or is directly responsible for) the price.

39 Unpaid seller's rights

(1) Subject to this and any other Act, notwithstanding that the property in the goods may have passed to the buyer, the unpaid seller of goods, as such, has by implication of law—

(a) a lien on the goods or right to retain them for the price while he is in possession of them;

(b) in the case of the insolvency of the buyer, a right of stopping the goods in transit after he has parted with the possession of them;

(c) a right of re-sale as limited by this Act.

(2) Where the property in goods has not passed to the buyer, the unpaid seller has (in addition to his other remedies) a right of withholding delivery similar to and coextensive with his rights of lien or retention and stoppage in transit where the property has passed to the buyer.

[. . .]

Unpaid seller's lien

41 Seller's lien

(1) Subject to this Act, the unpaid seller of goods who is in possession of them is entitled to retain possession of them until payment or tender of the price in the following cases:—

(a) where the goods have been sold without any stipulation as to credit;

(b) where the goods have been sold on credit but the term of credit has expired;

(c) where the buyer becomes insolvent.

(2) The seller may exercise his lien or right of retention notwithstanding that he is in possession of the goods as agent or bailee or custodier for the buyer.

42 Part delivery

Where an unpaid seller has made part delivery of the goods, he may exercise his lien or right of retention on the remainder, unless such part delivery has been made under such circumstances as to show an agreement to waive the lien or right of retention.

43 Termination of lien

(1) The unpaid seller of goods loses his lien or right of retention in respect of them—

(a) when he delivers the goods to a carrier or other bailee or custodier for the purpose of transmission to the buyer without reserving the right of disposal of the goods;

(b) when the buyer or his agent lawfully obtains possession of the goods;

(c) by waiver of the lien or right of retention.

(2) An unpaid seller of goods who has a lien or right of retention in respect of them does not lose his lien or right of retention by reason only that he has obtained judgment or decree for the price of the goods.

Stoppage in transit

44 Right of stoppage in transit

Subject to this Act, when the buyer of goods becomes insolvent the unpaid seller who has parted with the possession of the goods has the right of stopping them in transit, that is to say, he may resume possession of the goods as long as they are in course of transit, and may retain them until payment or tender of the price.

45 Duration of transit

(1) Goods are deemed to be in course of transit from the time when they are delivered to a carrier or other bailee or custodier for the purpose of transmission to the buyer, until the buyer or his agent in that behalf takes delivery of them from the carrier or other bailee or custodier.

(2)   If the buyer or his agent in that behalf obtains delivery of the goods before their arrival at the appointed destination, the transit is at an end.

(3)   If, after the arrival of the goods at the appointed destination, the carrier or other bailee or custodier acknowledges to the buyer or his agent that he holds the goods on his behalf and continues in possession of them as bailee or custodier for the buyer or his agent, the transit is at an end, and it is immaterial that a further destination for the goods may have been indicated by the buyer.

(4)   If the goods are rejected by the buyer, and the carrier or other bailee or custodier continues in possession of them, the transit is not deemed to be at an end, even if the seller has refused to receive them back.

(5)   When goods are delivered to a ship chartered by the buyer it is a question depending on the circumstances of the particular case whether they are in the possession of the master as a carrier or as agent to the buyer.

(6)   Where the carrier or other bailee or custodier wrongfully refuses to deliver the goods to the buyer or his agent in that behalf, the transit is deemed to be at an end.

(7)   Where part delivery of the goods has been made to the buyer or his agent in that behalf, the remainder of the goods may be stopped in transit, unless such part delivery has been made under such circumstances as to show an agreement to give up possession of the whole of the goods.

46   How stoppage in transit is effected

(1)   The unpaid seller may exercise his right of stoppage in transit either by taking actual possession of the goods or by giving notice of his claim to the carrier or other bailee or custodier in whose possession the goods are.

(2)   The notice may be given either to the person in actual possession of the goods or to his principal.

(3)   If given to the principal, the notice is ineffective unless given at such time and under such circumstances that the principal, by the exercise of reasonable diligence, may communicate it to his servant or agent in time to prevent a delivery to the buyer.

(4)   When notice of stoppage in transit is given by the seller to the carrier or other bailee or custodier in possession of the goods, he must re-deliver the goods to, or according to the directions of, the seller; and the expenses of the re-delivery must be borne by the seller.

Re-sale etc by buyer

47   Effect of sub-sale etc by buyer

(1)   Subject to this Act, the unpaid seller's right of lien or retention or stoppage in transit is not affected by any sale or other disposition of the goods which the buyer may have made, unless the seller has assented to it.

(2)   Where a document of title to goods has been lawfully transferred to any person as buyer or owner of the goods, and that person transfers the document to a person who takes it in good faith and for valuable consideration, then—

(a)   if the last-mentioned transfer was by way of sale the unpaid seller's right of lien or retention or stoppage in transit is defeated; and

(b)   if the last-mentioned transfer was made by way of pledge or other disposition for value, the unpaid seller's right of lien or retention of stoppage in transit can only be exercised subject to the rights of the transferee.

Rescission: and re-sale by seller

48   Rescission: and re-sale by seller

(1)   Subject to this section, a contract of sale is not rescinded by the mere exercise by an unpaid seller of his right of lien or retention or stoppage in transit.

(2)   Where an unpaid seller who has exercised his right of lien or retention or

stoppage in transit re-sells the goods, the buyer acquires a good title to them as against the original buyer.

(3)   Where the goods are of a perishable nature, or where the unpaid seller gives notice to the buyer of his intention to re-sell, and the buyer does not within a reasonable time pay or tender the price, the unpaid seller may re-sell the goods and recover from the original buyer damages for any loss occasioned by his breach of contract.

(4)   Where the seller expressly reserves the right of re-sale in case the buyer should make default, and on the buyer making default re-sells the goods, the original contract of sale is rescinded but without prejudice to any claim the seller may have for damages.

[PART VA
ADDITIONAL RIGHTS OF BUYER IN CONSUMER CASES

48A   Introductory

(1)   This section applies if—

(a)   the buyer deals as consumer or, in Scotland, there is a consumer contract in which the buyer is a consumer, and

(b)   the goods do not conform to the contract of sale at the time of delivery.

(2)   If this section applies, the buyer has the right—

(a)   under and in accordance with section 48B below, to require the seller to repair or replace the goods, or

(b)   under and in accordance with section 48C below—

(i)   to require the seller to reduce the purchase price of the goods to the buyer by an appropriate amount, or

(ii)   to rescind the contract with regard to the goods in question.

(3)   For the purposes of subsection (1)(b) above goods which do not conform to the contract of sale at any time within the period of six months starting with the date on which the goods were delivered to the buyer must be taken not to have so conformed at that date.

(4)   Subsection (3) above does not apply if—

(a)   it is established that the goods did so conform at that date;

(b)   its application is incompatible with the nature of the goods or the nature of the lack of conformity.

48B   Repair or replacement of the goods

(1)   If section 48A above applies, the buyer may require the seller—

(a)   to repair the goods, or

(b)   to replace the goods.

(2)   If the buyer requires the seller to repair or replace the goods, the seller must—

(a)   repair or, as the case may be, replace the goods within a reasonable time but without causing significant inconvenience to the buyer;

(b)   bear any necessary costs incurred in doing so (including in particular the cost of any labour, materials or postage).

(3)   The buyer must not require the seller to repair or, as the case may be, replace the goods if that remedy is—

(a)   impossible, or

(b)   disproportionate in comparison to the other of those remedies, or

(c)   disproportionate in comparison to an appropriate reduction in the purchase price under paragraph (a), or rescission under paragraph (b), of section 48C(1) below.

(4)   One remedy is disproportionate in comparison to the other if the one imposes costs on the seller which, in comparison to those imposed on him by the other, are unreasonable, taking into account—

(a)   the value which the goods would have if they conformed to the contract of sale,

(b)   the significance of the lack of conformity, and

(c)   whether the other remedy could be effected without significant inconvenience to the buyer.

(5)   Any question as to what is a reasonable time or significant inconvenience is to be determined by reference to—

(a)   the nature of the goods, and

(b)   the purpose for which the goods were acquired.

48C   Reduction of purchase price or rescission of contract

(1)   If section 48A above applies, the buyer may—

(a)   require the seller to reduce the purchase price of the goods in question to the buyer by an appropriate amount, or

(b)   rescind the contract with regard to those goods,

if the condition in subsection (2) below is satisfied.

(2)   The condition is that—

(a)   by virtue of section 48B(3) above the buyer may require neither repair nor replacement of the goods; or

(b)   the buyer has required the seller to repair or replace the goods, but the seller is in breach of the requirement of section 48B(2)(a) above to do so within a reasonable time and without significant inconvenience to the buyer.

(3)   For the purposes of this Part, if the buyer rescinds the contract, any reimbursement to the buyer may be reduced to take account of the use he has had of the goods since they were delivered to him.

48D   Relation to other remedies etc

(1)   If the buyer requires the seller to repair or replace the goods the buyer must not act under subsection (2) until he has given the seller a reasonable time in which to repair or replace (as the case may be) the goods.

(2)   The buyer acts under this subsection if—

(a)   in England and Wales or Northern Ireland he rejects the goods and terminates the contract for breach of condition;

(b)   in Scotland he rejects any goods delivered under the contract and treats it as repudiated;

(c)   he requires the goods to be replaced or repaired (as the case may be).

48E   Powers of the court

(1)   In any proceedings in which a remedy is sought by virtue of this Part the court, in addition to any other power it has, may act under this section.

(2)   On the application of the buyer the court may make an order requiring specific performance or, in Scotland, specific implement by the seller of any obligation imposed on him by virtue of section 48B above.

(3)   Subsection (4) applies if—

(a)   the buyer requires the seller to give effect to a remedy under section 48B or 48C above or has claims to rescind under section 48C, but

(b)   the court decides that another remedy under section 48B or 48C is appropriate.

(4)   The court may proceed—

(a)   as if the buyer had required the seller to give effect to the other remedy, or if the other remedy is rescission under section 48C; or

(b)   as if the buyer had claimed to rescind the contract under that section.

(5)   If the buyer has claimed to rescind the contract the court may order that any reimbursement to the buyer is reduced to take account of the use he has had of the goods since they were delivered to him.

(6)   The court may make an order under this section unconditionally or on such

terms and conditions as to damages, payment of the price and otherwise as it thinks just.

48F   Conformity with the contract
For the purposes of this Part, goods do not conform to a contract of sale if there is, in relation to the goods, a breach of an express term of the contract or a term implied by section 13, 14 or 15 above.]

PART VI
ACTIONS FOR BREACH OF THE CONTRACT

Seller's remedies

49   Action for price
(1)   Where, under a contract of sale, the property in the goods has passed to the buyer and he wrongfully neglects or refuses to pay for the goods according to the terms of the contract, the seller may maintain an action against him for the price of the goods.
(2)   Where, under a contract of sale, the price is payable on a day certain irrespective of delivery and the buyer wrongfully neglects or refuses to pay such price, the seller may maintain an action for the price, although the property in goods has not passed and the goods have not been appropriated to the contract.
(3)   Nothing in this section prejudices the right of the seller in Scotland to recover interest on the price from the date of tender of the goods, or from the date on which the price was payable, as the case may be.

50   Damages for non-acceptance
(1)   Where the buyer wrongfully neglects or refuses to accept and pay for the goods, the seller may maintain an action against him for damages for non-acceptance.
(2)   The measure of damages is the estimated loss directly and naturally resulting in the ordinary course of events, from the buyer's breach of contract.
(3)   Where there is an available market for the goods in question the measure of damages is prima facie to be ascertained by the difference between the contract price and the market or current price at the time or times when the goods ought to have been accepted or (if no time was fixed for acceptance) at the time of the refusal to accept.

Buyer's remedies

51   Damages for non-delivery
(1)   Where the seller wrongfully neglects or refuses to deliver the goods to the buyer, the buyer may maintain an action against the seller for damages for non-delivery.
(2)   The measure of damages is the estimated loss directly and naturally resulting, in the ordinary course of events, from the seller's breach of contract.
(3)   Where there is an available market for the goods in question the measure of damages is prima facie to be ascertained by the difference between the contract price and the market or current price of the goods at the time or times when they ought to have been delivered or (if no time was fixed) at the time of the refusal to deliver.

52   Specific performance
(1)   If any action for breach of contract to deliver specific or ascertained goods the court may, if it thinks fit, on the plaintiff's application, by its judgment or decree direct that the contract shall be performed specifically, without giving the defendant the option of retaining the goods on payment of damages.

(2)   The plaintiff's application may be made at any time before judgment or decree.

(3)   The judgment or decree may be unconditional, or on such terms and conditions as to damages, payment of the price and otherwise as seem just to the court.

(4)   The provisions of this section shall be deemed to be supplementary to, and not in derogation of, the right of specific implement in Scotland.

53   [*Does not apply to Scotland.*]

[53A   Measure of damages as respects Scotland
(1)   The measure of damages for the seller's breach of contract is the estimated loss directly and naturally resulting, in the ordinary course of events, from the breach.

(2)   Where the seller's breach consists of the delivery of goods which are not of the quality required by the contract and the buyer retains the goods, such loss as aforesaid is prima facie the difference between the value of the goods at the time of delivery to the buyer and the value they would have had if they had fulfilled the contract.

(3)   This section applies to Scotland only.]

Interest, etc

54   Interest, etc
Nothing in this Act affects the right of the buyer or the seller to recover interest or special damages in any case where by law interest or special damages may be recoverable, or to recover money paid where the consideration for the payment of it has failed.

PART VII
SUPPLEMENTARY

55   Exclusion of implied terms
(1)   Where a right, duty or liability would arise under a contract of sale of goods by implication of law, it may (subject to the Unfair Contract Terms Act 1977) be negatived or varied by express agreement, or by the course of dealing between the parties, or by such usage as binds both parties to the contract.

(2)   An express [term] does not negative a [term] implied by this Act unless inconsistent with it.

(3)   Paragraph 11 of Schedule 1 below applies in relation to a contract made on or after 18 May 1973 and before 1 February 1978, and paragraph 12 in relation to one made before 18 May 1973.

56   Conflict of laws
Paragraph 13 of Schedule 1 below applies in relation to a contract made on or after 18 May 1973 and before 1 February 1978, so as to make provision about conflict of laws in relation to such a contract.

57   Auction sales
(1)   Where goods are put up for sale by auction in lots, each lot is prima facie deemed to be the subject of a separate contract of sale.

(2)   A sale by auction is complete when the auctioneer announces its completion by the fall of the hammer, or in other customary manner; and until the announcement is made any bidder may retract his bid.

(3)   A sale by auction may be notified to be subject to a reserve or upset price, and a right to bid may also be reserved expressly by or on behalf of the seller.

(4)   Where a sale by auction is not notified to be subject to a right to bid by or on behalf of the seller, it is not lawful for the seller to bid himself or to employ any

person to bid at the sale, or for the auctioneer knowingly to take any bid from the seller or any such person.

(5) A sale contravening subsection (4) above may be treated as fraudulent by the buyer.

(6) Where, in respect of a sale by auction, a right to bid is expressly reserved (but not otherwise) the seller or any one person on his behalf may bid at the auction.

58 Payment into court in Scotland

In Scotland where a buyer has elected to accept goods which he might have rejected, and to treat a breach of contract as only giving rise to a claim for damages, he may, in an action by the seller for the price, be required, in the discretion of the court before which the action depends, to consign or pay into court the price of the goods, or part of the price, or to give other reasonable security for its due payment.

59 Reasonable time a question of fact

Where a reference is made in this Act to a reasonable time the question what is a reasonable time is a question of fact.

60 Rights etc enforceable by action

Where a right, duty or liability is declared by this Act, it may (unless otherwise provided by this Act) be enforced by action.

61 Interpretation

(1) In this Act, unless the context or subject matter otherwise requires,—

'action' includes counterclaim and set-off, and in Scotland condescendence and claim and compensation;

['bulk' means a mass or collection of goods of the same kind which—

(a)   is contained in a defined space or area; and

(b)   is such that any goods in the bulk are interchangeable with any other goods therein of the same number or quantity;]

'business' includes a profession and the activities of any government department (including a Northern Ireland department) or local or public authority;

'buyer' means a person who buys or agrees to buy goods;

['consumer contract' has the same meaning as in section 25(1) of the Unfair Contract Terms Act 1977; and for the purposes of this Act the onus of proving that a contract is not to be regarded as a consumer contract shall lie on the seller;]

'contract of sale' includes an agreement to sell as well as a sale;

'credit-broker' means a person acting in the course of a business of credit brokerage carried on by him, that is a business of effecting introductions of individuals desiring to obtain credit—

(a)   to persons carrying on any business so far as it relates to the provision of credit, or

(b)   to other persons engaged in credit brokerage;

'defendant' includes in Scotland defender, respondent, and claimant in a multiplepoinding;

'delivery' means voluntary transfer of possession from one person to another; [except that in relation to sections 20A and 20B above it includes such appropriation of goods to the contract as results in property in the goods being transferred to the buyer;]

'document of title to goods' has the same meaning as it has in the Factors Acts;

'Factors Acts' means the Factors Act 1889, the Factors (Scotland) Act 1890, and any enactment amending or substituted for the same;

'fault' means wrongful act or default;

'future goods' means goods to be manufactured or acquired by the seller after the making of the contract of sale;

'goods' includes all personal chattels other than things in action and money, and in Scotland all corporeal moveables except money; and in particular 'goods' includes emblements, industrial growing crops, and things attached to or forming part of the land which are agreed to be severed before sale or under the contract of sale; [and includes an undivided share in goods;]

'plaintiff' includes pursuer, complainer, claimant in a multiplepoinding and defendant or defender counter-claiming;

['producer' means the manufacturer of goods, the importer of goods into the European Economic Area or any person purporting to be a producer by placing his name, trade mark or other distinctive sign on the goods;]

'property' means the general property in goods, and not merely a special property;

['repair' means, in cases where there is a lack of conformity in goods for the purposes of section 48F of this Act, to bring the goods into conformity with the contract;]

'sale' includes a bargain and sale as well as a sale and delivery;

'seller' means a person who sells or agrees to sell goods;

'specific goods' means goods identified and agreed on at the time a contract of sale is made; [and includes an undivided share, specified as a fraction or percentage, of goods identified and agreed on as aforesaid;]

'warranty' (as regards England and Wales and Northern Ireland) means an agreement with reference to goods which are the subject of a contract of sale, but collateral to the main purpose of such contract, the breach of which gives rise to a claim for damages, but not to a right to reject the goods and treat the contract as repudiated.

[. . .]

(3)   A thing is deemed to be done in good faith within the meaning of this Act when it is in fact done honestly, whether it is done negligently or not.

(4)   A person is deemed to be insolvent within the meaning of this Act if he has either ceased to pay his debts in the ordinary course of business or he cannot pay his debts as they become due, [. . .]

(5)   Goods are in a deliverable state within the meaning of this Act when they are in such a state that the buyer would under the contract be bound to take delivery of them.

[(5A)   References in this Act to dealing as consumer are to be construed in accordance with Part I of the Unfair Contract Terms Act 1977; and, for the purposes of this Act, it is for a seller claiming that the buyer does not deal as consumer to show that he does not.]

(6)   As regards the definition of 'business' in subsection (1) above, paragraph 14 of Schedule 1 below applies in relation to a contract made on or after 18 May 1973 and before 1 February 1978, and paragraph 15 in relation to one made before 18 May 1973,

62   Savings: rules of law etc

(1)   The rules in bankruptcy relating to contracts of sale apply to those contracts, notwithstanding anything in this Act.

(2)   The rules of the common law, including the law merchant, except in so far as they are inconsistent with the provisions of this Act, and in particular the rules relating to the law of principal and agent and the effect of fraud, misrepresentation, duress or coercion, mistake, or other invalidating cause, apply to contracts for the sale of goods.

(3)   Nothing in this Act or the Sale of Goods Act 1893 affects the enactments relating to bills of sale, or any enactment relating to the sale of goods which is not expressly repealed or amended by this Act or that.

(4)   The provisions of this Act about contracts of sale do not apply to a transaction in the form of a contract of sale which is intended to operate by way of mortgage, pledge, charge, or other security.

(5)   Nothing in this Act prejudices or affects the landlord's right of hypothec [. . .] in Scotland.

64   Short title and commencement
(1)   This Act may be cited as the Sale of Goods Act 1979.
(2)   This Act comes into force on 1 January 1980.

SUPPLY OF GOODS AND SERVICES ACT 1982
(1982, c 29)

[PART IA
SUPPLY OF GOODS AS RESPECTS SCOTLAND

Contracts for the transfer of property in goods

11A   The contracts concerned
(1)   In this Act in its application to Scotland a 'contract for the transfer of goods' means a contract under which one person transfers or agrees to transfer to another the property in goods, other than an excepted contract.
(2)   For the purposes of this section an excepted contract means any of the following—
  (a)   a contract of sale of goods;
  (b)   a hire-purchase agreement;
  [. . .]
  (d)   a transfer or agreement to transfer for which there is no consideration;
  (e)   a contract intended to operate by way of mortgage, pledge, charge or other security.
(3)   For the purposes of this Act in its application to Scotland a contract is a contract for the transfer of goods whether or not services are also provided or to be provided under the contract, and (subject to subsection (2) above) whatever is the nature of the consideration for the transfer or agreement to transfer.

11B   Implied terms about title, etc
(1)   In a contract for the transfer of goods, other than one to which subsection (3) below applies, there is an implied term on the part of the transferor that in the case of a transfer of the property in the goods he has a right to transfer the property and in the case of an agreement to transfer the property in the goods he will have such a right at the time when the property is to be transferred.
(2)   In a contract for the transfer of goods, other than one to which subsection (3) below applies, there is also an implied term that—
  (a)   the goods are free, and will remain free until the time when the property is to be transferred, from any charge or encumbrance not disclosed or known to the transferee before the contract is made, and
  (b)   the transferee will enjoy quiet possession of the goods except so far as it may be disturbed by the owner or other person entitled to the benefit of any charge or encumbrance so disclosed or known.
(3)   This subsection applies to a contract for the transfer of goods in the case of which there appears from the contract or is to be inferred from its circumstances an intention that the transferor should transfer only such title as he or a third person may have.
(4)   In a contract to which subsection (3) above applies there is an implied term that all charges or encumbrances known to the transferor and not known to the transferee have been disclosed to the transferee before the contract is made.
(5)   In a contract to which subsection (3) above applies there is also an implied term that none of the following will disturb the transferee's quiet possession of the goods, namely—
  (a)   the transferor;

(b)   in a case where the parties to the contract intend that the transferor should transfer only such title as a third person may have, that person;

(c)   anyone claiming through or under the transferor or that third person otherwise than under a charge or encumbrance disclosed or known to the transferee before the contract is made.

(6)   [*amends Unfair Contract Terms Act 1977*]

11C   Implied terms where transfer is by description

(1)   This section applies where, under a contract for the transfer of goods, the transferor transfers or agrees to transfer the property in the goods by description.

(2)   In such a case there is an implied term that the goods will correspond with the description.

(3)   If the transferor transfers or agrees to transfer the property in the goods by reference to a sample as well as by description it is not sufficient that the bulk of the goods corresponds with the sample if the goods do not also correspond with the description.

(4)   A contract is not prevented from falling within subsection (1) above by reason only that, being exposed for supply, the goods are selected by the transferee.

11D   Implied terms about quality or fitness

(1)   Except as provided by this section and section 11E below and subject to the provisions of any other enactment, there is no implied term about the quality or fitness for any particular purpose of goods supplied under a contract for the transfer of goods.

(2)   Where, under such a contract, the transferor transfers the property in goods in the course of a business, there is an implied term that the goods supplied under the contract are of satisfactory quality.

(3)   For the purposes of this section and section 11E below, goods are of satisfactory quality if they meet the standard that a reasonable person would regard as satisfactory, taking account of any description of the goods, the price (if relevant) and all the other relevant circumstances.

[(3A)   If the contract for the transfer of goods is a consumer contract, the relevant circumstances mentioned in subsection (3) above include any public statements on the specific characteristics of the goods made about them by the transferor, the producer or his representative, particularly in advertising or on labelling.

(3B)   A public statement is not by virtue of subsection (3A) above a relevant circumstance for the purposes of subsection (3) above in the case of a contract for the transfer of goods, if the transferor shows that—

(a)   at the time the contract was made, he was not, and could not reasonably have been, aware of the statement,

(b)   before the contract was made, the statement had been withdrawn in public or, to the extent that it contained anything which was incorrect or misleading, it had been corrected in public, or

(c)   the decision to acquire the goods could not have been influenced by the statement.

(3C)   Subsections (3A) and (3B) above do not prevent any public statement from being a relevant circumstance for the purposes of subsection (3) above (whether or not the contract for the transfer of goods is a consumer contract) if the statement would have been such a circumstance apart from those subsections.]

(4)   The term implied by subsection (2) above does not extend to any matter making the quality of goods unsatisfactory—

(a)   which is specifically drawn to the transferee's attention before the contract is made,

(b)   where the transferee examines the goods before the contract is made, which that examination ought to reveal, or

(c)   where the property in the goods is, or is to be, transferred by reference to a sample, which would have been apparent on a reasonable examination of the sample.

(5)   Subsection (6) below applies where, under a contract for the transfer of goods, the transferor transfers the property in goods in the course of a business and the transferee, expressly or by implication, makes known—

(a)   to the transferor, or

(b)   where the consideration or part of the consideration for the transfer is a sum payable by instalments and the goods were previously sold by a credit-broker to the transferor, to that credit-broker,

any particular purpose for which the goods are being acquired.

(6)   In that case there is (subject to subsection (7) below) an implied term that the goods supplied under the contract are reasonably fit for the purpose, whether or not that is a purpose for which such goods are commonly supplied.

(7)   Subsection (6) above does not apply where the circumstances show that the transferee does not rely, or that it is unreasonable for him to rely, on the skill or judgment of the transferor or credit-broker.

(8)   An implied term about quality or fitness for a particular purpose may be annexed by usage to a contract for the transfer of goods.

(9)   The preceding provisions of this section apply to a transfer by a person who in the course of a business is acting as agent for another as they apply to a transfer by a principal in the course of a business, except where that other is not transferring in the course of a business and either the transferee knows that fact or reasonable steps are taken to bring it to the transferee's notice before the contract concerned is made.

[(10)   For the purposes of this section, 'consumer contract' has the same meaning as in section 11F(3) below.]

11E   Implied terms where transfer is by sample

(1)   This section applies where, under a contract for the transfer of goods, the transferor transfers or agrees to transfer the property in the goods by reference to a sample.

(2)   In such a case there is an implied term—

(a)   that the bulk will correspond with the sample in quality;

(b)   that the transferee will have a reasonable opportunity of comparing the bulk with the sample; and

(c)   that the goods will be free from any defect, making their quality unsatisfactory, which would not be apparent on reasonable examination of the sample.

(3)   For the purposes of this section a transferor transfers or agrees to transfer the property in goods by reference to a sample where there is an express or implied term to that effect in the contract concerned.

11F   Remedies for breach of contract

(1)   Where in a contract for the transfer of goods a transferor is in breach of any term of the contract (express or implied), the other party to the contract (in this section referred to as 'the transferee') shall be entitled—

(a)   to claim damages; and

(b)   if the breach is material, to reject any goods delivered under the contract and treat it as repudiated.

(2)   Where a contract for the transfer of goods is a consumer contract and the transferee is the consumer, then, for the purposes of subsection (1)(b) above, breach by the transferor of any term (express or implied)—

(a)   as to the quality of the goods or their fitness for a purpose;

(b)   if the goods are, or are to be, transferred by description, that the goods will correspond with the description;

(c)   if the goods are, or are to be, transferred by reference to a sample, that the bulk will correspond with the sample in quality,
shall be deemed to be a material breach.

(3)   In subsection (2) above, 'consumer contract' has the same meaning as in section 25(1) of the 1977 Act; and for the purposes of that subsection the onus of proving that a contract is not to be regarded as a consumer contract shall lie on the transferor.

Contracts for the hire of goods

11G   The contracts concerned

(1)   In this Act in its application to Scotland a 'contract for the hire of goods' means a contract under which one person ('the supplier') hires or agrees to hire goods to another, other than [a hire-purchase agreement].
[. . .]
(3)   For the purposes of this Act in its application to Scotland a contract is a contract for the hire of goods whether or not services are also provided or to be provided under the contract, and [. . .] whatever is the nature of the consideration for the hire or agreement to hire.

11H   Implied terms about right to transfer possession etc

(1)   In a contract for the hire of goods there is an implied term on the part of the supplier that—
   (a)   in the case of a hire, he has a right to transfer possession of the goods by way of hire for the period of the hire; and
   (b)   in the case of an agreement to hire, he will have such a right at the time of commencement of the period of the hire.
(2)   In a contract for the hire of goods there is also an implied term that the person to whom the goods are hired will enjoy quiet possession of the goods for the period of the hire except so far as the possession may be disturbed by the owner or other person entitled to the benefit of any charge or encumbrance disclosed or known to the person to whom the goods are hired before the contract is made.
(3)   The preceding provisions of this section do not affect the right of the supplier to repossess the goods under an express or implied term of the contract.

11I   Implied terms where hire is by description

(1)   This section applies where, under a contract for the hire of goods, the supplier hires or agrees to hire the goods by description.
(2)   In such a case there is an implied term that the goods will correspond with the description.
(3)   If under the contract the supplier hires or agrees to hire the goods by reference to a sample as well as by description it is not sufficient that the bulk of the goods corresponds with the sample if the goods do not also correspond with the description.
(4)   A contract is not prevented from falling within subsection (1) above by reason only that, being exposed for supply, the goods are selected by the person to whom the goods are hired.

11J   Implied terms about quality or fitness

(1)   Except as provided by this section and section 11K below and subject to the provisions of any other enactment, there is no implied term about the quality or fitness for any particular purpose of goods hired under a contract for the hire of goods.
(2)   Where, under such a contract, the supplier hires goods in the course of a business, there is an implied term that the goods supplied under the contract are of satisfactory quality.
(3)   For the purposes of this section and section 11K below, goods are of satis-

factory quality if they meet the standard that a reasonable person would regard as satisfactory, taking account of any description of the goods, the consideration for the hire (if relevant) and all the other relevant circumstances.

[(3A)   If the contract for the transfer of goods is a consumer contract, the relevant circumstances mentioned in subsection (3) above include any public statements on the specific characteristics of the goods made about them by the transferor, the producer or his representative, particularly in advertising or on labelling.

(3B)   A public statement is not by virtue of subsection (3A) above a relevant circumstance for the purposes of subsection (3) above in the case of a contract for the transfer of goods, if the transferor shows that—

(a)   at the time the contract was made, he was not, and could not reasonably have been, aware of the statement,

(b)   before the contract was made, the statement had been withdrawn in public or, to the extent that it contained anything which was incorrect or misleading, it had been corrected in public, or

(c)   the decision to acquire the goods could not have been influenced by the statement.

(3C)   Subsections (3A) and (3B) above do not prevent any public statement from being a relevant circumstance for the purposes of subsection (3) above (whether or not the contract for the transfer of goods is a consumer contract) if the statement would have been such a circumstance apart from those subsections.]

(4)   The term implied by subsection (2) above does not extend to any matter making the quality of goods unsatisfactory—

(a)   which is specifically drawn to the attention of the person to whom the goods are hired before the contract is made, or

(b)   where that person examines the goods before the contract is made, which that examination ought to reveal; or

(c)   where the goods are hired by reference to a sample, which would have been apparent on reasonable examination of the sample.

(5)   Subsection (6) below applies where, under a contract for the hire of goods, the supplier hires goods in the course of a business and the person to whom the goods are hired, expressly or by implication, makes known—

(a)   to the supplier in the course of negotiations conducted by him in relation to the making of the contract; or

(b)   to a credit-broker in the course of negotiations conducted by that broker in relation to goods sold by him to the supplier before forming the subject matter of the contract,

any particular purpose for which the goods are being hired.

(6)   In that case there is (subject to subsection (7) below) an implied term that the goods supplied under the contract are reasonably fit for that purpose, whether or not that is a purpose for which such goods are commonly supplied.

(7)   Subsection (6) above does not apply where the circumstances show that the person to whom the goods are hired does not rely, or that it is unreasonable for him to rely, on the skill or judgment of the hirer or credit-broker.

(8)   An implied term about quality or fitness for a particular purpose may be annexed by usage to a contract for the hire of goods.

(9)   The preceding provisions of this section apply to a hire by a person who in the course of a business is acting as agent for another as they apply to a hire by a principal in the course of a business, except where that other is not hiring in the course of a business and either the person to whom the goods are hired knows that fact or reasonable steps are taken to bring it to that person's notice before the contract concerned is made.

[(10)   For the purposes of this section, 'consumer contract' has the same meaning as in section 11F(3) above.]

11K   Implied terms where hire is by sample

(1)   This section applies where, under a contract for the hire of goods, the supplier hires or agrees to hire the goods by reference to a sample.

(2)   In such a case there is an implied term—

(a)   that the bulk will correspond with the sample in quality; and

(b)   that the person to whom the goods are hired will have a reasonable opportunity of comparing the bulk with the sample; and

(c)   that the goods will be free from any defect, making their quality unsatisfactory, which would not be apparent on reasonable examination of the sample.

(3)   For the purposes of this section a supplier hires or agrees to hire goods by reference to a sample where there is an express or implied term to that effect in the contract concerned.

Exclusion of implied terms, etc

11L   Exclusion of implied terms etc

(1)   Where a right, duty or liability would arise under a contract for the transfer of goods or a contract for the hire of goods by implication of law, it may (subject to subsection (2) below and the 1977 Act) be negatived or varied by express agreement, or by the course of dealing between the parties, or by such usage as binds both parties to the contract.

(2)   An express term does not negative a term implied by the preceding provisions of this Part of this Act unless inconsistent with it.

(3)   Nothing in the preceding provisions of this Part of this Act prejudices the operation of any other enactment or any rule of law whereby any term (other than one relating to quality or fitness) is to be implied in a contract for the transfer of goods or a contract for the hire of goods.]

[PART IB
ADDITIONAL RIGHTS OF TRANSFEREE IN CONSUMER CASES

11M   Introductory

(1)   This section applies if—

(a)   the transferee deals as consumer or, in Scotland, there is a consumer contract in which the transferee is a consumer, and

(b)   the goods do not conform to the contract for the transfer of goods at the time of delivery.

(2)   If this section applies, the transferee has the right—

(a)   under and in accordance with section 11N below, to require the transferor to repair or replace the goods, or

(b)   under and in accordance with section 11P below—

(i)   to require the transferor to reduce the amount to be paid for the transfer by the transferee by an appropriate amount, or

(ii)   to rescind the contract with regard to the goods in question.

(3)   For the purposes of subsection (1)(b) above, goods which do not conform to the contract for the transfer of goods at any time within the period of six months starting with the date on which the goods were delivered to the transferee must be taken not to have so conformed at that date.

(4)   Subsection (3) above does not apply if—

(a)   it is established that the goods did so conform at that date;

(b)   its application is incompatible with the nature of the goods or the nature of the lack of conformity.

(5)   For the purposes of this section, 'consumer contract' has the same meaning as in section 11F(3) above.

11N   Repair or replacement of the goods

(1)   If section 11M above applies, the transferee may require the transferor—

   (a)   to repair the goods, or

   (b)   to replace the goods.

(2)   If the transferee requires the transferor to repair or replace the goods, the transferor must—

   (a)   repair or, as the case may be, replace the goods within a reasonable time but without causing significant inconvenience to the transferee;

   (b)   bear any necessary costs incurred in doing so (including in particular the cost of any labour, materials or postage).

(3)   The transferee must not require the transferor to repair or, as the case may be, replace the goods if that remedy is—

   (a)   impossible,

   (b)   disproportionate in comparison to the other of those remedies, or

   (c)   disproportionate in comparison to an appropriate reduction in the purchase price under paragraph (a), or rescission under paragraph (b), of section 11P(1) below.

(4)   One remedy is disproportionate in comparison to the other if the one imposes costs on the transferor which, in comparison to those imposed on him by the other, are unreasonable, taking into account—

   (a)   the value which the goods would have if they conformed to the contract for the transfer of goods,

   (b)   the significance of the lack of conformity to the contract for the transfer of goods, and

   (c)   whether the other remedy could be effected without significant inconvenience to the transferee.

(5)   Any question as to what is a reasonable time or significant inconvenience is to be determined by reference to—

   (a)   the nature of the goods, and

   (b)   the purpose for which the goods were acquired.

11P   Reduction of purchase price or rescission of contract

(1)   If section 11M above applies, the transferee may—

   (a)   require the transferor to reduce the purchase price of the goods in question to the transferee by an appropriate amount, or

   (b)   rescind the contract with regard to those goods,

if the condition in subsection (2) below is satisfied.

(2)   The condition is that—

   (a)   by virtue of section 11N(3) above the transferee may require neither repair nor replacement of the goods, or

   (b)   the transferee has required the transferor to repair or replace the goods, but the transferor is in breach of the requirement of section 11N(2)(a) above to do so within a reasonable time and without significant inconvenience to the transferee.

(3)   If the transferee rescinds the contract, any reimbursement to the transferee may be reduced to take account of the use he has had of the goods since they were delivered to him.

11Q   Relation to other remedies etc

(1)   If the transferee requires the transferor to repair or replace the goods the transferee must not act under subsection (2) until he has given the transferor a reasonable time in which to repair or replace (as the case may be) the goods.

(2)   The transferee acts under this subsection if—

   (a)   in England and Wales or Northern Ireland he rejects the goods and terminates the contract for breach of condition;

   (b)   in Scotland he rejects any goods delivered under the contract and treats it as repudiated; or

(c) he requires the goods to be replaced or repaired (as the case may be).

11R Powers of the court
(1) In any proceedings in which a remedy is sought by virtue of this Part the court, in addition to any other power it has, may act under this section.
(2) On the application of the transferee the court may make an order requiring specific performance or, in Scotland, specific implement by the transferor of any obligation imposed on him by virtue of section 11N above.
(3) Subsection (4) applies if—
(a) the transferee requires the transferor to give effect to a remedy under section 11N or 11P above or has claims to rescind under section 11P, but
(b) the court decides that another remedy under section 11N or 11P is appropriate.
(4) The court may proceed—
(a) as if the transferee had required the transferor to give effect to the other remedy, or if the other remedy is rescission under section 11P,
(b) as if the transferee had claimed to rescind the contract under that section.
(5) If the transferee has claimed to rescind the contract the court may order that any reimbursement to the transferee is reduced to take account of the use he has had of the goods since they were delivered to him.
(6) The court may make an order under this section unconditionally or on such terms and conditions as to damages, payment of the price and otherwise as it thinks just.

11S Conformity with the contract
(1) Goods do not conform to a contract for the supply or transfer of goods if—
(a) there is, in relation to the goods, a breach of an express term of the contract or a term implied by section 3, 4 or 5 above or, in Scotland, by section 11C, 11D or 11E above, or
(b) installation of the goods forms part of the contract for the transfer of goods, and the goods were installed by the transferor, or under his responsibility, in breach of the term implied by section 13 below or (in Scotland) in breach of any term implied by any rule of law as to the manner in which the installation is carried out.]

BANKRUPTCY (SCOTLAND) ACT 1985
(1985, c 66)

1 Accountant in Bankruptcy
[(1) The Accountant in Bankruptcy shall be appointed by the Scottish Ministers.
[(1A) The Accountant in Bankruptcy shall be an officer of the court.]
(2) The Scottish Ministers may appoint a member of the staff of the Accountant in Bankruptcy to be Depute Accountant in Bankruptcy to exercise all of the functions of the Accountant in Bankruptcy at any time when the Accountant in Bankruptcy is unable to do so.]

[1A Supervisory functions of the Accountant in Bankruptcy
(1) The Accountant in Bankruptcy shall have the following general functions in the administration of sequestration and personal insolvency—
(a) the supervision of the performance by—
(i) interim trustees (not being the Accountant in Bankruptcy);
(ii) [trustees (not being the Accountant in Bankruptcy)];
[(iia) trustees under protected trust deeds;]
[(iib) orders made under subsection (2) of section 32 of this Act and agreements made under subsection (4B) of that section.]
(iii) commissioners,
of the functions conferred on them by this Act or any other enactment

(including an enactment contained in subordinate legislation) or any rule of law and the investigation of any complaints made against them;

[(aa)   the determination of debtor applications;]

(b)   the maintenance of a register (in this Act referred to as the 'register of insolvencies'), in such form as may be prescribed by the Court of Session by act of sederunt, which shall contain particulars of—

(i)   estates which have been sequestrated;

(ii)   trust deeds which have been sent to him for registration [. . .];

[(iia)   bankruptcy restrictions orders, interim bankruptcy restrictions orders and bankruptcy restrictions undertakings;]

[. . .]

[(iii) the winding up and receivership of business associations which the Court of Session has jurisdiction to wind up];

(c)   the preparation of an annual report which shall be presented to the Secretary of State and the Court of Session and shall contain—

(i)   statistical information relating to the state of all sequestrations [and the winding up and receiverships of business associations] of which particulars have been registered in the register of insolvencies during the year to which the report relates;

(ii)   particulars of trust deeds registered as protected trust deeds in that year; and

(iii)   particulars of the performance of the Accountant in Bankruptcy's functions under this Act;

(d)   such other functions as may from time to time be conferred on him by the Secretary of State [; and

(e)   in this subsection 'business association' has the meaning given in Section C2 of Part II of Schedule 5 to the Scotland Act 1998].

(2)   If it appears to the Accountant in Bankruptcy that a person mentioned in paragraph (a) of subsection (1) above has failed without reasonable excuse to perform a duty imposed on him by any provision of this Act or by any other enactment (including an enactment contained in subordinate legislation) or by any rule of law, he shall report the matter to the [sheriff who], after hearing that person on the matter, may remove him from office or censure him or make such other order as the circumstances of the case may require.

(3)   Where the Accountant in Bankruptcy has reasonable grounds to suspect that an offence has been committed—

(a)   by a person mentioned in paragraph (a) of subsection (1) above in the performance of his functions under this Act or any other enactment (including an enactment contained in subordinate legislation) or any rule of law; or

(b)   in relation to a sequestration, by the debtor in respect of his assets, his dealings with them or his conduct in relation to his business or financial affairs; or

(c)   in relation to a sequestration, by a person other than the debtor in that person's dealings with the debtor, the interim trustee or the [. . .] trustee in respect of the debtor's assets, business or financial affairs,

he shall report the matter to the Lord Advocate.

(4)   The Accountant in Bankruptcy shall—

(a)   make the register of insolvencies, at all reasonable times, available for inspection; and

(b)   provide any person, on request, with a certified copy of any entry in the register.]

[1B   Performance of certain functions of the Accountant in Bankruptcy

(1)   The functions of the Accountant in Bankruptcy, other than functions conferred by section 1A of this Act, may be carried out on his behalf by any member of his staff authorised by him to do so.

(2)   Without prejudice to subsection (1) above, the Accountant in Bankruptcy may appoint on such terms and conditions as he considers appropriate such persons as he considers fit to perform on his behalf any of his functions in respect of the sequestration of the estate of any debtor.

(3)   A person appointed under subsection (2) above shall comply with such general or specific directions as the Accountant in Bankruptcy may from time to time give to such person as to the performance of his functions in relation to any sequestration.

(4)   The Accountant in Bankruptcy may pay to a person appointed under subsection (2) above such fee as he may consider appropriate.]

[1C   Directions

(1)   The Secretary of State may, after consultation with the Lord President of the Court of Session, give to the Accountant in Bankruptcy general directions as to the performance of his functions under this Act.

(2)   Directions under this section may be given in respect of all cases or any class or description of cases, but may not be given in respect of any particular case.

(3)   The Accountant in Bankruptcy shall comply with any directions given to him under this section.]

2   Appointment and functions of [the trustee in the sequestration]

[(1)   Where the [sheriff] awards sequestration of the debtor's estate and the petition for the sequestration—

(a)   nominates a person to be [the] trustee;

(b)   states that the person satisfies the conditions mentioned in subsection (3) below; and

(c)   has annexed to it a copy of the undertaking mentioned in subsection (3)(c) below,

the [sheriff] may, if it appears to the [sheriff] that the person satisfies those conditions and if no interim trustee has been appointed in pursuance of subsection (5) below, appoint that person to be [the] trustee in the sequestration.

[(1A)   Subject to subsection (1C) below, where the Accountant in Bankruptcy awards sequestration of the debtor's estate and the debtor application—

(a)   nominates a person to be the trustee;

(b)   states that the person satisfies the conditions mentioned in subsection (3) below; and

(c)   has annexed to it a copy of the undertaking mentioned in subsection (3)(c) below,

the Accountant in Bankruptcy may, if it appears to him that the person satisfies those conditions, appoint that person to be the trustee in the sequestration.

(1B)   Where the Accountant in Bankruptcy awards sequestration of the debtor's estate and does not appoint a person to be the trustee in pursuance of subsection (1A) above, the Accountant in Bankruptcy shall be deemed to be appointed to be the trustee in the sequestration.

(1C)   Where—

(a)   the debtor application is made by a debtor to whom section 5(2B)(c)(ia) applies; and

(b)   the Accountant in Bankruptcy awards sequestration of the debtor's estate,

the Accountant in Bankruptcy shall be deemed to be appointed as trustee in the sequestration.]

(2)   Where the [sheriff] awards sequestration of the debtor's estate and—

(a)   [he] does not appoint a person to be [the] trustee in pursuance of subsection (1) above; and

(b)   no interim trustee has been appointed in pursuance of subsection (5) below, the [sheriff] shall appoint the Accountant in Bankruptcy to be [the] trustee in the sequestration.

[(2A)   Where the sheriff awards sequestration of the debtor's estate and an interim trustee has been appointed in pursuance of subsection (5) below, the sheriff may appoint—

(a)   the interim trustee; or

(b)   subject to subsection (2B) below, such other person as may be nominated by the petitioner,

to be the trustee in the sequestration.

(2B)   A person nominated under subsection (2A)(b) above may be appointed to be the trustee in the sequestration only if—

(a)   it appears to the sheriff that the person satisfies the conditions mentioned in subsection (3) below; and

(b)   a copy of the undertaking mentioned in subsection (3)(c) below has been lodged with the sheriff.

(2C)   Where the sheriff does not appoint a person to be trustee in pursuance of subsection (2A) above, the sheriff shall appoint the Accountant in Bankruptcy to be the trustee in the sequestration.]

(3)   The conditions referred to in subsection (1) above are that the person—

[. . .]

(b)   is qualified to act as an insolvency practitioner; and

(c)   has given an undertaking, in writing, that he will act [as the trustee [in the sequestration]].

[. . .]

(5)   Where a petition for sequestration is presented by a creditor or a trustee acting under a trust deed, the [sheriff] may appoint an interim trustee before sequestration is awarded—

(a)   if the debtor consents; or

(b)   if the trustee acting under the trust deed or any creditor shows cause.

(6)   For the purposes of the appointment of an interim trustee under subsection (5) above—

(a)   where a person is nominated as mentioned in subsection (1)(a) above and the provisions of that subsection apply, the [sheriff] may appoint that person; and

(b)   where such a person is not appointed, the [sheriff] shall appoint the Accountant in Bankruptcy.

[(6A)   The interim trustee's general function shall be to safeguard the debtor's estate pending the determination of the petition for sequestration.

(6B)   Whether or not the interim trustee is still acting in the sequestration, the interim trustee shall supply the Accountant in Bankruptcy with such information as the Accountant in Bankruptcy considers necessary to enable him to discharge his functions under this Act.]

(7)   Where—

[(a)   a trustee is appointed in a sequestration where the petition was presented by a creditor for the trustee acting under a trust deed; or

(b)   an interim trustee is appointed in pursuance of subsection (5) above,

he] shall, as soon as practicable, notify the debtor of his appointment.]

3   [Functions of the trustee]

(1)   In every sequestration there shall be a [. . .] trustee whose general functions shall be—

(a)   to recover, manage and realise the debtor's estate, whether situated in Scotland or elsewhere;

(b)   to distribute the estate among the debtor's creditors according to their respective entitlements;

(c)   to ascertain the reasons for the debtor's insolvency and the circumstances surrounding it;

(d)   to ascertain the state of the debtor's liabilities and assets;

(e)   to maintain a sederunt book during his term of office for the purpose of providing an accurate record of the sequestration process;

(f)   to keep regular accounts of his intromissions with the debtor's estate, such accounts being available for inspection at all reasonable times by the commissioners (if any), the creditors and the debtor; and

(g)   whether or not he is still acting in the sequestration, to supply the Accountant in Bankruptcy with such information as the Accountant in Bankruptcy considers necessary to enable him to discharge his functions under this Act.

(2)   A [. . .] trustee in performing his functions under this Act shall have regard to advice offered to him by the commissioners (if any).

(3)   If the [. . .] trustee has reasonable grounds to suspect that an offence has been committed in relation to a sequestration—

(a)   by the debtor in respect of his assets, his dealings with them or his conduct in relation to his business or financial affairs; or

(b)   by a person other than the debtor in that person's dealings with the debtor, the interim trustee or the [. . .] trustee in respect of the debtor's assets, business or financial affairs,

he shall report the matter to the Accountant in Bankruptcy.

[(3A)   If the trustee has reasonable grounds to believe that any behaviour on the part of the debtor is of a kind that would result in a sheriff granting, under section 56B(1) of this Act, an application for a bankruptcy restrictions order, he shall report the matter to the Accountant in Bankruptcy.]

(4)   A report under subsection (3) [or (3A)] above shall be absolutely privileged.

[(5)   Paragraph (g) of subsection (1) above and [subsections (3) and (3A)] above shall not apply in any case where the [. . .] trustee is the Accountant in Bankruptcy.]

[(6)   A [. . .] trustee may apply to the sheriff for directions in relation to any particular matter arising in the sequestration.]

[(7)   Where the debtor, a creditor or any other person having an interest is dissatisfied with any act, omission or decision of the [. . .] trustee, he may apply to the sheriff and, on such an application being made, the sheriff may confirm, annul or modify any act or decision of the [. . .] trustee or may give him directions or make such order as he thinks fit.]

[(8)   The trustee shall comply with the requirements of subsections (1)(a) to (d) and (2) above only in so far as, in his view, it would be of financial benefit to the estate of the debtor and in the interests of the creditors to do so.]

4   Commissioners
In any sequestration [. . .] commissioners, whose general functions shall be to supervise the intromissions of the [. . .] trustee with the sequestrated estate and to advise him, may be elected in accordance with section 30 of this Act.

Petitions for sequestration

5   Sequestration of the estate of living or deceased debtor
(1)   The estate of a debtor may be sequestrated in accordance with the provisions of this Act.

[(2)   The sequestration of the estate of a living debtor shall be—

(a)   by debtor application made by the debtor, if [subsection] below applies to the debtor; or

(b)   on the petition of—

(i)   subject to subsection (2D) below, a qualified creditor or qualified creditors, if the debtor is apparently insolvent;

(ii) a temporary administrator;

(iii) a member State liquidator appointed in main proceedings; or

(iv) the trustee acting under a trust deed if, and only if, one or more of the conditions in subsection (2C) below is satisfied.]

[. . .]

(2B) This subsection applies to the debtor where—

(a) the total amount of his debts (including interest) at the date [the debtor application is made] is not less than [£3,000 or such sum as may be prescribed];

(b) an award of sequestration has not been made against him in the period of 5 years ending on the day before the date [the debtor application is made]; and

(c) the debtor [. . .]—

(i) is apparently insolvent; or

[(ia) is unable to pay his debts and each of the conditions in section 5A of this Act is met;]

[(ib) has, within the prescribed period, been granted a certificate for sequestration of the debtor's estate in accordance with section 5B of this Act,]

(ii) has granted a trust deed [which is not a protected trust deed by reason of the creditors objecting, or not agreeing, in accordance with regulations under paragraph 5 of Schedule 5 to this Act, to the trust deed, and for the purposes of this paragraph a debtor shall not be apparently insolvent by reason only that he has granted a trust deed or that he has given notice to his creditors as mentioned in paragraph (b) of section 7(1) of this Act.]

(2C) The conditions mentioned in subsection [(2)(b)(iv)] above are—

(a) that the debtor has failed to comply—

(i) with any obligation imposed on him under the trust deed with which he could reasonably have complied; or

(ii) with any instruction or requirement reasonably given to or made of him by the trustee for the purposes of the trust deed; or

(b) that the trustee avers in his petition that it would be in the best interests of the creditors that an award of sequestration be made.

(2D) No petition may be presented under subsection (2)(b)(i) above unless the qualified creditor has provided, by such time prior to the presentation of the petition as may be prescribed, the debtor with a debt advice and information package.

(2E) In subsection (2D) above, 'debt advice and information package' means the debt advice and information package referred to in section 10(5) of the Debt Arrangement and Attachment (Scotland) Act 2002 (asp 17).]

[(2F) In subsection (2B)(c)(ib) above, 'the prescribed period' means such period, ending immediately before the debtor application is made, as may be prescribed under section 5B(5)(c) of this Act.]

(3) The sequestration of the estate of a deceased debtor shall be on the petition of—

(a) an executor or a person entitled to be appointed as executor on the estate;

(b) a qualified creditor or qualified creditors of the deceased debtor;

[(ba) a temporary administrator;

(bb) a member State liquidator appointed in main proceedings;] or

(c) the trustee acting under a trust deed.

(4) In this Act 'qualified creditor' means a creditor who, at the date of the presentation of the petition [or, as the case may be, the date the debtor application is made], is a creditor of the debtor in respect of liquid or illiquid debts (other than contingent or future debts [or amounts payable under a confiscation order]), whether secured or unsecured, which amount (or of one such debt which amounts) to not less than [£3,000] or such sum as may be prescribed; and 'qualified creditors' means creditors who at the said date are creditors of the debtor in respect of such debts as aforesaid amounting in aggregate to not less than [£3,000] or such sum as may be prescribed [; and in the foregoing provisions of this sub-

section 'confiscation order' [means a confiscation order under Part 2, 3, or 4 of the Proceeds of Crime Act 2002].

[(4A)   In this Act, 'trust deed' means a voluntary trust deed granted by or on behalf of the debtor whereby his estate (other than such of his estate as would not, under section 33(1) of this Act, vest in the [. . .] trustee if his estate were sequestrated) is conveyed to the trustee for the benefit of his creditors generally.

(4B)   A debtor application shall—

    (a)   be made to the Accountant in Bankruptcy; and

    (b)   be in such form as may be prescribed.

(4C)   The Scottish Ministers may, by regulations, make provision—

    (a)   in relation to the procedure to be followed in a debtor application (in so far as not provided for in this Act);

    (b)   prescribing the form of any document that may be required for the purposes of making a debtor application; and

    (c)   prescribing the fees and charges which may be levied by the Accountant in Bankruptcy in relation to debtor applications.]

(5)   Paragraphs 1(1) and (3), 2(1)(a) and (2) and 6 of Schedule 1 to this Act shall apply in order to ascertain the amount of the debt or debts for the purposes of subsection (4) above as they apply in order to ascertain the amount which a creditor is entitled to claim, but as if for any reference to the date of sequestration there were substituted a reference to the date of presentation of the petition [or, as the case may be, the date the debtor application is made].

(6)   The petitioner shall [on the day the petition for sequestration is presented under this section, send a copy of the petition] to the Accountant in Bankruptcy.

[(6A)   In the case of a debtor application, the debtor shall send a statement of assets and liabilities to the Accountant in Bankruptcy along with the application.]

(7)   Where, after a petition for sequestration has been presented but before the sequestration has been awarded, the debtor dies then—

    [. . .]

    (b)   if the petitioner is a creditor, the proceedings shall continue in accordance with this Act so far as circumstances will permit.

[(7A)   Where, after a debtor application is made but before the sequestration is awarded, the debtor dies, then the application shall fall.]

(8)   Where, after a petition for sequestration has been presented under this section but before the sequestration has been awarded, a creditor who—

    (a)   is the petitioner [. . .]; or

    (b)   has lodged answers to the petition,

withdraws or dies, there may be sisted in the place of—

      (i)   the creditor mentioned in paragraph (a) above, any creditor who was a qualified creditor at the date when the petition was presented and who remains so qualified at the date of the sist;

      (ii)   the creditor mentioned in paragraph (b) above, any other creditor.

[(8A)   Where, after a debtor application is made but before the sequestration is awarded, a creditor who concurs in the application withdraws or dies, any other creditor who was a qualified creditor at the date the debtor application was made and who remains so qualified may notify the Accountant in Bankruptcy that he concurs in the application in place of the creditor who has withdrawn or died.]

[(9)   If the debtor—

    (a)   fails to send to the Accountant in Bankruptcy in accordance with subsection [(6A)] above such statement of assets and liabilities; or

    (b)   fails to disclose any material fact in such statement of assets and liabilities; or

    (c)   makes a material misstatement in such statement of assets and liabilities,

he shall be guilty of an offence and liable on summary conviction to a fine not exceeding level 5 on the standard scale or to imprisonment for a term not exceeding 3 months or to both such fine and imprisonment.

(10)   In any proceedings for an offence under subsection (9) above, it shall be a defence for the accused to show that he had a reasonable excuse for—
   (a)   failing to send to the Accountant in Bankruptcy in accordance with subsection [(6A)] above such statement of assets and liabilities; or
   (b)   failing to disclose a material fact; or
   (c)   making a material misstatement.]

[5A   Debtor applications by low income, low asset debtors

   (1)   The conditions referred to in section 5(2B)(c)(ia) of this Act are as follows.
   (2)   The debtor's weekly income (if any) on the date the debtor application is made does not exceed £100 or such other amount as may be prescribed.
   (3)   The debtor does not own any land.
   (4)   The total value of the debtor's assets (leaving out of account any liabilities) on the date the debtor application is made does not exceed £1000 or such other amount as may be prescribed.
   (5)   The Scottish Ministers may by regulations—
   (a)   make provision as to how the debtor's weekly income is to be determined;
   (b)   provide that particular descriptions of income are to be excluded for the purposes of subsection (2) above;
   (c)   make provision as to how the value of the debtor's assets is to be determined;
   (d)   provide that particular descriptions of asset are to be excluded for the purposes of subsection (4) above;
   (e)   make different provision for different classes or description of debtor;
   (f)   add further conditions which must be met before a debtor application may be made by virtue of section 5(2B)(c)(ia) of this Act; and
   (g)   where such further conditions are added—
      (i)   remove; or
      (ii)   otherwise vary,
   those conditions.]

[5B   Certificate for sequestration

   (1)   A certificate for sequestration of a debtor's estate is a certificate granted by an authorised person certifying that the debtor is unable to pay debts as they become due.
   (2)   A certificate may be granted only on the application of the debtor.
   (3)   An authorised person must grant a certificate if, and only if, the debtor can demonstrate that the debtor is unable to pay debts as they become due.
   (4)   In this section 'authorised person' means a person falling within a class pre-scribed under subsection (5)(a).
   (5)   The Scottish Ministers may by regulations—
   (a)   prescribe classes of persons authorised to grant a certificate under this section;
   (b)   make provision about certification by an authorised person, including—
      (i)   the form and manner in which a certification must be made;
      (ii)   the fee, if any, which an authorised person is entitled to charge for or in connection with granting a certificate;
   (c)   prescribe a period for the purpose of section 5(2B)(c)(ib) of this Act;
   (d)   make different provision for different cases or classes of case.]

6   Sequestration of other estates

   (1)   Subject to subsection (2) below, the estate belonging to or held for or jointly by the members of any of the following entities may be sequestrated—
   (a)   a trust in respect of debts incurred by it;
   (b)   a partnership, including a dissolved partnership;
   (c)   a body corporate or an unincorporated body;

(d)   a limited partnership (including a dissolved partnership) within the meaning of the Limited Partnerships Act 1907.

(2)   It shall not be competent to sequestrate the estate of any of the following entities—

(a)   a company registered under the [Companies Act 2006]; or

(b)   an entity in respect of which an enactment provides, expressly or by implication, that sequestration is incompetent.

(3)   The sequestration of a trust estate in respect of debts incurred by the trust shall be [. . .]—

[(a)   by debtor application made by a majority of trustees, with the concurrence of a qualified creditor or qualified creditors; or

(b)   on the petition of—

(i)   a temporary administrator;

(ii)   a member State liquidator appointed in main proceedings; or

(iii)   a qualified creditor or qualified creditors, if the trustees as such are apparently insolvent.]

(4)   The sequestration of the estate of a partnership shall be [. . .]—

[(a)   by debtor application made by the partnership with the concurrence of a qualified creditor or qualified creditors; or

(b)   on the petition of—

(i)   a temporary administrator;

(ii)   a member State liquidator appointed in main proceedings;

(iii)   a trustee acting under a trust deed; or

(iv)   a qualified creditor or qualified creditors, if the partnership is apparently insolvent.]

(5)   A petition under [subsection (4)(b)] above may be combined with a petition for the sequestration of the estate of any of the partners as an individual where that individual is apparently insolvent.

(6)   The sequestration of the estate of a body corporate or of an unincorporated body shall be on the petition of—

[(a)   by debtor application made by a person authorised to act on behalf of the body, with the concurrence of a qualified creditor or qualified creditors; or

(b)   on the petition of—

(i)   a temporary administrator;

(ii)   a member State liquidator appointed in main proceedings; or

(iii)   a qualified creditor or qualified creditors, if the body is apparently insolvent.]

(7)   The application of this Act to the sequestration of the estate of a limited partnership shall be subject to such modifications as may be prescribed.

(8)   Subsections (6) [, (6A), (8) and (8A)] of section 5 of this Act shall apply for the purposes of this section as they apply for the purposes of that section.

[6A   Petition for sequestration of estate: provision of information

(1)   A petitioner for sequestration of a debtor's estate shall, insofar as it is within the petitioner's knowledge, state in the petition—

(a)   whether or not the debtor's centre of main interests is situated—

(i)   in the United Kingdom; or

(ii)   in another member State; and

(b)   whether or not the debtor possesses an establishment—

(i)   in the United Kingdom; or

(ii)   in any other member State.

(2)   If, to the petitioner's knowledge, there is a member State liquidator appointed in main proceedings in relation to the debtor, the petitioner shall, as soon as reasonably practicable, send a copy of the petition to that member State liquidator.]

[6B Debtor application: provision of information

(1) Where a debtor application is made, the debtor shall state in the application—

    (a) whether or not the debtor's centre of main interests is situated—

        (i) in the United Kingdom; or

        (ii) in another member State; and

    (b) whether or not the debtor possesses an establishment—

        (i) in the United Kingdom; or

        (ii) in any other member State.

(2) If, to the debtor's knowledge, there is a member State liquidator appointed in main proceedings in relation to the debtor, the debtor shall, as soon as reasonably practicable, send a copy of the debtor application to that member State liquidator.]

7 Meaning of apparent insolvency

(1) A debtor's apparent insolvency shall be constituted (or, where he is already apparently insolvent, constituted anew) whenever—

    (a) his estate is sequestrated, or he is adjudged bankrupt in England or Wales or Northern Ireland; or

    (b) [not being a person whose property is for the time being affected by a restraint order or subject to a confiscation, or charging, order,] he gives written notice to his creditors that he has ceased to pay his debts in the ordinary course of business; or

    [(ba) he becomes subject to main proceedings in a member State other than the United Kingdom.]

    (c) any of the following circumstances occurs—

        (i) he grants a trust deed;

        (ii) following the service on him of a duly executed charge for payment of a debt, the days of charge expire without payment;

        [. . .]

        (iv) a decree of adjudication of any part of his estate is granted, either for payment or in security;

        [. . .] [; or

        (vi) a debt payment programme under the Debt Arrangement and Attachment (Scotland) Act 2002 is revoked, where any debt being paid under the programme is constituted by a decree or document of debt as defined in section 10 (attachment) of that Act;]

        [(vii) where any debt being paid under a debt payment programme under the Debt Arrangement and Attachment (Scotland) Act 2002 is constituted by a decree or document of debt as defined in section 10 (attachment) of that Act and the programme is revoked,]

unless it is shown that at the time any such circumstance occurred, the debtor was able and willing to pay his debts as they became due [or that but for his property being affected by a restraint order or subject to a confiscation, or charging, order he would be able to do so]; or

    (d) a creditor of the debtor, in respect of a liquid debt which amounts (or liquid debts which in aggregate amount) to not less than £750 or such sum as may be prescribed, has served on the debtor, by personal service by an officer of court, a demand in the prescribed form requiring him either to pay the debt (or debts) or to find security for its (or their) payment, and within 3 weeks after the date of service of the demand the debtor has not—

        (i) complied with the demand; or

        (ii) intimated to the creditor, by recorded delivery, that he denies that there is a debt or that the sum claimed by the creditor as the debt is immediately payable.

[In paragraph (d) above, 'liquid debt' does not include a sum payable under a confiscation order; and in the foregoing provisions of this subsection—
    'charging order' has the meaning assigned by [section 78(2) of the Criminal Justice Act 1988 or by section 27(2) of the Drug Trafficking Act 1994];
    [. . .] 'restraint order' means a confiscation order or a restraint order under Part 2, 3, or 4 of the Proceeds of Crime Act 2002.]
(2) A debtor's apparent insolvency shall continue, if constituted under—
    (a) subsection (1)(a) above, until his discharge; [. . .]
    (b) subsection (1)(b), (c) or (d) above, until he becomes able to pay his debts and pays them as they become due [; or
    (c) subsection (i)(ba), [until] main proceedings have ended.]
(3) The apparent insolvency of—
    (a) a partnership shall be constituted either in accordance with the foregoing provisions of this section or if any of the partners is apparently insolvent for a debt of the partnership;
    (b) an unincorporated body shall be constituted if a person representing the body is apparently insolvent, or a person holding property of the body in a fiduciary capacity is apparently insolvent, for a debt of the body.
(4) Notwithstanding subsection (2) of section 6 of this Act, the apparent insolvency of an entity such as is mentioned in paragraph (a) or (b) of that subsection may be constituted (or as the case may be constituted anew) under subsection (1) above; and any reference in the foregoing provisions of this section to a debtor shall, except where the context otherwise requires, be construed as including a reference to such an entity.

8 Further provisions relating to presentation of petitions
(1) Subject to subsection (2) below, a petition for the sequestration of a debtor's estate (other than a deceased debtor's estate) may be presented—
    [(a) at any time by—
        [. . .]
        (ii) a trustee under a trust deed;
        (iii) a temporary administrator; or
        (iv) a member State liquidator appointed in main proceedings;]
    (b) by a qualified creditor or qualified creditors, only if the apparent insolvency founded on in the petition was constituted within 4 months before the petition is presented.
(2) A petition for the sequestration of the estate of a limited partnership may be presented within such time as may be prescribed.
(3) A petition for the sequestration of the estate of a deceased debtor may be presented—
    [(a) at any time by—
        (i) an executor;
        (ii) a person entitled to be appointed as executor of the estate;
        (iii) a trustee acting under a trust deed;
        (iv) a temporary administrator; or
        (v) a member State liquidator appointed in main proceedings;]
    (b) by a qualified creditor or qualified creditors of the deceased debtor—
        (i) in a case where the apparent insolvency of the debtor was constituted within 4 months before his death, at any time;
        (ii) in any other case (whether or not apparent insolvency has been constituted), not earlier than 6 months after the debtor's death.
(4) If an executor does not petition for sequestration of the deceased debtor's estate or for the appointment of a judicial factor to administer the estate within a reasonable period after he knew or ought to have known that the estate was absolutely insolvent and likely to remain so, any intromission by him with the estate

after the expiry of that period shall be deemed to be an intromission without a title.

(5)   The presentation of [. . .] a petition for sequestration shall bar the effect of any enactment or rule of law relating to the limitation of actions in any part of the United Kingdom.

(6)   Where before sequestration is awarded it becomes apparent that a petitioning [. . .] creditor was ineligible so to petition [. . .] he shall withdraw, or as the case may be withdraw from, the petition but another creditor may be sisted in his place.

[8A   **Further provisions relating to debtor applications**

(1)   Subject to subsection (2) below, a debtor application may be made at any time.

(2)   A debtor application made in relation to the estate of a limited partnership may be made within such time as may be prescribed.

(3)   The making of, or the concurring in, a debtor application shall bar the effect of any enactment or rule of law relating to the limitation of actions.

(4)   Where, before sequestration is awarded, it becomes apparent that a creditor concurring in a debtor application was ineligible to so concur the Accountant in Bankruptcy shall withdraw him from the application but another creditor may concur in the place of the ineligible creditor and that other creditor shall notify the Accountant in Bankruptcy of that fact.]

9   Jurisdiction

(1)   [Where a petition is presented for the sequestration of an estate,] the [sheriff] shall have jurisdiction in respect of the sequestration of the estate of a living debtor or of a deceased debtor if the debtor had an established place of business in [the sheriffdom], or was habitually resident there, at the relevant time.

[(1A)   The Accountant in Bankruptcy may determine a debtor application for the sequestration of the estate of a living debtor if the debtor had an established place of business in Scotland, or was habitually resident there, at the relevant time.]

(2)   [Where a petition is presented for the sequestration of an estate,] the [sheriff] shall have jurisdiction in respect of the sequestration of the estate of any entity which may be sequestrated by virtue of section 6 of this Act, if the entity—

(a)   had an established place of business in [the sheriffdom] at the relevant time; or

(b)   was constituted or formed under Scots law, and at any time carried on business in [the sheriffdom].

[(2A)   The Accountant in Bankruptcy may determine a debtor application for the sequestration of the estate of any entity which may be sequestrated by virtue of section 6 of this Act, if the entity—

(a)   had an established place of business in Scotland at the relevant time; or

(b)   was constituted or formed under Scots law, and at any time carried on business in Scotland.]

(3)   Notwithstanding that the partner of a firm, whether alive or deceased, does not fall within subsection (1) above, the [sheriff] shall have jurisdiction in respect of the sequestration of his estate if a petition has been presented for the sequestration of the estate of the firm of which he is, or was at the relevant time before his decease, a partner and the process of that sequestration is still current.

[(3A)   Any proceedings under this Act which—

(a)   relate to—

(i)   a debtor application; or

(ii) the sequestration of a debtor's estate awarded following such an application; and

(b)   may be brought before a sheriff,

shall be brought before the sheriff who would, under subsection (1) or (2) above, have had jurisdiction in respect of a petition for sequestration of the debtor's estate.]

[. . .]

(5)   In this section 'the relevant time' means at any time in the year immediately preceding the date of presentation of the petition [, the date the debtor application is made] or the date of death, as the case may be.

[(6)   This section is subject to Article 3 of the EC Regulation.]

[10   Duty to notify existence of concurrent proceedings for sequestration or analogous remedy

(1)   If, in the course of sequestration proceedings (referred to in this section and in section 10A of this Act as the 'instant proceedings')—

(a)   a petitioner for sequestration;

(b)   the debtor; or

(c)   a creditor concurring in a debtor application,

is, or becomes, aware of any of the circumstances mentioned in subsection (2) below, he shall as soon as possible take the action mentioned in subsection (3) below.

(2)   Those circumstances are that, notwithstanding the instant proceedings—

(a)   a petition for sequestration of the debtor's estate is before a sheriff or such sequestration has been awarded;

(b)   a debtor application has been made in relation to the debtor's estate or sequestration has been awarded by virtue of such an application;

(c)   a petition for the appointment of a judicial factor on the debtor's estate is before a court or such a judicial factor has been appointed;

(d)   a petition is before a court for the winding up of the debtor under Part IV or V of the Insolvency Act 1986 (c 45) or section 372 of the Financial Services and Markets Act 2000 (c 8); or

(e)   an application for an analogous remedy in respect of the debtor's estate is proceeding or such an analogous remedy is in force.

(3)   The action referred to in subsection (1) above is—

(a)   in a case where the instant proceedings are by petition for sequestration, to notify the sheriff to whom that petition was presented; and

(b)   in a case where the instant proceedings are by debtor application, to notify the Accountant in Bankruptcy,

of the circumstance referred to in subsection (2) above.

(4)   If a petitioner fails to comply with subsection (1) above, he may be made liable for the expenses of presenting the petition for sequestration.

(5)   If a creditor concurring in a debtor application fails to comply with subsection (1) above, he may be made liable for the expenses of making the debtor application.

(6)   If a debtor fails to comply with subsection (1) above, he shall be guilty of an offence and liable, on summary conviction, to a fine not exceeding level 5 on the standard scale.

(7)   In this section and in section 10A of this Act 'analogous remedy' means a bankruptcy order under the Bankruptcy Act 1914 (c 59) or an individual voluntary arrangement or bankruptcy order under the Insolvency Act 1986 (c 45) or an administration order under section 112 of the County Courts Act 1984 (c 28) in England and Wales or under any enactment having the like effect in Northern Ireland or a remedy analogous to any of the aforesaid remedies, or to sequestration, in any other country (including England, Wales and Northern Ireland).]

[10A   Powers in relation to concurrent proceedings for sequestration or analogous remedy

(1)   Where, in the course of instant proceedings which are by petition, any of the circumstances mentioned in paragraphs (a) to (d) of section 10(2) of this Act exists, the sheriff to whom the petition in the instant proceedings was presented may, on his own motion or at the instance of the debtor or any creditor or other person having an interest, allow that petition to proceed or may sist or dismiss it.

(2)   Without prejudice to subsection (1) above, where, in the course of instant proceedings which are by petition, any of the circumstances mentioned in paragraphs (a), (c) or (d) of section 10(2) of this Act exists, the Court of Session may, on its own motion or on the application of the debtor or any creditor or other person having an interest, direct the sheriff before whom the petition in the instant proceedings is pending, or the sheriff before whom the other petition is pending, to sist or dismiss the petition in the instant proceedings or, as the case may be, the other petition, or may order the petitions to be heard together.

(3)   Without prejudice to subsection (1) above, where, in the course of instant proceedings which are by petition, the circumstance mentioned in paragraph (b) of section 10(2) of this Act exists, the sheriff to whom the petition in the instant proceedings was presented may, on his own motion or at the instance of the debtor or any creditor or other person having an interest, direct the Accountant in Bankruptcy to dismiss the debtor application.

(4)   Where, in the course of instant proceedings which are by debtor application, any of the circumstances mentioned in paragraphs (a) to (d) of section 10(2) of this Act exists, the Accountant in Bankruptcy may dismiss the debtor application in the instant proceedings.

(5)   Where, in respect of the same estate—

   (a)   a petition for sequestration is pending before a sheriff; and

   (b)   an application for an analogous remedy is proceeding or an analogous remedy is in force,

the sheriff, on his own motion or at the instance of the debtor or any creditor or other person having an interest, may allow the petition for sequestration to proceed or may sist or dismiss it.

(6)   Where, in respect of the same estate—

   (a)   a debtor application has been made and has not been determined; and

   (b)   an application for an analogous remedy is proceeding or an analogous remedy is in force,

the Accountant in Bankruptcy may proceed to determine the application or may dismiss it.]

11   Creditor's oath

(1)   Every creditor, being a petitioner for sequestration, a creditor who concurs in a [debtor application] or a qualified creditor who becomes sisted under subsection (8)(i) of section 5 of this Act or under that subsection as applied by section 6(8) of this Act, shall produce an oath in the prescribed form made by him or on his behalf.

(2)   The oath may be made—

   (a)   in the United Kingdom, before any person entitled to administer an oath there;

   (b)   outwith the United Kingdom, before a British diplomatic or consular officer or any person authorised to administer an oath or affirmation under the law of the place where the oath is made.

(3)   The identity of the person making the oath and the identity of the person before whom the oath is made and their authority to make and to administer the oath respectively shall be presumed to be correctly stated, and any seal or signature on the oath shall be presumed to be authentic, unless the contrary is established.

(4)   If the oath contains any error or has omitted any fact, the [sheriff to whom] the petition for sequestration was presented [or, in the case of a creditor concurring in a debtor application, the Accountant in Bankruptcy] may, at any time before sequestration is awarded, allow another oath to be produced rectifying the original oath; and this section shall apply to the making of that other oath as it applies to the making of the original oath.

(5)   Every creditor must produce along with the oath an account or voucher (according to the nature of the debt) which constitutes *prima facie* evidence of the debt; and a petitioning creditor shall in addition produce such evidence as is available to him to show the apparent insolvency of the debtor.

Award of sequestration and appointment and resignation of interim trustee

12   When sequestration is awarded

[(1)   Where a [debtor application is made, the Accountant in Bankruptcy shall award sequestration forthwith if he is satisfied—

    (a)   that the application has been made in accordance with the provisions of this Act and any provisions made under this Act;]

    (b)   that [subsection] (2B) of section 5 of this Act applies to the debtor; and

    (c)   that the provisions of [subsection (6A)] of that section have been complied with.

[. . .]

(2)   Where a petition for sequestration of a debtor's estate is presented by a creditor or a trustee acting under a trust deed, the [sheriff to whom] the petition is presented shall grant warrant to cite the debtor to appear before [him] on such date as shall be specified in the warrant, being a date not less than 6 nor more than 14 days after the date of citation, to show cause why sequestration should not be awarded.

[(3)   Where, on a petition for sequestration presented by a creditor or a trustee acting under a trust deed, the [sheriff] is satisfied—

    (a)   that, if the debtor has not appeared, proper citation has been made of the debtor;

    (b)   that the petition has been presented in accordance with the provisions of this Act;

    (c)   that the provisions of subsection (6) of section 5 of this Act have been complied with;

    (d)   that, in the case of a petition by a creditor, the requirements of this Act relating to apparent insolvency have been fulfilled; and

    (e)   that, in the case of a petition by a trustee, the averments in his petition as to any of the conditions in subsection (2C) of the said section 5 are true,

[he] shall, subject to [subsections (3A) to (3C)] below, award sequestration forthwith.

[(3A)   Sequestration shall not be awarded in pursuance of subsection (3) above if—

    (a)   cause is shown why sequestration cannot competently be awarded; or

    (b)   the debtor forthwith pays or satisfies, or produces written evidence of the payment or satisfaction of, or gives or shows that there is sufficient security for the payment of—

        (i)   the debt in respect of which he became apparently insolvent; and

        (ii)   any other debt due by him to the petitioner and any creditor concurring in the petition.

(3B)   Where the sheriff is satisfied that the debtor shall, before the expiry of the period of 42 days beginning with the day on which the debtor appears before the sheriff, pay or satisfy—

    (a)   the debt in respect of which the debtor became apparently insolvent; and

(b)   any other debt due by the debtor to the petitioner and any creditor concurring in the petition,
the sheriff may continue the petition for a period of no more than 42 days.
    (3C)   Where the sheriff is satisfied—
        (a)   that a debt payment programme (within the meaning of Part 1 of the Debt Arrangement and Attachment (Scotland) Act 2002 (asp 17)) relating to—
            (i)   the debt in respect of which the debtor became apparently insolvent; and
            (ii)   any other debt due by the debtor to the petitioner and any creditor concurring in the petition,
has been applied for and has not yet been approved or rejected; or
        (b)   that such a debt payment programme will be applied for,
the sheriff may continue the petition for such period as he thinks fit.]
    [(4)   In this Act 'the date of sequestration' means—
        (a)   where [a debtor application is made], the date on which sequestration is awarded;
        (b)   where the petition for sequestration is presented by a creditor or a trustee acting under a trust deed—
            (i)   the date on which the [sheriff] grants warrant under subsection (2) above to cite the debtor; or
            (ii)   where more than one such warrant is granted, the date on which the first such warrant is granted.]

[13   Resignation, removal etc of interim trustee

    [(A1)   This section applies where an interim trustee is appointed under section 2(5) of this Act and the petition for sequestration has not been determined.]
    (1)   Where, under section 1A(2) of this Act, the [sheriff] removes from office an interim trustee, the [sheriff] shall, on the application of the Accountant in Bankruptcy, appoint a new interim trustee.
    (2)   Without prejudice to section 1A(2) of this Act or to subsection (1) above, where the [sheriff] is satisfied that an interim trustee—
        (a)   is unable to act [for any reason mentioned in subsection (2A) below or] by, under or by virtue of [any other] provision of this Act [. . .]; or
        (b)   has so conducted himself that he should no longer continue to act [. . .],
the [sheriff], on the application of the debtor, a creditor or the Accountant in Bankruptcy, shall remove from office the interim trustee and appoint a new interim trustee.
    [(2A)   the reasons referred to in subsection (2)(a) above are that the interim trustee—
        (a)   is incapable within the meaning of section 1(6) of the Adults with Incapacity (Scotland) Act 2000 (asp 4); or
        (b)   has some other incapacity by virtue of which he is unable to act as interim trustee.]
    (3)   An interim trustee (not being the Accountant in Bankruptcy) may apply to the [sheriff] for authority to resign office; and if the [sheriff] is satisfied that the grounds mentioned in paragraph (a) or (b) of subsection (2) above apply in relation to the interim trustee, [the sheriff] shall grant the application.
    (4)   Where, following an application under subsection (3) above, the interim trustee resigns office, the [sheriff] shall appoint a new interim trustee.
    (5)   Where the interim trustee has died, the [sheriff], on the application of the debtor, a creditor or the Accountant in Bankruptcy, shall appoint a new interim trustee.
    (6)   No one (other than the Accountant in Bankruptcy) shall act as interim trustee in a sequestration if he would, by virtue of section 24(2) of this Act, be [ineligible to be elected as replacement] trustee in that sequestration; but where an

interim trustee is, by virtue of this subsection, prohibited from so acting, he shall forthwith make an application under subsection (3) above.

(7)   Subsections (1) and (2) of section 2 of this Act shall apply as regards the appointment of an interim trustee under this section as if for any reference to—

(a)   the [sheriff] awarding sequestration of the debtor's estate, there was substituted a reference to the [sheriff] appointing a new interim trustee; and

(b)   the petition for sequestration there was substituted a reference to the application under this section for the appointment of a new interim trustee.]

[13A   Termination of interim trustee's functions where not appointed as trustee

(1)   This section applies where an interim trustee (not being the Accountant in Bankruptcy) is appointed under section 2(5) of this Act and the sheriff—

(a)   awards sequestration and appoints another person as trustee under subsection (2A) or (2C) of section 2 of this Act; or

(b)   refuses to award sequestration.

(2)   Where the sheriff awards sequestration and appoints another person as trustee, the interim trustee shall hand over to the trustee everything in his possession which relates to the sequestration and shall thereupon cease to act in the sequestration.

(3)   The sheriff may make such order in relation to liability for the outlays and remuneration of the interim trustee as may be appropriate.

(4)   Within 3 months of the sheriff awarding or, as the case may be, refusing to award sequestration, the interim trustee shall—

(a)   submit to the Accountant in Bankruptcy—

(i)   his accounts of his intromissions (if any) with the debtor's estate; and

(ii)   a claim for outlays reasonably incurred, and for remuneration for work reasonably undertaken, by him; and

(b)   send a copy of his accounts and the claim to—

(i)   the debtor;

(ii)   the petitioner; and

(iii)   in a case where sequestration is awarded, the trustee and all creditors known to the interim trustee.

(5)   On a submission being made to him under subsection (4)(a) above, the Accountant in Bankruptcy shall—

(a)   audit the accounts;

(b)   issue a determination fixing the amount of the outlays and remuneration payable to the interim trustee;

(c)   send a copy of the determination to—

(i)   the interim trustee; and

(ii)   the persons mentioned in subsection (4)(b) above; and

(d)   where a trustee (not being the Accountant in Bankruptcy) has been appointed in the sequestration, send a copy of the audited accounts and of the determination to the trustee, who shall insert them in the sederunt book.

(6)   Where the Accountant in Bankruptcy has been appointed as the trustee in the sequestration, the Accountant in Bankruptcy shall insert a copy of the audited accounts and the determination in the sederunt book.

(7)   The interim trustee or any person mentioned in subsection (4)(b) above may, within 14 days after the issuing of the determination under subsection (5)(b) above, appeal to the sheriff against the determination.

(8)   On receiving a copy of the Accountant in Bankruptcy's determination sent under subsection (5)(c)(i) above the interim trustee may apply to him for a certificate of discharge.

(9)   The interim trustee shall send notice of an application under subsection (8)

above to the persons mentioned in subsection (4)(b) above and shall inform
them—

(a)   that they may make written representations relating to the application to
the Accountant in Bankruptcy within the period of 14 days after such
notification; and

(b)   of the effect mentioned in subsection (16) below.

(10)   On the expiry of the period mentioned in subsection (9)(a) above the
Accountant in Bankruptcy, after considering any representations duly made to
him, shall—

(a)   grant or refuse to grant the certificate of discharge; and

(b)   notify the persons mentioned in subsection (4)(b) above accordingly.

(11)   The interim trustee or any person mentioned in subsection (4)(b) above
may, within 14 days after the issuing of the determination under subsection (10)
above, appeal therefrom to the sheriff.

(12)   If, following an appeal under subsection (11) above, the sheriff determines
that a certificate of discharge which has been refused should be granted he shall
order the Accountant in Bankruptcy to grant it.

(13)   If, following an appeal under subsection (11) above, the sheriff determines
that a certificate of discharge which has been granted should have been refused he
shall revoke the certificate.

(14)   The sheriff clerk shall send a copy of the decree of the sheriff following an
appeal under subsection (11) above to the Accountant in Bankruptcy.

(15)   The decision of the sheriff in an appeal under subsection (7) or (11) above
shall be final.

(16)   The grant of a certificate of discharge under this section by the Accountant
in Bankruptcy shall have the effect of discharging the interim trustee from all liability (other than any liability arising from fraud) to the debtor, to the petitioner or
to the creditors in respect of any act or omission of the interim trustee in exercising
the functions conferred on him by this Act.]

**[13B   Termination of Accountant in Bankruptcy's functions as interim trustee
where not appointed as trustee**

(1)   This section applies where the Accountant in Bankruptcy is appointed as
interim trustee under section 2(5) of this Act and the sheriff—

(a)   awards sequestration and appoints another person as trustee under
section 2(2A) of this Act; or

(b)   refuses to award sequestration.

(2)   Where the sheriff awards sequestration and appoints another person as
trustee, the Accountant in Bankruptcy shall hand over to the trustee everything in
his possession which relates to the sequestration and shall thereupon cease to act
in the sequestration.

(3)   The sheriff may make such order in relation to liability for the outlays and
remuneration of the Accountant in Bankruptcy as may be appropriate.

(4)   Within 3 months of the sheriff awarding or, as the case may be, refusing to
award sequestration, the Accountant in Bankruptcy shall—

(a)   send to the debtor and the petitioner—

(i)   his accounts of his intromissions (if any) with the debtor's estate;

(ii)   a determination of his fees and outlays calculated in accordance with
regulations made under section 69A of this Act; and

(iii)   the notice mentioned in subsection (5) below; and

(b)   in a case where sequestration is awarded, send a copy of his accounts,
the claim and the notice to all creditors known to him.

(5)   The notice referred to in subsection (4)(a)(iii) above is a notice in writing
stating—

(a)   that the Accountant in Bankruptcy has commenced procedure under this
Act leading to discharge in respect of his actings as interim trustee;

(b)   that an appeal may be made to the sheriff under subsection (7) below; and

(c)   the effect mentioned in subsection (9) below.

(6)   The Accountant in Bankruptcy shall, unless the sheriff refuses to award sequestration, insert a copy of the accounts and the determination in the sederunt book.

(7)   The debtor, the petitioner and any creditor may, within 14 days after the sending of the notice under subsection (4)(a)(iii) or, as the case may be, subsection (4)(b) above, appeal to the sheriff against—

(a)   the determination of the Accountant in Bankruptcy mentioned in subsection (4)(a)(ii) above;

(b)   the discharge of the Accountant in Bankruptcy in respect of his actings as interim trustee;

(c)   both such determination and discharge, and the sheriff clerk shall send a copy of the decree of the sheriff to the Accountant in Bankruptcy.

(8)   The decision of the sheriff in an appeal under subsection (7) above shall be final.

(9)   Where—

(a)   the requirements of this section have been complied with; and

(b)   no appeal is made to the sheriff under subsection (7) above or such an appeal is made but is refused as regards the discharge of the Accountant in Bankruptcy,

the Accountant in Bankruptcy shall be discharged from all liability (other than any liability arising from fraud) to the debtor, to the petitioner or to the creditors in respect of any act or omission of the Accountant in Bankruptcy in exercising the functions of interim trustee conferred on him by this Act.]

14   Registration of [warrant or determination of debtor application]

(1)   The [sheriff clerk] shall forthwith after the date of sequestration send—

(a)   a certified copy of the [order of the sheriff granting warrant under section 12(2) of this Act] to the keeper of the register of inhibitions and adjudications for recording in that register;

(b)   a copy of the order to the Accountant in Bankruptcy; [and

[(c)   a copy of the order to the DAS Administrator (as defined in regulation 2(1) of the Debt Arrangement Scheme (Scotland) Regulations 2011), where the debtor is taking part in a debt payment programme under Part 1 of the Debt Arrangement and Attachment (Scotland) Act 2002]

[(1A)   Where the Accountant in Bankruptcy awards sequestration on a debtor application he shall forthwith after the date of sequestration send a certified copy of his determination of the application to the keeper of the register of inhibitions for recording in that register.]

(2)   Recording under subsection (1)(a) [or (1A)] above shall have the effect as from the date of sequestration of an inhibition and of a citation in an adjudication of the debtor's heritable estate at the instance of the creditors who subsequently have claims in the sequestration accepted under section 49 of this Act.

(3)   The effect mentioned in subsection (2) above shall expire—

(a)   on the recording under section 15(5)(a) or 17(8)(a) of, or by virtue of paragraph 11 of Schedule 4 to, this Act of a certified copy of an order; or

[(aa)   on the recording under paragraph 11(4)(a) of Schedule 4 to this Act of a certified copy of a certificate;]

(b)   subject to subsection (4) below, if the effect has not expired by virtue of [paragraphs (a) and (aa)] above, at the end of the period of 3 years beginning with the date of sequestration.

(4)   The [. . .] trustee, if not discharged, [may] before the end of the period of 3 years mentioned in subsection (3)(b) above send a memorandum in a form pre-

scribed by the Court of Session by act of sederunt to the keeper of the register of inhibitions and adjudications for recording in that register, and such recording shall renew the effect mentioned in subsection (2) above; and thereafter the said effect shall continue to be preserved only if such a memorandum is so recorded before the expiry of every subsequent period of 3 years.

[. . .]

15 Further provisions relating to award of sequestration

[. . .]

(2) The [sheriff] may at any time after sequestration has been awarded, on application being made to [him and subject to subsection (2A) below], transfer the sequestration [. . .] to any other sheriff.

[(2A) The debtor may, with leave of the sheriff, appeal to the sheriff principal against a transfer under subsection (2) above.]

(3) Where the [sheriff] makes an order refusing to award sequestration, the petitioner [. . .] may appeal against the order within 14 days of the date of making of the order.

[(3A) Where the Accountant in Bankruptcy, on determining a debtor application, refuses to award sequestration, the debtor or a creditor concurring in the application may appeal against such a determination within 14 days of it being made to the sheriff.]

(4) Without prejudice to any right to bring an action of reduction of an award of sequestration, such an award shall not be subject to review otherwise than by recall under sections 16 and 17 of this Act.

(5) Where a petition for sequestration is presented by a creditor or a trustee acting under a trust deed, the [sheriff clerk] shall—

(a) on the final determination or abandonment of any appeal under subsection (3) above in relation to the petition, or if there is no such appeal on the expiry of the 14 days mentioned in that subsection, send a certified copy of an order refusing to award sequestration to the keeper of the register of inhibitions and adjudications for recording in that register;

[(b) forthwith send a copy of the order refusing or awarding sequestration—

(i) to the Accountant in Bankruptcy; and

(ii) where the debtor is taking part in a debt payment programme under Part 1 of the Debt Arrangement and Attachment (Scotland) Act 2002, to the DAS Administrator (as defined in regulation 2(1) of the Debt Arrangement Scheme (Scotland) Regulations 2011).]

. . .

(7) Where sequestration has been awarded, the process of sequestration shall not fall asleep.

(8) Where a debtor learns, whether before or after the date of sequestration, that he may derive benefit from another estate, he shall as soon as practicable after that date inform—

(a) the [. . .] trustee of that fact; and

(b) the person who is administering that other estate of the sequestration.

(9) If the debtor fails to comply with subsection (8) above, he shall be guilty of an offence and liable, on summary conviction, to a fine not exceeding level 5 on the standard scale.

16 Petitions for recall of sequestration

(1) A petition for recall of an award of sequestration may be presented to the [sheriff] by—

(a) the debtor, any creditor or any other person having an interest (notwithstanding that he was a petitioner, or concurred in the [debtor application], for the sequestration);

(b) the [. . .] trustee, or the Accountant in Bankruptcy.

(2)   The petitioner shall serve upon the debtor, any person who was a petitioner, or concurred in the [debtor application], for the sequestration, the [. . .] trustee and the Accountant in Bankruptcy, a copy of the petition along with a notice stating that the recipient of the notice may lodge answers to the petition within 14 days of the service of the notice.

(3)   At the same time as service is made under subsection (2) above, the petitioner shall publish a notice in the Edinburgh Gazette stating that a petition has been presented under this section and that any person having an interest may lodge answers to the petition within 14 days of the publication of the notice.

(4)   Subject to [sections 41(1)(b) and 41A(1)(b)] of this Act, a petition under this section may be presented—
  (a)   within 10 weeks after the date of [the award of] sequestration; but
  (b)   at any time if the petition is presented on any of the grounds mentioned in paragraphs (a) to (c) of section 17(1) of this Act.

(5)   Notwithstanding that a petition has been presented under this section, the proceedings in the sequestration shall continue (subject to section 17(6) of this Act) as if that petition had not been presented until the recall is granted.

(6)   Where—
  (a)   a petitioner under this section; or
  (b)   a person who has lodged answers to the petition,
withdraws or dies, any person entitled to present or, as the case may be, lodge answers to a petition under this section may be sisted in his place.

17   Recall of sequestration

(1)   The [sheriff] may recall an award of sequestration if [he] is satisfied that in all the circumstances of the case (including those arising after the date of the award of sequestration) it is appropriate to do so and, without prejudice to the foregoing generality, may recall the award if [he] is satisfied that—
  (a)   the debtor has paid his debts in full or has given sufficient security for their payment;
  (b)   a majority in value of the creditors reside in a country other than Scotland and that it is more appropriate for the debtor's estate to be administered in that other country; or
  (c)   one or more other awards of sequestration of the estate or analogous remedies (as defined in [section 10(7)] of this Act) have been granted.

(2)   Where one or more awards of sequestration of the debtor's estate have been granted, the [sheriff] may, after such intimation as [he] considers necessary, recall an award whether or not the one in respect of which the petition for recall was presented.

(3)   On recalling an award of sequestration, the [sheriff]—
  (a)   shall make provision for the payment of the outlays and remuneration of the interim trustee and [the] trustee by directing that such payment shall be made out of the debtor's estate or by requiring any person who was a party to the petition for sequestration [or, as the case may be, the debtor application,] to pay the whole or any part of the said outlays and remuneration;
  (b)   without prejudice to subsection (7) below, may direct that payment of the expenses of a creditor who was a petitioner, or concurred in the [debtor application], for sequestration shall be made out of the debtor's estate;
  (c)   may make any further order that [he] considers necessary or reasonable in all the circumstances of the case.

(4)   Subject to subsection (5) below, the effect of the recall of an award of sequestration shall be, so far as practicable, to restore the debtor and any other person affected by the sequestration to the position he would have been in if the sequestration had not been awarded.

(5)   A recall of an award of sequestration shall not—
  (a)   affect the interruption of prescription caused by the presentation of the

petition for sequestration [, the making of the debtor application] or the submission of a claim under section 22 or 48 of this Act;

(b)   invalidate any transaction entered into before such recall by the interim trustee or [the] trustee with a person acting in good faith;

[(c)   affect a bankruptcy restrictions order which has not been annulled under section 56J(1)(a) of this Act.]

(6)   Where the [sheriff] considers that it is inappropriate to recall or to refuse to recall an award of sequestration forthwith, [he] may order that the proceedings in the sequestration shall continue but shall be subject to such conditions as [he] may think fit.

(7)   The [sheriff] may make such order in relation to the expenses in a petition for recall as [he] thinks fit.

(8)   The [sheriff clerk] shall send—

(a)   a certified copy of any order recalling an award of sequestration to the keeper of the register of inhibitions and adjudications for recording in that register; and

(b)   a copy of any order recalling or refusing to recall an award of sequestration, or of any order under section 41(1)(b)(ii) [or 41A(1)(b)(ii)] of this Act, to—

(i)   the Accountant in Bankruptcy; and

(ii)   the [. . .] trustee (if any) who shall insert it in the sederunt book.

[Initial stages of sequestration]

18   Interim preservation of estate

(1)   The interim trustee may [, in pursuance of the function conferred on him by section 2(6A) of this Act,] give general or particular directions to the debtor relating to the management of the debtor's estate.

(2)   In exercising the [function] conferred on him by section [2(6A)] of this Act, an interim trustee may—

(a)   require the debtor to deliver up to him any money or valuables, or any document relating to the debtor's business or financial affairs, belonging to or in the possession of the debtor or under his control;

(b)   place in safe custody anything mentioned in paragraph (a) above;

(c)   require the debtor to deliver up to him any perishable goods belonging to the debtor or under his control and may arrange for the sale or disposal of such goods;

(d)   make or cause to be made an inventory or valuation of any property belonging to the debtor;

(e)   require the debtor to implement any transaction entered into by the debtor;

(f)   effect or maintain insurance policies in respect of the business or property of the debtor;

[. . .]

[(h)   carry on any business of the debtor or borrow money in so far as it is necessary for the interim trustee to do so to safeguard the debtor's estate].

[(2A)   Section 43 of this Act applies to an interim trustee as it applies to a trustee.]

(3)   The [sheriff], on the application of the interim trustee, may—

[. . .]

(b)   on cause shown, grant a warrant authorising the interim trustee to enter the house where the debtor resides or his business premises and to search for and take possession of anything mentioned in paragraphs (a) and (c) of subsection (2) above, if need be by opening shut and lock-fast places; or

(c)   make such other order to safeguard the debtor's estate as [he] thinks appropriate.

(4) The [sheriff], on an application by the debtor on the grounds that a direction under subsection (1) above is unreasonable, may—

(a) if [he] considers the direction to be unreasonable, set aside the direction; and

(b) in any event, give such directions to the debtor regarding the management of his estate as [he] considers appropriate;

but, subject to any interim order of the [sheriff], the debtor shall comply with the direction appealed against pending the final determination of the appeal.

(5) The debtor shall be guilty of an offence if—

(a) he fails without reasonable excuse to comply with—

(i) a direction under subsection (1) or (4)(b) above; or

(ii) a requirement under subsection 2(a), (c) or (e) above; or

(b) he obstructs the interim trustee where the interim trustee is acting in pursuance of subsection (3)(b) above.

(6) A person convicted of an offence under subsection (5) above shall be liable—

(a) on summary conviction to a fine not exceeding the statutory maximum or—

(i) to imprisonment for a term not exceeding 3 months; or

(ii) if he has previously been convicted of an offence inferring dishonest appropriation of property or an attempt at such appropriation, to imprisonment for a term not exceeding 6 months,

or (in the case of either sub-paragraph) to both such fine and such imprisonment; or

(b) on conviction on indictment to a fine or to imprisonment for a term not exceeding 2 years or to both.

19 [Statement of assets and liabilities etc

(1) Where the [debtor has made a debtor application] he shall, not later than 7 days after the appointment of the [trustee under section 2 of this Act] (where he is not the Accountant in Bankruptcy), send to the [. . .] trustee such statement of assets and liabilities as was [sent to the Accountant in Bankruptcy in pursuance of section 5(6A)] of this Act.

(2) Where the petitioner for sequestration is a creditor or a trustee acting under a trust deed, the debtor shall, not later than 7 days after having been notified by the [. . .] trustee as mentioned in section [2(7)(a)] of this Act, send to the [. . .] trustee a statement of assets and liabilities.

(3) If the debtor—

(a) fails to send to the [. . .] trustee in accordance with subsection (1) or (2) above such statement of assets and liabilities; or

(b) fails to disclose any material fact in such statement of assets and liabilities; or

(c) makes a material misstatement in such statement of assets and liabilities,

he shall be guilty of an offence and liable on summary conviction to a fine not exceeding level 5 on the standard scale or to imprisonment for a term not exceeding 3 months or to both such fine and imprisonment.

(4) In any proceedings for an offence under subsection (3) above, it shall be a defence for the accused to show that he had a reasonable excuse for—

(a) failing to send to the [. . .] trustee in accordance with subsection (1) or (2) above such statement of assets and liabilities; or

(b) failing to disclose a material fact; or

(c) making a material misstatement.]

20 Trustee's duties on receipt of list of assets and liabilities

[(1) When the [. . .] trustee has received the statement of assets and liabilities, he shall, as soon as practicable, prepare a statement of the debtor's affairs so far as within the knowledge of the [. . .] trustee and shall indicate in the statement of the

debtor's affairs whether, in his opinion, the debtor's assets are unlikely to be sufficient to pay any dividend whatsoever in respect of the debts mentioned in paragraphs (e) to (h) of section 51(1) of this Act.]
   (2)   The [. . .] trustee shall, not later than 4 days before the date fixed for the
statutory meeting, [or, where the trustee does not intend to hold such a meeting,
not later than 60 days after the date on which sequestration is awarded,] send to
the Accountant in Bankruptcy—
      (a)   [a statement] of assets and liabilities [(unless the statement has already
      been received by the Accountant in Bankruptcy by virtue of section 5(6A) of this
      Act)]; and
      (b)   [subject to subsection (2A) below] a copy of the [. . .] statement of the
      debtor's affairs; and
      (c)   written comments by the [. . .] trustee indicating what in his opinion are
      the causes of the insolvency and to what extent the conduct of the debtor may
      have contributed to the insolvency.
   [(2A)   The trustee need not send a statement of the debtor's affairs to the
Accountant in Bankruptcy in accordance with subsection (2)(b) above if the trustee
has sent a copy of the inventory and valuation to the Accountant in Bankruptcy in
accordance with section 38(1)(c) of this Act.]
   (3)   The written comments made under subsection (2)(c) above shall be absolutely privileged.
   [. . .]
   [(5A)   Subsections (2) and (3) above do not apply in any case where the
Accountant in Bankruptcy is the [. . .] trustee.]

[20A   Statutory meeting
A meeting of creditors called by the [. . .] trustee under section [. . .] 21A of this
Act shall, in this Act, be referred to as 'the statutory meeting'.]

[Statutory meeting of creditors and trustee vote]

[. . .]

[21A   Calling of statutory meeting [. . .]
   (1)   Subject to subsections (5) and (6) below, [. . .] the statutory meeting may be
held at such time and place as the [. . .] trustee may determine.
   (2)   Not later than 60 days after the date [on which sequestration is awarded],
or such longer period as the sheriff may on cause shown allow, the [. . .] trustee
shall give notice to every creditor known to him of whether he intends to call the
statutory meeting.
   (3)   A notice given under subsection (2) above shall—
      (a)   be accompanied by a copy of the [. . .] trustee's statement of the debtor's
      affairs; and
      (b)   where the [. . .] trustee is notifying his intention not to hold the statutory
      meeting, inform creditors—
         (i)   of the effect of subsections (4) and (5) below.
         [. . .]
   (4)   Within 7 days of the giving of notice under subsection (2) above, any creditor may request the [. . .] trustee to call the statutory meeting.
   (5)   Where a request or requests under subsection (4) above are made by not
less than one quarter in value of the debtor's creditors, the [. . .] trustee shall call
the statutory meeting not later than 28 days, or such other period as the sheriff
may on cause shown allow, after the giving of notice under subsection (2) above.
   (6)   Where the [. . .] trustee gives notice under subsection (2) above that he
intends to call the statutory meeting, such meeting shall be called not later than 28
days after the giving of such notice.
   (7)   Not less than 7 days before the date fixed for the statutory meeting, the

[. . .] trustee shall notify every creditor known to him of the date, time and place of the meeting, and shall in such notice invite the submission of such claims as have not already been submitted and inform them of his duties under section 23(3) of this Act.

(8)   The creditors may continue the statutory meeting to a date not later than 7 days after the end of the period mentioned in subsection (6) above or such longer period as the sheriff may on cause shown allow.]

[. . .]

[21B   Procedure where no statutory meeting called

(1)   Where the [. . .] trustee does not call the statutory meeting and the period mentioned in section 21A(4) of this Act has expired, he shall—

(a)   forthwith make a report to the [Accountant in Bankruptcy] on the circumstances of the sequestration.

[. . .]

[(1A)   This section does not apply in any case where the Accountant in Bankruptcy is the trustee.]

[. . .]

22   Submission of claims for voting purposes at statutory meeting

(1)   For the purposes of voting at the statutory meeting, a creditor shall submit a claim in accordance with this section to the [. . .] trustee at or before the meeting.

(2)   A creditor shall submit a claim under this section by producing to the [. . .] trustee—

(a)   a statement of claim in the prescribed form; and

(b)   an account or voucher (according to the nature of the debt) which constitutes *prima facie* evidence of the debt:

Provided that the [. . .] trustee may dispense with any requirement under this subsection in respect of any debt or any class of debt.

(3)   Where a creditor neither resides nor has a place of business in the United Kingdom, the [. . .] trustee—

(a)   shall, if he knows where the creditor resides or has a place of business and if no notification has been given to that creditor under section [21A(2)] of this Act, write to him informing him that he may submit a claim under this section;

(b)   may allow the creditor to submit an informal claim in writing.

(4)   A creditor who has produced a statement of claim in accordance with subsection (2) above may at any time before the statutory meeting produce in place of that statement of claim another such statement of claim specifying a different amount for his claim.

(5)   If a creditor produces under this section a statement of claim, account, voucher or other evidence which is false—

(a)   the creditor shall be guilty of an offence unless he shows that he neither knew nor had reason to believe that the statement of claim, account, voucher or other evidence was false;

(b)   the debtor shall be guilty of an offence if he—

(i)   knew or became aware that the statement of claim, account, voucher or other evidence was false; and

(ii)   failed as soon as practicable after acquiring such knowledge to report it to the [. . .] trustee or [. . .].

(6)   A creditor may, in such circumstances as may be prescribed, state the amount of his claim in foreign currency.

(7)   The [. . .] trustee shall, on production of any document to him under this section, initial the document and keep a record of it stating the date when it was produced to him, and, if requested by the sender, shall return it (if it is not a statement of claim) to him.

(8)   The submission of a claim under this section shall bar the effect of any

enactment or rule of law relating to the limitation of actions in any part of the United Kingdom.

(9)   Schedule 1 to this Act shall have effect for determining the amount in respect of which a creditor shall be entitled to claim.

(10)   A person convicted of an offence under subsection (5) above shall be liable—

(a)   on summary conviction to a fine not exceeding the statutory maximum or—

(i)   to imprisonment for a term not exceeding 3 months; or

(ii)   if he has previously been convicted of an offence inferring dishonest appropriation of property or an attempt at such appropriation, to imprisonment for a term not exceeding 6 months,

or (in the case of either sub-paragraph) to both such fine and such imprisonment; or

(b)   on conviction on indictment to a fine or to imprisonment for a term not exceeding 2 years or to both.

[23   Proceedings at statutory meeting before trustee vote]

(1)   At the commencement of the statutory meeting, the chairman shall be the [. . .] trustee who as chairman shall—

(a)   for the purposes of subsection (2) below, accept or reject in whole or in part the claim of each creditor, and, if the amount of a claim is stated in foreign currency, he shall convert that amount into sterling, in such manner as may be prescribed, at the rate of exchange prevailing at the close of business on the date of sequestration;

(b)   invite the creditors thereupon to elect one of their number as chairman in his place and shall preside over the election:

Provided that if a chairman is not elected in pursuance of this paragraph, the [. . .] trustee shall remain the chairman throughout the meeting; and

(c)   arrange for a record to be made of the proceedings at the meeting.

(2)   The acceptance of a claim in whole or in part under subsection (1) above shall, subject to section 24(3) of this Act, determine the entitlement of a creditor to vote at the statutory meeting.

(3)   On the conclusion of the proceedings under subsection (1) above, the [. . .] trustee—

[(a)   shall make available for inspection—

(i)   the statement of assets and liabilities; and

(ii)   his statement of the debtor's affairs prepared under section 20(1) of this Act;]; and

(b)   shall answer to the best of his ability any questions, and shall consider any representations, put to him by the creditors relating to the debtor's assets, business or financial affairs or his conduct in relation thereto;

(c)   shall, after considering any such representations as are mentioned in paragraph (b) above, indicate whether, in his opinion, the debtor's assets are unlikely to be sufficient as mentioned in section 20(1) of this Act; and

[(d)   shall determine whether it is necessary to revise his statement of the debtor's affairs and, if he determines that it is necessary to revise the statement, he shall do so either at, or as soon as possible after, the statutory meeting.]
[. . .]

[(5)   Where the [. . .] trustee has revised his statement of the debtor's affairs, he shall, as soon as possible after the statutory meeting, send a copy of the revised statement to every creditor known to him.]

[. . .]

24 [Trustee vote]
  [(1) At the statutory meeting, the creditors shall, at the conclusion of the proceedings under section 23(3) of this Act, proceed to [a vote at which they shall—
  (a) confirm the appointment of the trustee appointed under section 2 of this
Act (referred to in this section and in sections 25 to 27 of this Act as the 'original
trustee'); or
  (b) elect another person as the trustee in the sequestration (referred to in this
section and in sections 13 and 25 to 29 of this Act as the 'replacement trustee'),
such a vote being referred to in this Act as a 'trustee vote'].]
  (2) None of the following persons shall be eligible for election as [replacement]
trustee, nor shall anyone who becomes such a person after having been elected as
[replacement] trustee be qualified to continue to act as [. . .] trustee—
  (a) the debtor;
  (b) a person who is not qualified to act as an insolvency practitioner or who,
though qualified to act as an insolvency practitioner, is not qualified to act as
such in relation to the debtor;
  (c) a person who holds an interest opposed to the general interests of the
creditors;
  [. . .]
  [(e) a person who has not given an undertaking, in writing, to act as [. . .]
trustee;
  (f) the Accountant in Bankruptcy.]
  (3) The following persons shall not be entitled to vote in the [trustee vote]—
  (a) anyone acquiring a debt due by the debtor, otherwise than by succession,
after the date of sequestration;
  (b) any creditor to the extent that his debt is a postponed debt.
  [(3A) In any case where the Accountant in Bankruptcy is the [original] trustee,
if—
  (a) no creditor entitled to vote in the [trustee vote] attends the statutory
meeting; or
  (b) no [replacement] trustee is elected, the Accountant in Bankruptcy shall
forthwith report the proceedings at the statutory meeting to the sheriff and [shall
continue to act as the trustee].]
  [. . .]
  (4) [In any case where the Accountant in Bankruptcy is not the [original]
trustee] if no creditor entitled to vote in the [trustee vote] attends the statutory
meeting or if no [replacement] trustee is elected, the [original] trustee shall
forthwith—
  (a) so notify the Accountant in Bankruptcy; and
  (b) report the proceedings at the statutory meeting to the sheriff [and he
shall continue to act as the trustee].
  [. . .]

25 [Appointment of replacement trustee]
  [(A1) This section applies where a replacement trustee is elected by virtue of a
trustee vote.]
  (1) On the election of the [replacement] trustee—
  (a) the [original] trustee shall forthwith make a report of the proceedings at
the statutory meeting to the sheriff; and
  (b) the debtor, a creditor, the [original] trustee, the [replacement] trustee or
the Accountant in Bankruptcy may, within 4 days after the statutory meeting,
object to any matter connected with the election; and such objection shall be by
summary application to the sheriff, specifying the grounds on which the
objection is taken.
  (2) If there is no timeous objection under subsection (1)(b) above, the sheriff

shall forthwith declare the elected person to be the [trustee in the sequestration]; and the sheriff shall [make an order appointing him as such].

[. . .]

(3)   If there is a timeous objection under subsection (1)(b) above, the sheriff shall forthwith give parties an opportunity to be heard thereon and shall give his decision.

(4)   If in his decision under subsection (3) above the sheriff—

(a)   rejects the objection, subsection (2) above shall apply as if there had been no timeous objection;

(b)   sustains the objection, he shall order the [original] trustee to arrange a new meeting [at which a new trustee vote shall be held]; and sections 23 and 24 of this Act and this section shall apply in relation to such a meeting.

(5)   Any declaration, [appointment] or decision of the sheriff under this section shall be final, and no expense in objecting under this section shall fall on the debtor's estate.

[. . .]

26   [Provisions relating to termination of original trustee's functions]

[(A1)   This section applies where a replacement trustee is appointed under section 25 of this Act.]

(1)   [The original trustee shall, on the appointment of the replacement trustee,] hand over to him everything in his possession which relates to the sequestration (including [the statement of assets and liabilities, and a copy] of the statement prepared under section 23(3)(d), and of the written comments sent under section 20(2)(c) of this Act) and shall thereupon cease to act in the sequestration.

(2)   Within 3 months of the [appointment of the replacement trustee, the original] trustee shall—

(a)   submit to the Accountant in Bankruptcy—

(i)   his accounts of his intromissions (if any) with the debtor's estate; and

(ii)   a claim for outlays reasonably incurred, and for remuneration for work reasonably undertaken, by him; and

(b)   send to the [replacement] trustee [. . .], a copy of what is submitted to the Accountant in Bankruptcy under paragraph (a) above.

[(2A)   Where the original trustee was appointed under section 2(5) of this Act as the interim trustee in the sequestration, his accounts and the claim referred to in subsection (2)(a) above shall include accounts and a claim for the period of his appointment as interim trustee.]

(3)   On a submission being made to him under subsection (2) above, the Accountant in Bankruptcy—

(a)   shall—

(i)   audit the accounts; and

(ii)   issue a determination fixing the amount of the outlays and remuneration payable to the [original] trustee; and

(b)   shall send a copy of—

(i)   the said determination to the [original] trustee [. . .]; and

(ii)   the [original] trustee's audited accounts and of the said determination to the [replacement] trustee, who shall insert the copies in the sederunt book.

(4)   The [original] trustee, the [replacement] trustee, the debtor or any creditor may appeal to the sheriff against a determination under subsection (3)(a)(ii) above within 14 days of its issue [and the decision of the sheriff on such an appeal shall be final].

(5)   The [replacement] trustee, on being [appointed], shall make such insertions in the sederunt book as are appropriate to provide a record of the sequestration process before his [appointment], but he shall make no insertion therein relating to the written comments made by the [original] trustee under section 20(2)(c) of this Act.

[(5A)   This section does not apply in any case where the Accountant in Bankruptcy is the [original] trustee.]

[26A   Accountant in Bankruptcy to account for intromissions
(1)   This section applies in any case where the Accountant in Bankruptcy was the [original] trustee and some other person [is appointed as replacement trustee under section 25 of this Act].
(2)   The Accountant in Bankruptcy shall, on [the appointment of the replacement trustee], hand over to the [replacement] trustee everything in his possession which relates to the sequestration and which he obtained in his capacity as [original] trustee (including the statement of assets and liabilities); and thereupon he shall cease to act as [. . .] trustee.
(3)   The Accountant in Bankruptcy shall, not later than 3 months after the [appointment of the replacement trustee], supply to the [replacement] trustee—
   (a)   his accounts of his intromissions (if any) as [original] trustee with the debtor's estate;
   (b)   a determination of his fees and outlays calculated in accordance with regulations made under section 69A of this Act; and
   (c)   a copy of the notice mentioned in subsection (4)(b) below.
(4)   The Accountant in Bankruptcy shall send to the debtor and to all creditors known to him—
   (a)   a copy of the determination mentioned in subsection (3)(b) above; and
   (b)   a notice in writing stating—
      (i)   that the Accountant in Bankruptcy has commenced the procedure under this Act leading to discharge in respect of his actings as [. . .] trustee;
      (ii)   that the accounts of his intromissions (if any) with the debtor's estate are available for inspection at such address as the Accountant in Bankruptcy may determine;
      (iii)   that an appeal may be made to the sheriff under subsection (5) below; and
      (iv)   the effect of subsection (7) below.
(5)   The [replacement] trustee, the debtor and any creditor may appeal to the sheriff against—
   (a)   the determination of the Accountant in Bankruptcy mentioned in subsection (3)(b) above;
   (b)   the discharge of the Accountant in Bankruptcy in respect of his actings as [. . .] trustee; or
   (c)   both such determination and discharge.
(6)   An appeal under subsection (5) above shall be made not more than 14 days after the issue of the notice mentioned in subsection (4)(b) above; and the decision of the sheriff on such an appeal shall be final.
(7)   Where—
   (a)   the requirements of this section have been complied with; and
   (b)   no appeal is made to the sheriff under subsection (5) above or such an appeal is made but is refused as regards the discharge of the Accountant in Bankruptcy,
the Accountant in Bankruptcy shall be discharged from all liability (other than any liability arising from fraud) to the creditors or to the debtor in respect of any act or omission of the Accountant in Bankruptcy in exercising the functions of [. . .] trustee in the sequestration.
(8)   The [replacement] trustee, on being [appointed], shall make such insertions in the sederunt book as are appropriate to provide a record of the sequestration process before his [appointment].]

27   [Discharge of original trustee]
(1)   On receiving a copy of the Accountant in Bankruptcy's determination sent

under subsection (3)(b)(i) of section 26 of this Act the [original] trustee may apply to him for a certificate of discharge.

(2)   The [original] trustee shall send notice of an application under subsection (1) above to the debtor [, to all creditors known to the original trustee] and to the [replacement] trustee and shall inform the debtor—

(a)   that he, the [replacement] trustee or any creditor may make written representations relating to the application to the Accountant in Bankruptcy within a period of 14 days after such notification;

(b)   that the audited accounts of his intromissions (if any) with the debtor's estate are available for inspection at the office of the [original] trustee and that a copy of those accounts has been sent to the [replacement] trustee for insertion in the sederunt book; and

(c)   of the effect mentioned in subsection (5) below.

(3)   On the expiry of the period mentioned in subsection (2)(a) above the Accountant in Bankruptcy, after considering any representations duly made to him, shall—

(a)   grant or refuse to grant the certificate of discharge; and

(b)   notify (in addition to the [original] trustee) the debtor, the [replacement] trustee, and all creditors who have made such representations, accordingly.

(4)   The [original] trustee, the [replacement] trustee, the debtor or any creditor who has made representations under subsection (2)(a) above may, within 14 days after the issuing of the determination under subsection (3) above, appeal therefrom to the sheriff and if the sheriff determines that a certificate of discharge which has been refused should be granted he shall order the Accountant in Bankruptcy to grant it; and the sheriff clerk shall send a copy of the decree of the sheriff to the Accountant in Bankruptcy.

[(4A)   The decision of the sheriff in an appeal under subsection (4) above shall be final.]

(5)   The grant of a certificate of discharge under this section by the Accountant in Bankruptcy shall have the effect of discharging the [original] trustee from all liability (other than any liability arising from fraud) to the creditors or to the debtor in respect of any act or omission of the [original] trustee in exercising the functions conferred on him by this Act.

(6)   Where a certificate of discharge is granted under this section, the [replacement] trustee shall make an appropriate entry in the sederunt book.

[. . .]

[(7A)   This section does not apply in any case where the Accountant in Bankruptcy is the [original] trustee.]

Replacement of [. . .] trustee

28 Resignation and death of [. . .] trustee

[(1)   The [. . .] trustee may apply to the [Accountant in Bankruptcy] for authority to resign office and, where the [Accountant in Bankruptcy] is satisfied that [the trustee—

(a)   is unable to act (whether by, under or by virtue of a provision of this Act or from any other cause whatsoever); or

(b)   has so conducted himself that he should no longer continue to act, the Accountant in Bankruptcy] shall grant the application.]

[(1A)   The [Accountant in Bankruptcy] may make the granting of an application under subsection (1) above subject to the election of a new [. . .] trustee and to such conditions as he thinks appropriate in all the circumstances of the case.]

(2)   Where the [Accountant in Bankruptcy] grants an application under [. . .] subsection (1) above—

(a)   except where paragraph (b) below applies, the commissioners, or if there are no commissioners, the Accountant in Bankruptcy, shall call a meeting of the creditors, to be held not more than 28 days after the [. . .] trustee has resigned, for the election by them of a new [. . .] trustee;

    (b)   if the application has been granted subject to the election of a new [. . .] trustee, the resigning [. . .] trustee shall himself call a meeting of the creditors, to be held not more than 28 days after the granting of the application, for the purpose referred to in paragraph (a) above.

    (3)   Where the commissioners become, or if there are no commissioners, the Accountant in Bankruptcy becomes, aware that the [. . .] trustee has died, they or as the case may be the Accountant in Bankruptcy shall as soon as practicable after becoming so aware call a meeting of creditors for the election by the creditors of a new [. . .] trustee.

    (4)   The foregoing provisions of this Act relating to the election [of a replacement trustee and the appointment of that] trustee shall, subject to any necessary modifications, apply in relation to the election and [appointment] of a new [. . .] trustee in pursuance of subsection (1), [(1A)], (2) or (3) above.

    [(5)   Where no new [. . .] trustee is elected in pursuance of subsection (2) or (3) above—

    [(a)   the Accountant in Bankruptcy; or

    (b)   such person as may be nominated by the Accountant in Bankruptcy (being a person who is not ineligible for election as replacement trustee under section 24(2) of this Act) if that person consents to the nomination,

may apply to the sheriff for appointment as trustee in the sequestration; and, on such application, the sheriff shall make an order so appointing the Accountant in Bankruptcy or, as the case may be, the person nominated by him.]

    (6)   The new [. . .] trustee may require—

    (a)   delivery to him of all documents relating to the sequestration in the possession of the former trustee or his representatives, except the former trustee's accounts of which he shall be entitled to delivery of only a copy;

    (b)   the former trustee or his representatives to submit the trustee's accounts for audit to the commissioners or, if there are no commissioners, to the Accountant in Bankruptcy, and the commissioners or the Accountant in Bankruptcy shall issue a determination fixing the amount of the outlays and remuneration payable to the trustee or representatives in accordance with section 53 of this Act.

    (7)   The former trustee or his representatives, the new [. . .] trustee, the debtor or any creditor may appeal against a determination issued under subsection (6)(b) above within 14 days after it is issued—

    (a)   where it is a determination of the commissioners, to the Accountant in Bankruptcy; and

    (b)   where it is a determination of the Accountant in Bankruptcy, to the sheriff; and the determination of the Accountant in Bankruptcy under paragraph (a) above shall be appealable to the sheriff.

    [(8)   The decision of the sheriff on an appeal under subsection (7) above shall be final.]

[28A   Replacement of trustee acting in more than one sequestration

    (1)   This section applies where a trustee acting as such in two or more sequestrations—

    (a)   dies; or

    (b)   ceases to be qualified to continue to act as trustee by virtue of section 24(2) of this Act.

    (2)   The Accountant in Bankruptcy may, by a single petition to the Court of Session, apply—

    (a)   in a case where subsection (1)(b) above applies, for the removal of the trustee from office in each sequestration in which he has so ceased to be qualified; and

   (b)   for the appointment of—
        (i)   the Accountant in Bankruptcy; or
        (ii)   such person as may be nominated by the Accountant in Bankruptcy
(being a person who is not ineligible for election as replacement trustee under
section 24(2) of this Act) if that person consents to the nomination,
as the trustee in each sequestration in which the trustee was acting.
   (3)   The procedure in a petition under subsection (2) above shall be as the Court
of Session may, by act of sederunt, prescribe.
   (4)   An act of sederunt made under subsection (3) above may, in particular,
make provision as to the intimation to each sheriff who awarded sequestration or
to whom sequestration was transferred under section 15(2) of this Act of the
appointment by the Court of Session of a trustee in that sequestration.]

29   Removal of [. . .] trustee and trustee not acting
   (1)   The [. . .] trustee may be removed from office—
   (a)   by the creditors (other than any such person as is mentioned in section
24(3) of this Act) at a meeting called for the purpose if they also elect forthwith a
new [. . .] trustee; or
   (b)   without prejudice to section [1A(2)] of this Act, by order of the sheriff, on
the application of—
        (i)   the Accountant in Bankruptcy;
        (ii)   the commissioners; or
        (iii)   a person representing not less than one quarter in value of the creditors,
   if the sheriff is satisfied that cause has been shown on the basis of circumstances other than those to which subsection (9) below applies.
   (2)   The sheriff shall order any application under subsection (1)(b) above to be
served on the [. . .] trustee and intimated in the Edinburgh Gazette, and before disposing of the application shall give the [. . .] trustee an opportunity of being heard.
   (3)   On an application under subsection (1)(b) above, the sheriff may, in order-
ing the removal of the [. . .] trustee from office, make such further order as he
thinks fit or may, instead of removing the [. . .] trustee from office, make such
other order as he thinks fit.
   (4)   The [. . .] trustee, the Accountant in Bankruptcy, the commissioners or any
creditor may appeal against the decision of the sheriff on an application under
subsection (1)(b) above within 14 days after the date of that decision.
   (5)   If the [. . .] trustee has been removed from office under subsection (1)(b)
above or under section [1A(2)] of this Act or following an appeal under subsection
(4) above, the commissioners or, if there are no commissioners, the Accountant in
Bankruptcy shall call a meeting of creditors, to be held not more than 28 days after
such removal, for the election by them of a new [. . .] trustee.
   (6)   Without prejudice to section [1A(2)] of this Act, where the sheriff is satisfied
of any of the circumstances to which subsection (9) below applies he may, on the
application of a commissioner, the debtor, a creditor or the Accountant in Bankruptcy, and after such intimation as the sheriff considers necessary—
   (a)   declare the office of [. . .] trustee to have become or to be vacant; and
   (b)   make any necessary order to enable the sequestration to proceed or to
safeguard the estate pending the election of a new [. . .] trustee;
and thereafter the commissioners or, if there are no commissioners, the Accountant
in Bankruptcy shall call a meeting of creditors, to be held not more than 28 days
after such declaration, for the election by them of a new [. . .] trustee.
   (7)   The foregoing provisions of this Act relating to the election [of a replacement trustee and the appointment of that] trustee shall, subject to any necessary
modifications, apply in relation to the election and [appointment] of a new [. . .]
trustee in pursuance of subsection (5) or (6) above.
   (8)   Subsections (5) to (7) of section 28 of this Act shall apply for the purposes
of this section as they apply for the purposes of that section.

(9)   The circumstances to which this subsection applies are that the [. . .] trustee—

(a)   is unable to act (whether by, under or by virtue of a provision of this Act or from any other cause whatsoever other than death); or

(b)   has so conducted himself that he should no longer continue to act in the sequestration.

[(10)   This section does not apply in any case where the Accountant in Bankruptcy is the trustee.]

Election, resignation and removal of commissioners

30   Election, resignation and removal of commissioners

(1)   At the statutory meeting or any subsequent meeting of creditors, the creditors (other than any such person as is mentioned in section 24(3) of this Act) may, from among the creditors or their mandatories, elect one or more commissioners (or new or additional commissioners); but not more than 5 commissioners shall hold office in any sequestration at any one time.

(2)   None of the following persons shall be eligible for election as a commissioner, nor shall anyone who becomes such a person after having been elected as a commissioner be entitled to continue to act as a commissioner—

(a)   any person mentioned in paragraph (a) or (c) of section 24(2) of this Act as not being eligible for election;

(b)   a person who is an associate of the debtor or of the [. . .] trustee.

(3)   A commissioner may resign office at any time.

(4)   Without prejudice to section [1A(2)] of this Act, a commissioner may be removed from office—

(a)   if he is a mandatory of a creditor, by the creditor recalling the mandate and intimating in writing its recall to the [. . .] trustee;

(b)   by the creditors (other than any such person as is mentioned in section 24(3) of this Act) at a meeting called for the purpose.

[Vesting of estate in trustee]

31   Vesting of estate at date of sequestration

(1)   Subject to section 33 of this Act [and section 91(3) of the Pensions Act 1995], the whole estate of the debtor shall [by virtue of the trustee's appointment] vest [in the trustee] as at the date of sequestration [. . .] for the benefit of the creditors.

[. . .]

[(1A)   It shall not be competent for—

(a)   the trustee; or

(b)   any person deriving title from the trustee,

to complete title to any heritable estate in Scotland vested in the trustee by virtue of his appointment before the expiry of the period mentioned in subsection (1B) below.

(1B)   That period is the period of 28 days (or such other period as may be prescribed) beginning with the day on which—

(a)   the certified copy of the order of the sheriff granting warrant is recorded under subsection (1)(a) of section 14 of this Act; or

(b)   the certified copy of the determination of the Accountant in Bankruptcy awarding sequestration is recorded under subsection (1A) of that section,

in the register of inhibitions.]

(2)   The exercise by the [. . .] trustee of any power conferred on him by this Act in respect of any heritable estate vested in him by virtue of [his appointment] shall not be challengeable on the ground of any prior inhibition [. . .].

(3)   Where the debtor has an uncompleted title to any heritable estate in Scotland, the [. . .] trustee may complete title thereto either in his own name or in the name of the debtor, but completion of title in the name of the debtor shall not vali-

date by accretion any unperfected right in favour of any person other than the
[. . .] trustee.

(4)   Any moveable property, in respect of which but for this subsection—

(a)   delivery or possession; or

(b)   intimation of its assignation,

would be required in order to complete title to it, shall vest in the [. . .] trustee by
virtue of [his appointment] as if at the date of sequestration the [. . .] trustee had
taken delivery or possession of the property or had made intimation of its assignation to him, as the case may be.

(5)   Any non-vested contingent interest which the debtor has shall vest in the
[. . .] trustee as if an assignation of that interest had been executed by the debtor
and intimation thereof made at the date of sequestration.

[(5A)   Any non-vested contingent interest vested in the trustee by virtue of subsection (5) above shall, where it remains so vested in the trustee on the date on
which the debtor's discharge becomes effective, be reinvested in the debtor as if an
assignation of that interest had been executed by the trustee and intimation thereof
made at that date.]

(6)   Any person claiming a right to any estate claimed by the [. . .] trustee may
apply to the [sheriff] for the estate to be excluded from such vesting, a copy of the
application being served on the [. . .] trustee; and the [sheriff] shall grant the application if [he] is satisfied that the estate should not be so vested.

(7)   Where any successor of a deceased debtor whose estate has been sequestrated has made up title to, or is in possession of, any part of that estate, the
[sheriff] may, on the application of the [. . .] trustee, order the successor to convey
such estate to him.

(8)   In subsection (1) above [, subject to section 31A of this Act,] the 'whole
estate of the debtor' means [subject to subsection (9) below] [and to sections
71(10B) and 78(3B)]* his whole estate at the date of sequestration, wherever situated, including—

(a)   any income or estate vesting in the debtor on that date;

[(aa)   any property of the debtor, title to which has not been completed by
another person deriving right from the debtor;]

(b)   the capacity to exercise and to take proceedings for exercising, all such
powers in, over, or in respect of any property as might have been exercised by
the debtor for his own benefit as at, or on, the date of sequestration or might be
exercised on a relevant date (within the meaning of section 32(10) of this Act).

[(9)   Subject to subsection (10) below, the 'whole estate of the debtor' does not
include any interest of the debtor as tenant under any of the following tenancies—

(a)   a tenancy which is an assured tenancy within the meaning of Part II of
the Housing (Scotland) Act 1988, or

(b)   a protected tenancy within the meaning of the Rent (Scotland) Act 1984
in respect of which, by virtue of any provision of Part VIII of that Act, no
premium can lawfully be required as a condition of the assignation, or

(c)   a Scottish secure tenancy within the meaning of the Housing (Scotland)
Act 2001 (asp 10).

(10)   On the date on which the [. . .] trustee serves notice to that effect on the
debtor, the interest of this debtor as tenant under any of the tenancies referred to
in subsection (9) above shall form part of his estate and vest in the [. . .] trustee as
if it had vested in him under section 32(6) of this Act.]

*There is now no statutory basis for the words which should follow, namely, 'of the Social Security
Administration Act 1992', but these words are necessary to give meaning to the provisions!

[31ZA   Proceedings under EC Regulation: modified definition of 'estate'

In the application of this Act to insolvency proceedings under the EC Regulation, a
reference to 'estate' is a reference to estate which may be dealt with in those
proceedings.]

[31A   Property subject to restraint order

(1)   This section applies where—

(a)   property is excluded from the debtor's estate by virtue of section 420(2)(a) of the Proceeds of Crime Act 2002 (property subject to a restraint order),

(b)   an order under section 50, 52, 128, 198 or 200 of that Act has not been made in respect of the property, and

(c)   the restraint order is discharged.

(2)   On the discharge of the restraint order the property vests in the [. . .] trustee as part of the debtor's estate.

(3)   But subsection (2) does not apply to the proceeds of property realised by a management receiver under section 49(2)(d) or 197(2)(d) of that Act (realisation of property to meet receiver's remuneration and expenses).]

[31B   Property in respect of which receivership or administration order is made

(1)   This section applies where—

(a)   property is excluded from the debtor's estate by virtue of section 420(2)(b), (c) or (d) of the Proceeds of Crime Act 2002 (property in respect of which an order for the appointment of a receiver or administrator under certain provisions of that Act is in force),

(b)   a confiscation order is made under section 6, 92 or 156 of that Act,

(c)   the amount payable under the confiscation order is fully paid, and

(d)   any of the property remains in the hands of the receiver or administrator (as the case may be).

(2)   The property vests in the [. . .] trustee as part of the debtor's estate.]

[31C   Property subject to certain orders where confiscation order discharged or quashed

(1)   This section applies where—

(a)   property is excluded from the debtor's estate by virtue of section 420(2)(a), (b), (c) or (d) of the Proceeds of Crime Act 2002 (property in respect of which a restraint order or an order for the appointment of a receiver or administrator under that Act is in force),

(b)   a confiscation order is made under section 6, 92 or 156 of that Act, and

(c)   the confiscation order is discharged under section 30, 114 or 180 of that Act (as the case may be) or quashed under that Act or in pursuance of any enactment relating to appeals against conviction or sentence.

(2)   Any property in the hands of a receiver appointed under Part 2 or 4 of that Act or an administrator appointed under Part 3 of that Act vests in the [. . .] trustee as part of the debtor's estate.

(3)   But subsection (2) does not apply to the proceeds of property realised by a management receiver under section 49(2)(d) or 197(2)(d) of that Act (realisation of property to meet receiver's remuneration and expenses).]

32   Vesting of estate, and dealings of debtor, after sequestration

(1)   Subject to [subsections (2) and (4B)] below, any income of whatever nature received by the debtor on a relevant date, other than income arising from the estate which is vested in the [. . .] trustee, shall vest in the debtor.

(2)   [Notwithstanding anything in section 11 or 12 of the Welfare Reform and Pensions Act 1999] the sheriff, on the application of the [. . .] trustee, may, after having regard to all the circumstances, determine a suitable amount to allow for—

(a)   aliment for the debtor; and

(b)   the debtor's relevant obligations;

and if the debtor's income is in excess of the total amount so allowed the sheriff shall fix the amount of the excess and order it to be paid to the [. . .] trustee.

[(2WA)   Subject to subsection (4L) below, no application may be made under subsection (2) above after the date on which the debtor's discharge becomes effective.

(2XA) An order made by the sheriff under subsection (2) above shall specify the period during which it has effect and that period—

(a) may end after the date on which the debtor's discharge becomes effective; and

(b) shall end no later than 3 years after the date on which the order is made.

(2YA) An order made by the sheriff under subsection (2) above may provide that a third person is to pay to the trustee a specified proportion of money due to the debtor by way of income.

(2ZA) If the debtor fails to comply with an order made under subsection (2) above, he shall be guilty of an offence and liable on summary conviction to a fine not exceeding level 5 on the standard scale or to imprisonment for a term not exceeding 3 months or to both.]

[(2A) The amount allowed for the purposes specified in paragraphs (a) and (b) of subsection (2) above shall not be less than the total amount of any income received by the debtor—

(a) by way of guaranteed minimum pension; and

(b) in respect of his protected rights as a member of a pension scheme, 'guaranteed minimum pension' and 'protected rights' having the same meanings as in the Pension Schemes Act 1993.]

(3) The debtor's relevant obligations referred to in paragraph (b) of subsection (2) above are—

(a) any obligation of aliment owed by him ('obligation of aliment' having the same meaning as in the Family Law (Scotland) Act 1985);

(b) any obligation of his to make a periodical allowance to a former spouse [or civil partner];

[(c) any obligation of his to pay child support maintenance under the Child Support Act 1991;]

but any amount allowed under that subsection for the relevant obligations [referred to in paragraphs (a) and (b) above] need not be sufficient for compliance with a subsisting order or agreement as regards such aliment or periodical allowance.

(4) In the event of any change in the debtor's circumstances, the sheriff, on the application of the [. . .] trustee, the debtor or any other interested person, may vary or recall any order under subsection (2) above.

[(4A) The sheriff clerk shall send a copy of any order made under subsection (2) above (and a copy of any variation or recall of such an order) to the Accountant in Bankruptcy.

(4B) Where no order has been made under subsection (2) above, a debtor may enter into an agreement in writing with the trustee which provides—

(a) that the debtor is to pay to the trustee an amount equal to a specified part or proportion of his income; or

(b) that a third person is to pay to the trustee a specified proportion of money due to the debtor by way of income.

(4C) No agreement under subsection (4B) above may be entered into after the date on which the debtor's discharge becomes effective.

(4D) Subsection (2XA) above applies to agreements entered into under subsection (4B) above as it applies to orders made under subsection (2) above.

(4E) An agreement entered into under subsection (4B) above may, if subsection (4K) below has been complied with, be enforced, subject to subsection (4F) below, as if it were an order made under subsection (2) above.

(4F) Subsection (2ZA) above does not apply to an agreement entered into under subsection (4B) above.

(4G) An agreement entered into under subsection (4B) above may be varied—

(a) by written agreement between the parties; or

(b)   by the sheriff, on an application made by the trustee, the debtor or any other interested person.

(4H)   The sheriff—

(a)   may not vary an agreement entered into under subsection (4B) above so as to include provision of a kind which could not be included in an order made under subsection (2) above; and

(b)   shall grant an application to vary such an agreement if and to the extent that the sheriff thinks variation is necessary to determine a suitable amount to allow for the purposes specified in paragraphs (a) and (b) of subsection (2) above, being an amount which shall not be included in the amount to be paid to the trustee.

(4J)   Where a third person pays a sum of money to the trustee under subsection (2YA) or (4B)(b) above, that person shall be discharged of any liability to the debtor to the extent of the sum of money so paid.

(4K)   The trustee shall (unless he is the Accountant in Bankruptcy) send a copy of any agreement entered into under subsection (4B) above (and a copy of any variation of such an agreement) to the Accountant in Bankruptcy.

(4L)   If the debtor fails to comply with an agreement entered into under subsection (4B) above, the sheriff, on the application of the trustee, may make an order under subsection (2) above—

(a)   ending on the date on which the agreement would, had the debtor continued to comply with it, have ended; and

(b)   on the same terms as the agreement.]

(5)   Diligence [(which, for the purposes of this section, includes the making of a deduction from earnings order under the Child Support Act 1991)] in respect of a debt or obligation of which the debtor would be discharged under section 55 of this Act were he discharged under section 54 thereof shall not be competent against income vesting in him under subsection (1) above.

(6)   Without prejudice to subsection (1) above, any estate, wherever situated, which—

(a)   is acquired by the debtor on a relevant date; and

(b)   would have vested in the [. . .] trustee if it had been part of the debtor's estate on the date of sequestration,

shall vest in the [. . .] trustee for the benefit of the creditors as at the date of acquisition; and any person who holds any such estate shall, on production to him of a copy of the [order] certified by the sheriff clerk [or, as the case may be, by the Accountant in Bankruptcy appointing the trustee], convey or deliver the estate to the [. . .] trustee:

Provided that—

(i)   if such a person has in good faith and without knowledge of the sequestration conveyed the estate to the debtor or to anyone on the instructions of the debtor, he shall incur no liability to the [. . .] trustee except to account for any proceeds of the conveyance which are in his hands; and

(ii)   this subsection shall be without prejudice to any right or interest acquired in the estate in good faith and for value.

(7)   The debtor shall immediately notify the [. . .] trustee of any assets acquired by him on a relevant date or of any other substantial change in his financial circumstances; and, if the debtor fails to comply with this subsection, he shall be guilty of an offence and liable on summary conviction to a fine not exceeding level 5 on the standard scale or to imprisonment for a term not exceeding 3 months or to both.

(8)   Subject to subsection (9) below, any dealing of or with the debtor relating to his estate vested in the [. . .] trustee under [this section or] section 31 of this Act shall be of no effect in a question with the [. . .] trustee.

(9)   Subsection (8) above shall not apply where the person seeking to uphold the dealing establishes—

    (a)   that the [. . .] trustee—
        (i)   has abandoned to the debtor the property to which the dealing relates;
        (ii)   has expressly or impliedly authorised the dealing; or
        (iii)   is otherwise personally barred from challenging the dealing, or
    (b)   that the dealing is—
        (i)   the performance of an obligation undertaken before the date of sequestration by a person obliged to the debtor in the obligation;
        (ii)   the purchase from the debtor of goods for which the purchaser has given value to the debtor or is willing to give value to the [. . .] trustee; or
        (iii)   a banking transaction in the ordinary course of business between the banker and the debtor [; or
        (iv)   one which satisfies the conditions mentioned in subsection (9ZA) below.]
and that the person dealing with the debtor was, at the time when the dealing occurred, unaware of the sequestration and had at that time no reason to believe that the debtor's estate had been sequestrated or was the subject of sequestration proceedings.
[(9ZA)   The conditions are that—
    (a)   the dealing constitutes—
        (i)   the transfer of incorporeal moveable property; or
        (ii)   the creation, transfer, variation or extinguishing of a real right in heritable property,
for which the person dealing with the debtor has given adequate consideration to the debtor, or is willing to give adequate consideration to the trustee;
    (b)   the dealing requires the delivery of a deed; and
    (c)   the delivery occurs during the period beginning with the date of sequestration and ending on the day which falls 7 days after the day on which—
        (i)   the certified copy of the order of the sheriff granting warrant is recorded under subsection (1)(a) of section 14 of this Act; or
        (ii)   the certified copy of the determination of the Accountant in Bankruptcy awarding sequestration is recorded under subsection (1A) of that section,
in the register of inhibitions.
    (9A)   Where the trustee has abandoned to the debtor any heritable property, notice in such form as may be prescribed given to the debtor by the trustee shall be sufficient evidence that the property is vested in the debtor.
    (9B)   Where the trustee gives notice under subsection (9A) above, he shall, as soon as reasonably practicable after giving the notice, record a certified copy of it in the register of inhibitions.]
    (10)   In this section 'a relevant date' means a date after the date of sequestration and before the date on which the debtor's discharge becomes effective.

33 Limitations on vesting

    (1)   The following property of the debtor shall not vest in the [. . .] trustee—
    (a)   [any property kept outwith a dwellinghouse in respect of which attachment is, by virtue of section 11(1) of the Debt Arrangement and Attachment (Scotland) Act 2002 (asp 17), incompetent];
    [(aa)   any property kept in a dwellinghouse which is not a non-essential asset for the purposes of Part 3 of that Act;]
    (b)   property held on trust by the debtor for any other person.
    (2)   The vesting of a debtor's estate in a [. . .] trustee shall not affect the right of hypothec of a landlord.
    (3)   Sections 31 and 32 of this Act are without prejudice to the right of any secured creditor which is preferable to the rights of the [. . .] trustee.

Safeguarding of interests of creditors of insolvent persons

34 Gratuitous alienations

(1) Where this subsection applies, an alienation by a debtor shall be challengeable by—

(a) any creditor who is a creditor by virtue of a debt incurred on or before the date of sequestration, or before the granting of the trust deed or the debtor's death, as the case may be; or

(b) the [. . .] trustee, the trustee acting under the trust deed or the judicial factor, as the case may be.

(2) Subsection (1) above applies where—

(a) by the alienation, whether before or after the coming into force of this section, any of the debtor's property has been transferred or any claim or right of the debtor has been discharged or renounced; and

(b) any of the following has occurred—

(i) his estate has been sequestrated (other than, in the case of a natural person, after his death); or

(ii) he has granted a trust deed which has become a protected trust deed; or

(iii) he has died and within 12 months after his death, his estate has been sequestrated; or

(iv) he has died and within the said 12 months, a judicial factor has been appointed under section 11A of the Judicial Factors (Scotland) Act 1889 to administer his estate and the estate was absolutely insolvent at the date of death; and

(c) the alienation took place on a relevant day.

(3) For the purposes of paragraph (c) of subsection (2) above, the day on which an alienation took place shall be the day on which the alienation became completely effectual; and in that paragraph 'relevant day' means, if the alienation has the effect of favouring—

(a) a person who is an associate of the debtor, a day not earlier than 5 years before the date of sequestration, the granting of the trust deed or the debtor's death, as the case may be; or

(b) any other person, a day not earlier than 2 years before the said date.

(4) On a challenge being brought under subsection (1) above, the court shall grant decree of reduction or for such restoration of property to the debtor's estate or other redress as may be appropriate, but the court shall not grant such a decree if the person seeking to uphold the alienation establishes—

(a) that immediately, or at any other time, after the alienation the debtor's assets were greater than his liabilities, or

(b) that the alienation was made for adequate consideration; or

(c) that the alienation—

(i) was a birthday, Christmas or other conventional gift; or

(ii) was a gift made, for a charitable purpose, to a person who is not an associate of the debtor,

which having regard to all the circumstances, it was reasonable for the debtor to make:

Provided that this subsection shall be without prejudice to any right or interest acquired in good faith and for value from or through the transferee in the alienation.

(5) In subsection (4) above, 'charitable purpose' means any charitable, benevolent or philanthropic purpose whether or not it is charitable within the meaning of any rule of law.

(6) For the purposes of the foregoing provisions of this section, an alienation in implementation of a prior obligation shall be deemed to be one for which there was no consideration or no adequate consideration to the extent that the prior obligation was undertaken for no consideration or no adequate consideration.

(7) This section is without prejudice to the operation of section 2 of the Married Women's Policies of Assurance (Scotland) Act 1880 (policy of assurance may be effected in trust for spouse, future spouse and children) [including the operation of that section as applied by section 132 of the Civil Partnership Act 2004].

(8) A [. . .] trustee, the trustee acting under a protected trust deed and a judicial factor appointed under section 11A of the Judicial Factors (Scotland) Act 1889 shall have the same right as a creditor has under any rule of law to challenge an alienation of a debtor made for no consideration or for no adequate consideration.

(9) The [. . .] trustee shall insert in the sederunt book a copy of any decree under this section affecting the sequestrated estate.

35   Recalling of order for payment of capital sum on divorce

(1) This section applies where—
   (a)   a court has made an order, whether before or after the coming into force of this section, under section 5 of the Divorce (Scotland) Act 1976 or section 8(2) of the Family Law (Scotland) Act 1985, for the payment by a debtor of a capital sum or [a court has, under the said section 8(2), made an order for the transfer of property by him or made a pension sharing order];
   (b)   on the date of the making of the order the debtor was absolutely insolvent or was rendered so by implementation of the order; and
   (c)   within 5 years after the making of the order—
      (i)   the debtor's estate has been sequestrated other than after his death; or
      (ii)   he has granted a trust deed which has (whether or not within the 5 years) become a protected trust deed; or
      (iii)   he has died and, within 12 months after his death, his estate has been sequestrated; or
      (iv)   he has died and, within the said 12 months, a judicial factor has been appointed under section 11A of the Judicial Factors (Scotland) Act 1889 to administer his estate.

(2) Where this section applies, the court, on an application brought by the [. . .] trustee, the trustee acting under the trust deed or the judicial factor, may make an order for recall of the order made under the said section 5 or 8(2) and for the repayment to the applicant of the whole or part of any sum already paid, or as the case may be for the return to the applicant of all or part of any property already transferred, under that order, or, where such property has been sold, for payment to the applicant of all or part of the proceeds of sale:

Provided that before making an order under this subsection the court shall have regard to all the circumstances including, without prejudice to the generality of this proviso, the financial, and other, circumstances (in so far as made known to the court) of the person against whom the order would be made.

(3) Where an application is brought under this section in a case where the debtor's estate has been sequestrated, the [. . .] trustee shall insert a copy of the decree of recall in the sederunt book.

36   Unfair preferences

(1) Subject to subsection (2) below, subsection (4) below applies to a transaction entered into by a debtor, whether before or after the coming into force of this section, which has the effect of creating a preference in favour of a creditor to the prejudice of the general body of creditors, being a preference created not earlier than 6 months before—
   (a)   the date of sequestration of the debtor's estate (if, in the case of a natural person, a date within his lifetime); or
   (b)   the granting by him of a trust deed which has become a protected trust deed; or
   (c)   his death where, within 12 months after his death—
      (i)   his estate has been sequestrated, or

(ii) a judicial factor has been appointed under section 11A of the Judicial Factors (Scotland) Act 1889 to administer his estate and his estate was absolutely insolvent at the date of death.

(2)   Subsection (4) below shall not apply to any of the following transactions—

(a)   a transaction in the ordinary course of trade or business;

(b)   a payment in cash for a debt which when it was paid had become payable unless the transaction was collusive with the purpose of prejudicing the general body of creditors;

(c)   a transaction whereby the parties thereto undertake reciprocal obligations (whether the performance by the parties of their respective obligations occurs at the same time or at different times) unless the transaction was collusive as aforesaid;

(d)   the granting of a mandate by a debtor authorising an arrestee to pay over the arrested funds or part thereof to the arrester where—

(i)   there has been a decree for payment or a warrant for summary diligence; and

(ii)   the decree or warrant has been preceded by an arrestment on the dependence of the action or followed by an arrestment in execution.

(3)   For the purposes of subsection (1) above, the day on which a preference was created shall be the day on which the preference became completely effectual.

(4)   A transaction to which this subsection applies shall be challengeable by—

(a)   any creditor who is a creditor by virtue of a debt incurred on or before the date of sequestration, the granting of the protected trust deed or the debtor's death, as the case may be; or

(b)   the [. . .] trustee, the trustee acting under the protected trust deed, or the judicial factor, as the case may be.

(5)   On a challenge being brought under subsection (4) above, the court, if satisfied that the transaction challenged is a transaction to which this section applies, shall grant decree of reduction or for such restoration of property to the debtor's estate or other redress as may be appropriate:

Provided that this subsection shall be without prejudice to any right or interest acquired in good faith and for value from or through the creditor in whose favour the preference was created.

(6)   A [. . .] trustee, the trustee acting under a protected trust deed and a judicial factor appointed under section 11A of the Judicial Factors (Scotland) Act 1889 shall have the same right as a creditor has under any rule of law to challenge a preference created by a debtor.

(7)   The [. . .] trustee shall insert in the sederunt book a copy of any decree under this section affecting the sequestrated estate.

[36A   Recovery of excessive pension contributions

(1)   Where a debtor's estate has been sequestrated and he—

(a)   has rights under an approved pension arrangement, or

(b)   has excluded rights under an unapproved pension arrangement, the [. . .] trustee may apply to the court for an order under this section.

(2)   If the court is satisfied—

(a)   that the rights under the arrangement are to any extent, and whether directly or indirectly, the fruits of relevant contributions, and

(b)   that the making of any of the relevant contributions ('the excessive contributions') has unfairly prejudiced the debtor's creditors,

the court may make such order as it thinks fit for restoring the position to what it would have been had the excessive contributions not been made.

(3)   Subsection (4) applies where the court is satisfied that the value of the rights under the arrangement is, as a result of rights of the debtor under the arrangement or any other pension arrangement having at any time become subject

to a debit under section 29(1)(a) of the Welfare Reform and Pensions Act 1999 (debits giving effect to pension-sharing), less than it would otherwise have been.

(4)   Where this subsection applies—

(a)   any relevant contributions which were represented by the rights which became subject to the debit shall, for the purposes of subsection (2), be taken to be contributions of which the rights under the arrangement are the fruits, and

(b)   where the relevant contributions represented by the rights under the arrangement (including those so represented by virtue of paragraph (a)) are not all excessive contributions, relevant contributions which are represented by the rights under the arrangement otherwise than by virtue of paragraph (a) shall be treated as excessive contributions before any which are so represented by virtue of that paragraph.

(5)   In subsections (2) to (4) 'relevant contributions' means contributions to the arrangement or any other pension arrangement—

(a)   which the debtor has at any time made on his own behalf, or

(b)   which have at any time been made on his behalf.

(6)   The court shall, in determining whether it is satisfied under subsection (2)(b), consider in particular—

(a)   whether any of the contributions were made for the purpose of putting assets beyond the reach of the debtor's creditors or any of them, and

(b)   whether the total amount of any contributions—

(i)   made by or on behalf of the debtor to pension arrangements, and

(ii)   represented (whether directly or indirectly) by rights under approved pension arrangements or excluded rights under unapproved pension arrangements,

is an amount which is excessive in view of the debtor's circumstances when those contributions were made.

(7)   For the purposes of this section and sections 36B and 36C ('the recovery provisions'), rights of a debtor under an unapproved pension arrangement are excluded rights if they are rights which are excluded from his estate by virtue of regulations under section 12 of the Welfare Reform and Pensions Act 1999.

(8)   In the recovery provisions—

'approved pension arrangement' has the same meaning as in section 11 of the Welfare Reform and Pensions Act 1999;

'unapproved pension arrangement' has the same meaning as in section 12 of that Act.]

[36B   Orders under section 36A

(1)   Without prejudice to the generality of section 36A(2) an order under section 36A may include provision—

(a)   requiring the person responsible for the arrangement to pay an amount to the [. . .] trustee,

(b)   adjusting the liabilities of the arrangement in respect of the debtor,

(c)   adjusting any liabilities of the arrangement in respect of any other person that derive, directly or indirectly, from rights of the debtor under the arrangement,

(d)   for the recovery by the person responsible for the arrangement (whether by deduction from any amount which that person is ordered to pay or otherwise) of costs incurred by that person in complying in the debtor's case with any requirement under section 36C(1) or in giving effect to the order.

(2)   In subsection (1), references to adjusting the liabilities of the arrangement in respect of a person include (in particular) reducing the amount of any benefit or future benefit to which that person is entitled under the arrangement.

(3)   In subsection (1)(c), the reference to liabilities of the arrangement does not include liabilities in respect of a person which result from giving effect to an order or provision falling within section 28(1) of the Welfare Reform and Pensions Act 1999 (pension sharing orders and agreements).

(4)   The maximum amount which the person responsible for an arrangement may be required to pay by an order under section 36A is the lesser of—

(a)   the amount of the excessive contributions, and

(b)   the value of the debtor's rights under the arrangement (if the arrangement is an approved pension arrangement) or of his excluded rights under the arrangement (if the arrangement is an unapproved pension arrangement).

(5)   An order under section 36A which requires the person responsible for an arrangement to pay an amount ('the restoration amount') to the [. . .] trustee must provide for the liabilities of the arrangement to be correspondingly reduced.

(6)   For the purposes of subsection (5), liabilities are correspondingly reduced if the difference between—

(a)   the amount of the liabilities immediately before the reduction, and

(b)   the amount of the liabilities immediately after the reduction, is equal to the restoration amount.

(7)   An order under section 36A in respect of an arrangement—

(a)   shall be binding on the person responsible for the arrangement; and

(b)   overrides provisions of the arrangement to the extent that they conflict with the provisions of the order.]

[36C   Orders under section 36A: supplementary

(1)   The person responsible for—

(a)   an approved pension arrangement under which a debtor has rights,

(b)   an unapproved pension arrangement under which a debtor has excluded rights, or

(c)   a pension arrangement under which a debtor has at any time had rights, shall, on the [. . .] trustee making a written request, provide the [. . .] trustee with such information about the arrangement and rights as the [. . .] trustee may reasonably require for, or in connection with, the making of applications under section 36A.

(2)   Nothing in—

(a)   any provision of section 159 of the Pensions Schemes Act 1993 or section 91 of the Pensions Act 1995 (which prevent assignation and the making of orders that restrain a person from receiving anything which he is prevented from assigning),

(b)   any provision of any enactment (whether passed or made before or after the passing of the Welfare Reform and Pensions Act 1999) corresponding to any of the provisions mentioned in paragraph (a), or

(c)   any provision of the arrangement in question corresponding to any of those provisions, applies to a court exercising its powers under section 36A.

(3)   Where any sum is required by an order under section 36A to be paid to the [. . .] trustee, that sum shall be comprised in the debtor's estate.

(4)   Regulations may, for the purposes of the recovery provisions, make provision about the calculation and verification of—

(a)   any such value as is mentioned in section 36B(4)(b);

(b)   any such amounts as are mentioned in section 36B(6)(a) and (b).

(5)   The power conferred by subsection (4) includes power to provide for calculation or verification—

(a)   in such manner as may, in the particular case, be approved by a prescribed person; or

(b)   in accordance with guidance from time to time prepared by a prescribed person. [. . .]

(6)   References in the recovery provisions to the person responsible for a pension arrangement are to—

(a)   the trustees, managers or provider of the arrangement, or

(b)   the person having functions in relation to the arrangement corresponding to those of a trustee, manager or provider.

(7)   In this section and sections 36A and 36B—
   'the recovery provisions' means this section and sections 36A and 36B;
   'regulations' means regulations made by the Secretary of State.
(8)   Regulations under the recovery provisions may contain such incidental,
supplemental and transitional provisions as appear to the Secretary of State necessary or expedient.]

[36D   Recovery of excessive contributions in pension-sharing cases

(1)   For the purposes of section 34 of this Act, a pension-sharing transaction
shall be taken—
   (a)   to be a transaction, entered into by the transferor with the transferee, by
which the appropriate amount is transferred by the transferor to the transferee;
and
   (b)   to be capable of being an alienation challengeable under that section only
so far as it is a transfer of so much of the appropriate amount as is recoverable.
(2)   For the purposes of section 35 of this Act, a pension-sharing transaction
shall be taken—
   (a)   to be a pension sharing order made by the court under section 8(2) of the
Family Law (Scotland) Act 1985; and
   (b)   to be an order capable of being recalled under that section only so far as it
is a payment or transfer of so much of the appropriate amount as is recoverable.
(3)   For the purposes of section 36 of this Act, a pension-sharing transaction
shall be taken—
   (a)   to be something (namely a transfer of the appropriate amount to the
transferee) done by the transferor; and
   (b)   to be capable of being an unfair preference given to the transferee only
so far as it is a transfer of so much of the appropriate amount as is recoverable.
(4)   Where—
   (a)   an alienation is challenged under section 34;
   (b)   an application is made under section 35 for the recall of an order made
in divorce proceedings; or
   (c)   a transaction is challenged under section 36,
if any question arises as to whether, or the extent to which, the appropriate
amount in the case of a pension-sharing transaction is recoverable, the question
shall be determined in accordance with subsections (5) to (9).
(5)   The court shall first determine the extent (if any) to which the transferor's
rights under the shared arrangement at the time of the transaction appear to have
been (whether directly or indirectly) the fruits of contributions ('personal
contributions')—
   (a)   which the transferor has at any time made on his own behalf, or
   (b)   which have at any time been made on the transferor's behalf,
to the shared arrangement or any other pension arrangement.
(6)   Where it appears that those rights were to any extent the fruits of personal
contributions, the court shall then determine the extent (if any) to which those
rights appear to have been the fruits of personal contributions whose making has
unfairly prejudiced the transferor's creditors ('the unfair contributions').
(7)   If it appears to the court that the extent to which those rights were the fruits
of the unfair contributions is such that the transfer of the appropriate amount
could have been made out of rights under the shared arrangement which were not
the fruits of the unfair contributions, then the appropriate amount is not
recoverable.
(8)   If it appears to the court that the transfer could not have been wholly so
made, then the appropriate amount is recoverable to the extent to which it appears
to the court that the transfer could not have been so made.
(9)   In making the determination mentioned in subsection (6) the court shall
consider in particular—

(a)   whether any of the personal contributions were made for the purpose of putting assets beyond the reach of the transferor's creditors or any of them; and

(b)   whether the total amount of any personal contributions represented, at the time the pension sharing arrangement was made, by rights under pension arrangements is an amount which is excessive in view of the transferor's circumstances when those contributions were made.

(10)   In this section and sections 36E and 36F—

'appropriate amount', in relation to a pension-sharing transaction, means the appropriate amount in relation to that transaction for the purposes of section 29(1) of the Welfare Reform and Pensions Act 1999 (creation of pension credits and debits);

'pension-sharing transaction' means an order or provision falling within section 28(1) of the Welfare Reform and Pensions Act 1999 (orders and agreements which activate pension-sharing);

'shared arrangement', in relation to a pension-sharing transaction, means the pension arrangement to which the transaction relates;

'transferee', in relation to a pension-sharing transaction, means the person for whose benefit the transaction is made;

'transferor', in relation to a pension-sharing transaction, means the person to whose rights the transaction relates.]

[36E   Recovery orders

(1)   In this section and section 36F of this Act, 'recovery order' means—

(a)   a decree granted under section 34(4) of this Act;

(b)   an order made under section 35(2) of this Act;

(c)   a decree granted under section 36(5) of this Act,

in any proceedings to which section 36D of this Act applies.

(2)   Without prejudice to the generality of section 34(4), 35(2) or 36(5) a recovery order may include provision—

(a)   requiring the person responsible for a pension arrangement in which the transferee has acquired rights derived directly or indirectly from the pension-sharing transaction to pay an amount to the [. . .] trustee,

(b)   adjusting the liabilities of the pension arrangement in respect of the transferee,

(c)   adjusting any liabilities of the pension arrangement in respect of any other person that derive, directly or indirectly, from rights of the transferee under the arrangement,

(d)   for the recovery by the person responsible for the pension arrangement (whether by deduction from any amount which that person is ordered to pay or otherwise) of costs incurred by that person in complying in the debtor's case with any requirement under section 36F(1) or in giving effect to the order.

(3)   In subsection (2), references to adjusting the liabilities of a pension arrangement in respect of a person include (in particular) reducing the amount of any benefit or future benefit to which that person is entitled under the arrangement.

(4)   The maximum amount which the person responsible for an arrangement may be required to pay by a recovery order is the smallest of—

(a)   so much of the appropriate amount as, in accordance with section 36D of this Act, is recoverable,

(b)   so much (if any) of the amount of the unfair contributions (within the meaning given by section 36D(6)) as is not recoverable by way of an order under section 36A of this Act containing provision such as is mentioned in section 36B(1)(a), and

(c)   the value of the debtor's rights under the arrangement acquired by the transferee as a consequence of the transfer of the appropriate amount.

(5)   A recovery order which requires the person responsible for an arrangement

to pay an amount ('the restoration amount') to the [. . .] trustee must provide for the liabilities of the arrangement to be correspondingly reduced.

(6)   For the purposes of subsection (5), liabilities are correspondingly reduced if the difference between—

(a)   the amount of the liabilities immediately before the reduction, and

(b)   the amount of the liabilities immediately after the reduction is equal to the restoration amount.

(7)   A recovery order in respect of an arrangement—

(a)   shall be binding on the person responsible for the arrangement, and

(b)   overrides provisions of the arrangement to the extent that they conflict with the provisions of the order.]

[36F   Recovery orders: supplementary

(1)   The person responsible for a pension arrangement under which the transferee has, at any time, acquired rights by virtue of the transfer of the appropriate amount shall, on the [. . .] trustee making a written request, provide the trustee with such information about the arrangement and the rights under it of the transferor and transferee as the [. . .] trustee may reasonably require for, or in connection with, the making of an application for a recovery order.

(2)   Nothing in—

(a)   any provision of section 159 of the Pension Schemes Act 1993 or section 91 of the Pensions Act 1995 (which prevent assignation and the making of orders which restrain a person from receiving anything which he is prevented from assigning),

(b)   any provision of any enactment (whether passed or made before or after the passing of the Welfare Reform and Pensions Act 1999) corresponding to any of the provisions mentioned in paragraph (a), or

(c)   any provision of the arrangement in question corresponding to any of those provisions, applies to a court exercising its power to make a recovery order.

(3)   Regulations may, for the purposes of the recovery provisions, make provision about the calculation and verification of—

(a)   any such value as is mentioned in section 36E(4)(c);

(b)   any such amounts as are mentioned in section 36E(6)(a) and (b).

(4)   The power conferred by subsection (3) includes power to provide for calculation or verification—

(a)   in such manner as may, in the particular case, be approved by a prescribed person; or

(b)   in accordance with guidance from time to time prepared by a prescribed person. [. . .]

(5)   References in the recovery provisions to the person responsible for a pension arrangement are to—

(a)   the trustees, managers or provider of the arrangement, or

(b)   the person having functions in relation to the arrangement corresponding to those of a trustee, manager or provider.

(6)   In this section—

'prescribed' means prescribed by regulations;

'the recovery provisions' means this section and sections 34, 35, 36 and 36E of this Act;

'regulations' means regulations made by the Secretary of State.

(7)   Regulations under the recovery provisions may—

(a)   make different provision for different cases;

(b)   contain such incidental, supplemental and transitional provisions as appear to the Secretary of State necessary or expedient.

(8)   Regulations under the recovery provisions shall be made by statutory instrument subject to annulment in pursuance of a resolution of either House of Parliament.]

Effect of sequestration on diligence

37 Effect of sequestration on diligence

(1) The order of the [sheriff or, as the case may be, the determination of the debtor application by the Accountant in Bankruptcy] awarding sequestration shall as from the date of sequestration have the effect, in relation to diligence done (whether before or after the date of sequestration) in respect of any part of the debtor's estate, of—

(a) a decree of adjudication of the heritable estate of the debtor for payment of his debts which has been duly recorded in the register of inhibitions and adjudications on that date; and

(b) an arrestment in execution and decree of furthcoming, an arrestment in execution and warrant of sale, and [an attachment],

in favour of the creditors according to their respective entitlements.

(2) [Where an] inhibition on the estate of the debtor [. . .] takes effect within the period of 60 days before the date of sequestration [. . .] any relevant right of challenge shall, at the date of sequestration, vest in the [. . .] trustee as shall any right of the inhibitor to receive payment for the discharge of the inhibition:

Provided that this subsection shall neither entitle the trustee to receive any payment made to the inhibitor before the date of sequestration nor affect the validity of any thing done before that date in consideration of such payment.

(3) In subsection (2) above, 'any relevant right of challenge' means any right to challenge a deed voluntarily granted by the debtor if it is a right which vested in the inhibitor by virtue of the inhibition.

(4) No arrestment [, money attachment, interim attachment] or [attachment] of the estate of the debtor (including any estate vesting in the [. . .] trustee under section 32(6) of this Act) executed—

(a) within the period of 60 days before the date of sequestration and whether or not subsisting at that date; or

(b) on or after the date of sequestration,

shall be effectual to create a preference for the arrester or [attacher]; and the estate so arrested or [attached or any funds released under section 73J(2) of the Debtors (Scotland) Act 1987 (c 18) (automatic release of funds)], or the proceeds of sale thereof, shall be handed over to the [. . .] trustee.

(5) An arrester or [attacher] whose arrestment [, money attachment, interim attachment] or [attachment] is executed within the said period of 60 days shall be entitled to payment, out of the arrested or [attached] estate or out of the proceeds of the sale thereof, of the expenses incurred—

(a) in obtaining

[(i) warrant for interim attachment; or

(ii)] the extract of the decree or other document on which the arrestment or [attachment] proceeded;

(b) in executing the arrestment [, money attachment, interim attachment] or [attachment]; and

(c) in taking any further action in respect of the diligence.

[(5A) Nothing in subsection (4) or (5) above shall apply to an earnings arrestment, a current maintenance arrestment, a conjoined arrestment order or a deduction from earnings order under the Child Support Act 1991.]

[. . .]

(6) No poinding of the ground in respect of the estate of the debtor (including any estate vesting in the [. . .] trustee under section 32(6) of this Act) executed within the period of 60 days before the date of sequestration or on or after that date shall be effectual in a question with the [. . .] trustee, except for the interest on the debt of a secured creditor, being interest for the current half-yearly term and arrears of interest for one year immediately before the commencement of that term.

(7) The foregoing provisions of this section shall apply to the estate of a deceased debtor which—

(a)   has been sequestrated; or

(b)   was absolutely insolvent at the date of death and in respect of which a judicial factor has been appointed under section 11A of the Judicial Factors (Scotland) Act 1889,

within 12 months after his death, but as if for any reference to the date of sequestration and the debtor there were substituted respectively a reference to the date of the deceased's death and to the deceased debtor.

(8)   It shall be incompetent on or after the date of sequestration for any creditor to raise or insist in an adjudication against the estate of a debtor (including any estate vesting in the permanent trustee under section 32(6) of this Act) or to be confirmed as executor-creditor on the estate.

[(8A)   A notice of land attachment registered—

(a)   on or after the date of sequestration against land forming part of the heritable estate of the debtor (including any estate vesting in the trustee by virtue of section 32(6) of this Act); or

(b)   before that date in relation to which, by that date, no land attachment is created,

shall be of no effect.

(8B)   Subject to subsections (8C) to (8F) below, it shall not be competent for a creditor to insist in a land attachment—

(a)   created over heritable estate of the debtor before the beginning of the period of six months mentioned in subsection (5B) above; and

(b)   which subsists on the date of sequestration.

(8C)   Where, in execution of a warrant for sale, a contract to sell the land has been concluded—

(a)   the trustee shall concur in and ratify the deed implementing that contract; and

(b)   the appointed person shall account for and pay to the trustee any balance of the proceeds of sale which would, but for the sequestration, be due to the debtor after disbursing those proceeds in accordance with section 116 of the Bankruptcy and Diligence etc (Scotland) Act 2007 (asp 3) (disbursement of proceeds of sale of attached land).

(8D)   Subsection (8C) above shall not apply where the deed implementing the contract is not registered before the expiry of the period of 28 days beginning with the day on which—

(a)   the certified copy of the order of the sheriff granting warrant is recorded under subsection (1)(a) of section 14 of this Act; or

(b)   the certified copy of the determination of the Accountant in Bankruptcy awarding sequestration is recorded under subsection (1A) of that section, in the register of inhibitions.

(8E)   Where a decree of foreclosure has been granted but an extract of it has not registered, the creditor may proceed to complete title to the land by so registering that extract provided that the extract is registered before the expiry of the period mentioned in subsection (8D) above.

(8F)   The Scottish Ministers may—

(a)   prescribe such other period for the period mentioned in subsection (8D) above; and

(b)   prescribe different periods for the purposes of that subsection and subsection (8E) above,

as they think fit.]

(9)   Where—

(a)   a deceased debtor's estate is sequestrated; or

(b)   a judicial factor is appointed under section 11A of the Judicial Factors (Scotland) Act 1889 to administer his estate (in a case where the estate is absolutely insolvent),

within 12 months after the debtor's death, no confirmation as executor-creditor on that estate at any time after the debtor's death shall be effectual in a question with the [. . .] trustee or the judicial factor; but the executor-creditor shall be entitled out of that estate, or out of the proceeds of sale thereof, to the expenses incurred by him in obtaining the confirmation.

[(10)   Expressions used in subsections (5B), (5C) and (8A) to (8F) above which are also used in Chapter 2 of Part 4 of the Bankruptcy and Diligence etc (Scotland) Act 2007 (asp 3) have the same meanings in those subsections as they have in that Chapter.]

[Taking possession of estate by trustee]

38   Taking possession of estate by [. . .] trustee

(1)   The [. . .] trustee shall—

(a)   as soon as may be after his [appointment], for the purpose of recovering the debtor's estate under section 3(1)(a) of this Act, and subject to section 40 of this Act, take possession of the debtor's whole estate so far as vesting in the [. . .] trustee under sections 31 and 32 of this Act and any document in the debtor's possession or control relating to his assets or his business or financial affairs;

(b)   make up and maintain an inventory and valuation of the estate which he shall record in the sederunt book; and

(c)   forthwith thereafter send a copy of any such inventory and valuation to the Accountant in Bankruptcy.

(2)   The [. . .] trustee shall be entitled to have access to all documents relating to the assets or the business or financial affairs of the debtor sent by or on behalf of the debtor to a third party and in that third party's hands and to make copies of any such documents.

(3)   If any person obstructs a [. . .] trustee who is exercising, or attempting to exercise, a power conferred by subsection (2) above, the sheriff, on the application of the [. . .] trustee, may order that person to cease so to obstruct the [. . .] trustee.

(4)   The [. . .] trustee may require delivery to him of any title deed or other document of the debtor, notwithstanding that a right of lien is claimed over the title deed or document; but this subsection is without prejudice to any preference of the holder of the lien.

39   Management and realisation of estate

(1)   As soon as may be after his [appointment], the [. . .] trustee shall consult [. . .] with the Accountant in Bankruptcy concerning the exercise of his functions under section 3(1)(a) of this Act; and, subject to [subsections (1A), (6) and (9)] below, the [. . .] trustee shall comply with any general or specific directions given to him, as the case may be—

(a)   by the creditors;

(b)   on the application under this subsection of the commissioners, by the [sheriff]; or

(c)   [. . .] by the Accountant in Bankruptcy,

as to the exercise by him of such functions.

[(1A)   Subsection (1) above does not apply in any case where the Accountant in Bankruptcy is the trustee.]

(2)   The [. . .] trustee may [. . .] do any of the following things [. . .]—

(a)   carry on [or close down] any business of the debtor;

(b)   bring, defend or continue any legal proceedings relating to the estate of the debtor;

(c)   create a security over any part of the estate;

(d)   where any right, option or other power forms part of the debtor's estate, make payments or incur liabilities with a view to obtaining, for the benefit of the creditors, any property which is the subject of the right, option or power;

[(e)   borrow money in so far as it is necessary for the trustee to do so to safeguard the debtor's estate;

(f)   effect or maintain insurance policies in respect of the business or property of the debtor.]

(3)   Any sale of the debtor's estate by the [. . .] trustee may be by either public sale or private bargain.

(4)   The following rules shall apply to the sale of any part of the debtor's heritable estate over which a heritable security is held by a creditor or creditors if the rights of the secured creditor or creditors are preferable to those of the [. . .] trustee—

(a)   the [. . .] trustee may sell that part only with the concurrence of every such creditor unless he obtains a sufficiently high price to discharge every such security;

(b)   subject to paragraph (c) below, the following acts shall be precluded—

(i)   the taking of steps by a creditor to enforce his security over that part after the [. . .] trustee has intimated to the creditor that he intends to sell it;

(ii)   the commencement by the [. . .] trustee of the procedure for the sale of that part after a creditor has intimated to the [. . .] trustee that he intends to commence the procedure for its sale;

(c)   where the [. . .] trustee or a creditor has given intimation under paragraph (b) above, but has unduly delayed in proceeding with the sale, then, if authorised by the [sheriff] in the case of intimation under—

(i)   sub-paragraph (i) of that paragraph, any creditor to whom intimation has been given may enforce his security; or

(ii)   sub-paragraph (ii) of that paragraph,

the [. . .] trustee may sell that part.

(5)   The function of the [. . .] trustee under section 3(1)(a) of this Act to realise the debtor's estate shall include the function of selling, with or without recourse against the estate, debts owing to the estate.

(6)   The [. . .] trustee may sell any perishable goods without complying with any directions given to him under subsection (1)(a) or (c) above if the [. . .] trustee considers that compliance with such directions would adversely affect the sale.

(7)   The validity of the title of any purchaser shall not be challengeable on the ground that there has been a failure to comply with a requirement of this section.

(8)   It shall be incompetent for the [. . .] trustee or an associate of his or for any commissioner, to purchase any of the debtor's estate in pursuance of this section.

[(9)   The trustee—

(a)   shall comply with the requirements of subsection (4) of this section; and

(b)   may do anything permitted by this section,

only in so far as, in his view, it would be of financial benefit to the estate of the debtor and in the interests of the creditors to do so.]

[39A   Debtor's home ceasing to form part of sequestrated estate

(1)   This section applies where a debtor's sequestrated estate includes any right or interest in the debtor's family home.

(2)   At the end of the period of 3 years beginning with the date of sequestration the right or interest mentioned in subsection (1) above shall—

(a)   cease to form part of the debtor's sequestrated estate; and

(b)   be reinvested in the debtor (without disposition, conveyance, assignation or other transfer).

(3)   Subsection (2) above shall not apply if, during the period mentioned in that subsection—

(a)   the trustee disposes of or otherwise realises the right or interest mentioned in subsection (1) above;

(b)   the trustee concludes missives for sale of the right or interest;

(c)   the trustee sends a memorandum to the keeper of the register of inhibitions under section 14(4) of this Act;

(d)   the trustee registers in the Land Register of Scotland or, as the case may be, records in the Register of Sasines a notice of title in relation to the right or interest mentioned in subsection (1) above;

(e)   the trustee commences proceedings—

(i)   to obtain the authority of the sheriff under section 40(1)(b) of this Act to sell or dispose of the right or interest;

(ii)   in an action for division and sale of the family home; or

(iii)   in an action for the purpose of obtaining vacant possession of the family home;

(f)   the trustee and the debtor enter into an agreement such as is mentioned in subsection (5) below.

[(g)   the trustee has commenced an action under section 34 of this Act in respect of any right or interest mentioned in subsection (1) above or the trustee has not known about the facts giving rise to a right of action under section 34 of this Act, provided the trustee commences such an action reasonably soon after the trustee becomes aware of such right.]

(4)   The Scottish Ministers may, by regulations, modify paragraphs (a) to (f) of subsection (3) above so as to—

(a)   add or remove a matter; or

(b)   vary any such matter,

referred to in that subsection.

(5)   The agreement referred to in subsection (3)(f) above is an agreement that the debtor shall incur a specified liability to his estate (with or without interest from the date of the agreement) in consideration of which the right or interest mentioned in subsection (1) above shall—

(a)   cease to form part of the debtor's sequestrated estate; and

(b)   be reinvested in the debtor (without disposition, conveyance, assignation or other transfer).

(6)   If the debtor does not inform the trustee or the Accountant in Bankruptcy of his right or interest in the family home before the end of the period of 3 months beginning with the date of sequestration, the period of 3 years mentioned in subsection (2) above—

(a)   shall not begin with the date of sequestration; but

(b)   shall begin with the date on which the trustee or the Accountant in Bankruptcy becomes aware of the debtor's right or interest.

(7)   The sheriff may, on the application of the trustee, substitute for the period of 3 years mentioned in subsection (2) above a longer period—

(a)   in prescribed circumstances; and

(b)   in such other circumstances as the sheriff thinks appropriate.

(8)   The Scottish Ministers may, by regulations—

(a)   make provision for this section to have effect with the substitution, in such circumstances as the regulations may prescribe, of a shorter period for the period of 3 years mentioned in subsection (2) above;

(b)   prescribe circumstances in which this section does not apply;

(c)   prescribe circumstances in which a sheriff may disapply this section;

(d)   make provision requiring the trustee to give notice that this section applies or does not apply;

(e)   make provision about compensation;

(f)   make such provision as they consider necessary or expedient in consequence of regulations made under paragraphs (a) to (e) above.

(9)   In this section, 'family home' has the same meaning as in section 40 of this Act.]

40   Power of [. . .] trustee in relation to the debtor's family home

(1)   Before the [. . .] trustee [or the trustee acting under the trust deed] sells or disposes of any right or interest in the debtor's family home he shall—

(a)   obtain the relevant consent; or

    (b)   where he is unable to do so, obtain the authority of the [sheriff] in accordance with subsection (2) below.

    (2)   Where the [. . .] trustee [or the trustee acting under the trust deed] requires to obtain the authority of the [sheriff] in terms of subsection (1)(b) above, the [sheriff], after having regard to all the circumstances of the case, including—

    (a)   the needs and financial resources of the debtor's spouse or former spouse;

    [(aa)   the needs and financial resources of the debtor's civil partnership or former civil partner;]

    (b)   the needs and financial resources of any child of the family;

    (c)   the interests of the creditors;

    (d)   the length of the period during which (whether before or after the relevant date) the family home was used as a residence by any of the persons referred to in [paragraphs (a) to (b)] above,

may refuse to grant the application or may postpone the granting of the application for such period (not exceeding [3 years]) as [he] may consider reasonable in the circumstances or may grant the application subject to such conditions as [he] may prescribe.

    (3)   Subsection (2) above shall apply—

    (a)   to an action for division and sale of the debtor's family home; or

    (b)   to an action for the purpose of obtaining vacant possession of the debtor's family home,

brought by the [. . .] trustee [or the trustee acting under the trust deed] as it applies to an application under subsection (1)(b) above and, for the purposes of this subsection, any reference in the said subsection (2) to that granting of the application shall be construed as a reference to the granting of decree in the action.

    [(3A)   Before commencing proceedings to obtain the authority of the sheriff under subsection (1)(b) the trustee, or the trustee acting under the trust deed, must give notice of the proceedings to the local authority in whose area the home is situated.

    (3B)   Notice under subsection (3A) must be given in such form and manner as may be prescribed by the Scottish Ministers.]

    (4)   In this section—

    (a)   'family home' means any property in which, at the relevant date, the debtor had (whether alone or in common with any other person) a right or interest, being property which was occupied at that date as a residence by the debtor and his spouse [or civil partner] or by the debtor's spouse [or civil partner] or former spouse [or civil partner] (in any case with or without a child of the family) or by the debtor with a child of the family;

    (b)   'child of the family' includes any child or grandchild of either the debtor or his spouse [or civil partner] or former spouse [or civil partner], and any person who has been brought up or accepted by either the debtor or his spouse [or civil partner] or former spouse [or civil partner] as if he or she were a child of the debtor, spouse [or civil partner] or former spouse [or civil partner] whatever the age of such a child, grandchild or person may be;

    [(ba)   'local authority' means a council constituted under section 2 of the Local Government (Scotland) Act 1994 (c 39);]

    (c)   'relevant consent' means in relation to the sale or disposal of any right or interest in a family home—

        (i)   in a case where the family home is occupied by the debtor's spouse [or civil partner] or former spouse [or civil partner], the consent of the spouse [or civil partner], or, as the case may be, the former spouse [or civil partner], whether or not the family home is also occupied by the debtor;

        (ii)   where sub-paragraph (i) above does not apply, in a case where the family home is occupied by the debtor with a child of the family, the consent of the debtor; and

    (d)   'relevant date' means the day immediately preceding the date of sequestration [or, as the case may be, the day immediately preceding the date the trust deed was granted].

41 Protection of rights of spouse against arrangements intended to defeat them
(1) If a debtor's sequestrated estate includes a matrimonial home of which the debtor, immediately before the date [the order is made appointing] the [. . .] trustee (or, if more than one such [trustee is appointed] in the sequestration, of the first [order making such an appointment]) was an entitled spouse and the other spouse is a non-entitled spouse—
    (a)   the [. . .] trustee shall, where he—
        (i) is aware that the entitled spouse is married to the non-entitled spouse; and
        (ii) knows where the non-entitled spouse is residing,
inform the non-entitled spouse, within the period of 14 days beginning with that date, of the fact that sequestration of the entitled spouse's estate has been awarded, of the right of petition which exists under section 16 of this Act and of the effect of paragraph (b) below; and
    (b)   the [sheriff], on the petition under section 16 of this Act of the non-entitled spouse presented either within the period of 40 days beginning with that date or within the period of 10 weeks beginning with the date [of the award] of sequestration may—
        (i) under section 17 of this Act recall the sequestration; or
        (ii) make such order as [he] thinks appropriate to protect the occupancy rights of the non-entitled spouse;
if [he] is satisfied that the purpose of the petition for sequestration [or, as the case may be, the debtor application] was wholly or mainly to defeat the occupancy rights of the non-entitled spouse.
(2) In subsection (1) above—
'entitled spouse' and 'non-entitled spouse' have the same meanings as in section 6 of the Matrimonial Homes (Family Protection) (Scotland) Act 1981;
'matrimonial home' has the meaning assigned by section 22 of that Act as amended by the Law Reform (Miscellaneous Provisions) (Scotland) Act 1985; and
'occupancy rights' has the meaning assigned by section 1(4) of the said Act of 1981.

[41A Protection of rights of civil partner against arrangements intended to defeat them
(1) If a debtor's sequestrated estate includes a family home of which the debtor, immediately before the date [the order is made appointing] the [. . .] trustee (or, if more than one [trustee is appointed] in the sequestration, of the first [order making such an appointment]) was an entitled partner and the other partner in the civil partnership is a non-entitled partner—
    (a)   the [. . .] trustee shall, where he—
        (i) is aware that the entitled partner is in civil partnership with the non-entitled partner; and
        (ii) knows where the non-entitled partner is residing,
inform the non-entitled partner, within the period of 14 days beginning with that date, of the fact that sequestration of the entitled partner's estate has been awarded, of the right of petition which exists under section 16 of this Act and of the effect of paragraph (b) below; and
    (b)   the [sheriff], on the petition under section 16 of this Act of the non-entitled partner presented either within the period of 40 days beginning with that date or within the period of 10 weeks beginning with the date [of the award] of sequestration may—
        (i) under section 17 of this Act recall the sequestration; or

(ii) make such order as [he] thinks appropriate to protect the occupancy
rights of the non-entitled partner,
if [he] is satisfied that the purpose of the petition for sequestration [or, as the
case may be, the debtor application] was wholly or mainly to defeat the
occupancy rights of the non-entitled partner.

(2) In subsection (1) above—
'entitled partner' and 'non-entitled partner' have the same meanings as in
section 101 of the Civil Partnership Act 2004;
'family home' has the meaning assigned by section 135 of the 2004 Act; and
'occupancy rights' means the rights conferred by subsection (1) of that section 101.]

42 Contractual powers of [. . .] trustee

(1) Subject to subsections (2) and (3) below, the [. . .] trustee may adopt any
contract entered into by the debtor before the date of sequestration where he considers that its adoption would be beneficial to the administration of the debtor's
estate, except where the adoption is precluded by the express or implied terms of
the contract, or may refuse to adopt any such contract.

(2) The [. . .] trustee shall, within 28 days from the receipt by him of a request
in writing from any party to a contract entered into by the debtor or within such
longer period of that receipt as the [sheriff] on application by the [. . .] trustee may
allow, adopt or refuse to adopt the contract.

(3) If the [. . .] trustee does not reply in writing to the request under subsection
(2) above within the said period of 28 days or longer period, as the case may be, he
shall be deemed to have refused to adopt the contract.

(4) The [. . .] trustee may enter into any contract where he considers that this
would be beneficial for the administration of the debtor's estate.

43 Money received by [. . .] trustee

(1) Subject to [subsections (1A) and (2)] below, all money received by the [. . .]
trustee in the exercise of his functions shall be deposited by him in the name
of the debtor's estate in an [interest-bearing account in an] appropriate bank
or institution.

[(1A) In any case where the Accountant in Bankruptcy is the trustee, subject to
subsection (2) below, all money received by the Accountant in Bankruptcy in the
exercise of his functions as trustee shall be deposited by him in an interest-bearing
account in the name of the debtor's estate or in the name of the Scottish Ministers
in an appropriate bank or institution.]

(2) The [. . .] trustee may at any time retain in his hands a sum not exceeding
£200 or such other sum as may be prescribed.

[43A Debtor's requirement to give account of state of affairs

(1) This section applies to a debtor who—
   (a) has not been discharged under this Act; or
   (b) is subject to—
      (i) an order made by the sheriff under subsection (2) of section 32 of this
Act; or
      (ii) an agreement entered into under subsection (4B) of that section.

(2) The trustee shall, at the end of—
   (a) the period of 6 months beginning with the date of sequestration; and
   (b) each subsequent period of 6 months,
require the debtor to give an account in writing, in such form as may be prescribed, of his current state of affairs.]

Examination of debtor

44 Private examination

(1) The [. . .] trustee may request—

(a) the debtor to appear before him and to give information relating to his assets, his dealings with them or his conduct in relation to his business or financial affairs; or

(b) the debtor's spouse [or civil partner] or any other person who the [. . .] trustee believes can give such information (in this Act such spouse [, civil partner] or other person being referred to as a 'relevant person'), to give that information.

and, if he considers it necessary, the [. . .] trustee may apply to the sheriff for an order to be made under subsection (2) below.

(2) Subject to section 46(2) of this Act, on application to him under subsection (1) above the sheriff may make an order requiring the debtor or a relevant person to attend for private examination before him on a date (being not earlier than 8 days nor later than 16 days after the date of the order) and at a time specified in the order.

(3) A person who fails without reasonable excuse to comply with an order made under subsection (2) above shall be guilty of an offence and liable on summary conviction to a fine not exceeding level 5 on the standard scale or to imprisonment for a term not exceeding 3 months or to both.

(4) Where the debtor is an entity whose estate may be sequestrated by virtue of section 6(1) of this Act, the references in this section and in sections 45 to 47 of this Act to the debtor shall be construed, unless the context otherwise requires, as references to a person representing the entity.

45 Public examination

(1) Not less than 8 weeks before the end of the first accounting period, the [. . .] trustee—

(a) may; or

(b) if requested to do so by the Accountant in Bankruptcy or the commissioners (if any) or one quarter in value of the creditors, shall,

apply to the sheriff for an order for the public examination before the sheriff of the debtor or of a relevant person relating to the debtor's assets, his dealings with them or his conduct in relation to his business or financial affairs:

Provided that, on cause shown, such application may be made by the [. . .] trustee at any time.

(2) Subject to section 46(2) of this Act, the sheriff, on an application under subsection (1) above, shall make an order requiring the debtor or relevant person to attend for examination before him in open court on a date (being not earlier than 8 days nor later than 16 days after the date of the order) and at a time specified in the order.

(3) On the sheriff making an order under subsection (2) above, the [. . .] trustee shall—

(a) publish in the Edinburgh Gazette a notice in such form and containing such particulars as may be prescribed; and

(b) send a copy of the said notice—

(i) to every creditor known to the [. . .] trustee; and

(ii) where the order is in respect of a relevant person, to the debtor, and

inform the creditor and, where applicable, the debtor that he may participate in the examination.

(4) A person who fails without reasonable excuse to comply with an order made under subsection (2) above shall be guilty of an offence and liable on summary conviction to a fine not exceeding level 5 on the standard scale or to imprisonment for a term not exceeding 3 months or to both.

46   Provisions ancillary to sections 44 and 45
    (1)   If the debtor or relevant person is residing—
        (a)   in Scotland, the sheriff may, on the application of the [. . .] trustee, grant
    a warrant which may be executed by a messenger-at-arms or sheriff officer
    anywhere in Scotland [to apprehend]; or
        (b)   in any other part of the United Kingdom, [. . .] the sheriff may, on the
    application of the [. . .] trustee, [grant a warrant for the arrest of],
    [. . .] the debtor or relevant person to have him taken to the place of the
    examination:
        Provided that a warrant under [this subsection shall not be granted] unless the
    [sheriff] is satisfied that it is necessary to do so to secure the attendance of the
    debtor or relevant person at the examination.
    (2)   If the debtor or a relevant person is for any good reason prevented
    from attending for examination, the sheriff may, without prejudice to sub-
    section (3) below, grant a commission to take his examination (the commis-
    sioner being in this section and section 47 below referred to as an 'examining
    commissioner').
    (3)   The sheriff or the examining commissioner may at any time adjourn the
    examination to such day as the sheriff or the examining commissioner may fix.
    (4)   The sheriff or the examining commissioner may order the debtor or a rele-
    vant person to produce for inspection any document in his custody or control
    relating to the debtor's assets, his dealings with them or his conduct in relation to
    his business or financial affairs, and to deliver the document or a copy thereof to
    the [. . .] trustee for further examination by him.

47   Conduct of examination
    (1)   The examination, whether before the sheriff or an examining commissioner,
    shall be taken on oath.
    (2)   At the examination—
        (a)   the [. . .] trustee or a solicitor or counsel acting on his behalf and, in the
    case of public examination, any creditor may question the debtor or a relevant
    person; and
        (b)   the debtor may question a relevant person,
    as to any matter relating to the debtor's assets, his dealings with them or his con-
    duct in relation to his business or financial affairs.
    (3)   The debtor or a relevant person shall be required to answer any question
    relating to the debtor's assets, his dealings with them or his conduct in relation to
    his business or financial affairs and shall not be excused from answering any such
    question on the ground that the answer may incriminate or tend to incriminate
    him or on the ground of confidentiality:
        Provided that—
        (a)   a statement made by the debtor or a relevant person in answer to such a
    question shall not be admissible in evidence in any subsequent criminal
    proceedings against the person making the statement, except where the pro-
    ceedings are in respect of a charge of perjury relating to the statement;
        (b)   a person subject to examination shall not be required to disclose any
    information which he has received from a person who is not called for
    examination if the information is confidential between them.
    (4)   [The rules relating to the recording of evidence in ordinary causes specified
    in the First Schedule to the Sheriff Courts (Scotland) Act 1907] shall apply in re-
    lation to the recording of evidence at the examination before the sheriff or the
    examining commissioner.
    (5)   The debtor's deposition at the examination shall be subscribed by himself
    and by the sheriff (or, as the case may be, the examining commissioner) and shall
    be inserted in the sederunt book.
    (6)   The [. . .] trustee shall insert a copy of the record of the examination

in the sederunt book and send a copy of the record to the Accountant in Bankruptcy.

(7) A relevant person shall be entitled to fees or allowances in respect of his attendance at the examination as if he were a witness in an ordinary civil cause in the sheriff court:

Provided that, if the sheriff thinks that it is appropriate in all the circumstances, he may disallow or restrict the entitlement to such fees or allowances.

Submission and adjudication of claims

48 [Submission of claims to trustee]

(1) Subject to subsection (2) below and subsections (8) and (9) of section 52 of this Act, a creditor in order to obtain an adjudication as to his entitlement—

(a) to vote at a meeting of creditors other than the statutory meeting; or

(b) (so far as funds are available), to a dividend out of the debtor's estate in respect of any accounting period,

shall submit a claim in accordance with this section to the [. . .] trustee respectively—

(i) at or before the meeting; or

(ii) not later than 8 weeks before the end of the accounting period.

(2) A claim submitted by a creditor—

(a) under section 22 of this Act and accepted in whole or in part by the [. . .] trustee for the purpose of voting at the statutory meeting; or

(b) under this section [which has not been rejected in whole],

shall be deemed to have been re-submitted for the purpose of obtaining an adjudication as to his entitlement both to vote at any subsequent meeting and (so far as funds are available) to a dividend in respect of an accounting period, or, as the case may be, any subsequent accounting period.

(3) Subsections (2) and (3) of section 22 of this Act shall apply for the purposes of this section but as if in the proviso to subsection (2) [after the word 'trustee' there were inserted the words] 'with the consent of the commissioners, if any' [. . .].

(4) A creditor who has submitted a claim under this section (or under section 22 of this Act, a statement of claim which has been deemed re-submitted as mentioned in subsection (2) above) may at any time submit a further claim under this section specifying a different amount for his claim:

Provided that a secured creditor shall not be entitled to produce a further claim specifying a different value for the security at any time after the [. . .] trustee requires the creditor to discharge, or convey or assign, the security under paragraph 5(2) of Schedule 1 to this Act.

(5) The [. . .] trustee, for the purpose of satisfying himself as to the validity or amount of a claim submitted by a creditor under this section, may require—

(a) the creditor to produce further evidence; or

(b) any other person who he believes can produce relevant evidence, to produce such evidence,

and, if the creditor or other person refuses or delays to do so, the [. . .] trustee may apply to the sheriff for an order requiring the creditor or other person to attend for his private examination before the sheriff.

(6) Sections 44(2) and (3) and 47(1) of this Act shall apply, subject to any necessary modifications, to the examination of the creditor or other person as they apply to the examination of a relevant person; and references in this subsection and subsection (5) above to a creditor in a case where the creditor is an entity mentioned in section 6(1) of this Act shall be construed, unless the context otherwise requires, as references to a person representing the entity.

(7) Subsections (5) to (10) of section 22 of this Act shall apply for the purposes of this section but as if—

[. . .]

(b)   in subsection (7) for the words [. . .] 'keep a record of it' there were substituted [. . .] the words [. . .] 'make an insertion relating thereto in the sederunt book'.

(8)   At any private examination under subsection (5) above, a solicitor or counsel may act on behalf of the [. . .] trustee or he may appear himself.

49   Adjudication of claims

(1)   At the commencement of every meeting of creditors (other than the statutory meeting), the [. . .] trustee shall, for the purposes of section 50 of this Act so far as it relates to voting at that meeting, accept or reject the claim of each creditor.

(2)   Where funds are available for payment of a dividend out of the debtor's estate in respect of an accounting period, the [. . .] trustee for the purpose of determining who is entitled to such a dividend shall, not later than 4 weeks before the end of the period, accept or reject every claim submitted or deemed to have been re-submitted to him under this Act; and shall at the same time make a decision on any matter requiring to be specified under paragraph (a) or (b) of subsection (5) below.

[(2A)   On accepting or rejecting, under subsection (2) above, every claim submitted or deemed to have been re-submitted, the trustee shall, as soon as is reasonably practicable, send a list of every claim so accepted or rejected (including the amount of each claim and whether he has accepted or rejected it) to—
  (a)   the debtor; and
  (b)   every creditor known to the trustee.]

(3)   If the amount of a claim is stated in foreign currency the [. . .] trustee in adjudicating on the claim under subsection (1) or (2) above shall convert the amount into sterling, in such manner as may be prescribed, at the rate of exchange prevailing at the close of business on the date of sequestration.

(4)   Where the [. . .] trustee rejects a claim, he shall forthwith notify the creditor giving reasons for the rejection.

(5)   Where the [. . .] trustee accepts or rejects a claim, he shall record in the sederunt book his decision on the claim specifying—
  (a)   the amount of the claim accepted by him,
  (b)   the category of debt, and the value of any security, as decided by him, and
  (c)   if he is rejecting the claim, his reasons therefor.

(6)   The debtor [(subject to subsection (6A) below)] of any creditor may, if dissatisfied with the acceptance or rejection of any claim (or, in relation to such acceptance or rejection, with a decision in respect of any matter requiring to be specified under subsection (5)(a) or (b) above), appeal therefrom to the sheriff—
  (a)   if the acceptance or rejection is under subsection (1) above, within 2 weeks of that acceptance or rejection;
  (b)   if the acceptance or rejection is under subsection (2) above, not later than 2 weeks before the end of the accounting period,
and the [. . .] trustee shall record the sheriff's decision in the sederunt book.

[(6A)   A debtor may appeal under subsection (6) above if, and only if, he satisfies the sheriff that he has, or is likely to have, a pecuniary interest in the outcome of the appeal.]

(7)   Any reference in this section to the acceptance or rejection of a claim shall be construed as a reference to the acceptance or rejection of the claim in whole or in part.

Entitlement to vote and draw dividend

50   Entitlement to vote and draw dividend

[(1)]   A creditor who has had his claim accepted in whole or in part by the [. . .] trustee or on appeal under subsection (6) of section 49 of this Act shall be entitled—

(a)   subject to sections 29(1)(a) and 30(1) and (4)(b) of this Act, in a case where the acceptance is under (or on appeal arising from) subsection (1) of the said section 49, to vote on any matter at the meeting of creditors for the purpose of voting at which the claim is accepted; and

(b)   in a case where the acceptance is under (or on appeal arising from) subsection (2) of the said section 49, to payment out of the debtor's estate of a dividend in respect of the accounting period for the purposes of which the claim is accepted; but such entitlement to payment shall arise only in so far as that estate has funds available to make that payment, having regard to section 51 of this Act.

[(2)   No vote shall be cast by virtue of a debt more than once on any resolution put to a meeting of creditors.

(3)   Where a creditor—

(a)   is entitled to vote under this section;

(b)   has lodged his claim in one or more sets of other proceedings; and

(c)   votes (either in person or by proxy) on a resolution put to the meeting, only the creditor's vote shall be counted.

(4)   Where—

(a)   a creditor has lodged his claim in more than one set of other proceedings; and

(b)   more than one member State liquidator seeks to vote by virtue of that claim,

the entitlement to vote by virtue of that claim is exercisable by the member State liquidator in main proceedings, whether or not the creditor has lodged his claim in the main proceedings.

(5)   For the purposes of subsections (3) and (4) above, 'other proceedings' means main proceedings, secondary proceedings or territorial proceedings in a member State other than the United Kingdom.]

Distribution of debtor's estate

51   Order of priority in distribution

(1)   The funds of the debtor's estate shall be distributed by the [. . .] trustee to meet the following debts in the order in which they are mentioned—

(a)   the outlays and remuneration of the interim trustee in the administration of the debtor's estate;

(b)   the outlays and remuneration of the [. . .] trustee in the administration of the debtor's estate;

(c)   where the debtor is a deceased debtor, deathbed and funeral expenses reasonably incurred and expenses reasonably incurred in administering the deceased's estate;

(d)   the expenses reasonably incurred by a creditor who is a petitioner, or concurs in [a debtor application], for sequestration;

(e)   preferred debts (excluding any interest which has accrued thereon to the date of sequestration);

(f)   ordinary debts, that is to say a debt which is neither a secured debt nor a debt mentioned in any other paragraph of this subsection;

(g)   interest at the rate specified in subsection (7) below on—

(i)   the preferred debts;

(ii)   the ordinary debts,

between the date of sequestration and the date of payment of the debt;

(h)   any postponed debt.

(2)   In this Act 'preferred debt' means a debt listed in Part I of Schedule 3 to this Act; and Part II of that Schedule shall have effect for the interpretation of the said Part I.

(3)   In this Act 'postponed debt' means—

(a)   a loan made to the debtor, in consideration of a share of the profits in his business, which is postponed under section 3 of the Partnership Act 1890 to the claims of other creditors;

(b)   a loan made to the debtor by the debtor's spouse [or civil partner];

(c)   a creditor's right to anything vesting in the [. . .] trustee by virtue of a successful challenge under section 34 of this Act or to the proceeds of sale of such a thing.

(4)   Any debt falling within any of paragraphs (c) to (h) of subsection (1) above shall have the same priority as any other debt falling within the same paragraph and, where the funds of the estate are inadequate to enable the debts mentioned in the paragraph to be paid in full, they shall abate in equal proportions.

(5)   Any surplus remaining, after all the debts mentioned in this section have been paid in full, shall be made over to the debtor or to his successors or assignees; and in this subsection 'surplus' includes any kind of estate but does not include any unclaimed dividend.

[(5A)   Subsection (5) above is subject to Article 35 of the EC Regulation (surplus in secondary proceedings to be transferred to main proceedings).]

(6)   Nothing in this section shall affect—

(a)   the right of a secured creditor which is preferable to the rights of the [. . .] trustee; or

(b)   any preference of the holder of a lien over a title deed or other document which has been delivered to the [. . .] trustee in accordance with a requirement under section 38(4) of this Act.

(7)   The rate of interest referred to in paragraph (g) of subsection (1) above shall be whichever is the greater of—

(a)   the prescribed rate at the date of sequestration; and

(b)   the rate applicable to that debt apart from the sequestration.

52   Estate to be distributed in respect of accounting periods

[(1)   The [. . .] trustee shall make up accounts of his intromissions with the debtor's estate in respect of each accounting period.

(2)   In this Act 'accounting period' shall be construed as follows—

(a)   [subject to subsection (2ZA) below,] the first accounting period shall be the period of 6 months beginning with the date [on which sequestration is awarded]; and

(b)   any subsequent accounting period shall be the period of 6 months beginning with the end of the last accounting period; except that—

(i)   in a case where the Accountant in Bankruptcy is not the [. . .] trustee, the [. . .] trustee and the commissioners or, if there are no commissioners, the Accountant in Bankruptcy agree; or

(ii)   in a case where the Accountant in Bankruptcy is the [. . .] trustee, he determines,

that the accounting period shall be such other period beginning with the end of the last accounting period as may be agreed or, as the case may be determined, it shall be that other period.]

[(2ZA)   Where the trustee was appointed under section 2(5) of this Act as interim trustee in the sequestration, the first accounting period shall be the period beginning with the date of his appointment as interim trustee and ending on the date 12 months after the date on which sequestration is awarded.]

[(2A)   An agreement or determination under subsection (2)(b)(i) or (ii) above—

(a)   may be made in respect of one or more than one accounting period;

(b)   may be made before the beginning of the accounting period in relation to which it has effect and, in any event, shall not have effect unless made before the day on which such accounting period would, but for the agreement or determination, have ended;

(c)   may provide for different accounting periods to be of different durations,

and shall be recorded in the sederunt book by the [. . .] trustee.]

(3)   Subject to the following provisions of this section, the [. . .] trustee shall, if

the funds of the debtor's estate are sufficient and after making allowance for future contingencies, pay under section 53(7) of this Act a dividend out of the estate to the creditors in respect of each accounting period.

(4) The [. . .] trustee may pay—

(a) the debts mentioned in subsection (1)(a) to (d) of section 51 of this Act, other than his own remuneration, at any time;

(b) the preferred debts at any time but only with the consent of the commissioners or, if there are no commissioners, of the Accountant in Bankruptcy.

(5) If the [. . .] trustee—

(a) is not ready to pay a dividend in respect of an accounting period; or

(b) considers it would be inappropriate to pay such a dividend because the expense of doing so would be disproportionate to the amount of the dividend,

he may, with the consent of the commissioners, or if there are no commissioners of the Accountant in Bankruptcy, postpone such payment to a date not later than the time for payment of a dividend in respect of the next accounting period.

[. . .]

(7) Where an appeal is taken under section 49(6)(b) of this Act against the acceptance or rejection of a creditor's claim, the [. . .] trustee shall, at the time of payment of dividends and until the appeal is determined, set aside an amount which would be sufficient, if the determination in the appeal were to provide for the claim being accepted in full, to pay a dividend in respect of that claim.

(8) Where a creditor—

(a) has failed to produce evidence in support of his claim earlier than 8 weeks before the end of an accounting period on being required by the [. . .] trustee to do so under section 48(5) of this Act; and

(b) has given a reason for such failure which is acceptable to the [. . .] trustee,

the [. . .] trustee shall set aside, for such time as is reasonable to enable him to produce that evidence or any other evidence that will enable the [. . .] trustee to be satisfied under the said section 48(5), an amount which would be sufficient, if the claim were accepted in full, to pay a dividend in respect of that claim.

(9) Where a creditor submits a claim to the [. . .] trustee later than 8 weeks before the end of an accounting period but more than 8 weeks before the end of a subsequent accounting period in respect of which, after making allowance for contingencies, funds are available for the payment of a dividend, the [. . .] trustee shall, if he accepts the claim in whole or in part, pay to the creditor—

(a) the same dividend or dividends as has or have already been paid to creditors of the same class in respect of any accounting period or periods; and

(b) whatever dividend may be payable to him in respect of the said subsequent accounting period:

Provided that paragraph (a) above shall be without prejudice to any dividend which has already been paid.

[(10) In the declaration of and payment of a dividend, no payments shall be made more than once by virtue of the same debt.

(11) Any dividend paid in respect of a claim should be paid to the creditor.]

53 Procedure after end of accounting period

(1) Within 2 weeks after the end of an accounting period, the [. . .] trustee shall in respect of that period submit to the commissioners or, if there are no commissioners, to the Accountant in Bankruptcy—

(a) his accounts of his intromissions with the debtor's estate for audit and, where funds are available after making allowance for contingencies, a scheme of division of the divisible funds; and

(b) a claim for the outlays reasonably incurred by him and for his remuneration;

and, where the said documents are submitted to the commissioners, he shall send a copy of them to the Accountant in Bankruptcy.

[(2) Subject to subsection (2A) below, all accounts in respect of legal services incurred by the [. . .] trustee shall, before payment thereof by him, be submitted for taxation to the auditor of the court before which the sequestration is pending.]

[(2A)   Where—

(a)   any such account has been agreed between the [. . .] trustee and the person entitled to payment in respect of that account (in this subsection referred to as 'the payee');

(b)   the [. . .] trustee is not an associate of the payee; and

(c)   the commissioners [or, if there are no commissioners, the Accountant in Bankruptcy, have determined that the account need not] be submitted for taxation,

the [. . .] trustee may pay such account without submitting it for taxation.]

(3)   Within 6 weeks after the end of an accounting period—

(a)   the commissioners or, as the case may be, the Accountant in Bankruptcy—

(i)   [may] audit the accounts; and

(ii)   [shall] issue a determination fixing the amount of the outlays and the remuneration payable to the [. . .] trustee; and

(b)   the [. . .] trustee shall make the audited accounts, scheme of division and the said determination available for inspection by the debtor and the creditors.

(4)   The basis for fixing the amount of the remuneration payable to the [. . .] trustee may be a commission calculated by reference to the value of the debtor's estate which has been realised by the [. . .] trustee, but there shall in any event be taken into account—

(a)   the work which, having regard to that value, was reasonably undertaken by him; and

(b)   the extent of his responsibilities in administering the debtor's estate.

(5)   In fixing the amount of such remuneration in respect of [any] accounting period, the commissioners or, as the case may be, the Accountant in Bankruptcy may take into account any adjustment which the commissioners or the Accountant in Bankruptcy may wish to make in the amount of the remuneration fixed in respect of any earlier accounting period.

(6)   Not later than 8 weeks after the end of an accounting period, the [. . .] trustee, the debtor [(subject to subsection (6A) below)] or any creditor may appeal against a determination issued under subsection (3)(a)(ii) above—

(a)   where it is a determination of the commissioners, to the Accountant in Bankruptcy; and

(b)   where it is a determination of the Accountant in Bankruptcy, to the sheriff;

and the determination of the Accountant in Bankruptcy under paragraph (a) above shall be appealable to the sheriff [and the decision of the sheriff on such an appeal shall be final].

[(6A)   A debtor may appeal under subsection (6) above if, and only if, he satisfies the Accountant in Bankruptcy or, as the case may be, the sheriff that he has, or is likely to have, a pecuniary interest in the outcome of the appeal.

(6B)   Before—

(a)   a debtor; or

(b)   a creditor,

appeals under subsection (6) above, he must give notice to the trustee of his intention to appeal.]

(7)   On the expiry of the period within which an appeal may be taken under subsection (6) above or, if an appeal is so taken, on the final determination of the last such appeal, the [. . .] trustee shall pay to the creditors their dividends in accordance with the scheme of division.

(8)   Any dividend—
    (a)   allocated to a creditor which is not cashed or uplifted; or
    (b)   dependent on a claim in respect of which an amount has been set aside
under subsection (7) or (8) of section 52 of this Act,
shall be deposited by the [. . .] trustee in an appropriate bank or institution.
(9)   If a creditor's claim is revalued, the [. . .] trustee may—
    (a)   in paying any dividend to that creditor, make such adjustment to it as he
considers necessary to take account of that revaluation; or
    (b)   require the creditor to repay to him the whole or part of a dividend
already paid to him.
(10)   The [. . .] trustee shall insert in the sederunt book the audited accounts, the
scheme of division and the final determination in relation to the [. . .] trustee's outlays and remuneration.

[53A   Modification of procedure under section 53 where Accountant in Bankruptcy is trustee

(1)   In any case where the Accountant in Bankruptcy is the trustee, section 53 of
this Act shall have effect subject to the following modifications.
(2)   For subsections (1) to (7) of that section, there shall be substituted—

'(1)   At the end of each accounting period, the Accountant in Bankruptcy shall
prepare accounts of his intromissions with the debtor's estate and he shall make
a determination of his fees and outlays calculated in accordance with regulations
made under section 69A of this Act.
(2)   Such accounts and determination shall be available for inspection by the
debtor and the creditors not later than 6 weeks after the end of the accounting
period to which they relate.
(3)   In making a determination as mentioned in subsection (1) above, the
Accountant in Bankruptcy may take into account any adjustment which he may
wish to make in the amount of his remuneration fixed in respect of any earlier
accounting period.
(4)   Not later than 8 weeks after the end of an accounting period, the debtor
(subject to subsection (5) below) or any creditor may appeal to the sheriff against
the determination of the Accountant in Bankruptcy; and the decision of the
sheriff on such an appeal shall be final.
(5)   A debtor may appeal under subsection (4) above if, and only if, he
satisfies the sheriff that he has, or is likely to have, a pecuniary interest in the
outcome of the appeal.
(6)   Before—
    (a)   a debtor; or
    (b)   any creditor,
appeals under subsection (4) above, he must give notice to the Accountant in
Bankruptcy of his intention to appeal.
(7)   On the expiry of the period within which an appeal may be made under
subsection (4) above, the Accountant in Bankruptcy shall pay to the creditors
their dividends in accordance with the scheme of division.'
(3)   In subsection (10) for the words 'the audited' there shall be substituted the
word 'his'.]

Discharge of debtor

54   Automatic discharge [of debtor]

(1)   Subject to the following provisions of this section, the debtor shall be discharged on the expiry of [1 year] from the date of sequestration.
(2)   Every debtor who has been discharged under or by virtue of this
section or section 75(4) of this Act may apply to the Accountant in Bankruptcy for a certificate that he has been so discharged; and the Accountant in

Bankruptcy, if satisfied of such discharge, shall grant a certificate of discharge in the prescribed form.

(3)   The [. . .] trustee or any creditor may, not later than [. . .] 9 months after the date of sequestration, apply to the sheriff for a deferment of the debtor's discharge by virtue of subsection (1) above.

(4)   On an application being made to him under subsection (3) above, the sheriff shall order—

> (a)   the applicant to serve the application on the debtor and (if he is not himself the applicant and is not discharged) the [. . .] trustee; and
>
> (b)   the debtor to lodge in court a declaration—
>
> > (i)   that he has made a full and fair surrender of his estate and a full disclosure of all claims which he is entitled to make against other persons; and
> >
> > (ii)   that he has delivered to the [. . .] trustee every document under his control relating to his estate or his business or financial affairs;

and, if the debtor fails to lodge such a declaration in court within 14 days of being required to do so, the sheriff shall defer his discharge without a hearing for a period not exceeding 2 years.

(5)   If the debtor lodges the declaration in court within the said period of 14 days, the sheriff shall—

> (a)   fix a date for a hearing not earlier than 28 days after the date of the lodging of the declaration; and
>
> (b)   order the applicant to notify the debtor and the [. . .] trustee or (if he has been discharged) the Accountant in Bankruptcy of the date of the hearing;

and the [. . .] trustee or (if he has been discharged) the Accountant in Bankruptcy shall, not later than 7 days before the date fixed under paragraph (a) above, lodge in court a report upon the debtor's assets and liabilities, his financial and business affairs and his conduct in relation thereto and upon the sequestration and his conduct in the course of it.

(6)   After considering at the hearing any representations made by the applicant, the debtor or any creditor, the sheriff shall make an order either deferring the discharge for such period not exceeding 2 years as he thinks appropriate or dismissing the application:

Provided that the applicant or the debtor may appeal against an order under this subsection within 14 days after it is made.

(7)   Where the discharge is deferred under subsection (4) or (6) above, the clerk of the court shall send—

> (a)   a certified copy of the order of the sheriff deferring discharge to the keeper of the register of inhibitions and adjudications for recording in that register; and
>
> (b)   a copy of such order to—
>
> > (i)   the Accountant in Bankruptcy; and
> >
> > (ii)   the [. . .] trustee (if not discharged) for insertion in the sederunt book.

(8)   A debtor whose discharge has been deferred under subsection (4) or (6) above may, at any time thereafter and provided that he lodges in court a declaration as to the matters mentioned in sub-paragraphs (i) and (ii) of paragraph (b) of the said subsection (4), petition the sheriff for his discharge; and subsections (5) to (7) above shall, with any necessary modifications, apply in relation to the proceedings which shall follow the lodging of a declaration under this subsection as they apply in relation to the proceedings which follow the timeous lodging of a declaration under the said paragraph (b).

(9)   The [. . .] trustee or any creditor may, not later than 3 months before the end of a period of deferment, apply to the sheriff for a further deferment of the discharge; and subsections (4) to (8) above and this subsection shall apply in relation to that further deferment.

55 Effect of discharge under section 54

(1)   Subject to [subsections (2) and (3)] below, on the debtor's discharge under section 54 of this Act, the debtor shall be discharged within the United Kingdom of all debts and obligations contracted by him, or for which he was liable, at the date of sequestration.

(2)   The debtor shall not be discharged by virtue of subsection (1) above from—

(a)   any liability to pay a fine or other penalty due to the Crown;

[(aa)   any liability to pay a fine imposed on a district court;

(ab)   any liability under a compensation order within the meaning of section 249 of the Criminal Procedure (Scotland) Act 1995;]

(b)   any liability to forfeiture of a sum of money deposited in court under section 1(3) of the Bail etc (Scotland) Act 1980;

(c)   any liability incurred by reason of fraud or breach of trust;

(d)   any obligation to pay aliment or any sum of an alimentary nature under any enactment or rule of law or any periodical allowance payable on divorce by virtue of a court order or under an obligation, not—

(i)   being aliment or a periodical allowance which could be included in the amount of a creditor's claim under paragraph 2 of Schedule 1 to this Act; [or

(ii)   child support maintenance within the meaning of the Child Support Act 1991 which was unpaid in respect of any period before the date of sequestration of—(aa) any person by whom it was due to be paid; or (bb) any employer by whom it was, or was due to be, deducted under section 31(5) of that Act].

(e)   the obligation imposed on him by section 64 of this Act.

[(2A)   In subsection (2)(a) above the reference to a fine or other penalty due to the Crown includes a reference to a confiscation order made under Part 2, 3 or 4 of the Proceeds of Crime Act 2002.]

[(3)   The discharge of the debtor under the said section 54 shall not affect any right of a secured creditor—

(a)   for a debt in respect of which the debtor has been discharged to enforce his security for payment of the debt and any interest due and payable on the debt until the debt is paid in full; or

(b)   for an obligation in respect of which the debtor has been discharged to enforce his security in respect of the obligation.]

56 Discharge on composition

Schedule 4 to this Act shall have effect in relation to an offer of composition by or on behalf of the debtor to the [. . .] trustee in respect of his debts and his discharge and the discharge of the [. . .] trustee where the offer is approved.

[Bankruptcy restrictions orders and undertakings]

[56A Bankruptcy restrictions order

(1)   Where sequestration of a living debtor's estate is awarded, an order (known as a 'bankruptcy restrictions order') in respect of the debtor may be made by the sheriff.

(2)   An order may be made only on the application of the Accountant in Bankruptcy.]

[56B Grounds for making order

(1)   The sheriff shall grant an application for a bankruptcy restrictions order if he thinks it appropriate having regard to the conduct of the debtor (whether before or after the date of sequestration).

(2)   The sheriff shall, in particular, take into account any of the following kinds of behaviour on the part of the debtor—

(a)   failing to keep records which account for a loss of property by the debtor, or by a business carried on by him, where the loss occurred in the period beginning 2 years before the date of presentation of the petition for sequestration or, as the case may be, the date the debtor application was made and ending with the date of the application for a bankruptcy restrictions order;

    (b)   failing to produce records of that kind on demand by—

        (i)   the Accountant in Bankruptcy;

        (ii)   the interim trustee; or

        (iii)   the trustee;

    (c)   making a gratuitous alienation or any other alienation for no consideration or for no adequate consideration which a creditor has, under any rule of law, right to challenge;

    (d)   creating an unfair preference or any other preference which a creditor has, under any rule of law, right to challenge;

    (e)   making an excessive pension contribution;

    (f)   failing to supply goods or services which were wholly or partly paid for which gave rise to a claim submitted by a creditor under section 22 or 48 of this Act;

    (g)   trading at a time before the date of sequestration when the debtor knew or ought to have known that he was to be unable to meet his debts;

    (h)   incurring, before the date of sequestration, a debt which the debtor had no reasonable expectation of being able to pay;

    (j)   failing to account satisfactorily to—

        (i)   the sheriff;

        (ii)   the Accountant in Bankruptcy;

        (iii)   the interim trustee; or

        (iv)   the trustee,

for a loss of property or for an insufficiency of property to meet his debts;

    (k)   carrying on any gambling, speculation or extravagance which may have materially contributed to or increased the extent of his debts or which took place between the date of presentation of the petition for sequestration or, as the case may be, the date the debtor application was made and the date on which sequestration is awarded;

    (l)   neglect of business affairs of a kind which may have materially contributed to or increased the extent of his debts;

    (m)   fraud or breach of trust;

    (n)   failing to co-operate with—

        (i)   the Accountant in Bankruptcy;

        (ii)   the interim trustee; or

        (iii)   the trustee.

(3)   The sheriff shall also, in particular, consider whether the debtor—

    (a)   has previously been sequestrated; and

    (b)   remained undischarged from that sequestration at any time during the period of 5 years ending with the date of the sequestration to which the application relates.

(4)   For the purposes of subsection (2) above—

'excessive pension contribution' shall be construed in accordance with section 36A of this Act; and

'gratuitous alienation' means an alienation challengeable under section 34(1) of this Act.]

[56C Application of section 67(9)

(1)   Where the sheriff thinks it appropriate, the sheriff may specify in the bankruptcy restrictions order that subsection (9) of section 67 of this Act shall apply to the debtor during the period he is subject to the order as if he were a debtor within the meaning of subsection (10)(a) of that section.

(2)   For the purposes of subsection (1) above, section 67(10) of this Act shall have effect as if, for paragraph (c) of that subsection, there were substituted—

'(c)   the relevant information about the status of the debtor is the information that—

(i)   he is subject to a bankruptcy restrictions order; or

(ii)   where his estate has been sequestrated and he has not been discharged, that fact.'.]

[56D   Timing of application for order

(1)   An application for a bankruptcy restrictions order must be made, subject to subsection (2) below, within the period beginning with the date of sequestration and ending with the date on which the debtor's discharge becomes effective.

(2)   An application may be made after the end of the period referred to in subsection (1) above only with the permission of the sheriff.]

[56E   Duration of order and application for annulment

(1)   A bankruptcy restrictions order—

(a)   shall come into force when it is made; and

(b)   shall cease to have effect at the end of the date specified in the order.

(2)   The date specified in a bankruptcy restrictions order under subsection (1)(b) above must not be—

(a)   before the end of the period of 2 years beginning with the date on which the order is made; or

(b)   after the end of the period of 15 years beginning with that date.

(3)   On an application by the debtor the sheriff may—

(a)   annul a bankruptcy restrictions order; or

(b)   vary such an order, including providing for such an order to cease to have effect at the end of a date earlier than the date specified in the order under subsection (1)(b) above.]

[56F   Interim bankruptcy restrictions order

(1)   This section applies at any time between—

(a)   the making of an application for a bankruptcy restrictions order; and

(b)   the determination of the application.

(2)   The sheriff may make an interim bankruptcy restrictions order if he thinks that—

(a)   there are prima facie grounds to suggest that the application for the bankruptcy restrictions order will be successful; and

(b)   it is in the public interest to make an interim order.

(3)   An interim order may be made only on the application of the Accountant in Bankruptcy.

(4)   An interim order—

(a)   shall have the same effect as a bankruptcy restrictions order; and

(b)   shall come into force when it is made.

(5)   An interim order shall cease to have effect—

(a)   on the determination of the application for the bankruptcy restrictions order;

(b)   on the acceptance of a bankruptcy restrictions undertaking made by the debtor; or

(c)   if the sheriff discharges the interim order on the application of the Accountant in Bankruptcy or of the debtor.

(6)   Where a bankruptcy restrictions order is made in respect of a debtor who is subject to an interim order, section 56E(2) of this Act shall have effect in relation to the bankruptcy restrictions order as if the reference to the date on which the order is made were a reference to the date on which the interim order was made.]

[56G   Bankruptcy restrictions undertaking

(1)   A living debtor who is not subject to a bankruptcy restrictions order may offer an undertaking (known as a 'bankruptcy restrictions undertaking') to the Accountant in Bankruptcy.

(2)   In determining whether to accept a bankruptcy restrictions undertaking, the Accountant in Bankruptcy shall have regard to the matters specified in section 56B(2) and (3) of this Act.

(3)   A bankruptcy restrictions undertaking—

(a)   shall take effect on being accepted by the Accountant in Bankruptcy; and

(b)   shall cease to have effect at the end of the date specified in the undertaking.

(4)   The date specified under subsection (3)(b) above must not be—

(a)   before the end of the period of 2 years beginning with the date on which the undertaking is accepted; or

(b)   after the end of the period of 15 years beginning with that date.

(5)   On an application by the debtor the sheriff may—

(a)   annul a bankruptcy restrictions undertaking; or

(b)   vary such an undertaking, including providing for a bankruptcy restrictions undertaking to cease to have effect at the end of a date earlier than the date specified in the undertaking under subsection (3)(b) above.]

[56H   Bankruptcy restrictions undertakings: application of section 67(9)

(1)   A debtor may, with the agreement of the Accountant in Bankruptcy, specify in a bankruptcy restrictions undertaking that subsection (9) of section 67 of this Act shall apply to the debtor during the period the undertaking has effect as if he were a debtor within the meaning of subsection (10)(a) of that section.

(2)   For the purposes of subsection (1) above, section 67(10) of this Act shall have effect as if, for paragraph (c) of that subsection, there were substituted—

'(c)   the relevant information about the status of the debtor is the information that—

(i)   he is subject to a bankruptcy restrictions undertaking; or

(ii)   where his estate has been sequestrated and he has not been discharged, that fact.'.]

[56J   Effect of recall of sequestration

(1)   Where an award of sequestration of a debtor's estate is recalled under section 17(1) of this Act—

(a)   the sheriff may annul any bankruptcy restrictions order, interim bankruptcy restrictions order or bankruptcy restrictions undertaking which is in force in respect of the debtor;

(b)   no new bankruptcy restrictions order or interim order may be made in respect of the debtor; and

(c)   no new bankruptcy restrictions undertaking by the debtor may be accepted.

(2)   Where the sheriff refuses to annul a bankruptcy restrictions order, interim bankruptcy restrictions order or bankruptcy restrictions undertaking under subsection (1)(a) above the debtor may, no later than 28 days after the date on which the award of sequestration is recalled, appeal to the sheriff principal against such a refusal.

(3)   The decision of the sheriff principal on an appeal under subsection (2) above is final.]

[56K   Effect of discharge on approval of offer of composition

(1)   This section applies where a certificate of discharge is granted under paragraph 11(1) of Schedule 4 to this Act discharging a debtor.

(2)   Subject to sections 56E(3)(a), 56F(5)(c) and 56G(5)(a) of this Act, the debtor shall remain subject to any bankruptcy restrictions order, interim bankruptcy restrictions order or bankruptcy restrictions undertaking which is in force in respect of him.

(3)   The sheriff may make a bankruptcy restrictions order in relation to the debtor on an application made before the discharge.

(4)   The Accountant in Bankruptcy may accept a bankruptcy restrictions under-taking offered before the discharge.

(5)   No application for a bankruptcy restrictions order or interim order may be made in respect of the debtor.]]

Discharge of [. . .] trustee

57   Discharge of [. . .] trustee

(1)   After the [. . .] trustee has made a final division of the debtor's estate and has inserted his final audited accounts in the sederunt book, he—

(a)   shall deposit any unclaimed dividends and any unapplied balances in an appropriate bank or institution;

(b)   shall thereafter send to the Accountant in Bankruptcy the sederunt book, a copy of the audited accounts and a receipt for the deposit of the unclaimed dividends and unapplied balances; and

(c)   may at the same time as sending the said documents apply to the Accountant in Bankruptcy for a certificate of discharge.

(2)   The [. . .] trustee shall send notice of an application under subsection (1)(c) above to the debtor and to all the creditors known to the [. . .] trustee and shall inform the debtor and such creditors—

(a)   that they may make written representations relating to the application to the Accountant in Bankruptcy within a period of 14 days after such notification;

(b)   that the sederunt book is available for inspection at the office of the Accountant in Bankruptcy and contains the audited accounts of, and scheme of division in, the sequestration; and

(c)   of the effect mentioned in subsection (5) below.

(3)   On the expiry of the period mentioned in subsection (2)(a) above, the Accountant in Bankruptcy, after examining the documents sent to him and con-sidering any representations duly made to him, shall—

(a)   grant or refuse to grant the certificate of discharge; and

(b)   notify (in addition to the [. . .] trustee) the debtor and all creditors who have made such representations accordingly.

(4)   The [. . .] trustee, the debtor or any creditor who has made representations under subsection (2)(a) above, may within 14 days after the issuing of the deter-mination under subsection (3) above, appeal therefrom to the sheriff and if the sheriff determines that a certificate of discharge which has been refused should be granted he shall order the Accountant in Bankruptcy to grant it; and the sheriff clerk shall send a copy of the decree of the sheriff to the Accountant in Bankruptcy.

[(4A)   The decision of the sheriff on an appeal under subsection (4) above shall be final.]

(5)   The grant of a certificate of discharge under this section by the Accountant in Bankruptcy shall have the effect of discharging the [. . .] trustee from all liability (other than any liability arising from fraud) to the creditors or to the debtor in respect of any act or omission of the [. . .] trustee in exercising the functions con-ferred on him by this Act including, where he was also the interim trustee, the functions conferred on him as interim trustee.

(6)   Where a certificate of discharge is granted under this section, the Ac-countant in Bankruptcy shall make an appropriate entry in the register of insolven-cies and in the sederunt book.

(7)   Where the [. . .] trustee has died, resigned office or been removed from office, the provisions of this section shall, subject to any necessary modifications, apply in relation to that [. . .] trustee or, if he has died, to his executor as they apply to a [. . .] trustee who has made a final division of the debtor's estate in accordance with the foregoing provisions of this Act.

[(8)   This section does not apply in any case where the Accountant in Bank-ruptcy is the [. . .] trustee.]

58 Unclaimed dividends

(1) Any person, producing evidence of his right, may apply to the Accountant in Bankruptcy to receive a dividend deposited under section 57(1)(a) [or 58A(3)] of this Act, if the application is made not later than 7 years after the date of such deposit.

(2) If the Accountant in Bankruptcy is satisfied of the applicant's right to the dividend, he shall authorise the appropriate bank or institution to pay to the applicant the amount of that dividend and of any interest which has accrued thereon.

(3) The Accountant in Bankruptcy shall, at the expiry of 7 years from the date of deposit of any unclaimed dividend or unapplied balance under section 57(1)(a) [or 58A(3)] of this Act, hand over the deposit receipt or other voucher relating to such dividend or balance to the Secretary of State, who shall thereupon be entitled to payment of the amount due, principal and interest, from the bank or institution in which the deposit was made.

[58A Discharge of Accountant in Bankruptcy

(1) This section applies where the Accountant in Bankruptcy has acted as the [. . .] trustee in any sequestration [including, where the Accountant in Bankruptcy was the interim trustee, the functions of the interim trustee].

(2) After the Accountant in Bankruptcy has made a final division of the debtor's estate, he shall insert in the sederunt book—

    (a)   his final accounts of his intromissions (if any) with the debtor's estate;

    (b)   the scheme of division (if any); and

    (c)   a determination of his fees and outlays calculated in accordance with regulations made under section 69A of this Act.

(3) The Accountant in Bankruptcy shall deposit any unclaimed dividends and any unapplied balances in an appropriate bank or institution.

(4) The Accountant in Bankruptcy shall send to the debtor and to all creditors known to him—

    (a)   a copy of the determination mentioned in subsection (2)(c) above; and

    (b)   a notice in writing stating—

       (i) that the Accountant in Bankruptcy has commenced the procedure under this Act leading to discharge in respect of his actings as [. . .] trustee;

       (ii) that the sederunt book relating to the sequestration is available for inspection at such address as the Accountant in Bankruptcy may determine;

       (iii) that an appeal may be made to the sheriff under subsection (5) below; and

       (iv) the effect of subsection (7) below.

(5) The debtor and any creditor may appeal to the sheriff against—

    (a)   the determination of the Accountant in Bankruptcy mentioned in subsection (2)(c) above;

    (b)   the discharge of the Accountant in Bankruptcy in respect of his actings as [. . .] trustee; or

    (c)   both such determination and discharge.

(6) An appeal under subsection (5) above shall be made not more than 14 days after the issue of the notice mentioned in subsection (4)(b) above; and the decision of the sheriff on such an appeal shall be final.

(7) Where—

    (a)   the requirements of this section have been complied with; and

    (b)   no appeal to the sheriff is made under subsection (5) above or such an appeal is made but is refused as regards the discharge of the Accountant in Bankruptcy,

the Accountant in Bankruptcy shall be discharged from all liability (other than any liability arising from fraud) to the creditors or to the debtor in respect of any act or omission of the Accountant in Bankruptcy in exercising the functions of [. . .]

trustee in the sequestration [including, where the Accountant in Bankruptcy was the [. . .] trustee, the functions of the [. . .] trustee].

(8) Where the Accountant in Bankruptcy is discharged from all liability as mentioned in subsection (7) above, he shall make an entry in the sederunt book recording such discharge.]

[. . .]

Voluntary trust deeds for creditors

59 Voluntary trust deeds for creditors
Schedule 5 to this Act shall have effect in relation to trust deeds executed after the commencement of this section.

[59A Petition for conversion into sequestration
(1) Where a member State liquidator proposes to petition the [sheriff] for the conversion under Article 37 of the EC Regulation (conversion of earlier proceedings) of a protected trust deed into sequestration, an affidavit complying with section 59B of this Act must be prepared and sworn, and lodged in court in support of the petition.

(2) The petition and the affidavit required under subsection (1) above shall be served upon—
  (a) the debtor;
  (b) the trustee;
  (c) such other person as may be prescribed.]

[59B Contents of affidavit
(1) The affidavit shall—
  (a) state that main proceedings have been opened in relation to the debtor in a member State other than the United Kingdom;
  (b) state that the member State liquidator believes that the conversion of the trust deed into a sequestration would prove to be in the interests of the creditors in the main proceedings;
  (c) contain such other information the member State liquidator considers will be of assistance to the [sheriff]—
    (i) in deciding whether to make an order under section 59C; and
    (ii) if the [sheriff] were to do so, in considering the need for any consequential provision that would be necessary or desirable; and
  (d) contain any other matters as may be prescribed.
(2) An affidavit under this section shall be sworn by, or on behalf of, the member State liquidator.]

[59C Power of [sheriff]
(1) On hearing the petition for conversion of a trust deed into a sequestration the [sheriff] may make such order as [he] thinks fit.
(2) If the [sheriff] makes an order for conversion into sequestration the order may contain all such consequential provisions as the [sheriff] deems necessary or desirable.
  [(2A) The provisions of this Act shall apply to an order made by the sheriff under subsection (1) above as if it was a determination by the Accountant in Bankruptcy of a debtor application under section 12(1) of this Act and in relation to which the member State liquidator was a concurring creditor.]
(3) Where the [sheriff] makes an order for conversion into sequestration under subsection (1) above, any expenses properly incurred as expenses of the administration of the trust deed in question shall be a first charge on the debtor's estate.]]

Miscellaneous and supplementary

60   Liabilities and rights of co-obligants

(1)   Where a creditor has an obligant (in this section referred to as the 'co-obligant') bound to him along with the debtor for the whole or part of the debt, the co-obligant shall not be freed or discharged from his liability for the debt by reason of the discharge of the debtor or by virtue of the creditor's voting or drawing a dividend or assenting to, or not opposing—

  (a)   the discharge of the debtor; or

  (b)   any composition.

(2)   Where—

  (a)   a creditor has had a claim accepted in whole or in part; and

  (b)   a co-obligant holds a security over any part of the debtor's estate,

the co-obligant shall account to the [. . .] trustee so as to put the estate in the same position as if the co-obligant had paid the debt to the creditor and thereafter had had his claim accepted in whole or in part in the sequestration after deduction of the value of the security.

(3)   Without prejudice to any right under any rule of law of a co-obligant who has paid the debt, the co-obligant may require and obtain at his own expense from the creditor an assignation of the debt on payment of the amount thereof, and thereafter may in respect of that debt submit a claim, and vote and draw a dividend, if otherwise legally entitled to do so.

(4)   In this section a 'co-obligant' includes a cautioner.

[60A   Member State liquidator deemed creditor

For the purposes of this Act, and without prejudice to the generality of the right to participate referred to in paragraph 3 of Article 32 of the EC Regulation (exercise of creditors' rights) a member State liquidator appointed in relation to the debtor is deemed to be a creditor in the sum due to creditors in proceedings in relation to which he holds office.]

[60B   Trustee's duties concerning notices and copies of documents

(1)   This section applies where a member State liquidator has been appointed in relation to the debtor.

(2)   Where an interim [trustee or a] trustee is obliged to give notice to, or provide a copy of a document (including an order of court) to, the [sheriff] or the Accountant in Bankruptcy, the trustee shall give notice or provide copies, as appropriate, to the member State liquidator.

(3)   Subsection (2) above is without prejudice to the generality of the obligations imposed by Article 31 of the EC Regulation (duty to co-operate and communicate information).]

61   Extortionate credit transactions

(1)   This section applies where the debtor is or has been a party to a transaction for, or involving, the provision to him of credit and his estate is sequestrated.

(2)   The [sheriff] may, on the application of the [. . .] trustee, make an order with respect to the transaction if the transaction is or was extortionate and was not entered into more than three years before the date of sequestration.

(3)   For the purposes of this section a transaction is extortionate if, having regard to the risk accepted by the person providing the credit—

  (a)   the terms of it are or were such as to require grossly exorbitant payments to be made (whether unconditionally or in certain contingencies) in respect of the provision of the credit; or

  (b)   it otherwise grossly contravened ordinary principles of fair dealing; and

it shall be presumed, unless the contrary is proved, that a transaction with respect to which an application is made under this section is, or as the case may be was, extortionate.

(4)   An order under this section with respect to any transaction may contain such one or more of the following as the [sheriff] thinks fit—

(a)   provision setting aside the whole or part of any obligation created by the transaction;

(b)   provision otherwise varying the terms of the transaction or varying the terms on which any security for the purposes of the transaction is held;

(c)   provision requiring any person who is a party to the transaction to pay to the [. . .] trustee any sums paid to that person, by virtue of the transaction, by the debtor;

(d)   provision requiring any person to surrender to the [. . .] trustee any property held by him as security for the purposes of the transaction;

(e)   provision directing accounts to be taken between any persons.

(5)   Any sums or property required to be paid or surrendered to the [. . .] trustee in accordance with an order under this section shall vest in the [. . .] trustee.

(6)   [. . .] The powers conferred by this section shall be exercisable in relation to any transaction concurrently with any powers exercisable under this Act in relation to that transaction as a gratuitous alienation or unfair preference.

(7)   In this section 'credit' has the same meaning as in the said Act of 1974.

62   Sederunt book and other documents

(1)   Subject to subsection (2) below, whoever by virtue of this Act for the time being holds the sederunt book shall make it available for inspection at all reasonable hours by any interested person.

(2)   As regards any case in which the person on whom a duty is imposed by subsection (1) above is the Accountant in Bankruptcy, the Court of Session may by act of sederunt—

(a)   limit the period for which the duty is so imposed; and

(b)   prescribe conditions in accordance with which the duty shall be carried out.

(3)   Any entry in the sederunt book shall be sufficient evidence of the facts stated therein, except where it is founded on by the [. . .] trustee in his own interest.

(4)   Notwithstanding any provision of this Act, the [. . .] trustee shall not be bound to insert in the sederunt book any document of a confidential nature.

(5)   The [. . .] trustee shall not be bound to exhibit to any person other than a commissioner or the Accountant in Bankruptcy any document in his possession of a confidential nature.

(6)   An extract from the register of insolvencies bearing to be signed by the Accountant in Bankruptcy shall be sufficient evidence of the facts stated therein.

63   Power to cure defects in procedure

(1)   The sheriff may, on the application of any person having an interest—

(a)   if there has been a failure to comply with any requirement of this Act or any regulations made under it, make an order waiving any such failure and, so far as practicable, restoring any person prejudiced by the failure to the position he would have been in but for the failure;

(b)   if for any reason anything required or authorised to be done in, or in connection with, the sequestration process cannot be done, make such order as may be necessary to enable that thing to be done.

(2)   The sheriff, in an order under subsection (1) above, may impose such conditions, including conditions as to expenses, as he thinks fit and may—

(a)   authorise or dispense with the performance of any act in the sequestration process;

(b)   appoint as [. . .] trustee on the debtor's estate a person who would be eligible to be elected under section 24 of this Act, whether or not in place of an existing trustee;

(c)   extend or waive any time limit specified in or under this Act.

(3)   An application under subsection (1) above—

(a)   may at any time be remitted by the sheriff to the Court of Session, of his own accord or on an application by any person having an interest;

(b)   shall be so remitted, if the Court of Session so directs on an application by any such person,

if the sheriff or the Court of Session, as the case may be, considers that the remit is desirable because of the importance or complexity of the matters raised by the application.

(4)   The [. . .] trustee shall record in the sederunt book the decision of the sheriff or the Court of Session under this section.

64   Debtor to co-operate with [. . .] trustee

(1)   The debtor shall take every practicable step, and in particular shall execute any document, which may be necessary to enable the [. . .] trustee to perform the functions conferred on him by this Act.

(2)   If the sheriff, on the application of the [. . .] trustee, is satisfied that the debtor has failed—

(a)   to execute any document in compliance with subsection (1) above, he may authorise the sheriff clerk to do so; and the execution of a document by the sheriff clerk under this paragraph shall have the like force and effect in all respects as if the document had been executed by the debtor;

(b)   to comply in any other respect with subsection (1) above, he may order the debtor to do so.

(3)   If the debtor fails to comply with an order of the sheriff under subsection (2) above, he shall be guilty of an offence.

(4)   In this section 'debtor' includes a debtor discharged under this Act.

(5)   A person convicted of an offence under subsection (3) above shall be liable—

(a)   on summary conviction, to a fine not exceeding the statutory maximum or—

(i)   to imprisonment for a term not exceeding 3 months; or

(ii)   if he has previously been convicted of an offence inferring dishonest appropriation of property or an attempt at such appropriation, to imprisonment for a term not exceeding 6 months,

or (in the case of either sub-paragraph) to both such fine and such imprisonment; or

(b)   on conviction on indictment to a fine or to imprisonment for a term not exceeding 2 years or to both.

65   Arbitration and compromise

(1)   The [. . .] trustee may (but if there are commissioners only with the consent of the commissioners, the creditors or the [sheriff])—

(a)   refer to arbitration any claim or question of whatever nature which may arise in the course of the sequestration; or

(b)   make a compromise with regard to any claim of whatever nature made against or on behalf of the sequestrated estate;

and the decree arbitral or compromise shall be binding on the creditors and the debtor.

(2)   Where any claim or question is referred to arbitration under this section, the Accountant in Bankruptcy may vary any time limit in respect of which any procedure under this Act has to be carried out.

(3)   The [. . .] trustee shall insert a copy of the decree arbitral, or record the compromise, in the sederunt book.

66   Meetings of creditors and commissioners

Part I of Schedule 6 to this Act shall have effect in relation to meetings of creditors other than the statutory meeting; Part II of that Schedule shall have effect in relation to all meetings of creditors under this Act; and Part III of that Schedule shall have effect in relation to meetings of commissioners.

67 General offences by debtor etc

(1) A debtor who during the relevant period makes a false statement in relation to his assets or his business or financial affairs to any creditor or to any person concerned in the administration of his estate shall be guilty of an offence, unless he shows that he neither knew nor had reason to believe that his statement was false.

(2) A debtor, or other person acting in his interest whether with or without his authority, who during the relevant period destroys, damages, conceals [, disposes of] or removes from Scotland any part of the debtor's estate or any document relating to his assets or his business or financial affairs shall be guilty of an offence, unless the debtor or other person shows that he did not do so with intent to prejudice the creditors.

(3) A debtor who is absent from Scotland and who after the date of sequestration of his estate fails, when required by the court, to come to Scotland for any purpose connected with the administration of his estate, shall be guilty of an offence.

(4) A debtor, or other person acting in his interest whether with or without his authority, who during the relevant period falsifies any document relating to the debtor's assets or his business or financial affairs, shall be guilty of an offence, unless the debtor or other person shows that he had no intention to mislead the [. . .] trustee, a commissioner or any creditor.

(5) If a debtor whose estate is sequestrated—

(a) knows that a person has falsified any document relating to the debtor's assets or his business or financial affairs; and

(b) fails, within one month of the date of acquiring such knowledge, to report his knowledge to the [. . .] trustee,

he shall be guilty of an offence.

(6) A person who is absolutely insolvent and who during the relevant period transfers anything to another person for an inadequate consideration or grants any unfair preference to any of his creditors shall be guilty of an offence, unless the transferor or grantor shows that he did not do so with intent to prejudice the creditors.

(7) A debtor who is engaged in trade or business shall be guilty of an offence if at any time in the period of one year ending with the date of sequestration of his estate, he pledges or disposes of, otherwise than in the ordinary course of his trade or business, any property which he has obtained on credit and has not paid for unless he shows that he did not intend to prejudice his creditors.

[. . .]

(9) If a debtor, either alone or jointly with another person, obtains credit [—

(a) to the extent of £500 (or such other sum as may be prescribed) or more; or

(b) of any amount, where, at the time of obtaining credit, the debtor has debts amounting to £1,000 (or such other sum as may be prescribed) or more,] without giving the person from whom he obtained it the relevant information about his status he shall be guilty of an offence.

[(9A) For the purposes of calculating an amount of—

(a) credit mentioned in subsection (9) above; or

(b) debts mentioned in paragraph (b) of that subsection,

no account shall be taken of any credit obtained or, as the case may be, any liability for charges in respect of—

(i) any of the supplies mentioned in section 70(4) of this Act; and

(ii) any council tax within the meaning of section 99(1) of the Local Government Finance Act 1992 (c 14).]

(10)   For the purposes of subsection (9) above—
(a)   'debtor' means—
(i)   a debtor whose estate has been sequestrated,
(ii)   a person who has been adjudged bankrupt in England and Wales or Northern Ireland, [or
(iii)   a person subject to a bankruptcy restrictions order, or a bankruptcy restrictions undertaking, made in England or Wales,]
and who, in [the case mentioned in subparagraphs (i) or (ii) above], has not been discharged;
(b)   the reference to the debtor obtaining credit includes a reference to a case where goods are hired to him under a hire-purchase agreement or agreed to be sold to him under a conditional sale agreement; and
(c)   [the relevant information about the status of the debtor is the information that [—
(i)   his estate has been sequestrated and that he has not been discharged;
(ii)   he is an undischarged bankrupt in England and Wales or Northern Ireland; or
(iii)   he is subject to a bankruptcy restrictions order, or a bankruptcy restrictions undertaking, made in England or Wales, as the case may be.]
(11)   In this section—
(a)   'the relevant period' means the period commencing one year immediately before the date of sequestration of the debtor's estate and ending with his discharge;
(b)   references to intent to prejudice creditors shall include references to intent to prejudice an individual creditor.
[(11A)   A person shall be guilty of an offence under subsection (1), (2), (4), (5), (6) or (7) above if that person does or, as the case may be, fails to do, in any place in England and Wales or Northern Ireland, anything which would, if done or, as the case may be, not done in Scotland, be an offence under the subsection in question.]
(12)   A person convicted of any offence under this section shall be liable—
(a)   on summary conviction, to a fine not exceeding the statutory maximum or—
(i)   to imprisonment for a term not exceeding 3 months; or
(ii)   if he has previously been convicted of an offence inferring dishonest appropriation of property or an attempt at such appropriation, to imprisonment for a term not exceeding 6 months,
or (in the case of either sub-paragraph) to both such fine and such imprisonment; or
(b)   on conviction on indictment to a fine or—
(i)   in the case of an offence under subsection (1), (2), (4) or (7) above to imprisonment for a term not exceeding 5 years,
(ii)   in any other case to imprisonment for a term not exceeding 2 years,
or (in the case of either sub-paragraph) to both such fine and such imprisonment.

68   Summary proceedings

(1)   [Subject to subsection (1A) below] summary proceedings for an offence under this Act may be commenced at any time within the period of [12] months after the date on which evidence sufficient in the opinion of the Lord Advocate to justify the proceedings comes to his knowledge.
[(1A)   No such proceedings shall be commenced by virtue of this section more than three years after the commission of the offence.]
(2)   Subsection (3) of [section 136 of the Criminal Procedure (Scotland) Act 1995] (date of commencement of summary proceedings) shall have effect for the purposes of [this section] as it has effect for the purposes of that section.
(3)   For the purposes of subsection (1) above, a certificate of the Lord Advocate

as to the date on which the evidence in question came to his knowledge is conclusive evidence of the date on which it did so.

69 [Outlays of insolvency practitioner in actings as interim trustee or trustee]
The Secretary of State may, by regulations, provide for the premium (or a proportionate part thereof) of any bond of caution or other security required, for the time
being, to be given by an insolvency practitioner to be taken into account as part of
the outlays of the insolvency practitioner in his actings as an interim trustee or
[. . .] trustee.

[69A   Fees for the Accountant in Bankruptcy
The Secretary of State may prescribe—
(a)   the fees and outlays to be payable to the Accountant in Bankruptcy in
respect of the exercise of any of his functions under this Act [or the Insolvency
Act 1986];
(b)   the time and manner in which such fees and outlays are to be paid; and
(c)   the circumstances, if any, in which the Accountant in Bankruptcy may
allow exemption from payment or the remission or modification of payment of
any fees or outlays payable or paid to him.]

70   Supplies by utilities
(1)   This section applies where on any day ('the relevant day')—
(a)   sequestration is awarded in a case where [a debtor application was made],
(b)   a warrant is granted under section 12(2) of this Act in a case where the
petition was presented by a creditor or a trustee acting under a trust deed; or
(c)   the debtor grants a trust deed,
and in this section 'the office holder' means the interim trustee, the [. . .] trustee or
the trustee acting under a trust deed, as the case may be.
(2)   If a request falling within subsection (3) below is made for the giving after
the relevant day of any of the supplies mentioned in subsection (4) below, the
supplier—
(a)   may make it a condition of the giving of the supply that the office holder
personally guarantees the payment of any charges in respect of the supply; and
(b)   shall not make it a condition of the giving of the supply, or do anything
which has the effect of making it a condition of the giving of the supply, that
any outstanding charges in respect of a supply given to the debtor before the
relevant day are paid.
(3)   A request falls within this subsection if it is made—
(a)   by or with the concurrence of the office holder; and
(b)   for the purposes of any business which is or has been carried on by or on
behalf of the debtor.
(4)   The supplies referred to in subsection (2) above are—
(a)   [a [gas supplier] within the meaning of Part I of the Gas Act 1986];
(b)   a supply of electricity by [an electricity supplier] within the meaning of
Part I of the Electricity Act 1989;]
(c)   a supply of water by [Scottish Water];
[(d)   a supply of telecommunication services by a provider of a public
telecommunications service.
(5)   In subsection (4), 'communication services' do not include electronic communications services to the extent that they are used to broadcast or otherwise
transmit programme services (within the meaning of the Communications Act
2003).]

71   Edinburgh Gazette
The keeper of the Edinburgh Gazette shall, on each day of its publication, send a
free copy of it to—
(a)   the Accountant in Bankruptcy; and
(b)   the petition department of the Court of Session.

[71A Further duty of Accountant in Bankruptcy
The Accountant in Bankruptcy shall, on receiving any notice under section 109(1) of the Insolvency Act 1986 in relation to a community interest company, forward a copy of that notice to the Regulator of Community Interest Companies.]

[71B Disqualification provisions: power to make orders
  (1) The Scottish Ministers may make an order under this section in relation to a disqualification provision.
  (2) A 'disqualification provision' is a provision made by or under any enactment which disqualifies (whether permanently or temporarily and whether absolutely or conditionally) a relevant debtor or a class of relevant debtors from—
    (a) being elected or appointed to an office or position;
    (b) holding an office or position; or
    (c) becoming or remaining a member of a body or group.
  (3) In subsection (2) above, the reference to a provision which disqualifies a person conditionally includes a reference to a provision which enables him to be dismissed.
  (4) An order under subsection (1) above may repeal or revoke the disqualification provision.
  (5) An order under subsection (1) above may amend, or modify the effect of, the disqualification provision—
    (a) so as to reduce the class of relevant debtors to whom the disqualification provision applies;
    (b) so as to extend the disqualification provision to some or all individuals who are subject to a bankruptcy restrictions order;
    (c) so that the disqualification provision applies only to some or all individuals who are subject to a bankruptcy restrictions order;
    (d) so as to make the application of the disqualification provision wholly or partly subject to the discretion of a specified person, body or group.
  (6) An order by virtue of subsection (5)(d) above may provide for a discretion to be subject to—
    (a) the approval of a specified person or body;
    (b) appeal to a specified person, body, court or tribunal.
  (7) The Scottish Ministers may be specified for the purposes of subsection (5)(d) or (6)(a) or (b) above.
  (8) In this section—
'bankruptcy restrictions order' includes—
    (a) a bankruptcy restrictions undertaking;
    (b) a bankruptcy restrictions order made under paragraph 1 of Schedule 4A to the Insolvency Act 1986 (c 45); and
    (c) a bankruptcy restrictions undertaking entered into under paragraph 7 of that Schedule;
'relevant debtor' means a debtor—
    (a) whose estate has been sequestrated;
    (b) who has granted (or on whose behalf there has been granted) a trust deed;
    (c) who has been adjudged bankrupt by a court in England and Wales or in Northern Ireland; or
    (d) who, in England and Wales or in Northern Ireland, has made an agreement with his creditors for a composition in satisfaction of his debts or a scheme of arrangement of his affairs or for some other kind of settlement or arrangement.
  (9) An order under this section—
    (a) may make provision generally or for a specified purpose only;
    (b) may make different provision for different purposes; and
    (c) may make transitional, consequential or incidental provision.

(10)   An order under this section—
  (a)   shall be made by statutory instrument; and
  (b)   shall not be made unless a draft has been laid before and approved by a resolution of the Scottish Parliament.]

72   Regulations

[(1)   Subject to subsection (2) below] any power to make regulations under this Act shall be exercisable by statutory instrument subject to annulment in pursuance of a resolution of either House of Parliament; and the regulations may make different provision for different cases or classes of case.

[(2)   No regulations such as are mentioned in subsection (3) below may be made unless a draft of the statutory instrument containing the regulations has been laid before, and approved by a resolution of, the Scottish Parliament.

(3)   The regulations are—
  (a)   regulations made under—
      (i)   subsection (2B)(a) and (4) of section 5;
      (ii)   section 5A; and
  [(iia)   section 5B(5);]
      (iii)   section 39A(4),
  of this Act; and
  (b)   [. . .] regulations under paragraph 5 of Schedule 5 to this Act [. . .].]

[72ZA   Modification of regulation making powers

Any power in any provision of this Act to make regulations may, insofar as that provision relates to a matter to which the EC Regulation applies, be exercised for the purpose of making provision in consequence of the EC Regulation.]

[72A   Variation of references to time, money etc

For any reference in this Act to—
  (a)   a period of time;
  (b)   an amount of money; or
  (c)   a fraction,
there shall be substituted a reference to such other period or, as the case may be, amount or fraction as may be prescribed.]

73   Interpretation

(1)   In this Act, unless the context otherwise requires—
'Accountant in Bankruptcy' shall be construed in accordance with section 1 of this Act;
'accounting period' shall be construed in accordance with section [52(2)] of this Act;
'act and warrant' means an act and warrant issued under section 25(2) of, or paragraph 2(2) of Schedule 2 to, this Act;
'apparent insolvency' and 'apparently insolvent' shall be construed in accordance with section 7 of this Act;
['appropriate bank or institution' means—
  (a)   the Bank of England,
  (b)   a person who has permission under Part 4 of the Financial Services and Markets Act 2000 to accept deposits,
  (c)   an EEA firm of the kind mentioned in paragraph 5(b) of Schedule 3 to that Act which has permission under paragraph 15 of that Schedule (as a result of qualifying for authorisation under paragraph 12 of that Schedule) to accept deposits, or
  (d)   a person who is exempt from the general prohibition in respect of accepting deposits as a result of an exemption order made under section 38(1) of that Act,
and the expressions in this definition must be read with section 22 of the Financial

Services and Markets Act 2000, any relevant order under that section and Schedule 2 to that Act;]

'associate' shall be construed in accordance with section 74 of this Act;

['bankruptcy restrictions order' has the meaning given by section 56A(1) of this Act;

'bankruptcy restrictions undertaking' has the meaning given by section 56G(1) of this Act;]

'business' means the carrying on of any activity, whether for profit or not;

['centre of main interests' has the same meaning as in the EC Regulation;]

'commissioner', except in the expression 'examining commissioner', shall be construed in accordance with section 30(1) of this Act;

'court' means Court of Session or sheriff;

['creditor' includes a member State liquidator deemed to be a creditor under section 60A of this Act;]

'date of sequestration' has the meaning assigned by section 12(4) of this Act;

'debtor' includes, without prejudice to the expression's generality, an entity whose estate may be sequestrated by virtue of section 6 of this Act, a deceased debtor or his executor or a person entitled to be appointed as executor to a deceased debtor;

['debtor application' means an application for sequestration made to the Accountant in Bankruptcy under sections 5(2)(a) or 6(3)(a), (4)(a) or (6)(a) of this Act;]

['the EC Regulation' means Council Regulation (EC) No 1346/2000 of 29th May 2000 on insolvency proceedings;

['enactment' includes an Act of the Scottish Parliament and any enactment comprised in subordinate legislation under such an Act;]

'establishment' has the meaning given by Article 2(h) of the EC Regulation;]

'examination' means a public examination under section 45 of this Act or a private examination under section 44 of this Act;

'examining commissioner' shall be construed in accordance with section 46(2) of this Act;

'interim trustee' shall be construed in accordance with section [2(5)] of this Act;

[. . .]

['main proceedings' means proceedings opened in accordance with Article 3(1) of the EC Regulation and falling within the definition of insolvency proceedings in Article 2(a) of the EC Regulation and—

(a)   in relation to England and Wales and Scotland, set out in Annex A to the EC Regulation under the heading 'United Kingdom'; and

(b)   in relation to another member State, set out in Annex A to the EC Regulation under the heading relating to that member State;

'member State liquidator' means a person falling within the definition of liquidator in Article 2(b) of the EC Regulation appointed in proceedings to which it applies in a member State other than the United Kingdom;]

'ordinary debt' shall be construed in accordance with section 51(1)(f) of this Act;

['original trustee' shall be construed in accordance with section 24(1)(a) of this Act;]

[. . .]

'postponed debt' has the meaning assigned by section 51(3) of this Act;

'preferred debt' has the meaning assigned by section 51(2) of this Act;

'prescribed' means prescribed by regulations made by the Secretary of State;

['protected trust deed' means a trust deed which has been granted protected status in accordance with regulations made under paragraph 5 of Schedule 5 to this Act;]

'qualified creditor' and 'qualified creditors' shall be construed in accordance with section 5(4) of this Act;

'qualified to act as an insolvency practitioner' means being, in accordance with section 2 of the Insolvency Act 1985 (qualifications of insolvency practitioners), so qualified:

Provided that, until the coming into force of that section the expression shall instead mean satisfying such requirements (which, without prejudice to the generality of this definition, may include requirements as to the finding of caution) as may be prescribed for the purposes of this Act;

'register of insolvencies' has the meaning assigned by section [1A(1)(b)] of this Act;

'relevant person' has the meaning assigned by section 44(1)(b) of this Act;

['replacement trustee' shall be construed in accordance with section 24(1)(b) of this Act;]

['secondary proceedings' means proceedings opened in accordance with Articles 3(2) and 3(3) of the EC Regulation and falling within the definition of winding-up proceedings in Article 2(c) of the EC Regulation, and—

(a) in relation to England and Wales and Scotland, set out in Annex B to the EC Regulation under the heading 'United Kingdom'; and

(b) in relation to another member State, set out in Annex B to the EC Regulation under the heading relating to that member State;]

'secured creditor' means a creditor who holds a security for his debt over any part of the debtor's estate;

'security' means any security, heritable or moveable, or any right of lien, retention or preference;

'sederunt book' means the sederunt book maintained under section 3(1)(e) of this Act;

['sequestration proceedings' includes a debtor application and analogous expressions shall be construed accordingly;]

[. . .]

['statement of assets and liabilities' means a document (including a copy of a document) in such form as may be prescribed containing—

(i) a list of the debtor's assets and liabilities;

(ii) a list of his income and expenditure; and

(iii) such other information as may be prescribed;]

'statutory meeting' has the meaning assigned by [section 20A] of this Act;

[. . .]

['temporary administrator' means a temporary administrator referred to by Article 38 of the EC Regulation; and

'territorial proceedings' means proceedings opened in accordance with Articles 3(2) and 3(4) of the EC Regulation and falling within the definition of insolvency proceedings in Article 2(a) of the EC Regulation, and—

(a) in relation to England and Wales and Scotland, set out in Annex A to the EC Regulation under the heading 'United Kingdom'; and

(b) in relation to another member State, set out in Annex A to the EC Regulation under the heading relating to that member State.]

'trust deed' has the meaning assigned by section 5(4A) of this Act;

['trustee' means trustee in the sequestration;

'trustee vote' shall be construed in accordance with section 24(1) of this Act;]

'unfair preference' means a preference created as is mentioned in subsection (1) of section 36 of this Act by a transaction to which subsection (4) of that section applies.

(2) Any reference in this Act to a debtor being absolutely insolvent shall be construed as a reference to his liabilities being greater than his assets, and any reference to a debtor's estate being absolutely insolvent shall be construed accordingly.

(3) Any reference in this Act to value of the creditors is, in relation to any matter, a reference to the value of their claims as accepted for the purposes of that matter.

(4)   Any reference in this Act to 'the creditors' in the context of their giving consent or doing any other thing shall, unless the context otherwise requires, be construed as a reference to the majority in value of such creditors as vote in that context at a meeting of creditors.

(5)   Any reference in this Act to any of the following acts by a creditor barring the effect of any enactment or rule of law relating to the limitation of actions in any part of the United Kingdom, namely—

(a)   the presentation of a petition for sequestration;

(b)   the concurrence in [a debtor application]; and

(c)   the submission of a claim,

shall be construed as a reference to that act having the same effect, for the purposes of any such enactment or rule of law, as an effective acknowledgement of the creditor's claim; and any reference in this Act to any such enactment shall not include a reference to an enactment which implements or gives effect to any international agreement or obligation.

[(6)   Any reference in this Act, howsoever expressed, to the time when a petition for sequestration is presented shall be construed as a reference to the time when the petition is received by the [sheriff clerk].]

[(6A)   Any reference in this Act, howsoever expressed, to the time when a debtor application is made shall be construed as a reference to the time when the application is received by the Accountant in Bankruptcy.]

74   Meaning of 'associate'

(1)   Subject to subsection (7) below, for the purposes of this Act any question whether a person is an associate of another person shall be determined in accordance with the following provisions of this section (any reference, whether in those provisions or in regulations under the said subsection (7), to a person being an associate of another person being taken to be a reference to their being associates of each other).

(2)   A person is an associate of an individual if that person is the individual's [husband, wife or civil partner], or is a relative, or the [husband, wife or civil partner] of a relative, of the individual or of the individual's [husband, wife or civil partner].

(3)   A person is an associate of any person with whom he is in partnership, [and of any person who is an associate of any person with whom he is in partnership]; and a firm is an associate of any person who is a member of the firm.

(4)   For the purposes of this section a person is a relative of an individual if he is that individual's brother, sister, uncle, aunt, nephew, niece, lineal ancestor or lineal descendant treating—

(a)   any relationship of the half blood as a relationship of the whole blood and the stepchild or adopted child of any person as his child; and

(b)   an illegitimate child as the legitimate child of his mother and reputed father,

and references in this section to a [husband, wife or civil partner] include a former [husband, wife or civil partner] and a reputed [husband, wife or civil partner].

(5)   A person is an associate of any person whom he employs or by whom he is employed; and for the purposes of this subsection any director or other officer of a company shall be treated as employed by that company.

[(5A)   A company is an associate of another company—

(a)   if the same person has control of both, or a person has control of one and persons who are his associates, or he and persons who are his associates, have control of the other; or

(b)   if a group of two or more persons has control of each company, and the groups either consist of the same persons or could be regarded as consisting of the same persons by treating (in one or more cases) a member of either group as replaced by a person of whom he is an associate.

(5B)   A company is an associate of another person if that person has control of it or if that person and persons who are his associates together have control of it.

(5C)   For the purposes of this section a person shall be taken to have control of a company if—

(a)   the directors of the company or of another company which has control of it (or any of them) are accustomed to act in accordance with his directions or instructions; or

(b)   he is entitled to exercise, or control the exercise of, one third or more of the voting power at any general meeting of the company or of another company which has control of it,

and where two or more persons together satisfy either of the above conditions, they shall be taken to have control of the company.]

(6)   [In subsections (5), (5A), (5B) and (5C)] above, 'company' includes any body corporate (whether incorporated in Great Britain or elsewhere).

(7)   The Secretary of State may by regulations—

(a)   amend the foregoing provisions of this section so as to provide further categories of persons who, for the purposes of this Act, are to be associates of other persons; and

(b)   provide that any or all of subsections (2) to (6) above (or any subsection added by virtue of paragraph (a) above) shall cease to apply, whether in whole or in part, or shall apply subject to such modifications as he may specify in the regulations;

and he may in the regulations make such incidental or transitional provision as he considers appropriate.

75   [*Amendments, repeals and transitional provisions*]

76   Receipts and expenses

(1)   Any—

(a)   payments received by the Secretary of State under section 58(3) of this Act; or

(b)   amounts handed over to him in accordance with section 53 of this Act by virtue of the insertion provided for in paragraph 9 of Schedule 2 to this Act,

shall be paid by him into the Consolidated Fund.

(2)   There shall be paid out of moneys provided by Parliament—

(a)   any amount of outlays and remuneration payable in accordance with section 53 of this Act by virtue of the insertion mentioned in subsection (1)(b) above;

(b)   any administrative expenses incurred by the Secretary of State under this Act; and

(c)   any increase attributable to this Act in the sums so payable under any other Act.

77   Crown application

The application of this Act to the Crown is to the Crown as creditor only.

78   Short title, commencement and extent

(1)   This Act may be cited as the Bankruptcy (Scotland) Act 1985.

(2)   This Act, except this section, shall come into force on such day as the Secretary of State may by order made by statutory instrument appoint; and different days may be so appointed for different purposes and for different provisions.

(3)   An order under subsection (2) above may contain such transitional provisions and savings as appear to the Secretary of State necessary or expedient in connection with the provisions brought into force (whether wholly or partly) by the order.

(4)   Without prejudice to section 75(3) to (5) of this Act, this Act applies to sequestrations as regards which the petition—

(a)   is presented on or after the date of coming into force of section 5 of this Act; or

(b)   was presented before, but in respect of which no award of sequestration has been made by, that date.

(5)   This Act, except the provisions mentioned in subsection (6) below, extends to Scotland only.

(6)   The provisions referred to in subsection (5) above are sections 8(5), 22(8) (including that subsection as applied by section 48(7)), 46, 55 and 73(5), paragraph 16(b) of Schedule 4 and paragraph 3 of Schedule 5.

SCHEDULES

SCHEDULE 1
DETERMINATION OF AMOUNT OF CREDITOR'S CLAIM

Sections 5(5) and 22(9)

Amount which may be claimed generally

1—(1)   Subject to the provisions of this Schedule, the amount in respect of which a creditor shall be entitled to claim shall be the accumulated sum of principal and any interest which is due on the debt as at the date of sequestration.

(2)   If a debt does not depend on a contingency but would not be payable but for the sequestration until after the date of sequestration, the amount of the claim shall be calculated as if the debt were payable on the date of sequestration but subject to the deduction of interest at the rate specified in section 51(7) of this Act from the said date until the date for payment of the debt.

(3)   In calculating the amount of his claim, a creditor shall deduct any discount (other than any discount for payment in cash) which is allowable by contract or course of dealing between the creditor and the debtor or by the usage of trade.

Claims for aliment and periodical allowance on divorce

2—(1)   A person entitled to aliment, however arising, from a living debtor as at the date of sequestration, or from a deceased debtor immediately before his death, shall not be entitled to include in the amount of his claim—

(a)   any unpaid aliment for any period before the date of sequestration unless the amount of the aliment has been quantified by court decree or by any legally binding obligation which is supported by evidence in writing, and,

[(i)] in the case of spouses (or, where the aliment is payable to a divorced person in respect of a child, former spouses) they were living apart during that period;

[(ii) in the case of civil partners (or, where the aliment is payable to a former civil partner in respect of a child after dissolution of a civil partnership, former civil partners),]

(b)   any aliment for any period after the date of sequestration.

(2)   Sub-paragraph (1) above shall apply to a periodical allowance payable on divorce [or on dissolution of a civil partnership]—

(a)   by virtue of a court order; or

(b)   under any legally binding obligation which is supported by evidence in writing,

as it applies to aliment and as if for the words from 'in the case' to 'they' there were substituted the words 'the payer and payee'.

Debts depending on contingency

3—(1) Subject to sub-paragraph (2) below, the amount which a creditor shall be entitled to claim shall not include a debt in so far as its existence or amount depends upon a contingency.

(2) On an application by the creditor—

(a) to the [. . .] trustee; or

(b) if there is no [. . .] trustee, to the sheriff,

the [. . .] trustee or sheriff shall put a value on the debt in so far as it is contingent, and the amount in respect of which the creditor shall then be entitled to claim shall be that value but no more; and, where the contingent debt is an annuity, a cautioner may not then be sued for more than that value.

(3) Any interested person may appeal to the sheriff against a valuation under sub-paragraph (2) above by the [. . .] trustee, and the sheriff may affirm or vary that valuation.

Debts due under composition contracts

4 Where in the course of a sequestration the debtor is discharged following approval [. . .] of a composition offered by the debtor but the sequestration is subsequently revived, the amount in respect of which a creditor shall be entitled to claim shall be the same amount as if the composition had not been so approved less any payment already made to him under the composition contract.

Secured debts

5—(1) In calculating the amount of his claim, a secured creditor shall deduct the value of any security as estimated by him:

Provided that if he surrenders, or undertakes in writing to surrender, a security for the benefit of the debtor's estate, he shall not be required to make a deduction of the value of that security.

(2) The [. . .] trustee may, at any time after the expiry of 12 weeks from the date of sequestration, require a secured creditor at the expense of the debtor's estate to discharge the security or convey or assign it to the [. . .] trustee on payment to the creditor of the value specified by the creditor; and the amount in respect of which the creditor shall then be entitled to claim shall be any balance of his debt remaining after receipt of such payment.

(3) In calculating the amount of his claim, a creditor whose security has been realised shall deduct the amount (less the expenses of realisation) which he has received, or is entitled to receive, from the realisation.

Valuation of claims against partners for debts of the partnership

6 Where a creditor claims in respect of a debt of a partnership, against the estate of one of its partners, the creditor shall estimate the value of—

(a) the debt to the creditor from the firm's estate where that estate has not been sequestrated; or

(b) the creditor's claim against that estate where it has been sequestrated,

and deduct that value from his claim against the partner's estate; and the amount in respect of which he shall be entitled to claim on the partner's estate shall be the balance remaining after that deduction has been made.

[. . .]

SCHEDULE 3
PREFERRED DEBTS

Section 51

PART I
LIST OF PREFERRED DEBTS

[. . .]

Contributions to occupational pension schemes, etc

4   Any sum which is owed by the debtor and is a sum to which [Schedule 4 to the Pensions Schemes Act 1993] (contributions to occupational pension scheme and state scheme premiums) applies.

Remuneration of employees, etc

5—(1)   So much of any amount which—
    (a)   is owed by the debtor to a person who is or has been an employee of the debtor, and
    (b)   is payable by way of remuneration in respect of the whole or any part of the period of four months next before the relevant date,
as does not exceed the prescribed amount.
    (2)   An amount owed by way of accrued holiday remuneration, in respect of any period of employment before the relevant date, to a person whose employment by the debtor has been terminated, whether before, on or after that date.
    (3)   So much of any sum owed in respect of money advanced for the purpose as has been applied for the payment of a debt which, if it had not been paid, would have been a debt falling within sub-paragraph (1) or (2) above.

6   So much of any amount which—
    (a)   is ordered, whether before or after the relevant date, to be paid by the debtor under the Reserve Forces (Safeguard of Employment) Act 1985; and
    (b)   is so ordered in respect of a default made by the debtor before that date in the discharge of his obligations under that Act,
as does not exceed such amount as may be prescribed.

Levies on coal and steel production

[6A   Any sums due at the relevant date from the debtor in respect of—
    (a)   the levies on the production of coal and steel referred to in Articles 49 and 50 of the ECSC Treaty, or
    (b)   any surcharge for delay provided for in Article 50(3) of that Treaty and Article 6 of Decision 3/52 of the High Authority of the Coal and Steel Community.]

PART II
INTERPRETATION OF PART I

Meaning of 'the relevant date'

7   In Part I of this Schedule 'the relevant date' means—
    (a)   in relation to a debtor (other than a deceased debtor), the date of sequestration; and
    (b)   in relation to a deceased debtor, the date of his death.

[. . .]

Amounts payable by way of remuneration

9—(1)   For the purposes of paragraph 5 of Part I of this Schedule a sum is payable by the debtor to a person by way of remuneration in respect of any period if—

(a)   it is paid as wages or salary (whether payable for time or for piece work or earned wholly or partly by way of commission) in respect of services rendered to the debtor in that period; or

(b)   it is an amount falling within sub-paragraph (2) below and is payable by the debtor in respect of that period.

(2)   An amount falls within this sub-paragraph if it is—

(a)   a guarantee payment under section 12(1) of the Employment Protection (Consolidation) Act 1978 (employee without work to do for a day or part of a day),

(b)   remuneration on suspension on medical grounds under section 19 of that Act,

(c)   any payment for the time off under section 27(3) (trade-union duties), 31(3) (looking for work, etc) or 31A(4) (ante-natal care) of that Act,

(d)   [. . .]

(e)   remuneration under a protective award made by an industrial tribunal under section 101 of the Employment Protection Act 1975 (redundancy dismissal with compensation).

(3)   For the purposes of paragraph 5(2) of Part I of this Schedule, holiday remuneration shall be deemed, in the case of a person whose employment has been terminated by or in consequence of the award of sequestration of his employer's estate, to have accrued to that person in respect of any period of employment if, by virtue of that person's contract of employment or of any enactment (including an order made or direction given under any enactment), that remuneration would have accrued in respect of that period if that person's employment had continued until he became entitled to be allowed the holiday.

(4)   Without prejudice to the preceding provisions of this paragraph—

(a)   any remuneration payable by the debtor to a person in respect of a period of holiday or of absence from work through sickness or other good cause is deemed to be wages or, as the case may be, salary in respect of services rendered to the debtor in that period; and

(b)   references in this paragraph to remuneration in respect of a period of holiday include references to any sums which, if they had been paid, would have been treated for the purposes of the enactments relating to social services as earnings in respect of that period.

Transitional provisions

10   Regulations under paragraph 5 or 6 of Part I of this Schedule may contain such transitional provisions as may appear to the Secretary of State necessary or expedient.

SCHEDULE 4
DISCHARGE ON COMPOSITION
Section 56

1—(1)   At any time after the sheriff [*or, as the case may be, the Accountant in Bankruptcy appoints the*] trustee, an offer of composition may be made by or on behalf of the debtor, in respect of his debts, to the [. . .] trustee.

(2)   Any offer of composition shall specify caution or other security to be provided for its implementation.

2   The [. . .] trustee [where he is not the Accountant in Bankruptcy] shall submit the offer of composition along with a report thereon to the commissioners or, if there are no commissioners, to the Accountant in Bankruptcy.

3   The commissioners or, if there are no commissioners, the Accountant in Bankruptcy—
(a)   if they consider (or he considers) that the offer of composition will be timeously implemented and that, if the rules set out in section 51 of, and Schedule 1 to, this Act were applicable, its implementation would secure payment of a dividend of at least 25p in the £ in respect of the ordinary debts, and
(b)   if satisfied with the caution or other security specified in the offer,
shall recommend that the offer should be placed before the creditors.

4   Where a recommendation is made that the offer of composition should be placed before the creditors, the [. . .] trustee shall—
(a)   intimate the recommendation to the debtor and record it in the sederunt book;
(b)   publish in the Edinburgh Gazette a notice stating that an offer of composition has been made and where its terms may be inspected;
(c)   [not later than 1 week after the date of publication of such notice, send to every creditor known to him—
   (i)   a copy of the terms of offer; and
   (ii)   such other information as may be prescribed.]

[5   The notice mentioned in paragraph 4(b) of this Schedule shall be in the prescribed form and shall contain such information as may be prescribed.

6   Where, within the period of 5 weeks beginning with the date of publication of the notice under paragraph 4(b) of this Schedule, the trustee has not received notification in writing from a majority in number or not less than one third in value of the creditors that they reject the offer of composition, the offer of composition shall be approved by the trustee.

7   Where the trustee has received notification within the period and to the extent mentioned in paragraph 6 of this Schedule, the offer of composition shall be rejected by the trustee.

8   Any creditor who has been sent a copy of the terms of the offer as referred to in paragraph 4(c)(i) of this Schedule and who has not notified the trustee as mentioned in paragraph 6 of this Schedule that he objects to the offer shall be treated for all purposes as if he had accepted the offer.

8A—(1)   The Scottish Ministers may by regulations amend paragraphs 4 to 8 of this Schedule by replacing them, varying them or adding to or deleting anything from them.
(2)   Regulations made under sub-paragraph (1) above may contain such amendments of this Act as appear to the Scottish Ministers to be necessary in consequence of any amendment made by the regulations to the said paragraphs 4 to 8.
8B—(1)   Where an offer of composition is approved, a creditor who has not been sent a copy of the terms of the offer as mentioned in paragraph 4(c)(i) of this Schedule or who has notified the trustee of his rejection of the offer as mentioned in paragraph 6 of this Schedule may, not more than 28 days after the expiry of the period mentioned in said paragraph 6, appeal to the Accountant in Bankruptcy against such approval.
(2)   In determining an appeal under sub-paragraph (1) above, the Accountant in Bankruptcy may—
(a)   approve or reject the offer of composition; and
(b)   make such other determination in consequence of that approval or rejection as he thinks fit.]

9—(1)   Where the offer of composition is approved, the [. . .] trustee [where he is not the Accountant in Bankruptcy] shall—

(a)   submit to the commissioners or, if there are no commissioners, to the Accountant in Bankruptcy, his accounts of his intromissions with the debtor's estate for audit and a claim for the outlays reasonably incurred by him and for his remuneration; and where the said documents are submitted to the commissioners, he shall send a copy of them to the Accountant in Bankruptcy;

(b)   take all reasonable steps to ensure that the interim trustee (where he is a different person) has submitted, or submits, to the Accountant in Bankruptcy his accounts and his claim for his outlays and remuneration.

[(1A)   Where the offer of composition is approved and the [. . .] trustee is the Accountant in Bankruptcy, the [. . .] trustee shall prepare accounts of his intromissions with the debtor's estate and he shall make a determination of his fees and outlays calculated in accordance with regulations made under section 69A of this Act];

(2)   Subsections (3), (4), (6) and (10) of section 53 of this Act shall apply, subject to any necessary modifications, in respect of the accounts and claim submitted under sub-paragraph (1)(a) above as they apply in respect of the accounts and claim submitted under section 53(1) of this Act.

[(3)   Subsections (2), (3), (4), (5) and (10) of section 53 of this Act as adapted by [*section 53A of*] this Act shall apply, subject to any necessary modifications, in respect of the accounts and determination prepared under sub-paragraph (1A) above as they apply in respect of the accounts and determination prepared under the said section 53 as so adapted.]

10   As soon as the procedure under paragraph 9 of this Schedule has been completed, there shall be [*sent to the Accountant in Bankruptcy*]—

(a)   by the [*trustee (where he is not the Accountant in Bankruptcy)*], a declaration that all necessary charges in connection with the sequestration have been paid or that satisfactory provision has been made in respect of the payment of such charges;

(b)   by or on behalf of the debtor, the bond of caution or other security for payment of the composition.

[11—(1)   *Where the documents have been sent to the Accountant in Bankruptcy under paragraph 10 of this Schedule and either—*

(a)   *the period mentioned in paragraph 8B(1) of this Schedule has expired; or*

(b)   *the Accountant in Bankruptcy, in determining an appeal under said paragraph 8B(1), has approved the offer of composition,*

the Accountant in Bankruptcy shall grant the certificates of discharge referred to in sub-paragraph (2) below.

(2)   *Those certificates are—*

(a)   *a certificate discharging the debtor; and*

(b)   *a certificate discharging the trustee.*

(3)   *A certificate granted under sub-paragraph (1) above shall be in the prescribed form.*

(4)   *The Accountant in Bankruptcy shall—*

(a)   *send a certified copy of the certificate discharging the debtor to the keeper of the register of inhibitions for recording in that register; and*

(b)   *send a copy of that certificate to the trustee who shall insert it in the sederunt book or, where the Accountant in Bankruptcy is the trustee, insert a copy of that certificate in the sederunt book.]*

12   [*A certificate granted under paragraph 11(1)*] of this Schedule discharging the [. . .] trustee shall have the effect of discharging him from all liability (other than any liability arising from fraud) to the creditors or to the debtor in respect of any

act or omission of the [. . .] trustee in exercising the functions conferred on him, by this Act.

13 Notwithstanding that an offer of composition has been made, the sequestration shall proceed as if no such offer of composition has been made until the discharge of the debtor becomes effective; and the sequestration shall thereupon cease.

14 A creditor who has not submitted a claim under section 48 of this Act before [. . .] an offer of composition [*is approved*] shall not be entitled to make any demand against a person offering the composition on behalf of the debtor or against a cautioner in the offer; but this paragraph is without prejudice to any right of such a creditor to a dividend out of the debtor's estate equal to the dividend which creditors of the same class are entitled to receive under the composition.

15 A debtor may make two, but no more than two, offers of composition in the course of a sequestration.

16—(1) On [*the granting of a certificate under paragraph 11(1) of this Schedule discharging the debtor*]—
   (a)   the debtor shall be re-invested in his estate as existing at the date of the order;
   (b)   the debtor shall, subject to paragraph 14 of this Schedule, be discharged of all debts for which he was liable at the date of sequestration (other than any debts mentioned in section 55(2) of this Act); and
   (c)   the claims of creditors in the sequestration shall be converted into claims for their respective shares in the composition.
   [(2)   The discharge of the debtor by virtue of [*the granting of a certificate under paragraph 11(1) of this Schedule*] shall not affect any right of a secured creditor—
   (a)   for a debt in respect of which the debtor has been discharged to enforce his security for payment of the debt and any interest due and payable on the debt until the debt is paid in full; or
   (b)   for an obligation in respect of which the debtor has been discharged to enforce his security in respect of the obligation.]

17—(1) Without prejudice to any rule of law relating to the reduction of court decrees the Court of Session, on the application of any creditor, may recall the [order of the sheriff approving the offer of composition] discharging the debtor and the [. . .] trustee where it is satisfied—
   (a)   that there has been, or is likely to be, default in payment of the composition or of any instalment thereof; or
   (b)   that for any reason the composition cannot be proceeded with or cannot be proceeded with without undue delay or without injustice to the creditors.
   (2)   The effect of a decree of recall under this paragraph where the debtor has already been discharged shall be to revive the sequestration:
   Provided that the revival of the sequestration shall not affect the validity of any transaction which has been entered into by the debtor since his discharge with a person who has given value and has acted in good faith.
   (3)   Where the [. . .] trustee has been discharged, the Court may, on pronouncing a decree of recall under this paragraph, appoint a judicial factor to administer the debtor's estate, and give the judicial factor such order as it thinks fit as to that administration.
   (4)   The clerk of court shall send a copy of a decree of recall under this paragraph to the [. . .] trustee or judicial factor for insertion in the sederunt book.

18—(1) Without prejudice to any rule of law relating to the reduction of court decrees the Court of Session, on the application of any creditor, may reduce [an order under paragraph 11] of this Schedule discharging a debtor where it is satisfied that a payment was made or a preference granted or that a payment or preference was promised for the purpose of facilitating the obtaining of the debtor's discharge.

(2)   The Court may, whether or not it pronounces a decree of reduction under this paragraph, order a creditor who has received a payment or preference in connection with the debtor's discharge to surrender the payment or the value of the preference to the debtor's estate.

(3)   Where the [. . .] trustee has been discharged, the Court may, on pronouncing a decree of reduction under this paragraph, appoint a judicial factor to administer the debtor's estate, and give the judicial factor such order as it thinks fit as to that administration.

(4)   The clerk of court shall send a copy of a decree of reduction under this paragraph to the [. . .] trustee or judicial factor for insertion in the sederunt book.

SCHEDULE 5

VOLUNTARY TRUST DEEDS FOR CREDITORS

Section 59

Remuneration of trustee

1   Whether or not provision is made in the trust deed for auditing the trustee's accounts and for determining the method of fixing the trustee's remuneration or whether or not the trustee and the creditors have agreed on such auditing and the method of fixing the remuneration, the debtor, the trustee or any creditor may, at any time before the final distribution of the debtor's estate among the creditors, have the trustee's accounts audited by and his remuneration fixed by the Accountant in Bankruptcy.

[Accountant in Bankruptcy's power to carry out audit]

[1A   The Accountant in Bankruptcy may, at any time, audit the trustee's accounts and fix his remuneration.]

Registration of notice of inhibition

2—(1)   The trustee, from time to time after the trust deed has been delivered to him, may cause a notice in such form as shall be prescribed by the Court of Session by act of sederunt to be recorded in the register of inhibitions and adjudications; and such recording shall have the same effect as the recording in that register of letters of inhibition against the debtor.

(2)   The trustee, after the debtor's estate has been finally distributed among his creditors or the trust deed has otherwise ceased to be operative, shall cause to be so recorded a notice in such form as shall be prescribed as aforesaid recalling the notice recorded under sub-paragraph (1) above.

Lodging of claim to bar effect of limitation of actions

3   The submission of a claim by a creditor to the trustee acting under a trust deed shall bar the effect of any enactment or rule of law relating to limitation of actions in any part of the United Kingdom.

Valuation of claims

4   Unless the trust deed otherwise provides, Schedule 1 to this Act shall apply in relation to a trust deed as it applies in relation to a sequestration but subject to the following modifications—

(a)   in paragraphs 1, 2 and 5 for the word 'sequestration' wherever it occurs there shall be substituted the words 'granting of the trust deed';
(b)   in paragraph 3—
    (i)   in sub-paragraph (2), for the words from the beginning of paragraph (a) to 'or sheriff' there shall be substituted the words 'the trustee'; and
    [. . .]
(c)   paragraph 4 shall be omitted
[. . .]

Protected trust deeds

[5—(1)   The Scottish Ministers may by regulations make provision as to—
(a)   the conditions which require to be fulfilled in order for a trust deed to be granted the status of a protected trust deed;
(b)   the consequences of a trust deed being granted that status;
(c)   the rights of any creditor who does not accede to a trust deed which is granted protected status;
(d)   the extent to which a debtor may be discharged, by virtue of a protected trust deed, from his liabilities or from such liabilities or class of liabilities as may be prescribed in the regulations;
(e)   the circumstances in which a debtor may bring to an end the operation of a trust deed in respect of which the conditions provided for under sub-paragraph (a) above are not fulfilled;
(f)   the administration of the trust under a protected trust deed (including provision about the remuneration payable to the trustee).
(2)   Regulations under this paragraph may—
(a)   make provision enabling applications to be made to the court;
(b)   contain such amendments of this Act as appear to the Scottish Ministers to be necessary in consequence of any other provision of the regulations.]

SCHEDULE 7

PART II
RE-ENACTMENT OF CERTAIN PROVISIONS OF BANKRUPTCY (SCOTLAND) ACT 1913 (c 20)

Arrestments and poindings

24—(1)   Subject to sub-paragraph (2) below, all arrestments and [attachments] which have been executed within 60 days prior to the constitution of the apparent insolvency of the debtor, or within four months thereafter, shall be ranked *pari passu* as if they had all been executed on the same date.
(2)   Any such arrestment which is executed on the dependence of an action shall be followed up without undue delay.
(3)   Any creditor judicially producing in a process relative to the subject of such arrestment or [attachment] liquid grounds of debt or decree of payment within the 60 days or four months referred to in sub-paragraph (1) above shall be entitled to rank as if he had executed an arrestment or [an attachment]; and if the first or any subsequent arrester obtains in the meantime a decree of furthcoming, and recovers payment, or [an attaching] creditor carries through [an auction], he shall be accountable for the sum recovered to those who, by virtue of this Act, may be eventually found to have a right to a ranking *pari passu* thereon, and shall be liable in an action at their instance for payment to them proportionately, after allowing out of the fund the expense of such recovery.
(4)   Arrestments executed for attaching the same effects of the debtor after the period of four months subsequent to the constitution of his apparent insolvency

shall not compete with those within the said periods prior or subsequent thereto, but may rank with each other on any reversion of the fund attached in accordance with any enactment or rule of law relating thereto.

(5)   Any reference in the foregoing provisions of this paragraph to a debtor shall be construed as including a reference to any entity whose apparent insolvency may, by virtue of subsection [(4)] of section 7 of this Act, be constituted under subsection (1) of that section.

(6)   This paragraph shall apply in respect of arrestments and poindings which have been executed either before or after the coming into force of this paragraph.

(7)   The repeal of the Bankruptcy (Scotland) Act 1913 shall not affect the equalisation of arrestments and poindings (whether executed before or after the coming into force of this paragraph) in consequence of the constitution of notour bankruptcy under that Act.

[(8)   Nothing in this paragraph shall apply to an earnings arrestment, a current maintenance arrestment or a conjoined arrestment order.]

Exemptions from stamp duty or other duties for conveyances, deeds etc relating to sequestrated estates

25   Any—
   (a)   conveyance, assignation, instrument, discharge, writing, or deed relating solely to the estate of a debtor which has been or may be sequestrated, either under this or any former Act, being estate which after the execution of such conveyance, assignation, instrument, discharge, writing, or deed, shall be and remain the property of such debtor, for the benefit of his creditors, or the [. . .] trustee appointed or chosen under or by virtue of such sequestration,
   (b)   discharge to such debtor,
   (c)   deed, assignation, instrument, or writing for reinvesting the debtor in the estate,
   (d)   article of roup or sale, or submission,
   (e)   other instrument or writing whatsoever relating solely to the estate of any such debtor; and
   (f)   other deed or writing forming part of the proceedings ordered under such sequestration,
shall be exempt from all stamp duties or other Government duty.

DEBTORS (SCOTLAND) ACT 1987
(1987, c 18)

PART I
EXTENSION OF TIME TO PAY DEBTS

Time to pay directions on granting decree

1   Time to pay directions
   (1)   Subject to subsections (3) to (5) below and to section 14 of this Act, [on an application by the debtor,] the court, on granting decree for payment of any principal sum of money [shall, if satisfied that it is reasonable in all the circumstances to do so, and having regard in particular to the matters mentioned in subsection (1A) below,] direct that any sum decerned for in the decree (including any interest claimed in pursuance of subsections (6) and (7) below) or any expenses in relation to which the decree contains a finding as to liability or both such sum and such expenses shall be paid—
   (a)   by such instalments, commencing at such time after the date of intimation by the creditor to the debtor of an extract of the decree containing the direction, payable at such intervals; or

(b)   as a lump sum at the end of such period following intimation as mentioned in paragraph (a) above,
as the court may specify in the direction.

[(1A)   The matters referred to in subsection (1) above are—

(a)   the nature of and reasons for the debt in relation to which decree is granted;

(b)   any action taken by the creditor to assist the debtor in paying that debt;

(c)   the debtor's financial position;

(d)   the reasonableness of any proposal by the debtor to pay that debt; and

(e)   the reasonableness of any refusal by the creditor of, or any objection by the creditor to, and proposal by the debtor to pay that debt.]

(2)   A direction under subsection (1) above shall be known as a 'time to pay direction'.

(3)   Where a court grants a decree which contains a finding as to liability for expenses but does not at the same time make a time to pay direction, then (whether or not the decree also decerns for payment of the expenses), it shall not at any time thereafter be competent for the court to make a time to pay direction in relation to those expenses.

(4)   Where a court grants a decree which contains a finding as to liability for expenses and makes a time to pay direction in relation to those expenses but—

(a)   does not decern for payment of the expenses; or

(b)   decerns for payment of the expenses as taxed by the auditor of court but does not specify the amount of those expenses,
in relation to so much of the time to pay direction as relates to the expenses, the reference in subsection (1) above to the date of intimation of an extract of the decree containing the direction shall be treated as a reference to the date of intimation of an extract of a decree decerning for payment of the expenses, being an extract specifying their amount.

(5)   It shall not be competent for the court to make a time to pay direction—

(a)   where the sum of money (exclusive of any interest and expenses) decerned for exceeds [£25,000] or such amount as may be prescribed in regulations made by the Lord Advocate;

(b)   where the decree contains an award of a capital sum on divorce or on the granting of a declarator of nullity of marriage;

(c)   in connection with a maintenance order;

[(cc)   in connection with a liability order within the meaning of the Child Support Act 1991;]

(d)   in an action by or on behalf of [the Commissioners for Her Majesty's Revenue and Customs] for payment of any sum recoverable [under or by virtue of any enactment or under a contract settlement];

[. . .]

(f)   in an action for payment of—

[. . .]

(ii)   car tax due under the Car Tax Act 1983.

[. . .]

(6)   Without prejudice to section 2(5) of this Act, interest payable under a decree containing a time to pay direction (other than interest awarded as a specific sum in the decree) shall not be recoverable by the creditor except in accordance with subsection (7) below.

(7)   A creditor who wishes to recover interest to which subsection (6) above applies shall serve a notice on the debtor, not later than the date prescribed by Act of Sederunt occurring—

(a)   in the case of a direction under subsection (1)(a) above, before the date when the last instalment of the debt concerned (other than such interest) is payable under the direction;

(b)   in the case of a direction under subsection (1)(b) above, before the end of the period specified in the direction,

stating that he is claiming such interest and specifying the amount of the interest claimed.

(8)   Any sum paid by a debtor under a time to pay direction shall not be ascribed to interest claimed in pursuance of subsections (6) and (7) above until the debt concerned (other than such interest) has been discharged.

[(8A)   In paragraph (d) of subsection (5) above, 'contract settlement' means an agreement made in connection with any person's liability to make a payment to the Commissioners for Her Majesty's Revenue and Customs under or by virtue of any enactment.]

[. . .]

2   Effect of time to pay direction on diligence

(1)   While a time to pay direction is in effect, it shall not be competent—
   (a)   to serve a charge for payment; or
   (b)   to commence or execute any of the following diligences—
      (i)   an arrestment and action of furthcoming or sale;
      (ii)   [an attachment;]
      (iii)   an earnings arrestment;
      (iv)   an adjudication for debt;
      [(v)   a money attachment;]
      [(vi)   a land attachment;
      (vii)   a residual attachment]

to enforce payment of the debt concerned.

(2)   [Subject to subsection 2A below,] while a time to pay direction is in effect an arrestment used on the dependence of the action or in security of the debt concerned shall remain in effect—
   (a)   if it has not been recalled; and
   (b)   to the extent that it has not been restricted under subsection (3) below,

but, while the direction is in effect, it shall not be competent to commence an action of furthcoming or sale following on such an arrestment.

[(2A)   Where the arrestment which remains in effect as mentioned in subsection (2) above is an arrestment such as is mentioned in subsection (1) of section 73J of this Act, while the time to pay direction is in effect—
   (a)   it shall not be competent to release funds under subsection (2) of that section; and
   (b)   the period during which the direction is in effect shall be disregarded for the purposes of determining whether the period mentioned in subsection (3) of that section has expired.]

[(2B)   While a time to pay direction is in effect an interim attachment shall remain in effect—
   (a)   if it has not been recalled; or
   (b)   to the extent that it has not been restricted under subsection (3) below.]

(3)   The court may, on making a time to pay direction, recall or restrict [an interim attachment or] an arrestment of the kind described in subsection (2) above.

(4)   If [an interim attachment or] an arrestment of the kind described in subsection (2) above is in effect, the court may order that the making of a time to pay direction and the recall or restriction of the [interim attachment or] arrestment shall be subject to the fulfilment by the debtor of such conditions within such period as the court thinks fit; and, where the court so orders, it shall postpone granting decree until such fulfilment or the end of that period, whichever is the earlier.

(5)   Where a time to pay direction is recalled or ceases to have effect, otherwise than—

(a)   under section 12(2)(a) of this Act; or

(b)   by reason of the debt concerned being paid or otherwise extinguished,

the debt in so far as it remains outstanding and interest thereon, whether or not awarded as a specific sum in the decree, shall, subject to any enactment or rule of law to the contrary, become enforceable by any diligence mentioned in subsection (1)(b) above.

[(5A) Where—

(a)   a time to pay direction is recalled or ceases to have effect as mentioned in subsection (5) above; and

(b)   an arrestment such as is mentioned in section 73J(1) of this Act is in effect,

the clerk of court or sheriff clerk shall intimate the fact of that recall or cessation to the arrestee.]

3   Variation and recall of time to pay direction and arrestment

(1)   The court which granted a decree containing a time to pay direction may, on an application by the debtor or the creditor—

(a)   vary or recall the direction if it is satisfied that it is reasonable [in all the circumstances] to do so; or

(b)   if [an interim attachment or] an arrestment in respect of the debt concerned is in effect, recall or restrict the [interim attachment or] arrestment.

(2)   If [an interim attachment or] an arrestment in respect of the debt concerned is in effect, the court may order that any variation, recall or restriction under subsection (1) above shall be subject to the fulfilment by the debtor of such conditions as the court thinks fit.

(3)   The clerk of court or sheriff clerk shall as soon as is reasonably practicable intimate a variation under subsection (1) above to the debtor and to the creditor, and the variation shall come into effect on the date of such intimation.

4   Lapse of time to pay direction

(1)   If, on the day on which an instalment payable under a time to pay direction becomes due, there remains unpaid a sum, due under previous instalments, of not less than the aggregate of 2 instalments, the direction shall cease to have effect.

(2)   If at the end of the period of 3 weeks immediately following the day on which the last instalment payable under a time to pay direction becomes due, any part of the debt concerned remains outstanding, the direction shall cease to have effect.

(3)   If any sum payable under a time to pay direction under section 1(1)(b) of this Act remains unpaid 24 hours after the end of the period specified in the direction, the direction shall cease to have effect.

(4)   Where—

(a)   a decree for payment of a principal sum of money contains a finding as to liability for expenses and decree for payment of the expenses is subsequently granted; and

(b)   a time to pay direction is made in relation to both the principal sum and the expenses,

if under subsections (1) to (3) above the direction ceases to have effect in relation to the sum payable under either of the decrees, the direction shall also cease to have effect in relation to the sum payable under the other decree.

Time to pay orders following charge or diligence

5 Time to pay orders

(1) Subject to section 14 of this Act, this section applies to a debt due under a decree or other document in respect of which—

(a) a charge for payment has been served on the debtor;

(b) an arrestment has been executed; or

(c) an action of adjudication for debt has been commenced.

(2) Subject to subsections (4) and (5) below, the sheriff [, on an application by the debtor, shall, if satisfied that it is reasonable in all the circumstances to do so, and having regard in particular to the matters mentioned in subsection (2A) below,] make an order that a debt to which this section applies (including any interest claimed in pursuance of subsections (6) and (7) below) so far as outstanding, shall be paid—

(a) by such instalments, commencing at such time after the date of intimation in accordance with section 7(4) of this Act by the sheriff clerk to the debtor of the order under this subsection, payable at such intervals; or

(b) as a lump sum at the end of such period following intimation as mentioned in paragraph (a) above,

as the sheriff may specify in the order.

[(2A) The matters referred to in subsection (2) above are—

(a) the nature of and reasons for the debt in relation to which the order is sought;

(b) any action taken by the creditor to assist the debtor in paying that debt;

(c) the debtor's financial position;

(d) the reasonableness of any proposal by the debtor to pay that debt; and

(e) the reasonableness of the objection by the creditor to the offer by the debtor to pay that debt.]

(3) An order under subsection (2) above shall be known as a 'time to pay order'.

(4) It shall not be competent for the sheriff to make a time to pay order—

(a) where the amount of the debt outstanding at the date of the making of the application under subsection (2) above (exclusive of any interest) exceeds [£10,000] or such amount as may be prescribed in regulations made by the Lord Advocate;

(b) where, in relation to the debt, a time to pay direction or a time to pay order has previously been made (whether such direction or order is in effect or not);

[. . .]

(d) in relation to a debt including any sum recoverable by or on behalf of [the Commissioners of Her Majesty's Revenue and Customs [under or by virtue of any enactment or under a contract settlement]];

[. . .]

(f) in relation to a debt including—

[. . .]

(ii) car tax due under the Car Tax Act 1983.

[. . .]

(5) Where in respect of a debt to which this section applies—

(a) [articles belonging to the debtor have been attached and notice of an auction given under section 27(4) of the Debt Arrangement and Attachment (Scotland) Act 2002 (asp 17) but no auction has yet taken place;]

[(aa) money owned by the debtor has been attached and removed;]

(b) moveable property of the debtor has been arrested and in respect of the arrested property—

(i) a decree in an action of furthcoming has been granted but has not been enforced; or

(ii) a warrant of sale has been granted but the warrant has not been executed;

(c) a decree in an action of adjudication for debt has been granted and the creditor has, with the debtor's consent or acquiescence, entered into possession of any property adjudged by the decree or has obtained a decree of mails and duties, or a decree of removing or ejection, in relation to any such property.

(d) *property owned by the debtor has been attached by residual attachment and a satisfaction order under section 136(2) of the 2007 Act has been made but not yet executed,*]

it shall not be competent for the sheriff to make a time to pay order in respect of that debt until the diligence has been completed or has otherwise ceased to have effect.

[(5A) Where, in respect of a debt to which this section applies, an arrestment such as is mentioned in subsection (1) of section 73J of this Act has been executed, the sheriff may make a time to pay order in respect of that debt only if less than 8 weeks of the period mentioned in subsection (3) of that section have expired.]

(6) Without prejudice to section 9(12) of this Act, interest payable under a decree for payment of a debt in respect of which a time to pay order has been made (other than interest awarded as a specific sum in the decree) shall not be recoverable by the creditor except in accordance with subsection (7) below.

(7) A creditor who wishes to recover interest to which subsection (6) above applies shall serve a notice on the debtor not later than the date prescribed by Act of Sederunt occurring—

(a) in the case of an order under subsection (2)(a) above, before the date when the last instalment of the debt (other than such interest) is payable under the order;

(b) in the case of an order under subsection (2)(b) above, before the end of the period specified in the order,

stating that he is claiming such interest and specifying the amount of the interest claimed.

(8) Any sum paid by a debtor under a time to pay order shall not be ascribed to interest claimed in pursuance of subsections (6) and (7) above until the debt concerned (other than such interest) has been discharged.

[(8A) In paragraph (d) of subsection (4) above, 'contract settlement' means an agreement made in connection with any person's liability to make a payment to the Commissioners for Her Majesty's Revenue and Customs under or by virtue of any enactment.]

[. . .]

6 Application for time to pay order

(1) An application for a time to pay order shall specify, to the best of the debtor's knowledge, the amount of the debt outstanding as at the date of the making of the application and shall include an offer to pay it—

(a) by specified instalments, payable at specified intervals; or

(b) as a lump sum at the end of a specified period.

(2) The sheriff clerk's duty under section 96(2)(b) of this Act to assist the debtor in the completion of certain forms shall, in relation to a form of application for a time to pay order, consist of a duty to assist him in the completion of the form in accordance with proposals for payment made by the debtor.

(3) On receipt of an application for a time to pay order, the sheriff shall, if the application is properly made and unless it appears to him that the making of a time to pay order would not be competent, make an interim order sisting diligence as provided for in section 8(1) of this Act.

(4) The sheriff may, where the debtor is unable to furnish the necessary information, make an order requiring the creditor, within such period as may be specified therein, to furnish to the sheriff such particulars of the decree or other

document under which the debt is payable as may be prescribed by Act of Sederunt.

(5) If a creditor fails to comply with an order under subsection (4) above the sheriff may, after giving the creditor an opportunity to make representations, make an order recalling or extinguishing any existing diligence, and interdicting the creditor from executing diligence, for the recovery of the debt.

(6) Where the sheriff makes an interim order under subsection (3) above, the sheriff clerk shall as soon as is reasonably practicable—

(a) serve a copy of the application for the time to pay order on the creditor informing him that he may object to the granting of the application within a period of 14 days after the date of service;

[(b) serve on—

(i) the creditor; and

(ii) where an arrestment such as is mentioned in section 73J(1) of this Act is in effect, the arrestee,

a copy of the interim order; and

(c) serve on the creditor a copy of any order under subsection (4) above.]

7 Disposal of application

(1) If no objection is made in pursuance of section 6(6)(a) of this Act, the sheriff shall make a time to pay order in accordance with the application.

(2) If such an objection is made, the sheriff shall not dispose of the application without first—

(a) giving the debtor an opportunity to make representations; and

(b) if agreement is not reached as to whether a time to pay order should be made or as to its terms, giving the parties an opportunity to be heard.

(3) Where the sheriff refuses to make a time to pay order, he shall recall any interim order under section 6(3) of this Act.

(4) The sheriff clerk shall as soon as is reasonably practicable—

(a) intimate the decision of the sheriff on an application for a time to pay order (including any recall of an interim order under subsection (3) above) to the debtor [the creditor and, where an arrestment such as is mentioned in section 73J(1) of this Act is in effect, the arrestee]; and

(b) if the sheriff has made a time to pay order, inform the creditor of the date when he intimated that fact to the debtor.

8 Effect of interim order on diligence

(1) While an interim order under section 6(3) of this Act is in effect it shall not be competent in respect of the debt—

[(za) to attach in execution of the decree any articles which have been attached by interim attachment;]

(a) [to give, in relation to any articles which have been attached, notice of an auction under section 27(4) of the Debt Arrangement and Attachment (Scotland) Act 2002 (asp 17);]

[(aa) to execute a money attachment;]

(b) to execute an earnings arrestment;

(c) [subject to subsection (1A) below,] where an arrestment of property belonging to the debtor (other than an arrestment of earnings in the hands of his employer) has been executed before or after the making of the interim order, to commence an action of furthcoming or sale, or to grant decree in any such action which has already been commenced, in pursuance of that arrestment;

(d) to commence an action of adjudication for debt or, if such an action has already been commenced, to take any steps other than the registration of a notice of litigiosity in connection with the action, the obtaining and extracting of a decree in the action, the registration of an abbreviate of adjudication and the completion of title to property adjudged by the decree, [*(e) subject to subsection (1C) below, to apply, under section 130(1) of the 2007 Act, for a residual attachment order*].

[(1A)   Where the arrestment mentioned in subsection (1)(c) above is an arrestment such as is mentioned in subsection (1) of section 73J of this Act, while the interim order is in effect—

(a)   it shall not be competent to release funds under subsection (2) of that section; and

(b)   the period during which the order is in effect shall be disregarded for the purposes of determining whether the period mentioned in subsection (3) of that section has expired.

(1B)   Where, before the interim order is made—

(a)   a notice of land attachment is registered, it shall not be competent to take any steps other than—

(i)   serving, under subsection (5) of section 83 of the 2007 Act, a copy of that notice; and

(ii)   registering, under subsection (6) of that section, a certificate of service; or

(b)   a land attachment is created, it shall not be competent to make, under section 97(2) of the 2007 Act, an order granting a warrant for sale of the attached land.

(1C)   Where, before the interim order is made, a residual attachment order has been made, it shall not be competent—

(a)   to take any steps other than serving, under section 133(1) of the 2007 Act, a schedule of residual attachment; or

(b)   to make, under section 136(2) of the 2007 Act, a satisfaction order.]

(2)   An interim order under section 6(3) of this Act shall come into effect on intimation to the creditor under section 6(6)(b) of this Act and shall remain in effect until intimation of the sheriff's decision on the application for a time to pay order is made to the debtor and the creditor under section 7(4)(a) of this Act.

[. . .]

9 Effect of time to pay order on diligence

(1)   While a time to pay order is in effect, it shall not be competent—

(a)   to serve a charge for payment; or

(b)   to commence or execute any of the following diligences—

(i)   an arrestment and action of furthcoming or sale;

[(ii)   an attachment;]

(iii)   an earnings arrestment;

(iv)   an adjudication for debt;

[(v)   a money attachment;]

to enforce payment of the debt concerned.

(2)   On making a time to pay order, the sheriff in respect of the debt—

(a)   shall make an order recalling any existing earnings arrestment;

(b)   where the debt is being enforced by a conjoined arrestment order, shall—

(i)   if he, or another sheriff sitting in the same sheriff court, made the conjoined arrestment order, vary it so as to exclude the debt or, where no other debt or maintenance is being enforced by the order, recall the order;

(ii)   if a sheriff sitting in another sheriff court made the conjoined arrestment order, require intimation of the time to pay order to be made to a sheriff sitting there who shall so vary or, as the case may be, recall the conjoined arrestment order;

(c)   [where a notice of land attachment has been registered under section 83(1)(c) of the 2007 Act, shall make an order prohibiting the taking of any steps other than—

(i)   the serving, under subsection (5) of that section, of a copy of the notice; and

    (ii) the registration, under subsection (6) of that section, of a certificate of service;

    [(ca) where a residual attachment order has been made under section 132(2) of the 2007 Act, shall make an order prohibiting the taking of any steps other than the serving, under section 133(1) of the 2007 Act, of a schedule of residual attachment;

    (cb) may make an order recalling an interim attachment;]

    (d) may make an order recalling [an attachment];

    (e) may make an order recalling or restricting any arrestment other than an arrestment of the debtor's earnings in the hands of his employer.

    (3) If [an interim attachment, an attachment] or such an arrestment as is mentioned in subsection (2)(e) above is in effect, the sheriff may order that the making of a time to pay order [the recall of the interim attachment or the attachment] or the recall or restriction of the arrestment shall be subject to the fulfilment by the debtor of such conditions as the sheriff thinks fit.

    (4) [Subject to subsection (4A) below,] where the sheriff does not exercise the powers conferred on him by subsection [(2)(cb), (d) or (e)] above to recall a diligence, he shall order that no further steps shall be taken by the creditor in the diligence concerned other than, in the case of [an attachment, making a report of attachment under section 17 of the Debt Arrangement and Attachment (Scotland) Act 2002 (asp 17) or applying for an order under section 20(1) of that Act.]

    [(4A) Where, in relation to an arrestment such as is mentioned in subsection (1) of section 73J of this Act, the sheriff does not exercise the power conferred on him by subsection (2)(e) above to recall that arrestment, he shall make an order—

    (a) prohibiting, while the time to pay order is in effect, the release of funds under subsection (2) of section 73J of this Act; and

    (b) providing that the period during which the time to pay order is in effect shall be disregarded for the purposes of determining whether the period mentioned in subsection (3) of that section has expired.]

    (5) Any order made under subsection (2) or (4) above shall specify the diligence in relation to which it is made.

    (6) The sheriff shall not make an order under subsection [(2)(cb), (d) or (e)] above without first giving the creditor an opportunity to make representations.

    (7) The sheriff clerk shall, at the same time as he makes intimation under section 7(4)(a) of this Act—

    (a) intimate any order under subsection (2) or (4) above to the debtor and the creditor and the order shall come into effect on such intimation being made to the creditor;

    (b) intimate any order under subsection (2)(a) or (b) above to the employer [; and

    (c) where any order under subsection (4A) above is made in relation to an arrestment such as is mentioned in section 73J(1) of this Act is in effect, intimate that order to the arrestee.]

    (8) While an order under subsection (4) above is in effect it shall not be competent [. . .]—

    (a) [to sell articles which have been attached (other than by virtue of section 20(1) or 22(3) of the Debt Arrangement and Attachment (Scotland) Act (asp 17);]

    (b) [to grant] a decree of furthcoming or sale of arrested property.

    (9) For the purposes of section [24 of the Debt Arrangement and Attachment (Scotland) Act 2002 (asp 17)], the period during which an order under subsection (4) above is in effect shall be disregarded in calculating the period during which [an attachment] to which the order applies remains in effect.

    (10) Where, before the making of a time to pay order in respect of a debt, a charge to pay that debt has been served—

(a)   if the period for payment specified in the charge has not expired, the charge shall lapse on the making of the order;

(b)   if that period has expired, nothing in the time to pay order nor in any order under this section shall affect retrospectively the effect of the charge in the constitution of apparent insolvency within the meaning of section 7 of the Bankruptcy (Scotland) Act 1985.

(11)   If, when a time to pay order in relation to a debt is made, any diligence enforcing it is in effect which is not specified in an order under subsection (2) or (4) above, the diligence shall remain in effect unless and until it is recalled under section 10(4) of this Act.

(12)   Where a time to pay order is recalled or ceases to have effect, otherwise than—

(a)   under section 12(2)(a) of this Act; or

(b)   by the debt payable under the order being paid or otherwise extinguished, the debt in so far as it remains outstanding (including interest thereon, whether or not awarded as a specific sum in the decree) shall, subject to any enactment or rule of law to the contrary, become enforceable by any diligence mentioned in subsection (1)(b) above; and, notwithstanding section [25 of the Debt Arrangement and Attachment (Scotland) Act 2002 (asp 17)], in this subsection 'diligence' includes, where the debt was, immediately before the time to pay order was made, being enforced by [an attachment] in any premises, [another attachment] in those premises.

10   Variation and recall of time to pay order and arrestment

(1)   The sheriff may, on an application by the debtor or the creditor—

(a)   vary or recall a time to pay order if he is satisfied that it is reasonable [in all the circumstances] to do so; or

(b)   if [an interim attachment, an attachment] or an arrestment in respect of the debt is in effect,

recall [the attachment] or recall or restrict the arrestment.

(2)   If [an interim attachment, an attachment] or an arrestment in respect of the debt is in effect, the sheriff may order that any variation, recall or restriction under subsection (1) above shall be subject to the fulfilment by the debtor of such conditions as the sheriff thinks fit.

(3)   The sheriff clerk shall as soon as is reasonably practicable intimate a variation under subsection (1) above to the debtor and to the creditor, and the variation shall come into effect on the date of such intimation.

(4)   Where, after a time to pay order has been made, it comes to the knowledge of the sheriff that the debt to which the order applies is being enforced by any of the diligences mentioned in section 9(1)(b) of this Act which was in effect when the time to pay order was made, the sheriff, after giving all interested parties an opportunity to be heard, may make—

(a)   an order recalling the time to pay order; or

(b)   any of the orders mentioned in subsection (2) or (4) of section 9 of this Act; and that section shall, subject to any necessary modifications, apply for the purposes of an order made under this paragraph as it applies for the purposes of an order made under either of those subsections.

11   Lapse of time to pay order

(1)   If, on the day on which an instalment payable under a time to pay order becomes due, there remains unpaid a sum, due under previous instalments, of not less than the aggregate of 2 instalments, the order shall cease to have effect.

(2)   If at the end of the period of 3 weeks immediately following the day on which the last instalment payable under a time to pay order becomes due, any part of the debt payable under the order remains outstanding, the order shall cease to have effect.

(3)   If any sum payable under a time to pay order under section 5(2)(b) of this

Act remains unpaid 24 hours after the end of the period specified in the order, the order shall cease to have effect.

Miscellaneous

12 Sequestration and insolvency

(1)   While a time to pay direction or a time to pay order is in effect, the creditor shall not be entitled to found on the debt concerned in presenting, or in concurring in the presentation of, a petition for the sequestration of the debtor's estate.

(2)   A time to pay direction or a time to pay order shall cease to have effect—

(a)   on the granting of an award of sequestration of the debtor's estate;

(b)   on the granting by the debtor of a voluntary trust deed whereby his estate is conveyed to a trustee for the benefit of his creditors generally; or

(c)   on the entering by the debtor into a composition contract with his creditors.

13 Saving of creditor's rights and remedies

(1)   No right or remedy of a creditor to enforce his debt shall be affected by—

(a)   a time to pay direction;

(b)   a time to pay order; or

(c)   an interim order under section 6(3) of this Act,

except as expressly provided in this Part of this Act.

(2)   The recall—

(a)   on the making of a time to pay direction or an order under section 3(1) of this Act, of an arrestment; or

(b)   on the making of a time to pay order or an order under section 10(1) of this Act, of an arrestment or [an attachment],

shall not prevent the creditor therein from being ranked by virtue of that arrestment or [attachment] pari passu under paragraph 24 of Schedule 7 to the Bankruptcy (Scotland) Act 1985 on the proceeds of any other arrestment or [attachment].

14 Circumstances where direction or order not competent or no longer effective

(1)   It shall be competent to make a time to pay direction or a time to pay order only in relation to a debtor who is an individual and only if, and to the extent that, the debtor is liable for payment of the debt concerned in either or both of the following capacities—

(a)   personally;

(b)   as a tutor of an individual or as a judicial factor loco tutoris, curator bonis or judicial factor loco absentis on an individual's estate.

(2)   A time to pay direction or a time to pay order shall cease to have effect on the death of the debtor or on the transmission of the obligation to pay the debt concerned during his lifetime to another person.

(3)   Where a time order for the payment by instalments of a sum owed under a regulated agreement or a security has been made under section 129(2)(a) of the Consumer Credit Act 1974 it shall not thereafter be competent to make a time to pay direction or a time to pay order in relation to that sum.

15 Interpretation of Part I

(1)   In this Part of this Act—

'adjudication for debt' does not include—

(a)   an adjudication on a *debitum fundi*;

[. . .]

(2)   In sections 1 to 4 of this Act—

'the court' means the Court of Session or the sheriff;

'the debt concerned' means the sum or expenses in respect of which a time to pay direction is made.

(3)   In sections 5 to 14 of this Act—
'debt' means the sum due by a debtor under a decree or other document (including any interest thereon and any expenses decerned for), and any expenses of diligence used to recover such sum which are chargeable against the debtor, but does not include—

(a)   any sum due under an order of court in criminal proceedings;

(b)   maintenance, whether due at the date of application for the time to pay order or not, or any capital sum awarded on divorce or on the granting of a declarator of nullity of marriage or any other sum due under a decree awarding maintenance or such a capital sum; or

(c)   any fine imposed—

(i)   for contempt of court;

(ii)   under any enactment, for professional misconduct; or

(iii)   for failure to implement an order under section 91 of the Court of Session Act 1868 (orders for specific performance of statutory duty);
'decree or other document' means—

(a)   a decree of the Court of Session or the sheriff;

[(aa)   a summary warrant;]

(b)   an extract of a document which is registered for execution in the Books of Council and Session or the sheriff court books;

(c)   an order or determination which by virtue of any enactment is enforceable as if it were an extract registered decree arbitral bearing a warrant for execution issued by the sheriff;

(d)   a civil judgment granted outside Scotland by a court, tribunal or arbiter which by virtue of any enactment or rule of law is enforceable in Scotland; and

(e)   a document or settlement which by virtue of an Order in Council made under section 13 of the Civil Jurisdiction and Judgments Act 1982 is enforceable in Scotland,
but does not include a maintenance order [, a liability order within the meaning of the Child Support Act 1991] [. . .];
'sheriff'—

(a)   in relation to a debt constituted by decree granted by a sheriff, means that sheriff or another sheriff sitting in the same sheriff court;

(b)   in any other case, means the sheriff having jurisdiction—

(i)   in the place where the debtor is domiciled;

(ii)   if the debtor is not domiciled in Scotland, in a place in Scotland where he carries on business; or

(iii)   if the debtor does not carry on business in Scotland, in a place where he has property which is not exempt from diligence;
and, for the purposes of sub-paragraphs (i) and (ii) above, the debtor's domicile shall be determined in accordance with section 41 of the Civil Jurisdiction and Judgments Act 1982.

[PART 1A
DILIGENCE ON THE DEPENDENCE

Availability of diligence on the dependence

[**15A   Diligence on the dependence of action**
(1)   Subject to subsection (2) below and to sections 15C to 15F of this Act, the Court of Session or the sheriff may grant warrant for diligence by—

(a)   arrestment; or

(b)   inhibition,
on the dependence of an action.

(2)   Warrant for—

(a)   arrestment on the dependence of an action is competent only where the action contains a conclusion for payment of a sum other than by way of expenses; and

(b)   inhibition on the dependence is competent only where the action contains—

(i)   such a conclusion; or

(ii)   a conclusion for specific implement of an obligation to convey heritable property to the creditor or to grant in the creditor's favour a real right in security, or some other right, over such property.

(3)   In this Part of this Act, 'action' includes, in the sheriff court—

(a)   a summary cause;

(b)   a small claim; and

(c)   a summary application,

and references to 'summons', 'conclusion' and to cognate expressions shall be construed accordingly.]

[15B   Diligence on the dependence of petition

(1)   Subject to subsection (2) below and to sections 15C to 15F of this Act, the Court of Session may grant warrant for diligence by—

(a)   arrestment; or

(b)   inhibition,

on the dependence of a petition.

(2)   Warrant for—

(a)   arrestment on the dependence of a petition is competent only where the petition contains a prayer for payment of a sum other than by way of expenses; and

(b)   inhibition on the dependence is competent only where the petition contains—

(i)   such a prayer; or

(ii)   a prayer for specific implement of an obligation to convey heritable property to the creditor or to grant in the creditor's favour a real right in security, or some other right, over such property.

(3)   The provisions of this Act (other than section 15A), of any other enactment and of any rule of law relating to diligence on the dependence of actions shall, in so far as is practicable and unless the contrary intention appears, apply to petitions in relation to which it is competent to grant warrant for such diligence and to the parties to them as they apply to actions and to parties to them.]

[15C   Diligence on the dependence to secure future or contingent debts

(1)   It shall be competent for the court to grant warrant for diligence on the dependence where the sum concluded for is a future or contingent debt.

(2)   In this section and in sections 15D to 15M of this Act, the 'court' means the court before which the action is depending.]

Application for diligence on the dependence

[15D   Application for diligence on the dependence

(1)   A creditor may, at any time during which an action is in dependence, apply to the court for warrant for diligence by—

(a)   arrestment; or

(b)   inhibition,

on the dependence of the action.

(2)   An application under subsection (1) above shall—

(a)   be in (or as nearly as may be in) the form prescribed by Act of Sederunt;

(b)   subject to subsection (3) below, be intimated to and provide details of—

(i)   the debtor; and

(ii) any other person having an interest;
(c) state whether the creditor is seeking the grant, under section 15E(1) of this Act, of warrant for diligence on the dependence in advance of a hearing on the application under section 15F of this Act; and
(d) contain such other information as the Scottish Ministers may by regulations prescribe.
(3) An application under subsection (1) above need not be intimated where the creditor is seeking the grant, under section 15E(1) of this Act, of warrant in advance of a hearing on the application under section 15F of this Act.
(4) The court, on receiving an application under subsection (1) above, shall—
(a) subject to section 15E of this Act, fix a date for a hearing on the application under section 15F of this Act; and
(b) order the creditor to intimate that date to—
(i) the debtor; and
(ii) any other person appearing to the court to have an interest.]

[15E **Grant of warrant without a hearing**
(1) The court may, if satisfied as to the matters mentioned in subsection (2) below, make an order granting warrant for diligence on the dependence without a hearing on the application under section 15F of this Act.
(2) The matters referred to in subsection (1) above are—
(a) that the creditor has a prima facie case on the merits of the action;
(b) that there is a real and substantial risk enforcement of any decree in the action in favour of the creditor would be defeated or prejudiced by reason of—
(i) the debtor being insolvent or verging on insolvency; or
(ii) the likelihood of the debtor removing, disposing of, burdening, concealing or otherwise dealing with all or some of the debtor's assets,
were warrant for diligence on the dependence not granted in advance of such a hearing; and
(c) that it is reasonable in all the circumstances, including the effect granting warrant may have on any person having an interest, to do so.
(3) The onus shall be on the creditor to satisfy the court that the order granting warrant should be made.
(4) Where the court makes an order granting warrant for diligence on the dependence without a hearing on the application under section 15F of this Act, the court shall—
(a) fix a date for a hearing under section 15K of this Act; and
(b) order the creditor to intimate that date to—
(i) the debtor; and
(ii) any other person appearing to the court to have an interest.
(5) Where a hearing is fixed under subsection (4)(a) above, section 15K of this Act shall apply as if an application had been made to the court for an order under that section.
(6) Where the court refuses to make an order granting a warrant without a hearing under section 15F of this Act and the creditor insists in the application, the court shall—
(a) fix a date for such a hearing on the application; and
(b) order the creditor to intimate that date to—
(i) the debtor; and
(ii) any other person appearing to the court to have an interest.]

[15F **Hearing on application**
(1) At the hearing on an application for warrant for diligence on the dependence, the court shall not make any order without first giving—
(a) any person to whom intimation of the date of the hearing was made; and
(b) any other person the court is satisfied has an interest,
an opportunity to be heard.

(2)   The court may, if satisfied as to the matters mentioned in subsection (3) below, make an order granting warrant for diligence on the dependence.

(3)   The matters referred to in subsection (2) above are—

(a)   that the creditor has a prima facie case on the merits of the action;

(b)   that there is a real and substantial risk enforcement of any decree in the action in favour of the creditor would be defeated or prejudiced by reason of—

(i)   the debtor being insolvent or verging on insolvency; or

(ii)   the likelihood of the debtor removing, disposing of, burdening, concealing or otherwise dealing with all or some of the debtor's assets, were warrant for diligence on the dependence not granted; and

(c)   that it is reasonable in all the circumstances, including the effect granting warrant may have on any person having an interest, to do so.

(4)   The onus shall be on the creditor to satisfy the court that the order granting warrant should be made.

(5)   Where the court makes an order granting or, as the case may be, refusing warrant for diligence on the dependence, the court shall order the creditor to intimate that order to—

(a)   the debtor; and

(b)   any other person appearing to the court to have an interest.

(6)   Where the court makes an order refusing warrant for diligence on the dependence, the court may impose such conditions (if any) as it thinks fit.

(7)   Without prejudice to the generality of subsection (6) above, those conditions may require the debtor—

(a)   to consign into court such sum; or

(b)   to find caution or to give such other security, as the court thinks fit.]

Execution before service

[15G   Execution of diligence before service of summons

(1)   This section applies where diligence by—

(a)   arrestment; or

(b)   inhibition,

on the dependence of an action is executed before service of the summons on the debtor.

(2)   Subject to subsection (3) below, if the summons is not served on the debtor before the end of the period of 21 days beginning with the day on which the diligence is executed, the diligence shall cease to have effect.

(3)   The court may, on the application of the creditor, make an order extending the period referred to in subsection (2) above.

(4)   In determining whether to make such an order the court shall have regard to—

(a)   the efforts of the creditor to serve the summons within the period of 21 days; and

(b)   any special circumstances preventing or obstructing service within that period.]

Restriction on property attached

[15H   Sum attached by arrestment on dependence

(1)   The court may, subject to subsection (2) below, when granting warrant for arrestment on the dependence, limit the sum which may be attached to funds not exceeding such amount as the court may specify.

(2)   The maximum amount which the court may specify under subsection (1) above shall be the aggregate of—

(a)   the principal sum concluded for;

(b)   a sum equal to 20 per cent of that sum or such other percentage as the Scottish Ministers may, by regulations, prescribe;

(c)   a sum equal to 1 year's interest on the principal sum at the judicial rate; and

(d)   any sum prescribed under subsection (3) below.

(3)   The Scottish Ministers may, by regulations, prescribe a sum which appears to them to be reasonable having regard to the expenses likely to be—

(a)   incurred by a creditor; and

(b)   chargeable against a debtor,

in executing an arrestment on the dependence.

(4)   For the avoidance of doubt, section 73F of this Act applies to any sum attached under this section.]

[15J   Property affected by inhibition on dependence

Where the court grants warrant for diligence by inhibition on the dependence—

(a)   in a case where the action is brought for specific implement of an obligation—

(i)   to convey heritable property to the creditor;

(ii)   to grant in the creditor's favour a real right in security over such property; or

(iii)   to grant some other right over such property,

the court shall limit the property inhibited to that particular property; and

(b)   in any other case, the court may limit the property inhibited to such property as the court may specify.]

Recall etc of diligence on the dependence

[15K   Recall or restriction of diligence on dependence

(1)   This section applies where warrant is granted for diligence on the dependence.

(2)   The debtor and any person having an interest may apply to the court for an order—

(a)   recalling the warrant;

(b)   restricting the warrant;

(c)   if an arrestment or inhibition has been executed in pursuance of the warrant—

(i)   recalling; or

(ii)   restricting,

that arrestment or inhibition;

(d)   determining any question relating to the validity, effect or operation of the warrant; or

(e)   ancillary to any order mentioned in paragraphs (a) to (d) above.

(3)   An application under subsection (2) above shall—

(a)   be in (or as nearly as may be in) the form prescribed by Act of Sederunt; and

(b)   be intimated to—

(i)   the creditor; and

(ii)   any other person having an interest.

(4)   At the hearing on the application under subsection (2) above, the court shall not make any order without first giving—

(a)   any person to whom intimation of the application was made; and

(b)   any other person the court is satisfied has an interest,

an opportunity to be heard.

(5)   Where the court is satisfied that the warrant is invalid it—

(a)   shall make an order—

(i)   recalling the warrant; and

(ii) if an arrestment or inhibition has been executed in pursuance of the warrant, recalling that arrestment or inhibition; and

(b) may make an order ancillary to any order mentioned in paragraph (a) above.

(6) Where the court is satisfied that an arrestment or inhibition executed in pursuance of the warrant is incompetent, it—

(a) shall make an order recalling that arrestment or inhibition; and

(b) may make an order ancillary to any such order.

(7) Subject to subsection (8) below, where the court is satisfied that the warrant is valid but that—

(a) an arrestment or inhibition executed in pursuance of it is irregular or ineffective; or

(b) it is reasonable in all the circumstances, including the effect granting warrant may have had on any person having an interest, to do so,

the court may make any order such as is mentioned in subsection (2) above.

(8) If no longer satisfied as to the matters mentioned in subsection (9) below, the court—

(a) shall make an order such as is mentioned in subsection (5)(a) above; and

(b) may make an order such as is mentioned in subsection (5)(b) above.

(9) The matters referred to in subsection (8) above are—

(a) that the creditor has a prima facie case on the merits of the action;

(b) that there is a real and substantial risk enforcement of any decree in the action in favour of the creditor would be defeated or prejudiced by reason of—

(i) the debtor being insolvent or verging on insolvency; or

(ii) the likelihood of the debtor removing, disposing of, burdening, concealing or otherwise dealing with all or some of the debtor's assets; and

(c) that it is reasonable in all the circumstances, including the effect granting warrant may have had on any person having an interest, for the warrant or, as the case may be, any arrestment or inhibition executed in pursuance of it to continue to have effect.

(10) The onus shall be on the creditor to satisfy the court that no order under subsection (5), (6), (7) or (8) above should be made.

(11) In granting an application under subsection (2) above, the court may impose such conditions (if any) as it thinks fit.

(12) Without prejudice to the generality of subsection (11) above, the court may impose conditions which require the debtor—

(a) to consign into court such sum; or

(b) to find such caution or to give such other security,

as the court thinks fit.

(13) Where the court makes an order under this section, the court shall order the debtor to intimate that order to—

(a) the creditor; and

(b) any other person appearing to the court to have an interest.

(14) This section applies irrespective of whether warrant for diligence on the dependence is obtained, or executed, before this section comes into force.]

[15L Variation of orders and variation or recall of conditions

(1) Where—

(a) an order restricting warrant for diligence on the dependence is made under section 15K(7); or

(b) a condition is imposed by virtue of—

(i) section 15F(6); or

(ii) section 15K(11),

of this Act, the debtor may apply to the court for variation of the order or, as the case may be, variation or removal of the condition.

(2) An application under subsection (1) above shall—
(a) be in (or as nearly as may be in) the form prescribed by Act of Sederunt; and
(b) be intimated to—
(i) the creditor; and
(ii) any other person having an interest.
(3) At the hearing on the application under subsection (1) above, the court shall not make any order without first giving—
(a) any person to whom intimation of the application was made; and
(b) any other person the court is satisfied has an interest,
an opportunity to be heard.
(4) On an application under subsection (1) above, the court may if it thinks fit—
(a) vary the order; or
(b) vary or remove the condition.
(5) Where the court makes an order varying the order or, as the case may be, varying or removing the condition, the court shall order the debtor to intimate that order to—
(a) the creditor; and
(b) any other person appearing to the court to have an interest.]

General and miscellaneous

[15M Expenses of diligence on the dependence
(1) Subject to subsection (3)(a) below, a creditor shall be entitled to such expenses as the creditor incurs—
(a) in obtaining warrant for diligence on the dependence; and
(b) where an arrestment or inhibition is executed in pursuance of the warrant, in so executing the arrestment or inhibition.
(2) Subject to subsection (3)(b) below, a debtor shall be entitled, where—
(a) warrant for diligence on the dependence is granted; and
(b) the court is satisfied that the creditor was acting unreasonably in applying for it,
to the expenses incurred in opposing that warrant.
(3) The court may modify or refuse—
(a) such expenses as are mentioned in subsection (1) above if it is satisfied that—
(i) the creditor was acting unreasonably in applying for the warrant; or
(ii) such modification or refusal is reasonable in all the circumstances and having regard to the outcome of the action; and
(b) such expenses as are mentioned in subsection (2) above if it is satisfied as to the matter mentioned in paragraph (a)(ii) above.
(4) Subject to subsections (1) to (3) above, the court may make such finding as it thinks fit in relation to such expenses as are mentioned in subsections (1) and (2) above.
(5) Expenses incurred as mentioned in subsection (1) and (2) above in obtaining or, as the case may be, opposing an application for warrant shall be expenses of process.
(6) Subsections (1) to (5) above are without prejudice to any enactment or rule of law as to the recovery of expenses chargeable against a debtor as are incurred in executing an arrestment or inhibition on the dependence of an action.]

[15N Application of this Part to admiralty actions
This Part of this Act (other than sections 15H, 15J and 15M) shall apply, in so far as not inconsistent with the provisions of Part V of the Administration of Justice Act 1956 (c 46)(admiralty jurisdiction and arrestment of ships), to an arrestment on

the dependence of an admiralty action as it applies to any other arrestment on the dependence.]]

[PART 3A
ARRESTMENT AND ACTION OF FURTHCOMING

[73A Arrestment and action of furthcoming to proceed only on decree or document of debt
(1) Arrestment and action of furthcoming or sale shall be competent only in execution of—
    (a) subject to subsection (2) below, a decree; or
    (b) a document of debt.
(2) Arrestment and action of furthcoming or sale in execution of a summary warrant shall be competent only if—
    (a) the debtor has been charged to pay the debt due by virtue of the summary warrant; and
    (b) the period for payment specified in the charge has expired without payment being made.
(3) Any rule of law, having effect immediately before the coming into force of this section, as to the decrees or documents on which arrestment and action of furthcoming or sale can proceed shall, in so far as inconsistent with this section, cease to have effect.
(4) In this Part of this Act—
'decree' means—
    (a) a decree of the Court of Session, of the High Court of Justiciary or of the sheriff;
    (b) a decree of the Court of Teinds;
    (c) a summary warrant;
    (d) a civil judgment granted outside Scotland by a court, tribunal or arbiter which by virtue of any enactment or rule of law is enforceable in Scotland;
    (e) an order or determination which by virtue of any enactment is enforceable as if it were an extract registered decree arbitral bearing a warrant for execution issued by the sheriff;
    (f) a warrant granted, in criminal proceedings, for enforcement by civil diligence; or
    (g) a liability order within the meaning of section 33(2) of the Child Support Act 1991 (c 48),
being a decree, warrant, judgment, order or determination which, or an extract of which, authorises arrestment and action of furthcoming or sale; and
'document of debt' means—
    (a) a document registered for execution in the Books of Council and Session or the sheriff court books; or
    (b) a document or settlement which by virtue of an Order in Council under section 13 of the Civil Jurisdiction and Judgments Act 1982 (c 27) is enforceable in Scotland,
being a document or settlement which, or an extract of which, authorises arrestment and action of furthcoming or sale.
(5) The Scottish Ministers may, by order, modify the definitions of 'decree' and 'document of debt' in subsection (4) above so as to—
    (a) add or remove types of decree or document to or, as the case may be, from those referred to in that provision; or
    (b) vary any of the descriptions of the types of decree or document there referred to.]

[73B Schedule of arrestment to be in prescribed form
(1) This section applies where a creditor arrests in execution of—

(a) a decree and the creditor has not executed an arrestment on the dependence of the action; or

(b) a document of debt.

(2) The schedule of arrestment used in executing the arrestment shall be in (or as nearly as may be in) the form prescribed by the Scottish Ministers by regulations.]

[73C Arrestment on the dependence followed by decree

(1) This section applies where a creditor obtains a decree (in this Part of this Act referred to as a 'final decree') in an action on the dependence of which the creditor has executed an arrestment.

(2) The creditor shall, as soon as reasonably practicable, serve a copy of that final decree, in (or as nearly as may be in) the form prescribed by Act of Sederunt, on the arrestee.]

[73E Funds attached

(1) Subsections (2) to (5) below apply—

(a) where a creditor arrests in execution of—

(i) a decree and the creditor has not executed an arrestment on the dependence of the action; or

(ii) a document of debt; and

(b) only to the extent that the arrestee holds funds due to the debtor the value of which, at the time the arrestment is executed, is or can be ascertained (whether or not that arrestee also holds other moveable property of the debtor).

(2) Subject to subsection (4) below and to section 73F of this Act, the funds mentioned in subsection (1)(b) above attached by the arrestment shall be the lesser of—

(a) the sum due by the arrestee to the debtor; or

(b) the aggregate of—

(i) the principal sum, in relation to which the decree or document is executed, owed by the debtor to the creditor;

(ii) any judicial expenses chargeable against the debtor by virtue of the decree;

(iii) the expenses of executing the arrestment;

(iv) interest on the principal sum up to and including the date of service of the schedule of arrestment;

(v) the interest on the principal sum which would be accrued in the period of 1 year beginning with the day after the date mentioned in sub-paragraph (iv) above;

(vi) any interest on the expenses of executing the arrestment which is chargeable against the debtor; and

(vii) any sum prescribed under subsection (3) below.

(3) The Scottish Ministers may, by regulations, prescribe a sum which appears to them to be reasonable having regard to the average expenses likely to be incurred and chargeable against a debtor in a typical action of furthcoming.

(4) Where—

(a) the arrestee holds both funds due to and other moveable property of the debtor; and

(b) the sum mentioned in paragraph (b) of subsection (2) above exceeds the sum mentioned in paragraph (a) of that subsection,

the arrestment shall, in addition to the funds equal to the sum mentioned in that paragraph (a), attach the whole moveable property so held.

(5) Except as provided for in subsection (4) above, an arrestment to which this section applies shall not attach any moveable property of the debtor other than the sum attached under subsection (2) above.

(6)   Where, in a case to which subsections (2) to (5) above apply—

(a)   in addition to the funds mentioned in subsection (1)(b) above, the arrestee holds funds due to the debtor the value of which is not or cannot be ascertained; and

(b)   the sum mentioned in paragraph (a) of subsection (2) above exceeds the sum mentioned in paragraph (b) of that subsection,

the arrestment shall not attach any of the funds mentioned in paragraph (a) above.]

[73F   Protection of minimum balance in certain bank accounts

(1)   Subject to subsection (2) below, this section applies where—

(a)   a creditor arrests—

(i)   in pursuance of a warrant granted for diligence on the dependence of an action; or

(ii)   in execution of a decree or document of debt;

(b)   the arrestment attaches funds standing to the credit of a debtor in an account held by a bank or other financial institution; and

(c)   the debtor is an individual.

(2)   This section does not apply where the account is—

(a)   held in the name of a company, a limited liability partnership, a partnership or an unincorporated association; or

(b)   operated by the debtor as a trading account.

(3)   The arrestment shall—

(a)   in a case where the sum standing to the credit of the debtor exceeds the sum mentioned in subsection (4) below, attach only the balance above that sum; and

(b)   in any other case, attach no funds.

(4)   The sum referred to in subsection (3)(a) above is the sum first mentioned in column 1 of Table B in Schedule 2 to this Act (being the sum representing the net monthly earnings from which no deduction would be made under an earnings arrestment were such an arrestment in effect).

(5)   In subsection (1) above, 'bank or other financial institution' means—

(a)   the Bank of England;

(b)   a person who has permission under Part 4 of the Financial Services and Markets Act 2000 (c 8) to accept deposits;

(c)   an EEA firm of the kind mentioned in paragraph 5(b) of Schedule 3 to that Act which has permission under paragraph 15 of that schedule (as a result of qualifying for authorisation under paragraph 12 of that schedule) to accept deposits; or

(d)   a person who is exempt from the general prohibition in respect of accepting deposits as a result of an exemption order made under section 38(1) of that Act,

and the expressions in this definition shall be read with section 22 of that Act, any relevant order made under that section and Schedule 2 to that Act.

(6)   The Scottish Ministers may, by regulations—

(a)   modify subsection (2) above so as to—

(i)   add or remove types of account to or, as the case may be, from those referred to in that paragraph; or

(ii)   vary any of the descriptions of the types of account there referred to; and

(b)   modify the definition of 'bank or other financial institution' in subsection (5) above so as to—

(i)   add or remove types of financial institution to or, as the case may be, from those referred to in that provision; or

(ii)   vary any of the descriptions of the types of institution there referred to.]

[73G   Arrestee's duty of disclosure

(1)   This section applies where a creditor arrests—

(a)   in pursuance of a warrant granted for diligence on the dependence of an action; or

(b)   in execution of a decree or document of debt.

(2)   The arrestee shall, before the expiry of the period mentioned in subsection (3) below, send to the creditor in (or as nearly as may be in) the form prescribed by the Scottish Ministers by regulations, the information mentioned in subsection (4) below.

(3)   The period referred to in subsection (2) above is the period of 3 weeks beginning with the day on which the arrestment is executed.

(4)   The information referred to in subsection (2) above is—

(a)   where any property, other than funds due to the debtor, is attached—

(i)   the nature of that property; and

(ii)   the value of it in so far as known to the arrestee; and

(b)   where any such funds are attached, the nature and value of those funds.

(5)   The arrestee shall, at the same time as sending, under subsection (2) above, the information to the creditor, send a copy of it to—

(a)   the debtor; and

(b)   in so far as known to the arrestee, any person—

(i)   who owns or claims to own attached property; or

(ii)   to whom attached funds are or are claimed to be due,

solely or in common with the debtor.]

[73H   Failure to disclose information

(1)   Where an arrestee fails without reasonable excuse to send the prescribed form under section 73G(2) of this Act, the sheriff may, on the application of the creditor, make an order requiring the arrestee to pay to the creditor—

(a)   the sum due to the creditor by the debtor; or

(b)   the sum mentioned in section 73F(4) of this Act,

whichever is the lesser.

(2)   Where the arrestee fails to send the prescribed form in relation to an arrestment on the dependence of an action, the sheriff—

(a)   may not make an order under subsection (1) above until the creditor has served a copy of the final decree under section 73C(2) above; and

(b)   may deal with the failure as a contempt of court.

(3)   Where a sum is paid by virtue of an order under subsection (1) above—

(a)   the debt owed by the debtor to the creditor shall be reduced by that sum; and

(b)   the arrestee shall not be entitled to recover that sum from the debtor.

(4)   An arrestee aggrieved by an order under subsection (1) above may, before the expiry of the period of 2 weeks beginning with the day on which the order is made, appeal, on point of law only, to the sheriff principal, whose decision shall be final.]

[73J   Automatic release of arrested funds

(1)   This section applies where—

(a)   a creditor—

(i)   obtains a final decree in an action on the dependence of which the creditor has executed an arrestment; or

(ii)   arrests in execution of a decree or document of debt; and

(b)   the arrestment attaches funds which are due to the debtor (whether or not it also attaches other moveable property of the debtor).

(2)   Subject to section 73L of this Act, the arrestee—

(a)   shall, on the expiry of the period mentioned in subsection (3) below, release to the creditor, from the attached funds, a sum calculated in accordance with section 73K of this Act; and

(b)   may, where a mandate authorises the arrestee to do so, release that sum before the expiry of that period.

(3)   The period referred to in subsection (2) above is the period of 14 weeks beginning with the date of service of a copy of the final decree under section 73C(2) of this Act or, as the case may be, the date of service of the schedule of arrestment.

(4)   In this section and in sections 73K to 73P of this Act, references to funds or sums due to or by any person do not include references to funds or sums due in respect of future or contingent debts.]

[73K   Sum released under section 73J(2)

The sum released under section 73J(2) of this Act is the lowest of—

(a)   the sum attached by the arrestment;

(b)   the sum due by the arrestee to the debtor; or

(c)   the aggregate of—

(i)   the principal sum, in relation to which the decree or document is executed or, as the case may be, which is decerned for in the final decree, owed by the debtor to the creditor;

(ii)   any judicial expenses chargeable against the debtor by virtue of the decree or final decree;

(iii)   the expenses of executing the arrestment;

(iv)   interest on the principal sum up to and including the date of service of the schedule of arrestment or, as the case may be, the date of the final decree;

(v)   the interest on the principal sum which would be accrued in the period beginning with the day after the date mentioned in sub-paragraph (iv) above and ending on the day on which the funds are released under section 73J(2) of this Act; and

(vi)   any interest on the expenses of executing the arrestment which is chargeable against the debtor.]

[73L   Circumstances preventing automatic release

(1)   No funds may be released under section 73J(2) of this Act where—

(a)   a person mentioned in subsection (2) below applies, by notice of objection, to the sheriff under section 73M(1) of this Act;

(b)   the debtor applies to the sheriff under section 73Q(2) of this Act;

(c)   an action of multiplepoinding is raised in relation to the funds attached by the arrestment; or

(d)   the arrestment is—

(i)   recalled;

(ii)   restricted; or

(iii)   otherwise ceases to have effect.

(2)   The persons referred to in subsection (1)(a) above are—

(a)   the debtor;

(b)   the arrestee; and

(c)   any other person to whom the funds are due solely or in common with the debtor (in this section and in sections 73M and 73N of this Act, the 'third party').]

[73M   Notice of objection

(1)   Where section 73J of this Act applies—

(a)   the debtor;

(b)   the arrestee; or

(c)   a third party,

may, by notice of objection, apply to the sheriff for an order recalling or restricting the arrestment.

(2)   The notice of objection referred to in subsection (1) above shall—

(a)   be in (or as nearly as may be in) the form prescribed by Act of Sederunt;

(b)   be given to the persons mentioned in subsection (3) below before the expiry of the period of 4 weeks beginning with the date of service of a copy of the final decree under section 73C(2) of this Act or, as the case may be, the date of service of the schedule of arrestment; and

(c)   specify one or more of the grounds of objection mentioned in subsection (4) below.

(3)   The persons referred to in subsection (2)(b) above are—
  (a)   the creditor;
  (b)   the sheriff clerk;
  (c)   the debtor or, as the case may be, the arrestee; and
  (d)   in so far as known to the person objecting, any third party.

(4)   The grounds of objection referred to in subsection (2)(c) above are—
  (a)   the warrant in execution of which the arrestment is executed is invalid;
  (b)   the arrestment has been executed incompetently or irregularly;
  (c)   the funds attached are due to the third party solely or in common with the debtor.

(5)   Where a person applies by notice of objection under subsection (1) above, that person may not, subject to subsection (6) below, raise—
  (a)   an action of multiplepoinding; or
  (b)   subject to subsection (7) below, any other proceedings,
in relation to the funds attached.

(6)   Subsection (5) above is without prejudice to the right of the person—
  (a)   to enter any such action or proceedings raised by any other person; and
  (b)   to raise such an action or proceedings where the sheriff makes, under section 73N(5) of this Act, an order sisting the proceedings on the objection.

(7)   A debtor who applies by notice of objection under subsection (1) above may apply to the sheriff under section 73Q(2) of this Act and, in such a case, the sheriff may deal with both applications at one hearing.]

[73N   Hearings following notice of objection

(1)   Subject to subsection (5) below, before the expiry of the period of 8 weeks beginning with the day on which an application by notice of objection is made under section 73M(1) of this Act, the sheriff shall hold a hearing to determine the objection.

(2)   At the hearing under subsection (1) above, the sheriff shall not make any order without first giving—
  (a)   the creditor;
  (b)   the arrestee;
  (c)   the debtor; and
  (d)   any third party,
an opportunity to be heard.

(3)   Where the sheriff upholds the objection, the sheriff may make an order recalling or restricting the arrestment.

(4)   Where the sheriff rejects the objection, the sheriff may make an order requiring a sum determined in the order to be released to the creditor—
  (a)   in a case where the period mentioned in section 73J(3) of this Act has not expired, on the expiry of that period; or
  (b)   in any other case, as soon as reasonably practicable after the date on which the order is made.

(5)   Where—
  (a)   the sheriff is satisfied that it is more appropriate for the matters raised at the hearing to be dealt with by—
    (i)   an action of multiplepoinding; or
    (ii)   other proceedings,
raised in relation to the funds attached; or

(b)   at any time before a decision is made under subsections (3) or (4)
such an action is or other proceedings are raised,
the sheriff shall make an order sisting the proceedings on the objection.
(6)   The sheriff may make such other order as the sheriff thinks fit.
(7)   Where the sheriff makes an order under this section, the sheriff shall order
the person who objected to intimate that order to such of the persons mentioned in
subsection (2) above as the sheriff thinks fit.
(8)   A person aggrieved by a decision of the sheriff under this section may,
before the expiry of the period of 14 days beginning with the day on which the
decision is made, appeal, on point of law only, to the sheriff principal, whose
decision shall be final.]

[73P   Arrestee not liable for funds released in good faith
Where an arrestee releases funds under section 73J(2) of this Act in good faith
but—
(a)   the warrant in execution of which the arrestment was executed is invalid;
or
(b)   the arrestment was incompetently or irregularly executed,
the arrestee is not liable to the debtor or to any other person having an interest in
the funds for damages for patrimonial loss caused by the release of funds.]

[73Q   Application for release of property where arrestment unduly harsh
(1)   This section applies where—
(a)   a creditor—
(i)   obtains final decree in an action on the dependence of which the
creditor executed an arrestment; or
(ii)   arrests in execution of a decree or document of debt; and
(b)   the arrestment attaches funds due to or other moveable property of the
debtor.
(2)   The debtor may apply to the sheriff for an order—
(a)   providing that the arrestment ceases to have effect in relation to—
(i)   the funds or other property attached; or
(ii)   so much of those funds or that property as the sheriff specifies; and
(b)   requiring the arrestee to release the funds or property to the debtor.
(3)   An application under subsection (2) above shall be—
(a)   in (or as nearly as may be in) the form prescribed by Act of Sederunt;
(b)   made at any time during which the arrestment has effect; and
(c)   intimated to—
(i)   the creditor;
(ii)   the arrestee; and
(iii)   any other person appearing to have an interest.]

[73R   Hearing on application under section 73Q for release of property
(1)   At the hearing on an application under section 73Q(2) of this Act, the
sheriff shall not make any order without first giving—
(a)   the creditor;
(b)   the arrestee; and
(c)   any other person appearing to the court to have an interest,
an opportunity to be heard.
(2)   Subject to subsection (3) below, if the sheriff is satisfied that the arrestment
is unduly harsh—
(a)   to the debtor; or
(b)   where the debtor is an individual, to any person such as is mentioned in
subsection (4) below,
the sheriff shall make an order such as is mentioned in section 73Q(2) of this
Act.

ιn order under subsection (2) above the sheriff shall have
stances including, in a case where the debtor is an indivi-
ῃed—

ͻse funds; and

ᵗe of those funds is or includes earnings, whether an
ʳrent ·maintenance arrestment or conjoined arrestment
ιn to those earnings.

ᵤᵤ to in subsection (2)(b) above are—

. ᵤf the debtor;

᷁ person living together with the debtor as husband and wife;

(c) a civil partner of the debtor;

(d) a person living with the debtor in a relationship which has the characteristics of the relationship between a husband and wife except that the person and the debtor are of the same sex;

(e) a child of the debtor under the age of 16 years, including—

(i) a stepchild; and

(ii) any child brought up or treated by the debtor or any person mentioned in paragraph (b), (c) or (d) above as a child of the debtor or, as the case may be, that person.

(5) Where the sheriff refuses to make an order under subsection (2) above, the sheriff may, in a case where funds are attached, make an order requiring a sum determined in the order to be released to the creditor—

(a) in a case where the period mentioned in section 73J(3) of this Act has not expired, on the expiry of that period; or

(b) in any other case, as soon as reasonably practicable after the date on which the order is made.

(6) Where the sheriff makes an order under this section, the sheriff shall order the debtor to intimate that order to the persons mentioned in subsection (1) above.

(7) A person aggrieved by a decision of the sheriff under this section may, before the expiry of the period of 14 days beginning with the day on which the decision is made, appeal, on point of law only, to the sheriff principal, whose decision shall be final.]

[73S Mandate to be in prescribed form

(1) A mandate authorising an arrestee to pay over any funds or hand over other property attached by an arrestment shall be in (or as nearly as may be in) the form prescribed by the Scottish Ministers by regulations.

(2) A mandate which is not in (or as nearly as may be in) the prescribed form is invalid.

(3) Where—

(a) a mandate is invalid by virtue of subsection (2) above; but

(b) the arrestee pays over funds or hands over other property in accordance with that mandate,

the arrestee is not liable to the debtor or to any other person having an interest in the funds or property for damages for patrimonial loss caused by paying over the funds or handing over the property provided the arrestee acted in good faith.]

[73T Arrestment of ships etc

For the avoidance of doubt, this Part of this Act does not apply to the arrestment of a ship, cargo or other maritime property.]]

PART VI
WARRANTS FOR DILIGENCE AND CHARGES FOR PAYM

. . .

88 Warrants for diligence: special cases

(1) This section applies where a creditor has acquired by assignation in to the debtor, confirmation as executor, or otherwise a right to—

    (a) a decree;

    (b) an obligation contained in a document an extract of which, afte document has been registered in the Books of Council and Session or in sh court books, may be obtained containing warrant for execution;

    (c) an order or determination which by virtue of any enactment enforceable as if it were an extract registered decree arbitral bearing a warrar for execution issued by a sheriff,

either directly or through a third party from a person in whose favour the decree, order or determination was granted or who was the creditor in the obligation contained in the document.

(2) Where this section applies, the creditor who has acquired a right as mentioned in subsection (1) above may apply to the appropriate clerk for a warrant having the effect of authorising the execution at the instance of that creditor of any diligence authorised by an extract of the decree or document or by the order or determination, as the case may be.

(3) The applicant under subsection (2) above shall submit to the appropriate clerk—

    (a) an extract of the decree or of the document registered as mentioned in subsection (1)(b) above or a certified copy of the order or determination; and

    (b) the assignation (along with evidence of its intimation to the debtor), confirmation as executor or other document establishing the applicant's right.

(4) The appropriate clerk shall grant the warrant applied for under subsection (2) above if he is satisfied that the applicant's right is established.

(5) Where—

    (a) a charge has already been served in pursuance of the decree, order, determination or registered document; and

    (b) the applicant under subsection (2) above submits with his application the certificate of execution of the charge in addition to the documents mentioned in subsection (3) above,

a warrant granted under subsection (4) above shall authorise the execution at the instance of the applicant of diligence in pursuance of that charge.

(6) For the purposes of this section, 'the appropriate clerk' shall be—

    (a) in the case of a decree granted by the Court of Session or a document registered (whether before or after such acquisition) in the Books of Council and Session, a clerk of court of the Court of Session;

    (b) in the case of a decree granted by the High Court of Justiciary, a clerk of Justiciary;

    (c) in the case of a decree granted by a sheriff or a document registered (whether before or after such acquisition) in the books of a sheriff court, the sheriff clerk of that sheriff court;

    (d) in the case of such an order or determination as is mentioned in subsection (1)(c) above, any sheriff clerk.

89 Abolition of letters of horning, horning and poinding, poinding, and caption

The granting of letters of horning, letters of horning and poinding, letters of poinding and letters of caption shall cease to be competent.

for payment

earnings arrestment shall not be competent
⌐ved on the debtor and the period for pay-
ithout payment being made.
s section apply to any case where it is
charge for payment has been served on

pecified in any charge for payment served in
⌐tion shall be 14 days if the person on whom it is
⌐ngdom and 28 days if he is outside the United King-
⌐ unknown.
⌐hall be in the form prescribed by Act of Sederunt or Act

⌐section (6) below, where any such charge has been served, it
⌐tent to execute [diligence] by virtue of that charge more than 2
⌐ate of such service.
⌐tor may reconstitute his right to execute [diligence] by the service of
⌐arge for payment.
⌐o expenses incurred in the service of a further charge for payment within
⌐iod of 2 years after service of the first charge shall be chargeable against the
⌐or.

(8)   Registration of certificates of execution of charges for payment in a register of hornings shall cease to be competent.

91   Enforcement of certain warrants and precepts of sheriff anywhere in Scotland

(1)   The following may be executed anywhere in Scotland—

(a)   a warrant for execution contained in an extract of a decree granted by a sheriff;

(b)   a warrant for execution inserted in an extract of a document registered in sheriff court books;

(c)   a summary warrant;

(d)   a warrant of a sheriff for arrestment on the dependence of an action or in security;

(e)   a precept (issued by a sheriff clerk) of arrestment in security of a liquid debt the term of payment of which has not arrived.

(2)   A warrant or precept mentioned in subsection (1) above may be executed by a sheriff officer of—

(a)   the court which granted it; or

(b)   the sheriff court district in which it is to be executed.

PART VII
MISCELLANEOUS AND GENERAL

. . .

94   Ascription of sums recovered by diligence or while diligence is in effect

(1)   This section applies to any sums recovered by any of the following diligences—

[. . .]

(b)   an earnings arrestment;

(c)   an arrestment and action of furthcoming or sale; or

(d)   a conjoined arrestment order in so far as it enforces an ordinary debt,

or paid to account of the sums recoverable by the diligence while the diligence is in effect.

(2)   A sum to which this section applies shall be ascribed to the following in the order in which they are mentioned—
  (a)   the expenses already incurred in respect of—
    (i)   the diligence;
    (ii)   any previous diligence the expenses of which are chargeable against and recoverable from the debtor under section 93(5) of this Act;
    (iii)   the execution of a current maintenance arrestment;
  (b)   any interest, due under the decree or other document on which the diligence proceeds, which has accrued at the date of execution of the [. . .] earnings arrestment or arrestment, or in the case of an ordinary debt included in a conjoined arrestment order which has accrued at the date of application under section 60(2) or 62(5) of this Act;
  (c)   any sum (including any expenses) due under the decree or other document, other than any expenses or interest mentioned in paragraphs (a) and (b) above.

[95A   Prescription of arrestment

(1)   Subject to subsection (2) below, an arrestment which is not insisted in prescribes—
  (a)   where it is on the dependence of an action, at the end of the period of 3 years beginning with the day on which a final interlocutor is obtained by the creditor for payment of all or part of a principal sum concluded for; or
  (b)   where it is in execution of an extract decree or other extract registered document relating to a due debt, at the end of the period of 3 years beginning with the day on which the arrestment is executed.
(2)   Where the arrestment secures or enforces a future or contingent debt due to the creditor, it prescribes, if not insisted in, at the end of the period of 3 years beginning on the day on which the debt becomes due.
(3)   In a case where—
  (a)   a time to pay direction;
  (b)   an interim order under section 6(3) of this Act; or
  (c)   a time to pay order,
has been made, there shall be disregarded, in computing the period at the end of which the arrestment prescribes, the period during which the time to pay direction, interim order or time to pay order is in effect.
(4)   Nothing in this section shall apply to an earnings arrestment, a current maintenance arrestment or a conjoined arrestment order.
(5)   Subsections (1) to (3) above apply irrespective of whether the arrestment is executed, or warrant for it obtained, before this section comes into force.
(6)   For the purposes of subsection (1)(a) above, a final interlocutor is obtained when an interlocutor cannot be recalled or altered and is not subject to review.]

102   Procedure in diligence proceeding on extract of registered document etc

(1)   The Court of Session may by Act of Sederunt—
  (a)   regulate and prescribe the procedure and practice in; and
  (b)   prescribe the form of any document to be used in, or for the purposes of, diligence of a kind specified in subsection (2) below.
(2)   The diligences referred to in subsection (1) above are diligences proceeding—
  (a)   on an extract of a document which has been registered for execution in the Books of Council and Session or in sheriff court books; or
  (b)   on an order or a determination which by virtue of any enactment is to be treated as if it were so registered.

SCHEDULE   Regulation 2(b)

TABLE A: DEDUCTIONS FROM WEEKLY EARNINGS

Net earnings	Deduction*
Not exceeding £95.77	Nil
Exceeding £95.77 but not exceeding £346.15	£4 or 19% of earnings exceeding £95.77, whichever is the greater
Exceeding £346.15 but not exceeding £576.92	£47.57 plus 23% of earnings exceeding £346.15
Exceeding £576.92	£100.65 plus 50% of earnings exceeding £576.92

*When applying a percentage the calculation should be done to two decimal places of a penny and the result rounded to the nearest whole penny, with an exact half penny being rounded down.

TABLE B: DEDUCTIONS FROM MONTHLY EARNINGS

Net earnings	Deduction*
Not exceeding £415	Nil
Exceeding £415 but not exceeding £1,500	£15 or 19% of earnings exceeding £415, whichever is the greater
Exceeding £1,500 but not exceeding £2,500.00	£206.15 plus 23% of earnings exceeding £1,500
Exceeding £2,500	£436.15 plus 50% of earnings exceeding £2,500

*When applying a percentage the calculation should be done to two decimal places of a penny and the result rounded to the nearest whole penny, with an exact half penny being rounded down.

TABLE C: DEDUCTIONS FROM DAILY EARNINGS

Net earnings	Deduction*
Not exceeding £95.77	Nil
Exceeding £13.64 but not exceeding £49.32	£0.50 or 19% of earnings exceeding £13.64, whichever is the greater
Exceeding £49.32 but not exceeding £82.19	£6.78 plus 23% of earnings exceeding £49.32
Exceeding £82.19	£14.34 plus 50% of earnings exceeding £82.19

*When applying a percentage the calculation should be done to two decimal places of a penny and the result rounded to the nearest whole penny, with an exact half penny being rounded down.

CONSUMER PROTECTION ACT 1987
(1987, c 43)

PART I
PRODUCT LIABILITY

1 Purpose and construction of Part I

(1) This Part shall have effect for the purpose of making such provision as is necessary in order to comply with the product liability Directive and shall be construed accordingly.

(2) In this Part, except in so far as the context otherwise requires—

[. . .]

'dependant' and 'relative' have the same meaning as they have in, respectively, the Fatal Accidents Act 1976 and the Damages (Scotland) Act 1976;

'producer', in relation to a product, means—

(a) the person who manufactured it;

(b) in the case of a substance which has not been manufactured but has been won or abstracted, the person who won or abstracted it;

(c) in the case of a product which has not been manufactured, won or abstracted but essential characteristics of which are attributable to an industrial or other process having been carried out (for example, in relation to agricultural produce), the person who carried out that process;

'product' means any goods or electricity and (subject to subsection (3) below) includes a product which is comprised in another product, whether by virtue of being ̂component part or raw material or otherwise; and

'the product liability Directive' means the Directive of the Council of the European Communities, dated 25th July 1985, (No 85/374/EEC) on the approximation of the laws, regulations and administrative provisions of the member States concerning liability for defective products.

(3) For the purposes of this Part a person who supplies any product in which products are comprised, whether by virtue of being component parts or raw materials or otherwise, shall not be treated by reason only of his supply of that product as supplying any of the products so comprised.

2 Liability for defective products

(1) Subject to the following provisions of this Part, where any damage is caused wholly or partly by a defect in a product, every person to whom subsection (2) below applies shall be liable for the damage.

(2) This subsection applies to—

(a) the producer of the product;

(b) any person who, by putting his name on the product or using a trade mark or other distinguishing mark in relation to the product, has held himself out to be the producer of the product;

(c) any person who has imported the product into a member State from a place outside the member States in order, in the course of any business of his, to supply it to another.

(3) Subject as aforesaid, where any damage is caused wholly or partly by a defect in a product, any person who supplied the product (whether to the person who suffered the damage, to the producer of any product in which the product in question is comprised or to any other person) shall be liable for the damage if—

(a) the person who suffered the damage requests the supplier to identify one or more of the persons (whether still in existence or not) to whom subsection (2) above applies in relation to the product;

(b) that request is made within a reasonable period after the damage occurs and at a time when it is not reasonably practicable for the person making the request to identify all those persons; and

(c) the supplier fails, within a reasonable period after receiving the request, either to comply with the request or to identify the person who supplied the product to him.

[. . .]

(5) Where two or more persons are liable by virtue of this Part for the same damage, their liability shall be joint and several.

(6) This section shall be without prejudice to any liability arising otherwise than by virtue of this Part.

3 Meaning of 'defect'

(1) Subject to the following provisions of the section, there is a defect in a product for the purposes of this Part if the safety of the product is not such as persons generally are entitled to expect; and for those purposes 'safety', in relation to a product, shall include safety with respect to products comprised in that product and safety in the context of risks of damage to property, as well as in the context of risks of death or personal injury.

(2) In determining for the purposes of subsection (1) above what persons generally are entitled to expect in relation to a product all the circumstances shall be taken into account, including—

(a) the manner in which, and purposes for which, the product has been marketed, its get-up, the use of any mark in relation to the product and any instructions for, or warnings with respect to, doing or refraining from doing anything with or in relation to the product;

(b) what might reasonably be expected to be done with or in relation to the product; and

(c) the time when the product was supplied by its producer to another;

and nothing in this section shall require a defect to be inferred from the fact alone that the safety of a product which is supplied after that time is greater than the safety of the product in question.

4 Defences

(1) In any civil proceedings by virtue of this Part against any person ('the person proceeded against') in respect of a defect in a product it shall be a defence for him to show—

(a) that the defect is attributable to compliance with any requirement imposed by or under any enactment or with any Community obligation; or

(b) that the person proceeded against did not at any time supply the product to another; or

(c) that the following conditions are satisfied, that is to say—

(i) that the only supply of the product to another by the person proceeded against was otherwise than in the course of a business of that person's; and

(ii) that section 2(2) above does not apply to that person or applies to him by virtue only of things done otherwise than with a view to profit; or

(d) that the defect did not exist in the product at the relevant time; or

(e) that the state of scientific and technical knowledge at the relevant time was not such that a producer of products of the same description as the product in question might be expected to have discovered the defect if it had existed in his products while they were under his control; or

(f) that the defect—

(i) constituted a defect in a product ('the subsequent product') in which the product in question had been comprised; and

(ii) was wholly attributable to the design of the subsequent product or to compliance by the producer of the product in question with instructions given by the producer of the subsequent product.

(2) In this section 'the relevant time', in relation to electricity, means the time at which it was generated, being a time before it was transmitted or distributed, and in relation to any other product, means—

(a)   if the person proceeded against is a person to whom subsection (2) of section 2 above applies in relation to the product, the time when he supplied the product to another;

(b)   if that subsection does not apply to that person in relation to the product, the time when the product was last supplied by a person to whom that subsection does apply in relation to the product.

5   Damage giving rise to liability

(1)   Subject to the following provisions of this section, in this Part 'damages' means death or personal injury or any loss of or damage to any property (including land).

(2)   A person shall not be liable under section 2 above in respect of any defect in a product for the loss of or any damage to the product itself or for the loss of or any damage to the whole or any part of any product which has been supplied with the product in question comprised in it.

(3)   A person shall not be liable under section 2 above for any loss of or damage to any property which, at the time it is lost or damaged, is not—

(a)   of a description of property ordinarily intended for private use, occupation or consumption; and

(b)   intended by the person suffering the loss or damage mainly for his own private use, occupation or consumption.

(4)   No damages shall be awarded to any person by virtue of this Part in respect of any loss of or damage to any property if the amount which would fall to be so awarded to that person, apart from this subsection and any liability for interest, does not exceed £275.

. . .

(8)   Subsections (5) to (7) above shall not extend to Scotland.

6   Application of certain enactments etc

(1)   Any damage for which a person is liable under section 2 above shall be deemed to have been caused—

(a)   for the purposes of the Fatal Accidents Act 1976, by that person's wrongful act, neglect or default;

(b)   for the purposes of section 3 of the Law Reform (Miscellaneous Provisions) (Scotland) Act 1940 (contribution among joint wrongdoers), by that person's wrongful act or negligent act or omission;

(c)   for the purposes of section 1 of the Damages (Scotland) Act 1976 (rights of relatives of a deceased), by that person's act or omission, and

(d)   for the purposes of Part II of the Administration of Justice Act 1982 (damages for personal injuries, etc—Scotland), by an act or omission giving rise to liability in that person to pay damages.

(2)   Where—

(a)   a person's death is caused wholly or partly by a defect in a product, or a person dies after suffering damage which has been so caused;

(b)   a request such as mentioned in paragraph (a) of subsection (3) of section 2 above is made to a supplier of the product by that person's personal representatives or, in the case of a person whose death is caused wholly or partly by the defect, by any dependant or relative of that person; and

(c)   the conditions specified in paragraphs (b) and (c) of that subsection are satisfied in relation to that request,

this Part shall have effect for the purposes of the Law Reform (Miscellaneous Provisions) Act 1934, the Fatal Accidents Acts 1976 and the Damages (Scotland) Act 1976 as if liability of the supplier to that person under that subsection did not depend on that person having requested the supplier to identify certain persons or on the said conditions having been satisfied in relation to a request made by that person.

(3)   Section 1 of the Congenital Disabilities (Civil Liability) Act 1976 shall have effect for the purposes of this Part as if—

(a)   a person were answerable to a child in respect of an occurrence caused wholly or partly by a defect in a product if he is or has been liable under section 2 above in respect of any effect of the occurrence on a parent of the child, or would be so liable if the occurrence caused a parent of the child to suffer damage;

(b)   the provisions of this Part relating to liability under section 2 above applied in relation to liability by virtue of paragraph (a) above under the said section 1; and

(c)   subsection (6) of the said section 1 (exclusion of liability) were omitted.

(4)   Where any damage is caused partly by a defect in a product and partly by the fault of the person suffering the damage, the Law Reform (Contributory Negligence) Act 1945 and section 5 of the Fatal Accidents Act 1976 (contributory negligence) shall have effect as if the defect were the fault of every person liable by virtue of this Part for the damage caused by the defect.

(5)   In subsection (4) above 'fault' has the same meaning as in the said Act of 1945.

(6)   Schedule 1 to this Act shall have effect for the purpose of amending the Limitation Act 1980 and the Prescription and Limitation (Scotland) Act 1973 in their application in relation to the bringing of actions by virtue of this Part.

(7)   It is hereby declared that liability by virtue of this Part is to be treated as liability in tort for the purposes of any enactment conferring jurisdiction on any court with respect to any matter.

(8)   Nothing in this Part shall prejudice the operation of section 12 of the Nuclear Installations Act 1965 (rights to compensation for certain breaches of duties confined to rights under that Act).

7   Prohibition on exclusions from liability
The liability of a person by virtue of this Part to person who has suffered damage caused wholly or partly by a defect in a product, or to a dependant or relative of such a person, shall not be limited or excluded by any contract term, by any notice or by any other provision.

8   Power to modify Part I
(1)   Her Majesty may by Order in Council make such modifications of this Part and of any other enactment (including an enactment contained in the following Parts of this Act, or in an Act passed after this Act) as appear to Her Majesty in Council to be necessary or expedient in consequence of any modification of the product liability Directive which is made at any time after the passing of this Act.

(2)   An Order in Council under subsection (1) above shall not be submitted to Her Majesty in Council unless a draft of the Order has been laid before, and approved by a resolution of, each House of Parliament.

9   Application of Part I to Crown
(1)   Subject to subsection (2) below, this Part shall bind the Crown.

(2)   The Crown shall not, as regards the Crown's liability by virtue of this Part, be bound by this Part further than the Crown is made liable in tort or in reparation under the Crown Proceedings Act 1947, as that Act has effect from time to time.

PART II
CONSUMER SAFETY

[. . .]

11 Safety regulations

(1) The Secretary of State may by regulations under this section ('safety regulations') make such provision as he considers appropriate [. . .] for the purpose of securing—

(a) that goods to which this section applies are safe;

(b) that goods to which this section applies which are unsafe, or would be unsafe in the hands of persons of a particular description, are not made available to persons generally or, as the case may be, to persons of that description, and

(c) that appropriate information is, and inappropriate information is not, provided in relation to goods to which this section applies.

(2) Without prejudice to the generality of subsection (1) above, safety regulations may contain provision—

(a) with respect to the composition or contents, design, construction, finish or packing of goods to which this section applies, with respect to standards for such goods and with respect to other matters relating to such goods;

(b) with respect to the giving, refusal, alteration or cancellation of approvals of such goods, of descriptions of such goods or of standards for such goods;

(c) with respect to the conditions that may be attached to any approval given under the regulations;

(d) for requiring such fees as may be determined by or under the regulations to be paid on the giving or alteration of any approval under the regulations and on the making of an application for such an approval or alteration;

(e) with respect to appeals against refusals, alterations and cancellations of approvals given under the regulations and against the conditions contained in such approvals;

(f) for requiring goods to which this section applies to be approved under the regulations or to conform to the requirements of the regulations or to descriptions or standards specified in or approved by or under the regulations;

(g) with respect to the testing or inspection of goods to which this section applies (including provision for determining the standards to be applied in carrying out any test or inspection);

(h) with respect to the way of dealing with goods of which some or all do not satisfy a test required by or under the regulations or a standard connected with a procedure so required;

(i) for requiring a mark, warning or instruction or any other information relating to goods to be put on or to accompany the goods or to be used or provided in some other manner in relation to the goods, and for securing that inappropriate information is not given in relation to goods either by means of misleading marks or otherwise;

(j) for prohibiting persons from supplying, or from offering to supply, agreeing to supply, exposing for supply or possessing for supply, goods to which this section applies and component parts and raw materials for such goods;

(k) for requiring information to be given to any such person as may be determined by or under the regulations for the purpose of enabling that person to exercise any function conferred on him by the regulations.

(3) Without prejudice as aforesaid, safety regulations may contain provision—

(a) for requiring persons on whom functions are conferred by or under section 27 below to have regard, in exercising their functions so far as relating to any provision of safety regulations, to matters specified in a direction issued by the Secretary of State with respect to that provision;

(b) for securing that a person shall not be guilty of an offence under section

12 below unless it is shown that the goods in question do not conform to a particular standard;

(c)   for securing that proceedings for such an offence are not brought in England and Wales except by or with the consent of the Secretary of State or the Director of Public Prosecutions;

(d)   for securing that proceedings for such an offence are not brought in Northern Ireland except by or with consent of the Secretary of State or the Director of Public Prosecutions for Northern Ireland;

(e)   for enabling a magistrate's court in England and Wales or Northern Ireland to try an information or, in Northern Ireland, a complaint in respect of such an offence if the information was laid or the complaint made within twelve months from the time when the offence was committed;

(f)   for enabling summary proceedings for such an offence to be brought in Scotland at any time within twelve months from the time when the offence was committed; and

(g)   for determining the persons by whom, and the manner in which, anything required to be done by or under the regulations is to be done.

(4)   Safety regulations shall not provide for any contravention of the regulations to be an offence.

(5)   Where the Secretary of State proposes to make safety regulations it shall be his duty before he makes them—

(a)   to consult such organisations as appear to him to be representative of interests substantially affected by the proposal;

(b)   to consult such other persons as he considers appropriate; and

(c)   in the case of proposed regulations relating to goods suitable for use at work to consult [the Health and Safety Executive] in relation to the application of the proposed regulations to Great Britain;

but the preceding provisions of this subsection shall not apply in the case of regulations which provide for the regulations to cease to have effect at the end of a period of not more than twelve months beginning with the day on which they come into force and which contain a statement that it appears to the Secretary of State that the need to protect the public requires that the regulations should be made without delay.

(6)   The power to make safety regulations shall be exercisable by statutory instrument subject to annulment in pursuance of a resolution of either House of Parliament and shall include power—

(a)   to make different provision for different cases; and

(b)   to make such supplemental, consequential and transitional provision as the Secretary of State considers appropriate.

(7)   This section applies to any goods other than—

(a)   growing crops and things comprised in land by virtue of being attached to it;

(b)   water, food, feeding stuff and fertiliser;

(c)   gas which is, is to be or has been supplied by a person authorised to supply it by or under [section 7A of the Gas Act 1986 (licensing of gas suppliers and gas shippers)];

(d)   controlled drugs and licensed medicinal products.

12   Offences against the safety regulations

(1)   Where safety regulations prohibit a person from supplying or offering or agreeing to supply any goods or from exposing or possessing any goods for supply that person shall be guilty of an offence if he contravenes the prohibition.

(2)   Where safety regulations require a person who makes or processes any goods in the course of carrying on a business—

(a)   to carry out a particular test or use a particular procedure in connection with the making or processing of the goods with a view to ascertaining whether the goods satisfy any requirements of such regulations; or

(b) to deal or not to deal in a particular way with a quantity of the goods of which the whole or part does not satisfy such a test or does not satisfy standards connected with such a procedure,

that person shall be guilty of an offence if he does not comply with the requirement.

(3) If a person contravenes a provision of safety regulations which prohibits or requires the provision, by means of a mark or otherwise, of information of a particular kind in relation to goods, he shall be guilty of an offence.

(4) Where safety regulations require any person to give information to another for the purpose of enabling that other to exercise any function, that person shall be guilty of an offence if—

(a) he fails without reasonable cause to comply with the requirement; or

(b) in giving the information which is required of him—

(i) he makes any statement which he knows is false in a material particular; or

(ii) he recklessly makes any statement which is false in a material particular.

(5) A person guilty of an offence under this section shall be liable on summary conviction to imprisonment for a term not exceeding six months or to a fine not exceeding level 5 on the standard scale or to both.

13 Prohibition notices and notices to warn

(1) The Secretary of State may—

(a) serve on any person a notice ('a prohibition notice') prohibiting that person, except with the consent of the Secretary of State, from supplying, or from offering to supply, agreeing to supply or possessing for supply, any relevant goods which the Secretary of State considers are unsafe and which are described in the notice;

(b) serve on any person a notice ('a notice to warn') requiring that person at his own expense to publish, in a form and manner and on occasions specified in the notice, a warning about any relevant goods which the Secretary of State considers are unsafe, which that person supplies or has supplied and which are described in the notice.

(2) Schedule 2 to this Act shall have effect with respect to prohibition notices and notices to warn, and the Secretary of State may by regulations make provision specifying the manner in which information is to be given to any person under that Schedule.

(3) A consent given by the Secretary of State for the purposes of a prohibition notice may impose such conditions on the doing of anything for which the consent is required as the Secretary of State considers appropriate.

(4) A person who contravenes a prohibition notice or a notice to warn shall be guilty of an offence and liable on summary conviction to imprisonment for a term not exceeding six months or to a fine not exceeding level 5 on the standard scale or to both.

(5) The power to make regulations under subsection (2) above shall be exercisable by statutory instrument subject to annulment in pursuance of a resolution of either House of Parliament and shall include power—

(a) to make different provision for different cases; and

(b) to make such supplemental, consequential and transitional provision as the Secretary of State considers appropriate.

(6) In this section 'relevant goods' means—

(a) in relation to a prohibition notice, any goods to which section 11 above applies; and

(b) in relation to a notice to warn, any goods to which that section applies or any growing crops or things comprised in land by virtue of being attached to it.

[(7)   A notice may not be given under this section in respect of any aspect of the safety of goods, or any risk or category of risk associated with goods, concerning which provision is contained in the General Product Safety Regulations 2005.]

14   Suspension notices

(1)   Where an enforcement authority has reasonable grounds for suspecting that any safety provision has been contravened in relation to any goods, the authority may serve a notice ('suspension notice') prohibiting the person on whom it is served, for such period ending not more than six months after the date of the notice as is specified therein, from doing any of the following things without the consent of the authority, that is to say, supplying the goods, offering to supply them, agreeing to supply them or exposing them for supply.

(2)   A suspension notice served by an enforcement authority in respect of any goods shall—

(a)   describe the goods in a manner sufficient to identify them;

(b)   set out the grounds on which the authority suspects that a safety provision has been contravened in relation to the goods, and

(c)   state that, and the manner in which, the person on whom the notice is served may appeal against the notice under section 15 below.

(3)   A suspension notice served by an enforcement authority for the purpose of prohibiting a person for any period from doing the things mentioned in subsection (1) above in relation to any goods may also require that person to keep the authority informed of the whereabouts throughout that period of any of those goods in which he has an interest.

(4)   Where a suspension notice has been served on any person in respect of any goods, no further such notice shall be served on that person in respect of the same goods unless—

(a)   proceedings against that person for an offence in respect of a contravention in relation to the goods of a safety provision (not being an offence under this section); or

(b)   proceedings for the forfeiture of the goods under section 16 or 17 below, are pending at the end of the period specified in the first-mentioned notice.

(5)   A consent given by an enforcement authority for the purposes of subsection (1) above may impose such conditions on the doing of anything for which the consent is required as the authority considers appropriate.

(6)   Any person who contravenes a suspension notice shall be guilty of an offence and liable on summary conviction to imprisonment for a term not exceeding six months or to a fine not exceeding level 5 on the standard scale or to both.

(7)   Where an enforcement authority serves a suspension notice in respect of any goods, the authority shall be liable to pay compensation to any person having an interest in the goods in respect of any loss or damage caused by reason of the service of the notice if—

(a)   there has been no contravention in relation to the goods of any safety provision; and

(b)   the exercise of the power is not attributable to any neglect or default by that person.

(8)   Any disputed question as to the right to or the amount of any compensation payable under this section shall be determined by arbitration or, in Scotland, by a single arbiter appointed, failing agreement between the parties, by the sheriff.

15   Appeals against suspension notices

(1)   Any person having an interest in any goods in respect of which a suspension notice is for the time being in force may apply for an order setting aside the notice.

(2)   An application under this section may be made—

(a)   to any magistrates' court in which proceedings have been brought in England and Wales or Northern Ireland—

(i)   for an offence in respect of a contravention in relation to the goods of any safety provision; or

(ii)   for the forfeiture of the goods under section 16 below;

(b)   where no such proceedings have been so brought, by way of complaint to a magistrates' court; or

(c)   in Scotland, by summary application to the sheriff.

(3)   On an application under this section to a magistrates' court in England and Wales or Northern Ireland the court shall make an order setting aside the suspension notice only if the court is satisfied that there has been no contravention in relation to the goods of any safety provision.

(4)   On an application under this section to the sheriff he shall make an order setting aside the suspension notice only if he is satisfied that at the date of making the order—

(a)   proceedings for an offence in respect of a contravention in relation to the goods of any safety provision; or

(b)   proceedings for the forfeiture of the goods under section 17 below, have not been brought or, having been brought, have been concluded.

(5)   Any person aggrieved by an order made under this section by a magistrates' court in England and Wales or Northern Ireland, or by a decision of such a court not to make such an order, may appeal against that order or decision—

(a)   in England and Wales, to the Crown Court;

(b)   in Northern Ireland, to the county court;

and an order so made may contain such provision as appears to the court to be appropriate for delaying the coming into force of the order pending the making and determination of any appeal (including any application under section III of the Magistrates' Courts Act 1980 or Article 146 of the Magistrates' Courts (Northern Ireland) Order 1981 (statement of case)).

16   [*Does not apply to Scotland.*]

17   Forfeiture: Scotland

(1)   In Scotland a sheriff may make an order for forfeiture of any goods in relation to which there has been a contravention of a safety provision—

(a)   on an application by the procurator-fiscal made in the manner specified in [section 134 of the Criminal Procedure (Scotland) Act 1995]; or

(b)   where a person is convicted of any offence in respect of any such contravention, in addition to any other penalty which the sheriff may impose.

(2)   The procurator-fiscal making an application under subsection (1)(a) above shall serve on any person appearing to him to be the owner of, or otherwise to have an interest in, the goods to which the application relates a copy of the application, together with a notice giving him the opportunity to appear at the hearing of the application to show cause why the goods should not be forfeited.

(3)   Service under subsection (2) above shall be carried out, and such service may be proved, in the manner specified for citation of accused in summary proceedings under the [Criminal Procedure (Scotland) Act 1995].

(4)   Any person upon whom notice is served under subsection (2) above and any other person claiming to be the owner of, or otherwise to have an interest in, goods to which an application under this section relates shall be entitled to appear at the hearing of the application to show cause why the goods should not be forfeited.

(5)   The sheriff shall not make an order following an application under subsection (1)(a) above—

(a)   if any person on whom notice is served under subsection (2) above does not appear, unless service of the notice on that person is proved; or

(b)   if no notice under subsection (2) above has been served, unless the court is satisfied that in the circumstances it was reasonable not to serve notice on any person.

(6)   The sheriff shall make an order under this section only if he is satisfied that there has been a contravention in relation to those goods of a safety provision.

(7)   For the avoidance of doubt it is declared that the sheriff may infer for the purposes of this section that there has been a contravention in relation to any goods of a safety provision if he is satisfied that any such provision has been contravened in relation to any goods which are representative of those goods (whether by reason of being of the same design or part of the same consignment or batch or otherwise).

(8)   Where an order for the forfeiture of any goods is made following an application by the procurator-fiscal under subsection (1)(a) above, any person who appeared, or was entitled to appear, to show cause why goods should not be forfeited may, within twenty-one days of the making of the order, appeal to the High Court by Bill of Suspension on the ground of an alleged miscarriage of justice; [and section 182(5)(a) to (e) of the Criminal Procedure (Scotland) Act 1995 shall apply to an appeal under this subsection as it applies to a stated case under Part X of that Act].

(9)   An order following an application under subsection (1)(a) above shall not take effect—

(a)   until the end of the period of twenty-one days beginning with the day after the day on which the order is made; or

(b)   if an appeal is made under subsection (8) above within that period, until the appeal is determined or abandoned.

(10)   An order under subsection (1)(b) above shall not take effect—

(a)   until the end of the period within which an appeal against the order could be brought under the Criminal Procedure (Scotland) Act 1995; or

(b)   if an appeal is made within that period, until the appeal is determined or abandoned.

(11)   Subject to subsection (12) below, goods forfeited under this section shall be destroyed in accordance with such directions as the sheriff may give.

(12)   If he thinks fit the sheriff may direct that the goods be released, to such person as he may specify, on condition that that person does not supply those goods to any other person otherwise than as mentioned in section 46(7)(a) or (b) below.

18   Power to obtain information

(1)   If the Secretary of State considers that, for the purpose of deciding whether—

(a)   to make, vary or revoke any safety regulations; or

(b)   to serve, vary or revoke a prohibition notice; or

(c)   to serve or revoke a notice to warn,

he requires information which another person is likely to be able to furnish, the Secretary of State may serve on the other person a notice under this section.

(2)   A notice served on any person under this section may require that person—

(a)   to furnish to the Secretary of State, within a period specified in the notice, such information as is so specified;

(b)   to produce such records as are specified in the notice at a time and place so specified and to permit a person appointed by the Secretary of State for the purpose to take copies of the records at that time and place.

(3)   A person shall be guilty of an offence if he—

(a)   fails, without reasonable cause, to comply with a notice served on him under this section; or

(b)   in purporting to comply with a requirement which by virtue of paragraph (a) of subsection (2) above is contained in such a notice—

(i) furnishes information which he knows is false in a material particular; or
(ii) recklessly furnishes information which is false in a material particular.
(4) A person guilty of an offence under subsection (3) above shall—
(a) in the case of an offence under paragraph (a) of that subsection, be liable on summary conviction to a fine not exceeding level 5 on the standard scale; and
(b) in the case of an offence under paragraph (b) of that subsection be liable—
(i) on conviction on indictment, to a fine,
(ii) on summary conviction, to a fine not exceeding the statutory maximum.

19 Interpretation of Part II

(1) in this Part—
'controlled drug' means a controlled drug within the meaning of the Misuse of Drugs Act 1971;
'feeding stuff' and 'fertiliser' have the same meaning as in Part IV of the Agriculture Act 1970;
'food' does not include anything containing tobacco but, subject to that, has the same meaning as in the [Food Safety Act 1990] or, in relation to Northern Ireland, the same meaning as in the [Food (Northern Ireland) Order 1989];
'licensed medicinal product' means—
(a) any medicinal product within the meaning of the Medicines Act 1968 in respect of which a product licence within the meaning of that Act is for the time being in force;
(b) any other article or substance in respect of which any such licence is for the time being in force in pursuance of an order under section 104 or 105 of that Act (application of Act to other articles and substances); [or
(c) a veterinary medicinal product that has a marketing authorisation under the Veterinary Medicines Regulations 2006.]
'safe', in relation to any goods, means such that there is no risk, or no risk apart from one reduced to a minimum, that any of the following will (whether immediately or after a definite or indefinite period) cause the death of, or any personal injury to, any person whatsoever, that is to say—
(a) the goods;
(b) the keeping, use or consumption of the goods;
(c) the assembly of any of the goods which are, or are to be supplied unassembled;
(d) any emission or leakage from the goods or, as a result of the keeping, use or consumption of the goods, from anything else; or
(e) reliance on the accuracy of any measurement, calculation or other reading made by or by means of the goods,
and [. . .] 'unsafe' shall be construed accordingly;
'tobacco' includes any tobacco product within the meaning of the Tobacco Products Duty Act 1979 and any article or substance containing tobacco and intended for oral or nasal use.
(2) In the definition of 'safe' in subsection (1) above, references to the keeping, use or consumption of any goods are references to—
(a) the keeping, use or consumption of the goods by the persons by whom, and in all or any of the ways or circumstances in which, they might reasonably be expected to be kept, used or consumed; and
(b) the keeping, use or consumption of the goods either alone or in conjunction with other goods in conjunction with which they might reasonably be expected to be kept, used or consumed.

[. . .]

PART IV
ENFORCEMENT OF PARTS II AND III

27 Enforcement

(1) Subject to the following provisions of this section—

(a) it shall be the duty of every weights and measures authority in Great Britain to enforce within their area the safety provisions [. . .]; and

(b) it shall be the duty of every district council in Northern Ireland to enforce within their area the safety provisions.

(2) The Secretary of State may by regulations—

(a) wholly or partly transfer any duty imposed by subsection (1) above on a weights and measures authority or a district council in Northern Ireland to such other person who has agreed to the transfer as is specified in the regulations;

(b) relieve such an authority or council of any such duty so far as it is exercisable in relation to such goods as may be described in the regulations.

(3) The power to make regulations under subsection (2) above shall be exercisable by statutory instrument subject to annulment in pursuance of a resolution of either House of Parliament and shall include power—

(a) to make different provision for different cases; and

(b) to make such supplemental, consequential and transitional provision as the Secretary of State considers appropriate.

(4) Nothing in this section shall authorise any weights and measures authority, or any person on whom functions are conferred by regulations under subsection (2) above, to bring proceedings in Scotland for an offence.

28 Test purchases

(1) An enforcement authority shall have power, for the purpose of ascertaining whether any safety provision [. . .] has been contravened in relation to any goods, services, accommodation or facilities—

(a) to make, or to authorise an officer of the authority to make, any purchase of any goods; or

(b) to secure, or to authorise an officer of the authority to secure, the provision of any services, accommodation or facilities.

(2) Where—

(a) any goods purchased under this section by or on behalf of an enforcement authority are submitted to a test; and

(b) the test leads to—

(i) the bringing of proceedings for an offence in respect of a contravention in relation to the goods of any safety provision [. . .] or for the forfeiture of the goods under section 16 or 17 above; or

(ii) the serving of a suspension notice in respect of any goods; and

(c) the authority is requested to do so and it is practicable for the authority to comply with the request,

the authority shall allow the person from whom the goods were purchased or any person who is a party to the proceedings or has an interest in any goods to which the notice relates to have the goods tested.

(3) The Secretary of State may by regulations provide that any test of goods under this section by or on behalf of an enforcement authority shall—

(a) be carried out at the expense of the authority in a manner and by a person prescribed by or determined under the regulations; or

(b) be carried out either as mentioned in paragraph (a) above or by the authority in a manner prescribed by the regulations.

(4) The power to make regulations under subsection (3) above shall be exercisable by statutory instrument subject to annulment in pursuance of a resolution of either House of Parliament and shall include power—

(a)   to make different provision for different cases; and

(b)   to make such supplemental, consequential and transitional provision as the Secretary of State considers appropriate.

(5)   Nothing in this section shall authorise the acquisition by or on behalf of an enforcement authority of any interest in land.

29   Powers of search etc

(1)   Subject to the following provisions of this Part, a duly authorised officer of an enforcement authority may at any reasonable hour and on production, if required, of his credentials exercise any of the powers conferred by the following provisions of this section.

(2)   The officer may, for the purpose of ascertaining whether there has been any contravention of any safety provision [. . .], inspect any goods and enter any premises other than premises occupied only as a person's residence.

(3)   The officer may, for the purpose of ascertaining whether there has been any contravention of any safety provision, examine any procedure (including any arrangements for carrying out a test) connected with the production of any goods.

(4)   If the officer has reasonable grounds for suspecting that any goods are manufactured or imported goods which have not been supplied in the United Kingdom since they were manufactured or imported he may—

(a)   for the purpose of ascertaining whether there has been any contravention of any safety provision in relation to the goods, require any person carrying on a business, or employed in connection with a business, to produce any records relating to the business;

(b)   for the purpose of ascertaining (by testing or otherwise) whether there has been any such contravention, seize and detain the goods;

(c)   take copies of, or of any entry in, any records produced by virtue of paragraph (a) above.

(5)   If the officer has reasonable grounds for suspecting that there has been a contravention in relation to any goods of any safety provision [. . .], he may—

(a)   for the purpose of ascertaining whether there has been any such contravention, require any person carrying on a business, or employed in connection with a business, to produce any records relating to the business;

(b)   for the purpose of ascertaining (by testing or otherwise) whether there has been any such contravention, seize and detain the goods;

(c)   take copies of, or of any entry in, any records produced by virtue of paragraph (a) above.

(6)   The officer may seize and detain—

(a)   any goods or records which he has reasonable grounds for believing may be required as evidence in proceedings for an offence in respect of a contravention of any safety provision [. . .];

(b)   any goods which he has reasonable grounds for suspecting may be liable to be forfeited under section 16 or 17 above.

(7)   If and to the extent that it is reasonably necessary to do so to prevent a contravention of any safety provision [. . .], the officer may, for the purpose of exercising his power under subsection (4), (5) or (6) above to seize any goods or records—

(a)   require any person having authority to do so to open any container or to open any vending machine; and

(b)   himself open or break open any such container or machine where a requirement made under paragraph (a) above in relation to the container or machine has not been complied with.

30   Provisions supplemental to s 29

(1)   An officer seizing any goods or records under section 29 above shall inform the following persons that the goods or records have been so seized, that is to say—

(a)   the person from whom they are seized; and

(b)   in the case of imported goods seized on any premises under the control of the Commissioners of Customs and Excise, the importer of those goods (within the meaning of the Customs and Excise Management Act 1979).

(2)   If a justice of the peace—

(a)   is satisfied by any written information on oath that there are reasonable grounds for believing either—

(i)   that any goods or records which any officer has power to inspect under section 29 above are on any premises and that their inspection is likely to disclose evidence that there has been a contravention of any safety provision [. . .]; or

(ii)   that such a contravention has taken place, is taking place or is about to take place on any premises; and

(b)   is also satisfied by any such information either—

(i)   that admission to the premises has been or is likely to be refused and that notice of intention to apply for a warrant under this section has been given to the occupier; or

(ii)   that an application for admission, or the giving of such a notice, would defeat the object of entry or that the premises are unoccupied or that the occupier is temporarily absent and it might defeat the object of the entry to await his return, the justice may by warrant under his hand, which shall continue in force for a period of one month, authorise any officer of an enforcement authority to enter the premises, if need be by force.

(3)   An officer entering any premises by virtue of section 29 above or a warrant under subsection (2) above may take with him such other persons and such equipment as may appear to him necessary.

(4)   On leaving any premises which a person is authorised to enter by a warrant under subsection (2) above, that person shall, if the premises are unoccupied or the occupier is temporarily absent, leave the premises as effectively secured against trespassers as he found them.

(5)   If any person who is not an officer of an enforcement authority purports to act as such under section 29 above of this section he shall be guilty of an offence and liable on summary conviction to a fine not exceeding level 5 on the standard scale.

(6)   Where any goods seized by an officer under section 29 above are submitted to a test, the officer shall inform the persons mentioned in subsection (1) above of the result of the test and, if—

(a)   proceedings are brought for an offence in respect of a contravention in relation to the goods of any safety provision [. . .] or for the forfeiture of the goods under section 16 or 17 above, or a suspension notice is served in respect of any goods; and

(b)   the officer is requested to do so and it is practicable to comply with the request, the officer shall allow any person who is a party to the proceedings or, as the case may be, has an interest in the goods to which the notice relates to have the goods tested.

(7)   The Secretary of State may by regulations provide that any test of goods seized under section 29 above by an officer of an enforcement authority shall—

(a)   be carried out at the expense of the authority in a manner and by a person prescribed by or determined under the regulations; or

(b)   be carried out either as mentioned in paragraph (a) above or by the authority in a manner prescribed by the regulations.

(8)   The power to make regulations under subsection (7) above shall be exercisable by statutory instrument subject to annulment in pursuance of a resolution of either House of Parliament and shall include power—

(a)   to make different provision for different cases; and

(b)   to make such supplemental, consequential and transitional provisions as the Secretary of State considers appropriate.

(9)   In the application of this section to Scotland, the reference in subsection (2) above to a justice of the peace shall include a reference to a sheriff and the references to written information on oath shall be construed as references to evidence on oath.

(10)   In the application of this section to Northern Ireland, the references in subsection (2) above to any information on oath shall be construed as references to any complaint on oath.

31   Power of customs officer to detain goods

(1)   A customs officer may, for the purpose of facilitating the exercise by an enforcement authority or officer of such an authority of any functions conferred on the authority or officer by or under Part II of this Act, or by or under this Part in its application for the purposes of the safety provisions, seize any imported goods and detain them for not more than two working days.

(2)   Anything seized and detained under this section shall be dealt with during the period of its detention in such manner as the Commissioners of Customs and Excise may direct.

(3)   In subsection (1) above the reference to two working days is a reference to a period of forty-eight hours calculated from the time when the goods in question are seized but disregarding so much of any period as falls on a Saturday or Sunday or on Christmas Day, Good Friday or a day which is a bank holiday under the Banking and Financial Dealings Act 1971 in the part of the United Kingdom where the goods are seized.

(4)   In this section and section 32 below 'customs officer' means any officer within the meaning of the Customs and Excise Management Act 1979.

32   Obstruction of authorised officer

(1)   Any person who—

(a)   intentionally obstructs any officer of an enforcement authority who is acting in pursuance of any provision of this Part or any customs officer who is so acting; or

(b)   intentionally fails to comply with any requirements made of him by any officer of an enforcement authority under any provision of this Part, or

(c)   without reasonable cause fails to give any officer of an enforcement authority who is so acting any other assistance or information which the officer may reasonably require of him for the purposes of the exercise of the officer's functions under any provision of this Part,

shall be guilty of an offence and liable on summary conviction to a fine not exceeding level 5 on the standard scale.

(2)   A person shall be guilty of an offence if, in giving any information which is required of him by virtue of subsection (1)(c) above—

(a)   he makes any statement which he knows is false in a material particular, or

(b)   he recklessly makes a statement which is false in a material particular.

(3)   A person guilty of an offence under subsection (2) above shall be liable—

(a)   on conviction on indictment to a fine;

(b)   on summary conviction, to a fine not exceeding the statutory maximum.

33   Appeals against detention of goods

(1)   Any person having an interest in any goods which are for the time being detained under any provision of this Part by an enforcement authority or by an officer of such an authority may apply for an order requiring the goods to be released to him or to another person.

(2)   An application under this section may be made—

(a)   to any magistrates' court in which proceedings have been brought in England and Wales or Northern Ireland—
    (i)   for an offence in respect of a contravention in relation to the goods of any safety provision [. . .]; or
    (ii)   for the forfeiture of the goods under section 16 above;
(b)   where no such proceedings have been so brought, by way of complaint to a magistrates' court; or
(c)   in Scotland, by summary application to the sheriff [. . .].
(3)   On an application under this section to a magistrates' court or to the sheriff, an order requiring goods to be released shall be made only if the court or sheriff is satisfied—
    (a)   that proceedings—
    (i)   for an offence in respect of a contravention in relation to the goods of any safety provision [. . .]; or
    (ii)   for the forfeiture of the goods under section 16 or 17 above,
have not been brought or, having been brought, have been concluded without the goods being forfeited; and
    (b)   where no such proceedings have been brought, that more than six months have elapsed since the goods were seized.
(4)   *[Does not apply to Scotland.]*

34   Compensation for seizure and detention

(1)   Where an officer of an enforcement authority exercises any power under section 29 above to seize and detain goods, the enforcement authority shall be liable to pay compensation to any person having an interest in the goods in respect of any loss or damage caused by reason of the exercise of the power if—
    (a)   there has been no contravention in relation to the goods of any safety provision [. . .]; and
    (b)   the exercise of the power is not attributable to any neglect or default by that person [. . .].
(2)   Any disputed question as to the right to or the amount of any compensation payable under this section shall be determined by arbitration or, in Scotland, by a single arbiter appointed, failing agreement between the parties, by the sheriff.

35   Recovery of expenses of enforcement

(1)   This section shall apply where a court—
    (a)   convicts a person of an offence in respect of a contravention in relation to any goods of any safety provision [. . .]; or
    (b)   makes an order under section 16 or 17 above for the forfeiture of any goods [. . .].
(2)   The court may (in addition to any other order it may make as to costs or expenses) order the person convicted or, as the case may be, any person having an interest in the goods to reimburse an enforcement authority for any expenditure which has been or may be incurred by that authority—
    (a)   in connection with any seizure or detention of the goods by or on behalf of the authority; or
    (b)   in connection with any compliance by the authority with directions by the court for the purposes of any order for the forfeiture of the goods.

PART V
MISCELLANEOUS AND SUPPLEMENTAL

36 [*Amends Health and Safety at Work etc Act 1974*]

37 **[Power of Commissioners for Revenue and Customs to disclose information]**

(1) If they think it appropriate to do so for the purpose of facilitating the exercise by any person to whom subsection (2) below applies of any function conferred on that person by or under Part II of this Act, or by or under Part IV of this Act in its application for the purposes of the safety provisions, [the Commissioners for Her Majesty's Revenue and Customs] may authorise the disclosure to that person of any information obtained [or held] for the purposes of the exercise by [Her Majesty's Revenue and Customs] of their functions in relation to imported goods.

(2) This subsection applies to an enforcement authority and to any officer of an enforcement authority.

(3) A disclosure of information made to any person under subsection (1) above shall be made in such manner as may be directed by [Her Majesty's Revenue and Customs] and may be through such persons acting on behalf of that person as may be so directed.

(4) Information may be disclosed to a person under subsection (1) above whether or not the disclosure of the information has been requested by or on behalf of that person.

[. . .]

39 **Defence of due diligence**

(1) Subject to the following provisions of this section, in proceedings against any person for an offence to which this section applies it shall be a defence for that person to show that he took all reasonable steps and exercised all due diligence to avoid committing the offence.

(2) Where in any proceedings against any person for such an offence the defence provided by subsection (1) above involves an allegation that the commission of the offence was due—

　　(a)　to the act or default of another; or

　　(b)　to reliance on information given by another,

that person shall not, without the leave of the court, be entitled to rely on the defence unless, not less than seven clear days before the hearing of the proceedings, he has served a notice under subsection (3) below on the person bringing the proceedings.

(3) A notice under this subsection shall give such information identifying or assisting in the identification of the person who committed the act or default or gave the information as is in the possession of the person serving the notice at the time he serves it.

(4) It is hereby declared that a person shall not be entitled to rely on the defence provided by subsection (1) above by reason of his reliance on information supplied by another, unless he shows that it was reasonable in all the circumstances for him to have relied on the information, having regard in particular—

　　(a)　to the steps which he took, and those which might reasonably have been taken, for the purpose of verifying the information, and

　　(b)　to whether he had any reason to disbelieve the information.

(5) This section shall apply to an offence under section [. . .] 12(1), (2) or (3), 13(4) [, or 14(6)] above.

40 **Liability of persons other than principal offender**

(1) Where the commission by any person of an offence to which section 39 above applies is due to an act or default committed by some other person in the course of any business of his, the other person shall be guilty of the offence and

may be proceeded against and punished by virtue of this subsection whether or not proceedings are taken against the first-mentioned person.

(2)   Where a body corporate is guilty of an offence under this Act (including where it is so guilty by virtue of subsection (1) above) in respect of any act or default which is shown to have been committed with the consent or connivance of, or to be attributable to any neglect on the part of, any director, manager, secretary or other similar officer of the body corporate or any person who was purporting to act in any such capacity he, as well as the body corporate, shall be guilty of that offence and shall be liable to be proceeded against and punished accordingly.

(3)   Where the affairs of a body corporate are managed by its members, sub-section (2) above shall apply in relation to the acts and defaults of a member in connection with his functions of management as if he were a director of the body corporate.

41   Civil proceedings

(1)   An obligation imposed by safety regulations shall be a duty owed to any person who may be affected by a contravention of the obligation and, subject to any provisions to the contrary in the regulations and to the defences and other incidents applying to actions for breach of statutory duty, a contravention of any such obligation shall be actionable accordingly.

(2)   This Act shall not be construed as conferring any other right of action in civil proceedings, apart from the right conferred by virtue of Part I of this Act, in respect of any loss or damage suffered in consequence of a contravention of a safety provision [. . .].

(3)   Subject to any provision to the contrary in the agreement itself, an agree-ment shall not be void or unenforceable by reason only of a contravention of a safety provision [. . .].

(4)   Liability by virtue of subsection (1) above shall not be limited or excluded by any contract term, by any notice or (subject to the power contained in sub-section (1) above to limit or exclude it in safety regulations) by any other provision.

(5)   Nothing in subsection (1) above shall prejudice the operation of section 12 of the Nuclear Installations Act 1965 (rights to compensation for certain breaches of duties confined to rights under that Act).

(6)   In this section 'damage' includes personal injury and death.

42   Reports etc

(1)   It shall be the duty of the Secretary of State at least once in every five years to lay before each House of Parliament a report on the exercise during the period to which the report relates of the functions which under Part II of this Act, or under Part IV of this Act in its application for the purposes of the safety pro-visions, are exercisable by the Secretary of State, weights and measures authorities, district councils in Northern Ireland and persons on whom functions are conferred by regulations made under section 27(2) above.

(2)   The Secretary of State may from time to time prepare and lay before each House of Parliament such other reports on the exercise of those functions as he considers appropriate.

(3)   Every weights and measures authority, every district council in Northern Ireland and every person on whom functions are conferred by regulations under subsection (2) of section 27 above shall, whenever the Secretary of State so directs, make a report to the Secretary of State on the exercise of the functions exercisable by that authority or council under that section or by that person by virtue of any such regulations.

(4)   A report under subsection (3) above shall be in such form and shall contain such particulars as are specified in the direction of the Secretary of State.

(5)   The first report under subsection (1) above shall be laid before each House

of Parliament not more than five years after the laying of the last report under section 8(2) of the Consumer Safety Act 1978.

43 Financial provisions

(1) There shall be paid out of money provided by Parliament—

(a) any expenses incurred or compensation payable by a Minister of the Crown or Government department in consequence of any provision of this Act; and

(b) any increase attributable to this Act in the sums payable out of money so provided under any other Act.

(2) Any sums received by a Minister of the Crown or Government department by virtue of this Act shall be paid into the Consolidated Fund.

44 Service of documents etc

(1) Any documents required or authorised by virtue of this Act to be served on a person may be so served—

(a) by delivering it to him or by leaving it at his proper address or by sending it by post to him at that address; or

(b) if the person is a body corporate, by serving it in accordance with paragraph (a) above on the secretary or clerk of that body; or

(c) if the person is a partnership, by serving it in accordance with that paragraph on a partner or on a person having control or management of the partnership business.

(2) For the purposes of subsection (1) above, and for the purposes of section 7 of the Interpretation Act 1978 (which relates to the service of documents by post) in its application to that subsection, the proper address of any person on whom a document is to be served by virtue of this Act shall be his last known address except that—

(a) in the case of service on a body corporate or its secretary or clerk, it shall be the address of the registered or principal office of the body corporate;

(b) in the case of service on a partnership or a partner or a person having the control or management of a partnership business, it shall be the principal office of the partnership; and for the purposes of this subsection the principal office of a company registered outside the United Kingdom or of a partnership carrying on business outside the United Kingdom is its principal office within the United Kingdom.

(3) The Secretary of State may by regulations make provision for the manner in which any information is to be given to any person under any provision of Part IV of this Act.

(4) Without prejudice to the generality of subsection (3) above regulations made by the Secretary of State may prescribe the person, or manner of determining the person, who is to be treated for the purposes of section 28(2) or 30 above as the person from whom goods were purchased or seized where the goods were purchased or seized from a vending machine.

(5) The power to make regulations under subsection (3) or (4) above shall be exercisable by statutory instrument subject to annulment in pursuance of a resolution of either House of Parliament and shall include power—

(a) to make different provision for different cases; and

(b) to make such supplemental, consequential and transitional provision as the Secretary of State considers appropriate.

45 Interpretation

(1) In this Act, except in so far as the context otherwise requires—

'aircraft' includes gliders, balloons and hovercraft;

'business' includes a trade or profession and the activities of a professional or trade association or of a local authority or other public authority;

'conditional sale agreement', 'credit-sale agreement' and 'hire-purchase agreement' have the same meanings as in the Consumer Credit Act 1974 but as if in the definitions in that Act 'goods' had the same meaning as in this Act;

'contravention' includes a failure to comply and cognate expressions shall be construed accordingly;

'enforcement authority' means the Secretary of State, any other Minister of the Crown in charge of a Government department, any such department and any authority, council or other person on whom functions under this Act are conferred by or under section 27 above;

'gas' has the same meaning as in Part I of the Gas Act 1986;

'goods' includes substances, growing crops and things comprised in land by virtue of being attached to it and any ship, aircraft or vehicle;

'information' includes accounts, estimates and returns;

'magistrates' court', in relation to Northern Ireland, means a court of summary jurisdiction;

'modifications' includes additions, alterations and omissions, and cognate expressions shall be construed accordingly;

'motor vehicle' has the same meaning as in the Road Traffic Act 1972;

'notice' means a notice in writing;

'notice to warn' means a notice under section 13(1)(b) above;

'officer', in relation to an enforcement authority, means a person authorised in writing to assist the authority in carrying out its functions under or for the purposes of the enforcement of any of the safety provisions or of any of the provisions made by or under Part III of this Act;

'personal injury' includes any disease and any other impairment of a person's physical or mental condition;

'premises' includes any place and any ship, aircraft or vehicle;

'prohibition notice' means a notice under section 13(1)(a) above;

'records' includes any books or documents and any records in non-documentary form;

'safety provision' means [. . .] any provision of safety regulations, a prohibition notice or a suspension notice;

'safety regulations' means regulations under section 11 above;

'ship' includes any boat and any other description of vessel used in navigation;

'subordinate legislation' has the same meaning as in the Interpretation Act 1978;

'substance' means any natural or artificial substance, whether in solid, liquid or gaseous form or in the form of a vapour, and includes substances that are comprised in or mixed with other goods;

'supply' and cognate expressions shall be construed in accordance with section 46 below;

'suspension notice' means a notice under section 14 above.

(2)   Except in so far as the context otherwise requires, references in this Act to a contravention of a safety provision shall, in relation to any goods, include references to anything which would constitute such a contravention if the goods were supplied to any person.

(3)   References in this Act to any goods in relation to which any safety provision has been or may have been contravened shall include references to any goods which it is not reasonably practicable to separate from any such goods.

[. . .]

(5)   In Scotland, any reference in this Act to things comprised in land by virtue of being attached to it is a reference to moveables which have become heritable by accession to heritable property.

46   Meaning of 'supply'

(1)   Subject to the following provisions of this section, references in this Act to supplying goods shall be construed as references to doing any of the following, whether as principal or agent, that is to say—

(a)   selling, hiring out or lending the goods;

(b)   entering into a hire-purchase agreement to furnish the goods;

(c)   the performance of any contract for work and materials to furnish the goods;

(d)   providing the goods in exchange for any consideration [. . .] other than money;

(e)   providing the goods in or in connection with the performance of any statutory function; or

(f)   giving the goods as a prize or otherwise making a gift of the goods;

and, in relation to gas or water, those references shall be construed as including references to providing the service by which the gas or water is made available for use.

(2)   For the purposes of any reference in this Act to supplying goods, where a person ('the ostensible supplier') supplies goods to another person ('the customer') under a hire-purchase agreement, conditional sale agreement or credit-sale agreement or under an agreement for the hiring of goods (other than a hire-purchase agreement) and the ostensible supplier—

(a)   carries on the business of financing the provision of goods for others by means of such agreements; and

(b)   in the course of that business acquired his interest in the goods supplied to the customer as a means of financing the provision of them for the customer by a further person ('the effective supplier'),

the effective supplier and not the ostensible supplier shall be treated as supplying the goods to the customer.

(3)   Subject to subsection (4) below, the performance of any contract by the erection of any building or structure on any land or by the carrying out of any other building works shall be treated for the purposes of this Act as a supply of goods in so far as, but only in so far as, it involves the provision of any goods to any person by means of their incorporation into the building, structure or works.

(4)   Except for the purposes of, and in relation to, notices to warn [. . .], references in this Act to supplying goods shall not include references to supplying goods comprised in land where the supply is effected by the creation or disposal of an interest in the land.

(5)   Except in Part I of this Act references in this Act to a person's supplying goods shall be confined to references to that person's supplying goods in the course of a business of his, but for the purposes of this subsection it shall be immaterial whether the business is a business of dealing in the goods.

(6)   For the purposes of subsection (5) above goods shall not be treated as supplied in the course of a business if they are supplied, in pursuance of an obligation arising under or in connection with the insurance of the goods, to the person with whom they were insured.

(7)   Except for the purposes of, and in relation to, prohibition notices or suspension notices, references in [Part 2 or Part 4] of this Act to supplying goods shall not include—

(a)   references to supplying goods where the person supplied carries on a business of buying goods of the same description as those goods and repairing or reconditioning them,

(b)   references to supplying goods by a sale of articles as scrap (that is to say, for the value of materials included in the articles rather than for the value of the articles themselves).

(8)   Where any goods have at any time been supplied by being hired out or lent to any person, neither a continuation or renewal of the hire or loan (whether on the same or different terms) nor any transaction for the transfer after that time of any interest in the goods to the person to whom they were hired or lent shall be treated for the purposes of this Act as a further supply of the goods to that person.

(9)   A ship, aircraft or motor vehicle shall not be treated for the purposes of this

Act as supplied to any person by reason only that services consisting in the carriage of goods or passengers in that ship, aircraft or vehicle, or in its use for any other purpose, are provided to that person in pursuance of an agreement relating to the use of the ship, aircraft or vehicle for a particular period or for particular voyages, flights or journeys.

47 Savings for certain privileges
(1) Nothing in this Act shall be taken as requiring any person to produce any records if he would be entitled to refuse to produce those records in any proceedings in any court on the ground that they are the subject of legal professional privilege or, in Scotland, that they contain a confidential communication made by or to an advocate or solicitor in that capacity, or as authorising any person to take possession of any records which are in the possession of a person who would be so entitled.
(2) Nothing in this Act shall be construed as requiring a person to answer any question or give any information if to do so would incriminate that person or that person's spouse [or civil partner].

48 [*Minor and consequential amendments and repeals*]

49 [*Northern Ireland*]

50 Short title, commencement and transitional provision
(1) This Act may be cited as the Consumer Protection Act 1987.
(2) This Act shall come into force on such day as the Secretary of State may by order made by statutory instrument appoint, and different days may be so appointed for different provisions or for different purposes.
. . .

SCHEDULE 2
PROHIBITION NOTICES AND NOTICES TO WARN
Section 13

PART I
PROHIBITION NOTICES

1 A prohibition notice in respect of any goods shall—
(a) state that the Secretary of State considers that the goods are unsafe;
(b) set out the reasons why the Secretary of State considers that the goods are unsafe;
(c) specify the day on which the notice is to come into force; and
(d) state that the trader may at any time make representations in writing to the Secretary of State for the purpose of establishing that the goods are safe.
2—(1) If representations in writing about a prohibition notice are made by the trader to the Secretary of State, it shall be the duty of the Secretary of State to consider whether to revoke the notice and—
(a) if he decides to revoke it, to do so;
(b) in any other case, to appoint a person to consider those representations, any further representations made (whether in writing or orally) by the trader about the notice and the statements of any witnesses examined under this Part of this Schedule.
(2) Where the Secretary of State has appointed a person to consider representations about a prohibition notice, he shall serve a notification on the trader which—
(a) states that the trader may make oral representations to the appointed person for the purpose of establishing that the goods to which the notice relates are safe; and

(b) specifies the place and time at which the oral representations may be made.

(3) The time specified in a notification served under sub-paragraph (2) above shall not be before the end of the period of twenty-one days beginning with the day on which the notification is served, unless the trader otherwise agrees.

(4) A person on whom a notification has been served under sub-paragraph (2) above or his representative may, at the place and time specified in the notification—

(a) make oral representations to the appointed person for the purpose of establishing that the goods in question are safe; and

(b) call and examine witnesses in connection with representations.

3—(1) Where representations in writing about a prohibition notice are made by the trader to the Secretary of State at any time after a person has been appointed to consider representations about that notice, then, whether or not the appointed person has made a report to the Secretary of State, the following provisions of this paragraph shall apply instead of paragraph 2 above.

(2) The Secretary of State shall, before the end of the period of one month beginning with the day on which he receives the representations, serve a notification on the trader which states—

(a) that the Secretary of State has decided to revoke the notice, has decided to vary it or, as the case may be, has decided neither to revoke nor to vary it; or

(b) that, a person having been appointed to consider representations about the notice, the trader may, at a place and time specified in the notification, make oral representations to the appointed person for the purpose of establishing that the goods to which the notice relates are safe.

(3) The time specified in a notification served for the purposes of sub-paragraph (2)(b) above shall not be before the end of the period of twenty-one days beginning with the day on which the notification is served, unless the trader otherwise agrees or the time is the time already specified for the purposes of paragraph 2(2)(b) above.

(4) A person on whom a notification has been served for the purposes of sub-paragraph (2)(b) above or his representative may, at the place and time specified in the notification—

(a) make oral representations to the appointed person for the purpose of establishing that the goods in question are safe; and

(b) call and examine witnesses in connection with the representations.

4—(1) Where a person is appointed to consider representations about a prohibition notice, it shall be his duty to consider—

(a) any written representations made by the trader about the notice, other than those in respect of which a notification is served under paragraph 3(2)(a) above;

(b) any oral representations made under paragraph 2(4) or 3(4) above; and

(c) any statements made by witnesses in connection with the oral representations, and after considering any matters under this paragraph, to make a report (including recommendations) to the Secretary of State about the matters considered by him and the notice.

(2) It shall be the duty of the Secretary of State to consider any report made to him under sub-paragraph (1) above and, after considering the report, to inform the trader of his decision with respect to the prohibition notice to which the report relates.

5—(1) The Secretary of State may revoke or vary a prohibition notice by serving on the trader a notification stating that the notice is revoked or, as the case may be, is varied as specified in the notification.

(2) The Secretary of State shall not vary a prohibition notice so as to make the effect of the notice more restrictive for the trader.

(3) Without prejudice to the power conferred by section 13(2) of this Act, the service of a notification under sub-paragraph (1) above shall be sufficient to satisfy

the requirement of paragraph 4(2) above that the trader shall be informed of the Secretary of State's decision.

PART II
NOTICES TO WARN

6—(1) If the Secretary of State proposes to serve a notice to warn on any person in respect of any goods, the Secretary of State, before he serves the notice shall serve on that person a notification which—

(a)   contains a draft of the proposed notice;

(b)   states that the Secretary of State proposes to serve a notice in the form of the draft on that person;

(c)   states that the Secretary of State considers that the goods described in the draft are unsafe;

(d)   sets out the reasons why the Secretary of State considers that those goods are unsafe; and

(e)   states that that person may make representations to the Secretary of State for the purpose of establishing that the goods are safe if, before the end of the period of fourteen days beginning with the day on which the notification is served, he informs the Secretary of State—

(i) of his intention to make representations; and

(ii) whether the representations will be made only in writing or both in writing and orally.

(2)   Where the Secretary of State has served a notification containing a draft of a proposed notice to warn on any person, he shall not serve a notice to warn on that person in respect of the goods to which the proposed notice relates unless—

(a)   the period of fourteen days beginning with the day on which the notification was served expires without the Secretary of State being informed as mentioned in sub-paragraph (1)(e) above;

(b)   the period of twenty-eight days beginning with that day expires without any written representations being made by that person to the Secretary of State about the proposed notice; or

(c)   the Secretary of State has considered a report about the proposed notice by a person appointed under paragraph 7(1) below.

7—(1)   Where a person on whom a notification containing a draft of a proposed notice to warn has been served—

(a)   informs the Secretary of State as mentioned in paragraph 6(1)(e) above before the end of the period of fourteen days beginning with the day on which the notification was served; and

(b)   makes written representations to the Secretary of State about the proposed notice before the end of the period of twenty-eight days beginning with that day, the Secretary of State shall appoint a person to consider those representations, any further representations made by that person about the draft notice and the statements of any witnesses examined under this Part of this Schedule.

(2)   Where—

(a)   the Secretary of State has appointed a person to consider representations about a proposed notice to warn; and

(b)   the person whose representations are to be considered has informed the Secretary of State for the purposes of paragraph 6(1)(e) above that the representations he intends to make will include oral representations,

the Secretary of State shall inform the person intending to make the representations of the place and time at which oral representations may be made to the appointed person.

(3)   Where a person on whom a notification containing a draft of a proposed notice to warn has been served is informed of a time for the purposes of sub-paragraph (2) above, that time shall not be—

(a)   before the end of the period of twenty-eight days beginning with the day on which the notification was served; or

(b)   before the end of the period of seven days beginning with the day on which that person is informed of the time.

(4)   A person who has been informed of a place and time for the purposes of sub-paragraph (2) above or his representative may, at that place and time—

(a)   make oral representations to the appointed person for the purpose of establishing that the goods to which the proposed notice relates are safe; and

(b)   call and examine witnesses in connection with the representations.

8—(1)   Where a person is appointed to consider representations about a proposed notice to warn, it shall be his duty to consider—

(a)   any written representations made by the person on whom it is proposed to serve the notice; and

(b)   in a case where a place and time has been appointed under paragraph 7(2) above for oral representations to be made by that person or his representative, any representations so made and any statements made by witnesses in connection with those representations,

and, after considering those matters to make a report (including recommendations) to the Secretary of State about the matters considered by him and the proposal to serve the notice.

(2)   It shall be the duty of the Secretary of State to consider any report made to him under sub-paragraph (1) above, and after considering the report, to inform the person on whom it was proposed that a notice to warn should be served of his decision with respect to the proposal.

(3)   If at any time after serving a notification on a person under paragraph 6 above the Secretary of State decides not to serve on that person either the proposed notice to warn or that notice with modifications, the Secretary of State shall inform that person of the decision, and nothing done for the purposes of any of the preceding provisions of this Part of this Schedule before that person was so informed shall—

(a)   entitle the Secretary of State subsequently to serve the proposed notice or the notice with modifications; or

(b)   require the Secretary of State, or any person appointed to consider representations about the proposed notice, subsequently to do anything in respect of, or in consequence of, any such representations.

(4)   Where a notification containing a draft of a proposed notice to warn is served on a person in respect of any goods, a notice to warn served on him in consequence of a decision made under sub-paragraph (2) above shall either be in the form of the draft or shall be less onerous than the draft.

9   The Secretary of State may revoke a notice to warn by serving on the person on whom the notice was served a notification stating that the notice is revoked.

PART III
GENERAL

10—(1)   Where in a notification served on any person under this Schedule the Secretary of State has appointed a time for the making of oral representations or the examination of witnesses, he may, by giving that person such notification as the Secretary of State considers appropriate, change that time to a later time or appoint further times at which further representations may be made or the examination of witnesses may be continued; and paragraphs 2(4), 3(4) and 7(4) above shall have effect accordingly.

(2)   For the purposes of this Schedule the Secretary of State may appoint a person (instead of the appointed person) to consider any representations or statements, if the person originally appointed, or last appointed under this sub-

paragraph, to consider those representations or statements has died or appears
to the Secretary of State to be otherwise unable to act.

11   In this Schedule—
'the appointed person' in relation to a prohibition notice or a proposal to serve a
notice to warn, means the person for the time being appointed under this Schedule
to consider representations about the notice or, as the case may be, about the proposed notice;
   'notification' means a notification in writing;
   'trader', in relation to a prohibition notice, means the person on whom the notice
is or was served.

CARRIAGE OF GOODS BY SEA ACT 1992
(1992, c 50)

1   Shipping documents etc to which Act applies
   (1)   This Act applies to the following documents, that is to say—
      (a)   any bill of lading;
      (b)   any sea waybill; and
      (c)   any ship's delivery order.
   (2)   References in this Act to a bill of lading—
      (a)   do not include references to a document which is incapable of transfer
either by indorsement or, as a bearer bill, by delivery without indorsement; but
      (b)   subject to that, do include references to a received for shipment bill of
lading.
   (3)   References in this Act to a sea waybill are references to any document
which is not a bill of lading but—
      (a)   is such a receipt for goods as contains or evidences a contract for the
carriage of goods by sea; and
      (b)   identifies the person to whom delivery of the goods is to be made by the
carrier in accordance with that contract.
   (4)   References in this Act to a ship's delivery order are references to any document which is neither a bill of lading nor a sea waybill but contains an undertaking which—
      (a)   is given under or for the purposes of a contract for the carriage by sea of
the goods to which the document relates, or of goods which include those goods;
and
      (b)   is an undertaking by the carrier to a person identified in the document to
deliver the goods to which the document relates to that person.
   (5)   The Secretary of State may by regulations make provision for the
application of this Act to cases where [an electronic communications network] or
any other information technology is used for effecting transactions corresponding to—
      (a)   the issue of a document to which this Act applies;
      (b)   the indorsement, delivery or other transfer of such a document; or
      (c)   the doing of anything else in relation to such a document.
   (6)   Regulations under subsection (5) above may—
      (a)   make such modifications of the following provisions of this Act as the
Secretary of State considers appropriate in connection with the application of
this Act to any case mentioned in that subsection; and
      (b)   contain supplemental, incidental, consequential and transitional pro-
vision;
and the power to make regulations under that subsection shall be exercisable by
statutory instrument subject to annulment in pursuance of a resolution of either
House of Parliament.

2 Rights under shipping documents

(1)   Subject to the following provisions of this section, a person who becomes—

(a)   the lawful holder of a bill of lading;

(b)   the person who (without being an original party to the contract of carriage) is the person to whom delivery of the goods to which a sea waybill relates is to be made by the carrier in accordance with that contract; or

(c)   the person to whom delivery of the goods to which a ship's delivery order relates is to be made in accordance with the undertaking contained in the order,

shall (by virtue of becoming the holder of the bill or, as the case may be, the person to whom delivery is to be made) have transferred to and vested in him all rights of suit under the contract of carriage as if he had been a party to that contract.

(2)   Where, when a person becomes the lawful holder of a bill of lading, possession of the bill no longer gives a right (as against the carrier) to possession of the goods to which the bill relates, that person shall not have any rights transferred to him by virtue of subsection (1) above unless he becomes the holder of the bill—

(a)   by virtue of a transaction effected in pursuance of any contractual or other arrangements made before the time when such a right to possession ceased to attach to possession of the bill; or

(b)   as a result of the rejection to that person by another person of goods or documents delivered to the other person in pursuance of any such arrangements.

(3)   The rights vested in any person by virtue of the operation of subsection (1) above in relation to a ship's delivery order—

(a)   shall be so vested subject to the terms of the order; and

(b)   where the goods to which the order relates form a part only of the goods to which the contract of carriage relates, shall be confined to rights in respect of the goods to which the order relates.

(4)   Where, in the case of any document to which this Act applies—

(a)   a person with any interest or right in or in relation to goods to which the document relates sustains loss or damage in consequence of a breach of the contract of carriage; but

(b)   subsection (1) above operates in relation to that document so that rights of suit in respect of that breach are vested in another person,

the other person shall be entitled to exercise those rights for the benefit of the person who sustained the loss or damage to the same extent as they could have been exercised if they had been vested in the person for whose benefit they are exercised.

(5)   Where rights are transferred by virtue of the operation of subsection (1) above in relation to any document, the transfer for which that subsection provides shall extinguish any entitlement to those rights which derives—

(a)   where that document is a bill of lading, from a person's having been an original party to the contract of carriage; or

(b)   in the case of any document to which this Act applies, from the previous operation of that subsection in relation to that document;

but the operation of that subsection shall be without prejudice to any rights which derive from a person's having been an original party to the contract contained in, or evidenced by, a sea waybill and, in relation to a ship's delivery order, shall be without prejudice to any rights deriving otherwise than from the previous operation of that subsection in relation to that order.

3 Liabilities under shipping documents

(1)   Where subsection (1) of section 2 of this Act operates in relation to any document to which this Act applies and the person in whom rights are vested by virtue of that subsection—

(a)   takes or demands delivery from the carrier of any of the goods to which the document relates;

(b)   makes a claim under the contract of carriage against the carrier in respect of any of those goods; or

(c)   is a person who, at a time before those rights were vested in him, took or demanded delivery from the carrier of any of those goods,

that person shall (by virtue of taking or demanding delivery or making the claim or, in a case falling within paragraph (c) above, of having the rights vested in him) become subject to the same liabilities under that contract as if he had been a party to that contract.

(2)   Where the goods to which a ship's delivery order relates form a part only of the goods to which the contract of carriage relates, the liabilities to which any person is subject by virtue of the operation of this section in relation to that order shall exclude liabilities in respect of any goods to which the order does not relate.

(3)   This section, so far as it imposes liabilities under any contract on any person, shall be without prejudice to the liabilities under the contract of any person as an original party to the contract.

4   Representations in bills of lading

A bill of lading which—

(a)   represents goods to have been shipped on board a vessel or to have been received for shipment on board a vessel; and

(b)   has been signed by the master of the vessel or by a person who was not the master but had the express, implied or apparent authority of the carrier to sign bills of lading,

shall, in favour of a person who has become the lawful holder of the bill, be conclusive evidence against the carrier of the shipment of the goods or, as the case may be, of their receipt for shipment.

5   Interpretation etc

(1)   In this Act—

'bill of lading', 'sea waybill' and 'ship's delivery order' shall be construed in accordance with section 1 above;

'the contract of carriage'—

(a)   in relation to a bill of lading or sea waybill, means the contract contained in or evidenced by that bill or waybill; and

(b)   in relation to a ship's delivery order, means the contract under or for the purposes of which the undertaking contained in the order is given;

'holder', in relation to a bill of lading, shall be construed in accordance with subsection (2) below;

'information technology' includes any computer or other technology by means of which information or other matter may be recorded or communicated without being reduced to documentary form.

[. . .]

(2)   References in this Act to the holder of a bill of lading are references to any of the following persons, that is to say—

(a)   a person with possession of the bill who, by virtue of being the person identified in the bill, is the consignee of the goods to which the bill relates;

(b)   a person with possession of the bill as a result of the completion, by delivery of the bill, of any indorsement of the bill or, in the case of a bearer bill, of any other transfer of the bill;

(c)   a person with possession of the bill as a result of any transaction by virtue of which he would have become a holder falling within paragraph (a) or (b) above had not the transaction been effected at a time when possession of the bill no longer gave a right (as against the carrier) to possession of the goods to which the bill relates;

and a person shall be regarded for the purposes of this Act as having become the lawful holder of a bill of lading wherever he has become the holder of the bill in good faith.

(3)   References in this Act to a person's being identified in a document include references to his being identified by a description which allows for the identity of the person in question to be varied, in accordance with the terms of the document, after its issue; and the reference in section 1(3)(b) of this Act to a document's identifying a person shall be construed accordingly.

(4)   Without prejudice to sections 2(2) and 4 above, nothing in this Act shall preclude its operation in relation to a case where the goods to which a document relates—

(a)   cease to exist after the issue of the document; or

(b)   cannot be identified (whether because they are mixed with other goods or for any other reason);

and references in this Act to the goods to which a document relates shall be construed accordingly.

(5)   The preceding provisions of this Act shall have effect without prejudice to the application, in relation to any case, of the rules (the Hague-Visby Rules) which for the time being have the force of law by virtue of section 1 of the Carriage of Goods by Sea Act 1971.

6   Short title, repeal, commencement and extent

(1)   This Act may be cited as the Carriage of Goods by Sea Act 1992.

(2)   The Bills of Lading Act 1855 is hereby repealed.

(3)   This Act shall come into force at the end of the period of two months beginning with the day on which it is passed; but nothing in this Act shall have effect in relation to any document issued before the coming into force of this Act.

(4)   This Act extends to Northern Ireland.

CONTRACT (SCOTLAND) ACT 1997
(1997, c 34)

1   Extrinsic evidence of additional contract term etc

(1)   Where a document appears (or two or more documents appear) to comprise all the express terms of a contract or unilateral voluntary obligation, it shall be presumed, unless the contrary is proved, that the document does (or the documents do) comprise all the express terms of the contract or unilateral voluntary obligation.

(2)   Extrinsic oral or documentary evidence shall be admissible to prove, for the purposes of subsection (1) above, that the contract or unilateral voluntary obligation includes additional express terms (whether or not written terms).

(3)   Notwithstanding the foregoing provisions of this section, where one of the terms in the document (or in the documents) is to the effect that the document does (or the documents do) comprise all the express terms of the contract or unilateral voluntary obligation, that term shall be conclusive in the matter.

(4)   This section is without prejudice to any enactment which makes provision as respects the constitution, or formalities of execution, of a contract or unilateral voluntary obligation.

2   Supersession

(1)   Where a deed is executed in implement, or purportedly in implement, of a contract, an unimplemented, or otherwise unfulfilled, term of the contract shall not be taken to be superseded by virtue only of that execution or of the delivery and acceptance of the deed.

(2)   Subsection (1) above is without prejudice to any agreement which the parties to a contract may reach (whether or not an agreement incorporated into the contract) as to supersession of the contract.

3 Damages for breach of contract of sale

Any rule of law which precludes the buyer in a contract of sale of property from obtaining damages for breach of that contract by the seller unless the buyer rejects the property and rescinds the contract shall cease to have effect.

4 Short title, extent etc

. . .

(3) Section 1 of this Act applies only for the purposes of proceedings commenced on or after, and sections 2 and 3 only as respects contracts entered into on or after, the date on which this Act comes into force.

. . .

DATA PROTECTION ACT 1998
(1998, c 29)

7 Right of access to personal data*

(1) Subject to the following provisions of this section and to [sections 8, 9 and 9A], an individual is entitled—

    (a) to be informed by any data controller whether personal data of which that individual is the data subject are being processed by or on behalf of that data controller,

    (b) if that is the case, to be given by the data controller a description of—

      (i) the personal data of which that individual is the data subject,

      (ii) the purposes for which they are being or are to be processed, and

      (iii) the recipients or classes of recipients to whom they are or may be disclosed,

    (c) to have communicated to him in an intelligible form—

      (i) the information constituting any personal data of which that individual is the data subject, and

      (ii) any information available to the data controller as to the source of those data, and

    (d) where the processing by automatic means of personal data of which that individual is the data subject for the purpose of evaluating matters relating to him such as, for example, his performance at work, his creditworthiness, his reliability or his conduct, has constituted or is likely to constitute the sole basis for any decision significantly affecting him, to be informed by the data controller of the logic involved in that decision-taking.

(2) A data controller is not obliged to supply any information under subsection (1) unless he has received—

    (a) a request in writing, and

    (b) except in prescribed cases, such fee (not exceeding the prescribed maximum) as he may require.

[(3) Where a data controller—

    (a) reasonably requires further information in order to satisfy himself as to the identity of the person making a request under this section and to locate the information which that person seeks, and

    (b) has informed him of that requirement,

the data controller is not obliged to comply with the request unless he is supplied with that further information.]

(4) Where a data controller cannot comply with the request without disclosing information relating to another individual who can be identified from that information, he is not obliged to comply with the request unless—

---

*Section 7 is modified in relation to particular professions, namely health (SI 2000/413); education (SI 2000/414); and social work (SI 2000/415; SI 2005/467).

(a)   the other individual has consented to the disclosure of the information to the person making the request, or

(b)   it is reasonable in all the circumstances to comply with the request without the consent of the other individual.

(5)   In subsection (4) the reference to information relating to another individual includes a reference to information identifying that individual as the source of the information sought by the request; and that subsection is not to be construed as excusing a data controller from communicating so much of the information sought by the request as can be communicated without disclosing the identity of the other individual concerned, whether by the omission of names or other identifying particulars or otherwise.

(6)   In determining for the purposes of subsection (4)(b) whether it is reasonable in all the circumstances to comply with the request without the consent of the other individual concerned, regard shall be had, in particular, to—

(a)   any duty of confidentiality owed to the other individual,

(b)   any steps taken by the data controller with a view to seeking the consent of the other individual,

(c)   whether the other individual is capable of giving consent, and

(d)   any express refusal of consent by the other individual.

(7)   An individual making a request under this section may, in such cases as may be prescribed, specify that his request is limited to personal data of any prescribed description.

(8)   Subject to subsection (4), a data controller shall comply with a request under this section promptly and in any event before the end of the prescribed period beginning with the relevant day.

(9)   If a court is satisfied on the application of any person who has made a request under the foregoing provisions of this section that the data controller in question has failed to comply with the request in contravention of those provisions, the court may order him to comply with the request.

(10)   In this section—

'prescribed' means prescribed by the [Secretary of State] by regulations;

'the prescribed maximum' means such amount as may be prescribed;

'the prescribed period' means forty days or such other period as may be prescribed;

'the relevant day', in relation to a request under this section, means the day on which the data controller receives the request or, if later, the first day on which the data controller has both the required fee and the information referred to in subsection (3).

(11)   Different amounts or periods may be prescribed under this section in relation to different cases.

ELECTRONIC COMMUNICATIONS ACT 2000
(2000, c 7)

PART II
FACILITATION OF ELECTRONIC COMMERCE, DATA STORAGE, ETC

7   Electronic signatures and related certificates

(1)   In any legal proceedings—

(a)   an electronic signature incorporated into or logically associated with a particular electronic communication or particular electronic data, and

(b)   the certification by any person of such a signature,

shall each be admissible in evidence in relation to any question as to the authenticity of the communication or data or as to the integrity of the communication or data.

(2)   For the purposes of this section an electronic signature is so much of anything in electronic form as—
    (a)   is incorporated into or otherwise logically associated with any electronic
communication or electronic data; and
    (b)   purports to be so incorporated or associated for the purpose of being
used in establishing the authenticity of the communication or data, the integrity
of the communication or data, or both.

(3)   For the purposes of this section an electronic signature incorporated into or
associated with a particular electronic communication or particular electronic data
is certified by any person if that person (whether before or after the making of the
communication) has made a statement confirming that—
    (a)   the signature,
    (b)   a means of producing, communicating or verifying the signature, or
    (c)   a procedure applied to the signature,
is (either alone or in combination with other factors) a valid means of establishing
the authenticity of the communication or data, the integrity of the communication
or data, or both.

LIMITED LIABILITY PARTNERSHIPS ACT 2000
(2000, c 12)

Introductory

1   Limited liability partnerships
(1)   There shall be a new form of legal entity to be known as a limited liability
partnership.

(2)   A limited liability partnership is a body corporate (with legal personality
separate from that of its members) which is formed by being incorporated under
this Act; and—
    (a)   in the following provisions of this Act (except in the phrase 'oversea
limited liability partnership'), and
    (b)   in any other enactment (except where provision is made to the contrary
or the context otherwise requires),
references to a limited liability partnership are to such a body corporate.

(3)   A limited liability partnership has unlimited capacity.

(4)   The members of a limited liability partnership have such liability to contribute to its assets in the event of its being wound up as is provided for by virtue
of this Act.

(5)   Accordingly, except as far as otherwise provided by this Act or any other
enactment, the law relating to partnerships does not apply to a limited liability
partnership.

(6)   The Schedule (which makes provision about the names and registered
offices of limited liability partnerships) has effect.

Incorporation

2   Incorporation document etc
(1)   For a limited liability partnership to be incorporated—
    (a)   two or more persons associated for carrying on a lawful business with a
view to profit must have subscribed their names to an incorporation document,
    [(b)   the incorporation document or a copy of it must have been delivered to
the registrar, and]
    (c)   there must have been so delivered a statement [. . .], made by either a
solicitor engaged in the formation of the limited liability partnership or anyone
who subscribed his name to the incorporation document, that the requirement
imposed by paragraph (a) has been complied with.

(2)   The incorporation document must—

   [. . .]

   (b)   state the name of the limited liability partnership,

   (c)   state whether the registered office of the limited liability partnership is to be situated in England and Wales, in Wales [, in Scotland or in Northern Ireland],

   (d)   state the address of that registered office,

   [(e)   give the required particulars of each of the persons who are to be members of the limited liability partnership on incorporation, and]

   (f)   either specify which of those persons are to be designated members or state that every person who from time to time is a member of the limited liability partnership is a designated member.

[(2ZA)   The required particulars mentioned in subsection (2)(e) are the particulars required to be stated in the LLP's register of members and register of members' residential addresses.]

   [. . .]

(3)   If a person makes a false statement under subsection (1)(c) which he—

   (a)   knows to be false, or

   (b)   does not believe to be true, he commits an offence.

(4)   A person guilty of an offence under subsection (3) is liable—

   (a)   on summary conviction, to imprisonment for a period not exceeding six months or a fine not exceeding the statutory maximum, or to both, or

   (b)   on conviction on indictment, to imprisonment for a period not exceeding two years or a fine, or to both.

3   Incorporation by registration

   [(1)   The registrar, if satisfied that the requirements of section 2 are complied with, shall—

   (a)   register the documents delivered under that section, and

   (b)   give a certificate that the limited liability partnership is incorporated.]

   [(1A)   The certificate must state—

   (a)   the name and registered number of the limited liability partnership,

   (b)   the date of its incorporation, and

   (c)   whether the limited liability partnership's registered office is situated in England and Wales (or in Wales), in Scotland or in Northern Ireland.]

(2)   The registrar may accept the statement delivered under paragraph (c) of subsection (1) of section 2 as sufficient evidence that the requirement imposed by paragraph (a) of that subsection has been complied with.

(3)   The certificate shall either be signed by the registrar or be authenticated by his official seal.

(4)   The certificate is conclusive evidence that the requirements of section 2 are complied with and that the limited liability partnership is incorporated by the name specified in the incorporation document.

Membership

4   Members

(1)   On the incorporation of a limited liability partnership its members are the persons who subscribed their names to the incorporation document (other than any who have died or been dissolved).

(2)   Any other person may become a member of a limited liability partnership by and in accordance with an agreement with the existing members.

(3)   A person may cease to be a member of a limited liability partnership (as well as by death or dissolution) in accordance with an agreement with the other members or, in the absence of agreement with the other members as to cessation of membership, by giving reasonable notice to the other members.

(4)   A member of a limited liability partnership shall not be regarded for any

purpose as employed by the limited liability partnership unless, if he and the other members were partners in a partnership, he would be regarded for that purpose as employed by the partnership.

[4A   Minimum membership for carrying on business

(1)   This section applies where a limited liability partnership carries on business without having at least two members, and does so for more than 6 months.

(2)   A person who, for the whole or any part of the period that it so carries on business after those 6 months—

(a)   is a member of the limited liability partnership, and

(b)   knows that it is carrying on business with only one member,

is liable (jointly and severally with the limited liability partnership) for the payment of the limited liability partnership's debts contracted during the period or, as the case may be, that part of it.]

5   Relationship of members etc

(1)   Except as far as otherwise provided by this Act or any other enactment, the mutual rights and duties of the members of a limited liability partnership, and the mutual rights and duties of a limited liability partnership and its members, shall be governed—

(a)   by agreement between the members, or between the limited liability partnership and its members, or

(b)   in the absence of agreement as to any matter, by any provision made in relation to that matter by regulations under section 15(c).

(2)   An agreement made before the incorporation of a limited liability partnership between the persons who subscribe their names to the incorporation document may impose obligations on the limited liability partnership (to take effect at any time after its incorporation).

6   Members as agents

(1)   Every member of a limited liability partnership is the agent of the limited liability partnership.

(2)   But a limited liability partnership is not bound by anything done by a member in dealing with a person if—

(a)   the member in fact has no authority to act for the limited liability partnership by doing that thing, and

(b)   the person knows that he has no authority or does not know or believe him to be a member of the limited liability partnership.

(3)   Where a person has ceased to be a member of a limited liability partnership, the former member is to be regarded (in relation to any person dealing with the limited liability partnership) as still being a member of the limited liability partnership unless—

(a)   the person has notice that the former member has ceased to be a member of the limited liability partnership, or

(b)   notice that the former member has ceased to be a member of the limited liability partnership has been delivered to the registrar.

(4)   Where a member of a limited liability partnership is liable to any person (other than another member of the limited liability partnership) as a result of a wrongful act or omission of his in the course of the business of the limited liability partnership or with its authority, the limited liability partnership is liable to the same extent as the member.

7   Ex-members

(1)   This section applies where a member of a limited liability partnership has either ceased to be a member or—

(a)   has died,

(b)   has become bankrupt or had his estate sequestrated or has been wound up,

(c)   has granted a trust deed for the benefit of his creditors, or

(d)   has assigned the whole or any part of his share in the limited liability partnership (absolutely or by way of charge or security).

(2)   In such an event the former member or—

(a)   his personal representative,

(b)   his trustee in bankruptcy or permanent or interim trustee (within the meaning of the Bankruptcy (Scotland) Act 1985) or liquidator,

(c)   his trustee under the trust deed for the benefit of his creditors, or

(d)   his assignee,

may not interfere in the management or administration of any business or affairs of the limited liability partnership.

(3)   But subsection (2) does not affect any right to receive an amount from the limited liability partnership in that event.

8   Designated members

(1)   If the incorporation document specifies who are to be designated members—

(a)   they are designated members on incorporation, and

(b)   any member may become a designated member by and in accordance with an agreement with the other members,

and a member may cease to be a designated member in accordance with an agreement with the other members.

(2)   But if there would otherwise be no designated members, or only one, every member is a designated member.

(3)   If the incorporation document states that every person who from time to time is a member of the limited liability partnership is a designated member, every member is a designated member.

(4)   A limited liability partnership may at any time deliver to the registrar—

(a)   notice that specified members are to be designated members, or

(b)   notice that every person who from time to time is a member of the limited liability partnership is a designated member,

and, once it is delivered, subsection (1) (apart from paragraph (a)) and subsection (2), or subsection (3), shall have effect as if that were stated in the incorporation document.

[. . .]

(6)   A person ceases to be a designated member if he ceases to be a member.

9   Registration of membership changes

(1)   A limited liability partnership must ensure that—

(a)   where a person becomes or ceases to be a member or designated member, notice is delivered to the registrar within fourteen days, and

(b)   where there is any change in the [particulars contained in its register of members or its register of members' residential addresses], notice is delivered to the registrar within [14 days].

(2)   Where all the members from time to time of a limited liability partnership are designated members, subsection (1)(a) does not require notice that a person has become or ceased to be a designated member as well as a member.

[(3)   A notice delivered under subsection (1) that relates to a person becoming a member or designated member must contain—

(a)   a statement that the member or designated member consents to acting in that capacity, and

(b)   in the case of a person becoming a member, a statement of the particulars of the new member that are required to be included in the limited liability partnership's register of members and its register of residential addresses.]

[(3ZA)   Where—

(a)   a limited liability partnership gives notice of a change of a member's service address as stated in its register of members, and

(b)   the notice is not accompanied by notice of any resulting change in the particulars contained in its register of members' residential addresses,
the notice must be accompanied by a statement that no such change is required.]
[. . .]
(4)   If a limited liability partnership fails to comply with [this section], the partnership and every designated member commits an offence.
(5)   But it is a defence for a designated member charged with an offence under subsection (4) to prove that he took all reasonable steps for securing that [this section] was complied with.
(6)   A person guilty of an offence under subsection (4) is liable on summary conviction to a fine not exceeding level 5 on the standard scale.

Regulations

14   Insolvency and winding up
(1)   Regulations shall make provision about the insolvency and winding up of limited liability partnerships by applying or incorporating, with such modifications as appear appropriate, [—
(a)   in relation to a limited liability partnership registered in Great Britain, Parts 1 to 4, 6 and 7 of the Insolvency Act 1986;
(b)   in relation to a limited liability partnership registered in Northern Ireland, Parts 2 to 5 and 7 of the Insolvency (Northern Ireland) Order 1989, and so much of Part 1 of that Order as applies for the purposes of those Parts.]
(2)   Regulations may make other provision about the insolvency and winding up of limited liability partnerships, and provision about the insolvency and winding up of oversea limited liability partnerships, by—
(a)   applying or incorporating, with such modifications as appear appropriate, any law relating to the insolvency or winding up of companies or other corporations which would not otherwise have effect in relation to them, or
(b)   providing for any law relating to the insolvency or winding up of companies or other corporations which would otherwise have effect in relation to them not to apply to them or to apply to them with such modifications as appear appropriate.
(3)   In this Act 'oversea limited liability partnership' means a body incorporated or otherwise established outside [the United Kingdom] and having such connection with [the United Kingdom], and such other features, as regulations may prescribe.

15   Application of company law etc
Regulations may make provision about limited liability partnerships and oversea limited liability partnerships (not being provision about insolvency or winding up) by—
(a)   applying or incorporating, with such modifications as appear appropriate, any law relating to companies or other corporations which would not otherwise have effect in relation to them,
(b)   providing for any law relating to companies or other corporations which would otherwise have effect in relation to them not to apply to them or to apply to them with such modifications as appear appropriate, or
(c)   applying or incorporating, with such modifications as appear appropriate, any law relating to partnerships.

DEBT ARRANGEMENT AND ATTACHMENT (SCOTLAND) ACT 2002
(2002, asp 17)

PART 1
THE DEBT ARRANGEMENT SCHEME

1 Debt arrangement scheme
This Part of this Act constitutes a scheme (to be known as the 'debt arrangement scheme') under which individuals may arrange for their debts to be paid under debt payment programmes.

2 Debt payment programmes
(1) A debt payment programme is a programme which provides for the payment of money owed by a debtor.

[(1A) Subsection (1) above is subject to any provision in regulations made under section 7A(1) below.]

(2) The Scottish Ministers may, on an application by a debtor, approve any debt payment programme set out in the application.

(3) Such an application [. . .] shall—

(a) specify, to the best of the debtor's knowledge and belief, in relation to each debt which the debtor is proposing to be paid under the debt payment programme—

(i) the amount outstanding;

(ii) the creditor to whom the debt is due; and

(iii) the period for which the debt has been due;

(b) set out the arrangements under which those debts are, in accordance with the provisions of the programme, to be paid, in particular specifying—

(i) the amounts which the debtor proposes to pay under the programme;

(ii) the proposed regularity of those payments;

(iii) the manner in which those payments are to be made; and

(iv) the manner in which, and period over which, each of the debts included in the programme is to be paid;

(c) specify the name and address of the person (the 'payments distributor') who is to—

(i) receive payments from the debtor; and

(ii) pay, on behalf of the debtor, the debts included in the programme, in accordance with the provisions of the programme; and

(d) contain such other information (including information relating to the debtor's financial circumstances), and be in such form, as may be prescribed.

(4) Such an application shall, subject to any contrary provision in regulations made under section 7(1) [or 7A(1)] below, incorporate the consent, indicated in the prescribed form, of all the debtor's creditors.

(5) A person's name and address shall not be specified in an application for approval of a debt payment programme as a payments distributor unless that person has been approved by the Scottish Ministers as a person suitable to carry out the functions of a payments distributor.

3 Money advice
(1) A debtor is not entitled to make an application for the approval, or the variation, of a debt payment programme unless the debtor has obtained the advice of a money adviser in relation to—

(a) the debtor's financial circumstances;

(b) the effect of the proposed programme or, as the case may be, the proposed variation of the programme; and

(c) the preparation of the application.

(2) Such an application shall—

(a) contain a [. . .] declaration by the money adviser who provided the advice referred to in subsection (1) above that such advice has been given; and

(b)   specify the name and address of the money adviser.

[(3)   Subsections (1) and (2) above are subject to any contrary provision in regulations made under section 7(1) below.]

4   Effect of debt payment programmes

(1)   Where a debt payment programme has been approved or varied, the debts specified in the application for the approval or, as the case may be, the variation shall be paid in accordance with the programme.

(2)   It is not competent—

(a)   to serve a charge for payment in respect of; or

(b)   [subject to] subsection (2A),] to commence or execute any diligence to enforce payment of; or

[(c)   to commit a debtor to prison under section 4 of the Civil Imprisonment (Scotland) Act 1882, except for the purposes of section 40A of the Child Support Act 1991, in respect of,]

any debt owed by a debtor who has debts which are being paid under an approved debt payment programme.

[(2A)   Despite subsection (2)(b), it is competent to—

(a)   auction an attached article where—

(i)   notice has been given to the debtor under section 27(4) below; or

(ii)   an article has been removed, or notice of removal has been given, under section 53 below;

(b)   implement a decree of furthcoming;

(c)   implement a decree or order for sale of a ship (or a share of it) or cargo.

[. . .]

(3)   A creditor is not entitled to found on any debt owed by such a debtor in presenting, or concurring in the presentation of, a petition for the sequestration of the debtor's estate.

(4)   There is to be disregarded, for the purposes of the exercise by a creditor of any rights to enforce a debt or remedies to like effect, any period during which the debtor's debts were subject to an approved debt payment programme.

(5)   The debts referred to in subsections (2) to (4) above are restricted to—

(a)   those to which the debtor's debt payment programme relates; and

(b)   any other debts owed to creditors who have been given notice, in the prescribed form, of the approval of the debt payment programme.

5   Variation of debt payment programmes

(1)   The Scottish Ministers may, on an application by the debtor or by any creditor, approve the variation of a debt payment programme.

(2)   The Scottish Ministers may not consider an application for approval of a variation under subsection (1) above unless—

(a)   where the application is made by the debtor, a copy of the application has been given to each creditor who is owed a debt which is being paid under the debt payment programme; or

(b)   where the application is made by a creditor, a copy of the application has been given to the debtor and to each other creditor who is owed such a debt.

(3)   Such an application may seek the variation of any condition which is attached to the approval of the programme or, as the case may be, a previous variation of the programme.

(4)   An application for the variation of a debt payment programme shall—

(a)   contain such information, and be in such form, as may be prescribed;

[. . .]

6 Deduction from earnings

(1)   Where an approved debt payment programme requires sums to be paid to the payments distributor by way of deduction of the debtor's earnings from employment, the debtor shall provide an instruction, in the prescribed form, to the person by whom the debtor is employed to make—

(a)   deductions from the debtor's earnings; and

(b)   payments of the amounts deducted to the payments distributor, in accordance with the provisions of the debt payment programme.

(2)   It is the duty of the employer to comply with any instruction so provided.

7 Debt payment programmes: power to make further provision

(1)   The Scottish Ministers may, by regulations, make such further provision as they think fit in connection with—

(a)   applications for the approval, or for the variation, of debt payment programmes;

(b)   the manner in which such programmes are to operate, including conditions with which debtors, creditors, payments distributors or money advisers must comply;

(c)   the effect of such programmes; and

(d)   the effect of the failure of an employer to comply with the duty under section 6(2) above.

(2)   The regulations may, in particular, make provision about—

(a)   the class of person who may or may not make an application for the approval, or the variation, of a debt payment programme;

(b)   the class of debt in respect of which such an application may or may not be made;

[(ba)   circumstances in which some or all of the functions of a money adviser under section 3 above may instead be carried out by an approved intermediary;

(bb)   circumstances in which a debtor is entitled to make an application for the approval, or the variation, of a debt payment programme where the debtor has not obtained advice under section 3(1) above;

(bc)   the manner in which—

(i)   the seeking of the consent of creditors to applications for approval of debt payment programmes; or

(ii)   the making of such applications,

affects the rights and remedies of creditors or other third parties.]

(c)   the matters to which the Scottish Ministers are to have regard in determining whether to approve such an application;

(d)   the conditions which may or may not be attached to an approval of such an application;

(e)   circumstances in which such an application will not be approved;

(f)   appeals against determinations by the Scottish Ministers on such applications;

(g)   circumstances in which the consent for the purposes of section 2(4) above of a creditor or creditors generally may be dispensed with;

(h)   circumstances in which a creditor may object to—

(i)   the dispensation of the creditor's consent; or

(ii)   the approval of such an application, and the manner in which such objection may be made;

(i)   the remitting of any such application in respect of which a creditor has made an objection to the sheriff for determination;

(j)   the manner in which a debt payment programme may be varied;

(k)   the priority in which debts are to be paid under a debt payment programme;

(l)   the ingathering and sale or other disposal of assets and the distribution to creditors of amounts so realised;

(m)   the period for which a debt payment programme is to remain in operation;

(n)   circumstances in which, and the procedure under which, any such period can, in relation to a particular debt payment programme, be shortened or extended;

(o)   circumstances in which a debt payment programme is to cease to have effect;

(p)   subject to section 4 above, the manner in which a debt payment programme affects the rights or remedies of a creditor or other third party;

(q)   circumstances in which creditors are to notify debtors of the right to make such an application and the effect of the failure of a creditor to provide that notice;

(r)   the class of person who may act as a payments distributor;

(s)   the class of person who may act as a money adviser;

[(sa)   the class of person who may act as an approved intermediary;]

(t)   the functions of a payments distributor;

(u)   the functions of a money adviser;

[(ua)   the functions of an approved intermediary;]

(v)   the establishment and maintenance by the Scottish Ministers of a register of debt payment programmes and applications for the approval, and variation, of such programmes;

(w)   the information which is to be kept in such a register;

(x)   the manner in which that information is to be kept and in which it, or any part of it, is to be made available to the public; and

(y)   the determination, and charging, by the Scottish Ministers of fees in respect of—

(i)   the consideration of applications for the approval, or the variation, of a debt payment programme; and

(ii)   the provision of information recorded in the register of debt payment programmes.

(3)   The regulations may also—

(a)   make different provision in relation to such different types of debtors, debts or other matters as may be described by the Scottish Ministers;

(b)   provide that such different provision is to have effect only for such period as is specified by the Scottish Ministers; and

(c)   provide that, on the expiry of that period, the Scottish Ministers may determine that the different provision to which they relate is to—

(i)   continue to have effect without limit of time;

(ii)   continue to have effect for such further period as may be determined by the Scottish Ministers; or

(iii)   cease to have effect.

(4)   The regulations may also modify any enactment (including this Act), in-strument or document for the purposes of making such further provision as is mentioned in subsection (1) above.

[7A   Debt payment programmes: power to make provision about debt relief

(1)   The Scottish Ministers may, by regulations, make such further provision as they think fit in connection with debt payment programmes for the purposes of—

(a)   enabling such programmes to provide for the payment of part only of money owed by debtors; and

(b)   on the completion of such programmes or otherwise, enabling any liability of debtors to pay any part of such money owed as is outstanding to be discharged.

(2)   The regulations may, in particular, make provision about—

(a)   the minimum proportion or percentage of debts which shall be paid under such debt payment programmes;

(b)   without prejudice to section 7(2)(h) to (j) above, the consent of creditors for the purposes of section 2(4) above (including the circumstances in which consent by a majority by number or in value shall be sufficient);

(c)   the effect of such programmes on debtors' liabilities for interest, fees, penalties and other charges in relation to debts being paid under such programmes;

(d)   the effect of such programmes on the rights of creditors to charge interest, fees, penalties or other charges in relation to debts being paid under such programmes;

(e)   circumstances in which, on completion of such programmes or otherwise, any liability of debtors to pay—

(i)   part of any debts as are outstanding; or

(ii)   any interest, fees, penalties or other charges in relation to such debts,

is to be discharged.

(3)   Subsections (3) and (4) of section 7 above apply for the purposes of regulations under this section as they apply for the purposes of regulations under subsection (1) of that section.]

8   Functions of the Scottish Ministers

(1)   The Scottish Ministers may by order provide that their functions under this Part of this Act may be performed on their behalf by such other person as may be specified in the order.

(2)   Such an order does not allow regulations under this Part of this Act or any further order under this section to be made by any person other than the Scottish Ministers.

(3)   Such an order may make different provision for different functions.

9   Interpretation of Part

(1)   In this Part of this Act—

['approved intermediary' means any person, not being a money adviser, who has been approved by the Scottish Ministers as a person who may give advice to a debtor for the purposes of section 3(1) above.]

'money adviser' means any person who has been approved by the Scottish Ministers as a person who may give advice to a debtor for the purposes of section 3(1) above; and

'prescribed' means prescribed by regulations made by the Scottish Ministers.

(2)   The references in this Part of this Act to a debtor are references to a debtor who is a natural person.

[PART 1A
INTERIM ATTACHMENT

Interim attachment

[9A   Interim attachment
(1)   Subject to sections 9B to 9E below, the court may grant warrant for diligence by attachment of corporeal moveable property owned (whether alone or in
common) by the debtor on the dependence of an action (such attachment is to be
known as interim attachment).
(2)   Warrant for interim attachment is competent only where an action contains
a conclusion for payment of a sum other than by way of expenses.
(3)   This Part of this Act shall apply to petitions in the Court of Session and to
parties to them as it applies to actions and to parties to them.
(4)   In this Part of this Act—
'action' includes, in the sheriff court—
     (a)   a summary cause;
     (b)   a small claim; and
     (c)   a summary application,
and references to 'summons', 'conclusion' and to cognate expressions shall be construed accordingly;
'court' means—
     (a)   the court before which the action is in dependence; or
     (b)   where, by virtue of section 9L(1)(a) below, the interim attachment has
     effect after the creditor obtains a final interlocutor for payment, the court which
     granted that interlocutor;
'creditor' means the party who concludes for payment and who seeks, obtains or
executes warrant for interim attachment;
'debtor' means the party against whom the conclusion for payment is addressed;
and expressions used in this Part of this Act have, unless the context otherwise
requires, the same meanings as those expressions have in Part 2 of this Act.]

[9B   Articles exempt from interim attachment
It is not competent to attach by interim attachment—
     (a)   any article within a dwellinghouse;
     (b)   any article which, by virtue of section 11 below, it is not competent to
     attach;
     (c)   a mobile home which is the only or principal residence of a person other
     than the debtor;
     (d)   any article of a perishable nature or which is likely to deteriorate
     substantially and rapidly in condition or value; or
     (e)   where the debtor is engaged in trade, any article acquired by the
     debtor—
          (i)   to be sold by the debtor (whether or not after adaptation); or
          (ii)   as a material for a process of manufacturing for sale by the debtor,
     in the ordinary course of that trade.]

Application for interim attachment

[9C   Application for warrant for interim attachment
(1)   A creditor may, at any time during which an action is in dependence, apply
to the court for warrant for interim attachment.
(2)   An application under subsection (1) above shall—
     (a)   be in (or as nearly as may be in) the form prescribed by Act of Sederunt;
     (b)   subject to subsection (3) below, be intimated to and provide details of—
          (i)   the debtor; and
          (ii)   any other person having an interest;

(c)   state whether the creditor is seeking the grant, under section 9D(1) below, of warrant for interim attachment in advance of a hearing on the application under section 9E below; and

(d)   contain such other information as the Scottish Ministers may by regulations prescribe.

(3)   An application under subsection (1) above need not be intimated where the creditor is seeking the grant, under section 9D(1) below, of warrant in advance of a hearing on the application under section 9E below.

(4)   The court, on receiving an application under subsection (1) above, shall—

(a)   subject to section 9D below, fix a date for a hearing on the application under section 9E below; and

(b)   order the creditor to intimate that date to—

(i)   the debtor; and

(ii)   any other person appearing to the court to have an interest.]

[9D   Grant of warrant without a hearing

(1)   The court may, if satisfied as to the matters mentioned in subsection (2) below, make an order granting warrant for interim attachment without a hearing on the application under section 9E below.

(2)   The matters referred to in subsection (1) above are—

(a)   that the creditor has a prima facie case on the merits of the action;

(b)   that there is a real and substantial risk enforcement of any decree in the action in favour of the creditor would be defeated or prejudiced by reason of—

(i)   the debtor being insolvent or verging on insolvency; or

(ii)   the likelihood of the debtor removing, disposing of, burdening, concealing or otherwise dealing with all or some of the debtor's assets,

were warrant for interim attachment not granted in advance of such a hearing; and

(c)   that it is reasonable in all the circumstances, including the effect granting warrant may have on any person having an interest, to do so.

(3)   The onus shall be on the creditor to satisfy the court that the order granting warrant should be made.

(4)   Where the court makes an order granting warrant for interim attachment without a hearing on the application under section 9E below, the court shall—

(a)   fix a date for a hearing under section 9M below; and

(b)   order the creditor to intimate that date to—

(i)   the debtor; and

(ii)   any other person appearing to the court to have an interest.

(5)   Where a hearing is fixed under subsection (4)(a) above, section 9M (except subsection (11)) below shall apply as if an application had been made to the court for an order under that section.

(6)   Where the court refuses to make an order granting warrant without a hearing under section 9E below and the creditor insists in the application, the court shall—

(a)   fix a date for such a hearing on the application; and

(b)   order the creditor to intimate that date to—

(i)   the debtor; and

(ii)   any other person appearing to the court to have an interest.]

[9E   Hearing on application

(1)   At the hearing on an application for warrant for interim attachment, the court shall not make any order without first giving—

(a)   any person to whom intimation of the date of the hearing was made; and

(b)   any other person appearing to the court to have an interest,

an opportunity to be heard.

(2)   The court may, if satisfied as to the matters mentioned in subsection (3) below, make an order granting warrant for interim attachment.

(3)   The matters referred to in subsection (2) above are—
    (a)   that the creditor has a prima facie case on the merits of the action;
    (b)   that there is a real and substantial risk enforcement of any decree in the action in favour of the creditor would be defeated or prejudiced by reason of—
        (i)   the debtor being insolvent or verging on insolvency; or
        (ii)   the likelihood of the debtor removing, disposing of, burdening, concealing or otherwise dealing with all or some of the debtor's assets,
were warrant for interim attachment not granted; and
    (c)   that it is reasonable in all the circumstances, including the effect granting warrant may have on any person having an interest, to do so.
(4)   The onus shall be on the creditor to satisfy the court that the order granting warrant should be made.
(5)   Where the court makes an order granting or, as the case may be, refusing warrant for interim attachment, the court shall order the creditor to intimate that order to—
    (a)   the debtor; and
    (b)   any other person appearing to the court to have an interest.
(6)   Where the court makes an order refusing warrant for interim attachment, the court may impose such conditions (if any) as it thinks fit.
(7)   Without prejudice to the generality of subsection (6) above, those conditions may require the debtor—
    (a)   to consign into court such sum; or
    (b)   to find caution or to give such other security,
as the court thinks fit.]

Execution of interim attachment

[9F   Execution of interim attachment
(1)   Sections 12, 13, 15 and (subject to subsection (6) below) 17 below apply to execution of an interim attachment as they apply to execution of an attachment.
(2)   The officer shall, immediately after executing an interim attachment, complete a schedule such as is mentioned in subsection (3) below (in this Part of this Act, a 'schedule of interim attachment').
(3)   The schedule of interim attachment—
    (a)   shall be—
        (i)   in (or as nearly as may be in) the form prescribed by Act of Sederunt; and
        (ii)   signed by the officer; and
    (b)   shall specify—
        (i)   the articles attached; and
        (ii)   their value, so far as ascertainable.
(4)   The officer shall—
    (a)   give a copy of the schedule of interim attachment to the debtor; or
    (b)   where it is not practicable to do so—
        (i)   give a copy of the schedule to a person present at the place where the interim attachment was executed; or
        (ii)   where there is no such person, leave a copy of the schedule at that place.
(5)   References in this Part of this Act to the day on which an interim attachment is executed are references to the day on which the officer complies with subsection (4) above.
(6)   The application of section 17 below shall be subject to the following modifications—
    (a)   subsections (3)(b) and (4) shall not apply;
    (b)   in subsections (1), (5) and (6), the references to the sheriff shall be construed as references to the court; and

(c)   in subsection (6)(b), the reference to the sheriff clerk shall, in the case of an action in the Court of Session, be construed as a reference to the clerk of the court.]

[9G   Execution of interim attachment before service

(1)   This section applies where an interim attachment is executed before the service of the summons on the debtor.

(2)   Subject to subsection (3) below, if the summons is not served on the debtor before the end of the period of 21 days beginning with the day on which the interim attachment is executed, the attachment shall cease to have effect.

(3)   The court may, on the application of the creditor, make an order extending the period referred to in subsection (2) above.

(4)   In determining whether to make such an order the court shall have regard to—

(a)   the efforts of the creditor to serve the summons within the period of 21 days; and

(b)   any special circumstances preventing or obstructing service within that period.]

Interim attachment: further procedure

[9H   Order for security of attached articles

(1)   The court may, on an application, at any time after articles have been attached—

(a)   by the creditor;

(b)   the officer; or

(c)   the debtor,

make an order for the security of any of the attached articles.

(2)   An application for an order under subsection (1) above shall—

(a)   be in (or as nearly as may be in) the form prescribed by Act of Sederunt; and

(b)   be intimated—

(i)   where it is made by the creditor or the officer, to the debtor;

(ii)   where it is made by the debtor, to the creditor and the officer.

(3)   At the hearing on the application under subsection (1) above, the court shall not make any order without first giving—

(a)   any person to whom intimation of the application was made; and

(b)   any other person the court is satisfied has an interest,

an opportunity to be heard.]

Interim attachment: effects

[9J   Unlawful acts after interim attachment

Section 21 (except subsections (3) and (15)) below applies to an interim attachment as it applies to an attachment with the following modifications—

(a)   in subsections (10) and (11), the references to the sheriff shall be construed as references to the court; and

(b)   in subsection (12), the references to sections 51 and 54(1) below shall be of no effect.]

[9K   Articles belonging to or owned in common by a third party

(1)   Where—

(a)   a third party claims to own an article attached by interim attachment; and

(b)   the court, on the application of the third party, makes an order stating that it is satisfied that the claim is valid,

the interim attachment of that article shall cease to have effect.

(2)   Where—
   (a)   a third party claims to own an article attached by interim attachment in common with the debtor;
   (b)   the court, on the application of the third party, makes an order stating that it is satisfied—
      (i)   that the claim is valid; and
      (ii)   that the continued attachment of the article would be unduly harsh to the third party,
the interim attachment of that article shall cease to have effect.
   (3)   Subsection (2) of section 34 below applies where a third party makes an application for the purposes of subsection (1)(b) above as it applies where a third party makes an application for the purposes of subsection (1)(b)(ii) of that section.
   (4)   Where the attachment of an article ceases, by virtue of an order under subsection (1) or (2) above, to have effect, the officer may attach other articles which are owned by the debtor and kept at the place at which the original interim attachment was executed.]

[9L   Duration of interim attachment
   (1)   An interim attachment shall, unless recalled, have effect only until—
      (a)   subject to subsections (2), (4) and (7) below, where—
         (i)   the creditor obtains a final interlocutor for payment of all or part of a principal sum concluded for in the action on the dependence of which warrant for interim attachment was granted;
         (ii)   the creditor obtains a final interlocutor in the creditor's favour in respect of another remedy concluded for in that action; or
         (iii)   the final interlocutor is of absolvitor or dismissal and the court grants decree under and for the purposes of section 9Q(1)(b) below,
the expiry of the period of 6 months after the action is disposed of;
      (b)   where—
         (i)   the final interlocutor is of absolvitor or dismissal; and
         (ii)   no decree under and for the purposes of section 9Q(1)(b) below is granted,
the granting of that interlocutor; or
      (c)   the creditor consents, by virtue of subsection (3) below, to the interim attachment ceasing to have effect in relation to every article attached.
   (2)   An interim attachment shall have effect in relation to a specific article only until the article is attached by the creditor in execution of any such final interlocutor or decree as is mentioned in subsection (1)(a) above.
   (3)   The creditor may at any time consent in writing to the interim attachment ceasing to have effect in relation to a specific article attached; and the attachment shall cease to have effect when that consent is notified to the court.
   (4)   The court may, on an application by the creditor, extend the period mentioned in subsection (1)(a) above but only if—
      (a)   the application is made before the expiry of the period mentioned in that subsection; and
      (b)   the court is satisfied that exceptional circumstances make it reasonable to grant the application.
   (5)   An application under subsection (4) above shall—
      (a)   be in (or as nearly as may be in) the form prescribed by Act of Sederunt; and
      (b)   be intimated by the creditor to—
         (i)   the debtor; and
         (ii)   any other person having an interest.
   (6)   The court shall order the creditor to intimate any decision under subsection (4) above disposing of the application under that subsection to—
      (a)   the debtor; and

(b)   any other person appearing to the court to have an interest.

(7)   Where such an application is made but not disposed of before the date on which the interim attachment would, but for this subsection, cease to have effect, the interim attachment shall continue to have effect until the application is disposed of.

(8)   In calculating the period mentioned in subsection (1)(a) above, any period during which—

(a)   a time to pay direction under section 1(1) of the Debtors (Scotland) Act 1987 (c 18); or

(b)   an order under—

(i)   section 6(3) of that Act (interim order sisting diligence); or

(ii)   section 9(4) of that Act (diligence sisted if not recalled on making of time to pay order),

is in effect shall be disregarded.

(9)   For the purposes of subsection (1) above—

(a)   a final interlocutor is obtained when an interlocutor—

(i)   cannot be recalled or altered; and

(ii)   is not subject to review; and

(b)   an action is disposed of on the date on which the final interlocutor mentioned in paragraph (a) of that subsection is obtained unless, on a later date, the creditor obtains a final interlocutor for expenses in the action, in which case it is disposed of on that later date.]

Recall etc of interim attachment

[9M   Recall or restriction of interim attachment

(1)   This section applies where warrant is granted for interim attachment.

(2)   The debtor and any person having an interest may apply to the court for an order—

(a)   recalling the warrant;

(b)   restricting the warrant;

(c)   if an interim attachment has been executed in pursuance of the warrant—

(i)   recalling; or

(ii)   restricting,

that attachment;

(d)   determining any question relating to the validity, effect or operation of the warrant; or

(e)   ancillary to any order mentioned in paragraphs (a) to (d) above.

(3)   An application under subsection (2) above shall—

(a)   be in (or as nearly as may be in) the form prescribed by Act of Sederunt; and

(b)   be intimated to—

(i)   the creditor; and

(ii)   any other person having an interest.

(4)   At the hearing on the application under subsection (2) above, the court shall not make any order without first giving—

(a)   any person to whom intimation of the application was made; and

(b)   any other person the court is satisfied has an interest,

an opportunity to be heard.

(5)   Where the court is satisfied that the warrant is invalid it—

(a)   shall make an order—

(i)   recalling the warrant; and

(ii)   if interim attachment has been executed in pursuance of the warrant, recalling that interim attachment; and

(b)   may make an order ancillary to any order mentioned in paragraph (a) above.

(6)   Where the court is satisfied that an interim attachment executed in pursuance of the warrant is incompetent, it—

(a)   shall make an order recalling the interim attachment; and

(b)   may make an order ancillary to any such order.

(7)   Subject to subsection (8) below, where the court is satisfied that the warrant is valid but that—

(a)   an interim attachment executed in pursuance of it is irregular or ineffective; or

(b)   it is reasonable in all the circumstances, including the effect granting warrant may have had on any person having an interest, to do so,

the court may, subject to subsection (11) below, make any order such as is mentioned in subsection (2) above.

(8)   If no longer satisfied as to the matters mentioned in subsection (9) below, the court—

(a)   shall make an order such as is mentioned in subsection (5)(a) above; and

(b)   may make an order such as is mentioned in subsection (5)(b) above.

(9)   The matters referred to in subsection (8) above are—

(a)   that the creditor has a prima facie case on the merits of the action;

(b)   that there is a real and substantial risk enforcement of any decree in the action in favour of the creditor would be defeated or prejudiced by reason of—

(i)   the debtor being insolvent or verging on insolvency; or

(ii)   the likelihood of the debtor removing, disposing of, burdening, concealing or otherwise dealing with all or some of the debtor's assets; and

(c)   that it is reasonable in all the circumstances, including the effect granting warrant may have had on any person having an interest, for the warrant or, as the case may be, any interim attachment executed in pursuance of it to continue to have effect.

(10)   The onus shall be on the creditor to satisfy the court that no order under subsection (5), (6), (7) or (8) above should be made.

(11)   Where—

(a)   by virtue of section 9L(1)(a) above, the interim attachment continues to have effect after the creditor obtains a final interlocutor for payment; and

(b)   the period of six months mentioned in that paragraph has not expired, the court shall not make an order under subsection (7) above.

(12)   In granting an application under subsection (2) above, the court may impose such conditions (if any) as it thinks fit.

(13)   Without prejudice to the generality of subsection (12) above, those conditions may require the debtor—

(a)   to consign into court such sum; or

(b)   to find such caution or to give such other security,

as the court thinks fit.

(14)   Where the court makes an order under this section, the court shall order the debtor to intimate that order to—

(a)   the creditor; and

(b)   any other person appearing to the court to have an interest.]

[9N   **Variation of orders and variation or recall of conditions**

(1)   Where—

(a)   an order restricting warrant for interim attachment is made under section 9M(7) above; or

(b)   a condition is imposed under—

(i)   section 9E(6) above; or

(ii)   section 9M(12) above,

the debtor may apply to the court for variation of the order or, as the case may be, variation or removal of the condition.

(2)   An application under subsection (1) above shall—
(a)   be in (or as nearly as may be in) the form prescribed by Act of Sederunt; and
(b)   be intimated to—
(i)   the creditor; and
(ii)   any other person having an interest.

(3)   At the hearing on the application under subsection (1) above, the court shall not make any order without first giving—
(a)   any person to whom intimation of the application was made; and
(b)   any other person the court is satisfied has an interest,
an opportunity to be heard.

(4)   On an application under subsection (1) above, the court may if it thinks fit—
(a)   vary the order; or
(b)   vary or remove the condition.

(5)   Where the court makes an order varying the order or, as the case may be, varying or removing the condition, the court shall order the debtor to intimate that order to—
(a)   the creditor; and
(b)   any other person appearing to the court to have an interest.]

General and miscellaneous provisions

[9P   Expenses of interim attachment

(1)   Subject to subsection (3)(a) below, a creditor shall be entitled to the expenses incurred—
(a)   in obtaining warrant for interim attachment; and
(b)   where an interim attachment is executed in pursuance of the warrant, in so executing that attachment.

(2)   Subject to subsection (3)(b) below, a debtor shall be entitled, where—
(a)   warrant for interim attachment is granted; and
(b)   the court is satisfied that the creditor was acting unreasonably in applying for it,
to the expenses incurred in opposing that warrant.

(3)   The court may modify or refuse—
(a)   such expenses as are mentioned in subsection (1) above if it is satisfied that—
(i)   the creditor was acting unreasonably in applying for the warrant; or
(ii)   such modification or refusal is reasonable in all the circumstances and having regard to the outcome of the action; and
(b)   such expenses as are mentioned in subsection (2) above if it is satisfied as to the matter mentioned in paragraph (a)(ii) above.

(4)   Subject to subsections (1) to (3) above, the court may make such findings as it thinks fit in relation to such expenses as are mentioned in subsections (1) and (2) above.

(5)   Expenses incurred as mentioned in subsections (1) and (2) above in obtaining or, as the case may be, opposing an application for warrant shall be expenses of process.]

[9Q   Recovery of expenses of interim attachment

(1)   Subject to subsection (4) below, any expenses chargeable against the debtor which are incurred in executing an interim attachment shall be recoverable only by attachment—
(a)   in execution of a decree granted by virtue of—

(i) the conclusion for payment in the action on the dependence of which the warrant for interim attachment was granted; or

(ii) another conclusion in the creditor's favour in that action; or

(b) where the final interlocutor in the action is of absolvitor or dismissal, in execution of a decree granted under and for the purposes of this subsection.

(2) Where any such expenses cease to be recoverable in pursuance of subsection (1) above, they cease to be chargeable against the debtor.

(3) Subsection (4) below applies where interim attachment is—

(a) recalled under section 2(3), 3(1)(b), 9(2)(cb) or 10(1)(b) of the 1987 Act in relation to a time to pay direction or order;

(b) in effect immediately before the date of sequestration (within the meaning of the Bankruptcy (Scotland) Act 1985 (c 66)) of the debtor's estate;

(c) in effect immediately before the appointment of an administrator under Part II of the Insolvency Act 1986 (c 45);

(d) in effect against property of the debtor immediately before a floating charge attaches all or part of that property under section 53(7)(attachment on appointment of receiver by holder of charge) or 54(6)(attachment on appointment of receiver by court) of the 1986 Act;

(e) in effect immediately before the commencement of the winding up, under Part IV or V of the 1986 Act, of the debtor; or

(f) rendered unenforceable by virtue of the creditor entering into a composition contract or acceding to a trust deed for creditors or by virtue of the subsistence of a protected trust deed within the meaning of Schedule 5 to the 1985 Act.

(4) Where this subsection applies—

(a) the expenses of the interim attachment which were chargeable against the debtor remain so chargeable; and

(b) if the debtor's obligation to pay the expenses is not discharged under or by virtue of the time to pay direction or order, sequestration, appointment, receivership, winding up, composition contract or trust deed for creditors,

those expenses are recoverable in pursuance of subsection (1) above.]

[9R Ascription of sums recovered while interim attachment is in effect

(1) This section applies where—

(a) any amounts are—

(i) secured by an interim attachment; and

(ii) while the attachment is in effect, paid to account of the amounts recoverable from the debtor; and

(b) that interim attachment ceases to have effect.

(2) Such amounts shall be ascribed to the following in the order in which they are mentioned—

(a) the expenses incurred in—

(i) obtaining warrant for; and

(ii) executing,

the interim attachment;

(b) any interest which has accrued, in relation to a sum due under a decree granted by virtue of the conclusion in relation to which warrant for interim attachment was granted, as at the date of execution;

(c) any sum due under that decree together with such interest as has accrued after that date.

(3) Where an interim attachment is followed by an attachment in execution of a decree granted by virtue of the conclusion in relation to which the warrant for the interim attachment was granted, section 41 below shall apply to amounts to which this section applies as it applies to amounts to which that section applies.]

[9S   Ranking of interim attachment
For the purposes of any enactment or rule of law as to ranking or preference—
   (a)   where—
      (i)   an interim attachment has been executed; and
      (ii)   the creditor has, without undue delay, obtained an interlocutor for
   payment of all or part of the sum concluded for,
that interim attachment shall be treated as if it were an attachment by virtue of
section 10 below of the property attached, executed when the interim attachment
was executed; and
   (b)   where an interim attachment has ceased to have effect in relation to any
article by virtue of section 9L(2) above, the attachment of the article in question
shall be taken to have been executed when the interim attachment was
executed.]]

PART 2
ATTACHMENT

Attachment

10   Attachment
   (1)   There shall be a form of diligence over corporeal moveable property for
recovery of money owed; it is to be known as attachment.
   (2)   Attachment is exigible only in execution of a decree or document of debt
and only upon property owned (whether alone or in common) by the debtor.
   (3)   Attachment is competent only where—
   [(a)   the debtor has been charged to pay the debt;
   (b)   the period for payment specified in the charge has expired without
payment being made; and
   (c)   where the debtor is an individual, the creditor has, no earlier than 12
weeks before taking any steps to execute the attachment, provided the debtor
with a debt advice and information package.]
   [. . .]
   (5)   In this section—
'debt advice and information package' means a document or bundle of documents containing such information (including information regarding the availability of money advice within the debtor's locality), and in such form, as the
[Scottish Civil Enforcement Commission] may determine;
   'decree' means—
   (a)   a decree of the Court of Session, of the High Court of Justiciary or of the
sheriff;
   (b)   a decree of the Court of Teinds;
   (c)   a summary warrant;
   (d)   a civil judgment granted outside Scotland by a court, tribunal or
arbiter which by virtue of any enactment or rule of law is enforceable in
Scotland;
   (e)   an order or determination which by virtue of any enactment is
enforceable as if it were an extract registered decree arbitral bearing a warrant
for execution issued by the sheriff;
   (f)   a warrant granted, in criminal proceedings, for enforcement by civil
diligence;
   (g)   an order under section 114 of the Companies Clauses Consolidation
(Scotland) Act 1845 (c 17);
   (h)   a determination under section 46 of the Harbours, Docks and Piers
Clauses Act 1847 (c 27); or
   (i)   a liability order within the meaning of section 33(2) of the Child Support

Act 1991 (c 48), being a decree, warrant, judgment, order or determination which, or an extract of which, authorises attachment; and
'document of debt' means—
    (a)   a document registered for execution in the Books of Council and Session or the sheriff court books; or
    (b)   a document or settlement which by virtue of an Order in Council made under section 13 of the Civil Jurisdiction and Judgments Act 1982 (c 27) is enforceable in Scotland,
being a document, bill or settlement which, or an extract of which, authorises attachment.
    (6)   The Scottish Ministers may by order modify the definitions of 'decree' and 'document of debt' in subsection (5) above so as to—
    (a)   add or remove types of decree or document to or, as the case may be, from those referred to in that provision; or
    (b)   vary any of the descriptions of the types of decree or document there referred to.
    (7)   In this Act, references to attaching are references to the execution of attachment.

11   Articles exempt from attachment
    (1)   It is not competent to attach—
    (a)   any implements, tools of trade, books or other equipment reasonably required for the use of the debtor in the practice of the debtor's profession, trade or business and not exceeding in aggregate value £1,000 or such amount as may be prescribed in regulations made by the Scottish Ministers;
    (b)   any vehicle, the use of which is so reasonably required by the debtor, not exceeding in value £1,000 or such amount as may be prescribed in regulations made by the Scottish Ministers;
    (c)   a mobile home which is the debtor's only or principal residence;
    (d)   any tools or other equipment reasonably required for the purpose of keeping in good order and condition any garden or yard adjacent to, or associated with, a dwellinghouse in which the debtor resides;
    [(e)   any money.]
    (2)   The Scottish Ministers may by regulations modify subsection (1) above so as to—
    (a)   add or remove types of articles to or, as the case may be, from those referred to in that provision; or
    (b)   vary any of the descriptions of the types of articles there referred to.
    [(3)   It is not competent to attach cargo which it is competent to arrest by virtue of section 47C of the Administration of Justice Act 1965 (c 46) (competence of arresting cargo.)]*
    [(3)   In subsection (1)(e) above, 'money' has the same meaning as in section 175 of the Bankruptcy and Diligence etc (Scotland) Act 2007 (asp 3).]*
*Subsection (3) inserted twice, by Bankruptcy and Diligence etc (Scotland) Act 2007 Sch 4 para 11 and by Sch 5 para 11 respectively.

12   Times when attachment is not competent
    (1)   It is not competent to execute an attachment on—
    (a)   a Sunday;
    (b)   a day which is a public holiday in the area in which the attachment is to be executed; or
    (c)   such other day as may be prescribed by Act of Sederunt.
    (2)   The execution of an attachment shall not—
    (a)   begin before 8 am or after 8 pm; or
    (b)   be continued after 8 pm,

unless the officer has obtained prior authority from the sheriff for such commencement or continuation.

13 Presumption of ownership

(1)   An officer may, when executing an attachment, proceed on the assumption that the debtor owns, solely or in common with a third party, any article which is in the possession of the debtor.

(2)   The officer shall, before attaching any article, make enquiries of any person who is present at the place at which the article is situated as to the ownership of the article (and in particular shall enquire as to whether there is any person who owns the article in common with the debtor).

(3)   The officer may not proceed on the assumption mentioned in subsection (1) above where the officer knows or ought to know that the contrary is the case.

(4)   The officer is not precluded from relying on that assumption by reason only of one or both of the following circumstances—

(a)   that the article belongs to a class which is commonly held under a hire, hire-purchase or conditional sale agreement or on some other limited title of possession;

(b)   that an assertion has been made that the article is not owned by the debtor.

[13A   Schedule of attachment

(1)   The officer must, immediately after executing an attachment, complete a schedule such as is mentioned in subsection (2) below (in this section, the 'attachment schedule').

(2)   An attachment schedule—

(a)   must be in (or as nearly as may be in) the form prescribed by Act of Sederunt; and

(b)   must specify—

(i)   the articles attached; and

(ii)   their value, so far as ascertainable.

(3)   The officer must—

(a)   give a copy of the attachment schedule to the debtor; or

(b)   where it is not practicable to do so—

(i)   give a copy of the schedule to a person present at the place where the attachment was executed; or

(ii)   where there is no such person, leave a copy of it at that place.

(4)   An attachment is executed on the day on which the officer complies with subsection (3) above.]

Attachment of articles kept outwith dwellinghouses etc

14 Procedure for attachment of articles kept outwith dwellinghouses etc

Sections 15 to [19A] below apply only in relation to the attachment of articles which are—

(a)   kept outwith a dwellinghouse; or

(b)   mobile homes which are not the only or principal residence of the debtor.

15 [Valuation]

(1)   An officer may be open shut and lockfast places for the purposes of executing an attachment.

(2)   When executing an attachment the officer shall, subject to subsection (3) below, value the articles being attached at the price which they are likely to fetch if sold on the open market.

(3)   Where the officer considers that an article is such that a valuation by a professional valuer or other suitably skilled person is appropriate, the officer shall arrange for such a valuation and a valuation so arranged shall proceed on the basis set out in subsection (2) above.

16   Attachment of mobile homes

(1)   Where a mobile home which is the only or principal residence of a person other than the debtor has been attached—

(a)   the officer shall give notice to that other person of that fact; and

(b)   the sheriff may, on an application by the debtor or that other person, order that the attachment of the mobile home is to cease to have effect.

(2)   The sheriff—

(a)   shall consider any application for an order under subsection (1) above which is made before the date which is 14 days after the date on which the mobile home is attached; and

(b)   may, on cause shown, consider any such application which is made at any time after that date but before the date on which the attached mobile home is auctioned.

17   Report of attachment

(1)   The officer shall, within 14 days of the execution of an attachment (or such longer period as the sheriff on cause shown may allow on application by the officer), make to the sheriff a report of the attachment.

(2)   A report made under subsection (1) above shall—

(a)   be in the form prescribed by Act of Sederunt; and

(b)   be signed by the officer.

(3)   Such a report shall specify—

(a)   whether any person, in response to enquiries made under section 13(2) above, asserted that any attached article is not owned by the debtor (or is owned in common by the debtor and a third party);

(b)   whether any attached article has been redeemed under section 18(1) below.

(4)   Such a report need not be made in respect of any article or vehicle which has been sold in pursuance of an order made under section 20(1)(b) or, as the case may be, 22(3) below.

(5)   The sheriff may refuse to receive such a report on the ground that it has not been made and signed in accordance with subsections (1) and (2) above.

(6)   If the sheriff so refuses—

(a)   the attachment to which the report relates is to cease to have effect; and

(b)   the sheriff clerk shall intimate the refusal to—

(i)   the debtor; and

(ii)   if another person is in possession of the attached articles, that person.

18   Redemption

(1)   Subject to any order made under section 20(1)(b) below, the debtor is entitled, within 14 days of the date on which an article is attached, to redeem that article.

(2)   The amount for which such an article may be redeemed is the value fixed under subsection (2) or (3) of section 15 above.

(3)   The officer shall, on receiving payment from the debtor for the redemption of an attached article, grant a receipt in the form prescribed by Act of Sederunt to the debtor.

(4)   The attachment of the article is, on the grant of such a receipt, to cease to have effect.

(5)   Where an article is redeemed after the officer has made a report under section 17(1) above in respect of the attachment, the officer shall report the redemption as soon as is reasonably practicable to the sheriff.

19   Removal and auction of attached articles

(1)   [An officer] may, after the report of attachment has been received by the sheriff—

(a)   make arrangements for the auction of the attached articles; and

(b)   on the date specified in the notice given under section 27(4) below, remove the attached articles from the place at which they are kept.

(2)   The officer may open shut and lockfast places for the purpose of so removing the attached articles.

(3)   The officer may not remove any vehicle in respect of which an application for an order under subsection (1) or (3) of section 22 below has been made but not disposed of.

(4)   The officer may remove to the place at which the auction is to be held such attached articles as, if sold at their values fixed under subsection (2) or, as the case may be, (3) of section 15 above, would realise in aggregate the sum recoverable at the time of the auction.

(5)   The remaining attached articles will cease to be subject to attachment.

(6)   An attached article shall not, subject to any order made under section 20(1)(b) or 22(3) below, be auctioned before the date which is 7 days after the date on which the article is removed by the officer from the place at which it was attached.

[19A   Urgent removal of attached articles

(1)   The officer may at any time remove an attached article without notice if—
  (a)   the officer considers it necessary for—
    (i)   the security; or
    (ii)   the preservation of the value,
  of the article; and
  (b)   there is insufficient time to obtain an order under section 20(1)(a) below.

(2)   The officer shall remove an article under subsection (1) above—
  (a)   to the nearest convenient premises of the debtor or the person in possession of the articles; or
  (b)   if—
    (i)   no such premises are available; or
    (ii)   the officer considers such premises to be unsuitable,
  to the nearest suitable secure premises.

(3)   Subsections (2) and (6) of section 19 above shall apply to this section as they apply to that section.]

Attachment: further procedure

20   Order for security of articles or sale of articles which are perishable etc

(1)   The sheriff may, on an application by the creditor, the officer or the debtor, at any time after articles have been attached make an order—
  (a)   for the security of any of the attached articles;
  (b)   in relation to any of the articles which are of a perishable nature or which are likely to deteriorate substantially and rapidly in condition or value, for the creditor or the officer to make arrangements for their immediate sale and for any proceeds of the sale to be consigned in court.

(2)   An application for an order under subsection (1) above—
  (a)   by the creditor or the officer, shall be intimated by the creditor or, as the case may be, the officer to the debtor;
  (b)   by the debtor, shall be intimated to the creditor and the officer, [—
    (i)   who attached articles; or
    (ii)   who is authorised to arrange the auction,]
  at the time when it is made.

(3)   A decision of the sheriff to make an order under subsection (1)(b) above shall not be subject to appeal.

(4)   Any sum consigned in court in pursuance of an order made under subsection (1)(b) above shall, where an attachment ceases to have effect before the auction of attached articles is held, be paid to the creditor to the extent necessary to meet the sum recoverable, any surplus thereof being paid to the debtor.

21   Unlawful acts after attachment

(1)   The debtor or person in possession of an attached article shall not move it from the place at which it was attached.

(2)   If an article is so moved—

(a)   the debtor or, as the case may be, the person in possession of the attached articles is acting in breach of the attachment; and

(b)   the sheriff may, on an application by the creditor or by the officer, by order authorise the attachment of other articles which are owned by the debtor and kept at the place at which the original attachment was executed.

(3)   Subsection (1) above does not apply in relation to any vehicle in respect of which an application for an order under subsection (1) or (3) of section 22 below has been made but not disposed of.

(4)   The debtor shall not sell, make a gift of or otherwise relinquish ownership of any attached article.

(5)   If an attached article is so sold, gifted or otherwise disposed of the debtor is acting in breach of the attachment.

(6)   Any person who wilfully damages or destroys any article which that person knows has been attached is acting in breach of the attachment.

(7)   Where an attached article is stolen, the debtor shall give notice to the creditor and the officer [—

(i)   who attached articles; or

(ii)   who is authorised to arrange the auction,]

of that fact and of any related claim which the debtor makes, or intends to make, under a contract of insurance.

(8)   Any debtor who fails to give notice as required by subsection (7) above is acting in breach of the attachment.

(9)   Any act which is, under subsection (2), (5), (6) or (8) above, a breach of the attachment may be dealt with as a contempt of court.

(10)   Where attached articles are damaged, destroyed or stolen the sheriff, on an application by the creditor or by the officer, may by order authorise—

(a)   the attachment of other articles which are owned by the debtor and kept at the place at which the original attachment was executed;

(b)   the revaluation of any damaged article in accordance with subsection (2) or (3) of section 15 above.

(11)   Where the debtor or any third party who knows that an article is attached—

(a)   moves it from the place at which the attachment was executed, and it is—

(i)   damaged, destroyed, lost or stolen; or

(ii)   acquired from or through the debtor or, as the case may be, the third party by another person without knowledge of the attachment and for value; or

(b)   wilfully damages or destroys it,

the sheriff may order the debtor or, as the case may be, the third party to consign the sum set out in subsection (12) below in court.

(12)   That sum is—

(a)   where the article has been damaged but not so damaged as to make it worthless, a sum equal to the difference between the value of the article fixed under subsection (2) or (3) of section 15 above or, as the case may be, under section 51 or 54(1) below and the value of the article so damaged; or

(b)   in any other case, a sum equal to the value of the article as fixed under subsection (2) or (3) of section 15 above or, as the case may be, under section 51 or 54(1) below.

(13)   For the purposes of subsection (12)(a) above, the officer shall, subject to subsection (14) below, value a damaged article at the price which it is likely to fetch if sold in that condition on the open market.

(14)   Where the officer considers that a damaged article is such that a valuation

by a professional valuer or other suitably skilled person is appropriate, the officer shall arrange for such a valuation and a valuation so arranged shall proceed on the basis set out in subsection (13) above.

(15) Any sum consigned in court in pursuance of an order made under subsection (11) above shall, where the attachment of a damaged article ceases to have effect before it is auctioned, be paid to the creditor to the extent necessary to meet the sum recoverable, any surplus thereof being paid to the debtor.

22 Release of vehicle from attachment

(1) The sheriff may, on an application by the debtor and on being satisfied that the auction of any vehicle which has been attached would be unduly harsh in the circumstances, make an order—

(a) providing that the attachment of the vehicle is to cease to have effect; and

(b) where the vehicle has been removed by the officer from the place at which it was attached, requiring the officer to return the vehicle to that place.

(2) The sheriff may not make an order under subsection (1) above unless the value of the vehicle (as fixed under subsection (2) or (3) of section 15 above) does not exceed £1,000 or such other amount as may be prescribed in regulations made by the Scottish Ministers.

(3) Where the value (as fixed under subsection (2) or (3) of section 15 above) of an attached vehicle does exceed £1,000 or, as the case may be, such other prescribed amount the sheriff may, on an application by the debtor and on being satisfied that the auction of any vehicle which has been attached would be unduly harsh in the circumstances, make an order requiring the officer to—

(a) make arrangements for the immediate sale of the vehicle;

(b) pay to the debtor from any proceeds of such sale the sum of £1,000 (or such lesser amount as the sheriff may specify); and

(c) consign any surplus remaining in court.

(4) Where the amount realised on the sale of a vehicle in pursuance of an order has been made under subsection (3) above is less than the amount which the officer is required by that order to pay to the debtor, the order shall be deemed to have required the officer to pay the amount realised only.

(5) Where the officer is unable to sell the vehicle in pursuance of an order made under subsection (3) above within 14 days of the date on which the order was made, the attachment of that vehicle is to cease to have effect.

(6) The sheriff may consider an application for an order under subsection (1) or (3) above only where it is made within 14 days of the date on which the vehicle is attached.

23 Appeals against valuation

(1) Where the sheriff is satisfied that the aggregate of the values of attached articles fixed under section 15(2) or (3) above or, as the case may be, section 51 or 54(1) below is substantially below the aggregate of the prices which they are likely to fetch if sold on the open market, the sheriff may, on or before the day which immediately precedes the day on which the articles are to be auctioned, order that the attachment is to cease to have effect.

(2) The sheriff may make an order under subsection (1) above on the application of the debtor or on the sheriff's own accord.

(3) The sheriff shall not make such an order without first giving the debtor and the creditor—

(a) an opportunity to make representations; and

(b) if either party wishes to be heard, an opportunity to be heard.

24 Duration of attachment

(1) An attachment shall, subject to subsections (6), (7) and (8) below, have effect only until—

(a)   the earlier of—
(i)   the date which is six months after the date on which the article is attached; and
(ii)   the date which is 28 days after the date on which the attached article is removed by the officer from the place at which it was attached; or
(b)   such other date as may be specified in an order made under subsection (2) or section 29(4)(b) below or in an exceptional attachment order.
(2)   Where the sheriff is satisfied—
(a)   that, if the date on which an attachment is to cease to have effect were to be substituted with a later date, the debtor is likely to comply with an agreement between the creditor and the debtor for the payment of the sum recoverable by instalments or otherwise; or
(b)   that the auction of the attached articles cannot take place before the date on which the attachment is to cease to have effect due to circumstances for which the creditor cannot be held responsible and that the attachment ceasing to have effect on that date would prejudice the creditor,
the sheriff may, on an application by the creditor or by the officer, by order provide that the attachment is to remain in effect until such later date as the sheriff considers reasonable in the circumstances.
(3)   Where the period for which an attachment is to have effect is extended by an order made under subsection (2) above, an application may be made for another order under that subsection so as to further extend that period.
(4)   The sheriff may consider an application for an order under subsection (2) above only where it is made during the period in respect of which an extension is being sought.
(5)   A decision of the sheriff on such an application shall be intimated to the debtor by the sheriff clerk.
(6)   Where such an application is made but not disposed of before the date on which the attachment in respect of which it is made would, but for this subsection, cease to have effect, the attachment shall continue to have effect until the application is disposed of.
(7)   Where such an application is—
(a)   made on the ground referred to in paragraph (a) of subsection (2) above; and
(b)   refused by the sheriff within 14 days of the date on which the attachment in respect of which it is made would, but for this subsection, cease to have effect,
the attachment shall continue to have effect until the date which is 14 days after the date of the refusal.
(8)   Where—
(a)   arrangements for an auction of attached articles are, under section 29(1) below, cancelled; and
(b)   the agreement in respect of which the cancellation is made is breached by the debtor,
the period which begins with the date on which the report of agreement was made under section 29(3) below and which ends with the date on which the debtor breaches the agreement is to be disregarded in determining the date on which the attachment is, under subsection (1) above, to cease to have effect.

25   Second attachment at same place
(1)   Subject to—
(a)   section 9(12) (which provides that a debt which remains outstanding on the recall or cessation of a time to pay order may be enforced by certain diligences) of the Debtors (Scotland) Act 1987 (c 18);
(b)   any order made under subsection (2)(b) or (10)(a) of section 21 above; and

(c)   sections 34(3) and 35(4) below,

where articles are attached (or are purported to be attached) at any place, it is not competent to attach other articles kept at that place to enforce the same debt unless those other articles are brought to that place after the execution of the first attachment.

(2)   It is not competent to attach any article in respect of which an attachment has—

(a)   previously been executed in enforcement of the same debt; and

(b)   ceased, by virtue of section 16, 18(4), 22(1), 34(1), 35(3), 55(2) or 56(4) of this Act, to have effect.

26   Invalidity and cessation of attachment

(1)   Where, at any time before the auction of an article which has been or purports to have been attached, the sheriff is satisfied that—

(a)   the attachment has ceased to have effect; or, as the case may be

(b)   the purported attachment is invalid (by reason of the attachment being incompetent or otherwise),

the sheriff shall make an order declaring that to be the case and may make such consequential order as appears to the sheriff to be necessary in the circumstances.

(2)   An order under subsection (1) above may be made on an application by the debtor or on the sheriff's own initiative.

(3)   Where such an order is made on the sheriff's own initiative, the sheriff clerk shall intimate the order to the debtor.

(4)   The sheriff shall not make an order under subsection (1) above without first giving the debtor and the creditor—

(a)   an opportunity to make representations; and

(b)   if either party wishes to be heard, an opportunity to be heard.

(5)   Where—

(a)   an order is made under subsection (1) above; and

(b)   [an officer] has removed the article from the place at which it was, or purported to be, attached,

the officer shall return the article to the place from which it was removed.

(6)   The sheriff shall give reasons for a refusal to grant an order under subsection (1) above.

Auction of attached articles

27   Notice of public auction

(1)   The auction of attached articles shall, subject to subsections (2) and (3) below, be by public auction held in an auction room.

(2)   If it is impractical to hold the auction of an attached article in an auction room the auction may be held at such other place (other than the debtor's dwellinghouse) as the officer considers appropriate.

(3)   The auction of other articles which have been attached together with an article which is to be auctioned at a place other than an auction room may, if the officer considers it appropriate (having had regard, in particular, to the expenses which are likely to be incurred in connection with the auction), also be held at that other place.

(4)   The officer [. . .] shall give notice to the debtor and to any other person in possession of the attached articles of—

(a)   the date on which the auction is to be held;

(b)   the location of the auction room or, as the case may be, the other place at which the auction is to be held; and

(c)   where sections 15 to 19 above apply in relation to the attached articles, the date arranged for the removal of those attached articles from the place at which they are kept.

(5)   The officer shall advertise the auction by public notice.

28   Alteration of arrangements for removal or auction

(1)   Subject to subsection (2) below and without prejudice to section 29(4) below, the creditor or the officer is not, after notice has been given under section 27(4) above to the debtor, entitled to arrange—

   (a)   a new date for the auction; or

   (b)   where [sections 15 to 19A] above apply in relation to the attached articles, a new date for the removal of those articles from the place where they are kept.

(2)   Where, for any reason for which neither the creditor nor the officer is responsible, it is not possible—

   (a)   for the auction to be held on the date specified in the notice given under section 27(4) above; or

   (b)   for the attached articles to be removed from the place where they are kept on the date so specified,

the creditor may instruct the officer to arrange a new date for the auction or, as the case may be, a new date for the removal and the officer shall intimate the new date to the debtor and to any other person in possession of the attached articles.

(3)   A new date arranged under subsection (2) above shall not in any case be fewer than 7 days after the date of intimation under that subsection.

29   Cancellation of auctions

(1)   The officer may, for the purposes of enabling the sum recoverable to be paid in accordance with an agreement between the creditor and the debtor, cancel arrangements for an auction of attached articles.

(2)   The officer may not cancel the arrangements for such an auction on more than two occasions.

(3)   Where an auction has been cancelled the officer shall—

   (a)   make to the sheriff a report of the agreement reached; and

   (b)   arrange for the return of any attached articles which have been removed for auction to the place from which they were removed.

(4)   The sheriff, if satisfied on an application by the creditor that the debtor is in breach of any agreement which has been reported under subsection (3) above, may by order provide—

   (a)   if the arrangements for the auction of the attached articles can still be implemented in accordance with the provisions of this Part and Part 3 of this Act, that the officer may resume making arrangements for the auction in accordance with those provisions;

   (b)   if for any reason for which neither the creditor nor the officer is responsible arrangements for the auction cannot be implemented in accordance with those provisions, that the provisions of this Part and Part 3 of this Act which prevent such implementation are not to apply for the purposes of the attachment and auction of those articles.

(5)   The sheriff shall not make an order under subsection (4) above without first giving the debtor—

   (a)   an opportunity to make representations; and

   (b)   if the debtor so wishes, an opportunity to be heard.

30   Auction

(1)   The officer shall attend the auction and maintain a record of the attached articles which are sold.

(2)   Such a record shall specify the amount for which each attached article is sold.

(3)   The officer shall be accompanied at the auction by another person who shall witness the proceedings.

(4)   Any attached article exposed for sale in the auction may be purchased by—

   (a)   any creditor, including the creditor on whose behalf the article was attached;

   (b)   a third party who owns the attached article in common with the debtor.

31   Disposal of proceeds of auction

(1)   The officer shall, subject to section 37 (effect of sequestration on diligence) of the Bankruptcy (Scotland) Act 1985 (c 66), dispose of the proceeds of the auction by—

(a)   retaining such amount as necessary to meet the fees and outlays of the officer;

(b)   paying to the creditor the remainder of the proceeds of auction so far as necessary to meet the sum recoverable; and

(c)   paying to the debtor any surplus remaining.

[(1A)   Where an article is sold at the auction at a price below the value of the article, the difference between that price and that value shall, prior to the proceeds of the auction being disposed of under subsection (1) above, be credited against the sum recoverable.

(1B)   Where—

(a)   an article to which subsection (1A) above applies has been damaged and revalued under section 21(10)(b) above;

(b)   the damage was not caused by the fault of the debtor; and

(c)   no sum has been consigned into court by a third party under section 21(11) above,

the revaluation shall be disregarded for the purposes of subsection (1A) above.]

(2)   Where the sum recoverable is not realised by the proceeds of auction and any article remains unsold after being exposed for auction—

(a)   ownership of the article shall, without prejudice to the rights of any third party, pass to the creditor; and

(b)   the value of that article shall be credited against the sum recoverable.

(3)   Where the value of unsold articles exceeds the amount of the sum recoverable which remains outstanding, subsection (2) above shall operate only in relation to such of those articles which have, in aggregate, the value which is nearest to the amount which remains outstanding.

(4)   The references in subsections [(1A),] (2)(b) and (3) above to the value of an article are references to the value of the article as fixed under subsection (2) or (3) of section 15 above or, as the case may be, section 51 or 54(1) below.

(5)   Where the creditor does not uplift an article within 3 working days after the day on which the auction is held the ownership of the article shall revert to the person who owned the article before the operation of subsection (2)(a) above.

(6)   For the purposes of this section—

'proceeds of auction' include any amount—

(a)   consigned in court in pursuance of an order made under section 21(11), 20(1)(b), 22(3) or 50(5) of this Act;

(b)   received by the officer in respect of a transfer, under section 35(2) below, of the debtor's interest in any article owned in common by the debtor and a third party,

but do not include any amount which the officer is required to pay to the debtor in pursuance of an order under section 22(3) above; and

'working day' means a day which is not—

(a)   a Saturday;

(b)   a Sunday;

(c)   New Year's Day;

(d)   2nd January;

(e)   Good Friday;

(f)   Easter Monday;

(g)   Christmas Day;

(h)   Boxing Day; or

(i)   any other day which is a public holiday in the area in which the auction is held.

32   Report of auction

(1)   The officer who arranged the auction shall, within the period of 14 days after the date on which the auction is held, make to the sheriff a report in the form prescribed by Act of Sederunt (a 'report of auction').

(2)   A report of auction shall—

(a)   specify—

(i)   any attached articles which have been sold;

(ii)   the amount for which they have been sold;

(iii)   any attached articles which remain unsold;

[(iiia)   any sums paid by the debtor to account of the sum recoverable;]

(iv)   any chargeable expenses;

(v)   any surplus paid to the debtor; and

(vi)   any balance due by or to the debtor;

(b)   refer to any article in respect of which—

(i)   an attachment has, under section 34(1) below or in pursuance of an order made under section 35(3) below, ceased to have effect;

(ii)   the debtor's interest has, under section 35(2) below, transferred to a third party;

(c)   contain a declaration by the officer that all the information contained within it is, to the best of the officer's knowledge, true; and

(d)   be signed by the officer and the witness who attended the auction.

(3)   If the officer—

(a)   without reasonable excuse makes a report of auction after the expiry of the period mentioned in subsection (1) above; or

(b)   wilfully refuses to make, or delays making, a report of auction after the expiry of that period,

the sheriff may make an order providing that the officer is liable for the chargeable expenses, either in whole or in part.

(4)   An order made under subsection (3) above does not prejudice the right of the sheriff to report the matter to the [*Scottish Civil Enforcement Commission under section 67(1)(b) of the Bankruptcy and Diligence etc (Scotland) Act 2007 (asp 3)*].

33   Audit of report of auction

(1)   The sheriff shall remit the report of auction to the auditor of court who shall—

(a)   tax the chargeable expenses;

(b)   certify the balance due by or to the debtor following the auction; and

(c)   make a report to the sheriff.

(2)   The auditor of court shall not alter the report of auction without first providing all interested persons an opportunity to make representations.

(3)   The auditor of court shall not charge a fee in respect of the report made under subsection (1)(c) above.

(4)   On receipt of a report made under subsection (1)(c) above the sheriff shall make an order—

(a)   declaring the balance due by or to the debtor, as certified by the auditor of court;

(b)   declaring such a balance after making modifications to the balance so certified; or

(c)   where the sheriff is satisfied that there has been a substantial irregularity in the execution of the attachment (other than the timing of the report of auction), declaring the attachment and auction to be void.

(5)   An order made under subsection (4)(c) above may make such consequential provision as the sheriff thinks fit.

(6)   An order made under subsection (4)(c) above shall not affect the title of a person to any article acquired by that person at the auction, or subsequently, in good faith.

(7) The sheriff may not make an order under subsection (4)(b) or (c) above without first

[(a) giving—

(i) the debtor;

(ii) the creditor; and

(iii) any third party who claims ownership (whether alone or in common with the debtor) of any attached article,

an opportunity to make representations; or

(b) holding a hearing.]

(8) The sheriff clerk shall intimate the sheriff's order under subsection (4) above to the [persons mentioned in subsection (7)(a) above].

General and miscellaneous provisions

34 Articles belonging to a third party

(1) Where at any time before an attached article is auctioned—

(a) a third party claims to own the article; and

(b) either—

(i) the officer is satisfied that the claim is valid and neither the debtor nor any other person in possession of the article disputes the claim; or

(ii) the sheriff, on an application by the third party, makes an order stating that the sheriff is [satisfied that the claim is valid],

the attachment of that article is to cease to have effect.

(2) The making of an application to the sheriff for the purposes of subsection (1)(b)(ii) above does not preclude the third party making the application from taking any other proceedings for the recovery of an article which is owned by the third party.

(3) Where the attachment of an article ceases, under subsection (1) above, to have effect, the officer may attach other articles which are owned by the debtor and kept at the place at which the original attachment was executed.

35 Articles in common ownership

(1) Articles which are owned in common by a debtor and a third party may be attached and disposed of in satisfaction of the debts of the debtor.

(2) Where at any time before an attached article is auctioned—

(a) a third party claims to own the article in common with the debtor;

(b) either—

(i) the officer is satisfied that the claim is valid; or

(ii) the sheriff, on an application by the third party, makes an order stating that the sheriff is so satisfied; and

(c) the third party pays to the officer a sum equal to the value of the debtor's interest in the article,

the debtor's interest in the article shall transfer to the third party.

(3) Where the sheriff is satisfied—

(a) that an article which has been removed from the place at which it was attached is owned in common by the debtor and a third party; and

(b) that the auction of the article would be unduly harsh to the third party in the circumstances,

the sheriff may, on an application by the third party before the attached article is auctioned, order that the attachment of that article is to cease to have effect.

(4) Where—

(a) the debtor's interest in an article owned in common by the debtor and a third party is, under subsection (2) above, transferred to the third party; or

(b) the attachment of an article which is so owned ceases, in pursuance of an order made under subsection (3) above, to have effect,

the officer may attach other articles which are owned by the debtor and kept at the place at which the original attachment was executed.

36   Procedure where articles in common ownership are sold at auction

(1)   This subsection applies where—

   (a)   a third party claimed, before an attached article was auctioned, to own the article in common with the debtor;

   (b)   the debtor's interest in the article has not transferred to the third party under section 35(2) above;

   (c)   the attachment of the article has not, by virtue of an order made under section 35(3) above, ceased to have effect;

   (d)   the third party's interest in the article has, following the auction of the article, been transferred to another person; and

   (e)   either—

      (i)   the third party's claim is, after that transfer of interest, admitted by the creditor and the debtor; or

      (ii)   where the third party's claim is not so admitted, the sheriff, on an application by the third party after that transfer of interest, is satisfied that the claim is valid.

(2)   Where subsection (1) above applies, the creditor shall—

   (a)   where the article has been sold at the auction, pay to the third party the fraction of the proceeds of the sale of the article which corresponded to the third party's interest in the article; or

   (b)   where the ownership of the article has passed to the creditor under section 31(2)(a) above, pay to the third party the fraction of the value of the article which corresponded to the third party's interest in the article.

(3)   The reference in subsection (2)(b) above to the value of an article is a reference to the value of the article as fixed under subsection (2) or (3) of section 15 above or, as the case may be, section 51 or 54(1) below.

37   Attachment terminated by payment or tender of full amount owing

An attachment is to cease to have effect if the sum recoverable is—

   (a)   paid to the creditor, the officer or any other person who has authority to receive payment on behalf of the creditor; or

   (b)   tendered to any of those persons and the tender is not accepted within a reasonable time.

38   Assistance to debtor

The sheriff clerk shall, if requested by the debtor—

   (a)   provide the debtor with information as to the procedures available to him under any provision of this Part or Part 3 of this Act; and

   (b)   assist the debtor in the completion of any form required in connection with any proceedings under any provision of this Part or Part 3 of this Act,

but the sheriff clerk shall not be liable for any error or omission by him in performing the duties imposed on him by this section.

39   Expenses chargeable in relation to attachment etc

(1)   Schedule 1 to this Act has effect for the purposes of determining the liability, as between the creditor and the debtor, for expenses incurred in serving a charge and in the process of attachment and auction.

(2)   The Scottish Ministers may by order modify that schedule so as to—

   (a)   add or remove types of expenses to or, as the case may be, from those referred to in that schedule; or

   (b)   vary any of the descriptions of the types of expenses there referred to.

40   Recovery from debtor of expenses of attachment

(1)   Subject to subsections (2) and (4) below, any expenses chargeable against the debtor which are incurred in an attachment (including the service of the charge preceding it and the auction following it) are recoverable from the debtor by the attachment concerned but not by any other legal process, and any such expenses

which have not been recovered by the time the attachment and auction is completed will cease to be chargeable against the debtor.

(2)　The sheriff shall grant decree for payment of—

(a)　any expenses awarded by the sheriff against the debtor in favour of the creditor under paragraph 4 or 7 of schedule 1 to this Act; or

(b)　any additional sum of expenses awarded by the sheriff against the debtor in favour of the creditor under paragraph 5 of that schedule.

(3)　Subsection (4) below applies where an attachment is—

(a)　recalled under [section 9(2)(d) or (10)(b)] (effect of time to pay order on diligence) of the Debtors (Scotland) Act 1987 (c 18) in relation to a time to pay order;

(b)　in effect immediately before the date of sequestration (within the meaning of the Bankruptcy (Scotland) Act 1985 (c 66)) of the debtor's estate;

(c)　in effect immediately before the [appointment of an administrator] under Part II of the Insolvency Act 1986 (c 45);

(d)　in effect against property of the debtor immediately before a floating charge attaches to all or part of that property under section 53(7) (attachment on appointment of receiver by holder of charge) or 54(6) (attachment on appointment of receiver by court) of that Act of 1986;

(e)　in effect immediately before the commencement of the winding up, under Part IV or V of that Act of 1986, of the debtor; or

(f)　rendered unenforceable by virtue of the creditor entering into a composition contract or acceding to a trust deed for creditors or by virtue of the subsistence of a protected trust deed within the meaning of Schedule 5 to the Bankruptcy (Scotland) Act 1985 (c 66).

(4)　Where this subsection applies—

(a)　the expenses of the attachment which were chargeable against the debtor remain so chargeable; and

(b)　if the debtor's obligation to pay the expenses is not discharged under or by virtue of the time to pay order, sequestration, [appointment], receivership, winding up, composition contract or trust deed for creditors, those expenses are recoverable by further attachment.

41　Ascription of sums recovered by attachment or while attachment is in effect

(1)　This section applies to any amounts recovered by an attachment or paid to account of the amounts recoverable by the attachment while the attachment is in effect.

(2)　An amount to which this section applies shall be ascribed to the following in the order in which they are mentioned—

(a)　the expenses already incurred in respect of—

(i)　the attachment;

[(ia)　any previous interim attachment the expenses of which are chargeable against and recoverable from the debtor under section 9Q(1)(a) of this Act;]

(ii)　any previous diligence the expenses of which are chargeable against and recoverable from the debtor under section 40(4) above or section 93(5) of the Debtors (Scotland) Act 1987 (c 18);

(b)　any interest, due under the decree or other document of debt on which the attachment proceeds, which has accrued at the date of execution of the attachment;

(c)　any sum (including any expenses) due under the decree or other document of debt, other than any expenses or interest mentioned in paragraphs (a) and (b) above.

42　Restriction on fees payable by debtor

No fees shall be payable by a debtor in connection with—

(a)　any application by the debtor;

(b)   objections by the debtor to an application by any other person; or

(c)   a hearing held,

under any provision of this Part or Part 3 of this Act, to any officer of any office or department connected with the Court of Session or the sheriff court the expenses of which are paid wholly or partly out of the Scottish Consolidated Fund.

43, 44   [*Amending provisions*]

45   Interpretation of this Part and Parts 3 and 4

In this Part and in Parts 3 and 4 of this Act—

'chargeable expenses' means expenses chargeable against the debtor in accordance with this Part of this Act;

'dwellinghouse' does not include—

(a)   a garage, even although it forms part of the structure or building which consists of or includes the dwellinghouse; or

(b)   other structures or buildings used in connection with the dwellinghouse, but does include a mobile home or other place used as a dwelling;

'exceptional attachment order' has the meaning given by section 47(1) below;

'mobile home' means a caravan, houseboat or other moveable structure used as a dwelling;

'non-essential assets' has the meaning given by schedule 2 to this Act;

'officer' means [a judicial officer appointed by a creditor];

'sum recoverable' means the debt in respect of which the attachment is executed together with any interest thereon and any chargeable expenses; and

'summary warrant' means a summary warrant granted under, or by virtue of, any enactment.

PART 3

ATTACHMENT OF ARTICLES KEPT IN DWELLINGHOUSES:
SPECIAL PROCEDURE

46   Restriction on attachment of articles kept in dwellinghouses

Articles kept in a dwellinghouse may be attached but only—

(a)   in pursuance of an exceptional attachment order; and

(b)   otherwise in accordance with this Part of this Act.

47   Exceptional attachment order

(1)   The sheriff may, on an application by the creditor and on being satisfied that there are exceptional circumstances, order that an attachment of non-essential assets of the debtor's kept in any dwellinghouse specified in the application may take place; such an order shall be called an 'exceptional attachment order'.

(2)   An exceptional attachment order shall—

(a)   authorise the attachment, removal and auction of non-essential assets of the debtor's which are, at the time when an attachment is executed in pursuance of the order, kept in any dwellinghouse specified in the application for the order;

(b)   specify a period during which the order is to be executed; and

(c)   empower the officer to open shut and lockfast places for the purpose of executing the order.

(3)   In considering whether to make such an order the sheriff shall have regard to the matters set out in subsection (4) below.

(4)   Those matters are—

(a)   the nature of the debt (and, in particular, whether the debt incurred relates to any tax or duty or to any trade or business carried on by the debtor);

(b)   whether the debtor resides in the dwellinghouse specified in the application;

(c)   whether the debtor carries on a trade or business in that dwellinghouse;

(d)   whether money advice has been given to the debtor;

(e)   whether any direction made under section 1 (time to pay directions) of the Debtors (Scotland) Act 1987 (c 18), or order made under section 5 (time to pay orders) of that Act, in respect of the debt, or any other debt, has lapsed under section 4 (lapse of time to pay directions) or, as the case may be, section 11 (lapse of time to pay orders), of that Act of 1987;

(f)   any agreement between the debtor and creditor for the settlement of the debt;

(g)   any declaration or representation made, or document lodged, by or on behalf of the debtor which relates to—

(i)   the existence of any non-essential assets owned by the debtor;

(ii)   where they exist, their value; or

(iii)   the debtor's financial circumstances [; and

(h)   whether an application by the debtor for approval of a debt payment programme under Part 1 of this Act has been refused or approved, and if approved, whether that programme has been varied, or is revoked or completed.]

(5)   Before deciding whether to make an exceptional attachment order, the sheriff may make—

(a)   an order for a visit to the debtor by a person specified in the order for the purposes of giving money advice to the debtor; or

(b)   such other order as the sheriff thinks fit.

(6)   The Scottish Ministers may by order modify subsection (4) above so as to—

(a)   add or remove matters to or, as the case may be, from those referred to in that subsection; or

(b)   vary any of the descriptions of the matters there referred to.

48   Exceptional circumstances

(1)   The reference in section 47(1) above to the sheriff being satisfied that there are exceptional circumstances is to be regarded as a reference to the sheriff being satisfied—

(a)   that the creditor has taken reasonable steps to negotiate (or seek to negotiate) a settlement of the debt;

(b)   that the creditor has executed, or so far as it is reasonable to do so has attempted to execute—

(i)   an arrestment and action of forthcoming or sale; and

(ii)   an earnings arrestment, in order to secure payment of the debt;

(c)   that there is a reasonable prospect that the sum recovered from an auction of the debtor's non-essential assets would be at least equal to the aggregate of the following—

(i)   a reasonable estimate of any chargeable expenses; and

(ii)   £100 or such other amount as may be specified by order made by the Scottish Ministers; and

(d)   that, having had regard to the matters set out in section 47(4) above and any other matters which the sheriff considers appropriate, it would be reasonable in the circumstances to grant the exceptional attachment order.

(2)   For the purposes of subsection (1)(b) above, a creditor who has not proceeded with the diligences referred to in that subsection on the ground that so proceeding would be unlikely to recover the aggregate of—

(a)   a reasonable estimate of the expenses likely to be incurred by the creditor in exercising the diligences; and

(b)   £100 or such other amount as may be specified by order made by the Scottish Ministers, is to be treated as having attempted to execute those diligences in so far as it is reasonable to do so.

49   Power of entry

(1)   Notwithstanding the authorisation in an exceptional attachment order to

open shut and lockfast places, the officer shall not enter a dwellinghouse to execute the order unless the officer—

(a)   at the intended time of entry, is satisfied as to the condition set out in
subsection (2) below; or

(b)   has, at least 4 days before the intended date of entry, served notice on
the debtor setting out that intention and specifying that date.

(2)   That condition is that there appears to the officer to be a person present
who—

(a)   is aged 16 years or over; and

(b)   is not, because of the person's age, knowledge of English, mental illness,
mental or physical disability or otherwise, unable to understand the consequences of the procedure being carried out.

(3)   Where the sheriff is satisfied that the requirement of service under subsection (1)(b) above is likely to prejudice the execution of the order the sheriff may,
on an application by the officer, dispense with that requirement.

(4)   An application for a dispensation under subsection (3) above need not be
intimated to the debtor.

50   Unlawful acts before attachment

(1)   It shall be regarded as a breach of an exceptional attachment order—

(a)   for the debtor or any other person who knows that the order has been
made to, without the consent of the sheriff, move any article which forms part of
the debtor's non-essential assets from the dwellinghouse in which it is kept; or

(b)   for the debtor, without the consent of the sheriff, to sell, make a gift of or
otherwise relinquish ownership of any such article,
before an attachment is executed in pursuance of the order.

(2)   Any person who—

(a)   knows that an exceptional attachment order has been made; and

(b)   before an attachment is executed in pursuance of the order, wilfully
damages or destroys any article which forms part of the debtor's non-essential
assets,
shall be regarded as acting in breach of the order.

(3)   Where, at any time after an exceptional attachment order has been made,
an article which forms part of the debtor's non-essential assets is stolen, the debtor
shall give notice to the creditor, the officer and the sheriff who granted the order
of that fact and of any related claim which the debtor makes, or intends to make,
under a contract of insurance.

(4)   Any failure by the debtor to give notice as required by subsection (3) above
is to be regarded as acting in breach of the order.

(5)   Where a debtor or any third party who knows that an exceptional attachment order has been made and that an article forms part of the debtor's non-
essential assets—

(a)   moves it from the dwellinghouse in which it is kept before an attachment
is executed in pursuance of the order, and it is—

(i)   damaged, destroyed, lost or stolen; or

(ii)   acquired from or through the debtor or, as the case may be, the third
party by another person without knowledge of order and for value; or

(b)   wilfully damages or destroys it,
the sheriff may order the debtor or, as the case may be, the third party to consign
the sum set out in subsection (6) below in court.

(6)   That sum shall be—

(a)   where the article has been damaged but not so damaged as to make it
worthless, a sum equal to the difference between the value of the article before it
was damaged and the value of the article so damaged; or

(b)   where the damaged article is worthless, a sum equal to the value of the
article before it was so damaged.

(7) Any reference in subsection (6) above to the value of an article is a reference to the officer's best estimate of the amount which the article is or, as the case may be, was likely to realise on sale by auction.

(8) Any sum consigned in court in pursuance of an order made under subsection (5) above shall, where that order ceases to have effect before an auction is held in execution of the order, be paid to the creditor to the extent necessary to meet the sum recoverable, any surplus thereof being paid to the debtor.

51 Valuation

When executing an attachment in pursuance of an exceptional attachment order the officer shall value the articles being attached at the price which they are likely to fetch if sold on the open market.

52 Articles with sentimental value

(1) An officer may not, in executing an exceptional attachment order, attach any articles which the officer considers likely to be of sentimental value to the debtor.

(2) Subsection (1) above applies only where the aggregate of the values of articles considered likely to be of that type (as fixed by the officer under section 51 above) does not exceed £150 or such other amount as may be prescribed in regulations made by the Scottish Ministers.

53 Removal of articles attached in dwellinghouse

(1) The officer shall, unless the officer considers it impractical to do so, immediately remove any article which is attached in execution of an exceptional attachment order from the dwellinghouse in which it is attached.

(2) If an article is not immediately removed from the dwellinghouse in which it is attached, the officer shall give notice to the debtor and to any other person in possession of the article of the date arranged for the removal of the article from that dwellinghouse.

(3) The officer may remove from the dwellinghouse only such attached articles as, if sold at their values fixed under section 51 above, would realise in aggregate the sum recoverable.

54 Professional valuation

(1) The officer may, if the officer considers it appropriate, arrange for an attached article to be valued by a professional valuer or other suitably skilled person.

(2) Any such valuer or other person shall value an attached article at the price which it is likely to fetch if sold on the open market.

(3) If such a valuer or other person values an attached article at an amount other than the amount at which that article was valued by the officer when executing the attachment, the officer shall notify the debtor of the value arrived at by the valuer or other person.

55 Release of articles from attachment

(1) An article attached in execution of an exceptional attachment order shall not, subject to any order made under section 20(1)(b) above, be auctioned before the date which is 7 days after the date on which the article was removed by the officer from the dwellinghouse in which it was attached.

(2) The sheriff may, on an application by the debtor, make an order—

(a) providing that the attachment of an article attached in execution of an exceptional attachment order is to cease to have effect; and

(b) requiring the officer to return the article to the dwellinghouse at which it was attached.

(3) Where the sheriff is satisfied that—

(a) the attachment of an article is not competent; or

(b) the auction of an attached article would be unduly harsh in the circumstances,
the sheriff shall grant an order under subsection (2) above in respect of the article.

(4) Where the sheriff is satisfied that—

(a) articles likely to be of sentimental value to the debtor were kept in a dwellinghouse when an exceptional attachment order was executed in the dwellinghouse;

(b) those articles are likely to realise, on sale by auction, an aggregate amount not exceeding £150 or such other amount as may be prescribed in regulations made under section 52(2) above; and

(c) an article of that type has been attached in execution of the exceptional attachment order, the sheriff shall grant an order under subsection (2) above in respect of the attached article.

(5) The sheriff may consider an application for an order under subsection (2) above only where it is made during the period in which the article which is subject of the application may not, by virtue of subsection (1) above, be auctioned.

56 Redemption

(1) Subject to any order made under section 20(1)(b) above, the debtor is entitled, within 7 days of the date on which an article is attached, to redeem that article.

(2) The amount for which such an article may be redeemed is the value fixed under section 51 or 54(1) above.

(3) The officer shall, on receiving payment from the debtor for the redemption of an attached article, grant a receipt in the form prescribed by Act of Sederunt to the debtor.

(4) The attachment of the article is, on the grant of such a receipt, to cease to have effect.

57 Appeals

(1) An appeal made against any decision of a sheriff made under or for the purposes of this Part or, where the appeal relates to the attachment of articles kept in a dwellinghouse, under or for the purposes of Part 2 of this Act may be made only—

(a) to the sheriff principal;

(b) with the leave of the sheriff; and

(c) on a point of law.

(2) The decision of the sheriff principal on such an appeal is final.

PART 4
ABOLITION OF POINDINGS AND WARRANT SALES

58 Abolition of poindings and warrant sales

(1) It is not, subject to section 59 below, competent to enforce payment of a debt by poinding or warrant sale; and any enactment or rule of law allowing such enforcement shall cease to have effect.

(2) The following provisions of the Debtors (Scotland) Act 1987 (c 18) are repealed—

(a) Part II;

(b) section 74(2);

(c) Schedule 1; and

(d) Schedule 5.

59 Savings

(1) The provisions set out in subsection (5) below continue to have effect in relation to a poinding in respect of which a warrant sale has been completed before 30 December 2002 as if sections 58(2) above and 61 below had not come into force.

(2) Subject to subsection (3) below, those provisions also continue to have that

effect in relation to a poinding executed before that date in respect of which a warrant sale has not been completed before that date.

(3)   The saving provided for in subsection (2) above—

(a)   has effect only if the poinding was executed at a place other than a dwellinghouse; and

(b)   continues to have effect after 31 March 2003 only if a warrant sale is completed in respect of the poinding on or before that date.

(4)   A summary warrant which, before 30 December 2002, authorised a poinding and sale in accordance with Schedule 5 to the Debtors (Scotland) Act 1987 (c 18) is to be treated on and after that date as authorising an attachment.

(5)   The provisions referred to in subsections (1) and (2) above are—

(a)   paragraph 24 of Schedule 7 to the Bankruptcy (Scotland) Act 1985 (c 66);

(b)   the provisions of the Act of 1987 mentioned in section 58(2) above; and

(c)   the provisions of the Act of 2002 mentioned in paragraph 29 of schedule 3 to this Act.

PART 5
MISCELLANEOUS AND GENERAL

60   Application of this Act to sequestration for rent and arrestment

[. . .]

(2)   It is not competent for [the landlord's] hypothec to arise in any article—

(a)   of the type described in section 11(1);

[. . .]

(3)   An arrestment (other than an arrestment of a debtor's earnings in the hands of the debtor's employer) of any article of the type mentioned in paragraph (a) or (b) of subsection (2) above is incompetent.

[. . .]

[60A   Electronic signatures

(1)   This section applies where—

(a)   a report or declaration under this Act requires to be signed; and

(b)   provision is made by virtue of this Act or any other enactment permitting the report or declaration to be an electronic communication.

(2)   Where the report or declaration is an electronic communication, the requirement is satisfied by a certified electronic signature.

(3)   Subsection (2) above is to be read in accordance with section 7(2) and (3) of the Electronic Communications Act 2000 (c7) (electronic signatures and certification).]

61   [Minor and consequential amendments and repeals]

62   [Regulations and orders]

63   Crown application

This Act binds the Crown acting in its capacity as a creditor or employer.

64   Short title and commencement

(1)   This Act may be cited as the Debt Arrangement and Attachment (Scotland) Act 2002.

(2)   Subject to subsections (3) and (4) below, this Act (except this section and sections 43 and 62 above) comes into force on 30 December 2002.

. . .

SCHEDULE 2
NON-ESSENTIAL ASSETS

1 For the purposes of Part 3 of this Act, 'non-essential assets' are, subject to paragraph 2 below, corporeal moveable property of the debtor's which is kept in a dwellinghouse.

2 None of the following is a non-essential asset for the purposes of Part 3 of this Act—

(a)   an article specified in paragraph 3 below;

(b)   an article described in paragraph 4 below; and

(c)   an article the attachment of which is (by virtue of section 11(1) above or otherwise) incompetent.

3 The articles referred to in paragraph 2(a) above are—

(a)   clothing reasonably required for the use of the debtor or any member of the debtor's household;

(b)   implements, tools of trade, books or other equipment reasonably required for the use of any member of the debtor's household in the practice of such member's profession, trade or business, not exceeding in aggregate value £1,000 or such other amount as may be prescribed in regulations made by the Scottish Ministers;

(c)   medical aids or medical equipment reasonably required for the use of the debtor or any member of the debtor's household;

(d)   books or other articles reasonably required for the education or training of the debtor or any member of the debtor's household not exceeding in aggregate value £1,000 or such other amount as may be prescribed in regulations made by the Scottish Ministers;

(e)   articles reasonably required for the care or upbringing of a child who is a member of the debtor's household;

(f)   toys for the use of any child who is a member of the debtor's household.

4 The articles referred to in paragraph 2(b) above are the following so far as they are reasonably required, at the time of the attachment, for the use of the debtor or a member of the debtor's household—

(a)   beds or bedding;

(b)   household linen;

(c)   chairs or settees;

(d)   tables;

(e)   food;

(f)   lights or light fittings;

(g)   heating appliances;

(h)   curtains;

(i)   floor coverings;

(j)   furniture, equipment or utensils used for storing, cooking or eating food;

(k)   refrigerators;

(l)   articles used for cleaning, drying, mending, or pressing clothes;

(m)   articles used for cleaning the dwellinghouse;

(n)   furniture used for storing—

    (i)   clothing, bedding or household linen;

    (ii)   articles used for cleaning the dwellinghouse; or

    (iii)   utensils used for cooking or eating food;

(o)   articles used for safety in the dwellinghouse;

(p)   tools used for maintenance or repair of the dwellinghouse or of household articles;

(q)   computers and accessory equipment;

(r)   microwave ovens;

(s)   radios;

(t)   telephones;

(u)   televisions.

5   The Scottish Ministers may by regulations modify paragraph 4 above so as to—

   (a)   add or remove types of articles to or, as the case may be, from those referred to in that paragraph; or

   (b)   vary any of the descriptions of the types of articles there referred to.

. . .

ENTERPRISE ACT 2002
(2002, c 40)

PART 1
THE OFFICE OF FAIR TRADING

Establishment of OFT

1   The Office of Fair Trading

(1)   There shall be a body corporate to be known as the Office of Fair Trading (in this Act referred to as 'the OFT').

(2)   The functions of the OFT are carried out on behalf of the Crown.

(3)   Schedule 1 (which makes further provision about the OFT) has effect.

(4)   In managing its affairs the OFT shall have regard, in addition to any relevant general guidance as to the governance of public bodies, to such generally accepted principles of good corporate governance as it is reasonable to regard as applicable to the OFT.

2   The Director General of Fair Trading

(1)   The functions of the Director General of Fair Trading (in this Act referred to as 'the Director'), and his property, rights and liabilities, are transferred to the OFT.

(2)   The office of the Director is abolished.

(3)   Any enactment, instrument or other document passed or made before the commencement of subsection (1) which refers to the Director shall have effect, so far as necessary for the purposes of or in consequence of anything being transferred, as if any reference to the Director were a reference to the OFT.

3   Annual plan

(1)   The OFT shall, before each financial year, publish a document (the 'annual plan') containing a statement of its main objectives and priorities for the year.

(2)   The OFT shall for the purposes of public consultation publish a document containing proposals for its annual plan at least two months before publishing the annual plan for any year.

(3)   The OFT shall lay before Parliament a copy of each document published under subsection (2) and each annual plan.

4   Annual and other reports

(1)   The OFT shall, as soon as practicable after the end of each financial year, make to the Secretary of State a report (the 'annual report') on its activities and performance during that year.

(2)   The annual report for each year shall include—

   (a)   a general survey of developments in respect of matters relating to the OFT's functions;

   (b)   an assessment of the extent to which the OFT's main objectives and priorities for the year (as set out in the annual plan) have been met;

   (c)   a summary of the significant decisions, investigations or other activities made or carried out by the OFT during the year;

   (d)   a summary of the allocation of the OFT's financial resources to its various activities during the year; and

(e)   an assessment of the OFT's performance and practices in relation to its enforcement functions.

(3)   The OFT shall lay a copy of each annual report before Parliament and arrange for the report to be published.

(4)   The OFT may—

(a)   prepare other reports in respect of matters relating to any of its functions; and

(b)   arrange for any such report to be published.

General functions of OFT

5   Acquisition of information etc

(1)   The OFT has the function of obtaining, compiling and keeping under review information about matters relating to the carrying out of its functions.

(2)   That function is to be carried out with a view to (among other things) ensuring that the OFT has sufficient information to take informed decisions and to carry out its other functions effectively.

(3)   In carrying out that function the OFT may carry out, commission or support (financially or otherwise) research.

6   Provision of information etc to the public

(1)   The OFT has the function of—

(a)   making the public aware of the ways in which competition may benefit consumers in, and the economy of, the United Kingdom; and

(b)   giving information or advice in respect of matters relating to any of its functions to the public.

(2)   In carrying out those functions the OFT may—

(a)   publish educational materials or carry out other educational activities; or

(b)   support (financially or otherwise) the carrying out by others of such activities or the provision by others of information or advice.

7   Provision of information and advice to Ministers etc

(1)   The OFT has the function of—

(a)   making proposals, or

(b)   giving other information or advice,

on matters relating to any of its functions to any Minister of the Crown or other public authority (including proposals, information or advice as to any aspect of the law or a proposed change in the law).

(2)   A Minister of the Crown may request the OFT to make proposals or give other information or advice on any matter relating to any of its functions; and the OFT shall, so far as is reasonably practicable and consistent with its other functions, comply with the request.

8   Promoting good consumer practice

(1)   The OFT has the function of promoting good practice in the carrying out of activities which may affect the economic interests of consumers in the United Kingdom.

(2)   In carrying out that function the OFT may (without prejudice to the generality of subsection (1)) make arrangements for approving consumer codes and may, in accordance with the arrangements, give its approval to or withdraw its approval from any consumer code.

(3)   Any such arrangements must specify the criteria to be applied by the OFT in determining whether to give approval to or withdraw approval from a consumer code.

(4)   Any such arrangements may in particular—

(a)   specify descriptions of consumer code which may be the subject of an application to the OFT for approval (and any such description may be framed by reference to any feature of a consumer code, including the persons who are, or are to be, subject to the code, the manner in which it is, or is to be, operated and the persons responsible for its operation); and

(b)   provide for the use in accordance with the arrangements of an official symbol intended to signify that a consumer code is approved by the OFT.

(5)   The OFT shall publish any arrangements under subsection (2) in such manner it considers appropriate.

(6)   In this section 'consumer code' means a code of practice or other document (however described) intended, with a view to safeguarding or promoting the interests of consumers, to regulate by any means the conduct of persons engaged in the supply of goods or services to consumers (or the conduct of their employees or representatives).

Miscellaneous

9, 10   [*Amending provisions*]

11   Super-complaints to OFT

(1)   This section applies where a designated consumer body makes a complaint to the OFT that any feature, or combination of features, of a market in the United Kingdom for goods or services is or appears to be significantly harming the interests of consumers.

(2)   The OFT must, within 90 days after the day on which it receives the complaint, publish a response stating how it proposes to deal with the complaint, and in particular—

(a)   whether it has decided to take any action, or to take no action, in response to the complaint, and

(b)   if it has decided to take action, what action it proposes to take.

(3)   The response must state the OFT's reasons for its proposals.

(4)   The Secretary of State may by order amend subsection (2) by substituting any period for the period for the time being specified there.

(5)   'Designated consumer body' means a body designated by the Secretary of State by order.

(6)   The Secretary of State—

(a)   may designate a body only if it appears to him to represent the interests of consumers of any description, and

(b)   must publish (and may from time to time vary) other criteria to be applied by him in determining whether to make or revoke a designation.

(7)   The OFT—

(a)   must issue guidance as to the presentation by the complainant of a reasoned case for the complaint, and

(b)   may issue such other guidance as appears to it to be appropriate for the purposes of this section.

(8)   An order under this section—

(a)   shall be made by statutory instrument, and

(b)   shall be subject to annulment in pursuance of a resolution of either House of Parliament.

(9)   In this section—

(a)   references to a feature of a market in the United Kingdom for goods or services have the same meaning as if contained in Part 4, and

(b)   'consumer' means an individual who is a consumer within the meaning of that Part.

PART 8

ENFORCEMENT OF CERTAIN CONSUMER LEGISLATION

Introduction

210 Consumers

(1) In this Part references to consumers must be construed in accordance with this section.

(2) In relation to a domestic infringement a consumer is an individual in respect of whom the first and second conditions are satisfied.

(3) The first condition is that—

(a) goods are or are sought to be supplied to the individual (whether by way of sale or otherwise) in the course of a business carried on by the person supplying or seeking to supply them, or

(b) services are or are sought to be supplied to the individual in the course of a business carried on by the person supplying or seeking to supply them.

(4) The second condition is that—

(a) the individual receives or seeks to receive the goods or services otherwise than in the course of a business carried on by him, or

(b) the individual receives or seeks to receive the goods or services with a view to carrying on a business but not in the course of a business carried on by him.

(5) For the purposes of a domestic infringement it is immaterial whether a person supplying goods or services has a place of business in the United Kingdom.

(6) In relation to a Community infringement a consumer is a person who is a consumer for the purposes of—

(a) the Injunctions Directive, and

(b) the listed Directive [or the listed Regulation] concerned.

(7) A Directive is a listed Directive—

(a) if it is a Directive of the Council of the European Communities or of the European Parliament and of the Council, and

(b) if it is specified in Schedule 13 or to the extent that any of its provisions is so specified.

[(7A) A Regulation is a listed Regulation—

(a) if it is a Regulation of the Council of the European Parliament and of the Council, and

(b) if it is specified in Schedule 13 or to the extent that any of its provisions is so specified.]

(8) A business includes—

(a) a professional practice;

(b) any other undertaking carried on for gain or reward;

(c) any undertaking in the course of which goods or services are supplied otherwise than free of charge.

(9) The Secretary of State may by order modify Schedule 13.

(10) An order under this section must be made by statutory instrument subject to annulment in pursuance of a resolution of either House of Parliament.

211 Domestic infringements

(1) In this Part a domestic infringement is an act or omission which—

(a) is done or made by a person in the course of a business,

(b) falls within subsection (2), and

(c) harms the collective interests of consumers in the United Kingdom.

(2) An act or omission falls within this subsection if it is of a description specified by the Secretary of State by order and consists of any of the following—

(a) a contravention of an enactment which imposes a duty, prohibition or restriction enforceable by criminal proceedings;

(b)   an act done or omission made in breach of contract;

(c)   an act done or omission made in breach of a non-contractual duty owed to a person by virtue of an enactment or rule of law and enforceable by civil proceedings;

(d)   an act or omission in respect of which an enactment provides for a remedy or sanction enforceable by civil proceedings;

(e)   an act done or omission made by a person supplying or seeking to supply goods or services as a result of which an agreement or security relating to the supply is void or unenforceable to any extent;

(f)   an act or omission by which a person supplying or seeking to supply goods or services purports or attempts to exercise a right or remedy relating to the supply in circumstances where the exercise of the right or remedy is restricted or excluded under or by virtue of an enactment;

(g)   an act or omission by which a person supplying or seeking to supply goods or services purports or attempts to avoid (to any extent) liability relating to the supply in circumstances where such avoidance is restricted or prevented under an enactment.

(3)   But an order under this section may provide that any description of act or omission falling within subsection (2) is not a domestic infringement.

(4)   For the purposes of subsection (2) it is immaterial—

(a)   whether or not any duty, prohibition or restriction exists in relation to consumers as such;

(b)   whether or not any remedy or sanction is provided for the benefit of consumers as such;

(c)   whether or not any proceedings have been brought in relation to the act or omission;

(d)   whether or not any person has been convicted of an offence in respect of the contravention mentioned in subsection (2)(a);

(e)   whether or not there is a waiver in respect of the breach of contract mentioned in subsection (2)(b).

(5)   References to an enactment include references to subordinate legislation (within the meaning of the Interpretation Act 1978 (c 30)).

(6)   The power to make an order under this section must be exercised by statutory instrument.

(7)   But no such order may be made unless a draft of it has been laid before Parliament and approved by a resolution of each House.

212   Community infringements

(1)   In this Part a Community infringement is an act or omission which harms the collective interests of consumers and which—

(a)   contravenes a listed Directive as given effect by the laws, regulations or administrative provisions of an EEA State,

(b)   contravenes such laws, regulations or administrative provisions which provide additional permitted protections.

[(c)   contravenes a listed Regulation, or

(d)   contravenes any laws, regulations or administrative provisions of an EEA State which give effect to a listed Regulation.]

(2)   The laws, regulations or administrative provisions of an EEA State which give effect to a listed Directive provide additional permitted protections if—

(a)   they provide protection for consumers which is in addition to the minimum protection required by the Directive concerned, and

(b)   such additional protection is permitted by that Directive.

(3)   The Secretary of State may by order specify for the purposes of this section the law in the United Kingdom which—

(a)   gives effect to the listed Directives;

(b)   provides additional permitted protections [; or]

[(c) gives effect to a listed Regulation.]

(4)   References to a listed Directive [or listed Regulation] must be construed in accordance with section 210.

(5)   [EEA State has the meaning given by Schedule 1 to the Interpretation Act 1978.]

(6)   An order under this section must be made by statutory instrument subject to annulment in pursuance of a resolution of either House of Parliament.

213   Enforcers

(1)   Each of the following is a general enforcer—

    (a)   the OFT;

    (b)   every local weights and measures authority in Great Britain;

    (c)   the Department of Enterprise, Trade and Investment in Northern Ireland.

(2)   A designated enforcer is any person or body (whether or not incorporated) which the Secretary of State—

    (a)   thinks has as one of its purposes the protection of the collective interests of consumers, and

    (b)   designates by order.

(3)   The Secretary of State may designate a public body only if he is satisfied that it is independent.

(4)   The Secretary of State may designate a person or body which is not a public body only if the person or body (as the case may be) satisfies such criteria as the Secretary of State specifies by order.

(5)   A Community enforcer is a qualified entity for the purposes of the Injunctions Directive—

    (a)   which is for the time being specified in the list published in the Official Journal of the European Communities in pursuance of Article 4.3 of that Directive, but

    (b)   [which is not a general enforcer, a designated enforcer or a CPC enforcer].

[(5A)   Each of the following (being bodies or persons designated by the Secretary of State under Article 4(1) or 4(2) of the CPC Regulation) is a CPC enforcer—

    (a)   the OFT;

    (b)   the Civil Aviation Authority;

    (c)   the Financial Services Authority;

    (d)   the Secretary of State for Health;

    (e)   the Department of Health, Social Services and Public Safety in Northern Ireland;

    (f)   the Office of Communications;

    (g)   the Department of Enterprise, Trade and Investment in Northern Ireland;

    (h)   every local weights and measures authority in Great Britain;

    (i)   the Independent Committee for the Supervision of Standards of the Telephone Information Services.]

(6)   An order under this section may designate an enforcer in respect of—

    (a)   all infringements;

    (b)   infringements of such descriptions as are specified in the order.

(7)   An order under this section may make different provision for different purposes.

(8)   The designation of a body by virtue of subsection (3) is conclusive evidence for the purposes of any question arising under this Part that the body is a public body.

(9)   An order under this section must be made by statutory instrument subject to annulment in pursuance of a resolution of either House of Parliament.

(10)   If requested to do so by a designated enforcer which is designated in respect of one or more Community infringements the Secretary of State must notify the Commission of the European Communities—

    (a)   of its name and purpose;

(b)   of the Community infringements in respect of which it is designated.

(11)   The Secretary of State must also notify the Commission—

(a)   of the fact that a person or body in respect of which he has given notice under subsection (10) ceases to be a designated enforcer;

(b)   of any change in the name or purpose of a designated enforcer in respect of which he has given such notice;

(c)   of any change to the Community infringements in respect of which a designated enforcer is designated.

Enforcement procedure

214   Consultation

(1)   An enforcer must not make an application for an enforcement order unless he has engaged in appropriate consultation with—

(a)   the person against whom the enforcement order would be made, and

(b)   the OFT (if it is not the enforcer).

(2)   Appropriate consultation is consultation for the purpose of—

(a)   achieving the cessation of the infringement in a case where an infringement is occurring;

(b)   ensuring that there will be no repetition of the infringement in a case where the infringement has occurred;

(c)   ensuring that there will be no repetition of the infringement in a case where the cessation of the infringement is achieved under paragraph (a);

(d)   ensuring that the infringement does not take place in the case of a Community infringement which the enforcer believes is likely to take place.

(3)   Subsection (1) does not apply if the OFT thinks that an application for an enforcement order should be made without delay.

(4)   Subsection (1) ceases to apply—

(a)   for the purposes of an application for an enforcement order at the end of the period of 14 days beginning with the day after the person against whom the enforcement order would be made receives a request for consultation from the enforcer;

(b)   for the purposes of an application for an interim enforcement order at the end of the period of seven days beginning with the day after the person against whom the interim enforcement order would be made receives a request for consultation from the enforcer.

(5)   The Secretary of State may by order make rules in relation to consultation under this section.

(6)   Such an order must be made by statutory instrument subject to annulment in pursuance of a resolution of either House of Parliament.

(7)   In this section (except subsection (4)) and in sections 215 and 216 references to an enforcement order include references to an interim enforcement order.

215   Applications

(1)   An application for an enforcement order must name the person the enforcer thinks—

(a)   has engaged or is engaging in conduct which constitutes a domestic or a Community infringement, or

(b)   is likely to engage in conduct which constitutes a Community infringement.

(2)   A general enforcer may make an application for an enforcement order in respect of any infringement.

(3)   A designated enforcer may make an application for an enforcement order in respect of an infringement to which his designation relates.

(4)   A Community enforcer may make an application for an enforcement order in respect of a Community infringement.

[(4A)   A CPC enforcer may make an application for an enforcement order in respect of a Community infringement.]

(5)   The following courts have jurisdiction to make an enforcement order—

(a)   the High Court or a county court if the person against whom the order is sought carries on business or has a place of business in England and Wales or Northern Ireland;

(b)   the Court of Session or the sheriff if the person against whom the order is sought carries on business or has a place of business in Scotland.

(6)   If an application for an enforcement order is made by a Community enforcer the court may examine whether the purpose of the enforcer justifies its making the application.

(7)   If the court thinks that the purpose of the Community enforcer does not justify its making the application the court may refuse the application on that ground alone.

(8)   The purpose of a Community enforcer must be construed by reference to the Injunctions Directive.

(9)   An enforcer which is not the OFT must notify the OFT of the result of an application under this section.

216   Applications: directions by OFT

(1)   This section applies if the OFT believes that an enforcer other than the OFT intends to apply for an enforcement order.

(2)   In such a case the OFT may direct that if an application in respect of a particular infringement is to be made it must be made—

(a)   only by the OFT, or

(b)   only by such other enforcer as the OFT directs.

(3)   If the OFT directs that only it may make an application that does not prevent—

(a)   the OFT or any enforcer from accepting an undertaking under section 219, or

(b)   the OFT from taking such other steps it thinks appropriate (apart from making an application) for the purpose of securing that the infringement is not committed, continued or repeated.

(4)   The OFT may vary or withdraw a direction given under this section.

(5)   The OFT must take such steps as it thinks appropriate to bring a direction (or a variation or withdrawal of a direction) to the attention of enforcers it thinks may be affected by it.

(6)   But this section does not prevent an application for an enforcement order being made by a Community enforcer.

217   Enforcement orders

(1)   This section applies if an application for an enforcement order is made under section 215 and the court finds that the person named in the application has engaged in conduct which constitutes the infringement.

(2)   This section also applies if such an application is made in relation to a Community infringement and the court finds that the person named in the application is likely to engage in conduct which constitutes the infringement.

(3)   If this section applies the court may make an enforcement order against the person.

(4)   In considering whether to make an enforcement order the court must have regard to whether the person named in the application—

(a)   has given an undertaking under section 219 in respect of conduct such as is mentioned in subsection (3) of that section;

(b)   has failed to comply with the undertaking.

(5)   An enforcement order must—

(a)   indicate the nature of the conduct to which the finding under subsection (1) or (2) relates, and

    (b)   direct the person to comply with subsection (6).

(6)   A person complies with this subsection if he—

    (a)   does not continue or repeat the conduct;

    (b)   does not engage in such conduct in the course of his business or another business;

    (c)   does not consent to or connive in the carrying out of such conduct by a body corporate with which he has a special relationship (within the meaning of section 222(3)).

(7)   But subsection (6)(a) does not apply in the case of a finding under subsection (2).

(8)   An enforcement order may require a person against whom the order is made to publish in such form and manner and to such extent as the court thinks appropriate for the purpose of eliminating any continuing effects of the infringement—

    (a)   the order;

    (b)   a corrective statement.

(9)   If the court makes a finding under subsection (1) or (2) it may accept an undertaking by the person—

    (a)   to comply with subsection (6), or

    (b)   to take steps which the court believes will secure that he complies with subsection (6).

(10)   An undertaking under subsection (9) may include a further undertaking by the person to publish in such form and manner and to such extent as the court thinks appropriate for the purpose of eliminating any continuing effects of the infringement—

    (a)   the terms of the undertaking;

    (b)   a corrective statement.

(11)   If the court—

    (a)   makes a finding under subsection (1) or (2), and

    (b)   accepts an undertaking under subsection (9),

it must not make an enforcement order in respect of the infringement to which the undertaking relates.

(12)   An enforcement order made by a court in one part of the United Kingdom has effect in any other part of the United Kingdom as if made by a court in that part.

218 Interim enforcement order

(1)   The court may make an interim enforcement order against a person named in the application for the order if it appears to the court—

    (a)   that it is alleged that the person is engaged in conduct which constitutes a domestic or Community infringement or is likely to engage in conduct which constitutes a Community infringement,

    (b)   that if the application had been an application for an enforcement order it would be likely to be granted,

    (c)   that it is expedient that the conduct is prohibited or prevented (as the case may be) immediately, and

    (d)   if no notice of the application has been given to the person named in the application that it is appropriate to make an interim enforcement order without notice.

(2)   An interim enforcement order must—

    (a)   indicate the nature of the alleged conduct, and

    (b)   direct the person to comply with subsection (3).

(3)   A person complies with this subsection if he—

    (a)   does not continue or repeat the conduct;

    (b)   does not engage in such conduct in the course of his business or another business;

    (c)   does not consent to or connive in the carrying out of such conduct by a body corporate with which he has a special relationship (within the meaning of section 222(3)).

(4) But subsection (3)(a) does not apply in so far as the application is made in respect of an allegation that the person is likely to engage in conduct which constitutes a Community infringement.

(5) An application for an interim enforcement order against a person may be made at any time before an application for an enforcement order against the person in respect of the same conduct is determined.

(6) An application for an interim enforcement order must refer to all matters—
  (a) which are known to the applicant, and
  (b) which are material to the question whether or not the application is granted.

(7) If an application for an interim enforcement order is made without notice the application must state why no notice has been given.

(8) The court may vary or discharge an interim enforcement order on the application of—
  (a) the enforcer who applied for the order;
  (b) the person against whom it is made.

(9) An interim enforcement order against a person is discharged on the determination of an application for an enforcement order made against the person in respect of the same conduct.

(10) If it appears to the court as mentioned in subsection (1)(a) to (c) the court may instead of making an interim enforcement order accept an undertaking from the person named in the application—
  (a) to comply with subsection (3), or
  (b) to take steps which the court believes will secure that he complies with subsection (3).

(11) An interim enforcement order made by a court in one part of the United Kingdom has effect in any other part of the United Kingdom as if made by a court in that part.

[218A Unfair commercial practices: substantiation of claims

(1) This section applies where an application for an enforcement order or for an interim enforcement order is made in respect of a Community infringement involving a contravention of Directive 2005/29/EC of the European Parliament and of the Council of 11 May 2005 concerning unfair business-to-consumer commercial practices in the internal market.

(2) For the purposes of considering the application the court may require the person named in the application to provide evidence as to the accuracy of any factual claim made as part of a commercial practice of that person if, taking into account the legitimate interests of that person and any other party to the proceedings, it appears appropriate in the circumstances.

(3) If, having been required under subsection (2) to provide evidence as to the accuracy of a factual claim, a person—
  (a) fails to provide such evidence, or
  (b) provides evidence as to the accuracy of the factual claim that the court considers inadequate, the court may consider that the factual claim is inaccurate.

(4) In this section 'commercial practice' has the meaning given by regulation 2 of the Consumer Protection from Unfair Trading Regulations 2008.]

219 Undertakings

(1) This section applies if an enforcer has power to make an application under section 215.

(2) In such a case the enforcer may accept from a person to whom subsection (3) applies an undertaking that the person will comply with subsection (4).

(3) This subsection applies to a person who the enforcer believes—
  (a) has engaged in conduct which constitutes an infringement;

(b)   is engaging in such conduct;

(c)   is likely to engage in conduct which constitutes a Community infringement.

(4)   A person complies with this subsection if he—

(a)   does not continue or repeat the conduct;

(b)   does not engage in such conduct in the course of his business or another business;

(c)   does not consent to or connive in the carrying out of such conduct by a body corporate with which he has a special relationship (within the meaning of section 222(3)).

(5)   But subsection (4)(a) does not apply in the case of an undertaking given by a person in so far as subsection (3) applies to him by virtue of paragraph (c).

[(5A)   A CPC enforcer who has accepted an undertaking under this section may—

(a)   accept a further undertaking from the person concerned to publish the terms of the undertaking; or

(b)   take steps itself to publish the undertaking.

(5B)   In each case the undertaking shall be published in such form and manner and to such extent as the CPC enforcer thinks appropriate for the purpose of eliminating any continuing effects of the Community infringement.]

(6)   If an enforcer accepts an undertaking under this section it must notify the OFT—

(a)   of the terms of the undertaking;

(b)   of the identity of the person who gave it.

220   Further proceedings

(1)   This section applies if the court—

(a)   makes an enforcement order under section 217,

(b)   makes an interim enforcement order under section 218, or

(c)   accepts an undertaking under either of those sections.

(2)   In such a case the OFT has the same right to apply to the court in respect of a failure to comply with the order or undertaking as the enforcer who made the application for the order.

(3)   An application to the court in respect of a failure to comply with an undertaking may include an application for an enforcement order or for an interim enforcement order.

(4)   If the court finds that an undertaking is not being complied with it may make an enforcement order or an interim enforcement order (instead of making any other order it has power to make).

(5)   In the case of an application for an enforcement order or for an interim enforcement order as mentioned in subsection (3) sections 214 and 216 must be ignored and sections 215 and 217 or 218 (as the case may be) apply subject to the following modifications—

(a)   section 215(1)(b) must be ignored;

(b)   section 215(5) must be ignored and the application must be made to the court which accepted the undertaking;

(c)   section 217(9) to (11) must be ignored;

(d)   section 218(10) must be ignored.

(6)   If an enforcer which is not the OFT makes an application in respect of the failure of a person to comply with an enforcement order, an interim enforcement order or an undertaking given under section 217 or 218 the enforcer must notify the OFT—

(a)   of the application;

(b)   of any order made by the court on the application.

221   Community infringements: proceedings

(1)   Subsection (2) applies to—

(a)   every general enforcer;

(b)   every designated enforcer which is a public body.

(2)   An enforcer to which this subsection applies has power to take proceedings in EEA States other than the United Kingdom for the cessation or prohibition of a Community infringement.

(3)   Subsection (4) applies to—

(a)   every general enforcer;

(b)   every designated enforcer;

[(c)   every CPC enforcer].

(4)   An enforcer to which this subsection applies may co-operate with a Community enforcer—

(a)   for the purpose of bringing proceedings mentioned in subsection (2);

(b)   in connection with the exercise by the Community enforcer of its functions under this Part.

(5)   An EEA State is a State which is a contracting party to the Agreement on the European Economic Area signed at Oporto on 2nd May 1992 as adjusted by the Protocol signed at Brussels on 17th March 1993.

222   Bodies corporate: accessories

(1)   This section applies if the person whose conduct constitutes a domestic infringement or a Community infringement is a body corporate.

(2)   If the conduct takes place with the consent or connivance of a person (an accessory) who has a special relationship with the body corporate, the consent or connivance is also conduct which constitutes the infringement.

(3)   A person has a special relationship with a body corporate if he is—

(a)   a controller of the body corporate, or

(b)   a director, manager, secretary or other similar officer of the body corporate or a person purporting to act in such a capacity.

(4)   A person is a controller of a body corporate if—

(a)   the directors of the body corporate or of another body corporate which is its controller are accustomed to act in accordance with the person's directions or instructions, or

(b)   either alone or with an associate or associates he is entitled to exercise or control the exercise of one third or more of the voting power at any general meeting of the body corporate or of another body corporate which is its controller.

(5)   An enforcement order or an interim enforcement order may be made against an accessory in respect of an infringement whether or not such an order is made against the body corporate.

(6)   The court may accept an undertaking under section 217(9) or 218(10) from an accessory in respect of an infringement whether or not it accepts such an undertaking from the body corporate.

(7)   An enforcer may accept an undertaking under section 219 from an accessory in respect of an infringement whether or not it accepts such an undertaking from the body corporate.

(8)   Subsection (9) applies if—

(a)   an order is made as mentioned in subsection (5), or

(b)   an undertaking is accepted as mentioned in subsection (6) or (7).

(9)   In such a case for subsection (6) of section 217, subsection (3) of section 218 or subsection (4) of section 219 (as the case may be) there is substituted the following subsection—

'( ) A person complies with this subsection if he—

(a)   does not continue or repeat the conduct;

(b)   does not in the course of any business carried on by him engage in conduct such as that which constitutes the infringement committed by the body corporate mentioned in section 222(1);

(c)   does not consent to or connive in the carrying out of such conduct by another body corporate with which he has a special relationship (within the meaning of section 222(3)).'

(10)   A person is an associate of an individual if—

(a)   he is the spouse [or civil partner] of the individual;

(b)   he is a relative of the individual;

(c)   he is a relative of the individual's spouse [or civil partner];

(d)   he is the spouse [or civil partner] of a relative of the individual;

(e)   he is the spouse [or civil partner] of a relative of the individual's spouse;

(f)   he lives in the same household as the individual otherwise than merely because he or the individual is the other's employer, tenant, lodger or boarder;

(g)   he is a relative of a person who is an associate of the individual by virtue of paragraph (f);

(h)   he has at some time in the past fallen within any of paragraphs (a) to (g).

(11)   A person is also an associate of—

(a)   an individual with whom he is in partnership;

(b)   an individual who is an associate of the individual mentioned in paragraph (a);

(c)   a body corporate if he is a controller of it or he is an associate of a person who is a controller of the body corporate.

(12)   A body corporate is an associate of another body corporate if—

(a)   the same person is a controller of both;

(b)   a person is a controller of one and persons who are his associates are controllers of the other;

(c)   a person is a controller of one and he and persons who are his associates are controllers of the other;

(d)   a group of two or more persons is a controller of each company and the groups consist of the same persons;

(e)   a group of two or more persons is a controller of each company and the groups may be regarded as consisting of the same persons by treating (in one or more cases) a member of either group as replaced by a person of whom he is an associate.

(13)   A relative is a brother, sister, uncle, aunt, nephew, niece, lineal ancestor or lineal descendant.

223   Bodies corporate: orders

(1)   This section applies if a court makes an enforcement order or an interim enforcement order against a body corporate and—

(a)   at the time the order is made the body corporate is a member of a group of interconnected bodies corporate,

(b)   at any time when the order is in force the body corporate becomes a member of a group of interconnected bodies corporate, or

(c)   at any time when the order is in force a group of interconnected bodies corporate of which the body corporate is a member is increased by the addition of one or more further members.

(2)   The court may direct that the order is binding upon all of the members of the group as if each of them were the body corporate against which the order is made.

(3)   A group of interconnected bodies corporate is a group consisting of two or more bodies corporate all of whom are interconnected with each other.

(4)   Any two bodies corporate are interconnected—

(a)   if one of them is a subsidiary of the other, or

(b)   if both of them are subsidiaries of the same body corporate.

(5)   'Subsidiary' must be construed in accordance with section [1159 of the Companies Act 2006].

Information

224 OFT

(1) The OFT may for any of the purposes mentioned in subsection (2) give notice to any person requiring the person to provide it with the information specified in the notice.

(2) The purposes are—

(a) to enable the OFT to exercise or to consider whether to exercise any function it has under this Part;

(b) to enable a designated enforcer to which section 225 does not apply to consider whether to exercise any function it has under this Part;

(c) to enable a Community enforcer to consider whether to exercise any function it has under this Part;

(d) to ascertain whether a person has complied with or is complying with an enforcement order, an interim enforcement order or an undertaking given under section 217(9), 218(10) or 219.

225 Other enforcers

(1) This section applies to—

(a) every general enforcer (other than the OFT);

(b) every designated enforcer which is a public body.

[(c) every CPC enforcer (other than the OFT).]

(2) An enforcer to which this section applies may for any of the purposes mentioned in subsection (3) give notice to any person requiring the person to provide the enforcer with the information specified in the notice.

(3) The purposes are—

(a) to enable the enforcer to exercise or to consider whether to exercise any function it has under this Part;

(b) to ascertain whether a person has complied with or is complying with an enforcement order or an interim enforcement order made on the application of the enforcer or an undertaking given under section 217(9) or 218(10) (as the case may be) following such an application or an undertaking given to the enforcer under section 219.

226 Notices: procedure

(1) This section applies to a notice given under section 224 or 225.

(2) The notice must—

(a) be in writing;

(b) specify the purpose for which the information is required.

(3) If the purpose is as mentioned in section 224(2)(a), (b) or (c) or 225(3)(a) the notice must specify the function concerned.

(4) A notice may specify the time within which and manner in which it is to be complied with.

(5) A notice may require the production of documents or any description of documents.

(6) An enforcer may take copies of any documents produced in compliance with such a requirement.

[(6A) A notice may specify the form in which information is to be provided.]

(7) A notice may be varied or revoked by a subsequent notice.

(8) But a notice must not require a person to provide any information or produce any document which he would be entitled to refuse to provide or produce—

(a) in proceedings in the High Court on the grounds of legal professional privilege;

(b) in proceedings in the Court of Session on the grounds of confidentiality of communications.

227 Notices: enforcement

(1) If a person fails to comply with a notice given under section 224 or 225 the enforcer who gave the notice may make an application under this section.

(2) If it appears to the court that the person to whom the notice was given has failed to comply with the notice the court may make an order under this section.

(3) An order under this section may require the person to whom the notice was given to do anything the court thinks it is reasonable for him to do for any of the purposes mentioned in section 224 or 225 (as the case may be) to ensure that the notice is complied with.

(4) An order under this section may require the person to meet all the costs or expenses of the application.

(5) If the person is a company or association the court in proceeding under subsection (4) may require any officer of the company or association who is responsible for the failure to meet the costs or expenses.

(6) The court is a court which may make an enforcement order.

(7) In subsection (5) an officer of a company is a person who is a director, manager, secretary or other similar officer of the company.

[227A Power to enter premises without warrant

(1) An officer of a CPC enforcer who reasonably suspects that there has been, or is likely to be, a Community infringement may for any purpose relating to the functions of the CPC enforcer under this Part enter any premises to investigate whether there has been, or is likely to be, such an infringement.

(2) An officer of a CPC enforcer who reasonably suspects that there is, or has been, a failure to comply with a relevant enforcement measure may for any purpose relating to the functions of the CPC enforcer under this Part enter any premises to investigate whether a person is complying with, or has complied with, the relevant enforcement measure.

(3) An appropriate notice must be given to the occupier of the premises before an officer of a CPC enforcer enters them under subsection (1) and (2).

(4) An appropriate notice is a notice in writing given by an officer of a CPC enforcer which—

    (a) gives at least two working days' notice of entry on the premises;

    (b) sets out why the entry is necessary; and

    (c) indicates the nature of the offence created by section 227E.

(5) Subsection (3) does not apply if such a notice cannot be given despite all reasonably practicable steps having been taken to do so.

(6) In that case, the officer entering the premises must produce to any occupier that he finds on the premises a document setting out why the entry is necessary and indicating the nature of the offence created by section 227E.

(7) In all cases, the officer entering the premises must produce to any occupier evidence of—

    (a) his identity; and

    (b) in the case of an authorised officer of a CPC enforcer, his authorisation;

if asked to do so.

(8) In this section—

'give', in relation to the giving of a notice to the occupier of premises, includes delivering or leaving it at the premises or sending it there by post; and

'working day' means a day which is not—

    (a) Saturday or Sunday; or

    (b) Christmas Day, Good Friday or a day which is a bank holiday under the Banking and Financial Dealings Act 1971 in the part of the United Kingdom in which the premises are situated.

(9) In this section and sections 227B to 227F—

'authorised officer of a CPC enforcer' means an officer of a CPC enforcer who is authorised by that enforcer for the purposes of this Part;

'occupier' means any person whom the officer concerned reasonably suspects to be the occupier;

'officer of a CPC enforcer' means—

(a)   an officer of a local weights and measures authority in Great Britain; or

(b)   an authorised officer of a CPC enforcer which is not a local weights and measures authority in Great Britain;

'premises' includes vehicles but does not include any premises which are used only as a dwelling; and

'relevant enforcement measure' means—

(a)   an enforcement order made under section 217 on the application of the CPC enforcer;

(b)   an interim enforcement order made under section 218 on the application of the CPC enforcer;

(c)   an undertaking under section 217(9) in connection with an application made by the CPC enforcer for an enforcement order under section 217;

(d)   an undertaking under section 218(10) in connection with an application made by the CPC enforcer for an interim enforcement order under section 218; or

(e)   an undertaking under section 219 to the CPC enforcer.

227B   Powers exercisable on the premises

(1)   An officer of a CPC enforcer may, in the exercise of his powers under section 227A—

(a)   observe the carrying on of a business on the premises;

(b)   inspect goods or documents on the premises;

(c)   require any person on the premises to produce goods or documents within such period as the officer considers to be reasonable;

(d)   seize goods or documents to carry out tests on them on the premises or seize, remove and retain them to carry out tests on them elsewhere; or

(e)   seize, remove and retain goods or documents which he reasonably suspects may be required as evidence of a Community infringement or a breach of a relevant enforcement measure.

(2)   The power in subsection (1)(c) to require a person to produce goods or documents includes the power to require him—

(a)   to state, to the best of his knowledge and belief, where the goods or documents are;

(b)   to give an explanation of the goods or documents; and

(c)   to secure that any goods or documents produced are authenticated or verified in such manner as the officer considers appropriate.

(3)   An officer of a CPC enforcer may take copies of, or extracts from, any documents to which he has access by virtue of subsection (1).

(4)   But nothing in this section authorises action to be taken in relation to anything which, in proceedings in the High Court, a person would be entitled to refuse to produce on the grounds of legal professional privilege.

(5)   In this section document includes information recorded in any form.

(6)   The reference in subsection (1)(c) to the production of documents is, in the case of a document which contains information recorded otherwise than in legible form, a reference to the production of a copy of the information in legible form.

(7)   In its application to Scotland, this section has effect as if the reference in subsection (4)—

(a)   to proceedings in the High Court were a reference to proceedings in the Court of Session; and

(b)   to an entitlement on the grounds of legal professional privilege were a reference to an entitlement on the grounds of confidentiality of communications.

227C   Power to enter premises with warrant

(1)   A justice of the peace may issue a warrant authorising an officer of a CPC

enforcer to enter premises for purposes falling within section 227A(1) or (2) if the justice of the peace considers that there are reasonable grounds for believing that—

(a)   condition A is met; and

(b)   either condition B, C or D is met.

(2)   Condition A is that there are, on the premises, goods or documents to which an officer of a CPC enforcer would be entitled to have access under sections 227A and 227B.

(3)   Condition B is that an officer of a CPC enforcer acting under sections 227A and 227B has been, or would be likely to be, refused admission to the premises or access to the goods or documents.

(4)   Condition C is that the goods or documents would be likely to be concealed or interfered with if an appropriate notice were given under section 227A.

(5)   Condition D is that there is likely to be nobody at the premises capable of granting admission.

(6)   A warrant under this section authorises the officer of the CPC enforcer—

(a)   to enter the premises specified in the warrant (using reasonable force if necessary);

(b)   to do anything on the premises that an officer of the CPC enforcer would be able to do if he had entered the premises under section 227A;

(c)   to search for goods or documents which he has required a person on the premises to produce where that person has failed to comply with such a requirement;

(d)   to the extent that it is reasonably necessary to do so, to require any person to whom subsection (7) applies to break open a container and, if that person does not comply with the requirement, or if such a person cannot be identified after all reasonably practicable steps have been taken to identify such a person, to do so himself;

(e)   to take any other steps which he considers to be reasonably necessary to preserve, or prevent interference with, goods or documents to which he would be entitled to have access under sections 227A and 227B.

(7)   This subsection applies to a person who is responsible for discharging any of the functions of the business being carried on at the premises under inspection.

(8)   A warrant under this section—

(a)   is issued on information on oath given by an officer of a CPC enforcer;

(b)   ceases to have effect at the end of the period of one month beginning with the day of issue; and

(c)   must, on request, be produced to the occupier of the premises for inspection.

(9)   Any reference in this section to goods or documents being interfered with includes a reference to them being destroyed.

(10)   In its application to Scotland, this section has effect as if—

(a)   the references in subsection (1) to a justice of the peace included references to a sheriff; and

(b)   the reference in subsection (8) to information on oath were a reference to evidence on oath.

(11)   In its application to Northern Ireland, this section has effect as if the references in subsection (1) to a justice of the peace were references to a lay magistrate.

227D   Ancillary provisions about powers of entry

(1)   An officer of a CPC enforcer who enters premises by virtue of section 227A may only do so at a reasonable time.

(2)   An officer of a CPC enforcer who enters premises by virtue of section 227A or 227C may take with him such persons and equipment as he considers appropriate.

(3)   An officer of a CPC enforcer who enters premises by virtue of section 227A or 227C must, if the premises are unoccupied or the occupier is temporarily

absent, take reasonable steps to ensure that when he leaves the premises they are as secure as they were before he entered.

227E Obstructing, or failing to co-operate with, powers of entry

(1) A person commits an offence if, without reasonable excuse, he intentionally obstructs, or fails to co-operate with, an officer of a CPC enforcer who is exercising or seeking to exercise a power under sections 227A to 227D.

(2) A person guilty of an offence under subsection (1) is liable, on summary conviction, to a fine not exceeding level 5 on the standard scale.

227F Retention of documents and goods

(1) No documents seized under sections 227A to 227D may be retained for a period of more than three months.

(2) No goods seized under sections 227A to 227D may be retained for a period of more than three months unless they are reasonably required in connection with the exercise of any function of a CPC enforcer under this Part.

(3) Where goods are so required they may be retained for as long as they are so required.]

Miscellaneous

228 Evidence

(1) Proceedings under this Part are civil proceedings for the purposes of—

(a) section 11 of the Civil Evidence Act 1968 (c 64) (convictions admissible as evidence in civil proceedings);

(b) section 10 of the Law Reform (Miscellaneous Provisions) (Scotland) Act 1968 (c 70) (corresponding provision in Scotland);

(c) section 7 of the Civil Evidence Act (Northern Ireland) 1971 (c 36 (NI)) (corresponding provision in Northern Ireland).

(2) In proceedings under this Part any finding by a court in civil proceedings that an act or omission mentioned in section 211(2)(b), (c) or (d) or 212(1) has occurred—

(a) is admissible as evidence that the act or omission occurred;

(b) unless the contrary is proved, is sufficient evidence that the act or omission occurred.

(3) But subsection (2) does not apply to any finding—

(a) which has been reversed on appeal;

(b) which has been varied on appeal so as to negative it.

[(4) This section does not apply to proceedings for an offence under section 227E.]

229 Advice and information

(1) As soon as is reasonably practicable after the passing of this Act the OFT must prepare and publish advice and information with a view to—

(a) explaining the provisions of this Part to persons who are likely to be affected by them, and

(b) indicating how the OFT expects such provisions to operate.

(2) The OFT may at any time publish revised or new advice or information.

(3) Advice or information published in pursuance of subsection (1)(b) may include advice or information about the factors which the OFT may take into account in considering how to exercise the functions conferred on it by this Part.

(4) Advice or information published by the OFT under this section is to be published in such form and in such manner as it considers appropriate.

(5) In preparing advice or information under this section the OFT must consult such persons as it thinks are representative of persons affected by this Part.

(6) If any proposed advice or information relates to a matter in respect of which another general [or CPC] enforcer or a designated enforcer may act the persons to be consulted must include that enforcer.

230   Notice to OFT of intended prosecution

(1)   This section applies if a local weights and measures authority in England and Wales intends to start proceedings for an offence under an enactment or subordinate legislation specified by the Secretary of State by order for the purposes of this section.

(2)   The authority must give the OFT—

    (a)   notice of its intention to start the proceedings;

    (b)   a summary of the evidence it intends to lead in respect of the charges.

(3)   The authority must not start the proceedings until whichever is the earlier of the following—

    (a)   the end of the period of 14 days starting with the day on which the authority gives the notice;

    (b)   the day on which it is notified by the OFT that the OFT has received the notice and summary given under subsection (2).

(4)   The authority must also notify the OFT of the outcome of the proceedings after they are finally determined.

(5)   But such proceedings are not invalid by reason only of the failure of the authority to comply with this section.

(6)   Subordinate legislation has the same meaning as in section 21(1) of the Interpretation Act 1978 (c 30).

(7)   An order under this section must be made by statutory instrument subject to annulment in pursuance of a resolution of either House of Parliament.

231   Notice of convictions and judgments to OFT

(1)   This section applies if—

    (a)   a person is convicted of an offence by or before a court in the United Kingdom, or

    (b)   a judgment is given against a person by a court in civil proceedings in the United Kingdom.

(2)   The court may make arrangements to bring the conviction or judgment to the attention of the OFT if it appears to the court—

    (a)   having regard to the functions of the OFT under this Part or under the Estate Agents Act 1979 (c 38) that it is expedient for the conviction or judgment to be brought to the attention of the OFT, and

    (b)   without such arrangements the conviction or judgment may not be brought to the attention of the OFT.

(3)   For the purposes of subsection (2) it is immaterial that the proceedings have been finally disposed of by the court.

(4)   Judgment includes an order or decree and references to the giving of the judgment must be construed accordingly.

Interpretation

232   Goods and services

(1)   References in this Part to goods and services must be construed in accordance with this section.

(2)   Goods include—

    (a)   buildings and other structures;

    (b)   ships, aircraft and hovercraft.

(3)   The supply of goods includes—

    (a)   supply by way of sale, lease, hire or hire purchase;

    (b)   in relation to buildings and other structures, construction of them by one person for another.

(4)   Goods or services which are supplied wholly or partly outside the United Kingdom must be taken to be supplied to or for a person in the United Kingdom if they are supplied in accordance with arrangements falling within subsection (5).

(5)   Arrangements fall within this subsection if they are made by any means and—

(a)   at the time the arrangements are made the person seeking the supply is in the United Kingdom, or

(b)   at the time the goods or services are supplied (or ought to be supplied in accordance with the arrangements) the person responsible under the arrangements for effecting the supply is in or has a place of business in the United Kingdom.

233 Person supplying goods

(1)   This section has effect for the purpose of references in this Part to a person supplying or seeking to supply goods under—

(a)   a hire-purchase agreement;

(b)   a credit-sale agreement;

(c)   a conditional sale agreement.

(2)   The references include references to a person who conducts any antecedent negotiations relating to the agreement.

(3)   The following expressions must be construed in accordance with section 189 of the Consumer Credit Act 1974 (c 39)—

(a)   hire-purchase agreement;

(b)   credit-sale agreement;

(c)   conditional sale agreement;

(d)   antecedent negotiations.

234 Supply of services

(1)   References in this Part to the supply of services must be construed in accordance with this section.

(2)   The supply of services does not include the provision of services under a contract of service or of apprenticeship whether it is express or implied and (if it is express) whether it is oral or in writing.

(3)   The supply of services includes—

(a)   performing for gain or reward any activity other than the supply of goods;

(b)   rendering services to order;

(c)   the provision of services by making them available to potential users.

(4)   The supply of services includes making arrangements for the use of computer software or for granting access to data stored in any form which is not readily accessible.

(5)   The supply of services includes making arrangements by means of a relevant agreement (within the meaning of [paragraph 29 of Schedule 2 to the Telecommunications Act 1984]) for sharing the use of telecommunications apparatus.

(6)   The supply of services includes permitting or making arrangements to permit the use of land in such circumstances as the Secretary of State specifies by order.

(7)   The power to make an order under subsection (6) must be exercised by statutory instrument.

(8)   But no such order may be made unless a draft of it has been laid before Parliament and approved by a resolution of each House.

235 Injunctions Directive

In this Part the Injunctions Directive is Directive 98/27/EC of the European Parliament and of the Council on injunctions for the protection of consumers' interests.

[235A CPC Regulation

In this Part—

(a)   the CPC Regulation is Regulation (EC) No 2006/2004 of the European Parliament and of the Council of 27 October 2004 on cooperation between national authorities responsible for the enforcement of consumer protection laws as amended by the Unfair Commercial Practices Directive;

(b)   the Unfair Commercial Practices Directive is Directive 2005/29/EC of the European Parliament and of the Council of 11 May 2005 concerning unfair business-to-consumer commercial practices in the internal market.]

[235B   Dual enforcers

References in this Part to a general enforcer, a designated enforcer or a CPC enforcer are to be read, in the case of a person or body which is more than one kind of enforcer, as references to that person or body acting in its capacity as a general enforcer, designated enforcer or (as the case may be) CPC enforcer.]

Crown

236   Crown

[(1)]   This Part binds the Crown.

[(2)   But the powers conferred by sections 227A to 227D are not exercisable in relation to premises occupied by the Crown.]

SCHEDULE 13
LISTED DIRECTIVES AND REGULATIONS

Section 210

PART 1
DIRECTIVES

[. . .]

2   Council Directive 85/577/EEC of 20 December 1985 to protect the consumer in respect of contracts negotiated away from business premises.

[. . .]

4   Council Directive 90/314/EEC of 13 June 1990 on package travel, package holidays and package tours.

5   Council Directive 93/13/EEC of 5 April 1993 on unfair terms in consumer contracts.

6   Directive 94/47/EC of the European Parliament and of the Council of 26 October 1994 on the protection of purchasers in respect of certain aspects of contracts relating to the purchase of the right to use immovable properties on a time-share basis.

7   Directive 97/7/EC of the European Parliament and of the Council of 20 May 1997 on the protection of consumers in respect of distance contracts.

[. . .]

[7B   Directive 98/6/EC of the European Parliament and of the Council of 16 February 1998 on consumer protection in the indication of the prices of products offered to consumers.]

8   Directive 1999/44/EC of the European Parliament and of the Council of 25 May 1999 on certain aspects of the sale of consumer goods and associated guarantees.

9   Directive 2000/31/EC of the European Parliament and of the Council of 8 June 2000 on certain legal aspects of information society services, in particular electronic commerce, in the Internal Market ('Directive on electronic commerce').

[9A   Directive 2002/65/EC of the European Parliament and of the Council of 23 September 2002 concerning the distance marketing of consumer financial services and amending Council Directive 90/619/EEC and Directives 97/7/EC and 98/27/EC.

9B   Regulation (EC) No 261/2004 of the European Parliament and of the Council of 11 February 2004 establishing common rules on compensation and assistance to air passengers in the event of denied boarding and of cancellation or of long delay of flights.]

[9C   Directive 2005/29/EC of the European Parliament and of the Council of 11
May 2005 concerning unfair business-to-consumer commercial practices in the
internal market.
(9D)   Directive 2008/48/EC of the European Parliament and of the Council of
23 April 2008 on credit agreements for consumers and repealing Council Directive
87/102/EEC.]

PART 2
PROVISIONS OF DIRECTIVES

10   Articles 10 to 21 of Council Directive 89/552/EEC of 3 October 1989 on the
co-ordination of certain provisions laid down by law, regulation or administrative
action in Member States concerning the pursuit of television broadcasting activities
as amended by Directive 97/36/EC.
[11   [Articles 86 to 100] of the Directive 2001/83/EC of the European Parliament and of the Council of 6 November 2001 on the Community Code relating to
medicinal products for human use as read with—
    (a)   Directive 2004/24/EC of the European Parliament and of the Council
amending, as regards traditional herbal medicinal products, the code, and
    (b)   Directive 2004/27/EC of the European Parliament and of the Council
also amending the code.]

BANKRUPTCY AND DILIGENCE ETC (SCOTLAND) ACT 2007
(2007 asp 3)

PART 5
INHIBITION

Creation

**146   Certain decrees and documents of debt to authorise inhibition without
need for letters of inhibition**
(1)   Inhibition in execution is competent to enforce—
    (a)   payment of a debt constituted by a decree or document of debt;
    (b)   subject to subsection (2) below, an obligation to perform a particular act
(other than payment) contained in a decree.
(2)   Inhibition under subsection (1)(b) above is competent only if the decree is a
decree—
    (a)   in an action containing an alternative conclusion or crave for payment of
a sum other than by way of expenses; or
    (b)   for specific implement of an obligation to convey heritable property to
the creditor or to grant in the creditor's favour a real right in security, or some
other right, over such property.
(3)–(5)   [*amending provisions*]
(6)   It is not competent for the Court of Session to grant letters of inhibition.
(7)   In a case where inhibition is executed under subsection (1)(b) above—
    (a)   sections 165 and 166 of this Act do not apply; and
    (b)   sections 158, 159, 160 and 163 of this Act have effect as if references to a
'debtor' or 'creditor' were references to the debtor or creditor in the obligation.
(8)   In this Part—
'decree' has the meaning given by section 221 of this Act, except that paragraphs
(c), (g) and (h) of the definition of 'decree' in that section do not apply; and
    'document of debt' has the meaning given by section 221 of this Act.
(9)   The Scottish Ministers may by order modify the definitions of 'decree' and
'document of debt' in subsection (8) above by—

(a)   adding types of decree or document to;

(b)   removing types of decree or document from; or

(c)   varying the description of,

the types of decree or document to which those definitions apply.

147   Provision of debt advice and information package when executing inhibition

Where the debtor is an individual, a schedule of inhibition served in execution of an inhibition under section 146(1) of this Act (other than an inhibition such as is mentioned in section 146(2)(b)) must be accompanied with a debt advice and information package.

148   Registration of inhibition

(1)   An inhibition is registered only by registering—

(a)   the schedule of inhibition; and

(b)   the certificate of execution of the inhibition,

in the Register of Inhibitions.

(2)   References in any enactment to registering or, as the case may be, recording an inhibition must, unless the context otherwise requires, be construed as references to registration in accordance with subsection (1) above.

(3)   The—

(a)   schedule of inhibition; and

(b)   certificate of execution of the inhibition,

must be in (or as nearly as may be in) the form prescribed by the Scottish Ministers by regulations.

149   [Amends Titles to Land Consolidation (Scotland) Act 1868.]

Effect

150   Property affected by inhibition

(1)   Subject to section 153 of this Act, inhibition may affect any heritable property.

(2)   Any enactment or rule of law by virtue of which inhibition may affect other property ceases to have effect.

(3)   For the purposes of subsection (1) above and section 157 of the 1868 Act, a person acquires property at the beginning of the day on which the deed conveying or otherwise granting a real right in the property is delivered to that person.

151   Effect on inhibition to enforce obligation when alternative decree granted

Where—

(a)   an inhibition is executed to enforce a decree such as is mentioned in section 146(2)(a) of this Act; and

(b)   decree is subsequently granted in terms of the alternative conclusion or crave mentioned in that section,

the inhibition continues to have effect for the purposes of enforcing payment of the debt constituted by that subsequent decree.

152   Effect of conversion of limited inhibition on the dependence to inhibition in execution

[(1)]   [Subject to subsection (2) below,] where—

(a)   a creditor obtains a decree for payment of all or part of a principal sum concluded or craved for in proceedings on the dependence of which warrant for inhibition was granted; and

(b)   the warrant was limited to specified property by virtue of section 15J(b) of the 1987 Act (property affected by inhibition on dependence),

[any inhibition on the dependence which, on decree, becomes an inhibition in execution of that decree, is no longer limited to that property].

[(2) Subsection (1) above has effect from the beginning of the day on which—
(a) an extract of the decree (or a copy of the interlocutor certified by the clerk of court); and
(b) a notice in (or as nearly as may be in) the form set out in the Schedule to the Bankruptcy and Diligence etc (Scotland) Act 2007 (Inhibition) Order 2009,
are registered in the Register of Inhibitions.]

153 Property affected by inhibition to enforce obligation to convey heritable property

Where a decree such as is mentioned in section 146(2)(b) of this Act is granted, any inhibition executed to enforce that decree is limited to the property to which the decree relates.

154 Inhibition not to confer a preference in ranking

(1) An inhibition does not confer any preference in any—
(a) sequestration;
(b) insolvency proceedings; or
(c) other process in which there is ranking.
(2) Subsection (1) above does not affect any preference claimed in—
(a) a sequestration;
(b) insolvency proceedings; or
(c) any other process,
where the inhibition has effect before this section comes into force.
(3) For the avoidance of doubt, in this section, 'other process' includes the process, under section 27(1) of the Conveyancing and Feudal Reform (Scotland) Act 1970 (c 35), of applying the proceeds of sale where a creditor in a standard security has effected a sale of the security subjects.
(4) In this section, 'insolvency proceedings' means—
(a) winding up;
(b) receivership;
(c) administration; and
(d) proceedings in relation to a company voluntary arrangement,
within the meaning of the Insolvency Act 1986 (c 45).

Termination

. . .

157 Inhibition terminated by payment of full amount owing

(1) This section applies where—
(a) an inhibition executed to enforce payment of a debt has effect; and
(b) a sum is paid, in respect of the debt constituted by the decree or document of debt authorising the inhibition, to the creditor, a judicial officer or any other person who has authority to receive payment on behalf of the creditor.
(2) Where the sum paid amounts to the sum of—
(a) the debt (including any interest due under the decree or document of debt);
(b) the expenses incurred by the creditor in executing an inhibition (referred to in this section and in sections 165 and 166 as the 'inhibition expenses'); and
(c) the expenses of discharging the inhibition,
the inhibition ceases to have effect.
(3) Any rule of law to the effect that an inhibition ceases to have effect on payment or tender of the debt constituted by the decree or document of debt is abolished.
(4) This section and sections 165 and 166 of this Act do not apply to an inhibition on the dependence of an action.

158   Inhibition terminated by compliance with obligation to perform
Where—
    (a)   an inhibition executed to enforce an obligation to perform a particular act (other than payment) contained in a decree has effect; and
    (b)   the debtor has complied with the decree,
the inhibition ceases to have effect.

159   Termination of inhibition when property acquired by third party
    (1)   Notwithstanding section 160 of this Act, an inhibition ceases to have effect (and is treated as never having had effect) in relation to property if a person acquires the property (or a right in the property) in good faith and for adequate consideration.
    (2)   For the purposes of subsection (1) above, a person acquires property (or a right in the property) when the deed conveying (or granting the right in) the property is delivered to the person.
    (3)   An acquisition under subsection (1) above may be from the inhibited debtor or any other person who has acquired the property or right (regardless of whether that person acquired in good faith or for value).
    (4)   For the purposes of subsection (1) above, a person is presumed to have acted in good faith if the person—
    (a)   is unaware of the inhibition; and
    (b)   has taken all reasonable steps to discover the existence of an inhibition affecting the property.

Breach

160   Breach of inhibition
An inhibited debtor breaches the inhibition when the debtor delivers a deed—
    (a)   conveying; or
    (b)   otherwise granting a right in,
property over which the inhibition has effect to a person other than the inhibiting creditor.

161   Prescription of right to reduce transactions in breach of inhibition
For the avoidance of doubt, section 8(1) of the Prescription and Limitation (Scotland) Act 1973 (c 52) (extinction of certain rights relating to property by prescriptive period of 20 years) applies to the right of an inhibitor to have a deed granted in breach of an inhibition reduced.

163   Reduction of lease granted in breach of inhibition
    (1)   This section applies where an inhibited debtor grants a lease of property affected by the inhibition.
    (2)   A lease which, on the date an action of reduction of the lease is raised, has an unexpired duration of not less than 5 years is reducible.
    (3)   A lease which, on the date an action of reduction of the lease is raised, has an unexpired duration of less than 5 years may be reduced only if the Court of Session is satisfied that it would be fair and reasonable in all the circumstances to do so.
    (4)   In calculating the unexpired duration of a lease for the purposes of subsections (2) and (3) above—
    (a)   any provision in the lease (however expressed) enabling the lease to be terminated earlier than the date on which the lease would otherwise terminate must be disregarded; and
    (b)   where the lease includes provision (however expressed) requiring the landlord to renew it, the duration of any such renewed lease must be added to the duration of the original lease.

General and miscellaneous

165   Expenses of inhibition
(1)   Subject to subsection (3) below, the inhibition expenses are chargeable against the debtor.
(2)   Inhibition expenses are recoverable from the debtor by land attachment or residual attachment executed for the purpose of enforcing payment of the debt to which the inhibition relates but not by any other legal process.
(3)   Where a creditor has executed an inhibition, the expenses of only one further inhibition in relation to the debt to which the first inhibition relates are chargeable against the debtor as inhibition expenses.
(4)   For the purposes of a sequestration or other process in which there is ranking, the inhibition expenses must be treated as part of the debt constituted by the decree or document of debt authorising the inhibition.

166   Ascription
(1)   This section applies where—
   (a)   an inhibition has effect; and
   (b)   any sums are paid to account of the sums recoverable from the debtor by virtue of the decree or document of debt authorising the inhibition.
(2)   Such sums must be ascribed to the following in the order in which they are mentioned—
   (a)   the expenses which are chargeable against the debtor incurred in respect of any diligence (other than the inhibition) authorised by the decree or document of debt;
   (b)   the inhibition expenses;
   (c)   any interest which has accrued, at the date on which the inhibition takes effect, on the debt constituted by the decree or document of debt;
   (d)   the debt constituted by the decree or document of debt together with such interest as has accrued after the date on which the inhibition takes effect.

168   Inhibition effective against judicial factor
(1)   Notwithstanding the appointment of a judicial factor on a debtor's estate, an inhibition has effect.
(2)   But subsection (1) above does not apply in a case where—
   (a)   a judicial factor is appointed under section 11A of the Judicial Factors (Scotland) Act 1889 (c 39) (application for judicial factor on deceased person's estate); and
   (b)   the inhibition was effective against the debtor prior to the debtor's death.

PART 11
MAILLS AND DUTIES, SEQUESTRATION FOR RENT AND LANDLORD'S HYPOTHEC

. . .

Landlord's hypothec and sequestration for rent

208   Abolition of sequestration for rent and restriction of landlord's hypothec
(1)   The diligence of sequestration for rent is abolished and any enactment or rule of law enabling an action of sequestration for rent to be raised ceases to have effect.
(2)   Notwithstanding that abolition, the landlord's hypothec—
   (a)   continues, subject to subsections (3) to (9) below, as a right in security over corporeal moveable property kept in or on the subjects let; and—
   (b)   ranks accordingly in any—
      (i)   sequestration;

    (ii)   insolvency proceedings; or

    (iii) other process in which there is ranking,

in respect of that property.

(3)   The landlord's hypothec no longer arises in relation to property which is kept—

    (a)   in a dwellinghouse;

    (b)   on agricultural land; or

    (c)   on a croft.

(4)   It no longer arises in relation to property which is owned by a person other than the tenant.

(5)   Property which is acquired by a person from the tenant—

    (a)   in good faith; or

    (b)   where the property is acquired after an interdict prohibiting the tenant from disposing of or removing items secured by the hypothec has been granted in favour the landlord, in good faith and for value,

ceases to be subject to the hypothec upon acquisition by the person.

(6)   Subsection (5)(b) above does not affect the tenant's liability for breach of the interdict.

(7)   Where property is owned in common by the tenant and a third party, any right of hypothec arises only to the extent of the tenant's interest in that property.

(8)   The landlord's hypothec—

    (a)   is security for rent due and unpaid only; and

    (b)   subsists for so long as that rent remains unpaid.

(9)   Any enactment or rule of law relating to the landlord's hypothec ceases to have effect in so far as it is inconsistent with subsections (2) to (8) above.

(10)   Subsections (1) to (3), (8) and (9) above do not affect an action of sequestration for rent brought before this section comes into force.

(11)   Subsection (3) above does not affect a landlord's right of hypothec which arose before and subsists on the coming into force of this section.

(12)   In subsection (2) above, 'insolvency proceedings' means—

    (a)   winding up;

    (b)   receivership;

    (c)   administration; and

    (d)   proceedings in relation to a company voluntary arrangement,

within the meaning of the Insolvency Act 1986 (c 45).

(13)   In subsection (3) above—

'agricultural land' has the same meaning as in section 1(2) of the Agricultural Holdings (Scotland) Act 1991 (c 55);

'croft' has the same meaning as in section 3(1) of the Crofters (Scotland) Act 1993 (c 44); and

'dwellinghouse' includes—

    (a)   a mobile home or other place used as a dwelling; and

    (b)   any other structure or building used in connection with the dwellinghouse.

PART II
STATUTORY INSTRUMENTS

COMMERCIAL AGENTS (COUNCIL DIRECTIVE) REGULATIONS 1993
(SI 1993/3053)

PART I
GENERAL

2 Interpretation, application and extent

(1) In these Regulations—

'commercial agent' means a self-employed intermediary who has continuing authority to negotiate the sale or purchase of goods on behalf of another person (the 'principal'), or to negotiate and conclude the sale or purchase of goods on behalf of and in the name of that principal; but shall be understood as not including in particular:

(i) a person who, in his capacity as an officer of a company or association, is empowered to enter into commitments binding on that company or association;

(ii) a partner who is lawfully authorised to enter into commitments binding on his partners;

(iii) a person who acts as an insolvency practitioner (as that expression is defined in section 388 of the Insolvency Act 1986) or the equivalent in any other jurisdiction;

'commission' means any part of the remuneration of a commercial agent which varies with the number or value of business transactions;

['EEA Agreement' means the Agreement on the European Economic Area signed at Oporto on 2nd May 1992 as adjusted by the Protocol signed at Brussels on 17th March 1993;

'member State' includes a State which is a contracting party to the EEA Agreement;]

'restraint of trade clause' means an agreement restricting the business activities of a commercial agent following termination of the agency contract.

(2) These Regulations do not apply to—

(a) commercial agents whose activities are unpaid;

(b) commercial agents when they operate on commodity exchanges or in the commodity market;

(c) the Crown Agents for Overseas Governments and Administrations, as set up under the Crown Agents Act 1979, or its subsidiaries.

(3) The provisions of the Schedule to these Regulations have effect for the purpose of determining the persons whose activities as commercial agents are to be considered secondary.

(4) These Regulations shall not apply to the persons referred to in paragraph (3) above.

(5) These Regulations do not extend to Northern Ireland.

PART II
RIGHTS AND OBLIGATIONS

3 Duties of a commercial agent to his principal

(1)   In performing his activities a commercial agent must look after the interests of his principal and act dutifully and in good faith.

(2)   In particular, a commercial agent must—

    (a)   make proper efforts to negotiate and, where appropriate, conclude the transactions he is instructed to take care of;

    (b)   communicate to his principal all the necessary information available to him;

    (c)   comply with reasonable instructions given by his principal.

4 Duties of a principal to his commercial agent

(1)   In his relations with his commercial agent a principal must act dutifully and in good faith.

(2)   In particular, a principal must—

    (a)   provide his commercial agent with the necessary documentation relating to the goods concerned;

    (b)   obtain for his commercial agent the information necessary for the performance of the agency contract, and in particular notify his commercial agent within a reasonable period once he anticipates that the volume of commercial transactions will be significantly lower than that which the commercial agent could normally have expected.

(3)   A principal shall, in addition, inform his commercial agent within a reasonable period of his acceptance or refusal of, and of any non-execution by him of, a commercial transaction which the commercial agent has procured for him.

5 Prohibition on derogation from regulations 3 and 4 and consequence of breach

(1)   The parties may not derogate from regulations 3 and 4 above.

(2)   The law applicable to the contract shall govern the consequence of breach of the rights and obligations under regulations 3 and 4 above.

PART III
REMUNERATION

6 Form and amount of remuneration in absence of agreement

(1)   In the absence of any agreement as to remuneration between the parties, a commercial agent shall be entitled to the remuneration that commercial agents appointed for the goods forming the subject of his agency contract are customarily allowed in the place where he carries on his activities and, if there is no such customary practice, a commercial agent shall be entitled to reasonable remuneration taking into account all the aspects of the transaction.

(2)   This regulation is without prejudice to the application of any enactment or rule of law concerning the level of remuneration.

(3)   Where a commercial agent is not remunerated (wholly or in part) by commission, regulations 7 to 12 below shall not apply.

7 Entitlement to commission on transactions concluded during agency contract

(1)   A commercial agent shall be entitled to commission on commercial transactions concluded during the period covered by the agency contract—

    (a)   where the transaction has been concluded as a result of his action; or

    (b)   where the transaction is concluded with a third party whom he has previously acquired as a customer for transactions of the same kind.

(2)   A commercial agent shall also be entitled to commission on transactions concluded during the period covered by the agency contract where he has an

exclusive right to a specific geographical area or to a specific group of customers and where the transaction has been entered into with a customer belonging to that area or group.

8   Entitlement to commission on transactions concluded after agency contract has terminated
Subject to regulation 9 below, a commercial agent shall be entitled to commission on commercial transactions concluded after the agency contract has terminated if—
(a)   the transaction is mainly attributable to his efforts during the period covered by the agency contract and if the transaction was entered into within a reasonable period after that contract terminated; or
(b)   in accordance with the conditions mentioned in regulation 7 above, the order of the third party reached the principal or the commercial agent before the agency contract terminated.

9   Apportionment of commission between new and previous commercial agents
(1)   A commercial agent shall not be entitled to the commission referred to in regulation 7 above if that commission is payable, by virtue of regulation 8 above, to the previous commercial agent, unless it is equitable because of the circumstances for the commission to be shared between the commercial agents.
(2)   The principal shall be liable for any sum due under paragraph (1) above to the person entitled to it in accordance with that paragraph, and any sum which the other commercial agent receives to which he is not entitled shall be refunded to the principal.

10   When commission due and date for payment
(1)   Commission shall become due as soon as, and to the extent that, one of the following circumstances occurs:
(a)   the principal has executed the transaction; or
(b)   the principal should, according to his agreement with the third party, have executed the transaction; or
(c)   the third party has executed the transaction.
(2)   Commission shall become due at the latest when the third party has executed his part of the transaction or should have done so if the principal had executed his part of the transaction, as he should have.
(3)   The commission shall be paid not later than on the last day of the month following the quarter in which it became due, and, for the purposes of these Regulations, unless otherwise agreed between the parties, the first quarter period shall run from the date the agency contract takes effect, and subsequent periods shall run from that date in the third month thereafter or the beginning of the fourth month, whichever is the sooner.
(4)   Any agreement to derogate from paragraphs (2) and (3) above to the detriment of the commercial agent shall be void.

11   Extinction of right to commission
(1)   The right to commission can be extinguished only if and to the extent that—
(a)   it is established that the contract between the third party and the principal will not be executed; and
(b)   that fact is due to a reason for which the principal is not to blame.
(2)   Any commission which the commercial agent has already received shall be refunded if the right to it is extinguished.
(3)   any agreement to derogate from paragraph (1) above to the detriment of the commercial agent shall be void.

12   Periodic supply of information as to commission due and right of inspection of principal's books

(1)   The principal shall supply his commercial agent with a statement of the commission due, not later than the last day of the month following the quarter in which the commission has become due, and such statement shall set out the main components used in calculating the amount of the commission.

(2)   A commercial agent shall be entitled to demand that he be provided with all the information (and in particular an extract from the books) which is available to his principal and which he needs in order to check the amount of the commission due to him.

(3)   Any agreement to derogate from paragraphs (1) and (2) above shall be void.

(4)   Nothing in this regulation shall remove or restrict the effect of, or prevent reliance upon, any enactment or rule of law which recognises the right of an agent to inspect the books of a principal.

PART IV
CONCLUSION AND TERMINATION OF THE AGENCY CONTRACT

13   Right to signed written statement of terms of agency contract

(1)   The commercial agent and principal shall each be entitled to receive from the other, on request, a signed written document setting out the terms of the agency contract including any terms subsequently agreed.

(2)   Any purported waiver of the right referred to in paragraph (1) above shall be void.

14   Conversion of agency contract after expiry of fixed period

An agency contract for a fixed period which continues to be performed by both parties after that period has expired shall be deemed to be converted into an agency contract for an indefinite period.

15   Minimum periods of notice for termination of agency contract

(1)   Where an agency contract is concluded for an indefinite period either party may terminate it by notice.

(2)   The period of notice shall be—
   (a)   1 month for the first year of the contract;
   (b)   2 months for the second year commenced;
   (c)   3 months for the third year commenced and for the subsequent years;
and the parties may not agree on any shorter periods of notice.

(3)   If the parties agree on longer periods than those laid down in paragraph (2) above, the period of notice to be observed by the principal must not be shorter than that to be observed by the commercial agent.

(4)   Unless otherwise agreed by the parties, the end of the period of notice must coincide with the end of a calendar month.

(5)   The provisions of this regulation shall also apply to an agency contract for a fixed period where it is converted under regulation 14 above into an agency contract for an indefinite period subject to the proviso that the earlier fixed period must be taken into account in the calculation of the period of notice.

16   Savings with regard to immediate termination

These Regulations shall not affect the application of any enactment or rule of law which provides for the immediate termination of the agency contract—
   (a)   because of the failure of one party to carry out all or part of his obligations under that contract; or
   (b)   where exceptional circumstances arise.

17 Entitlement of commercial agent to indemnity or compensation on termination of agency contract

(1) This regulation has effect for the purpose of ensuring that the commercial agent is, after termination of the agency contract, indemnified in accordance with paragraphs (3) to (5) below or compensated for damage in accordance with paragraphs (6) and (7) below.

(2) Except where the agency [contract] otherwise provides, the commercial agent shall be entitled to be compensated rather than indemnified.

(3) Subject to paragraph (9) and to regulation 18 below, the commercial agent shall be entitled to an indemnity if and to the extent that—

(a) he has brought the principal new customers or has significantly increased the volume of business with existing customers and the principal continues to derive substantial benefits from the business with such customers; and

(b) the payment of this indemnity is equitable having regard to all the circumstances and, in particular, the commission lost by the commercial agent on the business transacted with such customers.

(4) The amount of the indemnity shall not exceed a figure equivalent to an indemnity for one year calculated from the commercial agent's average annual remuneration over the preceding five years and if the contract goes back less than five years the indemnity shall be calculated on the average for the period in question.

(5) The grant of an indemnity as mentioned above shall not prevent the commercial agent from seeking damages.

(6) Subject to paragraph (9) and to regulation 18 below, the commercial agent shall be entitled to compensation for the damage he suffers as a result of the termination of his relations with his principal.

(7) For the purpose of these Regulations such damage shall be deemed to occur particularly when the termination takes place in either or both of the following circumstances, namely circumstances which—

(a) deprive the commercial agent of the commission which proper performance of the agency contract would have procured for him whilst providing his principal with substantial benefits linked to the activities of the commercial agent; or

(b) have not enabled the commercial agent to amortize the costs and expenses that he had incurred in the performance of the agency contract on the advice of his principal.

(8) Entitlement to the indemnity or compensation for damage as provided for under paragraphs (2) to (7) above shall also arise where the agency contract is terminated as a result of the death of the commercial agent.

(9) The commercial agent shall lose his entitlement to the indemnity or compensation for damage in the instances provided for in paragraphs (2) to (8) above if within one year following termination of his agency contract he has not notified his principal that he intends pursuing his entitlement.

18 Grounds for excluding payment of indemnity or compensation under regulation 17

The [indemnity or] compensation referred to in regulation 17 above shall not be payable to the commercial agent where—

(a) the principal has terminated the agency contract because of default attributable to the commercial agent which would justify immediate termination of the agency contract pursuant to regulation 16 above; or

(b) the commercial agent has himself terminated the agency contract, unless such termination is justified—

(i) by circumstances attributable to the principal, or

(ii) on grounds of the age, infirmity or illness of the commercial agent in consequence of which he cannot reasonably be required to continue his activities; or

(c)   the commercial agent, with the agreement of his principal, assigns his rights and duties under the agency contract to another person.

19   Prohibition on derogation from regulations 17 and 18

The parties may not derogate from regulations 17 and 18 to the detriment of the commercial agent before the agency contract expires.

20   Restraint of trade clauses

(1)   A restraint of trade clause shall be valid only if and to the extent that—

(a)   it is concluded in writing; and

(b)   it relates to the geographical area or the group of customers and the geographical area entrusted to the commercial agent and to the kind of goods covered by his agency under the contract.

(2)   A restraint of trade clause shall be valid for not more than two years after termination of the agency contract.

(3)   Nothing in this regulation shall affect any enactment or rule of law which imposes other restrictions on the validity or enforceability of restraint of trade clauses or which enables a court to reduce the obligations on the parties resulting from such clauses.

PART V
MISCELLANEOUS AND SUPPLEMENTAL

21   Disclosure of information

Nothing in these Regulations shall require information to be given where such disclosure would be contrary to public policy.

22   Service of notice etc

(1)   Any notice, statement or other document to be given or supplied to a commercial agent or to be given or supplied to the principal under these Regulations may be so given or supplied:

(a)   by delivering it to him;

(b)   by leaving it at his proper address addressed to him by name;

(c)   by sending it by post to him addressed either to his registered address or to the address of his registered or principal office;

or by any other means provided for in the agency contract.

(2)   Any such notice, statement or document may—

(a)   in the case of a body corporate, be given or served on the secretary or clerk of that body;

(b)   in the case of a partnership, be given to or served on any partner or on any person having the control or management of the partnership business.

23   Transitional provisions

(1)   Notwithstanding any provision in an agency contract made before 1st January 1994, these Regulations shall apply to that contract after that date and, accordingly any provision which is inconsistent with these Regulations shall have effect subject to them.

(2)   Nothing in these Regulations shall affect the rights and liabilities of a commercial agent or a principal which have accrued before 1st January 1994.

THE SCHEDULE   Regulation 2(3)

1   The activities of a person as a commercial agent are to be considered
secondary where it may reasonably be taken that the primary purpose of the
arrangement with his principal is other than as set out in paragraph 2 below.

2   An arrangement falls within this paragraph if—
    (a)   the business of the principal is the sale, or as the case may be purchase,
of goods of a particular kind; and
    (b)   the goods concerned are such that—
        (i)   transactions are normally individually negotiated and concluded on
a commercial basis, and
        (ii)   procuring a transaction on one occasion is likely to lead to further
transactions in those goods with that customer on future occasions, or to
transactions in those goods with other customers in the same geographical
area or among the same group of customers, and
that accordingly it is in the commercial interests of the principal in developing the
market in those goods to appoint a representative to such customers with a view
to the representative devoting effort, skill and expenditure from his own resources
to that end.

3   The following are indications that an arrangement falls within paragraph 2
above, and the absence of any of them is an indication to the contrary—
    (a)   the principal is the manufacturer, importer or distributor of the goods;
    (b)   the goods are specifically identified with the principal in the market in
question rather than, or to a greater extent than, with any other person;
    (c)   the agent devotes substantially the whole of his time to representative
activities (whether for one principal or for a number of principals whose
interests are not conflicting);
    (d)   the goods are not normally available in the market in question other than
by means of the agent;
    (e)   the arrangement is described as one of commercial agency.

4   The following are indications that an arrangement does not fall within paragraph 2 above—
    (a)   promotional material is supplied direct to potential customers;
    (b)   persons are granted agencies without reference to existing agents in a
particular area or in relation to a particular group;
    (c)   customers normally select the goods for themselves and merely place
their orders through the agent.

5   The activities of the following categories of persons are presumed, unless the
contrary is established, not to fall within paragraph 2 above—
    Mail order catalogue agents for consumer goods.
    Consumer credit agents.

UNFAIR TERMS IN CONSUMER CONTRACTS REGULATIONS 1999
(SI 1999/2083)

3   Interpretation

(1)   In these Regulations—

'the Community' means the European Community;

'consumer' means any natural person who, in contracts covered by these Regulations, is acting for purposes which are outside his trade, business or profession;

'court' in relation to England and Wales and Northern Ireland means a county court or the High Court, and in relation to Scotland, the Sheriff or the Court of Session;

'Director' means the Director General of Fair Trading;*

'EEA Agreement' means the Agreement on the European Economic Area signed at Oporto on 2nd May 1992 as adjusted by the protocol signed at Brussels on 17th March 1993;

'Member State' means a State which is a contracting party to the EEA Agreement;

'notified' means notified in writing;

'qualifying body' means a person specified in Schedule 1;

'seller or supplier' means any natural or legal person who, in contracts covered by these Regulations, is acting for purposes relating to his trade, business or profession, whether publicly owned or privately owned;

'unfair terms' means the contractual terms referred to in regulation 5.

[(1A)   The references—

(a)   in regulation 4(1) to a seller or a supplier, and

(b)   in regulation 8(1) to a seller or supplier,

include references to a distance supplier and to an intermediary.

(1B)   In paragraph (1A) and regulation 5(6)—

'distance supplier' means—

(a)   a supplier under a distance contract within the meaning of the Financial Services (Distance Marketing) Regulations 2004, or

(b)   a supplier of unsolicited financial services within regulation 15 of those Regulations; and

'intermediary' has the same meaning as in those Regulations.]

(2)   In the application of these Regulations to Scotland for references to an 'injunction' or an 'interim injunction' there shall be substituted references to an 'interdict' or 'interim interdict' respectively.

4   Terms to which these Regulations apply

(1)   These Regulations apply in relation to unfair terms in contracts concluded between a seller or a supplier and a consumer.

(2)   These Regulations do not apply to contractual terms which reflect—

(a)   mandatory statutory or regulatory provisions (including such provisions under the law of any Member State or in Community legislation having effect in the United Kingdom without further enactment);

(b)   the provisions or principles of international conventions to which the Member States or the Community are party.

5   Unfair terms

(1)   A contractual term which has not been individually negotiated shall be regarded as unfair if, contrary to the requirement of good faith, it causes a significant imbalance in the parties' rights and obligations arising under the contract, to the detriment of the consumer.

(2)   A term shall always be regarded as not having been individually negotiated

---

*All references to 'the Director' have effect as if they were references to 'the OFT': Enterprise Act 2002, s 2.

where it has been drafted in advance and the consumer has therefore not been able to influence the substance of the term.

(3)   Notwithstanding that a specific term or certain aspects of it in a contract has been individually negotiated, these Regulations shall apply to the rest of a contract if an overall assessment of it indicates that it is a pre-formulated standard contract.

(4)   It shall be for any seller or supplier who claims that a term was individually negotiated to show that it was.

(5)   Schedule 2 to these Regulations contains an indicative and non-exhaustive list of the terms which may be regarded as unfair.

[(6)   Any contractual term providing that the consumer bears the burden of proof in respect of showing that the supplier complied with any or all of the obligations upon him resulting from the Directive and any rule or enactment implementing it shall always be regarded as unfair.

(7)   In paragraph (6)—

'the Directive' means Directive 2002/65/EC of the European Parliament and of the Council of 23 September 2002 concerning the distance marketing of consumer financial services and amending Council Directive 90/619/EEC and Directive 97/7/EC and 98/27/EC; and

'rule' means a rule made by the Financial Services Authority under the Financial Services and Markets Act 2000 or by a designated professional body within the meaning of section 326(2) of that Act.]

6   Assessment of unfair terms

(1)   Without prejudice to regulation 12, the unfairness of a contractual term shall be assessed, taking into account the nature of the goods or services for which the contract was concluded and by referring, at the time of conclusion of the contract, to all the circumstances attending the conclusion of the contract and to all the other terms of the contract or of another contract on which it is dependent.

(2)   In so far as it is in plain intelligible language, the assessment of fairness of a term shall not relate—

(a)   to the definition of the main subject matter of the contract, or

(b)   to the adequacy of the price or remuneration, as against the goods or services supplied in exchange.

7   Written contracts

(1)   A seller or supplier shall ensure that any written term of a contract is expressed in plain, intelligible language.

(2)   If there is doubt about the meaning of a written term, the interpretation which is most favourable to the consumer shall prevail but this rule shall not apply in proceedings brought under regulation 12.

8   Effect of unfair term

(1)   An unfair term in a contract concluded with a consumer by a seller or supplier shall not be binding on the consumer.

(2)   The contract shall continue to bind the parties if it is capable of continuing in existence without the unfair term.

9   Choice of law clauses

These Regulations shall apply notwithstanding any contract term which applies or purports to apply the law of a non-Member State, if the contract has a close connection with the territory of the Member States.

10   Complaints—consideration by Director

(1)   It shall be the duty of the Director to consider any complaint made to him that any contract term drawn up for general use is unfair, unless—

(a)   the complaint appears to the Director to be frivolous or vexatious; or

(b)   a qualifying body has notified the Director that it agrees to consider the complaint.

(2)   The Director shall give reasons for his decision to apply or not to apply, as the case may be, for an injunction under regulation 12 in relation to any complaint which these Regulations require him to consider.

(3)   In deciding whether or not to apply for an injunction in respect of a term which the Director considers to be unfair, he may, if he considers it appropriate to do so, have regard to any undertakings given to him by or on behalf of any person as to the continued use of such a term in contracts concluded with consumers.

11   Complaints—consideration by qualifying bodies

(1)   If a qualifying body specified in Part One of Schedule I notifies the Director that it agrees to consider a complaint that any contract term drawn up for general use is unfair, it shall be under a duty to consider that complaint.

(2)   Regulation 10(2) and (3) shall apply to a qualifying body which is under a duty to consider a complaint as they apply to the Director.

12   Injunctions to prevent continued use of unfair terms

(1)   The Director or, subject to paragraph (2), any qualifying body may apply for an injunction (including an interim injunction) against any person appearing to the Director or that body to be using, or recommending use of, an unfair term drawn up for general use in contracts concluded with consumers.

(2)   A qualifying body may apply for an injunction only where—
(a)   it has notified the Director of its intention to apply at least fourteen days before the date on which the application is made, beginning with the date on which the notification was given; or
(b)   the Director consents to the application being made within a shorter period.

(3)   The court on an application under this regulation may grant an injunction on such terms as it thinks fit.

(4)   An injunction may relate not only to use of a particular contract term drawn up for general use but to any similar term, or a term having like effect, used or recommended for use by any person.

13   Powers of the Director and qualifying bodies to obtain documents and information

(1)   The Director may exercise the power conferred by this regulation for the purpose of—
(a)   facilitating his consideration of a complaint that a contract term drawn up for general use is unfair; or
(b)   ascertaining whether a person has complied with an undertaking or court order as to the continued use, or recommendation for use, of a term in contracts concluded with consumers.

(2)   A qualifying body specified in Part One of Schedule 1 may exercise the power conferred by this regulation for the purpose of—
(a)   facilitating its consideration of a complaint that a contract term drawn up for general use is unfair; or
(b)   ascertaining whether a person has complied with—
(i)   an undertaking given to it or to the court following an application by that body, or
(ii)   a court order made on an application by that body,
as to the continued use, or recommendation for use, of a term in contracts concluded with consumers.

(3)   The Director may require any person to supply to him, and a qualifying body specified in Part One of Schedule 1 may require any person to supply to it—
(a)   a copy of any document which that person has used or recommended for use, at the time the notice referred to in paragraph (4) below is given, as a pre-formulated standard contract in dealings with consumers;

(b)   information about the use, or recommendation for use, by that person of that document or any other such document in dealings with consumers.

(4)   The power conferred by this regulation is to be exercised by a notice in writing which may—

(a)   specify the way in which and the time within which it is to be complied with; and

(b)   be varied or revoked by a subsequent notice.

(5)   Nothing in this regulation compels a person to supply any document or information which he would be entitled to refuse to produce or give in civil proceedings before the court.

(6)   If a person makes default in complying with a notice under this regulation, the court may, on the application of the Director or of the qualifying body, make such order as the court thinks fit for requiring the default to be made good, and any such order may provide that all the costs or expenses of and incidental to the application shall be borne by the person in default or by any officers of a company or other association who are responsible for its default.

14   Notification of undertakings and orders to Director

A qualifying body shall notify the Director—

(a)   of any undertaking given to it by or on behalf of any person as to the continued use of a term which that body considers to be unfair in contracts concluded with consumers,

(b)   of the outcome of any application made by it under regulation 12, and of the terms of any undertaking given to, or order made by, the court;

(c)   of the outcome of any application made by it to enforce a previous order of the court.

15   Publication, information and advice

(1)   The Director shall arrange for the publication in such form and manner as he considers appropriate, of—

(a)   details of any undertaking or order notified to him under regulation 14;

(b)   details of any undertaking given to him by or on behalf of any persons to the continued use of a term which the Director considers to be unfair in contracts concluded with consumers;

(c)   details of any application made by him under regulation 12, and of the terms of any undertaking given to, or order made by, the court;

(d)   details of any application made by the Director to enforce a previous order of the court.

(2)   The Director shall inform any person on request whether a particular term to which these Regulations apply has been—

(a)   the subject of an undertaking given to the Director or notified to him by a qualifying body; or

(b)   the subject of an order of the court made upon application by him or notified to him by a qualifying body;

and shall give that person details of the undertaking or a copy of the order, as the case may be, together with a copy of any amendments which the person giving the undertaking has agreed to make to the term in question.

(3)   The Director may arrange for the dissemination in such form and manner as he considers appropriate of such information and advice concerning the operation of these Regulations as may appear to him to be expedient to give to the public and to all persons likely to be affected by these Regulations.

[16   The functions of the Financial Services Authority

The functions of the Financial Services Authority under these Regulations shall be treated as functions of the Financial Services Authority under the [Financial Services and Markets Act 2000].]

Regulation 3   SCHEDULE 1
                                 QUALIFYING BODIES

                                      PART ONE

[1   The Information Commissioner.
2   The Gas and Electricity Markets Authority.
3   The Director General of Electricity Supply for Northern Ireland.
4   The Director General of Gas for Northern Ireland.
5   [The Office of Communications.]
6   [The Water Services Authority.]
7   The Rail Regulator.
8   Every weights and measures authority in Great Britain.
9   The Department of Enterprise, Trade and Investment in Northern Ireland.
10   The Financial Services Authority.

                                      PART TWO

11   Consumers' Association.]

Regulation 5(5)   SCHEDULE 2
INDICATIVE AND NON-EXHAUSTIVE LIST OF TERMS WHICH MAY BE
                            REGARDED AS UNFAIR

    1   Terms which have the object or effect of—
    (a)   excluding or limiting the legal liability of a seller or supplier in the event of
the death of a consumer or personal injury to the latter resulting from an act or
omission of that seller or supplier;
    (b)   inappropriately excluding or limiting the legal rights of the consumer vis-à-
vis the seller or supplier or another party in the event of total or partial non-performance or inadequate performance by the seller or supplier of any of the contractual obligations, including the option of offsetting a debt owed to the seller or
supplier against any claim which the consumer may have against him;
    (c)   making an agreement binding on the consumer whereas provision of ser-
vices by the seller or supplier is subject to a condition whose realisation depends
on his own will alone;
    (d)   permitting the seller or supplier to retain sums paid by the consumer
where the latter decides not to conclude or perform the contract, without providing for the consumer to receive compensation of an equivalent amount from the
seller or supplier where the latter is the party cancelling the contract;
    (e)   requiring any consumer who fails to fulfil his obligation to pay a dis-
proportionately high sum in compensation;
    (f)   authorising the seller or supplier to dissolve the contract on a discretionary
basis where the same facility is not granted to the consumer, or permitting the
seller or supplier to retain the sums paid for services not yet supplied by him
where it is the seller or supplier himself who dissolves the contract;
    (g)   enabling the seller or supplier to terminate a contract of indeterminate
duration without reasonable notice except where there are serious grounds for
doing so;
    (h)   automatically extending a contract of fixed duration where the consumer
does not indicate otherwise, when the deadline fixed for the consumer to express
his desire not to extend the contract is unreasonably early;
    (i)   irrevocably binding the consumer to terms with which he had no real
opportunity of becoming acquainted before the conclusion of the contract;

(j)   enabling the seller or supplier to alter the terms of the contract unilaterally without a valid reason which is specified in the contract;

(k)   enabling the seller or supplier to alter unilaterally without a valid reason any characteristics of the product or service to be provided;

(l)   providing for the price of goods to be determined at the time of delivery or allowing a seller of goods or supplier of services to increase their price without in both cases giving the consumer the corresponding right to cancel the contract if the final price is too high in relation to the price agreed when the contract was concluded;

(m)   giving the seller or supplier the right to determine whether the goods or services supplied are in conformity with the contract, or giving him the exclusive right to interpret any term of the contract;

(n)   limiting the seller's or supplier's obligation to respect commitments undertaken by his agents or making his commitments subject to compliance with a particular formality;

(o)   obliging the consumer to fulfil all his obligations where the seller or supplier does not perform his;

(p)   giving the seller or supplier the possibility of transferring his rights and obligations under the contract, where this may serve to reduce the guarantees for the consumer, without the latter's agreement,

(q)   excluding or hindering the consumer's right to take legal action or exercise any other legal remedy, particularly by requiring the consumer to take disputes exclusively to arbitration not covered by legal provisions, unduly restricting the evidence available to him or imposing on him a burden of proof which, according to the applicable law, should lie with another party to the contract.

2   Scope of paragraphs 1(g), (j) and (1)—

(a)   Paragraph 1(g) is without hindrance to terms by which a supplier of financial services reserves the right to terminate unilaterally a contract of indeterminate duration without notice where there is a valid reason provided that the supplier is required to inform the other contracting party or parties thereof immediately.

(b)   Paragraph 1(j) is without hindrance to terms under which a supplier of financial services reserves the right to alter the rate of interest payable by the consumer or due to the latter, or the amount of other charges for financial services without notice where there is a valid reason, provided that the supplier is required to inform the other contracting party or parties thereof at the earliest opportunity and that the latter are free to dissolve the contract immediately.

Paragraph 1(j) is also without hindrance to terms under which a seller or supplier reserves the right to alter unilaterally the conditions of a contract of indeterminate duration, provided that he is required to inform the consumer with reasonable notice and that the consumer is free to dissolve the contract.

(c)   Paragraphs 1(g), (j) and (l) do not apply to:

—transactions in transferable securities, financial instruments and other products or services where the price is linked to fluctuations in a stock exchange quotation or index or a financial market rate that the seller or supplier does not control;

—contracts for the purchase or sale of foreign currency, traveller's cheques or international money orders denominated in foreign currency;

(d)   Paragraph 1(l) is without hindrance to price indexation clauses, where lawful, provided that the method by which prices vary is explicitly described.

CONSUMER PROTECTION (DISTANCE SELLING) REGULATIONS 2000
(SI 2000/2334)

3   Interpretation

(1)   In these Regulations—

['the 2000 Act' means the Financial Services and Markets Act 2000;]

[. . .]

'breach' means contravention by a supplier of a prohibition in, or failure to comply with a requirement of, these Regulations;

'business' includes a trade or profession;

'consumer' means any natural person who, in contracts to which these Regulations apply, is acting for purposes which are outside his business;

'court' in relation to England and Wales and Northern Ireland means a county court or the High Court, and in relation to Scotland means the Sheriff Court or the Court of Session;

'credit' includes a cash loan and any other form of financial accommodation, and for this purpose 'cash' includes money in any form;

'Director' means the Director General of Fair Trading;*

'distance contract' means any contract concerning goods or services concluded between a supplier and a consumer under an organised distance sales or service provision scheme run by the supplier who, for the purpose of the contract, makes exclusive use of one or more means of distance communication up to and including the moment at which the contract is concluded;

'EEA Agreement' means the Agreement on the European Economic Area signed at Oporto on 2 May 1992 as adjusted by the Protocol signed at Brussels on 17 March 1993;

'enactment' includes an enactment comprised in, or in an instrument made under, an Act of the Scottish Parliament;

'enforcement authority' means the Director, every weights and measures authority in Great Britain, and the Department of Enterprise, Trade and Investment in Northern Ireland;

'excepted contract' means a contract such as is mentioned in regulation 5(1);

['financial service' means any service of a banking, credit, insurance, personal pension, investment or payment nature;]

'means of distance communication' means any means which, without the simultaneous physical presence of the supplier and the consumer, may be used for the conclusion of a contract between those parties; and an indicative list of such means is contained in Schedule 1;

'Member State' means a State which is a contracting party to the EEA Agreement;

'operator of a means of communication' means any public or private person whose business involves making one or more means of distance communication available to suppliers;

'period for performance' has the meaning given by regulation 19(2);

'personal credit agreement' has the meaning given by regulation 14(8);

['regulated activity' means an activity which is a regulated activity within the meaning of section 22 of the 2000 Act, read with any relevant order under that section and Schedule 2 to that Act;]

'related credit agreement' has the meaning given by regulation 15(5);

'supplier' means any person who, in contracts to which these Regulations apply, is acting in his commercial or professional capacity; and

---

* All references to 'the Director' have effect as if they were references to 'the OFT': Enterprise Act 2002, s 2.

'working days' means all days other than Saturdays, Sundays and public holidays.

(2) In the application of these Regulations to Scotland, for references to an 'injunction' or an 'interim injunction' there shall be substituted references to an 'interdict' or an 'interim interdict' respectively.

4   Contracts to which these Regulations apply

These Regulations apply, subject to regulation 6, to distance contracts other than excepted contracts.

5   Excepted contracts

(1) The following are excepted contracts, namely any contract—

(a) for the sale or other disposition of an interest in land except for a rental agreement;

(b) for the construction of a building where the contract also provides for a sale or other disposition of an interest in land on which the building is constructed, except for a rental agreement;

(c) relating to financial services; [. . .]

(d) concluded by means of an automated vending machine or automated commercial premises;

(e) concluded with a telecommunications operator through the use of a public pay-phone;

(f) concluded at an auction.

(2) References in paragraph (1) to a rental agreement—

(a) if the land is situated in England and Wales, are references to any agreement which does not have to be made in writing (whether or not in fact made in writing) because of section 2(5)(a) of the Law of Property (Miscellaneous Provisions) Act 1989;

(b) if the land is situated in Scotland, are references to any agreement for the creation, transfer, variation or extinction of an interest in land, which does not have to be made in writing (whether or not in fact made in writing) as provided for in section 1(2) and (7) of the Requirements of Writing (Scotland) Act 1995; and

(c) if the land is situated in Northern Ireland, are references to any agreement which is not one to which section II of the Statute of Frauds, (Ireland) 1695 applies.

(3) Paragraph (2) shall not be taken to mean that a rental agreement in respect of land situated outside the United Kingdom is not capable of being a distance contract to which these Regulations apply.

[. . .]

6   Contracts to which only part of these Regulations apply

(1) Regulations 7 to 20 shall not apply to a contract which is a 'timeshare agreement' within the meaning of the Timeshare Act 1992 and to which that Act applies.

(2) Regulations 7 to 19(1) shall not apply to—

(a) contracts for the supply of food, beverages or other goods intended for everyday consumption supplied to the consumer's residence or to his workplace by regular roundsmen; or

(b) contracts for the provision of accommodation, transport, catering or leisure services, where the supplier undertakes, when the contract is concluded, to provide these services on a specific date or within a specific period.

(3) Regulations 19(2) to (8) and 20 do not apply to a contract for a 'package' within the meaning of the Package Travel, Package Holidays and Package Tours

Regulations 1992 which is sold or offered for sale in the territory of the Member States.

[(4)   Regulations 7 to 14, 17 to 20 and 25 do not apply to any contract which is made, and regulation 24 does not apply to any unsolicited services which are supplied, by an unauthorised person where the making or performance of that contract or the supply of those services, as the case may be, constitutes or is part of a regulated activity carried on by him.

(5)   Regulations 7 to 9, 17 to 20 and 25 do not apply to any contract which is made, and regulation 24 does not apply to any unsolicited services which are supplied, by an appointed representative where the making or performance of that contract or the supply of those services, as the case may be, constitutes or is part of a regulated activity carried on by him.]

7   Information required prior to the conclusion of the contract

(1)   Subject to paragraph (4), in good time prior to the conclusion of the contract the supplier shall—

    (a)   provide to the consumer the following information—

        (i)   the identity of the supplier and, where the contract requires payment in advance, the supplier's address;

        (ii)   a description of the main characteristics of the goods or services;

        (iii)   the price of the goods or services including all taxes;

        (iv)   delivery costs where appropriate;

        (v)   the arrangements for payment, delivery or performance;

        (vi)   the existence of a right of cancellation except in the cases referred to in regulation 13;

        (vii)   the cost of using the means of distance communication where it is calculated other than at the basic rate;

        (viii)   the period for which the offer or the price remains valid; and

        (ix)   where appropriate, the minimum duration of the contract, in the case of contracts for the supply of goods or services to be performed permanently or recurrently;

    (b)   inform the consumer if he proposes, in the event of the goods or services ordered by the consumer being unavailable, to provide substitute goods or services (as the case may be) of equivalent quality and price; and

    (c)   inform the consumer that the cost of returning any such substitute goods to the supplier in the event of cancellation by the consumer would be met by the supplier.

(2)   The supplier shall ensure that the information required by paragraph (1) is provided in a clear and comprehensible manner appropriate to the means of distance communication used, with due regard in particular to the principles of good faith in commercial transactions and the principles governing the protection of those who are unable to give their consent such as minors.

(3)   Subject to paragraph (4), the supplier shall ensure that his commercial purpose is made clear when providing the information required by paragraph (1).

(4)   In the case of a telephone communication, the identity of the supplier and the commercial purpose of the call shall be made clear at the beginning of the conversation with the consumer.

8   Written and additional information

(1)   Subject to regulation 9, the supplier shall provide to the consumer in writing, or in another durable medium which is available and accessible to the consumer, the information referred to in paragraph (2), either—

    (a)   prior to the conclusion of the contract, or

    (b)   thereafter, in good time and in any event—

        (i)   during the performance of the contract, in the case of services;

(ii)   at the latest at the time of delivery where goods not for delivery to third parties are concerned;
[. . .]
(2)   The information required to be provided by paragraph (1) is—
(a)   the information set out in paragraphs (i) to (vi) of regulation 7(1)(a);
(b)   information about the conditions and procedures for exercising the right to cancel under regulation 10, including—
(i)   where a term of the contract requires (or the supplier intends that it will require) that the consumer shall return the goods to the supplier in the event of cancellation, notification of that requirement;
(ii)   information as to whether the consumer or the supplier would be responsible under these Regulations for the cost of returning any goods to the supplier, or the cost of his recovering them, if the consumer cancels the contract under regulation 10;
[(iii)   in the case of a contract for the supply of services, information as to how the right to cancel may be affected by the consumer agreeing to performance of the services beginning before the end of the seven working day period referred to in regulation 12;]
(c)   the geographical address of the place of business of the supplier to which the consumer may address any complaints;
(d)   information about any after-sales services and guarantees; and
(e)   the conditions for exercising any contractual right to cancel the contract, where the contract is of an unspecified duration or a duration exceeding one year.
[. . .]

9   Services performed through the use of a means of distance communication

(1)   Regulation 8 shall not apply to a contract for the supply of services which are performed through the use of a means of distance communication, where those services are supplied on only one occasion and are invoiced by the operator of the means of distance communication.
(2)   But the supplier shall take all necessary steps to ensure that a consumer who is a party to a contract to which paragraph (1) applies is able to obtain the supplier's geographical address and the place of business to which the consumer may address any complaints.

10   Right to cancel

(1)   Subject to regulation 13, if within the cancellation period set out in regulations 11 and 12, the consumer gives a notice of cancellation to the supplier, or any other person previously notified by the supplier to the consumer as a person to whom notice of cancellation may be given, the notice of cancellation shall operate to cancel the contract.
(2)   Except as otherwise provided by these Regulations, the effect of a notice of cancellation is that the contract shall be treated as if it had not been made.
(3)   For the purposes of these Regulations, a notice of cancellation is a notice in writing or in another durable medium available and accessible to the supplier (or to the other person to whom it is given) which, however expressed, indicates the intention of the consumer to cancel the contract.
(4)   A notice of cancellation given under this regulation by a consumer to a supplier or other person is to be treated as having been properly given if the consumer—
(a)   leaves it at the address last known to the consumer and addressed to the supplier or other person by name (in which case it is to be taken to have been given on the day on which it was left);
(b)   sends it by post to the address last known to the consumer and addressed to the supplier or other person by name (in which case, it is to be taken to have been given on the day on which it was posted);

(c)   sends it by facsimile to the business facsimile number last known to the consumer (in which case it is to be taken to have been given on the day on which it is sent); or

(d)   sends it by electronic mail, to the business electronic mail address last known to the consumer (in which case it is to be taken to have been given on the day on which it is sent).

(5)   Where a consumer gives a notice in accordance with paragraph (4)(a) or (b) to a supplier who is a body corporate or a partnership, the notice is to be treated as having been properly given if—

(a)   in the case of a body corporate, it is left at the address of, or sent to, the secretary or clerk of that body; or

(b)   in the case of a partnership, it is left with or sent to a partner or a person having control or management of the partnership business.

11   Cancellation period in the case of contracts for the supply of goods

(1)   For the purposes of regulation 10, the cancellation period in the case of contracts for the supply of goods begins with the day on which the contract is concluded and ends as provided in paragraphs (2) to (5).

(2)   Where the supplier complies with regulation 8, the cancellation period ends on the expiry of the period of seven working days beginning with the day after the day on which the consumer receives the goods.

(3)   Where a supplier who has not complied with regulation 8 provides to the consumer the information referred to in regulation 8(2), and does so in writing or in another durable medium available and accessible to the consumer, within the period of three months beginning with the day after the day on which the consumer receives the goods, the cancellation period ends on the expiry of the period of seven working days beginning with the day after the day on which the consumer receives the information.

(4)   Where neither paragraph (2) nor (3) applies, the cancellation period ends on the expiry of the period of three months and seven working days beginning with the day after the day on which the consumer receives the goods.

(5)   In the case of contracts for goods for delivery to third parties, paragraphs (2) to (4) shall apply as if the consumer had received the goods on the day on which they were received by the third party.

12   Cancellation period in the case of contracts for the supply of services

(1)   For the purposes of regulation 10, the cancellation period in the case of contracts for the supply of services begins with the day on which the contract is concluded and ends as provided in paragraphs (2) to (4).

(2)   [Subject to paragraph (3A)] where the supplier complies with regulation 8 on or before the day on which the contract is concluded, the cancellation period ends on the expiry of the period of seven working days beginning with the day after the day on which the contract is concluded.

(3)   Where a supplier who has not complied with regulation 8 on or before the day on which the contract is concluded provides to the consumer the information referred to in regulation 8(2) [. . .], and does so in writing or in another durable medium available and accessible to the consumer, within the period of three months beginning with the day after the day on which the contract is concluded, the cancellation period ends on the expiry of the period of seven working days beginning with the day after the day on which the consumer receives the information.

[(3A)   Where the performance of the contract has begun with the consumer's agreement before the expiry of the period of seven working days beginning with the day after the day on which the contract was concluded and the supplier has not complied with regulation 8 on or before the day on which performance began, but provides to the consumer the information referred to in regulation 8(2) in good time during the performance of the contract, the cancellation period ends—

(a)   on the expiry of the period of seven working days beginning with the day after the day on which the consumer receives the information; or

(b)   if the performance of the contract is completed before the expiry of the period referred to in sub-paragraph (a), on the day when the performance of the contract is completed.]

(4)   Where [none of paragraphs (2) to (3A) applies], the cancellation period ends on the expiry of the period of three months and seven working days beginning with the day after the day on which the contract is concluded.

13   Exceptions to the right to cancel

(1)   Unless the parties have agreed otherwise, the consumer will not have the right to cancel the contract by giving notice of cancellation pursuant to regulation 10 in respect of contracts—

[(a)   for the supply of services if the performance of the contract has begun with the consumer's agreement—

(i)   before the end of the cancellation period applicable under regulation 12(2); and

(ii)   after the supplier has provided the information referred to in regulation 8(2).]

(b)   for the supply of goods or services the price of which is dependent on fluctuations in the financial market which cannot be controlled by the supplier;

(c)   for the supply of goods made to the consumer's specifications or clearly personalised or which by reason of their nature cannot be returned or are liable to deteriorate or expire rapidly;

(d)   for the supply of audio or video recordings or computer software if they are unsealed by the consumer;

(e)   for the supply of newspapers, periodicals or magazines; or

(f)   for gaming, betting or lottery services.

14   Recovery of sums paid by or on behalf of the consumer on cancellation, and return of security

(1)   On the cancellation of a contract under regulation 10, the supplier shall reimburse any sum paid by or on behalf of the consumer under or in relation to the contract to the person by whom it was made free of any charge, less any charge made in accordance with paragraph (5).

(2)   The reference in paragraph (1) to any sum paid on behalf of the consumer includes any sum paid by a creditor who is not the same person as the supplier under a personal credit agreement with the consumer.

(3)   The supplier shall make the reimbursement referred to in paragraph (1) as soon as possible and in any case within a period not exceeding 30 days beginning with the day on which the notice of cancellation was given.

(4)   Where any security has been provided in relation to the contract, the security (so far as it is so provided) shall, on cancellation under regulation 10, be treated as never having had effect and any property lodged with the supplier solely for the purposes of the security as so provided shall be returned by him forthwith.

(5)   Subject to paragraphs (6) and (7), the supplier may make a charge, not exceeding the direct costs of recovering any goods supplied under the contract, where a term of the contract provides that the consumer must return any goods supplied if he cancels the contract under regulation 10 but the consumer does not comply with this provision or returns the goods at the expense of the supplier.

(6)   Paragraph (5) shall not apply where—

(a)   the consumer cancels in circumstances where he has the right to reject the goods under a term of the contract, including a term implied by virtue of any enactment, or

(b)   the term requiring the consumer to return any goods supplied if he cancels the contract is an 'unfair term' within the meaning of the Unfair Terms in Consumer Contracts Regulations 1999.

(7)   Paragraph (5) shall not apply to the cost of recovering any goods which were supplied as substitutes for the goods ordered by the consumer.

(8)   For the purposes of these Regulations, a personal credit agreement is an agreement between the consumer and any other person ('the creditor') by which the creditor provides the consumer with credit of any amount.

15   Automatic cancellation of a related credit agreement

(1)   Where a notice of cancellation is given under regulation 10 which has the effect of cancelling the contract, the giving of the notice shall also have the effect of cancelling any related credit agreement.

(2)   Where a related credit agreement is cancelled by virtue of paragraph (1), the supplier shall, if he is not the same person as the creditor under that agreement, forthwith on receipt of the notice of cancellation inform the creditor that the notice has been given.

(3)   Where a related credit agreement is cancelled by virtue of paragraph (1)—

(a)   any sum paid by or on behalf of the consumer under, or in relation to, the credit agreement which the supplier is not obliged to reimburse under regulation 14(1) shall be reimbursed, except for any sum which, if it had not already been paid, would have to be paid under sub-paragraph (b);

(b)   the agreement shall continue in force so far as it relates to repayment of the credit and payment of interest, subject to regulation 16; and

(c)   subject to sub-paragraph (b), the agreement shall cease to be enforceable.

(4)   Where any security has been provided under a related credit agreement, the security, so far as it is so provided, shall be treated as never having had effect and any property lodged with the creditor solely for the purposes of the security as so provided shall be returned by him forthwith.

(5)   For the purposes of this regulation and regulation 16, a 'related credit agreement' means an agreement under which fixed sum credit which fully or partly covers the price under a contract cancelled under regulation 10 is granted—

(a)   by the supplier, or

(b)   by another person, under an arrangement between that person and the supplier.

(6)   For the purposes of this regulation and regulation 16—

(a)   'creditor' is a person who grants credit under a related credit agreement;

(b)   'fixed sum credit' has the same meaning as in section 10 of the Consumer Credit Act 1974;

(c)   'repayment' in relation to credit means repayment of money received by the consumer, and cognate expressions shall be construed accordingly; and

(d)   'interest' means interest on money so received.

16   Repayment of credit and interest after cancellation of a related credit agreement

(1)   This regulation applies following the cancellation of a related credit agreement by virtue of regulation 15(1).

(2)   If the consumer repays the whole or a portion of the credit—

(a)   before the expiry of one month following the cancellation of the credit agreement, or

(b)   in the case of a credit repayable by instalments, before the date on which the first instalment is due,

no interest shall be payable on the amount repaid.

(3)   If the whole of a credit repayable by instalments is not repaid on or before the date referred to in paragraph (2)(b), the consumer shall not be liable to repay any of the credit except on receipt of a request in writing, signed by the creditor, stating the amounts of the remaining instalments (recalculated by the creditor as

nearly as may be in accordance with the agreement and without extending the repayment period), but excluding any sum other than principal and interest.

(4) Where any security has been provided under a related credit agreement the duty imposed on the consumer to repay credit and to pay interest shall not be enforceable before the creditor has discharged any duty imposed on him by regulation 15(4) to return any property lodged with him as security on cancellation.

17 Restoration of goods by consumer after cancellation

(1) This regulation applies where a contract is cancelled under regulation 10 after the consumer has acquired possession of any goods under the contract other than any goods mentioned in regulation 13(1)(b) to (e).

(2) The consumer shall be treated as having been under a duty throughout the period prior to cancellation—

(a) to retain possession of the goods, and

(b) to take reasonable care of them.

(3) On cancellation, the consumer shall be under a duty to restore the goods to the supplier in accordance with this regulation, and in the meanwhile to retain possession of the goods and take reasonable care of them.

(4) The consumer shall not be under any duty to deliver the goods except at his own premises and in pursuance of a request in writing, or in another durable medium available and accessible to the consumer, from the supplier and given to the consumer either before, or at the time when, the goods are collected from those premises.

(5) If the consumer—

(a) delivers the goods (whether at his own premises or elsewhere) to any person to whom, under regulation 10(1), a notice of cancellation could have been given; or

(b) sends the goods at his own expense to such a person,

he shall be discharged from any duty to retain possession of the goods or restore them to the supplier.

(6) Where the consumer delivers the goods in accordance with paragraph (5)(a), his obligation to take care of the goods shall cease; and if he sends the goods in accordance with paragraph (5)(b), he shall be under a duty to take reasonable care to see that they are received by the supplier and not damaged in transit, but in other respects his duty to take care of the goods shall cease when he sends them.

(7) Where, at any time during the period of 21 days beginning with the day notice of cancellation was given, the consumer receives such a request as is mentioned in paragraph (4), and unreasonably refuses or unreasonably fails to comply with it, his duty to retain possession and take reasonable care of the goods shall continue until he delivers or sends the goods as mentioned in paragraph (5), but if within that period he does not receive such a request his duty to take reasonable care of the goods shall cease at the end of that period.

(8) Where—

(a) a term of the contract provides that if the consumer cancels the contract, he must return the goods to the supplier, and

(b) the consumer is not otherwise entitled to reject the goods under the terms of the contract or by virtue of any enactment,

paragraph (7) shall apply as if for the period of 21 days there were substituted the period of 6 months.

(9) Where any security has been provided in relation to the cancelled contract, the duty to restore goods imposed on the consumer by this regulation shall not be enforceable before the supplier has discharged any duty imposed on him by regulation 14(4) to return any property lodged with him as security on cancellation.

(10) Breach of a duty imposed by this regulation on a consumer is actionable as a breach of statutory duty.

18   Goods given in part-exchange

(1)   This regulation applies on the cancellation of a contract under regulation 10 where the supplier agreed to take goods in part-exchange (the 'part-exchange goods') and those goods have been delivered to him.

(2)   Unless, before the end of the period of 10 days beginning with the date of cancellation, the part-exchange goods are returned to the consumer in a condition substantially as good as when they were delivered to the supplier, the consumer shall be entitled to recover from the supplier a sum equal to the part-exchange allowance.

(3)   In this regulation the part-exchange allowance means the sum agreed as such in the cancelled contract, or if no such sum was agreed, such sum as it would have been reasonable to allow in respect of the part-exchange goods if no notice of cancellation had been served.

(4)   Where the consumer recovers from the supplier a sum equal to the part-exchange allowance, the title of the consumer to the part-exchange goods shall vest in the supplier (if it has not already done so) on recovery of that sum.

19   Performance

(1)   Unless the parties agree otherwise, the supplier shall perform the contract within a maximum of 30 days beginning with the day after the day the consumer sent his order to the supplier.

(2)   Subject to paragraphs (7) and (8), where the supplier is unable to perform the contract because the goods or services ordered are not available, within the period for performance referred to in paragraph (1) or such other period as the parties agree ('the period for performance'), he shall—

(a)   inform the consumer; and

(b)   reimburse any sum paid by or on behalf of the consumer under or in relation to the contract to the person by whom it was made.

(3)   The reference in paragraph (2)(b) to any sum paid on behalf of the consumer includes any sum paid by a creditor who is not the same person as the supplier under a personal credit agreement with the consumer.

(4)   The supplier shall make the reimbursement referred to in paragraph (2)(b) as soon as possible and in any event within a period of 30 days beginning with the day after the day on which the period for performance expired.

(5)   A contract which has not been performed within the period for performance shall be treated as if it had not been made, save for any rights or remedies which the consumer has under it as a result of the non-performance.

(6)   Where any security has been provided in relation to the contract, the security (so far as it is so provided) shall, where the supplier is unable to perform the contract within the period for performance, be treated as never having had any effect and any property lodged with the supplier solely for the purposes of the security as so provided shall be returned by him forthwith.

(7)   Where the supplier is unable to supply the goods or services ordered by the consumer, the supplier may perform the contract for the purposes of these Regulations by providing substitute goods or services (as the case may be) of equivalent quality and price provided that—

(a)   this possibility was provided for in the contract;

(b)   prior to the conclusion of the contract the supplier gave the consumer the information required by regulation 7(1)(b) and (c) in the manner required by regulation 7(2).

(8)   In the case of outdoor leisure events which by their nature cannot be rescheduled, paragraph 2(b) shall not apply where the consumer and the supplier so agree.

20   Effect of non-performance on related credit agreement

Where a supplier is unable to perform the contract within the period for performance—

(a)   regulations 15 and 16 shall apply to any related credit agreement as if the consumer had given a valid notice of cancellation under regulation 10 on the expiry of the period for performance; and

(b)   the reference in regulation 15(3)(a) to regulation 14(1) shall be read, for the purposes of this regulation, as a reference to regulation 19(2).

[. . .]

24   Inertia selling

(1)   Paragraphs (2) and (3) apply if—

(a)   unsolicited goods are sent to a person ('the recipient') with a view to his acquiring them;

(b)   the recipient has no reasonable cause to believe that they were sent with a view to their being acquired for the purposes of a business; and

(c)   the recipient has neither agreed to acquire nor agreed to return them.

(2)   The recipient may, as between himself and the sender, use, deal with or dispose of the goods as if they were an unconditional gift to him.

(3)   The rights of the sender to the goods are extinguished.

[. . .]

(6)   In this regulation—

'acquire' includes hire;

'send' includes deliver;

'sender', in relation to any goods, includes—

(a)   any person on whose behalf or with whose consent the goods are sent;

(b)   any other person claiming through or under the sender or any person mentioned in paragraph (a); and

(c)   any person who delivers the goods; and

'unsolicited' means, in relation to goods sent or services supplied to any person, that they are sent or supplied without any prior request made by or on behalf of the recipient.

[. . .]

(10)   This regulation applies only to goods sent and services supplied after the date on which it comes into force.

25   No contracting-out

(1)   A term contained in any contract to which these Regulations apply is void if, and to the extent that, it is inconsistent with a provision for the protection of the consumer contained in these Regulations.

(2)   Where a provision of these Regulations specifies a duty or liability of the consumer in certain circumstances, a term contained in a contract to which these Regulations apply, other than a term to which paragraph (3) applies, is inconsistent with that provision if it purports to impose, directly or indirectly, an additional duty or liability on him in those circumstances.

(3)   This paragraph applies to a term which requires the consumer to return any goods supplied to him under the contract if he cancels it under regulation 10.

(4)   A term to which paragraph (3) applies shall, in the event of cancellation by the consumer under regulation 10, have effect only for the purposes of regulations 14(5) and 17(8).

(5)   These Regulations shall apply notwithstanding any contract term which applies or purports to apply the law of a non-Member State if the contract has a close connection with the territory of a Member State.

26   Consideration of complaints

(1)   It shall be the duty of an enforcement authority to consider any complaint made to it about a breach unless—

(a)   the complaint appears to the authority to be frivolous or vexatious; or

(b)   another enforcement authority has notified the Director that it agrees to consider the complaint.

(2)   If an enforcement authority notifies the Director that it agrees to consider a complaint made to another enforcement authority, the first mentioned authority shall be under a duty to consider the complaint.

(3)   An enforcement authority which is under a duty to consider a complaint shall give reasons for its decision to apply or not to apply, as the case may be, for an injunction under regulation 27.

(4)   In deciding whether or not to apply for an injunction in respect of a breach an enforcement authority may, if it considers it appropriate to do so, have regard to any undertaking given to it or another enforcement authority by or on behalf of any person as to compliance with these Regulations.

27   Injunctions to secure compliance with these Regulations

(1)   The Director or, subject to paragraph (2), any other enforcement authority may apply for an injunction (including an interim injunction) against any person who appears to the Director or that authority to be responsible for a breach.

(2)   An enforcement authority other than the Director may apply for an injunction only where—

(a)   it has notified the Director of its intention to apply at least fourteen days before the date on which the application is to be made, beginning with the date on which the notification was given; or

(b)   the Director consents to the application being made within a shorter period.

(3)   The court on an application under this regulation may grant an injunction on such terms as it thinks fit to secure compliance with these Regulations.

28   Notification of undertakings and orders to the Director

An enforcement authority other than the Director shall notify the Director—

(a)   of any undertaking given to it by or on behalf of any person who appears to it to be responsible for a breach;

(b)   of the outcome of any application made by it under regulation 27 and of the terms of any undertaking given to or order made by the court;

(c)   of the outcome of any application made by it to enforce a previous order of the court.

29   Publication, information and advice

(1)   The Director shall arrange for the publication in such form and manner as he considers appropriate of—

(a)   details of any undertaking or order notified to him under regulation 28;

(b)   details of any undertaking given to him by or on behalf of any person as to compliance with these Regulations;

(c)   details of any application made by him under regulation 27, and of the terms of any undertaking given to, or order made by, the court;

(d)   details of any application made by the Director to enforce a previous order of the court.

(2)   The Director may arrange for the dissemination in such form and manner as he considers appropriate of such information and advice concerning the operation of these Regulations as it may appear to him to be expedient to give to the public and to all persons likely to be affected by these Regulations.

Regulation 3   SCHEDULE 1
          INDICATIVE LIST OF MEANS OF DISTANCE COMMUNICATION

1   Unaddressed printed matter.
2   Addressed printed matter.
3   Letter.
4   Press advertising with order form.
5   Catalogue.

6   Telephone with human intervention.

7   Telephone without human intervention (automatic calling machine, audio-text).

8   Radio.

9   Videophone (telephone with screen).

10   Videotext (microcomputer and television screen) with keyboard or touch screen.

11   Electronic mail.

12   Facsimile machine (fax).

13   Television (teleshopping).

LIMITED LIABILITY PARTNERSHIPS REGULATIONS 2001
(SI 2001/1090)

PART VI
DEFAULT PROVISION

7   Default provision for limited liability partnerships

The mutual rights and duties of the members and the mutual rights and duties of the limited liability partnership and the members shall be determined, subject to the provisions of the general law and to the terms of any limited liability partnership agreement, by the following rules:

(1)   All the members of a limited liability partnership are entitled to share equally in the capital and profits of the limited liability partnership.

(2)   The limited liability partnership must indemnify each member in respect of payments made and personal liabilities incurred by him—

    (a)   in the ordinary and proper conduct of the business of the limited liability partnership; or

    (b)   in or about anything necessarily done for the preservation of the business or property of the limited liability partnership.

(3)   Every member may take part in the management of the limited liability partnership.

(4)   No member shall be entitled to remuneration for acting in the business or management of the limited liability partnership.

(5)   No person may be introduced as a member or voluntarily assign an interest in a limited liability partnership without the consent of all existing members.

(6)   Any difference arising as to ordinary matters connected with the business of the limited liability partnership may be decided by a majority of the members, but no change may be made in the nature of the business of the limited liability partnership without the consent of all the members.

(7)   The books and records of the limited liability partnership are to be made available for inspection at the registered office of the limited liability partnership or at such other place as the members think fit and every member of the limited liability partnership may when he thinks fit have access to and inspect and copy any of them.

(8)   Each member shall render true accounts and full information of all things affecting the limited liability partnership to any member or his legal representatives.

(9)   If a member, without the consent of the limited liability partnership, carries on any business of the same nature as and competing with the limited liability partnership, he must account for and pay over to the limited liability partnership all profits made by him in that business.

(10)   Every member must account to the limited liability partnership for any benefit derived by him without the consent of the limited liability partnership from any transaction concerning the limited liability partnership, or from any use

by him of the property of the limited liability partnership, name or business connection.

8 Expulsion

No majority of the members can expel any member unless a power to do so has been conferred by express agreement between the members.

SALE AND SUPPLY OF GOODS TO CONSUMERS REGULATIONS 2002
(SI 2002/3045)

15 Consumer guarantees

(1) Where goods are sold or otherwise supplied to a consumer which are offered with a consumer guarantee, the consumer guarantee takes effect at the time the goods are delivered as a contractual obligation owed by the guarantor under the conditions set out in the guarantee statement and the associated advertising.

(2) The guarantor shall ensure that the guarantee sets out in plain intelligible language the contents of the guarantee and the essential particulars necessary for making claims under the guarantee, notably the duration and territorial scope of the guarantee as well as the name and address of the guarantor.

[(2A) The guarantor shall also ensure that the guarantee contains a statement that the consumer has statutory rights in relation to the goods which are sold or supplied and that those rights are not affected by the guarantee.]

(3) On request by the consumer to a person to whom paragraph (4) applies, the guarantee shall within a reasonable time be made available in writing or in another durable medium available and accessible to him.

(4) This paragraph applies to the guarantor and any other person who offers to consumers the goods which are the subject of the guarantee for sale or supply.

(5) Where consumer goods are offered with a consumer guarantee, and where those goods are offered within the territory of the United Kingdom, then the guarantor shall ensure that the consumer guarantee is written in English.

(6) If the guarantor fails to comply with the provisions of paragraphs (2) or (5) above, or a person to whom paragraph (4) applies fails to comply with paragraph (3) then the enforcement authority may apply for an injunction or (in Scotland) an order of specific implement against that person requiring him to comply.

(7) The court on application under this Regulation may grant an injunction or (in Scotland) an order of specific implement on such terms as it thinks fit.

CANCELLATION OF CONTRACTS MADE IN A CONSUMER'S HOME OR PLACE OF WORK ETC REGULATIONS 2008
(SI 2008/1816)

2 Interpretation

(1) In these Regulations:

'the 1974 Act' means the Consumer Credit Act 1974;

'cancellable agreement' has the same meaning as in section 189(1) of the 1974 Act;

'cancellation notice' means a notice in writing given by the consumer which indicates that he wishes to cancel the contract;

'cancellation period' means the period of 7 days starting with the date of receipt by the consumer of a notice of the right to cancel;

'consumer' means a natural person who in making a contract to which these Regulations apply is acting for purposes which can be regarded as outside his trade or profession;

'consumer credit agreement' means an agreement between the consumer and any other person by which the other person provides the consumer with credit of any amount;

'credit' includes a cash loan and any other form of financial accommodation, and for this purpose 'cash' includes money in any form;

'enforcement authority' means any person mentioned in regulation 21;

'fixed sum credit' has the same meaning as in section 10(1) of the 1974 Act;

'notice of the right to cancel' means a notice given in accordance with regulation 7;

'related credit agreement' means a consumer credit agreement under which fixed sum credit which fully or partly covers the price under a contract which may be cancelled under regulation 7 is granted—

 (i) by the trader; or

 (ii) by another person, under an arrangement made between that person and the trader;

'solicited visit' has the meaning given in regulation 6(3);

'specified contract' has the meaning given in regulation 9; and

'trader' means a person who, in making a contract to which these Regulations apply, is acting in his commercial or professional capacity and anyone acting in the name or on behalf of a trader.

(2) Paragraph 8(2) of Schedule 3 has effect for the purposes of paragraphs 7 and 8(1).

4 ...

(2) The Consumer Protection (Cancellation of Contracts Concluded away from Business Premises) Regulations 1987 ('the 1987 Regulations') shall continue to have effect in relation to a contract to which they applied before their revocation by these Regulations.

(3) These Regulations shall not apply to a contract to which the 1987 Regulations applied before their revocation.

5 Scope of application

These Regulations apply to a contract, including a consumer credit agreement, between a consumer and a trader which is for the supply of goods or services to the consumer by a trader and which is made—

 (a) during a visit by the trader to the consumer's home or place of work, or to the home of another individual;

 (b) during an excursion organised by the trader away from his business premises; or

 (c) after an offer made by the consumer during such a visit or excursion.

6 — (1) These Regulations do not apply to—

 (a) any contracts listed in Schedule 3 (Excepted Contracts);

 (b) a cancellable agreement;

 (c) a consumer credit agreement which may be cancelled by the consumer in accordance with the terms of the agreement conferring upon him similar rights as if the agreement were a cancellable agreement; or

 [(ca) a consumer credit agreement regulated under the 1974 Act to which the right of withdrawal applies under section 66A of that Act;]

 (d) a contract made during a solicited visit or a contract made after an offer made by a consumer during a solicited visit where the contract is—

  (i) a regulated mortgage, home purchase plan or home reversion plan if the making or performance of such a contract constitutes a regulated activity for the purposes of the Financial Services and Markets Act 2000;

  (ii) a consumer credit agreement secured on land which is—

   (aa) regulated under the 1974 Act; or

   (bb) to the extent that it is not regulated under the 1974 Act, exempt under that Act; or

(iii)   any other consumer credit agreement regulated under the 1974 Act.

(2)   Where any agreement referred to in paragraph (1)(b), [*(c), (ca) or (d)(iii)*] is a related credit agreement the provisions of regulations 11 and 12 shall apply to the cancellation of that agreement.

(3)   A solicited visit means a visit by a trader, whether or not he is the trader who supplies the goods or services, to a consumer's home or place of work or to the home of another individual, which is made at the express request of the consumer but does not include—

(a)   a visit by a trader which is made after he, or a person acting in his name or on his behalf—

(i)   telephones the consumer (otherwise than at the consumer's express request) and indicates during the course of the telephone call (either expressly or by implication) that he, or the trader in whose name or on whose behalf he is acting, is willing to visit the consumer; or

(ii)   visits the consumer (otherwise than at the consumer's express request) and indicates during the course of that visit (either expressly or by implication) that he, or the trader in whose name or on whose behalf he is acting, is willing to make a subsequent visit to the consumer; or

(b)   a visit during which the contract which is made relates to goods and services other than those concerning which the consumer requested the visit of the trader, provided that when the visit was requested the consumer did not know, or could not reasonably have known, that the supply of such goods or services formed part of the trader's commercial or professional activities.

Right to cancel a contract to which these Regulations apply

7 — (1)   A consumer has the right to cancel a contract to which these Regulations apply within the cancellation period.

(2)   The trader must give the consumer a written notice of his right to cancel the contract and such notice must be given at the time the contract is made except in the case of a contract to which regulation 5(c) applies in which case the notice must be given at the time the offer is made by the consumer.

(3)   The notice must—

(a)   be dated;

(b)   indicate the right of the consumer to cancel the contract within the cancellation period;

(c)   be easily legible;

(d)   contain—

(i)   the information set out in Part I of Schedule 4; and

(ii)   a cancellation form in the form set out in Part II of that Schedule provided as a detachable slip and completed by or on behalf of the trader in accordance with the notes; and

(e)   indicate if applicable—

(i)   that the consumer may be required to pay for the goods or services supplied if the performance of the contract has begun with his written agreement before the end of the cancellation period;

(ii)   that a related credit agreement will be automatically cancelled if the contract for goods or services is cancelled.

(4)   Where the contract is wholly or partly in writing the notice must be incorporated in the same document.

(5)   If incorporated in the contract or another document the notice of the right to cancel must—

(a)   be set out in a separate box with the heading 'Notice of the Right to Cancel'; and

(b)   have as much prominence as any other information in the contract or document apart from the heading and the names of the parties to the contract and any information inserted in handwriting.

(6)   A contract to which these Regulations apply shall not be enforceable against the consumer unless the trader has given the consumer a notice of the right to cancel and the information required in accordance with this regulation.

Exercise of the right to cancel a contract

8 — (1)   If the consumer serves a cancellation notice within the cancellation period then the contract is cancelled.

(2)   A contract which is cancelled shall be treated as if it had never been entered into by the consumer except where these Regulations provide otherwise.

(3)   The cancellation notice must indicate the intention of the consumer to cancel the contract and does not need to follow the form of cancellation notice set out in Part II of Schedule 4.

(4)   The cancellation notice must be served on the trader or another person specified in the notice of the right to cancel as a person to whom the cancellation notice may be given.

(5)   A cancellation notice sent by post is taken to have been served at the time of posting, whether or not it is actually received.

(6)   Where a cancellation notice is sent by electronic mail it is taken to have been served on the day on which it is sent.

Cancellation of specified contracts commenced before expiry of the right to cancel

9 — (1)   Where the consumer enters into a specified contract and he wishes the performance of the contract to begin before the end of the cancellation period, he must request this in writing.

(2)   Where the consumer cancels a specified contract in accordance with regulation 8 he shall be under a duty to pay in accordance with the reasonable requirements of the cancelled contract for goods or services that were supplied before the cancellation.

(3)   If the consumer fails to provide the request in writing referred to in paragraph (1) then—

(a)   the trader is not obliged to begin performance of the specified contract before the end of the cancellation period; and

(b)   the consumer is not bound by the duty referred to in paragraph (2) if he cancels the contract in accordance with regulation 8.

(4)   For the purposes of this regulation and regulation 13, a 'specified contract' means a contract for any of the following—

(a)   the supply of newspapers, periodicals or magazines;

(b)   advertising in any medium;

(c)   the supply of goods the price of which is dependent on fluctuations in the financial markets which cannot be controlled by the trader;

(d)   the supply of goods to meet an emergency;

(e)   the supply of goods made to a customer's specifications or clearly personalised and any services in connection with the provision of such goods;

(f)   the supply of perishable goods;

(g)   the supply of goods which by their nature are consumed by use and which, before the cancellation, were so consumed;

(h)   the supply of goods which, before the cancellation, had become incorporated in any land or thing not comprised in the cancelled contract;

(i)   the supply of goods or services relating to a funeral; or

(j)   the supply of services of any other kind.

Recovery of money paid by consumer

10 — (1)   On the cancellation of a contract under regulation 8 any sum paid by or on behalf of the consumer in respect of the contract shall become repayable except where these Regulations provide otherwise.

(2)   If the consumer or any person on his behalf is in possession of any goods

under the terms of the cancelled contract then he shall have a lien on them for any sum repayable to him under paragraph (1).

(3) Where any security has been provided in relation to the cancelled contract, the security shall be treated as never having had effect for that purpose and the trader must immediately return any property lodged with him solely as security for the purposes of the cancelled contract.

Automatic cancellation of related credit agreement

11 — (1) A cancellation notice which cancels a contract for goods or services shall have the effect of cancelling any related credit agreement.

(2) Subject to paragraphs (3) and (4), where a related credit agreement has been cancelled under paragraph (1)—

(a) the trader must, if he is not the same person as the creditor under that agreement, immediately on receipt of the cancellation notice inform the creditor that the notice has been given;

(b) any sum paid by or on behalf of the consumer in relation to the credit agreement must be reimbursed, except for any sum which would have to be paid under sub-paragraph (c);

(c) the agreement shall continue in force so far as it relates to repayment of the credit and payment of interest in accordance with regulation 12, but shall otherwise cease to be enforceable; and

(d) any security provided under the related credit agreement shall be treated as never having had effect for that purpose and the creditor must immediately return any property lodged with him solely as security for the purposes of the related credit agreement.

(3) Where a related credit agreement is a cancellable agreement—

(a) its cancellation under paragraph (1) shall take effect as if a notice of cancellation within the meaning of the 1974 Act had been served;

(b) that Act shall apply in respect of the consequences of such cancellation;

(c) paragraph (2)(b) to (d) and regulation 12 shall not apply in respect of its cancellation; and

(d) regulations 13 and 14 shall not apply in respect of the cancellation of the related contract for goods or services.

(4) Where a related credit agreement of a kind referred to in regulation 6(1)(c) is cancelled under paragraph (1)—

(a) paragraph (2)(b) to (d) and regulation 12 shall not apply in respect of its cancellation; and

(b) regulations 13 and 14 shall not apply in respect of the cancellation of the related contract for goods or services.

(5) Where a related credit agreement of a kind referred to in [regulation 6(1)(ca), 6(1)(d)(iii)] is cancelled under paragraph (1)—

(a) the provisions of this regulation and regulation 12 shall apply in respect of its cancellation; and

(b) the provisions of regulations 13 and 14 shall apply in respect of the cancellation of the related contract for goods or services.

(6) For the purposes of this regulation and regulation 12 'creditor' is the person who grants credit under a related credit agreement.

Repayment of credit and interest

12 — (1) Where—

(a) a contract under which credit is provided to the consumer is cancelled under regulation 8; or

(b) a related credit agreement (other than a cancellable agreement or an agreement of a kind referred to in regulation 6(1)(c)) is cancelled as a result of the cancellation of a contract for goods or services,

the contract or agreement shall continue in force so far as it relates to repayment of the credit and payment of interest.

(2) If, following the cancellation of a contract or related credit agreement to which paragraph (1) applies, the consumer repays the whole or a portion of the credit—

(a) before the expiry of one month following service of the cancellation notice; or

(b) in the case of a credit repayable by instalments, before the date on which the first instalment is due,

no interest shall be payable on the amount repaid.

(3) If the whole of a credit repayable by instalments is not repaid on or before the date specified in paragraph (2)(b), the consumer shall not be liable to repay any of the credit except on receipt of a request in writing signed by the trader stating the amounts of the remaining instalments (recalculated by the trader as nearly as may be in accordance with the contract and without extending the repayment period), but excluding any sum other than principal and interest.

(4) Repayment of a credit, or payment of interest, under a cancelled contract or related credit agreement shall be treated as duly made if it is made to any person on whom, under regulation 8(4), a cancellation notice could have been served.

(5) Where any security has been provided in relation to the contract or consumer credit agreement, the duty imposed on the consumer by this regulation shall not be enforceable before the trader or creditor has discharged any duty imposed on him by regulation 10(3) or 11(2)(d) respectively.

Return of goods by consumer after cancellation

13 — (1) A consumer who has acquired possession of any goods by virtue of the contract shall on the cancellation of that contract be under a duty, subject to any lien, to restore the goods to the trader and meanwhile to retain possession of the goods and take reasonable care of them.

(2) The consumer shall not be under a duty to restore goods supplied under a specified contract in circumstances where—

(a) he is required to pay, in accordance with the reasonable requirements of the cancelled contract, for the supply of such goods before cancellation; or

(b) the trader has begun performance of the contract before the end of the cancellation period without a prior request in writing by the consumer.

(3) The consumer shall not be under any duty to deliver the goods except at his own premises and following a request in writing signed by the trader and served on the consumer either before, or at the time when, the goods are collected from those premises.

(4) If the consumer—

(a) delivers the goods (whether at his own premises or elsewhere) to any person on whom, under regulation 8(4), a cancellation notice could have been served; or

(b) sends the goods at his own expense to such a person,

he shall be discharged from any duty to retain possession of the goods or restore them to the trader.

(5) Where the consumer delivers the goods as mentioned in paragraph (4)(a), his obligation to take care of the goods shall cease; and if he send the goods as mentioned in paragraph (4)(b), he shall be under a duty to take reasonable care to see that they are received by the trader and not damaged in transit, but in other respects his duty to take care of the goods shall cease.

(6) Where, at any time during the period of 21 days following the cancellation, the consumer receives such a request as is mentioned in paragraph (3) and unreasonably refuses or unreasonably fails to comply with it, his duty to retain possession and take reasonable care of the goods shall continue until he delivers or sends the goods as mentioned in paragraph (4); but if within that period he does not receive such a request his duty to take reasonable care of the goods shall cease at the end of that period.

(7)   Where any security has been provided in relation to the cancelled contract, the duty imposed on the consumer to restore goods shall not be enforceable before the trader has discharged any duty imposed on him by regulation 10(3).

(8)   Breach of a duty imposed on a consumer by this regulation is actionable as a breach of statutory duty.

Goods given in part-exchange

14 — (1)   This regulation applies on the cancellation of a contract where the trader agreed to take goods in part-exchange (the 'part-exchange goods') and those goods have been delivered to him.

(2)   Unless, before the end of the period of ten days beginning with the date of cancellation, the part-exchange goods are returned to the consumer in a condition substantially as good as when they were delivered to the trader, the consumer shall be entitled to recover from the trader a sum equal to the part-exchange allowance.

(3)   During the period of ten days beginning with the date of cancellation, the consumer, if he is in possession of goods to which the cancelled contract relates, shall have a lien on them for—

(a)   delivery of the part-exchange goods in a condition substantially as good as when they were delivered to the trader; or

(b)   a sum equal to the part-exchange allowance,

and if the lien continues to the end of that period it shall thereafter subsist only as a lien for a sum equal to the part-exchange allowance.

(4)   In this regulation the part-exchange allowance means the sum agreed as such in the cancelled contract, or if no such sum was agreed, such sum as it would have been reasonable to allow in respect of the part-exchange goods if no notice of cancellation had been served.

No contracting-out of contracts to which these Regulations apply

15 — (1)   A term contained in a contract is void if, and to the extent that, it is inconsistent with a provision for the protection of the consumer contained in these Regulations.

(2)   Where a provision of these Regulations specifies the duty or liability of the consumer in certain circumstances, a term contained in a contract is inconsistent with that provision if it purports to impose, directly or indirectly, an additional or different duty or liability on the consumer in those circumstances.

Service of documents

16 — (1)   A document to be served under these Regulations on a person may be so served—

(a)   by delivering it to him, or by leaving it at his proper address or by sending it to him at that address;

(b)   if the person is a body corporate, by serving it in accordance with sub-paragraph (a) on the secretary or clerk of that body;

(c)   if the person is a partnership, by serving it in accordance with sub-paragraph (a) on a partner or on a person having the control or management of the partnership business; and

(d)   if the person is an unincorporated body, by serving it in accordance with sub-paragraph (a) on a person having control or management of that body.

(2)   For the purposes of paragraph (1), the proper address of any person on whom a document is to be served under these Regulations is his last known address except that—

(a)   in the case of service on a body corporate or its secretary or clerk, it is the address of the registered or principal office of the body corporate in the United Kingdom; and

(b)   in the case of service on a partnership or partner or person having the control or management of a partnership business, it is the partnership's principal place of business in the United Kingdom.

(3)   A person's electronic mail address may also be his proper address for the purposes of paragraph (1).

Enforcement

Offence relating to the failure to give notice of the right to cancel
17 — (1)   A trader is guilty of an offence if he enters into a contract to which these Regulations apply but fails to give the consumer a notice of the right to cancel in accordance with regulation 7.

(2)   A person who is guilty of an offence under paragraph (1) shall be liable on summary conviction to a fine not exceeding level 5 on the standard scale.

Defence of due diligence
18 — (1)   In any proceedings against a person for an offence under regulation 17 it is a defence for that person to prove—
    (a)   that the commission of the offence was due to—
        (i)   the act or default of another, or
        (ii)   reliance on information given by another, and
    (b)   that he took all reasonable precautions and exercised all due diligence to avoid the commission of such an offence by himself or any person under his control.

(2)   A person shall not be entitled to rely on the defence provided by paragraph (1) without leave of the court unless—
    (a)   he has served on the prosecutor a notice in writing giving such information identifying or assisting in the identification of that other person as was in his possession; and
    (b)   the notice is served on the prosecutor not less than seven clear days before the hearing of the proceedings or, in Scotland, the diet of trial.

Liability of persons other than the principal offender
19   Where the commission by a person of an offence under regulation 17 is due to the act or default of another person, that other person is guilty of the offence and may be proceeded against and punished whether or not proceedings are taken against the first person.

Offences committed by bodies of persons
20 — (1)   Where an offence under regulation 17 committed by a body corporate is proved—
    (a)   to have been committed with the consent or connivance of an officer of the body corporate or
    (b)   to be attributable to any neglect on his part,
the officer, as well as the body corporate shall be guilty of the offence and liable to be proceeded against and punished accordingly.

(2)   In paragraph (1) a reference to an officer of a body corporate includes a reference to—
    (a)   a director, manager, secretary or other similar officer; and
    (b)   a person purporting to act as a director, manager, secretary or other similar officer.

(3)   Where an offence under regulation 17 committed in Scotland by a Scottish partnership is proved—
    (a)   to have been committed with the consent or connivance of a partner; or
    (b)   to be attributable to any neglect on his part,
that partner, as well as the partnership shall be guilty of the offence and liable to be proceeded against and punished accordingly.

(4)   In paragraph (3) a reference to a partner includes a person purporting to act as a partner.

Duty to enforce
21 — (1)   Subject to paragraphs (2) and (3)—
     (a)   it shall be the duty of every weights and measures authority in Great Britain to enforce regulation 17 within its area; and
     (b)   it shall be the duty of the Department of Enterprise Trade and Investment in Northern Ireland to enforce regulation 17 within Northern Ireland.
     (2)   No proceedings for an offence under these Regulations may be instituted in England and Wales except by or on behalf of an enforcement authority.
     (3)   Nothing in paragraph (1) shall authorise any weights and measures authority to bring proceedings in Scotland for an offence.

Powers of investigation
22 — (1)   If a duly authorised officer of an enforcement authority has reasonable grounds for suspecting that an offence has been committed under regulation 17, he may require a person carrying on or employed in a business to produce any document relating to the business, and take copies of it or any entry in it for the purposes of ascertaining whether such an offence has been committed.
     (2)   If the officer has reasonable grounds for believing that any documents may be required as evidence in proceedings for such an offence, he may seize and detain them and shall, if he does so, inform the person from whom they are seized.
     (3)   In this regulation 'document' includes information recorded in any form.
     (4)   The reference in paragraph (1) to production of documents is, in the case of a document which contains information recorded otherwise than in a legible form, a reference to the production of a copy of the information in a legible form.
     (5)   An officer seeking to exercise a power under this regulation must do so only at a reasonable hour and on production (if required) of his identification and authority.
     (6)   Nothing in this regulation requires a person to produce, or authorises the taking from a person of, a document which the other person would be entitled to refuse to produce in proceedings in the High Court on the grounds of legal professional privilege or (in Scotland) in the Court of Session on the grounds of confidentiality of communications.
     (7)   In paragraph (6) 'communications' means—
     (a)   communications between a professional legal adviser and his client; or
     (b)   communications made in connection with, or in contemplation of legal proceedings and for the purpose of those proceedings.

Obstruction of authorised officers
23 — (1)   A person is guilty of an offence if he—
     (a)   intentionally obstructs an officer of an enforcement authority acting in pursuance of his functions under these Regulations;
     (b)   without reasonable cause fails to comply with any requirement properly made of him by such an officer under regulation 22; or
     (c)   without reasonable cause fails to give such an officer any other assistance or information which he may reasonably require of him for the purpose of the performance of his functions under these Regulations.
     (2)   A person is guilty of an offence if, in giving any information which is required of him under paragraph (1)(c), he makes any statement which he knows to be false in a material particular.
     (3)   A person guilty of an offence under paragraph (1) or (2) shall be liable on summary conviction to a fine not exceeding level 3 on the standard scale.

24   Nothing in regulation 22 or 23 shall be construed as requiring a person to answer any question or give any information if to do so might incriminate him.

SCHEDULE 3
EXCEPTED CONTRACTS

Regulations 2(2) and 6(1)(a)

1   A contract for the construction, sale or rental of immovable property or a contract concerning other rights relating to immovable property other than—

(a)   a contract for the construction of extensions, patios, conservatories or driveways;

(b)   a contract for the supply of goods and their incorporation in immovable property; and

(c)   a contract for the repair, refurbishment or improvement of immovable property.

2   A contract for the supply of foodstuffs or beverages or other goods intended for current consumption in the household and supplied by a regular roundsman.

3   A contract for the supply of goods or services provided that each of the following conditions is met:

(a)   the contract is concluded on the basis of a trader's catalogue which the consumer has a proper opportunity of reading in the absence of the trader's representative;

(b)   there is intended to be continuity of contact between the trader's representative and the consumer in relation to that or any subsequent transaction; and

(c)   both the catalogue and the contract contain a prominent notice informing the consumer of his rights to return goods to the supplier within a period of not less than seven days of receipt or otherwise to cancel the contract within that period without obligation of any kind other than to take reasonable care of the goods.

4   A contract of insurance.

5   Any contract under which credit within the meaning of the 1974 Act is provided not exceeding £35 other than a hire purchase or conditional sale agreement.

6   Any contract not falling within paragraph 5 under which the total payments to be made by the consumer do not exceed £35.

7   Any agreement the making or performance of which by either party constitutes a relevant regulated activity.

8 — (1)   For the purposes of paragraph 7—

(a)   'a relevant regulated activity' means an activity of the following kind—

(i)   dealing in investments, as principal or as agent;

(ii)   arranging deals in investments;

(iii)   operating a multilateral trading facility;

(iv)   managing investments;

(v)   safeguarding and administering investments;

(vi)   establishing, operating or winding up a collective investment scheme; and

(b)   for these purposes 'investment' means—

(i)   shares;

(ii)   instruments creating or acknowledging indebtedness;

(iii)   instruments giving entitlement to investments

(iv)   certificates representing securities;

(v)   units in a collective investment scheme;

(vi)   options;

(vii)   futures;

(viii)   contracts for differences; and

(ix)   rights to or interests in investments.

(2)   Paragraph 7 and this paragraph must be read with—

(a)   section 22 of the Financial Services and Markets Act 2000;

(b)   any relevant order under that section; and

(c)   Schedule 2 to that Act,

but any restriction on or exclusion from the meaning of a regulated activity for the purposes of paragraph 7 which arises from the identity of the person carrying on such activity is to be disregarded.

SCHEDULE 4
NOTICE OF THE RIGHT TO CANCEL

Regulation 7(3)

PART I
INFORMATION TO BE CONTAINED IN NOTICE OF THE RIGHT TO CANCEL

1   The identity of the trader including trading name if any.

2   The trader's reference number, code or other details to enable the contract or offer to be identified.

3   A statement that the consumer has a right to cancel the contract if he wishes and that this right can be exercised by delivering, or sending (including by electronic mail) a cancellation notice to the person mentioned in the next paragraph at any time within the period of 7 days starting with the day of receipt of a notice in writing of the right to cancel the contract.

4   The name and address, (including any electronic mail address as well as the postal address), of a person to whom a cancellation notice may be given.

5   A statement that notice of cancellation is deemed to be served as soon as it is posted or sent to a trader or in the case of an electronic communication from the day it is sent to the trader.

6   A statement that the consumer can use the cancellation form provided if he wishes.

PART II
CANCELLATION NOTICE TO BE INCLUDED IN NOTICE OF THE RIGHT TO CANCEL

If you wish to cancel the contract you MUST DO SO IN WRITING and deliver personally or send (which may be by electronic mail) this to the person named below. You may use this form if you want to but you do not have to.

(Complete, detach and return this form ONLY IF YOU WISH TO CANCEL THE CONTRACT.)

To.. [trader to insert name and address of person to whom notice may be given.]

I/We (delete as appropriate) hereby give notice that I/we (delete as appropriate) wish to cancel my/our (delete as appropriate) contract.. [trader to insert reference number, code or other details to enable the contract or offer to be identified. He may also insert the name and address of the consumer.]

Signed

Name and Address

Date

BANKRUPTCY AND DILIGENCE ETC (SCOTLAND) ACT 2007
(COMMENCEMENT NO 4, SAVINGS AND TRANSITIONALS) ORDER 2009
(SSI 2009/67)

5 Transitional modification of the Act—references to the Registers of Inhibitions

(1) Any reference to 'the Register of Inhibitions' in, or having effect by virtue of, any provision of the Act commenced by this Order is to be read as a reference to the Register of Inhibitions and Adjudications.

(2) This article ceases to have effect on the day to be appointed for the coming into force of section 80 of the Act (renaming of the Register of Inhibitions and Adjudications).

CONSUMER CREDIT (EU DIRECTIVE) REGULATIONS 2010
(SI 2010/1010)

PART 4
COMMENCEMENT, TRANSITIONAL AND SAVING PROVISION

. . .

100 Application of regulations to agreements entered into before 1st February 2011

(1) Subject to paragraphs (2) to (5) [regulations 101 and 101A] these Regulations apply only to a regulated consumer credit agreement entered into on or after 1st February 2011.

(2) The following regulations apply (from 1st February 2011) to a regulated consumer credit agreement which is an open-end agreement and is entered into before 11th June 2010—

[(za) regulation 22 (information to be provided on significant overdrawing without prior arrangement);]

(a) regulations 27 and 28 (information on change of interest rate etc);

(b) regulation 36 (assignment);

(c) regulations 37 to 39 (open-end agreements);

(d) regulation 46(b)(amendments to Enterprise Act 2002);

(e) regulation 63 (amendments to Consumer Credit (Running-Account Credit Information) Regulations 1983);

(f) regulation 69(b)(amendments to Enterprise Act 2002 (Part 8 Community Infringements Specified UK Laws) Order 2003);

(g) regulation 97 (amendments to Payment Services Regulations 2009).

(3) The following regulations apply (from 1st February 2011) to a regulated consumer credit agreement which is an open-end agreement and is entered into on or after 11th June 2010 and before 1st February 2011—

[(za) regulation 22 (information to be provided on significant overdrawing without prior arrangement);]

(a) regulation 25 (linked credit agreements);

(b) regulations 27 and 28 (information on change of interest rate etc);

(c) regulations 29 to 35 (early repayment);

(d) regulation 36 (assignment);

(e) regulations 37 to 39 (open-end agreements);

(f) regulation 46 (amendments to Enterprise Act 2002);

(g) regulations 59 to 62 (amendments to Consumer Credit (Settlement Information) Regulations 1983);

(h) regulation 63 (amendments to Consumer Credit (Running-Account Credit Information) Regulations 1983);

(i)   regulation 69 (amendments to Enterprise Act 2002 (Part 8 Community Infringements Specified UK Laws) Order 2003);

(j)   regulations 77 to 84 (amendments to Consumer Credit (Early Settlement) Regulations 2004);

(k)   regulation 97 (amendments to Payment Services Regulations 2009).

(4)   The following regulations apply (from 1st February 2011) to a regulated consumer credit agreement which not an open-end agreement and is entered into on or after 11th June 2010 and before 1st February 2011—

(a)   regulation 25 (linked credit agreements);

(b)   regulation 26 (statement of account);

(c)   regulations 29 to 35 (early repayment);

(d)   regulation 36 (assignment);

(e)   regulation 46 (amendments to Enterprise Act 2002);

(f)   regulations 59 to 62 (amendments to Consumer Credit (Settlement Information) Regulations 1983);

(g)   regulation 69 (amendments to Enterprise Act 2002 (Part 8 Community Infringements Specified UK Laws) Order 2003);

(h)   regulations 77 to 84 (amendments to Consumer Credit (Early Settlement) Regulations 2004).

(5)   Section 95A of the Consumer Credit Act 1974 (compensation for early repayment) applies in relation to an agreement by virtue of sub-paragraph (3)(c) or (4)(c) only where the debtor's entitlement to discharge his indebtedness arises by virtue of a notice made on or after 1st February 2011.

101   Early application of regulations to certain agreements before 1st February 2011

(1)   Where one of the conditions A to E is satisfied in relation to a prospective regulated consumer credit agreement on a date on or after 30th April 2010 and before 1st February 2011, Parts 1 to 3 of these Regulations apply to that agreement (and to any subsequent regulated consumer credit agreement entered into before 1st February 2011), from the date and time that the condition is satisfied.

(2)   Condition A is that information relating to the agreement is disclosed by a creditor or a credit intermediary before the agreement is made in compliance or in purported compliance with the Information Regulations 2010.

(3)   Condition B is that—

(a)   the agreement would, if made, be an agreement entered into at the debtor's request using a means of distance communication (other than voice telephony) which does not enable the provision before the agreement is made of the information referred to in regulation 3(4) of the Information Regulations 2010, and

(b)   the debtor is informed by the creditor before the agreement is made that the information referred to in regulation 3(4) of the Information Regulations 2010 will be disclosed immediately after the agreement is made in accordance with regulation 5 of those Regulations.

(4)   Condition C is that—

(a)   the agreement would, if made, be a distance agreement entered into by the debtor wholly or predominantly for the purposes of a business carried on, or intended to be carried on, by him, and

(b)   the debtor is informed by the creditor before the agreement is made that information referred to in regulation 3(4) of the Information Regulations 2010 will be disclosed immediately after the agreement is made in accordance with regulation 6 of those Regulations.

(5)   Condition D is that —

(a)   the agreement would, if made, be an authorised non-business overdraft agreement (other than a qualifying overdraft agreement referred to in paragraph (7)(b)),

(b)   the agreement would, if made, be one made at the debtor's request using a means of distance communication which does not enable the provision before the agreement is made of the information referred to in regulation 10(2) of the Information Regulations 2010, and

(c)   the creditor has informed the debtor before the agreement is made that a document containing the terms of the agreement will be provided immediately after the agreement is made as though the amendment made by regulation 9 of these Regulations (insertion of section 61B in the Consumer Credit Act 1974) applied.

(6)   Condition E is that the agreement would, if made, be a qualifying overdraft agreement and—

(a)   the creditor has provided a document containing the terms of the agreement before the agreement is made as though the amendment made by regulation 9 (insertion of section 61B in the Consumer Credit Act 1974) applied, or

(b)   the creditor has informed the debtor before the agreement is made that a document containing the terms of the agreement will be provided at, or immediately after, the time the agreement is made as though the amendment made by regulation 9 applied.

(7)   In paragraph (6) 'qualifying overdraft agreement' means—

(a)   an authorised business overdraft agreement, or

(b)   an authorised non-business overdraft agreement under which the creditor provides the debtor with credit exceeding £60,260 or which is secured on land.

[101A—(1)   Where condition F is satisfied on a date on or after 26th August 2010 and before 1st February 2011 in relation to a prospective regulated consumer credit agreement falling within paragraph (2), Parts 1 to 3 of these Regulations apply to that agreement (and to any subsequent regulated consumer credit agreement entered into before 1st February 2011), from the date and time that the condition is satisfied.

(2)   An agreement falls within this paragraph if it is an agreement which would, if made, be—

(a)   an agreement under which the creditor provides the debtor with credit exceeding £60,260 and is not an authorised non-business overdraft agreement, or

(b)   an agreement entered into by the debtor wholly or predominantly for the purposes of a business carried on, or intended to be carried on, by him.

(3)   Condition F is that the Consumer Credit (Disclosure of Information) Regulations 2004 apply to the agreement, but the creditor—

(a)   does what would be required by regulations 3(1)(a) and (c) of those Regulations (pre-contractual information requirement to disclose information and statements required by the Consumer Credit (Agreements) Regulations 1983) if the amendments to the Consumer Credit (Agreements) Regulations 1983 made by regulations 52 to 56 were in force; and

(b)   also provides the debtor with a statement before the agreement is made that, if the creditor decides not to proceed with the agreement on the basis of information obtained from a credit reference agency, the creditor will, when informing the debtor of the decision—

(i)   inform the debtor that this decision has been reached on the basis of information from a credit reference agency, and

(ii)   provide the debtor with the particulars of the agency including its name, address and telephone number.]

102   Interpretation
In this Part—

(a)   'authorised business overdraft agreement', 'authorised non-business overdraft agreement', 'consumer credit agreement', 'creditor', 'debtor', 'open-end' and 'regulated' have the meanings given by section 189(1) of the Consumer Credit Act 1974;

(b) 'distance agreement' means any regulated consumer credit agreement made under an organised distance sales or service-provision scheme run by the creditor or on behalf of the creditor who, in any such case, for the purpose of that agreement makes exclusive use of one or more means of distance communication up to and including the time at which the agreement is made;

(c) 'Information Regulations 2010' means the Consumer Credit (Disclosure of Information) Regulations 2010;

(d) 'means of distance communication' means any means which, without the simultaneous physical presence of the creditor or a person acting on behalf of the creditor and of the debtor, may be used for the making of a regulated consumer credit agreement between the parties to that agreement.

CONSUMER CREDIT (DISCLOSURE OF INFORMATION) REGULATIONS 2010
(SI 2010/1013)

1   Citation, commencement and interpretation

(1) These Regulations may be cited as the Consumer Credit (Disclosure of Information) Regulations 2010 and shall come into force on 30th April 2010.

(2)   In these Regulations—

'the Act' means the Consumer Credit Act 1974;

'advance payment' includes any deposit and in relation to a regulated consumer credit agreement includes also any part-exchange allowance in respect of any goods agreed in antecedent negotiations [. . .] to be taken by the creditor in part exchange but does not include a repayment of credit or any insurance premium or any amount entering into the total charge for credit;

'ancillary service' means a service that relates to the provision of credit under the agreement and includes in particular an insurance or payment protection policy;

'the APR' means the annual percentage rate of charge for credit determined in accordance with Schedule 2 to these Regulations and the Total Charge for Credit Regulations;

'cash price' in relation to any goods, services, land or other things means the price or charge at which the goods, services, land or other things may be purchased by, or supplied to, the debtor for cash account being taken of any discount generally available from the dealer or supplier in question;

'credit intermediary' has the same meaning as in section 160A of the Act;

'distance contract' means any regulated agreement made under an organised distance sales or service-provision scheme run by or on behalf of the creditor who, in any such case, for the purpose of that agreement makes exclusive use of one or more means of distance communication up to and including the time at which the agreement is made. For this purpose, 'means of distance communication' means any means which, without the simultaneous physical presence of the creditor or a person acting on behalf of the creditor and of the debtor, may be used for the making of a regulated agreement between the parties to that agreement;

'excluded pawn agreement' means a pawn agreement—

(a) where the debtor is not a new customer of the creditor (see [paragraph (6)]), and

(b) where, before the agreement is made, the creditor has not received a request from the debtor for the pre-contract credit information (see regulation 9);

'linked credit agreement' means a regulated consumer credit agreement which—

(a) serves exclusively to finance an agreement for the supply of specific goods or the provision of a specific service or land, and

(b) (i) where the supplier or service provider himself finances the credit for the debtor, or if it is financed by a third party, where the creditor uses the services of the supplier or service provider in connection with the preparation or making of the credit agreement, or

> (ii) where the specific goods or land or the provision of a specific service are explicitly specified in the credit agreement;

'pawn agreement' means a consumer credit agreement under which the creditor takes an article in pawn;

'pre-contract credit information' means the information specified in regulation 3(4);

'total amount of credit' means the credit limit or the total sums made available under a consumer credit agreement;

'total amount payable' means the sum of the total charge for credit and the total amount of credit payable under the agreement as well as any advance payment;

'total charge for credit' means the total charge for credit determined in accordance with the Total Charge for Credit Regulations and the Schedule to these Regulations;

'the Total Charge for Credit Regulations' means the Consumer Credit (Total Charge for Credit) Regulations 2010.

(3) In these Regulations, a reference to a repayment is a reference to—

> (a) a repayment of the whole or any part of the credit,
> (b) a payment of the whole or any part of the total charge for credit, or
> (c) a combination of such repayments and payments.

(4) In these Regulations, a reference to rate of interest is a reference to the interest rate expressed as a fixed or variable percentage applied on an annual basis to the amount of credit drawn down.

(5) In these Regulations, a reference to an agreement includes a reference to a prospective agreement.

(6) For the purposes of the definition of 'excluded pawn agreement' and regulation 8 the debtor is a new customer if the debtor has not entered into a pawn agreement with the creditor in the three years preceding the start of the negotiations antecedent to the agreement.

(7) In relation to a regulated consumer credit agreement secured on land and to which these Regulations do not apply, the definition of Total Charge for Credit Regulations shall apply as if for the words 'Consumer Credit (Total Charge for Credit) Regulations 2010' there were substituted 'Consumer Credit (Total Charge for Credit) Regulations 1980'.

2 Agreements to which these Regulations apply

(1) These Regulations apply in respect of a regulated consumer credit agreement, except as provided for in paragraphs (2) to (4).

(2) These regulations do not apply to an agreement to which section 58 of the Act (opportunity for withdrawal from prospective land mortgage) applies.

(3) These Regulations do not apply to an authorised non-business overdraft agreement which is—

> (a) for credit which exceeds £60,260, or
> (b) secured on land.

(4) Except as provided for in paragraph (5) these Regulations do not apply to an agreement—

> (a) under which the creditor provides the debtor with credit exceeding £60,260,
> (b) secured on land,
> (c) entered into by the debtor wholly or predominantly for the purposes of a business also carried on, or intended to be carried on, by him, or
> (d) made before 1st February 2011.

(5) These Regulations apply to an agreement mentioned in paragraph (4) (which is not also an agreement mentioned in paragraph (2) or (3)) where a cred-

itor or, where applicable a credit intermediary, discloses or purports to disclose the pre-contract credit information in accordance with these Regulations rather than in accordance with the Consumer Credit (Disclosure of Information) Regulations 2004 or the Financial Services (Distance Marketing) Regulations 2004 (as the case may be).

(6)   Subsections (2) to (5) of section 16B of the Act (declaration by the debtor as to the purposes of the agreement) apply for the purposes of [paragraph (4)(c)].

3   Information to be disclosed: agreements other than telephone contracts, non-telephone distance contracts, excluded pawn agreements and overdraft agreements

(1)   This regulation applies to an agreement other than—

[(a)   an agreement made by voice telephone communication where it is a distance contract and the debtor consents to the disclosure of the information referred to in regulation 4(2);

(aa)   an agreement made by voice telephone communication where it is not a distance contract (see regulation 4(3));]

(b)   an agreement made using a means of distance communication other than a voice telephone communication, which does not enable the provision of the pre-contract credit information before the agreement is made (see regulation 5);

(c)   an excluded pawn agreement;

(d)   an authorised non-business overdraft agreement (see regulations 10 and 11).

(2)   In good time before the agreement is made, the creditor must disclose to the debtor, in the manner set out in regulation 8, the pre-contract credit information.

(3)   Paragraph (2) does not require a creditor to disclose the pre-contract credit information where it has already been disclosed to the debtor by a credit intermediary in a manner which complies with paragraph (2).

(4)   For the purposes of these Regulations, the pre-contract credit information comprises—

(a)   the type of credit,

(b)   the identity and geographical address of the creditor and, where applicable, of the credit intermediary,

(c)   the total amount of credit to be provided under the agreement and the conditions governing the draw down of credit. In the case of an agreement for running-account credit, the total amount of credit may be expressed as a statement indicating the manner in which the credit limit will be determined where it is not practicable to express the limit as a sum of money,

(d)   the duration or minimum duration of the agreement or a statement that the agreement has no fixed or minimum duration,

(e)   in the case of—

(i)   credit in the form of deferred payment for specific goods, services or land, or

(ii)   a linked credit agreement,

a description of the goods, services or land and the cash price of each and the total cash price,

(f)   the rate of interest charged, any conditions applicable to that rate, where available, any reference rate on which that rate is based and any information on any changes to the rate of interest (including the periods that the rate applies, and any conditions or procedure applicable to changing the rate),

(g)   where different rates of interest are charged in different circumstances the creditor must provide the information in paragraph (f) in respect of each rate,

(h)   the APR and the total amount payable under the agreement illustrated (if not known) by way of a representative example mentioning all the assumptions used in order to calculate that rate and amount,

(i) the amount (expressed as a sum of money), number (if applicable) and frequency of repayments to be made by the debtor and, where appropriate, the order in which repayments will be allocated to different outstanding balances charged at different rates of interest,

(j) in the case of an agreement for running-account credit, the amount of each repayment is to be expressed as (a) a sum of money; (b) a specified proportion of a specified amount; (c) a combination of (a) or (b); or (d) in a case where the amount of any repayment cannot be expressed in accordance with (a), (b) or (c), a statement indicating the manner in which the amount will be determined,

(k) if applicable, any charges for maintaining an account recording both payment transactions and draw downs, unless the opening of an account is optional, and any charge payable for using a method of payment in respect of payment transactions or draw downs,

(l) any other charges payable deriving from the credit agreement and the conditions under which those charges may be changed,

(m) if applicable, a statement that fees will be payable by the debtor to a notary on conclusion of the credit agreement,

(n) the obligation, if any, to enter into a contract for ancillary services relating to the consumer credit agreement, in particular insurance services, where the conclusion of such a contract is compulsory in order to obtain the credit or to obtain it on the terms and conditions marketed,

(o) the rate of interest applicable in the case of late payments and the arrangements for its adjustment, and, where applicable, any charges payable for default,

(p) a warning regarding the consequences of missing payments (for example, the possibility of legal proceedings and the possibility that the debtor's home may be repossessed),

(q) where applicable, any security to be provided by the debtor or on behalf of the debtor,

(r) the existence or absence of a right of withdrawal,

(s) the debtor's right of early repayment under section 94 of the Act, and where applicable, information concerning the creditor's right to compensation and the way in which that compensation will be determined,

(t) the requirement for a creditor to inform a debtor in accordance with section 157(A1) of the Act that a decision not to proceed with a prospective regulated consumer credit agreement has been reached on the basis of information from a credit reference agency and of the particulars of that agency,

(u) the debtor's right to be supplied under section 55C of the Act on request and free of charge, with a copy of the draft agreement except where—

(i) the creditor is at the time of the request unwilling to proceed to the making of the agreement, or

(ii) the agreement is an agreement referred to in regulation 2(4)(a) to (c) or a pawn agreement, and

(v) if applicable, the period of time during which the creditor is bound by the pre-contract credit information.

(5) For the purpose of the representative example referred to in paragraph (4)(h)—

(a) (i) where the debtor has informed the creditor or credit intermediary of one or more components of his preferred credit, such as the duration of the consumer credit agreement or the total amount of credit, and

(ii) where the creditor would in principle agree to offer credit on such terms, the creditor or credit intermediary must take those components into account when calculating the representative APR and the total amount payable;

(b)   where the creditor uses the assumption set out in regulation 6(g) of the Consumer Credit (Total Charge for Credit) Regulations 2010 the creditor must indicate that other draw down mechanisms for this type of consumer credit agreement may result in a higher APR;

(c)   subject to paragraph (a), in the case of an agreement for running-account credit, where the credit limit is not known at the date on which the pre-contract credit information is disclosed, the total amount of credit is to be assumed to be £1,200 or in a case where credit is to be provided subject to a maximum credit limit of less than £1,200, an amount equal to that maximum limit.

(6)   In the case of a consumer credit agreement under which repayments do not give rise to an immediate reduction in the total amount of credit advanced but are used to constitute capital as provided for under the agreement or under an ancillary agreement, the creditor or credit intermediary must provide a clear and concise statement that such agreements do not provide for a guarantee of repayment of the total amount of credit drawn down under the credit agreement unless such a guarantee is given.

4   Information to be disclosed: telephone contracts

(1)   This regulation applies to an agreement (other than an authorised non-business overdraft agreement) made by way of a voice telephone communication (whether or not it is a distance contract).

(2)   Where the agreement is a distance contract and where the debtor explicitly consents, the creditor must disclose the following information before the agreement is made—

(a)   the identity of the person in contact with the debtor and that person's link with the creditor,

(b)   a description of the main characteristics of the credit agreement which includes the information set out in regulation 3(4)(c), (d), (e), (f), (g), (h), (i) and (j),

(c)   the total price to be paid by the debtor to the creditor for the credit including all taxes paid via the creditor or, if an exact price cannot be indicated, the basis for the calculation of the price enabling the debtor to verify it,

(d)   notice of the possibility that other taxes or costs may exist that are not paid via the creditor or imposed by the creditor,

(e)   whether or not there is—

(i)   a right to withdraw under section 66A of the Act, or

(ii)   a right to cancel under regulation 9 of the Financial Services (Distance Marketing) Regulations 2004 and, where there is such a right, its duration and the conditions for exercising it, including information on the amount which the consumer may be required to pay in accordance with regulation 13 of those Regulations, as well as the consequences of not exercising that right,

(f)   that other information is available on request and the nature of that information.

(3)   Where the agreement is not a distance contract the creditor must disclose the information in paragraph (2)(b) before the agreement is made.

(4)   The creditor must disclose the pre-contract credit information in the manner set out in regulation 8 immediately after the agreement is made.

5   Information to be disclosed: non-telephone distance contracts

(1)   This regulation applies to an agreement (other than an authorised non-business overdraft agreement) made—

(a)   at the debtor's request, and

(b)   using a means of distance communication other than a voice telephone communication which does not enable the provision before the agreement is made of the pre-contract credit information.

(2)   The creditor must disclose the pre-contract credit information in the manner set out in regulation 8 immediately after the agreement is made.

6   Information to be disclosed: distance contracts for the purpose of a business

(1)   This regulation applies to an agreement that is a distance contract entered into by the debtor wholly or predominantly for the purposes of a business carried on, or intended to be carried on by him.

(2)   Where the agreement is an agreement to which [regulations 3, 4 or 5] would otherwise apply the creditor may comply with those regulations by disclosing the pre-contract credit information immediately after the agreement is entered into.

(3)   Subsections (2) to (5) of section 16B of the Act (declaration by the debtor as to the purposes of the agreement) apply for the purposes of paragraph (1).

7   Information about contractual terms and conditions: [regulations 3, 4 and 5]

(1)   This regulation applies to an agreement which is—
   (a)   a distance contract to which [regulations 3, 4 or 5] applies, and
   (b)   which is not entered into by the debtor wholly or predominantly for the purposes of a business carried on, or intended to be carried on, by him.

(2)   The creditor must ensure that—
   (a)   the information provided to the debtor pursuant to [regulations 3, 4 or 5] includes the contractual terms and conditions, and
   (b)   the information provided to the debtor in relation to the contractual obligations which would arise if the distance contract were made accurately reflects the contractual obligations which would arise under the law presumed to be applicable to that contract.

(3)   Subsections (2) to (5) of section 16B of the Act (declaration by the debtor as to the purposes of the agreement) apply for the purposes of paragraph (1).

8   Manner of disclosure

(1)   The pre-contract credit information must be disclosed by means of the form contained in Schedule 1.

(2)   The form must be—
   (a)   in writing, and
   (b)   of a nature that enables the debtor to remove it from the place where it is disclosed to him.

(3)   The form must be completed as specified in this paragraph—
   (a)   the relevant pre-contract credit information is to be provided in the appropriate row,
   (b)   the form is to be completed in accordance with the notes to that form,
   (c)   the asterisks and notes may be deleted,
   (d)   gridlines and boxes may be omitted, and
   (e)   any information contained in the form must be clear and easily legible.

(4)   Any additional information relating to the credit which is provided in writing by the creditor to the debtor must be provided in a separate document to the form.

(5)   Where a consumer credit agreement is a multiple agreement containing more than one part for the purposes of section 18 of the Act, the pre-contract credit information in respect of each part may be provided in the same form provided that—
   (a)   information that is not common to each part of the agreement is disclosed separately within the relevant section of the form, and
   (b)   it is clear which information relates to which part.

9   Information to be disclosed: pawn agreements

(1)   This Regulation applies to a pawn agreement.

(2)   In good time before a pawn agreement is made (unless the debtor is a new

customer), the creditor must inform the debtor of his right to receive the pre-contract credit information in the form contained in Schedule 1, free of charge, on request.

10 Information to be disclosed: overdraft agreements

(1) This regulation applies to an agreement which is an authorised non-business overdraft agreement.

(2) In good time before an authorised non-business overdraft agreement is made, the creditor must disclose to the debtor, the information in paragraph (3) in the manner set out in regulation 11.

(3) The information referred to in paragraph (2) is as follows—

(a) the type of credit,

(b) the identity and geographical address of the creditor and, where applicable, of the credit intermediary,

(c) the total amount of credit,

(d) the duration of the agreement,

(e) the rate of interest charged, any conditions applicable to that rate, any reference rate on which that rate is based and any information on any changes to the rate of interest (including the periods that the rate applies, and any conditions or procedure applicable to changing the rate),

(f) where different rates of interest are charged in different circumstances the creditor must provide the information in paragraph (e) in respect of each rate,

(g) the conditions and procedure for terminating the agreement,

(h) where applicable, an indication that the debtor may be requested to repay the amount of credit in full on demand at any time,

(i) the rate of interest applicable in the case of late payments and the arrangements for its adjustment, and, where applicable, any charges payable for default,

(j) the requirement for a creditor to inform a debtor in accordance with section 157(A1) of the Act that a decision not to proceed with a prospective regulated consumer credit agreement has been reached on the basis of information from a credit reference agency and of the particulars of that agency,

(k) the charges, other than the rates of interest, payable by the debtor under the agreement (and the conditions under which those charges may be varied),

(l) if applicable, the period of time during which the creditor is bound by the information set out in this paragraph.

(4) Paragraph (2) does not apply to—

(a) an agreement made by a voice telephone communication (whether or not it is a distance contract),

(b) an agreement made at the debtor's request using a means of distance communication, other than a voice telephone communication, which does not enable the provision of the information required by paragraph (2) before the agreement is made, or

(c) an agreement that does not come within sub-paragraph (a) or (b) but where the debtor requests the overdraft be made available with immediate effect.

(5) In the case of an agreement that falls within paragraph (4)(a) that is also a distance contract, where the debtor explicitly consents the creditor must disclose the following information before the agreement is made—

(a) the identity of the person in contact with the debtor and that person's link with the creditor,

(b) a description of the main characteristics of the financial service including at least the information in paragraph (3)(c), (e), (f), (h) and (k),

(c) the total price to be paid by the debtor to the creditor for the credit including all taxes paid via the creditor or, if an exact price cannot be indicated, the basis for the calculation of the price enabling the debtor to verify it,

(d)   notice of the possibility that other taxes or costs may exist that are not paid via the creditor or imposed by the creditor,

(e)   whether or not there is a right to cancel under regulation 9 of the Financial Services (Distance Marketing) Regulations 2004 and where there is such a right, its duration and the conditions for exercising it including information on the amount which the consumer may be required to pay in accordance with regulation 13 of those regulations, as well as the consequences of not exercising that right, and

(f)   that other information is available on request and the nature of that information.

[(5A)   In the case of an agreement that falls within paragraph (4)(a) that is also a distance contract, where the debtor does not explicitly consent to the disclosure of the information in paragraph (5), the creditor must disclose the information in paragraph (3) to the debtor before the regulation is made.]

(6)   In the case of an agreement that falls within paragraph (4)(a) that is not a distance contract the creditor must disclose the information in paragraph (5)(b) before the agreement is made.

(7)   In the case of an agreement that is a distance contract to which this regulation applies the creditor must ensure that the information he provides to the debtor pursuant to this regulation regarding the contractual obligations which would arise if the distance contract were concluded, accurately reflects the contractual obligations which would arise under the law presumed to be applicable to that contract.

(8)   In the case of an agreement that falls within paragraph (4)(c), the creditor must disclose the information in paragraph (3)(c), (e), (f), (h), and (k) to the debtor before the agreement is made in the manner set out in regulation 11.

(9)   Where a current account is an agreement for two or more debtors jointly the creditor may comply with paragraphs (5), [(5A),] (6) or (8) by disclosing the information to one debtor provided that each of the debtors have given the creditor their consent that the creditor may not comply in each debtor's case with the relevant paragraph.

11—(1)   Where regulation 10(2) applies, the creditor must comply with that regulation by—

(a)   disclosing the information by means of the European Consumer Credit Information form set out in Schedule 3 to these Regulations and as specified in paragraph (2), or

(b)   disclosing the information in writing so that all information is equally prominent.

(2)   The specifications referred to in paragraph (1)(a) are that—

(a)   the relevant information must be provided in the appropriate row,

(b)   the form must be completed in accordance with the notes to that form,

(c)   the asterisks and notes may be deleted,

(d)   gridlines and boxes may be omitted, and

(e)   any information contained in the form must be clear and easily legible.

(3)   Where regulation 10(8) applies, the creditor may provide the information orally.

12   Modifying agreements

(1)   Subject to paragraphs (2) to (4), these Regulations apply to a modifying agreement which varies or supplements an earlier agreement and which is, or is treated under section 82(3) of the Act as, a regulated agreement.

[(2)   Where a modifying agreement modifies an earlier consumer credit agreement, the requirements of regulations 3, 4 and 10 will be deemed to be satisfied if—

(a)   in good time before the modifying agreement is made—

(i)   the information specified by regulations 3(4) and 10(3) is disclosed to the debtor in respect of any provision of the earlier agreement which is varied or supplemented, and

(ii)   the creditor informs the debtor in writing that the other information in the earlier agreement remains unchanged, and

(b)   where the Financial Services (Distance Marketing) Regulations 2004 apply, the creditor complies with regulations 7 and 8 of those Regulations.]

(3)   Where a modifying agreement is made in a manner that does not allow the creditor to comply with the requirement in [paragraph (2)(a)(ii)], the creditor is deemed to have complied with that requirement if—

(a)   before the agreement is made the creditor informs the debtor orally that the other information in the earlier agreement remains unchanged, and

(b)   this is confirmed to the debtor in writing immediately after the agreement is made.

(4)   This regulation does not apply to an excluded pawn agreement.

Regulation 8(1)   SCHEDULE 1

PRE-CONTRACT CREDIT INFORMATION

(Standard European Consumer Credit Information)

1. Contact details

Creditor. Address. Telephone number(s).* E-mail, address.* Fax number.* Web address.*	[Identity.] [Geographical address of the creditor to be used by the debtor.]
If applicable Credit intermediary. Address. Telephone number(s).* E-mail address.* Fax number.* Web address.*	[Identity.] [Geographical address of the credit intermediary to be used by the debtor.]

*This information is optional for the creditor. The row may be deleted if the information is not provided.

Wherever "if applicable" is indicated, the creditor must give the information relevant to the credit product or, if the information is not relevant for the type of credit considered, delete the respective information or the entire row, or indicate that the information is not applicable.

Indications between square brackets provide explanations for the creditor and must be replaced with the corresponding information.

2. Key features of the credit product

The type of credit.	
The total amount of credit. This means the amount of credit to be provided under the proposed credit agreement or the credit limit.	[The amount is to be expressed as a sum of money. In the case of running-account credit, the total amount may be expressed as a statement indicating the manner in which the credit limit will be determined where it is not practicable to express the limit as a sum of money.]
How and when credit would be provided.	[Details of how and when any credit being advanced is to be drawn down.]
The duration of the credit agreement.	[The duration or minimum duration of the agreement or a statement that the agreement has no fixed or minimum duration.]
Repayments. If applicable: Your repayments will pay off what you owe in the following order.	[The amount (expressed as a sum of money), number (if applicable) and frequency of repayments to be made by the debtor. In the case of an agreement for running-account credit, the amount may be expressed as a sum of money or a specified proportion of a specified amount or both, or in a case where the amount of any repayment cannot be expressed as a sum of

	money or a specified proportion, a statement indicating the manner in which the amount will be determined. [The order in which repayments will be allocated to different outstanding balances charged at different rates of interest.]
The total amount you will have to pay. This means the amount you have borrowed plus interest and other costs.	[The amount payable by the debtor under the agreement (where necessary, illustrated by means of a representative example). The total amount payable will be the sum of the total amount of credit and the total charge for credit payable under the agreement as well as any advance payment where required. In the case of running account credit, where it is not practicable to express the limit as a sum of money, a credit limit of £1200 should be assumed. In a case where credit is to be provided subject to a maximum credit limit of less than £1200, an amount equal to that maximum limit. The total charge for credit is to be calculated using the relevant APR assumptions set out in Schedule 2 to the Consumer Credit (Disclosure of Information) Regulations 2010 and the Total Charge for Credit Regulations, and where appropriate the relevant components of the debtor's preferred credit.]
If applicable [The proposed credit will be granted in the form of a deferred payment for goods or service.] or [The proposed credit will be linked to the supply of specific goods or the provision of a service.] Description of goods/services/land (as applicable). Cash price.	[A list or other description] [Cash price of goods or service.] [Total cash price.]
If applicable Security required. This is a description of the security to be provided by you in relation to the credit agreement.	[Description of any security to be provided by or on behalf of the debtor.]
If applicable Repayments will not immediately reduce the amount you owe.	[In the case of a credit agreement under which repayments do not give rise to an immediate reduction in the total amount of credit advanced but are used to constitute capital as provided by the agreement (or an ancillary agreement a clear and concise statement) where applicable, that the agreement does not provide for a guarantee of the repayment of the total amount of credit drawn down under the credit agreement.]

3. Costs of the credit

The rates of interest which apply to the credit agreement	[Details of the rate of interest charged, any conditions applicable to that rate, where available, any reference rate on which that rate is based and any information on changes to the rate of interest (including the periods that the rate applies, and any conditions or procedure applicable to changing the rate). Where different rates of interest are charged in different circumstances, the creditor must provide the above information in respect of each rate.]
Annual Percentage Rate of Charge (APR). This is the total cost expressed as an annual percentage of the total amount of credit. The APR is there to help you compare different offers.	[% if known. If the APR is not known a representative example (expressed as a %) mentioning all the necessary assumptions used for calculating the rate (as set out in Schedule 2 to the Consumer Credit (Disclosure of Information) Regulations 2010, the Total Charge for Credit Regulations and, where appropriate, the relevant components of the debtor's preferred credit). Where the creditor uses the assumption set out in regulation 6(g) of the Total Charge for Credit Regulations, the creditor shall indicate that other draw down mechanisms for this type of agreement may result in a higher APR.]
If applicable In order to obtain the credit or to obtain it on the terms and conditions marketed, you must take out: —an insurance policy securing the credit, or —another ancillary service contract. If we do not know the costs of these services they are not included in the APR.	[Nature and description of any insurance or other ancillary service contract required.]
Related costs	
If applicable You must have a separate account for recording both payment transactions and drawdowns.	[Details of any account or accounts that the creditor requires to be set up in order to obtain the credit together with the amount of any charge for this.]
If applicable Charge for using a specific payment method.	[Specify means of payment and the amount of charge.]
If applicable Any other costs deriving from the credit agreement. If applicable Conditions under which the above charges can be changed.	[Description and amount of any other charges not otherwise referred to in this form.] [Details of the conditions under which any of the charges mentioned above can be changed.]

If applicable You will be required to pay notarial fees.	[Description and amount of any fee.]
Costs in the case of late payments	Either [A statement that there are no charges for late or missed payments.] Or [Applicable rate of interest in the case of late payments and arrangements for its adjustment and, where applicable any charges payable for default.]
Consequences of missing payments.	[A statement warning about the consequences of missing payments, including: —a reference to possible legal proceedings and repossession of the debtor's home where this is a possibility, and —the possibility of missing payments making it more difficult to obtain credit in the future.]

4. Other important legal aspects

Right of withdrawal.	Either: [A statement that the debtor has the right to withdraw from the credit agreement before the end of 14 days beginning with the day after the day on which the agreement is made, or if information is provided after the agreement is made, the day on which the debtor receives a copy of the executed agreement under sections 61A or 63 of the Consumer Credit Act 1974, the day on which the debtor receives the information required in section 61A(3) of that Act or the day on which the creditor notifies the debtor of the credit limit, the first time it is provided, whichever is the latest.] Or [There is no right to withdraw from this agreement—if there is a right to cancel the agreement this should be stated.](a) [If the right to cancel is under the Financial Services (Distance Marketing) Regulations 2004 refer to section 5 of the form.]
Early repayment. If applicable Compensation payable in the case of early repayment.	[A statement that the debtor has the right to repay the credit early at any time in full or partially.](b). [Determination of the compensation (calculation method) in accordance with section 95A of the Consumer Credit Act 1974.]

Consultation with a Credit Reference Agency(c).	[A statement that if the creditor decides not to proceed with a prospective regulated consumer credit agreement on the basis of information from a credit reference agency the creditor must, when informing the debtor of the decision, inform the debtor that it has been reached on the basis of information from a credit reference agency and of the particulars of that agency.]
Right to a draft credit agreement(d).	[A statement that the debtor has the right, upon request, to obtain a copy of the draft credit agreement free of charge, unless the creditor is unwilling at the time of the request to proceed to the conclusion of the credit agreement.]
If applicable The period of time during which the creditor is bound by the pre-contractual information.	[This information is valid from [—] until [—].] or [Period of time during which the information on this form is valid.]

(a) i.e. If there is a cancellation right in respect of an agreement involving credit in excess of £60,260.

(b) The words "or partially" may be excluded in the case of agreements secured on land.

(c) This requirement does not apply in the case of agreements secured on land.

(d) This requirement does not apply in the case of agreements secured on land, agreements for credit agreements exceeding £60,260, pawn agreements and business purpose agreements.

If applicable

5. Additional information in the case of distance marketing of financial services

(a) concerning the creditor	
If applicable The creditor's representative in your Member State of residence. Address. Telephone number(s). E-mail address.* Fax number.* Web address.*	[i.e. where different from section 1.] [Identity.] [Geographical address to be used by the debtor.]
If applicable Registration number.	[Consumer credit licence number and any other relevant registration number of the creditor.]
If applicable The supervisory authority.	[The Office of Fair Trading or any other relevant supervisory authority or both.]
(b) concerning the credit agreement	

If applicable(a) Right to cancel the credit agreement.	[Practical instructions for exercising the right to cancel indicating, amongst other things, the period for exercising the right, the address to which notification of exercise of the right to cancel should be sent and the consequences of non- exercise of that right.]
If applicable The law taken by the creditor as a basis for the establishment of relations with you before the conclusion of the credit agreement.	[English/other law]
If applicable The law applicable to the credit agreement and/or the competent court.	[A statement concerning the law which governs the contract and the courts to which disputes may be referred.]
If applicable Language to be used in connection with the credit agreement.	[Details of the language that the information and contractual terms will be supplied in and used, with your consent, for communication during the duration of the credit agreement.]
(c) concerning redress	
Access to out-of-court complaint and redress mechanism.	[Whether or not there is an out-of-court complaint and redress mechanism for the debtor and, if so, the methods of access to it.]

*This information is optional for the creditor. The row may be deleted if the information is not provided.
(a) If the right to withdraw referred to in section 4 does not apply.

SCHEDULE 2 PROVISIONS RELATING TO CALCULATION AND
DISCLOSURE OF THE TOTAL CHARGE FOR CREDIT AND APR

1. Assumptions about running-account credit

(a)   In the case of an agreement for running-account credit, the assumption in paragraph (b) shall have effect for the purpose of calculating the total charge for credit and any APR in place of any assumptions in regulation 6(o) of the Consumer Credit (Total Charge for Credit) Regulations 2010 that might otherwise apply—

(b)   in a case where the credit limit applicable to the credit is not known at the time the pre-contract credit information is disclosed but it is known that it will be subject to a maximum limit of less than £1,200, the credit limit shall be assumed to be an amount equal to that maximum limit.

2. Permissible tolerances in disclosure of an APR

For the purposes of these Regulations, it shall be sufficient compliance with the requirement to show an APR if there is included in the pre-contract credit information—

(a)   a rate which exceeds the APR by not more than one,

(b)   a rate which falls short of the APR by not more than 0.1, or

(c)   in a case to which paragraph 3 or 4 of this Schedule applies, a rate determined in accordance with those paragraphs or whichever of them applies to that case.

3. Tolerance where repayments are nearly equal

In the case of an agreement under which all repayments but one are equal and that one repayment does not differ from any other repayment by more whole pence than there are repayments of credit, there may be included in the pre-contract credit information a rate found under regulation 5 of the Consumer Credit (Total Charge for Credit) Regulations 2010 as if that one repayment were equal to the other repayments to be made under the agreement.

4. Tolerance where interval between relevant date and first repayment is greater than interval between repayments

In the case of an agreement under which-

(a)   three or more repayments are to be made at equal intervals, and

(b)   the interval between the relevant date and the first repayment is greater than the interval between the repayments,

there may be included in the pre-contract credit information a rate found under regulation 5 of the Consumer Credit (Total Charge for Credit) Regulations 2010 as if the interval between the relevant date and the first repayment were shortened so as to be equal to the interval between repayments.

SCHEDULE 3   Regulation 11(1)

EUROPEAN CONSUMER CREDIT INFORMATION

1. Contact details

Creditor. Address. Telephone number(s).* E-mail address.* Fax number.* Web address.*	[Identity.] [Geographical address of the creditor to be used by the debtor.]
If applicable Credit intermediary. Address. Telephone number(s).* E-mail address.* Fax number.* Web address.*	[Identity.] [Geographical address of the credit intermediary to be used by the debtor.]

*This information is optional for the creditor. The row may be deleted if the information is not provided.

Wherever "if applicable" is indicated, the creditor must give the information relevant to the credit product or, if the information is not relevant for the type of credit considered, delete the respective information or the entire row or indicate that the information is not applicable.

Indications between square brackets provide explanations for the creditor and must be replaced with the corresponding information.

2. Description of the main features of the credit product

The type of credit.	
The total amount of credit. This means the amount of credit to be provided under the agreement or the credit limit.	[The amount is to be expressed as a sum of money. In the case of running account credit, the total amount may be expressed as a statement indicating the manner in which the credit limit will be determined where it is not practicable to express the limit as a sum of money.]
The duration of the credit agreement.	[The duration or minimum duration of the agreement or a statement that the agreement has no fixed or minimum duration.]
If applicable Repayment of the credit.	[A statement informing the debtor that the debtor may be required to repay the amount of credit in full on demand at any time.]

3. Costs of the credit

The rates of interest which apply to the credit agreement.	[Details of the rates of interest charged, any conditions applicable to that rate, where available any reference rate on which that rate is based and any information on changes to the rate of interest (including the periods that the rate applies and any conditions or procedure applicable to changing the rate). Where different rates of interest are charged in different circumstances, the creditor must provide the above information in respect of each rate.]
If applicable Costs. If applicable The conditions under which those costs may be changed.	[The costs applicable from the time the credit agreement is concluded.]
Costs in the case of late payments.	Either [A statement that there are no charges for late or missed payments.] Or [Applicable rate of interest, in the case of late payments and arrangements for its adjustment and, where applicable, any charges payable for default.]

4. Other important legal aspects

Termination of the credit agreement.	[The conditions and procedure for termination of the credit agreement.]
Consultation with a credit reference agency.	[A statement that if the creditor decides not to proceed with a prospective regulated consumer credit agreement on the basis of information from a credit reference agency the creditor must, when informing the debtor of that decision, inform the debtor that it has been reached on the basis of information from a credit reference agency and of the particulars of that agency.]
If applicable The period of time during which the creditor is bound by the pre-contractual information.	[This information is valid from [—] until [—] or [Period of time during which the information on this form is valid.]

If applicable

5. Additional information to be given in the case of distance marketing of financial services

(a) concerning the creditor	
If applicable The creditor's representative in [the UK] [your Member State of residence.] Address. Telephone number.* E-mail address.* Fax number.* Web address.*	[i.e. where different from section 1.] [Identity.] [Geographical address to be used by the debtor.]
If applicable Registration number.	[Consumer credit licence number and any other relevant registration number of the creditor.]
If applicable The supervisory authority.	[The Office of Fair Trading or any other relevant supervisory authority or both.]
(b) concerning the credit agreement	
If applicable The law taken by the creditor as a basis for the establishment of relations with you before the conclusion of the credit contract.	[English/other law.]
If applicable The law applicable to the credit agreement and/or the competent court.	[A statement concerning the law which governs the contract and the courts to which disputes may be referred.]
If applicable Language to be used in connection your agreement.	[Details of the language that the information and contractual terms will be supplied in and used, with the debtor's consent, for communication during the duration of the credit agreement.]
(c) concerning redress	
Access to out- of-court complaint and redress mechanism.	[Whether or not there is an out-of-court complaint and redress mechanism for the debtor who is party to the distance contract and, if so, the methods of access to it.]

* This information is optional for the creditor. The row may be deleted if the information is not provided.

PART III
EC MATERIALS

COUNCIL REGULATION (EC) NO 1346/2000 OF 29 MAY ON INSOLVENCY PROCEEDINGS

Official Journal L 160, 30/06/2000 pp 1–18

THE COUNCIL OF THE EUROPEAN UNION,

Having regard to the Treaty establishing the European Community, and in particular Articles 61(c) and 67(1) thereof,
Having regard to the initiative of the Federal Republic of Germany and the Republic of Finland,
Having regard to the opinion of the European Parliament,
Having regard to the opinion of the Economic and Social Committee,

HAS ADOPTED THIS REGULATION:

CHAPTER I
GENERAL PROVISIONS

Article 1. Scope
1.   This Regulation shall apply to collective insolvency proceedings which entail the partial or total divestment of a debtor and the appointment of a liquidator.
2.   This Regulation shall not apply to insolvency proceedings concerning insurance undertakings, credit institutions, investment undertakings which provide services involving the holding of funds or securities for third parties, or to collective investment undertakings.

Article 2. Definitions
For the purposes of this Regulation:
(a)   'insolvency proceedings' shall mean the collective proceedings referred to in Article 1(1). These proceedings are listed in Annex A;
(b)   'liquidator' shall mean any person or body whose function is to administer or liquidate assets of which the debtor has been divested or to supervise the administration of his affairs. Those persons and bodies are listed in Annex C;
(c)   'winding-up proceedings' shall mean insolvency proceedings within the meaning of point (a) involving realising the assets of the debtor, including where the proceedings have been closed by a composition or other measure terminating the insolvency, or closed by reason of the insufficiency of the assets. Those proceedings are listed in Annex B;
(d)   'court' shall mean the judicial body or any other competent body of a Member State empowered to open insolvency proceedings or to take decisions in the course of such proceedings;
(e)   'judgment' in relation to the opening of insolvency proceedings or the

appointment of a liquidator shall include the decision of any court empowered to open such proceedings or to appoint a liquidator;

(f)   'the time of the opening of proceedings' shall mean the time at which the judgment opening proceedings becomes effective, whether it is a final judgment or not;

(g)   'the Member State in which assets are situated' shall mean, in the case of:
- tangible property, the Member State within the territory of which the property is situated,
- property and rights ownership of or entitlement to which must be entered in a public register, the Member State under the authority of which the register is kept,
- claims, the Member State within the territory of which the third party required to meet them has the centre of his main interests, as determined in Article 3(1);

(h)   'establishment' shall mean any place of operations where the debtor carries out a non-transitory economic activity with human means and goods.

Article 3. International jurisdiction

1.   The courts of the Member State within the territory of which the centre of a debtor's main interests is situated shall have jurisdiction to open insolvency proceedings. In the case of a company or legal person, the place of the registered office shall be presumed to be the centre of its main interests in the absence of proof to the contrary.

2.   Where the centre of a debtor's main interests is situated within the territory of a Member State, the courts of another Member State shall have jurisdiction to open insolvency proceedings against that debtor only if he possesses an establishment within the territory of that other Member State. The effects of those proceedings shall be restricted to the assets of the debtor situated in the territory of the latter Member State.

3.   Where insolvency proceedings have been opened under paragraph 1, any proceedings opened subsequently under paragraph 2 shall be secondary proceedings. These latter proceedings must be winding-up proceedings.

4.   Territorial insolvency proceedings referred to in paragraph 2 may be opened prior to the opening of main insolvency proceedings in accordance with paragraph 1 only:

(a)   where insolvency proceedings under paragraph 1 cannot be opened because of the conditions laid down by the law of the Member State within the territory of which the centre of the debtor's main interests is situated; or

(b)   where the opening of territorial insolvency proceedings is requested by a creditor who has his domicile, habitual residence or registered office in the Member State within the territory of which the establishment is situated, or whose claim arises from the operation of that establishment.

Article 4. Law applicable

1.   Save as otherwise provided in this Regulation, the law applicable to insolvency proceedings and their effects shall be that of the Member State within the territory of which such proceedings are opened, hereafter referred to as the 'State of the opening of proceedings'.

2.   The law of the State of the opening of proceedings shall determine the conditions for the opening of those proceedings, their conduct and their closure. It shall determine in particular:

(a)   against which debtors insolvency proceedings may be brought on account of their capacity;

(b)   the assets which form part of the estate and the treatment of assets acquired by or devolving on the debtor after the opening of the insolvency proceedings;

(c)   the respective powers of the debtor and the liquidator;

(d)   the conditions under which set-offs may be invoked;

(e)   the effects of insolvency proceedings on current contracts to which the debtor is party;

(f)   the effects of the insolvency proceedings on proceedings brought by individual creditors, with the exception of lawsuits pending;

(g)   the claims which are to be lodged against the debtor's estate and the treatment of claims arising after the opening of insolvency proceedings;

(h)   the rules governing the lodging, verification and admission of claims;

(i)   the rules governing the distribution of proceeds from the realisation of assets, the ranking of claims and the rights of creditors who have obtained partial satisfaction after the opening of insolvency proceedings by virtue of a right in rem or through a set-off;

(j)   the conditions for and the effects of closure of insolvency proceedings, in particular by composition;

(k)   creditors' rights after the closure of insolvency proceedings;

(l)   who is to bear the costs and expenses incurred in the insolvency proceedings;

(m)   the rules relating to the voidness, voidability or unenforceability of legal acts detrimental to all the creditors.

Article 5. Third parties' rights in rem

1.   The opening of insolvency proceedings shall not affect the rights in rem of creditors or third parties in respect of tangible or intangible, moveable or immoveable assets – both specific assets and collections of indefinite assets as a whole which change from time to time – belonging to the debtor which are situated within the territory of another Member State at the time of the opening of proceedings.

2.   The rights referred to in paragraph 1 shall in particular mean:

(a)   the right to dispose of assets or have them disposed of and to obtain satisfaction from the proceeds of or income from those assets, in particular by virtue of a lien or a mortgage;

(b)   the exclusive right to have a claim met, in particular a right guaranteed by a lien in respect of the claim or by assignment of the claim by way of a guarantee;

(c)   the right to demand the assets from, and/or to require restitution by, anyone having possession or use of them contrary to the wishes of the party so entitled;

(d)   a right in rem to the beneficial use of assets.

3.   The right, recorded in a public register and enforceable against third parties, under which a right in rem within the meaning of paragraph 1 may be obtained, shall be considered a right in rem.

4.   Paragraph 1 shall not preclude actions for voidness, voidability or unenforceability as referred to in Article 4(2)(m).

Article 6. Set-off

1.   The opening of insolvency proceedings shall not affect the right of creditors to demand the set-off of their claims against the claims of the debtor, where such a set-off is permitted by the law applicable to the insolvent debtor's claim.

2.   Paragraph 1 shall not preclude actions for voidness, voidability or unenforceability as referred to in Article 4(2)(m).

Article 7. Reservation of title

1.   The opening of insolvency proceedings against the purchaser of an asset shall not affect the seller's rights based on a reservation of title where at the time of the opening of proceedings the asset is situated within the territory of a Member State other than the State of opening of proceedings.

2.   The opening of insolvency proceedings against the seller of an asset, after

delivery of the asset, shall not constitute grounds for rescinding or terminating the sale and shall not prevent the purchaser from acquiring title where at the time of the opening of proceedings the asset sold is situated within the territory of a Member State other than the State of the opening of proceedings.

3.   Paragraphs 1 and 2 shall not preclude actions for voidness, voidability or unenforceability as referred to in Article 4(2)(m).

Article 8. Contracts relating to immoveable property
The effects of insolvency proceedings on a contract conferring the right to acquire or make use of immoveable property shall be governed solely by the law of the Member State within the territory of which the immoveable property is situated.

Article 9. Payment systems and financial markets
1.   Without prejudice to Article 5, the effects of insolvency proceedings on the rights and obligations of the parties to a payment or settlement system or to a financial market shall be governed solely by the law of the Member State applicable to that system or market.

2.   Paragraph 1 shall not preclude any action for voidness, voidability or unenforceability which may be taken to set aside payments or transactions under the law applicable to the relevant payment system or financial market.

Article 10. Contracts of employment
The effects of insolvency proceedings on employment contracts and relationships shall be governed solely by the law of the Member State applicable to the contract of employment.

Article 11. Effects on rights subject to registration
The effects of insolvency proceedings on the rights of the debtor in immoveable property, a ship or an aircraft subject to registration in a public register shall be determined by the law of the Member State under the authority of which the register is kept.

Article 12. Community patents and trade marks
For the purposes of this Regulation, a Community patent, a Community trade mark or any other similar right established by Community law may be included only in the proceedings referred to in Article 3(1).

Article 13. Detrimental acts
Article 4(2)(m) shall not apply where the person who benefited from an act detrimental to all the creditors provides proof that:
  – the said act is subject to the law of a Member State other than that of the State of the opening of proceedings, and
  – that law does not allow any means of challenging that act in the relevant case.

Article 14. Protection of third-party purchasers
Where, by an act concluded after the opening of insolvency proceedings, the debtor disposes, for consideration, of:
  – an immoveable asset, or
  – a ship or an aircraft subject to registration in a public register, or
  – securities whose existence presupposes registration in a register laid down by law,
the validity of that act shall be governed by the law of the State within the territory of which the immoveable asset is situated or under the authority of which the register is kept.

Article 15. Effects of insolvency proceedings on lawsuits pending
The effects of insolvency proceedings on a lawsuit pending concerning an asset or a right of which the debtor has been divested shall be governed solely by the law of the Member State in which that lawsuit is pending.

CHAPTER II
RECOGNITION OF INSOLVENCY PROCEEDINGS

Article 16. Principle

1.   Any judgment opening insolvency proceedings handed down by a court of a Member State which has jurisdiction pursuant to Article 3 shall be recognised in all the other Member States from the time that it becomes effective in the State of the opening of proceedings.

This rule shall also apply where, on account of his capacity, insolvency proceedings cannot be brought against the debtor in other Member States.

2.   Recognition of the proceedings referred to in Article 3(1) shall not preclude the opening of the proceedings referred to in Article 3(2) by a court in another Member State. The latter proceedings shall be secondary insolvency proceedings within the meaning of Chapter III.

Article 17. Effects of recognition

1.   The judgment opening the proceedings referred to in Article 3(1) shall, with no further formalities, produce the same effects in any other Member State as under this law of the State of the opening of proceedings, unless this Regulation provides otherwise and as long as no proceedings referred to in Article 3(2) are opened in that other Member State.

2.   The effects of the proceedings referred to in Article 3(2) may not be challenged in other Member States. Any restriction of the creditors' rights, in particular a stay or discharge, shall produce effects vis-à-vis assets situated within the territory of another Member State only in the case of those creditors who have given their consent.

Article 18. Powers of the liquidator

1.   The liquidator appointed by a court which has jurisdiction pursuant to Article 3(1) may exercise all the powers conferred on him by the law of the State of the opening of proceedings in another Member State, as long as no other insolvency proceedings have been opened there nor any preservation measure to the contrary has been taken there further to a request for the opening of insolvency proceedings in that State. He may in particular remove the debtor's assets from the territory of the Member State in which they are situated, subject to Articles 5 and 7.

2.   The liquidator appointed by a court which has jurisdiction pursuant to Article 3(2) may in any other Member State claim through the courts or out of court that moveable property was removed from the territory of the State of the opening of proceedings to the territory of that other Member State after the opening of the insolvency proceedings. He may also bring any action to set aside which is in the interests of the creditors.

3.   In exercising his powers, the liquidator shall comply with the law of the Member State within the territory of which he intends to take action, in particular with regard to procedures for the realisation of assets. Those powers may not include coercive measures or the right to rule on legal proceedings or disputes.

Article 19. Proof of the liquidator's appointment

The liquidator's appointment shall be evidenced by a certified copy of the original decision appointing him or by any other certificate issued by the court which has jurisdiction.

A translation into the official language or one of the official languages of the Member State within the territory of which he intends to act may be required. No legalisation or other similar formality shall be required.

Article 20. Return and imputation

1.   A creditor who, after the opening of the proceedings referred to in Article 3(1) obtains by any means, in particular through enforcement, total or partial satis-

faction of his claim on the assets belonging to the debtor situated within the territory of another Member State, shall return what he has obtained to the liquidator, subject to Articles 5 and 7.

2.   In order to ensure equal treatment of creditors a creditor who has, in the course of insolvency proceedings, obtained a dividend on his claim shall share in distributions made in other proceedings only where creditors of the same ranking or category have, in those other proceedings, obtained an equivalent dividend.

Article 21. Publication

1.   The liquidator may request that notice of the judgment opening insolvency proceedings and, where appropriate, the decision appointing him, be published in any other Member State in accordance with the publication procedures provided for in that State. Such publication shall also specify the liquidator appointed and whether the jurisdiction rule applied is that pursuant to Article 3(1) or Article 3(2).

2.   However, any Member State within the territory of which the debtor has an establishment may require mandatory publication. In such cases, the liquidator or any authority empowered to that effect in the Member State where the proceedings referred to in Article 3(1) are opened shall take all necessary measures to ensure such publication.

Article 22. Registration in a public register

1.   The liquidator may request that the judgment opening the proceedings referred to in Article 3(1) be registered in the land register, the trade register and any other public register kept in the other Member States.

2.   However, any Member State may require mandatory registration. In such cases, the liquidator or any authority empowered to that effect in the Member State where the proceedings referred to in Article 3(1) have been opened shall take all necessary measures to ensure such registration.

Article 23. Costs

The costs of the publication and registration provided for in Articles 21 and 22 shall be regarded as costs and expenses incurred in the proceedings.

Article 24. Honouring of an obligation to a debtor

1.   Where an obligation has been honoured in a Member State for the benefit of a debtor who is subject to insolvency proceedings opened in another Member State, when it should have been honoured for the benefit of the liquidator in those proceedings, the person honouring the obligation shall be deemed to have discharged it if he was unaware of the opening of proceedings.

2.   Where such an obligation is honoured before the publication provided for in Article 21 has been effected, the person honouring the obligation shall be presumed, in the absence of proof to the contrary, to have been unaware of the opening of insolvency proceedings; where the obligation is honoured after such publication has been effected, the person honouring the obligation shall be presumed, in the absence of proof to the contrary, to have been aware of the opening of proceedings.

Article 25. Recognition and enforceability of other judgments

1.   Judgments handed down by a court whose judgment concerning the opening of proceedings is recognised in accordance with Article 16 and which concern the course and closure of insolvency proceedings, and compositions approved by that court shall also be recognised with no further formalities. Such judgments shall be enforced in accordance with Articles 31 to 51, with the exception of Article 34(2), of the Brussels Convention on Jurisdiction and the Enforcement of Judgments in Civil and Commercial Matters, as amended by the Conventions of Accession to this Convention.

The first subparagraph shall also apply to judgments deriving directly from the insolvency proceedings and which are closely linked with them, even if they were handed down by another court.

The first subparagraph shall also apply to judgments relating to preservation measures taken after the request for the opening of insolvency proceedings.

2.   The recognition and enforcement of judgments other than those referred to in paragraph 1 shall be governed by the Convention referred to in paragraph 1, provided that that Convention is applicable.

3.   The Member States shall not be obliged to recognise or enforce a judgment referred to in paragraph 1 which might result in a limitation of personal freedom or postal secrecy.

Article 26. Public policy

Any Member State may refuse to recognise insolvency proceedings opened in another Member State or to enforce a judgment handed down in the context of such proceedings where the effects of such recognition or enforcement would be manifestly contrary to that State's public policy, in particular its fundamental principles or the constitutional rights and liberties of the individual.

CHAPTER III
SECONDARY INSOLVENCY PROCEEDINGS

Article 27. Opening of proceedings

The opening of the proceedings referred to in Article 3(1) by a court of a Member State and which is recognised in another Member State (main proceedings) shall permit the opening in that other Member State, a court of which has jurisdiction pursuant to Article 3(2), of secondary insolvency proceedings without the debtor's insolvency being examined in that other State. These latter proceedings must be among the proceedings listed in Annex B. Their effects shall be restricted to the assets of the debtor situated within the territory of that other Member State.

Article 28. Applicable law

Save as otherwise provided in this Regulation, the law applicable to secondary proceedings shall be that of the Member State within the territory of which the secondary proceedings are opened.

Article 29. Right to request the opening of proceedings

The opening of secondary proceedings may be requested by:
  (a)   the liquidator in the main proceedings;
  (b)   any other person or authority empowered to request the opening of insolvency proceedings under the law of the Member State within the territory of which the opening of secondary proceedings is requested.

Article 30. Advance payment of costs and expenses

Where the law of the Member State in which the opening of secondary proceedings is requested requires that the debtor's assets be sufficient to cover in whole or in part the costs and expenses of the proceedings, the court may, when it receives such a request, require the applicant to make an advance payment of costs or to provide appropriate security.

Article 31. Duty to cooperate and communicate information

1.   Subject to the rules restricting the communication of information, the liquidator in the main proceedings and the liquidators in the secondary proceedings shall be duty bound to communicate information to each other. They shall immediately communicate any information which may be relevant to the other proceedings, in particular the progress made in lodging and verifying claims and all measures aimed at terminating the proceedings.

2.   Subject to the rules applicable to each of the proceedings, the liquidator in the main proceedings and the liquidators in the secondary proceedings shall be duty bound to cooperate with each other.

3.   The liquidator in the secondary proceedings shall give the liquidator in the main proceedings an early opportunity of submitting proposals on the liquidation or use of the assets in the secondary proceedings.

Article 32. Exercise of creditors' rights

1.   Any creditor may lodge his claim in the main proceedings and in any secondary proceedings.

2.   The liquidators in the main and any secondary proceedings shall lodge in other proceedings claims which have already been lodged in the proceedings for which they were appointed, provided that the interests of creditors in the latter proceedings are served thereby, subject to the right of creditors to oppose that or to withdraw the lodgement of their claims where the law applicable so provides.

3.   The liquidator in the main or secondary proceedings shall be empowered to participate in other proceedings on the same basis as a creditor, in particular by attending creditors' meetings.

Article 33. Stay of liquidation

1.   The court, which opened the secondary proceedings, shall stay the process of liquidation in whole or in part on receipt of a request from the liquidator in the main proceedings, provided that in that event it may require the liquidator in the main proceedings to take any suitable measure to guarantee the interests of the creditors in the secondary proceedings and of individual classes of creditors. Such a request from the liquidator may be rejected only if it is manifestly of no interest to the creditors in the main proceedings. Such a stay of the process of liquidation may be ordered for up to three months. It may be continued or renewed for similar periods.

2.   The court referred to in paragraph 1 shall terminate the stay of the process of liquidation:
   – at the request of the liquidator in the main proceedings,
   – of its own motion, at the request of a creditor or at the request of the liquidator in the secondary proceedings if that measure no longer appears justified, in particular, by the interests of creditors in the main proceedings or in the secondary proceedings.

Article 34. Measures ending secondary insolvency proceedings

1.   Where the law applicable to secondary proceedings allows for such proceedings to be closed without liquidation by a rescue plan, a composition or a comparable measure, the liquidator in the main proceedings shall be empowered to propose such a measure himself.

Closure of the secondary proceedings by a measure referred to in the first subparagraph shall not become final without the consent of the liquidator in the main proceedings; failing his agreement, however, it may become final if the financial interests of the creditors in the main proceedings are not affected by the measure proposed.

2.   Any restriction of creditors' rights arising from a measure referred to in paragraph 1 which is proposed in secondary proceedings, such as a stay of payment or discharge of debt, may not have effect in respect of the debtor's assets not covered by those proceedings without the consent of all the creditors having an interest.

3.   During a stay of the process of liquidation ordered pursuant to Article 33, only the liquidator in the main proceedings or the debtor, with the former's consent, may propose measures laid down in paragraph 1 of this Article in the secondary proceedings; no other proposal for such a measure shall be put to the vote or approved.

Article 35. Assets remaining in the secondary proceedings

If by the liquidation of assets in the secondary proceedings it is possible to meet all claims allowed under those proceedings, the liquidator appointed in those proceedings shall immediately transfer any assets remaining to the liquidator in the main proceedings.

Article 36. Subsequent opening of the main proceedings
Where the proceedings referred to in Article 3(1) are opened following the opening of the proceedings referred to in Article 3(2) in another Member State, Articles 31 to 35 shall apply to those opened first, in so far as the progress of those proceedings so permits.

Article 37. Conversion of earlier proceedings
The liquidator in the main proceedings may request that proceedings listed in Annex A previously opened in another Member State be converted into winding-up proceedings if this proves to be in the interests of the creditors in the main proceedings.

The court with jurisdiction under Article 3(2) shall order conversion into one of the proceedings listed in Annex B.

Article 38. Preservation measures
Where the court of a Member State which has jurisdiction pursuant to Article 3(1) appoints a temporary administrator in order to ensure the preservation of the debtor's assets, that temporary administrator shall be empowered to request any measures to secure and preserve any of the debtor's assets situated in another Member State, provided for under the law of that State, for the period between the request for the opening of insolvency proceedings and the judgment opening the proceedings.

. . .

CHAPTER V
TRANSITIONAL AND FINAL PROVISIONS

Article 43. Applicability in time
The provisions of this Regulation shall apply only to insolvency proceedings opened after its entry into force. Acts done by a debtor before the entry into force of this Regulation shall continue to be governed by the law which was applicable to them at the time they were done.

Article 44. Relationship to Conventions
1.   After its entry into force, this Regulation replaces, in respect of the matters referred to therein, in the relations between Member States, the Conventions concluded between two or more Member States, in particular:

(a)   the Convention between Belgium and France on Jurisdiction and the Validity and Enforcement of Judgments, Arbitration Awards and Authentic Instruments, signed at Paris on 8 July 1899;

(b)   the Convention between Belgium and Austria on Bankruptcy, Winding-up, Arrangements, Compositions and Suspension of Payments (with Additional Protocol of 13 June 1973), signed at Brussels on 16 July 1969;

(c)   the Convention between Belgium and the Netherlands on Territorial Jurisdiction, Bankruptcy and the Validity and Enforcement of Judgments, Arbitration Awards and Authentic Instruments, signed at Brussels on 28 March 1925;

(d)   the Treaty between Germany and Austria on Bankruptcy, Winding-up, Arrangements and Compositions, signed at Vienna on 25 May 1979;

(e)   the Convention between France and Austria on Jurisdiction, Recognition and Enforcement of Judgments on Bankruptcy, signed at Vienna on 27 February 1979;

(f)   the Convention between France and Italy on the Enforcement of Judgments in Civil and Commercial Matters, signed at Rome on 3 June 1930;

(g)   the Convention between Italy and Austria on Bankruptcy, Winding-up, Arrangements and Compositions, signed at Rome on 12 July 1977;

(h)   the Convention between the Kingdom of the Netherlands and the Federal Republic of Germany on the Mutual Recognition and Enforcement of Judgments and other Enforceable Instruments in Civil and Commercial Matters, signed at The Hague on 30 August 1962;

(i)   the Convention between the United Kingdom and the Kingdom of Belgium providing for the Reciprocal Enforcement of Judgments in Civil and Commercial Matters, with Protocol, signed at Brussels on 2 May 1934;

(j)   the Convention between Denmark, Finland, Norway, Sweden and Iceland on Bankruptcy, signed at Copenhagen on 7 November 1933;

(k)   the European Convention on Certain International Aspects of Bankruptcy, signed at Istanbul on 5 June 1990.

2.   The Conventions referred to in paragraph 1 shall continue to have effect with regard to proceedings opened before the entry into force of this Regulation.

3.   This Regulation shall not apply:

(a)   in any Member State, to the extent that it is irreconcilable with the obligations arising in relation to bankruptcy from a convention concluded by that State with one or more third countries before the entry into force of this Regulation;

(b)   in the United Kingdom of Great Britain and Northern Ireland, to the extent that is irreconcilable with the obligations arising in relation to bankruptcy and the winding-up of insolvent companies from any arrangements with the Commonwealth existing at the time this Regulation enters into force.

Article 45. Amendment of the Annexes
The Council, acting by qualified majority on the initiative of one of its members or on a proposal from the Commission, may amend the Annexes.

Article 46. Reports
No later than 1 June 2012, and every five years thereafter, the Commission shall present to the European Parliament, the Council and the Economic and Social Committee a report on the application of this Regulation. The report shall be accompanied if need be by a proposal for adaptation of this Regulation.

Article 47. Entry into force
This Regulation shall enter into force on 31 May 2002.

This Regulation shall be binding in its entirety and directly applicable in the Member States in accordance with the Treaty establishing the European Community.

Done at Brussels, 29 May 2000.

ANNEX A

Insolvency proceedings referred to in Article 2(a)

. . .
UNITED KINGDOM
– Winding up by or subject to the supervision by the court,
– Creditors' voluntary winding up (with confirmation by the court),
– Administration, including appointments made by filing prescribed documents with the court,
– Voluntary arrangements under insolvency legislation,
– Bankruptcy or sequestration.

ANNEX B

Winding up proceedings referred to in Article 2(c)

. . .

UNITED KINGDOM
- Winding up by or subject to the supervision of the court,
- Winding up through administration, including appointments made by filing pre-scribed documents with the court,
- Creditors' voluntary winding up (with confirmation by the court),
- Bankruptcy or sequestration.

ANNEX C

Liquidators referred to in Article 2(b)

. . .

UNITED KINGDOM
- Liquidator,
- Supervisor of a voluntary arrangement,
- Administrator,
- Official Receiver,
- Trustee,
- Provisional liquidator,
- Judicial factor.

REGULATION (EC) NO 593/2008 OF THE EUROPEAN PARLIAMENT AND OF THE COUNCIL OF 17 JUNE 2008 ON THE LAW APPLICABLE TO CONTRACTUAL OBLIGATIONS (ROME I)

Official Journal L 177, 04/07/2008 pp 6-16

THE EUROPEAN PARLIAMENT AND THE COUNCIL OF THE EUROPEAN UNION,

Having regard to the Treaty establishing the European Community, and in parti-cular Article 61(c) and the second indent of Article 67(5) thereof,
    Having regard to the proposal from the Commission,
    Having regard to the opinion of the European Economic and Social Committee,
    Acting in accordance with the procedure laid down in Article 251 of the Treaty,

HAVE ADOPTED THIS REGULATION:

CHAPTER I
SCOPE

Article 1. Material scope

1.   This Regulation shall apply, in situations involving a conflict of laws, to con-tractual obligations in civil and commercial matters.
    It shall not apply, in particular, to revenue, customs or administrative matters.
2.   The following shall be excluded from the scope of this Regulation:
    (a)   questions involving the status or legal capacity of natural persons, without prejudice to Article 13;
    (b)   obligations arising out of family relationships and relationships deemed by the law applicable to such relationships to have comparable effects, including maintenance obligations;
    (c)   obligations arising out of matrimonial property regimes, property regimes

of relationships deemed by the law applicable to such relationships to have comparable effects to marriage, and wills and succession;

(d)   obligations arising under bills of exchange, cheques and promissory notes and other negotiable instruments to the extent that the obligations under such other negotiable instruments arise out of their negotiable character;

(e)   arbitration agreements and agreements on the choice of court;

(f)   questions governed by the law of companies and other bodies, corporate or unincorporated, such as the creation, by registration or otherwise, legal capacity, internal organisation or winding-up of companies and other bodies, corporate or unincorporated, and the personal liability of officers and members as such for the obligations of the company or body;

(g)   the question whether an agent is able to bind a principal, or an organ to bind a company or other body corporate or unincorporated, in relation to a third party;

(h)   the constitution of trusts and the relationship between settlors, trustees and beneficiaries;

(i)   obligations arising out of dealings prior to the conclusion of a contract;]

(j)   insurance contracts arising out of operations carried out by organisations other than undertakings referred to in Article 2 of Directive 2002/83/EC of the European Parliament and of the Council of 5 November 2002 concerning life assurance the object of which is to provide benefits for employed or self-employed persons belonging to an undertaking or group of undertakings, or to a trade or group of trades, in the event of death or survival or of discontinuance or curtailment of activity, or of sickness related to work or accidents at work.

3.   This Regulation shall not apply to evidence and procedure, without prejudice to Article 18.

4.   In this Regulation, the term 'Member State' shall mean Member States to which this Regulation applies. However, in Article 3(4) and Article 7 the term shall mean all the Member States.

Article 2. Universal application
Any law specified by this Regulation shall be applied whether or not it is the law of a Member State.

CHAPTER II
UNIFORM RULES

Article 3. Freedom of choice
1.   A contract shall be governed by the law chosen by the parties. The choice shall be made expressly or clearly demonstrated by the terms of the contract or the circumstances of the case. By their choice the parties can select the law applicable to the whole or to part only of the contract.

2.   The parties may at any time agree to subject the contract to a law other than that which previously governed it, whether as a result of an earlier choice made under this Article or of other provisions of this Regulation. Any change in the law to be applied that is made after the conclusion of the contract shall not prejudice its formal validity under Article 11 or adversely affect the rights of third parties.

3.   Where all other elements relevant to the situation at the time of the choice are located in a country other than the country whose law has been chosen, the choice of the parties shall not prejudice the application of provisions of the law of that other country which cannot be derogated from by agreement.

4.   Where all other elements relevant to the situation at the time of the choice are located in one or more Member States, the parties' choice of applicable law other than that of a Member State shall not prejudice the application of provisions of Community law, where appropriate as implemented in the Member State of the forum, which cannot be derogated from by agreement.

5.   The existence and validity of the consent of the parties as to the choice of the

applicable law shall be determined in accordance with the provisions of Articles 10, 11 and 13.

Article 4. Applicable law in the absence of choice

1. To the extent that the law applicable to the contract has not been chosen in accordance with Article 3 and without prejudice to Articles 5 to 8, the law governing the contract shall be determined as follows:

(a) a contract for the sale of goods shall be governed by the law of the country where the seller has his habitual residence;

(b) a contract for the provision of services shall be governed by the law of the country where the service provider has his habitual residence;

(c) a contract relating to a right in rem in immovable property or to a tenancy of immovable property shall be governed by the law of the country where the property is situated;

(d) notwithstanding point (c), a tenancy of immovable property concluded for temporary private use for a period of no more than six consecutive months shall be governed by the law of the country where the landlord has his habitual residence, provided that the tenant is a natural person and has his habitual residence in the same country;

(e) a franchise contract shall be governed by the law of the country where the franchisee has his habitual residence;

(f) a distribution contract shall be governed by the law of the country where the distributor has his habitual residence;

(g) a contract for the sale of goods by auction shall be governed by the law of the country where the auction takes place, if such a place can be determined;

(h) a contract concluded within a multilateral system which brings together or facilitates the bringing together of multiple third-party buying and selling interests in financial instruments, as defined by Article 4(1), point (17) of Directive 2004/39/EC, in accordance with non-discretionary rules and governed by a single law, shall be governed by that law.

2. Where the contract is not covered by paragraph 1 or where the elements of the contract would be covered by more than one of points (a) to (h) of paragraph 1, the contract shall be governed by the law of the country where the party required to effect the characteristic performance of the contract has his habitual residence.

3. Where it is clear from all the circumstances of the case that the contract is manifestly more closely connected with a country other than that indicated in paragraphs 1 or 2, the law of that other country shall apply.

4. Where the law applicable cannot be determined pursuant to paragraphs 1 or 2, the contract shall be governed by the law of the country with which it is most closely connected.

Article 5. Contracts of carriage

1. To the extent that the law applicable to a contract for the carriage of goods has not been chosen in accordance with Article 3, the law applicable shall be the law of the country of habitual residence of the carrier, provided that the place of receipt or the place of delivery or the habitual residence of the consignor is also situated in that country. If those requirements are not met, the law of the country where the place of delivery as agreed by the parties is situated shall apply.

2. To the extent that the law applicable to a contract for the carriage of passengers has not been chosen by the parties in accordance with the second subparagraph, the law applicable shall be the law of the country where the passenger has his habitual residence, provided that either the place of departure or the place of destination is situated in that country. If these requirements are not met, the law of the country where the carrier has his habitual residence shall apply.

The parties may choose as the law applicable to a contract for the carriage of passengers in accordance with Article 3 only the law of the country where:

    (a)   the passenger has his habitual residence; or
    (b)   the carrier has his habitual residence; or
    (c)   the carrier has his place of central administration; or
    (d)   the place of departure is situated; or
    (e)   the place of destination is situated.
    3.   Where it is clear from all the circumstances of the case that the contract, in the absence of a choice of law, is manifestly more closely connected with a country other than that indicated in paragraphs 1 or 2, the law of that other country shall apply.

Article 6. Consumer contracts

    1.   Without prejudice to Articles 5 and 7, a contract concluded by a natural person for a purpose which can be regarded as being outside his trade or profession (the consumer) with another person acting in the exercise of his trade or profession (the professional) shall be governed by the law of the country where the consumer has his habitual residence, provided that the professional:
    (a)   pursues his commercial or professional activities in the country where the consumer has his habitual residence, or
    (b)   by any means, directs such activities to that country or to several countries including that country,
and the contract falls within the scope of such activities.
    2.   Notwithstanding paragraph 1, the parties may choose the law applicable to a contract which fulfils the requirements of paragraph 1, in accordance with Article 3. Such a choice may not, however, have the result of depriving the consumer of the protection afforded to him by provisions that cannot be derogated from by agreement by virtue of the law which, in the absence of choice, would have been applicable on the basis of paragraph 1.
    3.   If the requirements in points (a) or (b) of paragraph 1 are not fulfilled, the law applicable to a contract between a consumer and a professional shall be determined pursuant to Articles 3 and 4.
    4.   Paragraphs 1 and 2 shall not apply to:
    (a)   a contract for the supply of services where the services are to be supplied to the consumer exclusively in a country other than that in which he has his habitual residence;
    (b)   a contract of carriage other than a contract relating to package travel within the meaning of Council Directive 90/314/EEC of 13 June 1990 on package travel, package holidays and package tours;
    (c)   a contract relating to a right in rem in immovable property or a tenancy of immovable property other than a contract relating to the right to use immovable properties on a timeshare basis within the meaning of Directive 94/47/EC;
    (d)   rights and obligations which constitute a financial instrument and rights and obligations constituting the terms and conditions governing the issuance or offer to the public and public take-over bids of transferable securities, and the subscription and redemption of units in collective investment undertakings in so far as these activities do not constitute provision of a financial service;
    (e)   a contract concluded within the type of system falling within the scope of Article 4(1)(h)

Article 7. Insurance contracts*

    1.   This Article shall apply to contracts referred to in paragraph 2, whether or not the risk covered is situated in a Member State, and to all other insurance con-

---

*Art 7 applies in the case of conflicts between (a) the laws of the different parts of the UK, or (b) the laws of one or more parts of the UK and Gibraltar: SI 2009/3075, Art 3.

tracts covering risks situated inside the territory of the Member States. It shall not apply to reinsurance contracts.

2. An insurance contract covering a large risk as defined in Article 5(d) of the First Council Directive 73/239/EEC of 24 July 1973 on the coordination of laws, regulations and administrative provisions relating to the taking-up and pursuit of the business of direct insurance other than life assurance shall be governed by the law chosen by the parties in accordance with Article 3 of this Regulation.

To the extent that the applicable law has not been chosen by the parties, the insurance contract shall be governed by the law of the country where the insurer has his habitual residence. Where it is clear from all the circumstances of the case that the contract is manifestly more closely connected with another country, the law of that other country shall apply.

3. In the case of an insurance contract other than a contract falling within paragraph 2, only the following laws may be chosen by the parties in accordance with Article 3:

(a) the law of any Member State where the risk is situated at the time of conclusion of the contract;

(b) the law of the country where the policy holder has his habitual residence;

(c) in the case of life assurance, the law of the Member State of which the policy holder is a national;

(d) for insurance contracts covering risks limited to events occurring in one Member State other than the Member State where the risk is situated, the law of that Member State;

(e) where the policy holder of a contract falling under this paragraph pursues a commercial or industrial activity or a liberal profession and the insurance contract covers two or more risks which relate to those activities and are situated in different Member States, the law of any of the Member States concerned or the law of the country of habitual residence of the policy holder.

Where, in the cases set out in points (a), (b) or (e), the Member States referred to grant greater freedom of choice of the law applicable to the insurance contract, the parties may take advantage of that freedom.

To the extent that the law applicable has not been chosen by the parties in accordance with this paragraph, such a contract shall be governed by the law of the Member State in which the risk is situated at the time of conclusion of the contract.

4. The following additional rules shall apply to insurance contracts covering risks for which a Member State imposes an obligation to take out insurance:

(a) the insurance contract shall not satisfy the obligation to take out insurance unless it complies with the specific provisions relating to that insurance laid down by the Member State that imposes the obligation. Where the law of the Member State in which the risk is situated and the law of the Member State imposing the obligation to take out insurance contradict each other, the latter shall prevail;

(b) by way of derogation from paragraphs 2 and 3, a Member State may lay down that the insurance contract shall be governed by the law of the Member State that imposes the obligation to take out insurance.

5. For the purposes of paragraph 3, third subparagraph, and paragraph 4, where the contract covers risks situated in more than one Member State, the contract shall be considered as constituting several contracts each relating to only one Member State.

6. For the purposes of this Article, the country in which the risk is situated shall be determined in accordance with Article 2(d) of the Second Council Directive 88/357/EEC of 22 June 1988 on the coordination of laws, regulations and administrative provisions relating to direct insurance other than life assurance and

laying down provisions to facilitate the effective exercise of freedom to provide services and, in the case of life assurance, the country in which the risk is situated shall be the country of the commitment within the meaning of Article 1(1)(g) of Directive 2002/83/EC.

Article 8. Individual employment contracts

1. An individual employment contract shall be governed by the law chosen by the parties in accordance with Article 3. Such a choice of law may not, however, have the result of depriving the employee of the protection afforded to him by provisions that cannot be derogated from by agreement under the law that, in the absence of choice, would have been applicable pursuant to paragraphs 2, 3 and 4 of this Article.

2. To the extent that the law applicable to the individual employment contract has not been chosen by the parties, the contract shall be governed by the law of the country in which or, failing that, from which the employee habitually carries out his work in performance of the contract. The country where the work is habitually carried out shall not be deemed to have changed if he is temporarily employed in another country.

3. Where the law applicable cannot be determined pursuant to paragraph 2, the contract shall be governed by the law of the country where the place of business through which the employee was engaged is situated.

4. Where it appears from the circumstances as a whole that the contract is more closely connected with a country other than that indicated in paragraphs 2 or 3, the law of that other country shall apply.

Article 9. Overriding mandatory provisions

1. Overriding mandatory provisions are provisions the respect for which is regarded as crucial by a country for safeguarding its public interests, such as its political, social or economic organisation, to such an extent that they are applicable to any situation falling within their scope, irrespective of the law otherwise applicable to the contract under this Regulation.

2. Nothing in this Regulation shall restrict the application of the overriding mandatory provisions of the law of the forum.

3. Effect may be given to the overriding mandatory provisions of the law of the country where the obligations arising out of the contract have to be or have been performed, in so far as those overriding mandatory provisions render the performance of the contract unlawful. In considering whether to give effect to those provisions, regard shall be had to their nature and purpose and to the consequences of their application or non-application.

Article 10. Consent and material validity

1. The existence and validity of a contract, or of any term of a contract, shall be determined by the law which would govern it under this Regulation if the contract or term were valid.

2. Nevertheless, a party, in order to establish that he did not consent, may rely upon the law of the country in which he has his habitual residence if it appears from the circumstances that it would not be reasonable to determine the effect of his conduct in accordance with the law specified in paragraph 1.

Article 11. Formal validity

1. A contract concluded between persons who, or whose agents, are in the same country at the time of its conclusion is formally valid if it satisfies the formal requirements of the law which governs it in substance under this Regulation or of the law of the country where it is concluded.

2. A contract concluded between persons who, or whose agents, are in different countries at the time of its conclusion is formally valid if it satisfies the formal requirements of the law which governs it in substance under this Regulation, or of the law of either of the countries where either of the parties or their agent is pre-

sent at the time of conclusion, or of the law of the country where either of the parties had his habitual residence at that time.

3.   A unilateral act intended to have legal effect relating to an existing or contemplated contract is formally valid if it satisfies the formal requirements of the law which governs or would govern the contract in substance under this Regulation, or of the law of the country where the act was done, or of the law of the country where the person by whom it was done had his habitual residence at that time.

4.   Paragraphs 1, 2 and 3 of this Article shall not apply to contracts that fall within the scope of Article 6. The form of such contracts shall be governed by the law of the country where the consumer has his habitual residence.

5.   Notwithstanding paragraphs 1 to 4, a contract the subject matter of which is a right in rem in immovable property or a tenancy of immovable property shall be subject to the requirements of form of the law of the country where the property is situated if by that law:

(a)   those requirements are imposed irrespective of the country where the contract is concluded and irrespective of the law governing the contract; and

(b)   those requirements cannot be derogated from by agreement.

Article 12. Scope of the law applicable

1.   The law applicable to a contract by virtue of this Regulation shall govern in particular:

(a)   interpretation;

(b)   performance;

(c)   within the limits of the powers conferred on the court by its procedural law, the consequences of a total or partial breach of obligations, including the assessment of damages in so far as it is governed by rules of law;

(d)   the various ways of extinguishing obligations, and prescription and limitation of actions;

(e)   the consequences of nullity of the contract.

2.   In relation to the manner of performance and the steps to be taken in the event of defective performance, regard shall be had to the law of the country in which performance takes place.

Article 13. Incapacity

In a contract concluded between persons who are in the same country, a natural person who would have capacity under the law of that country may invoke his incapacity resulting from the law of another country, only if the other party to the contract was aware of that incapacity at the time of the conclusion of the contract or was not aware thereof as a result of negligence.

Article 14. Voluntary assignment and contractual subrogation

1.   The relationship between assignor and assignee under a voluntary assignment or contractual subrogation of a claim against another person (the debtor) shall be governed by the law that applies to the contract between the assignor and assignee under this Regulation.

2.   The law governing the assigned or subrogated claim shall determine its assignability, the relationship between the assignee and the debtor, the conditions under which the assignment or subrogation can be invoked against the debtor and whether the debtor's obligations have been discharged.

3.   The concept of assignment in this Article includes outright transfers of claims, transfers of claims by way of security and pledges or other security rights over claims.

Article 15. Legal subrogation

Where a person (the creditor) has a contractual claim against another (the debtor) and a third person has a duty to satisfy the creditor, or has in fact satisfied the creditor in discharge of that duty, the law which governs the third person's duty to satisfy the creditor shall determine whether and to what extent the third person is entitled to exercise against the debtor the rights which the creditor had against the debtor under the law governing their relationship.

Article 16. Multiple liability

If a creditor has a claim against several debtors who are liable for the same claim, and one of the debtors has already satisfied the claim in whole or in part, the law governing the debtor's obligation towards the creditor also governs the debtor's right to claim recourse from the other debtors. The other debtors may rely on the defences they had against the creditor to the extent allowed by the law governing their obligations towards the creditor.

Article 17. Set-off

Where the right to set-off is not agreed by the parties, set-off shall be governed by the law applicable to the claim against which the right to set-off is asserted.

Article 18. Burden of proof

1.   The law governing a contractual obligation under this Regulation shall apply to the extent that, in matters of contractual obligations, it contains rules which raise presumptions of law or determine the burden of proof.

2.   A contract or an act intended to have legal effect may be proved by any mode of proof recognised by the law of the forum or by any of the laws referred to in Article 11 under which that contract or act is formally valid, provided that such mode of proof can be administered by the forum.

CHAPTER III
OTHER PROVISIONS

Article 19. Habitual residence

1.   For the purposes of this Regulation, the habitual residence of companies and other bodies, corporate or unincorporated, shall be the place of central administration.

The habitual residence of a natural person acting in the course of his business activity shall be his principal place of business.

2.   Where the contract is concluded in the course of the operations of a branch, agency or any other establishment, or if, under the contract, performance is the responsibility of such a branch, agency or establishment, the place where the branch, agency or any other establishment is located shall be treated as the place of habitual residence.

3.   For the purposes of determining the habitual residence, the relevant point in time shall be the time of the conclusion of the contract.

Article 20. Exclusion of renvoi

The application of the law of any country specified by this Regulation means the application of the rules of law in force in that country other than its rules of private international law, unless provided otherwise in this Regulation.

Article 21. Public policy of the forum

The application of a provision of the law of any country specified by this Regulation may be refused only if such application is manifestly incompatible with the public policy (ordre public) of the forum.

Article 22. States with more than one legal system*

1.   Where a State comprises several territorial units, each of which has its own

---

*Reg 4 of The Law Applicable to Contractual Obligations (Scotland) Regulations 2009 (SSI 2009/410) provides that, notwithstanding Art 22(2), the Regulation, with the exception of Art 7, applies in the case of conflicts between (a) the laws of different parts of the UK; or (b) the laws of one or more parts of the UK and Gibraltar.

rules of law in respect of contractual obligations, each territorial unit shall be considered as a country for the purposes of identifying the law applicable under this Regulation.

2.   A Member State where different territorial units have their own rules of law in respect of contractual obligations shall not be required to apply this Regulation to conflicts solely between the laws of such units.

Article 23. Relationship with other provisions of Community law

With the exception of Article 7, this Regulation shall not prejudice the application of provisions of Community law which, in relation to particular matters, lay down conflict-of-law rules relating to contractual obligations.

Article 24. Relationship with the Rome Convention

1.   This Regulation shall replace the Rome Convention in the Member States, except as regards the territories of the Member States which fall within the territorial scope of that Convention and to which this Regulation does not apply pursuant to Article 299 of the Treaty.

2.   In so far as this Regulation replaces the provisions of the Rome Convention, any reference to that Convention shall be understood as a reference to this Regulation.

Article 25. Relationship with existing international conventions

1.   This Regulation shall not prejudice the application of international conventions to which one or more Member States are parties at the time when this Regulation is adopted and which lay down conflict-of-law rules relating to contractual obligations.

2.   However, this Regulation shall, as between Member States, take precedence over conventions concluded exclusively between two or more of them in so far as such conventions concern matters governed by this Regulation.

Article 26. List of Conventions

1.   By 17 June 2009, Member States shall notify the Commission of the conventions referred to in Article 25(1). After that date, Member States shall notify the Commission of all denunciations of such conventions.

2.   Within six months of receipt of the notifications referred to in paragraph 1, the Commission shall publish in the Official Journal of the European Union:

(a)   a list of the conventions referred to in paragraph 1;

(b)   the denunciations referred to in paragraph 1.

Article 27. Review clause

1.   By 17 June 2013, the Commission shall submit to the European Parliament, the Council and the European Economic and Social Committee a report on the application of this Regulation. If appropriate, the report shall be accompanied by proposals to amend this Regulation. The report shall include:

(a)   a study on the law applicable to insurance contracts and an assessment of the impact of the provisions to be introduced, if any; and

(b)   an evaluation on the application of Article 6, in particular as regards the coherence of Community law in the field of consumer protection.

2.   By 17 June 2010, the Commission shall submit to the European Parliament, the Council and the European Economic and Social Committee a report on the question of the effectiveness of an assignment or subrogation of a claim against third parties and the priority of the assigned or subrogated claim over a right of another person. The report shall be accompanied, if appropriate, by a proposal to amend this Regulation and an assessment of the impact of the provisions to be introduced.

Article 28. Application in time

This Regulation shall apply to contracts concluded as from 17 December 2009.

INDEX OF STATUTES